ANCIENT MAGIC
AND RITUAL POWER

RELIGIONS IN
THE GRAECO-ROMAN WORLD

EDITORS

R. VAN DEN BROEK   H.J.W. DRIJVERS
H.S. VERSNEL

VOLUME 129

ANCIENT MAGIC AND RITUAL POWER

EDITED BY

MARVIN MEYER

AND

PAUL MIRECKI

E.J. BRILL

LEIDEN · NEW YORK · KÖLN

1995

This series *Religions in the Graeco-Roman World* presents a forum for studies in the social and cultural function of religions in the Greek and the Roman world, dealing with pagan religions both in their own right and in their interaction with and influence on Christianity and Judaism during a lengthy period of fundamental change. Special attention will be given to the religious history of regions and cities which illustrate the practical workings of these processes.

Enquiries regarding the submission of works for publication in the series may be directed to Professor H.J.W. Drijvers, Faculty of Letters, University of Groningen, 9712 EK Groningen, The Netherlands.

The paper in this book meets the guidelines for permanence and durability of the Committee on Production Guidelines for Book Longevity of the Council on Library Resources

BF
1591
.A55
1995

Library of Congress Cataloging-in-Publication Data

Ancient magic and ritual power / by Marvin Meyer and Paul Mirecki, editors.
    p.   cm. — (Religions in the Graeco-Roman world, ISSN 0927-7633 ; v. 129)
    Includes bibliographical references.
    ISBN 9004104062 (cloth : alk. paper)
    1. Magic, Ancient.   2. Rites and ceremonies—Rome.   3. Power (Social sciences)—Rome.   4. Rome—Religion.   I. Meyer, Marvin, W.   II. Mirecki, Paul Allan.   III. Series.
BF1591.A55   1995
133.4'3'0936—dc20

95-26114
CIP

Die Deutsche Bibliothek - CIP-Einheitsaufnahme

Ancient magic and ritual power / by Marvin Meyer and Paul Mirecki (eds). – Leiden ; New York ; Köln : Brill, 1995
    (Religions in the Graeco-Roman world ; Vol. 129)
    ISBN 90-04-10406-2
NE: Meyer, Marvin [Hrsg.]; GT

ISSN 0927-7633
ISBN 90 04 10406 2

PRINTED IN THE NETHERLANDS

TABLE OF CONTENTS

PART ONE

DEFINING MAGIC AND RITUAL POWER

PART TWO

MAGIC AND RITUAL POWER
IN THE ANCIENT NEAR EAST

PART THREE

MAGIC AND RITUAL POWER
IN JUDAISM AND EARLY CHRISTIANITY

CONTRIBUTORS

Richard H. Beal
Jason David BeDuhn
William M. Brashear
Todd Breyfogle
Leda Jean Ciraolo
Billie Jean Collins
Christopher A. Faraone
David Frankfurter
Fritz Graf
Sarah Iles Johnston
Roy Kotansky
Rebecca Lesses

David Martinez
Marvin Meyer
Paul Mirecki
Oliver Phillips
Stephen D. Ricks
Robert K. Ritner
Brian B. Schmidt
J. A. Scurlock
Jonathan Seidel
Jonathan Z. Smith
Michael D. Swartz
Jacques van der Vliet

MANAGING EDITOR
Neal Kelsey

PREFACE

The essays in this volume derive from the conference on "Magic in the Ancient World," held in August 1992 at the University of Kansas. We would like to acknowledge the support provided for this conference by the Department of Religious Studies at the University of Kansas, the Kansas School of Religion, the College Lecture Fund, and the Office of International Studies and Programs. Additional encouragement for the conference and the volume has been offered by the Coptic Magical Texts Project of the Institute for Antiquity and Christianity, Claremont Graduate School. Through the Coptic Magical Texts Project and the Institute, the J. W. and Ida M. Jameson Foundation and the Board of Higher Education of the United Methodist Church have given financial assistance, as has the Griset Chair Fund of Chapman University. The essays themselves, diverse as they are, incorporate the different approaches and even the different styles typical of the disciplines represented. We have allowed some of this diversity to remain, and readers may anticipate that they will have the opportunity to savor the flavors of the several disciplines.

Marvin Meyer
Professor of Religion, Chapman University
Director, Coptic Magical Texts Project, Institute for Antiquity and Christianity

Paul Mirecki
Associate Professor of Religious Studies, University of Kansas

INTRODUCTION

Marvin Meyer
Paul Mirecki

Over the past couple of decades there has been a dramatic resurgence of interest in the study of what has usually been called "ancient magic." We may take the appearance, in 1973-74, of the second edition of Karl Preisendanz' *Papyri Graecae Magicae: Die griechischen Zauberpapyri,* edited by Albert Henrichs, as a convenient point of reference for this renewed enthusiasm on the part of scholars to examine ancient magic. Since then, scholars have published a substantial number of individual magical texts in journals and have produced several new collections of magical texts in translation. For example, if we cite only collections in English translation, we can list the following: *The Greek Magical Papyri in Translation, Including the Demotic Spells* (1986, 2nd ed. 1992), edited by Hans Dieter Betz; *Ancient Egyptian Magical Texts* (1978), edited by J. F. Borghouts; *Curse Tablets and Binding Spells from the Ancient World* (1992), edited by John G. Gager; *Ancient Christian Magic: Coptic Texts of Ritual Power* (1994), edited by Marvin Meyer and Richard Smith; *Amulets and Magical Bowls: Aramaic Incantations of Late Antiquity* (1985), edited by Joseph Naveh and Shaul Shaked; *Hebrew and Aramaic Incantation Texts from the Cairo Genizah* (1992), edited by Lawrence H. Schiffman and Michael D. Swartz; and so on. Beyond these, a plethora of articles and monographs has appeared as scholarly studies and evaluations of magical texts and traditions from the ancient world. Fritz Graf is certainly right in calling this "the modern boom of magical studies."

The present volume, *Ancient Magic and Ritual Power,* provides a series of essays that disclose "the state of the art" in the study of ancient magic. These essays derive from an international conference on "Magic in the Ancient World," convened in August 1992 by Marvin Meyer and Paul Mirecki, at the University of Kansas. The essays, like the papers presented at the conference, are authored by scholars, from a variety of disciplines, who represent the renaissance in the study of ancient magic. At the conference and in this volume these scholars have intentionally been brought

together to employ the approaches of their own disciplines as they
investigate the phenomena of ancient magic.

Apart from the many positive contributions, what emerges
from these essays is a clear sense of scholarly discomfort with
some traditional ways of describing and classifying magic, including
ancient magic. At times this discomfort extends to the very use of
a term that may be as loaded and prejudicial as "magic." Jonathan
Z. Smith's assertion—"I see little merit in continuing the use of
the substantive term 'magic' in second-order, theoretical, academic
discourse"—is strongly put, but it represents one way of articulating this sense of dis-ease with what has been dubbed "magic." For
often "magic" has been discussed in comparison with, and in sharp
contrast to, religion, science, and medicine, and "magic" has got-
ten the worst of such comparisons. Various theories—at times
theologically biased, culturally one-sided, chronologically self-
congratulatory—have been advanced to show that "magic" is bad
religion, bad science, bad medicine. "Magic" is an old, immature,
underdeveloped form of religion and science; or it is a degraded
form of true religion and pure science; or it is a partial, unfulfilled
form of the more complete expression of religion and science that
we modern folks wish to consider characteristic of our own way of
life. As the essays in this volume show, such biased descriptions and
definitions of magic may be seen in the likes of Sir James G. Frazer
(*The Golden Bough*, 1910) and many others, but they are ultimately rooted in Greco-Roman polemic and Protestant anti-
Roman Catholic statements. (See especially the essays by Jonathan
Z. Smith, Fritz Graf, Robert K. Ritner, and Stephen D. Ricks.) It
has become a part of Western conceit to think of religion and
science as what "we" do and magic as what others ("they") do.
Ritner puts it very succinctly: "Magic is a category of exclusion"—
and it has been such, in some Western circles in particular, for a
long time.

A large part of the problem of describing and defining magic
comes from our preoccupation with classifying. We scholars are
unrepentant taxonomists, and taxonomy entails comparison and
contrast. In his essay in this volume Smith mentions the problems
of comparison and the taxa used in comparison, most notably the
problem of dichotomous taxa. Elsewhere, in his book *Drudgery
Divine: On the Comparison of Early Christianities and the Religions of Late Antiquity* (1990), he expands upon this issue. In the
book he observes that the statement "x resembles y" is invariably
triadic: "there is always an implicit 'more than,' and there is
always a 'with respect to'" (51). The implications of this observa-

tion, including the political implications, Smith continues, are striking:

> comparison does not necessarily tell us how things "are" (the far from latent presupposition that lies behind the notion of the "genealogical" with its quest for "real" historical connections); like models and metaphors, comparison tells us how things might be conceived, how they might be "redescribed," in Max Black's useful term. A comparison is a disciplined exaggeration in the service of knowledge. It lifts out and strongly marks certain features within difference as being of possible intellectual significance, expressed in the rhetoric of their being "like" in some stipulated fashion. Comparison provides the means by which we "revision" phenomena as our data in order to solve our theoretical problems (52).

Applying this idea of comparison and the hidden agenda of comparison to the scholarly study of ancient magic, we may conclude that many of the scholars represented in this volume seek to identify the "exaggerations" of previous ways of describing "magic" and suggest new, "revisionist" means of viewing "magical" phenomena. It is no surprise that essays in this volume express a profound concern for paradigms and paradigm-shifts.

*   *   *

The title of this volume, *Ancient Magic and Ritual Power,* has been chosen with paradigmatic concerns in mind. In these essays we encounter what traditionally has been depicted as "ancient magic," but we may prefer to apply different labels or taxa in our task of "re-visioning"—hence the phrase "ritual power." A common feature of the texts and traditions under consideration, as highlighted in the essays, is *empowerment.* A quick survey of these essays discloses powers supernal and infernal being summoned, i.e., deities, supernatural assistants, angels, and demons; powers coming to expression in the lives of people for divination, healing, protection, exorcism of evil, and love; powers being employed to marginalize others who are judged to be deviant or even diabolical; powers being retained in a person, and sometimes worn in the form of amulets or phylacteries. The texts and traditions examined here claim to empower people, in ways similar to those commonly assigned to religious texts and traditions, by channeling, summoning, adjuring, realizing powers without and within.

Yet the sort of empowerment discussed in this volume is achieved specifically through *ritual.* There are numerous ways to

characterize ritual, and many of the essays published here describe
ritual and rituals. In *Ancient Christian Magic* Marvin Meyer and
Richard Smith offer the following overview of rituals in magical
texts, that is, texts of ritual power:

> They direct the user to engage in activities that are marked off from nor-
> mal activity by framing behavior through rules, repetitions, and other
> formalities. Ritual instructions pervade these texts. Stand over here, hold
> a pebble, tie seven threads in seven knots, say the names seven times,
> draw the figure in the bottom of the cup, write the spell with the finger of
> a mummy, write it with bat's blood, with menstrual blood, on papyrus,
> on clay, on lead, on tin, or a rib bone, on a parchment shaped like a
> sword, fold it, burn it, tie it to your arm, your thumb, drive a nail in it,
> bury it with a mummy, bury it under someone's doorstep, mix this rec-
> ipe, drink it. Or simply "do the usual" (4).

In the present volume the essays similarly study the
"repetitions" and "formalities" of ritual. As these essays also
indicate, such ritual comes to expression variously, for instance
through sacrifices and cultic meals, often miniaturized, and commonly through the repetitions of words, written or spoken, in the
form of incantations, formulae, *historiolae, voces magicae,* and
divine names of power. Myths and names, when performed ritually, may produce an eruption of power in the present moment. It
is entirely appropriate that David Frankfurter's essay on *historiolae,* or stories of mythic precedent, should close the volume in a
conclusion with the rubric "Myth, Magic, and the Power of the
Word."

An understanding of "magic" as "ritual power," then, permeates
many of the essays in this volume. In the first essay Jonathan Z.
Smith sets the tone for the discussion by re-defining the Greek
"magical" papyri in these terms as "one of the largest collections
of functioning ritual texts, largely in Greek, produced by ritual
specialists that has survived from late antiquity." Yet, we know all
too well, paradigm-changes are slippery and often difficult to
accomplish. If "magic" is taken as "ritual power," then "magical"
phenomena may need to be described anew and the lines of demar-
cation redrawn. Precisely what the possibilities and problems are
for the category "ritual power" may need to be explored. For these
reasons we have cast the interpretive net in this volume as widely
as we could, in order to explore the options for "ritual" and
"power," broadly conceived, in antiquity and late antiquity. Sometimes the investigation of "ritual" may go beyond what we might
intuit to be "magical ritual"; at other times the analysis of "power"

may include rituals and texts that we judge to be on the periphery of the discussion of "magical power." Such breadth, reflecting the state of the scholarly discussion, is important if we are to attempt to designate helpful and telling criteria for our discussion of "magic" and "ritual power."

* * *

The texts and traditions of magic and ritual power addressed here are represented in the volume title as "ancient," and this term, too, merits attention. The essays in this volume and the papers from the conference that preceded the volume have been prepared by scholars from a wide range of disciplines, all of whom are still concerned with magic and ritual power in Mediterranean and Near Eastern antiquity and late antiquity. The scholars thus assembled are students of Egyptology, ancient Near Eastern studies, the Hebrew Bible, Judaica, classical Greek and Roman studies, early Christianity and patristics, and Coptology, and the chronological period they consider begins with the early civilizations of Egypt and Mesopotamia and extends into the Middle Ages. The methods of these scholars include historical-critical, textual, papyrological, descriptive, interpretive, exegetical, theoretical, and rhetorical approaches to the subject matter. It is unusual for such a diverse assemblage of scholars and their essays to be brought together to investigate ancient magical traditions, and herein lies some of the unique value of this volume. In these essays we have the opportunity to explore these traditions with scholars who exemplify the manifold approaches that are appropriate if we are to do justice to the study of magic and ritual power in antiquity.

The essays have been carefully organized into five sections plus a conclusion. Apart from the first section and the conclusion, which bracket the rest of the essays, the sections are organized with chronological and cultural considerations in mind.

In Part 1, "Defining Ancient Magic and Ritual Power," Jonathan Z. Smith, Fritz Graf, and Robert K. Ritner lay the foundation for the volume by examining second-order, academic descriptions as well as first-order, "native" descriptions of ancient magic and ritual power. From this examination comes a clarification of "magic" as a polemical term of exclusion, as we have already noted, but also an understanding of the classical Egyptian and early Greek conceptions of "magic" as a more neutral category of inclusion. With a deliberately ambiguous title, "Trading Places," Smith not only suggests trading places between generic labels used to describe "magic" and "ritual power"; he also adds a set of reflections on the function of ritual "place" in the Greek magical papyri.

In Part 2, "Magic and Ritual Power in the Ancient Near East," Richard H. Beal, Billie Jean Collins, and J. A. Scurlock describe and interpret several ancient Hittite and Mesopotamian rituals that empowered the Hittite military, structured Hittite sacrifice and cultic meals, and made opportunistic use of the power available from ghosts who were traveling at the time of annual Mesopotamian festivals of the dead. These three essays show how the ancient Near Eastern folks who participated in these rituals were able to live out of the power they had invoked: the Hittite military and the Hittite kingdom thrived for centuries "in a tough neighborhood," the participants in sacrifice and cultic feasting communed with and curried the favor of the gods and goddesses, and people conjuring ghosts got rid of illnesses and personal problems while also divining the future.

Brian B. Schmidt opens Part 3, "Magic and Ritual Power in Judaism and Early Christianity," by building upon this same tradition of ancient Near Eastern necromancy as he interprets the story of the "witch" of En-Dor in the Hebrew Bible. The subsequent essays in this section likewise reflect upon the place of magic in Jewish and Christian traditions. Stephen D. Ricks surveys the role of the magician in these traditions, and his thesis, that the term "magician" is used in a pejorative way to distinguish those who are to be considered outsiders, coheres well with a basic perspective of many of the essays in this volume. The next three essays, by Jonathan Seidel, Michael D. Swartz, and Rebecca Lesses, all evaluate issues in Jewish magic: Seidel seeks to untangle the Talmudic classification of illicit and licit "magical" acts, Swartz underscores the ambivalent status of magic in ancient and medieval Judaism, and Lesses applies a theory of the performative use of language to an important text (also discussed by Swartz) from the Hekhalot literature of Jewish mysticism.

Part 4, "Magic and Ritual Power in Greek Antiquity," begins with a lively papyrological essay, by William M. Brashear, in which he presents eight previously unpublished magical and divinatory texts from Berlin. Such textual work, crucial for making available the primary texts, spells, and amulets of ancient magic, is taken a step further by Roy Kotansky, who identifies a series of Greek exorcistic amulets and traces the language of adjuration through these and other exorcistic texts. Leda Jean Ciraolo focuses her attention upon the classic collection of Greek magical texts, *Papyri Graecae Magicae,* and examines the activities of supernatural assistants in these Greek texts, just as others examine angels and demons in Judeo-Christian texts elsewhere in the volume. Christopher A. Faraone studies the same classic collection of Greek texts in his wide-ranging essay, but he investigates a portion of *PGM* XX in order to illustrate "the continual cultural give-and-take" that characterizes the multiculturism of magical texts. David Martinez is equally wide-ranging in his study of Greek texts when he turns his attention to vows of abstinence in all kinds of contexts, and particularly in love magic. Sarah Iles Johnston concludes this section (and anticipates the next) by "defining the dreadful" according to Greek ways of describing and averting the demonic and the liminal, or the deviant, in society.

The four essays in Part 5, "Magic and Ritual Power in Roman and Late Antiquity," carry the discussion of magical traditions through some of the late sources from the Mediterranean world. Oliver Phillips and Jacques van der Vliet continue "defining the dreadful": Phillips inquires into cures for poisonous snakebite, and describes Libyans (again, those who are the "others" from a Roman point of view) who know how to cope with snakebite through the application of what we might call magical and medical techniques; van der Vliet discusses Satan and demons in Coptic Christian texts, and analyzes the potpourri of accounts of Satan's fall in Coptic myth and magic. Jason David BeDuhn introduces the magical bowls from late-antique Mesopotamia, and asks whether—and how—such bowls might have been used by Manichaean Gnostics. Todd R. Breyfogle closes this section by questioning the circumstances that led to the execution of the Christian bishop Priscillian in 385 in Trier, Germany, on the charges of practicing sorcery, participating in nocturnal orgies, and praying naked.

The volume ends with a conclusion given the designation "Myth, Magic, and the Power of the Word." In this conclusion David Frankfurter draws together many of the themes discussed throughout the other essays (note especially that of Lesses) by investigating the *historiola* in magical texts. Frankfurter maintains that through the narration of myth and the performance of the word, the magical power of ritual came to authoritative expression for practitioners of ancient magic.

* * *

Ancient Magic and Ritual Power offers a fresh look at ancient magical phenomena. As the essays suggest, comfortable, sometimes self-serving categories like "magic"—or, for that matter, "religion" and "science"—cannot be used uncritically. Instead, new, self-critical approaches may prove more adequate in illuminating texts and traditions in our cultural heritage. Like the essays in the present volume, such new approaches may raise more questions than answers, but these questions themselves may help us "re-vision" and "re-imagine" the ancient roots of our traditions. Finally, these questions may remind us of our own biases and presuppositions, and thus they may teach us a goodly amount about ourselves and the "magic" of scholarly inquiry.

SELECTED BIBLIOGRAPHY

Aune, David E. "Magic in Early Christianity." In *Aufstieg und Niedergang der römischen Welt*, edited by Hildegard Temporini and Wolfgang Haase, II.23.2, 1507-57. Berlin and New York: Walter de Gruyter, 1980.

Betz, Hans Dieter, ed. *The Greek Magical Papyri in Translation, Including the Demotic Spells*. Chicago: University of Chicago Press, 1986. Second ed., 1992.

Borghouts, J. F. *Ancient Egyptian Magical Texts*. Nisaba 9. Leiden: E. J. Brill, 1978.

Brashear, William M. "The Greek Magical Papyri: an Introduction and Survey; Annotated Bibliography (1928-1994) [Indices in vol. II 18.6]." In *Aufstieg und Niedergang der römischen Welt*, edited by Hildegard Temporini and Wolfgang Haase, II.18.5, 3380-3684. Berlin and New York: Walter de Gruyter, 1995.

Daniel, Robert W., and Franco Maltomini, eds. *Supplementum Magicum*. 2 vols. Papyrologica Coloniensia, vol. 16. Abhandlungen der Rheinisch-Westfälischen Akademie der Wissenschaften. Opladen: Westdeutscher Verlag, 1990-92.

Faraone, Christopher A., and Dirk Obbink, eds. *Magika Hiera: Ancient Greek Magic and Religion*. New York and Oxford: Oxford University Press, 1991.

Frazer, James George. *The Golden Bough: A Study in Magic and Religion*. London: Macmillan, 1910.

Gager, John G., ed. *Curse Tablets and Binding Spells from the Ancient World*. New York and Oxford: Oxford University Press, 1992.

Hopfner, Theodor. *Griechisch-ägyptischer Offenbarungszauber*. 2 vols. Studien zur Palaeographie und Papyruskunde 21 & 23. Leipzig: Haessel, 1921, 1923.

Kropp, Angelicus M. *Ausgewählte koptische Zaubertexte*. 3 vols. Brussels: Fondation égyptologique reine Elisabeth, 1930-31.

Leclercq, H. "Magie." In *Dictionnaire d'archéologie chrétienne et de liturgie*, 10.1067-1114. Paris: Librairie Letouzey et Ané, 1931-53.

Meyer, Marvin, and Richard Smith, eds. *Ancient Christian Magic: Coptic Texts of Ritual Power*. San Francisco: Harper San Francisco, 1994.

Naveh, Joseph, and Shaul Shaked, eds. *Amulets and Magical Bowls: Aramaic Incantations of Late Antiquity*. Leiden: E. J. Brill, 1985.

Pernigotti, Sergio. "La magia copta: i testi." In *Aufstieg und Niedergang der römischen Welt*, edited by Hildegard Temporini and Wolfgang Haase, II.18.5, 3685-3730. Berlin and New York: Walter de Gruyter, 1995.

Preisendanz, Karl, ed. *Papyri Graecae Magicae: Die griechischen Zauberpapyri*. 2 vols. Second ed., edited by Albert Henrichs. Stuttgart: B. G. Teubner, 1973.

Remus, Harold. "Does Terminology Distinguish Early Christian from Pagan Miracles?" *Journal of Biblical Literature* 101 (1982): 531-51.

Ritner, Robert. "Egyptian Magical Practice Under the Roman Empire: the Demotic Spells and their Religious Context." In *Aufstieg und Niedergang der römischen Welt*, edited by Hildegard Temporini and Wolfgang Haase, II.18.5, 3333-79. Berlin and New York: Walter de Gruyter, 1995.

————. *The Mechanics of Ancient Egyptian Magical Practice*. Studies in Ancient Oriental Civilization, no. 54, edited by Thomas A. Holland. Chicago: Oriental Institute of the University of Chicago, 1993.

Schiffman, Lawrence H., and Michael D. Swartz. *Hebrew and Aramaic Incantation Texts from the Cairo Genizeh*. Semitic Texts and Studies, vol. 1. Sheffield: JSOT, 1992.

Segal, Alan F. "Hellenistic Magic: Some Questions of Definition." In *Studies in Gnosticism and Hellenistic Religions*, edited by R. van den Broek and M. J. Vermaseren, 349-75. Etudes préliminaires aux religions orientales dans l'Empire romain, vol. 91. Leiden: E. J. Brill, 1981.

Smith, Jonathan Z. *Drudgery Divine: On the Comparison of Early Christianities and the Religions of Late Antiquity*. Chicago Studies in the History of Judaism. Chicago: University of Chicago Press, 1990.

Smith, Morton. *Jesus the Magician.* New York: Harper & Row, 1978.

PART ONE

DEFINING MAGIC AND RITUAL POWER

CHAPTER ONE

TRADING PLACES

Jonathan Z. Smith

As the novelist, Tom Robbins, has observed, all human beings may be divided into just two classes: those who think that everything can be divided into just two classes, and those who don't. The putative category "magic" is a prime example of such duality. Indeed, in the history of its imagination, it has been doubly dual, being counter-distinguished from *both* elements in another persistent and strong duality—from both "science" *and* "religion." On logical grounds alone, this reduplicated dualism should give rise to some suspicion of duplicity, for, if something is the opposite of one member of another opposition, it ought to have, at the very least, a close affinity to the second member of the pair. But, in the "pre-logical" modes of thought which so often characterize anthropological and religious studies discourse within the human sciences (and so rarely characterize the thought of those peoples they claim to study), the law of the excluded middle has long since been repealed, most commonly by means of a shift from a logical to a chronological rhetoric. Employing an evolutionary hierarchy, the one ("magic") is encompassed by either one of its opposites ("religion" or "science"), with "magic" invariably labeled "older" and "religion" or "science" labeled "newer." (Note that this same hierarchy is often applied to the relations between "religion" and "science.") In this strategic model, as Rick Shweder describes it,

> The image is one of subsumption, progress and hierarchical inclusion. Some forms of understanding are described as though they were incipient forms of other understandings, and those other forms of understanding are described as though they can do everything the incipient forms can do plus more.[1]

Hence, many accounts of "magic" adopt a *privative* definition of their subject matter. "Magic" resembles "religion" (e.g., Rodney

---

[1] R. A. Shweder, *Thinking Through Cultures* (Cambridge: Harvard University Press, 1991), 118.

Stark and William Bainbridge[2]) or "science" (e.g., Robin Horton[3])
lacking only some of the latter's traits. In such formulations, a
promised difference in kind turns out to be a postulated difference
of degree—or, more pointedly, of development—and one is entitled to ask what sort of difference that sort of difference makes?

This is, perhaps, the largest single family of theoretical, substantive definitions of "magic": "magic" is "religion" or "science,"
or an incipient form of "religion" or "science," but for the lack of
this or that—or, less commonly, but for an excess of this or that.
(More popular in early apologetic accounts, but still present in
scholars such as H. D. Betz,[4] is the reverse ploy which sees
"magic" as a degraded form of "religion" or "science.")

This dominant understanding is an odd sort of definition. Not
only does it break the conventional definitory rules (especially
those against the use of a negative definiens), but also because it is
typically inconsistent in its application of differentia. For example, many phenomena that we unhestitatingly label "religious" or
understand to be "religions" (notwithstanding the long and tortured
debates over how those terms are to be defined) differ among
themselves, on some scale of absent or excessive characteristics, at
least as much, if not more, than "magic" does from "religion" in
many theories. What privileges the characteristics chosen for the
"magic/religion" duality? Or, to ask this question another way, if
the purpose of a model in academic discourse—if the heart of its
explanatory power—is that it does *not* accord exactly with any
cluster of phenomena ("map is not territory"), by what measurement is the incongruency associated with those phenomena labeled
"magical" by scholars (rather than, say, "religious") judged to be so
great as to require the design and employment of another model?

This becomes clearer if we turn to the second major family of
theoretical, substantive definitions of "magic." While exhibiting
many of the strategic features of the first, this second group adopts
an atemporal rather than an explicit (or implicit) developmental
perspective. This approach holds that "magic" is essentially *synonymous* with this or that aspect of the total ensemble of
"religion." (Note that this understanding mimics the first family in

---

[2] R. Stark and W. S. Bainbridge, *A Theory of Religion* (New York: P. Lang,
1987), 40 *et passim*.

[3] R. Horton, "African Traditional Thought and Western Science," *Africa* 37
(1967): 50-71, 159-87.

[4] See, for example, H. D. Betz, "Magic and Mystery in the Greek Magical Papyri," in C. A. Faraone and D. Obbink, eds., *Magika Hiera: Ancient Greek Magic
and Religion* (Oxford: Oxford University Press, 1991), 244-59, esp. 253-54.

viewing "magic" as encompassed by "religion" and as exhibiting either a lack or an excess. The old notion of magic as "compulsion," for example, judges "magic" to be either an inadequacy or an exaggeration, depending on the overall theoretical [and apologetic] stance of the scholar.) Thus, Stanley J. Tambiah, in his recently published Morgan Lectures, *Magic, Science, Religion and the Scope of Rationality*, reviews and criticizes the usual roundup of suspects—from Tylor and Frazer to Malinowski and Evans-Pritchard—in order to make his main point, that magic is essentially "performative utterance."[5] True, but even leaving aside the on-going arguments with and reformulations of Austin's original proposals in differing ways by both philosophers and linguists, so are a whole host of human utterances in a wide variety of concrete, pragmatic contexts, including a large number of expressions, as Tambiah would acknowledge, usually classified as "religious" rituals.

The second family of theoretical, substantive definitions depends, as has been already suggested, upon a notion of some aspect of "magic" being synonymous with some aspect of "religion" (albeit often with a different valence). Synonymy is theoretically useful precisely in that two (or more) terms are thought to be so close that their micro-distinctions take on enormous clarificatory power. While of no use whatever for scholarly purposes, I refer, for a sense of what I mean, to the entry "magic" in *Webster's New Dictionary of Synonyms* (1968 edition):

> Magic, sorcery, witchcraft, witchery, wizardry, alchemy, thaumaturgy are comparable rather than synonymous in their basic senses. In extended use they are sometimes employed indifferently without regard to the implications of their primary senses and with little distinction from the most inclusive term, magic, but all are capable of being used discriminatingly and with quite distinctive implications.

But if one cannot specify the distinctions with precision, as is usually the case in definitions of this second type, the difference makes no difference at all.

From E. B. Tylor's notion of "magic" as misapplied logic (a strong example of the first family) to Claude Lévi-Strauss's under-

---

[5] S. J. Tambiah, *Magic, Science, Religion and the Scope of Rationality* (New York and Cambridge: Cambridge University Press, 1990), 58, 82-83, *et passim*. Cf. Tambiah, "The Magical Power of Words," *Man*, n.s. 3 (1968): 175-208, and Tambiah, "A Performative Approach to Ritual," *Proceedings of the British Academy* 65 (1979): 113-69. These latter two articles are a more sophisticated presentation of his thesis than that in *Magic, Science, Religion*.

standing of magic as an exaggeration of human analogies (an equally strong example of the second family), substantive definitions of "magic" have proven empty in concrete instances and worthless when generalized to characterize entire peoples, whole systems of thought or world-views. Such substantive definitions have failed for the logical and procedural reasons already suggested (among others). In their turn, these flaws have been brought about by the fact that in academic discourse "magic" has almost always been treated as a *contrast* term, a shadow reality known only by looking at the reflection of its opposite ("religion," "science") in a distorting fun-house mirror. Or, to put this another way, within the academy, "magic" has been made to play the role of an evaluative rather than an interpretative term, and, as such, usually bears a negative valence.

While such negative valuations can, at times, be traced to specific ideologies, causality is rarely that clear. The notion of "magic" as "other" is far more deeply engrained. It is already present, to be used rather than created by these ideologies. As is the case with the majority of our most disturbing and mischievous hegemonic formulations, the negative valence attributed to "magic" has been, and continues to be, an element in our common-sense—and, therefore, apparently unmotivated—way of viewing cultural affairs.

Consider the shifting taxonomies and genealogies we employ (without ever troubling to account for the shift). For example, in most late 19th and early 20th century works, shamanism is the very type of "magic." In more recent treatments, shamanism has been transferred to the "religious." (For Mircea Eliade it is the most transcendent form of "archaic religion"; for Tom Overholt it is the very type of "prophetic religion.") What has changed is *not* the data—by and large, the old, circumpolar ethnographies continue to be the prime sources—what has changed is the attitude of the scholar.

For these (and for other) reasons, I see little merit in continuing the use of the substantive term "magic" in second-order, theoretical, academic discourse. We have better and more precise scholarly taxa for each of the phenomena commonly denotated by "magic" which, among other benefits, create more useful categories for comparison. For any culture I am familiar with, we can trade places between the corpus of materials conventionally labeled "magical" and corpora designated by other generic terms (e.g., healing, divining, execrative) with no cognitive loss. Indeed, there would be a gain in that this sort of endeavor promises to yield a set of middle-range typologies—always the most useful kind—more adequate than the highly general, usually dichotomous, taxa commonly employed ("sympathetic/contagious," "witchcraft/sorcery," "benevolent/malevolent"—or even Christina Larner's more sophisticated typology of three types with two sub-types[6]). Similarly, such mid-range taxa would be more adequate than the highly specific categories employed for particular cultures, usually constructed either anthropologically by function, or philologically by native vocabulary, formulae, or text-type.

John Middleton was right in his meditation on Lévi-Strauss, although he shrunk from its consequences:

> If magic is a subjective notion . . . then it can have little or no meaning in cross-cultural analysis or understanding. The concept of magic is in itself empty of meaning and thus susceptible to the recognition of any meaning we care to give it; following this, Lévi-Strauss has implied that the category of magic must be "dissolved."[7]

The matter, however, will not be so simply disposed of. As with a large class of religious studies vocabulary (e.g., "myth"), the name will not be easily rectified. Abstention, "just say 'No'," will not settle "magic." For, unlike a word such as "religion," "magic" is not only a second-order term, located in academic discourse. It is as well, cross-culturally, a native, first-order category, occurring in ordinary usage which has deeply influenced the evaluative language of the scholar. Every sort of society appears to have a term (or, terms) designating some modes of ritual activities, some beliefs, and some ritual practitioners as dangerous, and/or illegal, and/or deviant. (Even some texts, conventionally labeled "magical" by scholars, themselves contain charms and spells against what the text labels "magic."[8])

These ethnoclassifications differ widely and can be quite complex. Moreover, it is far from clear that, in many cases, these native distinctions as to dangerous, illicit, and/or deviant practitioners and practices can be properly rendered, in all their nuances, by the common English terms "magic," "witchcraft," "sorcery."

---

[6] C. Larner, *Witchcraft and Religion: The Politics of Popular Belief* (Oxford: Blackwell, 1985), 80-82.

[7] J. Middleton, "Theories of Magic," in M. Eliade, ed., *Encyclopedia of Religion* (New York: Macmillan, 1987), 9.88.

[8] See, for example, the well-known "Moses Phylactery" from Acre, most recently edited by R. D. Kotansky, "Texts and Studies in the Greco-Egyptian Magic Lamellae" (diss., University of Chicago, 1988), text no. 36 (esp. 220-22) and his general treatment of "counter-magic" in the "Introduction" (8-10).

Nevertheless, the observation of these native categories has generated a number of important interpretative strategies, although it is
now becoming clear, despite earlier enthusiasms, that these have
often complicated rather than simplified the problem.

First, as pioneered by Africanists, the focus on native categories
has shifted attention away from the act and actor to the accuser
and the accusation. "Magic," in this sense, is almost always a third-
person attribution rather than a first-person self-designation, and it
becomes essential for the interpreter to explain the charge. Note
that this presents a set of extraordinary documentary problems
which have been overcome in only a relatively few areas of research. Pay attention to one Africanist's research protocol which
catalogues the kinds of data required:

> The significant point about a given instance of accusation is not that it is
> made . . . but that it is made in a given field situation. (An account of)
> this situation would include not only the structure of the groups and sub-
> groups to which the accuser and accused belong but also their extant divi-
> sion into transient alliances and factions on the basis of immediate inter-
> ests, ambitions, moral aspirations, and the like. It would also include as
> much of the history of these groups, subgroups, alliances and factions as
> would be considered relevant to the understanding of the accusation . . . .
> It would further include . . . demographic data about subgroup and fac-
> tional fluctuations over the relevant time period together with information
> about the biological and sociological factors bearing on these such as epi-
> demics, rise and fall in the birth and death rates, labor migrations, wars
> and feuds . . . .[9]

Due, in large part, to the absence of the sorts of data required, I
know of *no* convincing application of this interpretative strategy,
for example, to ancient accusations of magic. In this latter area of
research, generalities abound concerning power relations—many of
which I find intuitively satisfying—but they lack the sociological
specificity, the documentary gravity that confers plausibility to
some of the work of colleagues in African, European, and American studies, to name the most obvious examples.

Second, focus on the accusation and the accuser implies that one
can usually speak only of the "magician" rather than of "magic."
Almost any act, or, in some cases, no act at all (this latter possibility alluding to the long-standing discussion engendered by Evans-

---

    [9] V. Turner, "Witchcraft and Sorcery: Taxonomy versus Dynamics" (1964),
reprinted in Turner, *The Forest of Symbols* (Ithaca: Cornell University Press,
1967), 115.

Pritchard's Zande materials[10]) can give rise to the accusation. It is the accused individual or group, and their network of social relations and loci in relation to the accusing individual or group, that is held to be the prime motivation for the charge. The "evidence" adduced by the native accuser is held by the scholar to be secondary, and usually utterly conventional.

This has led to a noticeable bias in the literature towards the powerless. But this is an unwarranted simplification. While the accusation of "magic" may well be a power ploy that marginalizes the accused, the accusation may equally well be between members of elite groups (as the practice of "magic" may well be directed by the marginal against elites).

One cannot have it both ways. The shift to a social understanding of the relations between the accuser and the accused *forbids* any attempt at a substantive, theoretical definition of "magic." As Victor Turner has observed,

> Almost every society recognizes such a wide variety of mystically harmful techniques that it may be positively misleading to impose on them a dichotomous classification. Their name is legion, their form is protean for the very reason that individual *spite* is capricious.[11]

I wish I could share the confidence of some scholars that, although a substantive definition of "magic" is rendered impossible by a sociological approach, the sorts of social fissures and conflicts revealed by the accusations are generalizable. A review of the ethnographic, historical and analytic literature makes clear that they are not. Any form of *ressentiment*, for real or imagined reasons (see Aberle on "relative deprivation"[12]), *may* trigger a language of alienating displacement of which the accusation of magic is *just one possibility* in any given culture's rich vocabulary of alterity.

---

[10] E. E. Evans-Pritchard, *Witchcraft, Oracles and Magic among the Azande* (Oxford: Clarendon, 1937), 21: "A witch performs no rite, utters no spell and possesses no medicines. An act of witchcraft is a psychic act." If this distinction be accepted as generalizable beyond the Zande (by no means an uncontroversial proposal), then so much for Christian apologetic New Testament scholars who would acquit Jesus of magic on the grounds that he employed no spells or magic *materia*. In Zande terms, Jesus may be no sorcerer, but might well be a witch!

[11] Turner, "Witchcraft and Sorcery," 124-25, emphasis added.

[12] D. Aberle, "A Note on Relative Deprivation Theory as Applied to Millenarian and Other Cult Movements," in S. Thrupp, ed., *Millennial Dreams in Action* (The Hague: Mouton, 1962), 209-14.

Third, by focusing scholarly attention on the accusation, and given most scholars' work-a-day common-sense positivism, it is all too easy to reduce the charge of "magic" to one of mere social placement. One can read entire monographs, especially on European materials, without gaining the sense that anyone might have "actually" practiced "magic" or "witchcraft." As an example, I would call attention to the lively debate which has exercised social historians of Salem for the past decade and a half. While their social analyses agree to a significant degree, they sharply disagree over the question as to whether the accused (or others) "actually" practiced "magic."[13]

Fourth, and closely related to the above, the social approach, ironically, cannot seem to handle those cultural instances where "magicians" function as a craft, as a profession, either as an hereditary office or as a guild with procedures for both training and incorporation. The accusatory model's bias towards the powerless often ignores the positive association of native conceptions of "magic" with power. (The latter was one of the strengths of the evolutionary understanding which stressed, although often in naive or polemical forms, the power relations between what it termed "magic" and priestcraft or kingship.) The same issue recurs in those cultural instances where "magic" is a "high class" phenomenon, or where its practice confers social prestige.

A fifth and final caution is more strictly methodological in nature. Giving primacy to native terminology yields, at best, *lexical* definitions which, historically and statistically, tell how a word is used. But, lexical definitions are almost always useless for scholarly work. To remain content with how "they" understand "magic" may yield a proper description, but little explanatory power. How "they" use a word cannot substitute for the *stipulative* procedures by which the academy contests and controls second-order, specialized usage. However, this returns us to the beginning of this essay and the problematics of a proper, theoretical definition of "magic."

*   *   *

I should now like to turn to the Preisendanz corpus, as modified and translated in Betz's edition, and offer some reflections by a generalist for whom the label "Greek Magical Papyri" constitutes

---

[13] This debate was largely engendered by the publication of Chadwick Hansen's *Witchcraft at Salem* (New York: Braziller, 1969).

something of a distraction.[14] After all, compared with the fragments, contextless quotations, literary descriptions and artistic representations, the corpus, even as it now stands, represents something quite precious: *one of the largest collections of functioning ritual texts, largely in Greek, produced by ritual specialists that has survived from late antiquity.* The fact that the size of the collection could have been more than doubled by the inclusion of parallel materials from other Greek and Greek-based corpora only serves to reinforce its importance.[15]

My own interest in late antique "magical" texts has stemmed, primarily, from my long-standing preoccupation with themes related to place, especially the shift in the locus of religious experience and expression from a permanent sacred center, the archaic temple, to a place of temporary sacrality sanctified by a mobile religious specialist (in this case, the so-called "magician").[16] I propose to continue that meditation by calling attention to some features of the Preisendanz-Betz corpus which have little to do with issues of "magic" as conventionally perceived.

---

[14] K. Preisendanz, *Papyri Graecae Magicae* (Leipzig and Berlin: B. G. Teubner, 1928-41); K. Preisendanz and A. Henrichs, *Papyri Graecae Magicae*, 2nd ed. (Stuttgart: Verlag Teubner, 1973-74); H. D. Betz, ed., *The Greek Magical Papyri in Translation* (Chicago: University of Chicago Press, 1986-). All citations will be to the Betz translation with occasional small emendations.

[15] Additional "handbook" materials could have been included from the Byzantine documents published by A. Delatte, *Anecdota Atheniensia* (Paris: E. Champion; Liège: Imp. H. Vaillant-Carmaune, 1927), and the Coptic materials published by A. M. Kropp, *Ausgewählte koptische Zaubertexte* (Brussels: Edition de la Fondation égyptologique reine Elisabeth, 1930-33), cf. P. A. Mirecki, "The Coptic Hoard of Spells from the University of Michigan," in M. Meyer and R. Smith, eds., *Ancient Christian Magic: Coptic Texts of Ritual Power* (San Francisco: HarperSanFrancisco, 1994), 293-310, and the greatly expanded version in Mirecki, "The Coptic Wizard's Hoard," *HTR* 87 (in press). Likewise the amuletic materials collected by R. D. Kotansky, "Texts and Studies in the Greco-Egyptian Magic Lamellae" (diss., University of Chicago, 1988). But such expansions accept whatever commonsense criteria for inclusion Preisendanz-Betz had in mind. There are, as well, individual pieces in *PGM* which could trade places with individual items in other Greek collections, and vice versa, especially, M. Bertholet, *Collection des anciens alchemistes grecs* (Paris: Ch. - Em Ruelle, 1887-88) and the *Catalogus codicum astrologorum graecorum* (Brussels: Lamertin, 1898-), not to speak of the relations of individual items in *PGM* to even wider circles of texts from herbaria and oracles to Gnostica and Hermetica.

[16] See, among others, J. Z. Smith, *Map Is Not Territory* (Leiden: E. J. Brill, 1978), 172-207; Smith, "Towards Interpreting Demonic Powers in Hellenistic and Roman Antiquity," in *ANRW*, 2.16.1: 425-39.

As part of a larger pattern of religious persistence and change in late antiquity, and for a diversity of reasons ranging from the economic to the aesthetic, from the political and demographic to the ethical and theological, in a number of traditions, temple sacrifice, especially that requiring animal victims, declined. As sacrifice was the raison d'etre of the archaic temple, the chief currency of both its divine and human economies, this meant that temples must either be revalorized or abandoned. A temple, an altar, without sacrifice is a mere monument. (See, already, the admittedly polemic account in Joshua 22:10-34.) This meant, as well, that sacrifice would have either to be dis-placed or re-placed.

The rationales and strategies for these latter processes were varied. Sometimes, as in the case of Orphic, Neoplatonic and Neo-Pythagorean traditions, a moral cast—no bloodshed—was given to older cultic rules prohibiting pollution by dead animal products, corpses and blood with a consequent recovery and refocus on archaic practices of cereal and incense offerings. (See, for example, the fumigation recipes which form part of the titula of seventy-eight of the eighty-seven late 3rd century *"Orphic" Hymns.*)

In the case of the emergent Judaisms and Christianities, spurred only in part by the destruction of the Temple in Jerusalem, the locus of sacrifice was shifted from Temple to domicile, and the act of sacrifice was wholly replaced by narrative and discourse. Early rabbinic traditions talked endlessly about sacrifices no longer performed, in many cases, never experienced, and, in its ritual praxis, substituted speech for deed. The best known example is the dictum attributed to Rabbi Gamliel: "Whoever does not say these three things on Passover has not fulfilled his obligations," with the first of the three being the sacrifice of the Paschal lamb (M. *Pesahim* 10.5). This is a sentence *about* ritual speech which, by virtue of its inclusion in the later *Passover Haggadah,* has itself *become* ritual speech.

Some early Christians developed the utterly rhetorical metaphor of sacrifice as an important component of their narrative understanding of Jesus' death. Over time, the Christian use of the sacrificial analogy was extended to characterize a whole host of human phenomena by traditions that never "actually" sacrificed, including the sacrament of marriage post-Vatican II.

Christian liturgy maintained the language of "altar," "smoke," and of the sacrificial elements—now wholly metaphorized; the eucharistic flesh and blood was subsumed to a narrative of paradigmatic institution which was set in a domestic, non-sacrificial context.

Of all the documents from late antiquity, I know of *none* more filled with the general and technical terminology and the praxis of sacrifice than those texts collected by modern scholars under the title Greek Magical Papyri. They are all the more important because they display, as well, a thoroughly domesticated understanding of sacrifice.

Within the papyri,[17] while a small number of the ritual *topoi* are outside—in an open place (IV.900), a deserted place (III.616), a tomb (III.25,286) or by a river (III.286; IV.27)[18]—the vast majority of rituals which give a locale are set in domestic space, in the practitioner's house (e.g., I.83,84; II.148; III.193; IV.2188), or more rarely in the client's place of business or home (VIII.59; XII.104; cf. IV.2373-2440 where it is implied). As a substantial number of rituals are for procuring some sort of dream oracle, "your bedroom" predominates (e.g., II.1-182; IV.62; VII.490, 593-619, 628-42, 664-85). There are, as well, a number of references to rituals performed on "your housetop" (I.70; IV.2711; LXI.6), "lofty roof" (I.56; IV.2469, 2711), or upper room (IV.171), chiefly as a place for receiving a celestial power who is then conducted to "the room in which you reside" (e.g., I.80-84).

Within this domestic space, there is a high concern for purity in both the rituals of preparation and reception. The practitioner is to abstain from sex, from animal food (including fish), and from "all uncleanness" (I.40-1, 54, 290-92, *et passim*). The ritual site is to be a "clean room" (IV.2189), a "pure room" (VII.875[?])—"let your place be cleaned of all pollution" (II.148).

Within the "clean," domestic place, the chief ritual is that of sacrifice, most commonly of generic incense (e.g., IV.215; V.395; VIII.58), with frankincense the most frequently specified (e.g., I.63; IV.908, 1269, 1909). Some dozen other aromatic plant substances, from gums (e.g., III.23) to spices (e.g., III.308; IV.919), were also employed. Other vegetable offerings include roses (IV.2235), sumac (IV.2235), mulberries (III.611), beets (III.614), moss (LXXII.3), cakes (XII.22) and fruits (XII.22), along with libations of wine and/or milk (e.g., III.694).

By contrast to these common vegetable offerings, sacrifices *wholly* made up of animal victims or products are rare. The largest

---

[17] Please note that my citations from the Betz edition are exemplary and not exhaustive.

[18] Other outside loci include: a bathhouse (II.49); a stadium (II.43); the eastern section of a village (IV.58-9); a bean field (IV.769); "a place where grass grows" (IV.3091); a crossroad (LXX.16).

group requires the sacrifice of a white cock (IV.26-51,2189-92, 2359-72; XIII.364-82 [+ pigeon]). The only instance of the whole offering of a mammal remains an editorial conjecture (IV.2394-99).

More common than purely animal sacrifices, though less common than purely vegetable offerings, are sacrifices of mixed animal and plant substances. Their usual form is a series of plants plus one animal part, usually its dung or an organ (e.g., I.285; IV.1309-15, 3092). If it is a vegetable series plus a whole animal, the latter is invariably a bird (e.g., IV.2892). Some of the animal *materia* (e.g., dung, eggs, a snake's shed skin) do not require the killing of the animal, while other *materia*—"wolf's eye" (I.285), "frog's tongue" (V.203)—may well be code names for plants (see XII.401-44), as is certainly the case for the ingredient, "pig's snout" (III.468; V.198, 371). Other texts appear to place differing valences on animal and plant offerings, for example IV.2873-79:

> For doing good, offer storax, myrrh, sage, frankincense, a fruit pit. But for doing harm, offer magical material of a dog and dappled goat [(gloss:) or, in a similar way, of a virgin untimely dead].[19]

The impression that animal offerings were not the central focus is strengthened by the fact that a sharp knife, the one, indispensible requirement in animal sacrifice, is mentioned as an implement just three times in the corpus (XIII.91-96, 373-75, 646-51).

The other ritual implements mentioned introduce another important and highly characteristic element. They are not only highly portable, but appear to be *miniaturized*. The table, the throne, the tripod, and the censer seem, themselves, to be small and to hold relatively small objects. The sacrificial altar—most often constructed of two or more (unbaked) bricks, but never more than seven—seems especially so. What must be the scale of an altar on which is sacrificed "on grapevine charcoal, one sesame seed and [one] black cumin seed" (IV.919)?

In addition to these common, though miniaturized, implements is a set of small wooden shrines. Eight appear to be mentioned in the corpus: a juniper wood shrine that holds a mummified falcon (I.21-26); a small, wooden shrine, set up on a table covered with pure linen, enclosing a tripod, censer and small figurine (III.290-320); a lime wood shrine in which lies a small figurine of Hermes made of dough (V.370-99); a shrine of olive wood containing a

---

[19] For a most complex example of differing evaluation, in several recensions, see the slander spells involving "hostile" offerings, IV.2571-2707.

statuette of Selene (VII.866-79); a small temple, standing on a table, into which a small dish is placed in which the first morsels of food from a meal are offered (X.1-9); two small (?) temples connected by a single sheet of papyrus (V.159-60, admittedly obscure); and, most suggestive of all, IV.3125-71, which contains a ritual for fashioning a phylactery which will cause any "place or temple" to flourish, to become a "marvel," and to be "talked about throughout the whole world." (It would appear that this "place or temple," for which favor is being asked, is the shop of the ritual's patron [IV.3170, editorial conjecture].) The ritual involves the construction of a small, three-headed wax statue, "three handbreadths high," which is deified by animal (?) sacrifice and placed within a "little juniper wood temple" wreathed with olive. The practitioner is enjoined, "Now feast [with the god], singing to him all night long."

As this last text makes plain, the "little" temples and shrines, in this latter case one housing a figure 0.3 meters high, are treated as if they were major edifices housing a divine image and a cult table. Sacrifice is held before them; a cultic meal follows with a liturgy sung. In other cases, incubation is practiced before the miniature (e.g., V.390-423) rather than sleeping within the large temple precincts. In still other rituals, the divine being is conducted to a small throne, in an ordinary but purified room, from which it gives oracles or provides a powerful guiding presence (e.g., I.293-347; cf. I.74-90), just as in the throne room of a major temple complex. These quite typical procedures within the Greek Magical Papyri suggest that the practitioner's "clean room" and the rituals performed therein are to be understood, to no small degree, as *replacements* of (and for) temple space and rituals.

Alternatively, while the small shrines resemble the portable *naiskoi* commonly carried in religious processions, the little shrines, ritual implements, small statues and ritual practices have their closest parallels, as Fritz Graf has convincingly argued, in small-scale, private, domestic rituals conducted by ordinary householders for their household deities and/or ancestors[20] (a comparison that deserves further detailed study). From this point of view, the domestication of ritual has *already* occurred. What is different about the Greek Magical Papyri is that these practices have been divorced from a familial setting, becoming both highly mobile and professionalized.

---

[20] F. Graf, "Prayer in Magic and Religious Ritual," in Faraone and Obbink, eds., *Magika Hiera*, 195f.

In either case, the sacrality of the place is established, *tempo-rarily*, through ritual activities, and by virtue of the direct experi-ence of a mobile, professional ritualist (the "magician") with an equally mobile deity.

One further matter. If one reads through the entire corpus with an eye towards ritual activities, it is not purification, nor incuba-tion, nor even sacrifice that predominates. Rather, the chief ritual activity within the Greek Magical Papyri appears to be *the act of writing itself.* The vocabulary of inscription constitutes one of the larger groups. Alongside the evident concern for the accurate transmission of a professional literature marked, among other features, by scribal glosses and annotations is an overwhelming belief in the efficacy of writing, especially in the recipes which focus on the fashioning of amulets and phylacteries—themselves, miniaturized, portable, powerful written texts of papyrus, metal, stone and bone.

The most common writing material is a sheet of papyrus, often described as "clean," "pure," "choice," or "hieratic." While blood and other *magica materia* occasionally function as writing fluids (most dramatically, VIII.70-72), most of the inks, some of which are quite complex, are variants of the common, everyday combi-nation of a burnt substance for pigment (e.g., charcoal, soot, lampblack) and a gum as a fixative. The most frequent combina-tion is "myrrh ink" (*smurnomelan*, or *zmurnomelan*).

The technology of ink mimics the technology of the vegetable sacrifice, with burning and aromatic gums serving as their common denominators:

> The (preparation of the) ink is as follows: In a purified container, burn myrrh, cinquefoil, and wormwood; grind them to a paste and use them (II.36; cf. I.244-46).

Within the corpus, the instructions for the preparation of ink are often given a liturgical rubric, *skeuē melanos* (e.g., I.243; IV.3199; VII.998), at times in immediate juxtaposition to the rubric for the sacrificial offering.

The ritual of writing is more than a replacement of the archaic temple as a major site of scribal activities and library of ritual books—although, at times, use is made of the familiar motif of allegedly finding a book or spell in a prestigious temple, as in one of the older, surviving papyri, CXXII.1-4. It is, rather, a displace-ment of ritual practice into writing, analogous, in important re-spects, to the displacement of sacrifice into speech in the emergent Judaisms and Christianities (discussed above), as well as a continuation of the impulse towards miniaturization.

In a difficult analogy in *La Pensée sauvage*, Lévi-Strauss has written of "the intrinsic value of a small scale model" as a process of compensating "for the renunciation of sensible dimensions by the acquisition of intelligible dimensions."[21] In a somewhat similar vein, the literary critic and folklorist, Susan Stewart, who has written the most extended meditation on miniaturization,[22] insists that small does not equal insignificant (in both senses of the term), that:

> a reduction in the physical dimension of an object depicted can, in fact, increase the dimension of significance .... The miniature always tends towards exaggeration—it is a selection of detail that magnifies detail in the same movement by which it reduces detail.[23]

If ritual, with its characteristic strategies for achieving focus, with its typical concern for "microadjustment," often is, itself, a miniaturization that is, at one and the same time, an exaggeration of everyday actions, as major theorists of ritual from Freud to Lévi-Strauss have rightly maintained,[24] then miniaturization, when applied *to* ritual, as is the case in the Greek Magical Papyri, becomes a sort of *ritual of ritual*, existing, among other loci, in a space best described as discursive or intellectual.[25]

---

[21] C. Lévi-Strauss, *La Pensée sauvage* (Paris: Plon, 1962), 34-36; English translation, *The Savage Mind* (Chicago: University of Chicago Press, 1966), 23-24, esp. 24.

[22] S. Stewart, *On Longing: Narratives of the Miniature, the Gigantic, the Souvenir, the Collection* (Baltimore: Johns Hopkins University Press, 1984), chapter 2.

[23] S. Stewart, *Nonsense: Aspects of Intertextuality in Folklore and Literature* (Baltimore: John Hopkins University Press, 1980), 100-01.

[24] Cf. J. Z. Smith, *To Take Place: Toward Theory in Ritual* (Chicago: Chicago University Press, 1987), 103-12 *et passim*.

[25] The second part of this essay has been adopted from my paper, "Constructing a Small Place," delivered at the Joshua Prawer Memorial Conference, "Sacred Space: Shrine, City, Land," sponsored by the Israel Academy of Sciences and Humanities, Jerusalem, June 1992.

CHAPTER TWO

EXCLUDING THE CHARMING:
THE DEVELOPMENT OF THE GREEK CONCEPT OF MAGIC

Fritz Graf

Academic and other interest in magic is rapidly growing.[1] We are already quite close to the state of affairs described, in about 1550, by Agostino Nifo, a then famous Italian philosopher and necromancer: "Magic is taught in many universities, and terrible things happen there, and it is difficult to explain all this by Aristotelian principles alone." Nifo presumably would have had equal difficulties in explaining the modern boom of magical studies.[2]

In our society, in religious, ethnographical or psychological studies as well as in daily life, magic tends to be taken as a human universal: all societies have their magical tradition, as they have their myths and their rituals. This is an attitude which should be adopted with more caution than is customarily the case. The term magic belongs primarily to our own intellectual tradition, where it has been handed down through the teaching of the church to those people (often missionaries) who detected magic among the "savage" non-Western peoples, and from them to the fathers of social and religious anthropology. It is no surprise, then, that in the past not a few anthropologists contended that magic was an ethnocentric concept whose helpfulness when applied outside of Western societies would be highly questionable[3]—though that might be an all too naive Whorfian approach.

This essay does not intend to renew the debate, nor will it really enter into the related subject of how to define magic in ancient societies. Henk Versnel recently asserted that any definition other

---

[1] This paper takes up some ideas which are more fully treated in my *La magie dans l'antiquité gréco-romaine. Idéologie et pratiques* (Paris: Belles Lettres, 1994).

[2] Agostino Nifo, *De daemonibus*, Venice 1553, f 72^V; the citation stems from Paola Zambelli, *L'ambigua natura della magia. Filosofi, streghe, riti nel Rinascimento* (Milan: Mondadori, 1991), 212.

[3] Most prominent: M. and R. Wax, "The notion of magic," *Current Anthropology* 4 (1963): 495-513; often reprinted.

than an "outside" (*etic*) definition would be impossible[4]; my position here will become implicitly clear during this essay. My aim rather is to show how both in Greece and later (and not independently) in Rome the concept of magic as something different from religion was developed in a quite specific historical situation—in the course of the Sophist enlightenment in Athens and in Ciceronian Rome. This development would influence deeply our own modern conception of magic.

*　　*　　*

Some lexicological considerations may serve as a starting point for larger issues. Ancient Greek had several terms to denote magic and the magicians: *magos* (and *mageia*), *goēs* (and *goēteia*), *agurtēs*, and terms deriving from *pharmakon*. Most are attested early; only the terms related to *magos* seem comparably recent.

Magos appears for the first time in a Greek text of the end of the 6th century BCE and becomes more frequent during the classical period; it is a non-Greek word with an indisputed origin in the religious language of Persia,[5] where the *magos* is a priest or religious specialist.[6] Herodotus is the first to speak about the *magoi*, as a tribe or secret society (Herodotus is somewhat ambiguous here) whose members perform the royal sacrifices and the funeral rites and who practice divination and the interpretation of dreams.[7] A generation later, Xenophon calls them "technicians in matters divine."[8] Plato takes over this ethnographic definition in the *Major Alcibiades* when, speaking about the instrúction of a young Persian nobleman, he gives a list of his foremost teachers, among them one who "teaches the art of the *magoi* (*mageia*) which derives from Zoroaster, the son of Oromasdes: it comprises the

---

[4] H. S. Versnel, "Some reflections on the relationship magic-religion," *Numen* 38 (1991): 177-97.

[5] Among the discussions, the contribution of A. D. Nock, "Paul and the Magus," in Nock, *Essays on Religion and the Ancient World*, ed. Zeph Stewart (Oxford: Clarendon Press, 1972), 308-30, is indispensable.

[6] For the Persian material and its Greek transformations, see J. Bidez and F. Cumont, *Les mages hellénisés. Zoroastre, Ostanes et Hystaspe d'après la tradition grecque* (Paris: Belles Lettres, 1938), and, for the classical age, the synthesis of E. J. Bickerman, "Darius I, Pseudo-Smerdis, and the Magi," in Bickerman, *Religions and Politics in the Hellenistic and Roman Periods*, ed. E. Gabba and M. Smith (Como: Athenaeum, 1985), 619-41.

[7] See F. Mora, *Religione e religioni nelle storie di Erodoto* (Milan: Jaca, 1985), 152.

[8] Xenophon, *Cyr.* 8,3,11.

cult of the gods."[9] Much later, Apuleius will use this passage, somewhat playfully, to revalorize the accusation of magic brought forward against him: Greeks and Romans could always remember that the *magoi* were basically priests from Persia; it is only Apollonius of Tyana who belittles their celebrity in the name of his own superior wisdom.[10]

But already in 5th-century Greece there is more to the *magoi*: they are not quite the ideal sages of Platonic tradition. The first attestation of the term is found already in the fragments of Heraclitus of Ephesus, himself a subject of the Persian King of Kings. Clement of Alexandria cites the text: "To whom does Heraclitus of Ephesus prophesy? To those who err in the night—to the *magoi*, the bacchants, the maenads, the *mystai* ... : to all those he threatens tortures after death, he threatens the fire, since what people think to be mysteries are impious deeds."[11] The slightly aberrant semantics of *magos*, which in Clement's time could only mean "sorcerer," guarantees the authenticity: in the list, the *magoi* range among adherents of different ecstatic cults, especially Dionysian ones, strange company for a wizard and sorcerer. *Magos*, then, must mean something else in this text, one of those itinerant priests whom Plato calls "seers and begging priests" (*manteis kai agurteis*) and which the Derveni Papyrus, an intriguing document from about 320 BCE, calls "professionals of ritual,"[12] specialists, that is, for secret and private rituals and initiations. Because their rituals are secret and mysterious, they are called *nuktipoloi*, "erring in the night." To an Ionian of the late 6th century BCE, a *magos* was not so much a wizard as a ritual specialist at the margins of society, with wide-ranging functions, ridiculed by some, secretly dreaded by many others.[13]

Half a century later, the word is used with the same semantics by Sophocles, in his *Oedipus Turannos* (397ss). Oedipus is angry about Creon and the seer Tiresias (whom he believes to be Creon's creature): furiously, he calls the seer "this *magos*, plotter of

---

[9] Plato, *Alc.mai.* 122 A.

[10] Apuleius, *Metamorph.* 25, 10; Philostratus, *vita Apollonii* 1, 26. Among Renaissance Neoplatonist magicians, this became a topos in order to justify their interest in magic; see Zambelli (1991), 27.

[11] Heraclitus, DK 12 B 14, from Clement, *Protr.* 22,2.

[12] Plato, *Rep.* 364 B; papyrus from Derveni: *Zeitschrift für Papyrologie und Epigraphik* 47 (1982): col. 16, 3s.

[13] For these itinerant priests, see W. Burkert, *The Orientalizing Revolution. Near Eastern Influence on Greek Culture in the Early Archaic Age* (Cambridge: Harvard University Press, 1991), chap. 2.

stratagems, crafty begging priest (*agurtēs*), who only sees the profit and is blind towards the rules of his art"; a few verses later, Oedipus calls him *mantis* ("seer"), another aspect of this same composite figure. The same two terms, *mantis* and *agurtēs*, appear in Plato's *Republic* (2,364B): *manteis kai agurtai* visit the doors of the rich and convince them "that they would possess a faculty which they obtained from the gods though sacrifices and incantations, to heal them through joy and feasts in case their ancestors or they themselves had committed some injustice; and in case they would like to harm an enemy, they would be able, at low cost, to injure righteous people as well as unrighteous ones through some incantation and *defixion* because they were able, as they brag about, to persuade the gods to help them." The passage is very significant: it presents a religious specialist who combines initiation into private mystery cults with "black magic." To heal the consequences of injustice is one of the aims of private "Orphic" and Bacchic mystery cults. From Plato to a fragment of Orpheus cited in Olympiodoros, psychic troubles (*mania*) are viewed as resulting from the crimes of ancestors, and what heals them are purificatory rituals (*katharmoi kai teletai*) in Plato and mystery rites (*orgia*) in Orpheus. These *manteis kai agurtai* are the prophets and initiators of Bacchic mystery rituals.[14] If one remembers that, in those circles, the ritual rested upon a complicated eschatology with rewards and punishments in the after-life, the passage of Heraclitus becomes highly ironic: the philosopher threatens those performing initiations with the same punishments from which they claimed to be able to free their clients.

On the other hand, these same practitioners also are specialists in "black magic," incantations and *defixiones*, which are intended to hurt an enemy. They are, thus, specialists also in those rites which we discern behind the many *defixiones* from Athenian wells and graves, the Attic voodoo dolls, some of which were detected in an archeological context contemporary to Plato.[15]

Another aspect of this usage of *magos* is its combination with *goēs*. A *goēs* is a complicated figure, combining ecstasy and ritual lament, healing rites and divination; the *goēs* has been connected with the world of the shamans.[16] But this connection would belong

---

[14] Plato, *Phaedr.* 244e; Orphicorum Fragmenta no. 232 Kern.

[15] See Chr. A. Faraone, "Talismans, Voodoo Dolls and Other Apotropaic Statues in Ancient Greece" (diss., Stanford University, 1988).

[16] W. Burkert, "Goēs. Zum griechischen Schamanismus," *Rheinisches Museum* 105 (1962): 36ss.

rather to prehistory. Plato, in his *Symposium*, connects the *goēs* with the phenomena which interest us here: Eros, according to Plato, is the intermediary between the divine and the human world, "therefore, divination belongs to him entirely and the devices of those priests who occupy themselves with sacrifices, initiations, incantation and with every sort of divination and sorcery (*goēteia*)."[17] Here, Plato collects all those rituals which have to do with the passage between the human and the divine realm, without taking notice of their widely differing valuation in society. In other passages, the *goēs* is nearly as badly regarded as the *magos*. Menon, in the dialogue named after him, blames Socrates for having him "enchanted and drugged and totally bewitched." Socrates, he continues, must have been happy to live in Athens, because in many other Greek poleis he would have been arrested and accused of being a sorcerer (*goēs*).[18] Athens, we learn incidentally, had less severe legislation against sorcery than other Greek cities— this might explain the amount of *defixiones* and voodoo-dolls found in 5th and 4th century BCE Athens. Only much later, in his *Laws*, Plato pleads for the introduction of severe laws against those "who, having lost their humanity, think that the gods do not exist or that they were careless or venal and who despise their fellow human beings and seduce (*psuchagōgōsi*) many of the living by pretending that they could seduce (*psuchagōgein*) the souls of the dead, and promise to persuade the gods through the magic of offerings and prayers and incantations (*thusiais kai euchais kai epōidais goēteuein*), thus proposing, in order to make money, to destroy individuals, families and entire cities." We have here the same three activities already mentioned in the *Republic*: (1) seducing the soul of the living and the dead, (2) healing the rich from the consequences of their own misdeeds and of those of their ancestors and, (3) practicing sorcery by means of divine help obtained through rituals at least partly parallel to the polis rituals (sacrifices and prayers) and, more specifically magical, through incantations.

To the old Plato, thus, all these religious practices which the begging priests and marginal mystagogues performed well outside the world of polis religion were punishable offenses. The reason is clear: the sorcerer is seen as a danger to the polis comparable to the *atheos*, one who denies the existence of the gods. Both jeopardize the just relation between human beings and gods. This would

---

[17] Plato, *Symp.* 202 E.
[18] Plato, *Meno* 80 B.

cause the loss of what is specifically human—therefore, Plato calls
the sorcerer *thēriōdēs*, "beastlike," with a term used to characterize
precultural humankind, from the theories of Prodicus, Plato's
senior, to late Greek philosophy.[19]

The combination, finally, of *goēteia* and *mageia* occurs for the
first time with Gorgias, in his *Encomium of Helena*. Here, the
sophist speaks about the power of rhetorically effective words:
"The ecstatic incantations of words bring joy and drive away
gloom; because, when the power of incantation enters our soul with
the help of belief, it charms and persuades and transforms the soul
through goetic art. There are two techniques of goetic and magic
art (*goēteia kai mageia*): both are the error of the soul and the
illusion of belief." Magic is an art of deception, and the power of
incantation rests on illusion—the negative connotations are evident. In the context of the text, this makes perfect sense: Gorgias
intends to exonerate Helen from the charge of adultery by presenting her as an innocent victim of Paris' overpowering magical
persuasion. To serve this end, flattering persuasion and magical
incantation are identified—in other contexts, Gorgias is perfectly
able to differentiate the two.[20]

This somewhat condensed analysis of Greek terminology of sorcery—*gōes*; *agurtēs*; *mageia*; *goeteia*; *mageuein*; *goēteuein*—
yields interesting results:

(1) What this lexical complex denotes is not identical to what
we would call magic in our contemporary definition. The Greek
terminology connects private mystery rituals with initiatory
sacrifices as well as divination and sorcery; their common denominator is that they do not belong to civic religion.

(2) The evaluation is ambiguous. Heraclitus and Plato despise
both magic and the mysteries, in the name of a spiritualized conception of religion and the divine which they share but which is
somewhat at odds with religious tradition. On the other hand, there
were those Athenian citizens of the upper classes who believed in
the efficacy of magic and who therefore used the services offered
by the seers and begging priests; and the vast majority of Athenians must have shared their attitude. On a more panhellenic level,
one discerns a difference in the juridical assessment of these rituals:
in classical times, there were many Greek poleis in which sorcery

---

[19] Plato, *legg.* 10, 909 A.
[20] Gorgias, DK 82 B 11, 10. For rhetoric and magic, see Jaqueline de Romilly,
Magic and Rhetoric in Ancient Greece (Cambridge: Harvard University Press,
1975).

was severely punished. Plato joins this negative assessment, not for juridical reasons, but from a more severe theological position.

Thus, we see that the Frazerian dichotomy between magic and religion is already present in Heraclitus and in Plato: in the *Laws*, *goēteia* is characterized by the intention to persuade the gods, while the proper conduct would be to leave them free choice; they know better than we what will prove useful to us. This comes close to Frazer's view that magic forces the gods, while religion prays submissively. Keith Thomas had argued that the Frazerian dichotomy had its roots in Protestant theology of the 17th century[21]; even though correct, this is somewhat shortsighted, since the dichotomy is deeply entrenched in the continuum of our cultural heritage.

*   *   *

Among all those terms, only *magos* and related terms are not attested before the 6th century BCE. *Goēs*, a word without a good Greek pedigree, preserves traces of more archaic functions well attuned to its etymology: it derives from *goos*, ritual lament, and the *goēs* is a socially marginal figure connected with the passage of the dead between the worlds. At least in Aeschylus, he is the one who calls the souls from their graves, which can be seen as an inversion of the more usual function implied in *goos*,[22] to accompany the dead to their grave. *Goēs* then must have a long past existence in Greece, although its first literary attestation does not predate that of *magos*.

Thus the term which was to displace all concurring terms, the Persian word *magos* (and its family of terms), is the most recent one, introduced in the 5th century BCE. To Greeks and Romans alike, the new word never lost its original association: *mageia* always was the art of the Persian priests. But already in the later 4th century BCE, this art has lost its historically correct relations with Persian ethnological realities. A fragment of Pseudo-Aristotle's dialogue *Magikos* points to this development: here the author opposes the then current view that *mageia* was sorcery, in the name of objective ethnography, asserting instead that "the

---

[21] K. Thomas, *Religion and the Decline of Magic. Studies in Popular Beliefs in Sixteenth and Seventeenth Century England* (London: Weidenfeld & Nicolson, 1971); see his "An anthropology of religion and magic II," *The Journal of Interdisciplinary History* 6 (1975): 91-109.

[22] Aeschylus, *Pers.* 687.

magoi do not know magical sorcery"; the ethnographer judges this a defamation of Persian religion. He is not alone in Plato's school in doing this: the above mentioned definition of *mageia* in the *First Alcibiades* (*therapeia tōn theōn*, "service of the gods") must have had the same polemical purpose.

Magic as something practiced by the priests of the Persians means not only a foreign, exotic and barbarian practice, it also means a practice emphatically opposed and hostile to the Greek tradition. Its appearance in 5th century Athens goes together with other signs for self-demarcation towards foreigners or outright xenophobia.[23] It also fits into a much wider mental structure which has been pointed out by Tylor: in many different cultures, sorcery and magic were thought to be the art of the hostile (or feared) neighbors and were named accordingly, from "primitive" and ancient Near Eastern cultures to the contemporary Swedes.[24]

Thus, the term *magos* originated not so much from real observation of Persian religion or from the presence of Persian priests on Greek soil, but from the desire to designate certain ritual and ideological attachments as foreign, unwanted, and dangerous, from inside Greek (or Athenian) religion, not from outside it.

* * *

To understand the forces behind what was going on when the Ionians and Athenians coined the term "Persian priests," *magoi*, for those religious specialists, one has to look back at the role magic and related phenomena played in Archaic Greece. Again, terminology is helpful.

Among the earliest terms is *pharmakon* and its verb *pharmattein*. In Archaic Greece, the word is not confined to what we would call magic. Helen uses an Egyptian *pharmakon* to drive away the gloomy mood of Menelaos and Telemachos, and Circe transforms Ulysses' crew into swine with the help of a *pharmakon*.[25] Ancient scholars already explained this by referring to witchcraft, and seen from their much later point of view, they might be right; but to the members of Homeric society, these *pharmaka* were potent drugs with supernatural, "magical" effects, but they were not used

---

[23] See Edith Hall, *Inventing the Barbarian* (Oxford: Clarendon Press, 1989); R. Garland, *Introducing New Gods* (London: Duckworth, 1992), 145-50.

[24] E. B. Tylor, *Primitive Culture. Researches Into the Development of Mythology, Philosophy, Religion, Art and Custom* (London: John Murray, 1873), 1.113-17.

[25] Helen: Homer, *Od.* 4,221; Circe: *ibid.* 10, 388ss.

for sorcery and witchcraft. The same word indicates a drug for healing wounds or for poison which ends a life in an unexpected way; Ulysses has to find a *pharmakon* to poison his arrows, and the suitors are afraid that Telemachos went away to procure himself a *pharmakon* which could kill them secretly.[26] Again, here we see substances whose effect goes beyond ordinary power—but here, we would categorize them not as magical but as medical or criminal.

Another Homeric term is *epaoidē/epoidē*, "incantation," a verbal utterance with supernatural effect. The only Homeric attestation values it positively: Ulysses' uncles use an *epaoidē* to stop the bleeding from his wound after he has been attacked by a boar. The word keeps its healing connotations as late as Plato, who uses it in long lists of medical therapies, drugs, burning, cutting, and incantation.[27] Plato also knows its negative "magical" connotation, but in his time, the differentiation between magical and scientific medicine has barely begun.

Thus, in Archaic Greece, no differentiation is made in the wider sphere of sorcery, healing and surreptitious killing. A myth told as late as Pindar, in his 4th *Pythian Ode* of 462 BCE, confirms this. Pindar narrates the well-known myth of how Jason seduced the young Medea in Kolchis and adds an otherwise unattested detail: in order to attain his goal, Jason used erotic magic, in a ritual which made use of a well-attested magical wheel, the iynx. If the description of an epic hero taking refuge in magic would strike us as odd, even more so does the etiological myth which Pindar narrates: Jason had been taught this magical art by none other than Aphrodite; for Jason, the goddess "brought the first time the mad bird (the iynx) to men and taught incantations and prayers to the wise son of Aison." Pindar tells a myth about the origin of a specific item of our present culture. Aphrodite taught Jason erotic magic, as Dionysus had taught the use of wine to Icarius, and as Demeter taught the cultivation of domestic crops to Triptolemos. The myth tells its story quite neutrally, and we do not seem faced with something special or even unwanted. Erotic magic is just an integral part of the archaic cultural outfit.[28]

---

[26] Healing: Homer, *Iliad* 4,190. 11,846. 13,392; *Od.* 4,230. 11,741. 22,94; Odysseus: *Od.* 1,261; the suitors: *Od.* 2,329.

[27] Odysseus: *Od.* 19,450s.; Plato: *Rep.* 426 B; see also Pindar, *Pyth.* 4,217; Sophocles, *Aias* 582.

[28] Pindar, *Pyth.* 4,213ss. See now also V. Pirenne-Delforge, "L'iynge dans le discours mythique et les procédures magiques," *Kernos* 6 (1993): 277-89.

*   *   *

Thus, the introduction of *magos* and related terms during the 5th century BCE and its consequent success indicates a deep and radical change in the attitude towards magic. Even more, this change results from the constitution of what will finally be, in our Western cultural matrix, the province of magic as opposed to religion.

This development in terminology corresponds to a major change in religious mentality, the evolution of magic (or rather *mageia*) as an autonomous domain among religious phenomena. In Greece, there were two main forces at work to bring about this change of paradigm.

One of these forces is the development of what we would call a philosophical theology, already discussed in the analysis of Plato. In traditional cosmology and theology, there was no doubt that communication between humans and gods (or rather, between humans and the superhuman forces, the *daimones, hērōes, theoi*) was easy. Humans were able to communicate with them through ritual; sacrifice and prayer persuaded the gods to help human beings fulfill their aims. Criticism of this view began in the generation of Heraclitus. The Ephesian philosopher censured traditional ritual practices, not only those of the mystery cults and of the *magoi*, but also traditional purification and Bacchic ritual, which to him were either blasphemous or obscene, or both.[29] Plato was even more explicit. In the *Laws*, he counts the sorcerers among those who think that the gods either do not exist or are careless and mercenary, a belief which contradicts the Platonic concept of divinity as pure good, as a supreme being which cares for humankind in a perfect way and to which humankind surrenders happily.

The other force at work is medical science, which also in the later 5th century begins to constitute itself as an autonomous domain. The key text for this development is the treatise *On the Sacred Disease*, whose author, an unknown Hippocratean physician from the late 5th century, vehemently opposes the idea that epilepsy (the "sacred disease") had supernatural causes. The physician attacks on two fronts. On the one hand, he opposes the traditional etiology of the disease as resulting from divine interference and possession. He accuses "men like the sorcerers (*magoi*), purification priests (*kathartai*), begging priests (*agurtai*) and quacks (*alazones*) of today" to have brought forward this religious expla-

---

[29] Heraclitus, DK 12 B 15, 5.

nation "in order to hide their own weakness" in healing it. The religious explanation of epilepsy is just a pretense of bungling quacks. Even more, this explanation is a fraud: "By inventing this explanation, they pretend to know more, and they deceive people (*exapatōsi anthrōpous*) by prescribing purificatory and cathartic rituals."[30] Therefore, they do not adhere to true religion (*eusebeia*), but to a punishable aberration (*asebeia*), a sort of atheism. Plato's position in the *Laws* springs to mind: the physician embraces the same spiritualized theology as Plato or, before him, Heraclitus. He persists on this accusation: the priests pretend to be able to influence the course of nature through their magical sacrifices (*mageuōn kai thuōn*), but by doing so they make claim to powers which belong to the gods only, to powers superior even to those of the gods, since they claim to be able to force the gods and to use them like their slaves. "Thus, to me, they seem to be impious and to suppose that there are no gods," since the divine defines itself as absolutely superior to any human being.[31]

There is a second line of attack within ancient medical science. The therapy of the physicians makes use of the same rationality as that of the seers: both first observe the symptoms, in order to arrive at the adequate therapy. But the two sorts of therapists start from different symptoms and therefore arrive at different therapies. The cathartic priests, who understand epilepsy as spirit possession, look for signs which would allow them to recognize the superhuman power at work in the patient: if he should bleat like a goat, it is the Mother of the Gods who is responsible; if he should neigh like a horse, it would be Poseidon. All this is perfectly within the laws of causality: the divine agent is recognized by a sound of a sacred animal which in turn reveals the divine agent at work. This immediately leads to therapy: one possessed by the Mother of the Gods has to abstain from all the products of the goat, from its milk, its cheese, and its leather. To this, physicians oppose their own etiology, which starts from the bodily functions and is based in a series of somatic observations, and from them the physicians recommend a particular medical therapy.

What separates the seer and the physician is not rationality but cosmology. Whereas for the seer the disease is the result of divine intervention, for the physician all diseases have natural causes.

---

[30] Pseudo-Hippocrates, *De morbo sacro* 4. See esp. G. E. R. Lloyd, *Magic, Reason, and Experience. Studies in the Origin and Development of Greek Science* (Cambridge: Cambridge University Press, 1979), chap. 1.
[31] Pseudo-Hippocrates, *De morbo sacro* 31.

Nature is a closed system, homogeneous and radically separated
from the divine world; never and nowhere do gods, demons and
heroes interfere with the course of nature. Concomitantly, on the
level of theology, people are not able to penetrate into the divine
world.

Thus, two intellectual developments in the Greek world caused
magic to become a proper domain inside religion, a domain attributed to specialists, *magoi*, *goētes*, *agurtai*: the rise of philosophical
theology as a radicalization and purification of traditional, civic
theology, and the rise of scientific medicine, based on the conception of nature as a homogeneous and closed system. Both of these
developments have a similar result: they stress the separation
between the world of nature (humans included) and the divine
realm. Philosophers and physicians become the enemies of the
sorcerers, and *magos*, in this debate, becomes a term of polemic
and denigration.

Three final remarks come to mind:
(1) Once again, one has to underline that we have to do with
more than what is commonly called magic: the philosophical and
medical opposition concerns an entire set of ritual practices and
beliefs outside civic religion—Bacchic mysteries, private ecstasy
rituals, purifications, and "black magic."
(2) The opposition to magic has nothing to do with civic religion. It is not the polis which opposes the *magoi*, it is on the contrary a debate among marginals. Philosophers and physicians are
barely less marginal towards the polis than itinerant priests: philosophers and physicians have their own associations, and philosophical theology is different and often at odds with civic theology. The towns can oppose magic, as the *Menon* passage demonstrates, but this opposition concerns only the damage done, never
the entire complex of *mageia* which philosophers and physicians
attacked.
(3) Finally, we saw that the Frazerian opposition between magic
and religion and the tendency to separate the two through their
differing attachment towards the superhuman world is present
already in Plato. We now see that the other Frazerian dichotomy,
between magic and science, is present in the late 5th century: for
the Hippocratic thinker, as for Frazer, magic and science share
their rationality—but the magician starts from the wrong premises,
and the Hippocratic thinker adds that the *magoi* constrain the

gods. Obviously, the Frazerian categories are not simply ethnocentric, they are so in very fundamental ways.[32]

* * *

Before becoming our modern term "magic," Greek *mageia* and *magos* had to become Latin *magia* and *magus*—terms which occur relatively late and at the same moment when consciousness of and reflection about magic as something essentially different sets in.[33] First, in the age of Cicero, the terms denote Persian ethnographical facts, as in Herodotus' Greek, and only later, in the famous history of magic in the 30th book of Pliny's *Natural History*, they signify more or less what we would call magic.[34]

In Republican Rome, as in Archaic Greece, magic was never thought as something special and radically different from religion or medicine. Already at the time of the Twelve Tablets, Roman authorities were opposed to sorcery, to *incantamenta*, "spells"— but only to those which threatened established rights of possession; there were other *incantamenta* used for healing which even the severe Cato recommended. And the law which Imperial Rome used against sorcery, the *lex Cornelia de sicariis et veneficis* (promulgated by the dictator Sulla in 81 BCE) was originally not aimed at sorcerers but at murderers: *sicarii* are those who kill openly, by force of a weapon, *venefici* are those who kill secretly, through poison or magic. Again, what we would call magic is not thought as something different.

In contrast to Greece, it is more difficult to explain why, at about the time of the Emperor Augustus, Roman society started to differentiate between magic on the one hand and both religion and science on the other, in order to marginalize it. One important factor must have been the overwhelming influence of Greek thinking conspicuous in Pliny's account and in the invasion of

---

[32] For another attestation of the dichotomy well before the age of the Reformation, see Galeotto Marzio, "Culturae et religionis nomen potius quam scientiae et magia et alchimia subibunt," in *De doctrina promiscua*, ed. M. Frezza (Naples: R. Pironti, 1949), 11.

[33] Fundamental for Roman magic is the essay by R. Garosi, "Indagini sulla formazione del concetto di magia nella cultura romana," in Paolo Xella, ed., *Magia. Studi di storia delle religioni in memoria di R. Garosi* (Rome: Bulzoni, 1976), 13-79; see also Anne-Marie Tupet, "Rites magiques dans l'antiquité romaine," in *ANRW*, 2.16.3: 2591-2675.

[34] Cicero, *divin.* 1,46 and 1,91, *legg.* 2,26; Catullus, *c.* 90; Pliny, *nat. hist.* 30, 1ss.

Eastern magical practice evident from Tacitus' account of the
death of Germanicus.[35] Another factor was political. The reigns of
Augustus' heirs, from Tiberius to Nero, were littered with the
victims of witchcraft accusation: it proved a horribly efficient
weapon for the removal of unwanted opponents.[36] Thus, the
combination of enlightenment and political ruthlessness might, in
the end, have laid the foundation of the concept of magic as we
now use it.

---

[35] Tacitus, *ann.* 2,69; it has close parallels in Near Eastern practice.
[36] See especially R. MacMullen, *Enemies of the Roman Order. Treason, Unrest, and Alienation in the Empire* (Cambridge: Harvard University Press,
1966).

CHAPTER THREE

THE RELIGIOUS, SOCIAL, AND LEGAL PARAMETERS OF TRADITIONAL EGYPTIAN MAGIC

Robert K. Ritner

To set the stage for this discussion,[1] I would ask you to consider a recent advertisement for a volume entitled *Religion, Science, and Magic*:

> Every culture makes the distinction between "true religion" and magic. A particular action and its result may be termed "miraculous" while another is rejected as the work of the devil.[2]

The implications of this sweeping declaration are transparent: every society contrasts religion and magic, and religion produces miracles while magic is the work of a devil. While it is hardly fair to hold advertising copy to the critical standards of scholarship, the statement does express—quite succinctly—the traditional assumptions surrounding the concept of "magic" and those of the volume's editors.[3] In scholarly discussions, just these assumptions have been held explicitly, or more often implicitly, since Sir James G. Frazer's *Golden Bough* of 1910.[4] What is most clear, however, in this statement and its underlying assumptions is its Western bias (Greco-Roman and Judeo-Christian), assuming distinctions between

---

[1] This essay is an expanded adaptation of the author's note entitled "Egyptian Magic: Questions of Legitimacy, Religious Orthodoxy and Social Deviance," published in Alan B. Lloyd, ed., *Religion and Society in Ancient Egypt*, J. Gwyn Griffiths Festschrift (Swansea, Wales: University College of Swansea, 1993), 189-200.

[2] Advance flier for J. Neusner, E. Frerichs and P. McCracken Flesher, eds., *Religion, Science and Magic* (Oxford: Oxford University Press, 1989); now published inside the volume's dust jacket.

[3] Cf. Neusner, *ibid.*, vii: "fairly well-accepted and clearly defined distinction between religion in the form of miracle and magic," and p. 4: "Religious systems of thought mark the boundary and center of a community, defining its identity, in part through making a distinction between true religion and magic. They do so, for example, by designating one act and its result as a miracle, and another as the work of the devil."

[4] Sir J. G. Frazer, *The Golden Bough*, Part I, *The Magic Art and the Evolution of Kings* (New York: The Macmillan Company, 1910).

magic and religion because we *in the West* have made such a distinction, and even dragging the specifically Judeo-Christian devil into the picture. In the following essay, I wish to confront such "general theories of magic" with the explicit evidence of Egypt, and see to what extent one may reasonably espouse universal definitions of magic.

At the outset, a definition of "magic" is critical for any discussion of the problem since there is no consensus on the meaning of the term *in English*, leaving aside the wider problem of concepts equated with "magic" in other cultures. Most often, the English term is bandied about as if an implicit consensus existed, yet this can easily be proved to be false, not only by widespread contemporary scholarly disagreement on the topic, but by the unstandardized ways in which the term has been used historically.[5] Thus, the Romans prosecuted the early Christians for practicing magic. In turn, the politically secure Catholic Church prosecuted pagan Romans for magic, only to be charged again with magic by schismatic Protestant critics during the Reformation.[6] Are we to believe that all these groups were accused of performing the same acts? Certainly not. The later Protestants thought the Catholics openly performed rites before idols, which is exactly what would have exonerated them from the charge of magic in the eyes of the Romans. Magic here is simply the religious practices of one group viewed with disdain by another. As in the quoted advertisement, the concept "magic" serves to distinguish "us" from "them," but it has no universal content. Your religion is my magic, and thus in English, Africa has no priests but "witchdoctors." Any understanding of the *Western* concept of magic must acknowledge this inherent negative connotation and trace it to its roots: the Greek

---

[5] For an overview of conflicting theories of magic, see W. Gutekunst, "Zauber," in W. Helck and E. Otto, eds., *Lexikon der Ägyptologie* (Wiesbaden: Otto Harrassowitz, 1986), 6.1320-55. An extended discussion of the various Western uses of "magic" and its relationship to Egyptian concepts is contained in R. Ritner, *The Mechanics of Ancient Egyptian Magical Practice*, SAOC 54 (Chicago: The Oriental Institute, 1993). See also *idem*, "Horus on the Crocodiles: A Juncture of Religion and Magic in Late Dynastic Egypt," in W. K. Simpson, ed., *Religion and Philosophy in Ancient Egypt*, Yale Egyptological Studies 3 (New Haven: Yale University, 1989), 103-16.

[6] See Peter Brown, "Sorcery, Demons and the Rise of Christianity from Late Antiquity into the Middle Ages," in Mary Douglas, ed., *Witchcraft Confessions and Accusations* (London: Tavistock Publications, 1970), 17-45, and Keith V. Thomas, *Religion and the Decline of Magic* (London: Weidenfeld and Nicholson, 1971), 51-77 *et passim* .

terms *mageia* (practitioner: *magos*) and *goēteia* (practitioner: *goēs*).[7]

The latter term *goēteia*, which originally may have described native priestly or shamanistic practices among the earliest Greeks, is consistently employed in historical periods to express "trickery, fraud, hucksterism," or "evil sorcery." At odds with contemporary cult, *goēteia* was no longer religion, whatever its origins. By contrast, the term *mageia* (> English "magic") originally designated the alien religious practices of Medean priests, the Magi. By the 3rd century BCE, however, Aristotle uses *mageia* and *goēteia* as comparable expressions, and though the original meaning as "Persian religion" survives, *mageia* had been popularly stigmatized as alien "non-religion," or "magic."[8] In post-Socratic philosophical circles, *mageia* was held to make use of good *daimones* (spirits lower than the gods of religion), while *goēteia* utilized evil *daimones*, thus producing the categories of good and evil ("white" and "black") magic. In Roman society, the cognate Latin category of *magia* underwent the same "demonization" as the Greek *mageia*, and subsumed as well the evil overtones of *goēteia*. Bequeathed to the Judeo-Christian world, these terms were readily serviceable, since all "paganism" was "non-religion" in the service of demons, not God. As a label for unacceptable or outmoded pseudo-religion, "magic" was equally useful for Reformation Protestants and early ethnographers. Modern Western terms for "magic" are all dependent upon this stemma of meanings, and function primarily as designations for that which we as a society do not accept, and which has overtones of the supernatural or the démonic (but not of the divine). It is important to stress that this pejorative connotation has not been grafted onto the notion of magic as the result of any recent theoretical fancy, but is inherent in Western terminology virtually from its beginning. It constitutes *the essential core* of the Western concept of magic.

---

[7] For the evolution of these terms, see Eugene Tavenner, *Studies in Magic from Latin Literature* (New York: Columbia University Press, 1916), 1-5; Morton Smith, *Jesus the Magician* (San Francisco: Harper and Row, 1978), 69-74; *idem*, "On the Lack of a History of Greco-Roman Magic," in Heinz Heinen, ed., *Althistorische Studien*, Hermann Bengston Festschrift, Historia Einzelschriften 40 (Wiesbaden: Franz Steiner Verlag, 1983), 251-57; and A. F. Segal, "Hellenistic Magic: Some Questions of Definition," in R. Van den Broek and M. J. Vermaseren, eds., *Studies in Gnosticism and Hellenistic Religions Presented to Gilles Quispel* (Leiden: E. J. Brill, 1981), 349-75.

[8] See E. Tavenner, *Studies in Magic*, 3.

Despite this underlying bond between Western terms, however, in actual practice it has often proved difficult (if not impossible) to make clear determinations of magic in specific cases, even from the perspective of Western society. Depending upon an individual's predilection, the same text or act may be classified as "magical," "religious," or (most evasively) "magico-religious."[9] The problem, especially for secular scholars, has been to determine just what factors should constitute the unacceptable "non-us," the necessary and sufficient quotient which separates magic from religion, medicine and science. In my own volume on Egyptian magical techniques, I adopted a specific working definition of magic from the modern Western perspective as comprising "any activity which seeks to obtain its goal by methods outside the simple laws of cause and effect."[10] This definition of "magic" is serviceable for analyzing elements of our own and other cultures *from our cultural perspective*; it does not, however, make any pretence of being universally valid from the perspectives of those other cultures. This is in direct contrast to most designations of magic, which proclaim universal applicability at all times and in all places.

The oldest, and most common, 19th century "universal" definition of magic was obtained by generalizing (Protestant) Judeo-Christian theological assumptions about piety vs. rote ritual, seen as a contrast between "higher" ethics vs. "lower" mechanistic practices. Best summarized by W. J. Goode in 1949, this approach distinguishes "religion" by the pious attitude of its practitioner, the humble supplications of its prayers, and the noble, all-inclusive world view of its rituals and theology.[11] In contrast, "magic" demanded *hubris* and blasphemy of its devotees, its spells (not called prayers) did not beg but threatened, and its goals were immediate, limited and personal. This view still has its devotees and is cited with approval in David E. Aune's 1980 discussion of "Magic in Early Christianity."[12] As we shall see with regard to Egypt, problems with this definition are legion, not least because it requires the investigator to intuit subjectively the attitude of the ancient practitioner. This is not often easy or even possible. This approach is also of limited scholarly value as a descriptive tool,

---

9 See the references in R. Ritner, "Horus on the Crocodiles," 103 n. 4.

10 R. Ritner, *The Mechanics of Ancient Egyptian Magical Practice* , 67-72.

11 W. J. Goode, "Magic and Religion: A Continuum," *Ethnos* 14 (1949): 172-82.

12 David E. Aune, "Magic in Early Christianity," in *ANRW*, 2.23.2: 1512-16.

since it usually merely demonstrates that non-Judeo-Christian societies function in ways non-Judeo-Christian. In any case, the posed dichotomy is clear: magic is outside of religion; it is inherently unorthodox.

An alternate, sociological approach to defining a "universal" concept of magic is to be found in the early theories of Emile Durkheim and Marcel Mauss, who generalize Latin legal codes and thus stigmatize magic as anti-social and illegal behavior.[13] Seizing upon the latter characteristic, Jonathan Z. Smith, Peter Brown, and Morton Smith have argued that illegality is "the one universal characteristic" of magic.[14] On the other hand, the notion of anti-social behavior was selected by David Aune, who views magic within the framework of recent studies on "social deviance." Aune considers magic to be "universally regarded as a form of deviant behavior," that is to say, "conduct that departs significantly from the norms set for people in their social statuses."[15] A similar distinction is assumed by Jacob Neusner, who opposes religion and magic as "what is normative and what is aberrational in religious situations."[16] Unlike the absolute theological categories posited by Goode, such theories do acknowledge the varying content of magic according to cultural bias ("what I do is a miracle, but what you do is magic").[17] Like the previous theory, however, they assume that the *distinction* between magic and religion is itself universal. Again the dichotomies are clear; magic is not legal and not socially normative.

One final set of theories should be mentioned before addressing the Egyptian evidence, and those are the varying anthropological approaches. At base indistinguishable from theological approaches (higher piety vs. lower mechanics), the early work of Frazer focused on its sympathetic character, adding the distinctions of homeopathic magic (like makes like) and contagious magic (items in contact form permanent bonds, i.e., act as relics). All magic was

---

[13] See Emile Durkheim, *The Elementary Forms of the Religious Life* (New York: The Macmillan Company, 1915); and Marcel Mauss, *A General Theory of Magic* (New York: W. W. Norton and Co., 1975; reprint, Paris: L'Année sociologique, 1902-03).

[14] Jonathan Z. Smith, *Map is not Territory* (Leiden: E. J. Brill, 1978), 192; following Peter Brown, "Sorcery, Demons and the Rise of Christianity," 17-45; and Morton Smith, *Clement of Alexandria and a Secret Gospel of Mark* (Cambridge: Harvard University Press, 1973), 220-37.

[15] David E. Aune, "Magic in Early Christianity," 1515.

[16] Jacob Neusner, "Introduction," in *Religion, Science and Magic*, 5.

[17] Neusner, *ibid.*, 4-5.

reduced to these terms, and once designated, there was nothing
more to be said.[18] In response to this reductionism, E. E. Evans-
Pritchard devised a new vocabulary sensitive to cultural distinctions
based upon and devised for a single culture: the Zande of the Sudan.
From Zande concepts Evans-Pritchard distinguished two forms of
hostile magic: (1) the conscious performance of illegal rites and
spells, and (2) *mangu*, an innate psychic emanation from an
internal bodily substance which produces injury. The former he
called "sorcery," the latter "witchcraft."[19] Though expressly
designed as a reaction against general theories of magic, Evans-
Pritchard's terms have now been granted universal validity by his
successors, and this ironic turn of events has produced the only
"universal" theory of magic based on African preconceptions
rather than Greco-Roman or Judeo-Christian ones. Under the guise
of "witchcraft," *mangu* is now sought in Europe, the Middle East
and ancient Egypt.[20]

*   *   *

Armed with this plethora of theories, it is to Egypt that we may
at last turn. Fortunately for studies of Egyptian magic, a native
term and concept are readily at hand, since in the Coptic Christian
period *magia* and its biblical cognates were equated with Coptic
ϩⲓⲕ, as can be demonstrated by a representative passage from the
"Martyrdom of Saint George":

This man is a magician ("a man who does ϩⲓⲕ") because by means of
his ⲙⲁⲅⲓⲁ he set demons before us.[21]

Coptic ϩⲓⲕ derives from Pharaonic *ḥk3*, and about pagan *ḥk3*
we are very well informed indeed.[22] At the beginning of time,

---

[18] Sir J. G. Frazer, *The Golden Bough*, 1.52 ff.

[19] E. E. Evans-Pritchard, *Witchcraft, Oracles, and Magic among the Azande*
(Oxford: Clarendon Press, 1937), 8-12.

[20] Cf. Max Marwick, ed., *Witchcraft and Sorcery* (Middlesex: Penguin Books,
1970), 19 *et passim*; S. Walters, "The Sorceress and her Apprentice," *JCS* 23
(1970-71): 27-38; and J. F. Borghouts, "Magie," in *Lexikon der Ägyptologie*,
3.1144.

[21] I. Balestri and H. Hyvernant, eds., *Acta Martyrum II*, CSCO 6 (Paris: Im-
primerie Nationale, 1924), 292.

[22] The following discussion of *ḥk3* is primarily indebted to H. Te Velde, "The
God Heka in Egyptian Theology," *JEOL* 21 (1969-70): 175-86. See further the
literature gathered in L. Kákosy, "Heka," in *Lexikon der Ägyptologie*, 2.1108-
10, and the analysis in R. Ritner, *The Mechanics of Ancient Egyptian Magical
Practice* , 14-28.

before the creation of the world, the creator conceived in his heart the force of ḥk3, at once creative *logos* and source of all cosmic dynamics. Reminiscent of the Christian Logos of the Gospel of John, ḥk3 became embodied as a divine personality, Heka, and the recipient of a cult in his capacity as first emanation (*ba*) from the creator. All subsequent creation (the universe with its gods and men) was subject to this first-born son. As Heka himself states in an address to the gods in Coffin Text Spell 261,

> I am he whom the Unique Lord made before duality had yet come into being . . . I am the son of Him who gave birth to the universe . . . I am the protection of that which the Unique Lord has ordained . . . I am he who gave life to the Ennead of gods . . . I have come to take my position that I might receive my dignity, for to me belonged the universe before you gods had come into being. Down, you who have come afterward. I am Heka.[23]

The threatening posture which Heka adopts in his final remarks is characteristic, for as a Berlin hymn declares, "Everyone trembles when his [*scil.* "the creator's"] *ba* comes into being, Heka who has power over the gods."[24] As Heka, "magic" is accorded primary divine status with which subsequent deities identify by means of the epithet wr-ḥk3(.w) "great of magic."[25] A similar identification motivated the Coffin Text passage quoted above, which was to be recited by a private individual who thereby *became* the god Heka and controlled the gods.[26] To understand Egyptian "magic," one must understand the nature of Heka.

Late speculation explained the name Heka as "The First Work," but the original significance of ḥk3 seems rather to be "The One who Consecrates Imagery" (< ḥwy-k3).[27] As the creator called the world into being by word or deed, it was the force of ḥk3 which empowered his actions, translating divine "ideal" speech and action into its "tangible" reflection here below. Every temple ritual which reenacts or supports these actions entails the "real

[23] A. De Buck and A. Gardiner, *The Egyptian Coffin Texts III*, OIP 64 (Chicago: University of Chicago Press, 1947), 382-89.

[24] W. Wolf, "Der Berliner Ptah-Hymnus," *Zeitschrift für Ägyptische Sprache und Altertumskunde* 64 (1929): 40-41, ll. 8-9 (col. 11, 7).

[25] Bibliographical summary in Ingrid Nebe, "Werethekau," *Lexikon der Ägyptologie*, 6.1221-24. By this affiliation with ḥk3, various gods, kings, crowns, and staves are affirmed in their abilities to coerce yet other deities, events, etc.

[26] The spell is entitled "To Become the God Heka."

[27] H. Te Velde, "The God Heka in Egyptian Theology," 179-80.

presence" of ḥkꜣ, and consequently that of the creator of whom ḥkꜣ is an emanation. Thus in discussing spells (rꜣ.w), the sun god Re states,

> Behold, Heka himself is in them. As for him who swallows/knows them, there am I.[28]

This statement contains within itself an example of the "imagistic" nature of the magical process, for the Egyptian word ꜥm, "to swallow," comes to mean "to know." Thus, by the act of swallowing the dissolved ink of a text one acquires the reflex of the action, innate knowledge of the text's content.[29] If the force of ḥkꜣ is to be understood as functioning through "consecrated imagery," then it would represent the fundamental principle underlying all orthodox temple cult, indeed all ritual—whether state or private, public or clandestine. The same force would be felt to animate both beneficent and hostile "magic" as well. Gods and demons both use ḥkꜣ; the term "magician" (ḥkꜣy) is morally neutral, equally applicable to heroes and villains, Egyptians and foreigners.[30] It is significant that Re's acknowledgement of the true efficacy of spells appears within a context describing the work of hostile "magicians." There is no distinction here of authentic "miracle" vs. debased or fraudulent "magic."

The "imagistic" process is shown repeatedly on Egyptian temple reliefs in which the king's ritual presentation of food, diadems and prisoners is a *reflection* of the god's granting of life, prosperity, and victory, each object offered being a tangible image of its abstract counterpart. The essential unity of the divine and royal actor is concretely embodied in the person of the Pharaoh, who is

---

[28] *The Book of the Heavenly Cow*, ll. 218-20; see E. Hornung, *Der ägyptische Mythos von der Himmelskuh* (Freiburg: Universitätsverlag, 1982), 20 and 44.

[29] R. Ritner, "Horus on the Crocodiles," 107-08.

[30] For the use of ḥkꜣ by demons, see the description of Apep in Papyrus Bremner-Rhind, col. 29/19: "his utterance, his magic (ḥkꜣ), and his spells are caused to withdraw." The "amoral" nature of "magician" is easily shown, for the term is applied equally to the king (e.g., Pyramid Text spell 472), the gods, temple personnel, and foreign "sorcerers." For the profession, see the literature gathered in J. F. Borghouts, "Magie," *Lexikon der Ägyptologie*, 3.1146. For hostile magicians, cf. n. 28, above, and the numerous examples gathered in I. E. S. Edwards, *Oracular Amuletic Decrees of the Late New Kingdom*, HPBM 4 (London: British Museum, 1960), 124 (index, *s.v.* ḥkꜣ). A supposed distinction between creative magic (ꜣḫw) and destructive magic (ḥkꜣ) has been suggested by Borghouts in *Lexikon der Ägyptologie*, 3.1139. A full refutation of this suggestion appears in R. Ritner, *The Mechanics of Ancient Egyptian Magical Practice*, 30-35.

at once god and living image, expressed theologically in such names as Twt-^cnh-$\textit{'}mn$, Shm-^cnh-$\textit{'}mn$, or $T\textit{'}.t$-^cnh-R^c "The living image of Amon/Re." Obviously, Pharaoh cannot perform every rite in all temples, and thus these were performed by *his* image, the priest. It is the priesthood which composed, collected and performed rites and spells for both public and private ceremonies, not merely imitating gods, but becoming them. By an intricate series of consciously elaborated imagery, humans may exploit the powers of the primordial gods.

The very notions of divinity and imagery are conjoined in Egyptian thought; the conventional term for "god" (*nṯr*) has as its root meaning "image," as is revealed by an Old Kingdom relief from the tomb of Nefermaat that is now in the Oriental Institute Museum in Chicago.[31] Gods, humans, animals, objects, actions, and words are all part-of a fluid continuum of projected divine images without sharp divisions. Humans in particular were formed from the creator's tears, are instructed to confront "the god who is within you,"[32] regularly become gods at death, and in exceptional cases during life. By virtue of this "Great Chain of Being," humans are justified in equating themselves with one, several or all of the gods, and, following divine prototypes, may *or must* threaten other gods during ritual performance.[33] This practice is without *hubris* (a specifically *Greek* cultural notion), and in complete orthodoxy. Such "magic" was the express gift of the creator, and a list of god's benefactions for humanity concludes the mention of the creation of heaven, earth, air, food and government by stating,

It was in order to be weapons to ward off the blow of events that he (god) made magic for them (humanity).[34]

Consider the implications of this weapon in Pyramid Text Spell 539:

---

[31] Oriental Institute Museum 9002; see W. Spiegelberg, "'*n ṯr.w*' 'Götter' = 'Bilder'," *Zeitschrift für Ägyptische Sprache und Altertumskunde* 65 (1930): 120-21.

[32] Adolf Erman and Hermann Grapow, *Wörterbuch der ägyptischen Sprache*, 2nd edition (Berlin and Leipzig: Akademie-Verlag, 1957), 2.359/3.

[33] S. Sauneron, "Aspects et sort d'un thème magique égyptien: les menaces incluant les dieux," *Bulletin de la Société Française d'Égyptologie* 8 (1951): 11-21; and H. Grapow, "Bedrohungen der Götter durch Verstorbenen," *Zeitschrift für Ägyptische Sprache und Altertumskunde* 49 (1911): 48-54.

[34] A. Volten, *Zwei altägyptische politische Schriften*, AnAe 4 (Copenhagen: Einar Munksgaard, 1945), 75 and 78.

Every god who will not build this stairway of the king for him . . . will
have no offering bread, will have no sunshade . . . It is not the king who
says this against you, O gods, it is Heka who says this against you, O
gods.[35]

In the same light should be understood the common greeting formula of New Kingdom letters: "I say to all the gods, 'Make you
healthy,'" *using the imperative.*[36] Such religious practices provided
a ready source of confusion and scandal to late, contemporary
Greek theologians whose religious norms and expectations were
quite alien.[37] As our modern theological preconceptions are largely
derived from Greek categories, it is hardly surprising that contemporary theory is equally ill at ease with a system incorporating
ritualized divinization, blessing and cursing: a *single system* for
gods, men and "devils," cultural "insiders" and "outsiders" (both
"us" *and* "them").

All of these complexities are entailed in the concept of ḥk3,
and notions of "sympathetic magic," piety vs. ritual, or unorthodoxy are either woefully inadequate to describe the situation, or
simply wrong. Heka cannot be opposed to Egyptian religion, since
it is the force which animates Egyptian religion. The techniques of
ḥk3 are in every case those of temple ritual, serving for both
public and private concerns. General calendrical rituals and personal "crisis rites" overlap and should not be contrasted.[38] Nor is
there a real distinction between public and private practitioner, for
Egypt had no itinerant magicians who acted outside of orthodox
religion, no witches or warlocks on the social fringe. With literacy
restricted to 1% of the population, only the scribally-trained
priesthood could compose and use the complex magical texts.[39]

---

[35] K. Sethe, *Die altägyptischen Pyramidentexte* (Leipzig: J. C. Hinrichs,
1908-10), 2.234-35.

[36] ỉmy snbⲫk; e.g., A. Gardiner, *Late Egyptian Miscellanies*, Bib Aeg 7
(Brussels: Fondation égyptologique reine Élisabeth, 1937), 5/16, 7/2, 8/12, etc.

[37] Cf. the response of Iamblichus to Porphyry in *De mysteriis Aegyptiorum*,
in Edouard des Places, ed. and trans., *Jamblique, Les Mystères d'Égypte* (Paris:
Société d'Edition <<Belles Lettres>>, 1966), 146 ff. and 186-88.

[38] This dichotomy is suggested in M. Titiev, "A Fresh Approach to the Problem of Magic and Religion," *Southwestern Journal of Anthropology* 16 (1960):
292-98; and followed in Jørgen P. Sørensen, "The Argument in Ancient Egyptian Magical Formulae," *Acta Orientalia* 45 (1984): 6. Cf., however, the Apep
ritual of Papyrus Bremner-Rhind, col. 23/6-9, performed without modification at
specific public festivals and for private use "likewise any day."

[39] J. Baines and C. J. Eyre, "Four Notes on Literacy," *Göttingen Miszellen* 61
(1983): 65-96. The only exceptions to priestly control of magical texts occur at
the aberrant, restricted community of Deir el-Medineh where, in the absence of a

Like "religious" hymns and prayers, "magical" recitations of healing and cursing were drafted, compiled, edited and stored in the temple scriptorium (pr-ᶜnḫ).[40] Thus it is intrinsically logical that the literate lector-priest (ḫry-ḥb.t) should be the most commonly designated magical practitioner in ancient Egypt.[41] As priests served in the temples in rotation, it was the off-duty priest who acted as community magician and guardian of temple secrets. The complete kit of one such priest has been found from the 18th-17th century BCE, labeled with his title ḥry-sštȝ "Chief of mysteries."[42] The "mysteries" are the spells themselves, the property of the temple scriptorium.[43]

From the foregoing remarks, it should be clear that "magic" (as either ḥkȝ or as "activity not based on the simple laws of cause and effect") was by no means illegal or socially deviant in Egypt. Even hostile magic was not inherently illegal. Using images of wax and clay, priests regularly performed rites for cursing gods, men and demons with perfect legality, and the famous execration texts of the 3rd to 2nd millennia BCE include sections for Egyptians as well as foreigners.[44] One 4th century BCE temple ritual contains provisions for cursing personal enemies, declaring, "If this spell is

---

professional priesthood, workers acted as their own priests, and thus had access to material restricted elsewhere.

[40] See A. Gardiner, "The House of Life," *JEA* 24 (1938): 157-79; L. Habachi and P. Ghalioungui, "The <<House of Life>> of Bubastis," *Chronique d'Égypte* 46 (1971): 59-71; and P. Derchain, *Le Papyrus Salt 825 (B.M. 10051)* (Paris: Palais des Académies, 1965), 48-61 and 96-108.

[41] Eberhard Otto, "Cheriheb," *Lexikon der Ägyptologie*, 1.940-43; A. Gardiner, "Professional Magicians in Ancient Egypt," *Proceedings of the Society of Biblical Archaeology* 39 (1917): 31-43; Jan Quaegebeur, "On the Egyptian Equivalent of Biblical ḤARṬUMMÎM," in S. Groll, ed., *Pharaonic Egypt, the Bible and Christianity* (Jerusalem: Hebrew University, 1985), 162-72.

[42] J. E. Quibell, *The Ramesseum* (Egyptian Research Account, 1896; London: Bernard Quaritch, 1898), 3. The lid of the "magician's box" is decorated with a depiction of a crouching jackal, thus forming the common writing of ḥry-sštȝ (*Wörterbuch der ägyptischen Sprache*, 4.298-99). The significance of this label is unrecognized in both Quibell's report, and the recent, popularized retelling in Bob Brier, *Ancient Egyptian Magic* (New York: William Morrow, 1980), 48.

[43] Cf. the title to spell K of the Harris Magical Papyrus: "The first spell of enchanting all within the water, concerning which the lector-priests say, 'Do not reveal it to others.' A veritable mystery (sštȝ) of the temple scriptorium"; in H. O. Lange, *Der magische Papyrus Harris* (Copenhagen: Andr. Fred. Høst & Søn, 1927), 53.

[44] General bibliography in S. Schoske, "Vernichtungsrituale," *Lexikon der Ägyptologie*, 6.1009-12.

recited against any enemy of NN, evil will happen to him for 7 days."[45] Unlike traditional Western concepts, Egyptian magic was amoral, not immoral. No term distinguished hostile from good magic, "black" vs. "white."[46] There was no devil for one, and god for another. The same principle was invoked; all was ḥkȝ. Only when this weapon was directed against King Ramses III in a harem conspiracy (12th century BCE) do we have what has been called a "trial for sorcery," but this was not a trial against sorcery *per se*, but a trial for treason.[47] Had a sword been used as the weapon rather than wax dolls, the trial would have occurred nonetheless. The magical rite was hardly illegal in itself, since the culprit, a disaffected priest, was said to have acquired it from the royal archives.[48] That the priest should practice such a rite entails no "social deviance," no activity outside expected social norms. Act and actor are typical; it is only the recipient of the curse that distinguishes this case—the name consciously inserted in the standard text.

From the perspective of modern theories of "witchcraft," this conscious nature of Egyptian hostile magic is significant. In 1980, a decade after appearing in Mesopotamian studies, Evans-Pritchard's Zande-inspired terminology was introduced to Egyptology to little purpose.[49] Though Heka, like *mangu* or "witchcraft," can be said to reside within the body, it is activated by special words, acts and ingredients. Only the late and presumably imported notion of the "evil eye" approximates the innate evil of Zande *mangu*; otherwise "Egyptian witchcraft" is a category without content.

As hostile magic need not be the "work of the devil," so "miracle" need not be contrasted with "magic." Indeed, the

---

[45] S. Schott, *Urkunden mythologischen Inhalts. Bücher und Sprüche gegen den Gott Seth* (Leipzig: J. C. Hinrichs'sche Buchhandlung, 1929), 61, ll. 17-18.

[46] On occasion, ḥkȝ may be qualified by the adjectives ḏw or bỉn "bad/evil/hostile," but these designations only reflect the relative perspective of the threatened party, and do not constitute a separate, absolute "category" of magic. The same texts which promise safety from "all evil magic" (ḥkȝ nb ḏw) also promise safety from "every transgressing god" (nṯr nb thỉ). As such gods include Horus, Osiris, etc., they are hardly inherently "evil," but merely ill-disposed to their victim. "Magic" may be similarly "ill-disposed," cf. I. E. S. Edwards, *Oracular Amuletic Decrees of the Late New Kingdom*, 31-32 (L 5, v. 11 & 15-16). See also n. 30, above.

[47] General bibliography in Manfred Weber, "Harimsverschwörung," *Lexikon der Ägyptologie,* 2.989-91.

[48] Papyrus Lee, col. 1/2-3.

[49] See above, n. 20.

"magician" Heka is equally the patron of the closest Egyptian lexical approximations to the English term "miracle." In an Esna litany, the god is hymned as *nb šmw nb bì3 sr ḫpr* "lord of oracles, lord of miracles/wonders, who predicts what will happen."[50] While the term *bì3* is generally rendered as "miracle" or "wonder,"[51] *šmw* is the unrecognized ancestor of Coptic ϢⲎⲘ, "sign/oracle/wonder,"[52] and from *ḫpr* derives the common Coptic word ϢⲠⲎⲢⲈ, "sign/wonder/miracle."[53] If native terms of "magic" and "miracle" are thus easily associated within *pre-Christian* religious texts, it is readily apparent that their Coptic descendants are used quite differently. Within Coptic literature, a sharp division does appear in the usage of ϢⲠⲎⲢⲈ, "miracle" and ϨⲒⲔ, "magic," with "miracles" being the work of God, Jesus, angels and saints, while "magic" is demonic or pagan. How, then, did this new dichotomy arise?

The answer to this question is best illustrated by the fate of the official, "miraculous omens" or "oracles" said to be sanctioned by Heka. While oracles may have been associated with temple cult from the earliest times,[54] their significance and popularity increase, especially in the form of revelations known by the name *pḥ-nṯr* or "petitioning the god."[55] Conducted privately with priestly aid via lamps, bowls and images, or publicly during regular

---

[50] S. Sauneron, *Le Temple d'Esna*, Esna 3 (Cairo: IFAO, 1968), 113-14; and *idem*, *L'écriture figurative dans les textes d'Esna*, Esna 8 (Cairo: IFAO, 1982), 31-32.

[51] Cf. R. O. Faulkner, *Concise Dictionary of Middle Egyptian* (Oxford: Griffith Institute, 1972), 80; and *Wörterbuch der ägyptischen Sprache*, 1.440-41. For the term's additional nuance of "oracle," see G. Posener, "Aménémopé 21, 13 et *bì3j.t* au sens d'<<oracle>>," *Zeitschrift für Ägyptische Sprache und Altertumskunde* 90 (1963): 98-102.

[52] W. E. Crum, *A Coptic Dictionary* (Oxford: Clarendon Press, 1939), 564a; cf. W. Erichsen, *Demotisches Glossar* (Copenhagen: Einar Munksgaard, 1954), 508 ("Verbum"). Further examples are gathered in Ritner, *The Mechanics of Ancient Egyptian Magical Practice*, 20, 36-37 and 202.

[53] Crum, *A Coptic Dictionary*, p. 581a; J. Černý, *Coptic Etymological Dictionary* (Cambridge: Cambridge University Press, 1976), 250.

[54] A Pre-dynastic attestation is suggested in anon., "The Nodding Falcon of the Guennol Collection at the Brooklyn Museum," *The Brooklyn Museum Annual* 9 (1969): 69-87; and W. K. Simpson, "A Horus-of-Nekhen Statue of Amunhotpe III from Soleb," *Boston Museum Bulletin* 69 (1971): 152-64. A bibliographical overview (beginning only with the New Kingdom) is found in L. Kákosy, "Orakel," *Lexikon der Ägyptologie*, 4.600-06.

[55] J.-M. Kruchten, *Le grand texte oraculaire de Djéhoutymose*, Monographies Reine Elisabeth 5 (Brussels: Fondation égyptologique reine Élisabeth, 1986), 63-65 and 329-32, and J. Johnson, "Louvre E. 3229: A Demotic Magical Text," *Enchoria* 7 (1977): 90-91.

processions of statues, these divine confrontations (literally, "reaching god") are a regular feature of Egyptian religious life from the New Kingdom onward. The manifestation of the god was addressed directly, and by appropriate signs or documents an oracular response was granted.[56]

Like other facets of Egyptian "magic," the $ph-ntr$ was morally neutral.[57] Thus, while the harem conspiracy against Ramses III was furthered by means of a $ph-ntr$, royal workers under Ramses IX could be excused from work to attend a $ph-ntr$, and the ceremonies increasingly became standard arbiters of justice, fully equivalent to a court of law. Magic is here not only legal, but the very author of legality. With the conquest of Egypt by Rome, however, a very different attitude prevailed, and the history of the $ph-ntr$, and $hk3$ itself, takes a new turn.

Rome long had a suspicious attitude toward foreign religious practices, as is evident from its well-known restrictions upon the imported cults of the Magna Mater, Isis, and Christianity. Attempts to expel Egyptian religion from Rome were made in 59, 58, 53, and 48 BCE, and it was inevitable that Roman preconceptions would clash with Egyptian practice. The most direct expression of this cultural conflict is found in a decree of Q. Aemilius Saturninus, prefect of Egypt under Septimius Severus, in 199 CE:

> [Since I have come across many people] who consider themselves to be beguiled by the means of divination [I quickly considered it necessary], in order that no danger should ensue upon their foolishness, clearly herein to enjoin all people to abstain from this hazardous (or "misleading") superstition. Therefore, let no man through oracles, that is, by means of written documents supposedly granted in the presence of the deity, nor by means of the procession of cult images or suchlike charlatanry, pretend to have knowledge of the supernatural, or profess to know the obscurity of future events. Nor let any man put himself at the disposal of those who enquire about this nor answer in any way whatsoever. If any person is detected adhering to this profession, let him be sure that he will be handed over for capital punishment.[58]

---

[56] See J. Černý, "Egyptian oracles," in R. Parker, *A Saite Oracle Papyrus from Thebes* (Providence: Brown University, 1962), 35-48.

[57] In company with "ill-disposed" $hk3$ (above, n. 46), the $ph-ntr$ can also be qualified as potentially "unfavorable" (*bin*) to a client purchasing safety from every variety of misfortune; see Edwards, *Oracular Amuletic Decrees of the Late New Kingdom*, 39 (Papyrus BM 10587, ll. 90-98).

[58] Papyrus Yale inv. 299, translation adapted from John Rea, "A New Version of P. Yale Inv. 299," *Zeitschrift für Papyrologie und Epigraphik* 27 (1977):

Apparently promulgated only within Egypt, this prohibition of oracles was aimed unmistakably at the techniques of the traditional *pḥ-nṯr,* here dismissed as nonreligious "charlatanry"—despite its fundamental role in later Egyptian religion. Without any change in action or actors, a pious, religious arbiter of legality has become illegal superstition. The change is entirely one of cultural perspective. As in Rome itself, the prohibition was unsuccessful, for in 359 an Egyptian oracle (of Bes at Abydos) again troubled Roman authority, prompting Constantius to decree a general abolition of oracles throughout the empire.[59] Coptic evidence shows that even this attempt was without success.[60] At the Theban temple of Luxor, the processional ceremony continues even today in the annual festival of the Moslem saint Abu el-Hagag.

Nonetheless, official Roman condemnation did produce a significant change. The decree of Saturninus, whatever its immediate effect upon temple ritual, was but part of a larger pattern of restrictive "supervision" by Roman authority over Egyptian theology, intrusions based upon a perceived priestly threat to Roman morals, social control, and financial dominance.[61] The cumulative effect of many such "supervisory" restrictions was to cripple the traditional institution of the Egyptian temple. Much of what had constituted public religion was driven underground, becoming secretive and "private" practice.[62] Though still of priestly origin,

---

151-56; and G. H. R. Horsley, *New Documents Illustrating Early Christianity* (North Ryde, Australia: Macquarie University, 1981), 1.47-51. For the text, see also George M. Parássoglou, "Circular from a Prefect: Sileat Omnibus Perpetuo Divinandi Curiositas," in Ann Ellis Hanson, ed., *Collectanea Papyrologica, Youtie Festschrift* (Bonn: Rudolf Habelt Verlag, 1976), 261-74 and plate 12; and Naphtali Lewis, "A Ban on False Prophets: P. Coll. Youtie 30," *Chronique d'Egypte* 52 (1977): 143-46.

[59] Ammianus Marcellinus, 19.12.3-16; ed. John C. Rolfe, Loeb Library (Cambridge: Harvard University Press, 1971), 535-43. See also A. Piankoff, "The Osireion of Seti I at Abydos during the Greco-Roman Period and the Christian Occupation," *Bulletin de la Société d'Archéologie Copte* 15 (1958-60): 125-49.

[60] J. Černý, "Egyptian oracles," 47-48 (7th - 8th century).

[61] A convenient summation of such interference is found in Richard Gordon, "Religion in the Roman Empire: the civic compromise and its limits," in Mary Beard and John North, eds., *Pagan Priests* (New York: Cornell University Press, 1990), 241-42.

[62] The need for secrecy led also to the development of a cipher in which to write magical manuals; see F. Ll. Griffith and H. Thompson, *The Demotic Magical Papyrus of London and Leiden* (Oxford: Clarendon Press, 1904), 1.8-9, and 3.105-112; and J. Johnson, "Louvre E. 3229: A Demotic Magical Text," *Enchoria* 7 (1977): 93.

all Demotic examples of the *pḥ-nṯr* (as well as the related Greek σύστασις and αὐτόπτος) are for private use only, performed secretly in secluded quarters.[63] *Only now* could the practice be termed "magic" in the Western sense (i.e., "illegal" and "clandestine") and *then only from the Roman perspective* .

Egyptian reaction to the Roman prohibition is epitomized in the second century Greek tale of Thessalos, a physician from Asia Minor who travelled to Upper Egypt to supplement his philosophical studies.[64] Having sought out priests in Thebes, Thessalos asked them if anything remained of Egyptian magical power (τι τῆς μαγικῆς ἐνεργείας) to conduct an audience with the gods or the dead. Although most appeared scandalized (φερόντων) by the question, one old priest agreed to conduct the rite with the aid of a bowl filled with water. After preparations and fasting, Thessalos was led to a secluded (temple?) room[65] where in a vision he confronted Aesclepius/Imhotep who answered his questions. The techniques of this procedure (bowl, fasting, seclusion) accord perfectly with those in contemporary "private" Demotic (and Greek) papyri.

Traditionally, the priests' initial shock at the question of Thessalos has been interpreted in light of Roman prohibitions of magic that entailed capital punishment for both performer and teacher. Jonathan Z. Smith, however, has argued that it is rather an indication of their disbelief in the efficacy of magical power.[66] This reinterpretation is unconvincing, given (1) the centrality of *ḥk3* to Egyptian religion even in the latest periods (which would entail priests professing disbelief in the religion which they serve), (2) the severity of Roman punishment for magic, and (3) the fact that Thessalos was a stranger to the priests, and a foreign Greek stranger at that. The most likely interpretation would be that the priests were unwilling to risk capital punishment for imparting secret (and sacred) knowledge to a foreigner who could not be

---

[63] Demotic examples appear in Papyrus Louvre E 3229, cols. 6/6, 6/11, 6/26, and 7/13; and in the Demotic Magical Papyrus of London and Leiden, cols. 4/3, 8/12,27/29, and 28/32-33.

[64] A. J. Festugière, "L'expérience religieuse du médecin Thessalos," *RB* 48 (1939): 45-77; A. D. Nock, *Conversion* (London: Oxford University Press, 1933), 108-09; and Jonathan Z. Smith, "The Temple and the Magician," in *idem, Map is Not Territory* (Leiden: E. J. Brill, 1978), 172-89.

[65] The term is οἰκός, which (like the word *ꜥ.wy* found in corresponding Demotic rites) may signify either a sacred or profane room. For the Greek term, see A. J. Festugière, "L'expérience religieuse du médecin Thessalos," 61-62 n. 21; vs. J. Z. Smith, "The Temple and the Magician," 180.

[66] J. Z. Smith, *ibid.*, 179-82.

trusted, and who should be excluded from such knowledge in any case.

Smith's suggestion of priestly disbelief was intended to bolster his contention that the epiphany in this text represents a reversal of the traditional priestly/temple context in favor of "temporary sacrality sanctified by a magician's power."[67] This is not correct. The rite may well have taken place in a temple, and the magician responsible for the vision was definitely not Thessalos, but the traditional Egyptian priest trained in traditional temple practice. Fear of Roman punishment for *magia* may have made the priests wary and the rite secretive, but the *ph-ntr* experienced by Thessalos was still administered by an Egyptian *priest* as an orthodox religious rite.[68]

Despite imperial sanctions, Egyptian and Roman conceptions of "magic" did not merge until the Coptic period, when Christian hostility stigmatized all pagan practices—Roman as well as Egyptian—with the derogatory *magia*. With the abandonment of its native religion, Egypt might maintain its religious vocabulary, but not its religious perspective. The cultural gulf which separates *ḥk3* from ϩικ is paralleled by that which divides Egyptian *ỉmnt.t*, the abode of Osiris and the blessed dead, from Coptic ⲁⲙⲉⲛⲧⲉ, the devil's hell. Stripped of its ancient theological significance, Coptic ϩικ was now reduced to a designation for *alien and demonic* religion, at once illegal, unorthodox, and socially deviant.

The irony of this designation, and its innate limitations, could not be clearer. By regularly casting disparate concepts together as an expression for "non-us," the label of "magic" tells us far more about the cultural biases of the society which applies it than it does about the practices to which it is applied. There can be no universal concept of magic precisely because "magic" is a Western concept, laden with "our" innate value judgments. As a term for defining what we do not accept, it can be useful, but the content of magic, that which comprises "what it is we do not accept," cannot be generalized to other cultures. Egyptian *ḥk3* was a most complex theological concept; only the superimposition of Christian theology demoted it to "magic." Magic and *ḥk3* are fundamentally incompatible notions. *Ḥk3* is a category of inclusion, defined by

---

[67] J. Z. Smith, *ibid.*, 182.

[68] Cf. also the temple-sponsored incubation vision of Aesclepius/Imhotep recorded in Papyrus Oxyrhynchus XI.1381 (equally 2d century), translated in Frederick C. Grant, *Hellenistic Religions* (Indianapolis: Bobbs-Merrill, 1953), 124-27.

specific, invariable content. The transfer of a blessing by water is always ḥk3. Magic is a category of exclusion, defined by what it does *not* contain: piety, legality, etc. The transfer of blessing by water is sometimes magic, sometimes "baptism." The Demotic magical papyri were illegal, socially deviant, impious documents in the eyes of the Romans; they were illegal but perfectly pious in the eyes of their users, and their antecedents had been both pious and legal.

One must always be on guard against the underlying social biases of classification lest we, in the words of the 16th century philosopher Giordano Bruno, "in vain attempt to contain water in nets and catch fish with a shovel."[69] Bruno had attempted to defend Egyptian religion from the charges of "superstition" and "magic"; his recommendation went unheeded. Bruno himself was burned for heresy, the conceptual stepchild of "magic," connoting illegality, unorthodoxy, and social deviance.

As a concept, "heresy" provides a convenient and useful scholarly category. One may meaningfully study the elements and effects of heresy, the methods by which a society defines it and reacts to it. Yet none would assume the existence of a universal approach to the concept. What might constitute "heresy" is clearly not identical within the competing Christian denominations alone, not to mention the distinct systems of Judaism or Islam. Indeed, for non-dogmatic religions the very notion of "heresy" would be either meaningless or irrelevant. The inherent bias of this category has long been recognized. The same recognition must now be extended to that of magic.

---

[69] Arthur D. Imerti, ed. and trans., Giordano Bruno, *The Expulsion of the Triumphant Beast* (New Brunswick: Rutgers University Press, 1964), 238.

PART TWO

MAGIC AND RITUAL POWER IN
THE ANCIENT NEAR EAST

CHAPTER FOUR

HITTITE MILITARY RITUALS

Richard H. Beal

From approximately 1800 to 1175 BCE the Hittites were one of the great kingdoms of the ancient Near East, ruling much of Anatolia and often Syria, and successfully holding their own against such kingdoms as Egypt, Assyria and Babylonia.[1] Their records are preserved on cuneiform tablets, largely excavated from the royal archives at the site of their capital Ḫattuša, modern Boğazkale. Alongside annals, treaties, letters, instructions, land-deeds, literature, prayers, oracular results and festival instructions are found numerous magic rituals devoted to such diverse subjects as birth, healing, impotence, insomnia, counter-magic, family dissension, building, and infertile grapevines. Some are well preserved, some poorly preserved. It is not my aim here to discuss Hittite magical techniques[2] but rather the use made of magic in one important aspect of Hittite life: the military. I shall list and discuss the various rituals employed by the army to deal with the situations that it would encounter during the course of doing its duty to preserve the Hittite state.[3]

When soldiers were inducted into the Hittite army, they and/or their junior officers had to take an elaborate oath. In actions and in words, soldiers subjected themselves to a series of conditional curses that would take effect if they were disloyal. Here is a quotation from such an oath: "[The officiant] places wax and mutton-fat into their hands. Then he throws them into a fire, and says, 'As this wax melts and mutton-fat fries, so may he who breaks the oath and deceives the Hittite king melt like wax and fry like mut-

---

[1] I wish to thank H. A. Hoffner and J. A. Scurlock for reading and making many valuable suggestions on this paper. Any mistakes which remain are, of course, my own responsibility.

[2] For which see D. Engelhard, "Hittite Magical Practices: An Analysis" (Ph.D. diss., Brandeis University, 1970).

[3] I am preparing English translations of all of these rituals, together with transliterations and philological commentary where appropriate, as "Hittite Military Ritual Texts in Translation." Text numbers in the footnotes refer to this work.

ton-fat.' (The soldiers) reply, 'So be it!' ... They bring in women's clothing, and a distaff and a spindle (symbols of woman-hood); and they break an arrow (symbol of manhood). You speak to them (the troops) as follows: 'What are these? Are these not the dresses of a woman, which we have here for (your) oath? Whoever breaks these oaths and does evil to the king and the queen and the royal princes, let these oath-gods change him from a man into a woman. Let them change his soldiers into women. Let them dress them like women and cover their heads with kerchiefs. Let them break their bows, arrows and (other) weapons in their hands and put in their hands distaff and spindle.'[4] ... He places in their hands a [male] figurine, its belly filled with water.[5] He says, 'See the man who previously took this oath before the gods and then broke it. The oath-gods seized him. His belly is swollen. He holds up his swollen belly in front with his hands. May the oath-gods seize whoever breaks these oaths. May his belly swell.[6] May the sons of Išhara[7] [live] in him and feed on him.'"[8]

---

[4] For this type of magic see H. A. Hoffner, "Symbols for Masculinity and Femininity: Their Use in Ancient Near Eastern Sympathetic Magic Rituals," *JBL* 85 (1966): 326-34. For parallels from Ḫatti and an Arabic chronicle dealing with the Persians, see N. Oettinger, *Die militärischen Eide der Hethiter*, Studien zu den Boğazköy Texten (=StBoT) 22 (Wiesbaden: Otto Harrassowitz, 1976), 75f. with n. 19.

[5] Such statuettes have been found archeologically, see J. Börker-Klähn, "Illustrationen zum hethitischen Eidritual," in *Hittite and Other Anatolian and Near Eastern Studies in Honour of Sedat Alp*, ed. H. Otten et al. (Ankara: Türk Tarih Kurumu, 1992), 69-72.

[6] For the association of innards filled with water (dropsy=edema) in other ancient cultures, esp. Kassite and later Mesopotamia, Israel and Vedic India, see N. Oettinger, StBoT 22, 71-73.

[7] Išhara is called the "Queen of the Oath" in the curse formula of an edict (KUB 26.43 + KBo 22.56 rev. 19, edited and translated by F. Imparati, "Una concessione di terre da parte di Tudhaliya IV," *Revue hittite et asianique* XXXII [1974]: 36f.). She is also known to inflict disease. The goddess is often associated with the Moongod Kušuḫ, "lord of the oath." Išhara, as well as the Moongod as "lord of the oath," seem most at home in Kizzuwatna (= Cilicia) and N. Syria. (See G. Frantz-Szabó, "Išhara," *Reallexikon der Assyriologie*, 5.177f.) H. Kronasser's (*Etymologie der hethitischen Sprache* 1 [Wiesbaden: Otto Harrassowitz, 1963-66], 186) and Oettinger's (StBoT 22, 74) contention that the presence of Išhara in the Middle Hittite 1st Military Oath, well before the Hurrianization of the Hittite cult (late New Hittite), shows these deities to be natively Hittite can be ignored since there was an earlier stage of imports from Syria and Kizzuwatna after the conquest of these places by the Middle Hittite king Tudhaliya II. (Note especially that the newly found Hittite/Hurrian bilingual ritual—KBo 32:10-104, ed. E. Neu, StBoT 32 [forthcoming] is in Middle Hittite/Middle Script. See H. Otten, "Die Tontafelfunde aus Haus 16," *Archäologischer Anzeiger* (1984): 372-75. Išhara is mentioned in KBo 32.11, KBo 32:37

As can be seen from this quotation, what would happen to the oathbreaker was illustrated with a graphic analogy. The oathtaker subjected himself to potential punishment by holding, touching or licking the objects used in the analogy, thus establishing a physical link between himself and the oath. The whole exercise was simultaneously explained with words. The words of the oath were also linked to the troops by having them orally add, "So be it." The multiple punishments of the person who broke the oath were usually seen as being carried out by "oath-deities" or by the oaths themselves, although sometimes "the Stormgod," "the Moongod" or "the gods of Ḫatti" were asked to carry out the punishment. In the briefer paragraphs the punisher is not mentioned; if comparative evidence is any indication, the objects used in the oath ceremony would have been capable, by themselves, of enforcing the oath.[9]

The analogies that we have seen above were to wax and mutton-fat, melting in heat, conveying a threat of melting; a broken arrow and the wearing of women's clothing and the carrying of women's stereotypical objects: spindle and distaff conveying a threat of being turned into women; and a figurine of a man with swollen belly and filled with water conveying a threat of looking like this due to disease. Other oaths in the same text include an analogy to a blind and a deaf man; to a figurine (?) thrown face-down on the ground and squashed underfoot; to the crackling of rock-salt and sinews thrown into a fire; to the grinding, cooking and mashing of the malt and grains used in making beer—the malt here and the salt in the previous example do double duty since it is also pointed out that they cannot reproduce. There is also an analogy to yeast in breadmaking, with the threat that disease will make the oathbreaker crumble and puff up; and to a bladder-balloon squashed underfoot and emptied of air, with the threat that the oathbreaker's house will similarly be emptied of people and animals. Water poured on a fire, extinguishing it, is used on analogy with

---

and KBo 32:64). For the widespread worship of Isḫara in both Semitic and Hurrian cultures and the antiquity of this worship, see A. Archi, "Substrate: Some remarks on the formation of the west Hurrian pantheon," in *Hittite and Other Anatolian and Near Eastern Studies in Honour of Sedat Alp*, ed. H. Otten et al., (Ankara, Türk Tarih Kurumu, 1992), 9-10.

[8] Translation of the last sentence follows A. Goetze, in J. Pritchard, *ANET*[3], 354, against Oettinger, StBoT 22, 41f. For the texts quoted see below n. 11.

[9] E.g., E. Westermarck, *Ritual and Belief in Morocco* 1 (London: Macmillan, 1926), 518-69—reference courtesy of J. A. Scurlock.

oathgods similarly extinguishing the lives of the oathbreaker, his family, animals and crops. Water is also poured onto the ground, where it is swallowed up by the ground, with the threat that the same thing will happen to oathbreakers. The same act with wine represents the ground swallowing up the oathbreaker's blood.[10] The persistence of the reddish-brown color of tanned leather is used to illustrate the persistence of the pursuing oath-gods. The officiants break models of plow, wagon and chariot, with the threat that the oathbreaker's plow, wagon and chariot will be smashed. An oven is used due to the fact that nothing grows on the ground that is inside it. The heaviness of a rock is analogous to the heaviness of the disease that will be in the oathbreaker's innards, and the mixing of wine and water illustrate that the illness and innards of an oath-breaker cannot be unmixed. Broken sections involve torches, cedar splints, oxhide, clay and the smashing of jars.[11]

Before a campaign, the officers were given magical help. According to the ritual of Azzari, the Hurrian female physician, she would recite an incantation over some fine oil and then anoint with it the commanding "lord of the army," his horses, his chariot and implements of war.[12]

There was also a long ritual called "When the soldiers go away from the land to campaign and [they go] to the enemy land to fight." In this ritual, the practitioner lights a fire in the plain, sacrifices bread and wine and summons the gods to eat and drink. How exactly this was intended to protect the army and give them

---

[10] The spoken words here make an even stronger equation between the oath-takers' blood and the wine: "This is not wine. It is your blood." For a similar phrase in a Neo-Assyrian treaty see Oettinger, StBoT 22, 74f. Note also *Iliad* 3:292ff.

[11] "Ritual for When They Lead the Troops for the Oath" (= Text 1) = *CTH* 427, see N. Oettinger, *Die militärischen Eide der Hethiter*, StBoT 22 (Wiesbaden: Otto Harrassowitz, 1976), with edition of the Hittite, German translation, and extensive notes and commentary.

1st oath, 1st tablet: D: KBo 21.10, C: KUB 40.13 obv.!, E: Bo 6881.

1st oath, 2nd tablet: A: KBo 6.34 + KUB 48.76; B: KUB 40.16 + KUB 7.59 ++; C: KUB 40.13 rev.!; F: KBo 27.12, old tr. by A. Goetze, in *ANET*[3] (ed. J. Pritchard), 353f.

2nd Oath: KUB 43.38.

A number of oaths with similar use of analogous magic from the Greco-Roman and medieval Christian world are listed by J. Friedrich, "Der hethitische Soldateneid," *ZA* 35 (1924): 170-72. See also C. Faraone, "Molten Wax, Spilt Wine, and Mutilated Animals," *Journal of Hellenic Studies* 113 (1993): 60-80.

[12] (Text no. 3 =) KUB 30.42 i 8-14 (catalog entry), transliteration and French translation by E. Laroche, *Catalogue des textes hittites*[2] (= *CTH*) (Paris: Klincksieck, 1971), 162.

victory is unknown since the remainder of the ritual is broken away.[13]

Since chariot horses were nearly as important to the success of the Hittite army as the fighting men, it is not surprising that before a campaign chariot horses went through a purification ritual designed to remove, burn away and wash off evils from them.[14]

Another woman, Nikkaluzzi, wrote a ritual designed to protect the Hittite general and ensure that it was his opponent who was killed. "We made two figurines, [one of cedar] and one of clay. [On the one] of cedar we placed the name of the enemy of His Majesty, but on the one of clay [we put] the name of Ḫismi-Šarruma." The figures were presumably both thrown into a fire, whereupon the cedar figure of the enemy burned up while the clay figure of the Hittite was baked solid.[15] The Hittites had a strong concept of the just war; only if one's cause was legitimate would the gods give one victory in battle. By throwing both figurines into the fire, both underwent a sort of trial by fire. In this way, the war was symbolically transformed into a judicial ordeal by battle in which the injured party (the Hittites) was vindicated and the aggressors (the enemy) were found guilty and punished.

When the army reached the enemy's land, another ritual would be performed, in which the Hittites presented to the gods a legal justification for the war, together with a number of offerings. "They sacrifice one sheep to Zitḫariya. They say as follows: 'The god Zitḫariya keeps prostrating himself to all the gods. That which was Zitḫariya's perpetual share,[16] the lands which he wandered,[17]

---

[13] (Text no. 2) A: KBo 34.38; B: KUB 57.20; C: KUB 9.1 iii 31-iv 12; D: KBo 34.39; E: KUB 30.51 rev. 7'-8' (library catalogue entry), transliterated S. Košak, review of A. Archi, KUB 57, ZA 78 (1988): 310f.

[14] (Text no. 8) A: KBo 10.44, B: KUB 29.56, C: KUB 51.14, = CTH 644, transliteration and German translation by B. Rosenkranz, "Ein neues hethitisches Ritual für ᵈLAMA ᴷᵁˢ̌kuršaš," Or, n.s. 33 (1964): 253-55; A obv. 13-21 by B. J. Collins, "The Puppy in Hittite Ritual," Journal of Cuneiform Studies 42 (1990): 220 with n. 49 (into English).

[15] (Text no. 4) KUB 7.61 = CTH 417.1, partial English translation by H. G. Güterbock, "The Hurrian Element in the Hittite Empire," Cahiers d'Histoire Mondiale 2 (1954): 387 n. 44. Contrary to Güterbock, PU-Šarruma cannot be a Hittite king, since in another text, KBo 4.14 iii 40, it is said that PU-Šarruma "died." Hittite kings did not "die"; they "became gods."

[16] The word translated "perpetual share" is ukturi-. As an adjective this means "perpetual" and as a noun "incinerator, pyre" (cf. H. Otten, Hethitische Totenrituale, Veröffentlichungen des Instituts für Orientforschung der Deutschen Akademie der Wissenschaften 37 [1958], 141), a place where among other things corpses and impurities were safely disposed. In this text Von Schuler and Goetze (see below n. 19) have translated the term "Kultplätze" and "place of worship,"

where they used to give him great festivals,[18] now the Kaškeans
have taken them for themselves. The Kaškeans began the hostili-
ties. They continually boast of their power and strength. They
belittle you gods. Now Zithariya keeps prostrating himself to all
the gods. He keeps bringing you (his) lawsuit. All you gods, judge
his lawsuit. Let it be a considerable revenge for the gods. Those
(lands) are not taken away from Zithariya alone. They are taken
away from all you gods—from the Sungoddess of Arinna, the
[Storm]god of Nerik, the Stormgod, the Protective Deity, Telipinu
and from all the gods. His cities are taken from you. Now Zithariya
keeps bringing his lawcase to you gods. [Take] your own lawcase to
heart for yourselves. Judge your own lawcase. Judge the lawcase for
Zithariya. O gods, destroy the land of the Kaška. Let each deity
look after his own perpetual (allotment?) and take it back for
himself.'" Afterwards the enemy's gods were summoned: "O gods
of Kaška-land, we have called you to assembly. Come, eat, drink
and listen to the lawcase which we now are bringing to you. The
gods of Hatti have <taken> nothing from you gods of Kaška. They
have done nothing oppressing against you. And you gods of Kaška
made trouble and expelled the gods of Hatti from the land. You
took their land for yourselves. The Kaškeans started the trouble.
They took away the cities from the Hittites. They expelled them
from fields, pastures, and their vineyards. The gods and men of
Hatti are calling for the shedding of blood." After a lacuna the text
ends with a rousing statement: "Eat and drink. G[o (?)] back and
defe[at] the enemy."[19]

Ensuring victory in battle, however, did not necessarily guarantee a successful conclusion to the war. On a typical campaign, most
of the army's time would have been spent on the march, in camp,

---

respectively.

[17] From the resumption in i 41-42, this must be *weh-* + acc., "to wander
lands." Differently, E. Neu, *Interpretation der hethitischen mediopassiven
Verbalformen*, StBoT 5 (Wiesbaden: Otto Harrassowitz, 1968), 198 "vorhanden
sein" ("exist"), E. von Schuler, *Die Kaškäer* (Berlin: Walter de Gruyter, 1965),
168f. "zuwenden" ("bestowed upon"), A. Goetze, *ANET*[3], 354 "fall into tur-
moil." Other examples of *weh-* "to wander," cited by Neu, take datives, not
accusatives: *dankuwai takanzipi weh-*, HUR.SAG.MEŠ-*aš anda weh-*.

[18] *iške-* must here be the iterative of *iya-*; note the resumption in i 41 with
išša- the durative of *iya-*.

[19] (Text no. 10) A: KUB 4.1 i-iii 14; B: KUB 31.146; C: KUB 48.86 iv; D:
Bo 7960 (H. Otten & Chr. Rüster, *ZA* 67 [1977]: 59); E: 26/r = *CTH* 422, A&B
transliterated and translated into German in E. von Schuler, *Die Kaškäer*, 168-74,
English tr. A. Goetze, *ANET*[3], 354f.

or besieging an enemy city. Although no texts mention it, one can presume, based on records of other wars, that military camps could be as hazardous for the troops as actual combat and that, during prolonged sieges, more people, both besiegers and besieged, would have died of disease than from battle. At least six different rituals attempted magically to rid army camps of devastating diseases and to pass them to the enemy.

The best preserved is Ašhella's ritual. This ritual begins in the army camp in the evening. The generals and colonels each are given a ram and white, red, and green strands of yarn. The exorcist braids the yarn into a single strand for each officer and attaches a bead and rings of iron and lead. The officers each tie their yarn to their rams' horns and necks. Then they tie the rams up in front of their tents for the night, orally promising them to whatever deity is causing the plague. The next morning the officers place their hands on the rams and recite, Whatever deity made this plague, now see—rams are standing. They are fat with liver, heart and limbs. Let the flesh of humankind then become distasteful to him. Be satisfied with these rams. An adorned woman is seated before the king's tent. Each ram is matched with a jug of beer and a loaf of thick-bread. The woman is matched with a jug and three loaves. The officers bow behind the rams and the king bows behind the woman. The rams and the woman, the thick-bread and the beer are carried through the army. The woman and the sheep are then encouraged to flee Hittite territory, while the soldiers say, "What evil exists in the people, oxen, horses, mules and donkeys of this army—now, see those rams and woman have removed it from the army; whatever land meets them, let that one take this evil plague."

The second day is spent in a different place in the plain sacrificing rams, billy goats, beer, bread, and various vessels, trying to get on the good side of the deity who caused the plague. The food is cooked and offered, and the deity summoned to see his or her dinner, to "eat and drink like a deity" and "not forsake (a single) person." They abandon the knives used for the sacrifice, thus leaving behind the evil that they contain in the place where the sacrifice was performed. When they depart from the place of the ritual, they wash their hands in salty water and walk between two fires to wash and burn away residual evil. There is then a sacrifice of more billy goats, bread and wine to the Protective Deity of the Implements used and abandoned in the ritual earlier in the day. After this, all concerned eat and depart.

At dawn on the third day, again out on the plain, a billy goat, a

wether, a pig, three thick-breads and a pot of beer are offered to
the deity who caused the plague, and he is begged to come enjoy
himself by eating and drinking and to be at peace with the land and
army of Ḫatti. After this all concerned eat, drink and depart.

At dawn on the fourth day, at yet another place on the plain,
they sacrifice a bull and virgin ewe to the divine pair of the Hittite
pantheon, the Stormgod and the Sungoddess, and several sheep to
all the other gods.[20]

In this ritual, by means of various colors of wool, various
strands of the evil were transferred from the officers to the ram.[21]
By spending the night in the camp, the ram absorbed yet more
evils. Other evils were transferred when the officers put their hands
on the rams and bowed to them. Finally, carrying the rams, the
woman, bread and beer through the army was intended to draw out
evil from the rest of the army. When the participants drove the
rams and woman across the border, the evil now resident in the
rams and the woman was commanded to leave Ḫatti and go to the
enemy. It is interesting to note that the rams were matched one to
one with each high officer, with an even tastier morsel matched
with the king. Was each animal (or woman) intended to serve as a
personal substitute for one of the commanders and the king? or,
was the woman a scapegoat for the army as a whole, and did the
rams take the evils of each individual regiment/brigade? or were all
of the above true? While serving as scapegoats, the same rams (and
woman) simultaneously served as a sacrifice to propitiate the god
who had caused the plague in the first place. The efficacy of this
procedure was assured by further offerings and prayers to the deity
who had caused the plague. The intent of the sacrifices to the chief
gods of the pantheon and to all the other gods on the last day was
presumably that these gods, by accepting their share of the sacrifices, would agree to put social pressure on the god causing the
plague so that he would desist and accept the sacrifices. Presumably
it was also hoped that the gods would act as guarantors of the
plague god's decision to terminate the plague.

---

[20] (Text no. 11) A: KUB 9.32 + Bo 4445 (ZA 64:244); B: KUB 9.31 iii 14ff.;
C: HT 1 iii 1 - iv 43; D: KUB 41.18 ii 2-iii; E: KUB 41.17 iii-iv 25; F: KBo
13.212 rev.; G: FHL 95; H: 218/q = CTH 394, edited and translated into Turkish
by A. Dinçol, "Ašḫella Rituali (CTH 394) ve Hititlerde salgın hastalıklara karsı
yapılan majik ısemlere toplu bir bakıs," Belleten XLIX/193 (1985): 11-26,
German translation by H. M. Kümmel, in Religiöse Texte: Rituale und Besch-
wörungen, Texten aus der Umwelt des Alten Testaments 2 (Gütersloh: Güterslo-
her Verlagshaus Gerd Mohn, 1987), 285-88.
[21] See Engelhard, "Hittite Magical Practices" (Ph.D. diss.), 136-40, esp. 140.

In a second ritual, the officiant scatters a bit of straw and crumbles a bit of bread, apparently inside his room/tent. In the evening he gathers these fragments up into a basket and carries them outside. A woman stands in the entranceway and screams. The offerings are carried away, while the officiant says, "See, I've brought you [foo]d (?), O deity, and I've brought food for your dogs." The same ritual is performed for any person whose tent is affected. The ritual is repeated on a second and probably on a third day as well.[22] Apparently the image employed here is that of collecting up the day's table-scraps and throwing them out to the dogs lurking around the house. The scream of the woman presumably was part of the image of throwing out the table-scraps, namely, chasing the dogs away from the yard. Startled, the dogs could have been expected to grab the food and run off into the blackness.[23] Presumably, these scraps were thought to have been sitting out all day collecting the evils of the house. The intent of the ritual is that the scraps be carried from the affected dwelling, thrown away at a distance, picked up by the god's dogs and carried far away. This is an appropriate image since this plague deity apparently had a court of hounds. The scraps thus have an explicit second meaning, as an offering to the plague deity and his hounds.

A third, badly broken ritual was authored by an auspex named Maddunani. The ritual mentions two puppies, a pig, a clay statue, offerings, prayers, an uncultivated place, and the act of going through the army, all, in so far as can be seen, in a relatively standard way for these rituals. The ritual is unusual in that it was intended to be performed not by an exorcist/liver-diviner or "old woman," but rather by an auspex and an old man. The ritual is also unusual in that during the ritual and again at the end, a specific auspicial sign is looked for.[24] This presumably was designed to assure those performing the ritual that the deity concerned was

---

[22] (Text no. 12) A: KUB 41.17 i; C: 283/q, = CTH 424; edited and translated into German by V. Souček, "Ein neues hethitisches Ritual gegen die Pest," *Mitteilungen des Instituts für Orientforschung* 9 (1963): 167-72.

[23] For a very similar use of dogs in a rite in China used to get rid of ghosts see E. Ahern, *The Cult of the Dead in a Chinese Village* (Stanford: Stanford University, 1973), 198—reference courtesy of J. A. Scurlock.

[24] Ritual of Maddunani against Plague in the Army (Text no. 14) *CTH* 425.1 = A: KUB 7.54 i 1-ii 6; B: KUB 54.65 + IBoT 4.16 rt. col. 1'-6' + KUB 56.59; A i 5-9 transliterated with English translation, H. A. Hoffner, *Alimenta Hethaeorum: Food Production in Hittite Asia Minor*, American Oriental Series 55 (New Haven: American Oriental Society, 1974), 71; ii 1-6 transliterated by H. Otten & Chr. Rüster, *ZA* 72 (1982): 139f.; D: KUB 57.114 (+) KUB 55.9 rt. col. 3-8.

accepting the ritual.

A fourth ritual against plague in the army was authored by a certain Dandanku, also an auspex. In this ritual the participants mix straw and red, blue, black, green and white wool together and scatter them at a crossroads. It is explained that the straw is for the horses of the horsemen who accompany the god Yarri, and the wool is for his female attendants. The god Yarri was an archer who was occasionally thanked for giving the army victory. At other times he and his associates, the underworld heptad, were blamed for plague in the army.[25] The participants are to move to an uncultivated place to offer to this heptad a cut-up kid, piglet and puppy and to libate beer and wine three times to them. This is repeated in its entirety on the second day. On the third day the ritual takes place in the plain. Here a billy goat is sacrificed to Yarri, his heptad and attendants, and is cooked and eaten with bread and wine. Then a donkey is brought in and faced toward the enemy with the request, "Yo, Yarri, you made evil in this land and army. Lift up this donkey and carry it to the land of the enemy." This, unlike the other rituals against plague in the army, requires the participation of the client who requested and paid for the ritual. This client did not have to be the king or a general since the ritual adds that if the client is poor, a clay donkey can be substituted for the real donkey. After the participants are finished with the donkey, they string a bow and place an arrow in it. But then he (the officiant? the client?) pours the remaining arrows out from the quiver onto the ground, saying, "O god, keep shooting the enemy land with these arrows. But when you come into the land of Ḫatti, let your quiver be closed. Let your bow be unstrung." Then everyone returns from the plain. The fourth and last day contains more offerings and drinking to Yarri and his heptad but is largely broken away.[26]

A short ritual against plague in a fortress simply tells one to tie up a sheep at the edge of the fortress, and tell the deity who made the plague that the sheep is for him and that he should go to the enemy land and not into the fortress.[27]

---

[25] See H. Otten, "Jarri," *Reallexikon der Assyriologie*, 5.267f.

[26] (Text no. 15) *CTH* 425.2 = A:KUB 7.54 ii 7- iv, B: IBoT 4.16 rt. col. 7' + KUB 56.59 ii 7-iii + KUB 54.65 ii-iii!, partially edited and translated into German by H. Klengel, "Zu einem Ablenkungszauber bei Krankheit im hethitischen Heer (KUB LIV 65)," *Altorientalische Forschungen* 11 (1984): 175f.

[27] (Text no. 13) A: KUB 41.17 ii 1-17; B: KBo 22.121 i 1-16 = *CTH* 424, ed. V. Souček, "Ein neues hethitisches Ritual gegen die Pest," *Mitteilungen des*

One of the rituals specifies that when the army recovers, the king and the troops are to give an exaltation ritual to whatever deity has been causing the plague, and that the king, the generals and the captains are to give whatever presents to the deity that they wish.[28]

If things were going badly for the army, a ritual could be performed to turn things around: "When it gets scary in the field for a 'lord of the army,' or when all goes right for the enemy in battle, and it doesn't go right for our boys, (one performs the following ritual)."[29] The ritual itself unfortunately is broken away. Another ritual on the same tablet and presumably for the same purpose reads, "Throw hot fir cones and a hot stone into water. As the fir cones and the stone hiss and then cool and become silent, so may the manhood, battle, and renown[30] of you and your troops likewise grow cold and be extinguished. Like the stone, let them become deaf and dumb. Let their bowstring and arrow and slingstone (?)[31] be put (down). And let it grow cold. The gods march on our side. The (former) kings speak on our behalf. The multitude has hurried to our side. The gods have given boys to our army with manhood and bravery (?)."[32]

As the enemy closed in on a Hittite city, another ritual was performed which had the title "The Ritual of Heaven and Earth." The ritual is unusual and badly broken. The ritual involved the king, who would have been expected in most cases to be personally commanding an army in the field, the other officers, the non-commissioned officers, and even the scribe. The first paragraph involves seeking a male horse and bringing it to a mare of "the place of procreation."[33] The horse is eventually released toward the enemy, and it is said that it will bring the destruction of the enemy land. Dare one suggest that the returned enemy male horse is supposed to plant thoughts of mares in the minds of the other

---

Instituts für Orientforschung 9 (1963): 169-73.

[28] (Text no. 16) KUB 17.16 iv.

[29] (Text no. 19) KUB 7.58 i 18-22 (NS), transliterated and translated into English in the *Chicago Hittite Dictionary* L-N (Chicago: The Oriental Institute, 1980-89), 116b.

[30] Literally "news."

[31] Literally "stone of Alminala-town."

[32] (Text no. 18) A: KUB 7.58 i 1-17; B: KUB 45.20 i 1-32; C: IBoT 2.118 lf.col.; E. KUB 23.112 ii? = *CTH* 426.1; A i 1-12 transliterated and translated into German by E. Neu, *Interpretation der hethitischen mediopassiven Verbalformen,* StBoT 5 (Wiesbaden: Otto Harrassowitz, 1968), 68.

[33] Presumably meaning either "a brood mare" or "a mare in heat."

enemy stallions, thoughts that will distract them from their military duties? Next the participants take a wheel and say it is from
the land of Zidapara.[34] The king grasps the wheel and sets it in
motion while asking the gods to roll it against the (enemy) Hurrian
land and to follow it there.[35] After a long lacuna, there is an offering of a sheep and some thick-breads. Then the participants
wash out the braziers. After they perform a libation of wine and
bow three times to heaven and earth, the wash water goes through
some unusual type of object, is carried away in a leather bucket and
is eventually dumped into ox stomachs. Then "the entire (army)
libates away the enemy troops with what they washed out of the
braziers" and simultaneously asks the "seven deities" (perhaps the
seven underworld deities addressed in anti-plague rituals) to carry
away plague and to do evil to the enemy.[36] The prominence of
horses and wheels leads me to suspect that this ritual was designed
to help the Hittite chariotry defeat the enemy chariotry, but any
parallels that might help elucidate this sadly broken text would be
most welcome.

Of course, despite the best efforts of strategists and magicians,
defeats did occur. "If the troops are defeated by the enemy, they
perform the far-side-of-the-river ritual. On the far side of the
river, they cut in half a person, a billy goat, a puppy and a piglet.
Half of each they place on this side and half on that side. In front
they build a gate of hawthorn. Overtop they draw a rope. In front
of this, on either side, they light a fire. The troops go through the
middle. When they reach the river, they splash them with water.
Afterwards they perform the ritual of the battlefield for them in
the usual way." That is, whatever impurity caused the defeat was
magically removed from the troops by the hawthorn's scraping,
the fire's burning, the water's purification and the power of the
severed corpses. The soldiers were then magically reinducted into
soldiering, using the standard battlefield ritual.[37] They could thus

---

[34] Otherwise unknown.

[35] For a parallel to this wheel rolling against the enemy land, note the dream
in which a disk (Hebr. *kikkar*, cf. Akk. *kakkaru*) of bread rolls into the Midianite
camp and flattens a Midianite tent; the disk of bread is then explained as the
sword of Gideon into whose hand Yahweh has given the Midianites (Judges
7:13-14—reference courtesy of H. Hoffner).

[36] (Text no. 7) KUB 9.1 ii 13- iii 30.

[37] (Text no. 17) KUB 17.28 iv 45-56 = *CTH* 426.2, edited and translated into
German by H. M. Kümmel, *Ersatzrituale für den hethitischen König*, StBoT 3
(Wiesbaden: Otto Harrassowitz, 1967), 151-52, and into English by B. J. Col-
lins, "The Puppy in Hittite Ritual," *JCS* 42 (1990): 219f. with n. 44. Cf. C.
Faraone, *Journal of Hellenic Studies* 113 (1993): 71 n. 45, 79 with n. 73.

put their defeat behind them and, with morale high again, look
forward to their next victory.

It is interesting to note that the ritual actions performed in this
ritual are nearly identical to those performed in the ritual to purify
the army's chariot horses, which I mentioned earlier.[38]

After a victory, it was time to give thanks to the gods. Usually a
percentage of the booty was dedicated to them. Sometimes an
entire town and its hinterland would be emptied of its gods and
people and dedicated to the Hittite Stormgod as pasture for the
divine bulls who pulled his chariot. Removing the people was easy.
The gods of the enemy were more of a problem. Removing the
gods was accomplished by using an evocation ritual. Tables were set
up to the right and left and offerings put on them. Included was a
jug of beer with the enemy gods' names on it. A fire-pan and
brazier burned incense. From the tables long scarves of red, white
and blue material were rolled out and declared to be roads for the
gods. These were extended into nine roads of fine oil, nine roads of
honey and nine roads of pap. The gods were summoned to follow
the roads to the table. A sheep was then sacrificed to the male gods
of the city and another to the goddesses of the city, and the
roasted liver and heart were put on the offering table. After the
gods were out of the city, the king, dressed in the robes of kingship, made the enemy city sacrosanct; this was symbolized by
pouring out a vessel of wine while saying, "This city was hateful to
me." The king then summoned the Stormgod, thanked him for
giving it to him, and explained that he had now consecrated it and
was laying a curse on any person who would resettle it.[39] This could
be symbolically indicated by sowing the site with fennel (a weed
that grew particularly well on abandoned settlements). The latter

---

[38] For other Hittite rituals involving the severing of puppies see B. J. Collins,
"The Puppy in Hittite Ritual," *JCS* 42 (1990): 211-26. Cited there are similar
rituals known from the Bible and classical authors. The latter appear to be the
closest to the Hittite: Livy XL 6 describing a purification of the Macedonian
army; Hdt VII 41 describing a ritual of the Persian army, but misunderstood by
Herodotos and turned into a typical Greek tyrant story. In the biblical examples
the ritual is similar but the object is entirely different. Here those who pass
between the parts of the severed animal(s) (Yahweh himself in Gen 15:9-10 and
the notables of Judah in Jer 34:18-20) subject themselves to conditional curses;
that is, the Hebrew rituals are more like the Hittite military oath than the Hittite
and Greek military purification rituals.

[39] (Text no. 21) KUB 7.60 = *CTH* 423, edited and translated into German by
V. Haas & G. Wilhelm, "Hurritische und luwische Riten aus Kizzuwatna," *AOAT
Sonderreihe* 3 (1974): 234-39, and edited and translated into French by R.
Lebrun, "Le fragment KUB VII 60 = CTH 423," *Hethitica* 11 (1992): 103-15.

part of this ritual must have somehow been reversible, since an
early Hittite king, Anitta of Kuššara and Neša, emptied and laid
such a curse on the city of Ḫattuš,[40] which one of his successors
was to later make the Hittite capital.

In summary, in the military, as in every other facet of Hittite
life, magic played an important role. It helped ensure loyalty and
gave soldiers the confidence to go into battle; it supported morale
and, when necessary, rebuilt it. That it was successful can be seen
from the fact that Hittite armies ranged from the Hellespont to
the Ḫabur for two and a half centuries and that their kingdom
lasted some 600 years in a tough neighborhood.

---

[40] KBo 3.22:48-51 (Anitta's annals, Old Hittite Script), ed. E. Neu, *Der
Anitta-Text*, StBoT 18 (Wiesbaden: Otto Harrassowitz, 1974), 12f.

CHAPTER FIVE

RITUAL MEALS IN THE HITTITE CULT

Billie Jean Collins

In a prayer composed in the 15th century BCE by the Hittite king Arnuwanda I and his queen Ašmunikal, the royal pair lament the loss of their cult centers to Kaškaean raiders from the north.[1] The temples have been plundered, their contents and holdings taken. "Thus, in those lands no one any longer invokes your names, O gods. No one performs for you the rituals of the day, the month or the year. No one celebrates your festivals and ceremonies (ḫazziwi-)."[2] The Hittites took seriously their fundamental obligation to care for the gods. This prayer ends with a promise to send offerings through enemy lines to the cult centers.

Because of their importance to Hittite society, festivals and rituals from all over Anatolia were collected in the archives at Boghazköy and supply much information about religious life in the second millennium BCE. The ritual texts, which are prescriptive in nature,[3] give an abundance of detail about each part of the sacrificial procedure and the meal that follows it. They are our only major source of information about blood sacrifices, but they are more detailed than any of the Greek sources. These consist of descriptions of sacrifice in literary texts, vase-paintings and other iconographical evidence, and the so-called *leges sacrae*, which are

[1] I am grateful to the editors of the *Chicago Hittite Dictionary*, Harry Hoffner and Hans Güterbock, who have generously made their files available to me. The Dictionary is supported by a grant from the National Endowment for the Humanities. I also wish to thank Christopher Faraone, Richard Beal, Joanne Scurlock, Harry Hoffner and Gary Beckman who read the manuscript in its various forms and offered valuable comments.
[2] KUB 17.21 iii 12-16 (MH/MS) w. dupls. KUB 31.124 ii 22-25 (MH/MS), KUB 48.108 iii 6-10 (MH) (CTH 375.1), ed. Einar von Schuler, *Die Kaškäer* (Berlin: de Gruyter, 1965), 158-59, trans. Albrecht Goetze, "Hittite Prayers" in J. B. Pritchard, ed., *Ancient Near Eastern Texts Relating to the Old Testament*, 3rd edition (Princeton: Princeton University Press, 1969), 399.

[3] See Baruch Levine, "Ugaritic Descriptive Rituals," *JCS* 17 (1963): 105. See also Baruch A. Levine and William W. Hallo, "Offerings to the Temple Gates at Ur," *HUCA* 38 (1967): 17-58, and A. F. Rainey, "The Order of Sacrifices in Old Testament Ritual Texts," *Bib* 51 (1970): 485-98.

religious statutes, usually inscribed on stone, that stipulate calendrical sacrifice and other ritual activities. The Hittite ritual texts are
also a far richer source, both in quantity and in detail, than has
been left behind in either Mesopotamia or Egypt.[4] Thus, it is fair
to say that the implications of a discussion of Hittite cultic meals
for the study of ancient magic and ritual power may be considerable.

In investigating this topic, I have examined only those ritual
meals that include meat, which are less frequent than ritual meals
without meat.[5] Moreover, I have limited myself largely to those
rituals where eating is specifically mentioned. Many blood sacrifices occur that do not mention ritual feasting, and although it
seems likely in many instances that there was ritual feasting, we
cannot assume in these cases that a shared ritual meal followed the
sacrifice. The following study will address first the procedure leading to the meal, then the participants in the meal, and finally the
sacrificial victims.

It is difficult to talk about a typical procedure for the consumption of the sacrificed animal in Hittite ritual since no two instances
are exactly alike, the amount of detail varies greatly from description to description, and the most detailed descriptions are not
necessarily the most typical. In broadest terms, we may reconstruct an outline as follows: (1) preparation, (2) killing and butch-
ering, (3) setting the table, (4) calling the god(s) to eat, (5) feasting, and (6) withdrawal.

The ritual feast could take place in a number of locations: in the
temple before the altar of the deity, or at a *ḫuwaši-* , which was a

---

[4] For Mesopotamia see B. A. Levine and W. W. Hallo, *HUCA* 38 (1967): 17-
58, and W. W. Hallo, "The Origins of the Sacrificial Cult: New Evidence from
Mesopotamia and Israel," *Ancient Israelite Religion: Essays in Honor of Frank
Moore Cross,* ed. Patrick Miller et al. (Philadelphia: Fortress Press, 1987), 3-13:
for Egypt see Hermann Kees, "Bemerkungen zum Tieropfer der Ägypter und
seiner Symbolik," *Nachrichten von der Gesellschaft der Wissenschaften zu
Göttingen Philologisch-Historische Klasse* (1942): 71-88; Harold H. Nelson,
"Certain Reliefs at Karnak and Medinet Habu and the Ritual of Amenophis I,"
JNES 8 (1949): 201-32; Philippe Derchain, *Le sacrifice de l'oryx,* Rites Egyp-
tiens, I (Bruxelles: Fondation égyptologique reine Elisabeth, 1962), and
Françoise de Cenival, *Les Associations Religieuses en Egypte: d'après les
documents démotiques* (Bibliothèque d'Etude 46, 1972), 143-97, esp. 181-87.

[5] Bread and fruit offerings were less expensive and therefore more frequent than
meat offerings. For similar Greek practices see Michael H. Jameson, "Sacrifice and
Ritual: Greece," in Michael Grant and Rachel Kitzinger, eds., *Civilization of the
Ancient Mediterranean: Greece and Rome* (New York: Scribner's Sons, 1988),
963.

rock formation or stele made sacred by the presence of a deity. When no *ḫuwaši-* or temple was nearby, a tent could be constructed. Lacking even these luxuries, rituals could be held "on the steppe," away from human habitation, in which case greenery spread out on the ground would serve as an altar.

The preparation includes consecrating the animal and the sacred space in which the sacrifice will occur. The consecration can involve an incantation.[6] Washing the statue of the deity and anointing the altar are also a part of the preparations.[7] If the ritual occurred outside the god's temple, then his statue had to be set up. The critical personnel also had to be cleansed.[8] At least one ritual mentions the burning of incense prior to the offering.[9] In the ritual for the Stormgod of Kuliwišna, the victims were led to the place of the sacrifice in a procession: "As the yearly slaughter, they drive one ram and one bull to the pyres of the deity. In front of them the singers of Kaniš play the *ISTAR*-instrument and sing. The [c]ook consecrates [them] (the animals) [with] *tuḫḫueššar*.[10] The

---

[6] "The chief cook consecrates the altar with *tuḫḫueššar*. He consecrates the cattle and sheep. The chief cook speaks the words of consecration: 'J[ust a]s heaven is pure, let [the altar of] ⌜the gods,⌝ the jugular veins (of the victims), [the thick-bread] and the [lib]ation [vessel] ⌜be⌝ pu[r]e [in the same way].'" KUB 25.20 + KUB 46.23 iv 17'-23' (CTH 618), restored from the par. KUB 11.23 vi 1-3 (OH/NS).

[7] "They bring in the single goat and then wash it. They sweep the rooms (lit. houses) of the palace into which they drive it (the goat). Further, they spray them." KBo 13.179 ii 6'-10' (CTH 683.2). Cf. KUB 25.24 ii 8-9 (CTH 524, NH), ed. Volkert Haas, *Der Kult von Nerik* (Rome: Pontificium Institutum Biblicum, 1970), 244-45. In this and similar contexts, the substance sprayed is not named, although, more likely than not, it was water sprinkled on the floor to keep the dust down after sweeping.

[8] For example, in a ritual for the Stormgod of Kuliwišna, the master of the estate bathes in the bathhouse prior to the ceremony (KBo 15.33 ii 35, 39 [CTH 330, MH/MS], ed. George C. Moore, "The Disappearing Deity Motif in Hittite Texts: A Study in Religious History" [B.A. thesis, Oxford: Faculty of Oriental Studies, 1975], 75, 84). Cf. LÚSANGA-*za* ŠE.NAGA-*zi* KUB 17.35 i 1 (CTH 525.2, NH), ed. Charles Carter, "Hittite Cult-Inventories" (Ph.D. diss., University of Chicago, 1962), 123, 136.

[9] "When it is light the master of the deity goes before the deity and burns first-quality incense, recites an invocation and makes the offering rounds three times." KUB 53.20 rev. 14'-15', w. dupl. VBoT 58 iv 40-41 (OH/NS) (CTH 323).

[10] The substance *tuḫḫueššar* may be a kind of purificatory lotion that is made from a resin. Sedat Alp ("Zum Wesen der kultischen Reinigungssubstanz *tuḫḫueššar* und die Verbal form *tuḫša*," *Or* 52 [FsKammenhuber, 1983]: 14-19) believes that *tuḫḫueššar* is related to the noun *tuḫḫuwai-* "smoke," hence his translation "Räucher(harz)lotion." Hans G. Güterbock ("A Religious Text from Masat," *Anadolu Arastırmaları* 10 [1986]: 211) believes instead that *tuḫḫueššar* is a solid object and tentatively translates "resin."

master of the estate bows [behin]d them. They lead them forth to the master of the estate."[11]

As the following examples show, a consecrated animal produced consecrated meat, unless the meat was consecrated separately after the slaughter: "These birds, lambs and the single calf are consecrated. No one may eat them"[12]; "He puts the consecrated liver (dupl.: and heart) on top (of a broken loaf of soldier-bread) and sets (them) at the ḫuwaši- for the Stormgod of the town of Išdanuwa and for the Sungod."[13]

After the preparations are made, the victim is presented (šipant-) to the deity and then killed.[14] The words used for the slaughter are ḫuek- "kill" and ḫattai- "slit the throat." Later the animal might be butchered (mark-),[15] gutted (ark-)[16], and/or dismembered (arḫa ḫappešnai-).[17] Often the ritual omits direct reference to the slaughter, stating only—in a kind of shorthand—that the animal is presented, but meaning that it is presented, slaughtered and butchered.[18] The narrative then jumps to the next stage, which is the cooking and/or setting out of the meat.

Notably, there is never any mention of examining the exta of the dead animal as in Greek ritual. Perhaps we should assume that this is an omission of the obvious since numerous Boghazköy texts

---

[11] KBo 15.33 iii 4-8 (CTH 330, MH/MS), ed. G. C. Moore, B.A. thesis (1975), 76, 85.

[12] KBo 8.86 obv. 13'-14' (CTH 785), ed. Volkert Haas and Gernot Wilhelm, *Hurritische und luwische Riten aus Kizzuwatna*, AOATS 3 (Neukirchen-Vluyn: Neukirchener Verlag, 1974), 262f.

[13] KUB 32.123 iii 38-40 (NH) w. dupl. KBo 8.107:19'-21' (CTH 772.3).

[14] In virtually all of the contexts adduced here (with an animal as object), *šipant-* clearly does not refer to the killing of the animal. I have translated "present" in these sacrificial contexts because the animals are being brought before the god, presumably to be viewed (and approved [?]) by the god, prior to the slaughter. At the same time, I recognize that "present" is an inadequate translation for other contexts where *šipant-* is used.

[15] KUB 53.4 rev. 15'-16' (CTH 638); VBoT 24 ii 42 (CTH 393, MH/NS), ed. E. H. Sturtevant and G. Bechtel, *A Hittite Chrestomathy* (Philadelphia: Linguistic Society of America, 1935), 112-13; KUB 17.23 ii 20 (CTH 439, NS).

[16] IBoT 1.29 rev. 38 (CTH 633, OH/MS?); KBo 12.96 iv 15 (CTH 433, MH/NS); KUB 32.123 iii 35 (CTH 772.3, NH).

[17] VBoT 24 ii 2-3 (CTH 393, MH/NS), ed. E. H. Sturtevant and G. Bechtel, *Chrest.* (1935), 108f.

[18] On the concise nature of Hittite ritual prescriptions see now Cord Kühne, "Zum Vor-Opfer im alten Anatolien," in Bernd Janowski, Klaus Koch and Gernot Wilhelm, eds., *Religionsgeschichtliche Beziehungen zwischen Kleinasien, Nordsyrien und dem Alten Testament. Internationales Symposion Hamburg 17.-21. März 1990* (Orbis Biblicus et Orientalis, 129; Göttingen: Vandenhoeck & Ruprecht, 1993), 225-83.

record the results of extispicy. In addition, a recent study of Hittite "šumma immeru" texts has brought to light some evidence that the Hittites may have observed the victim's behavior as it was led to slaughter and examined its entrails afterwards.[19] However, since neither these texts nor any other text of oracular results mention that the particular oracle was taken during a ritual and no ritual mentions the taking of oracles, it is possible that in Ḫatti these were quite separate procedures.

When a location is specified, the slaughter is said to take place on an altar, or at a ḫuwaši-.[20] A wicker table (or a mat of greenery [GISlaḫḫurnuzi]) is generally used to hold the meal. The altar can also serve in this way. In the Festival for Telipinu in Ḫanḫana and Kašḫa, the slaughter occurs at a hearth on one occasion[21] and at a ḫuwaši- on another.[22] (Neither of these precludes the use of an altar as well.) In a ritual for the Stormgod of Kuliwišna, we are told that the slaughter takes place on the altar. This text provides us with what is perhaps the most detailed description of a blood sacrifice that we have:

---

[19] Harry A. Hoffner, Jr., "Akkadian šumma immeru Texts and Their Hurro-Hittite Counterparts," *The Tablet and the Scroll. Near Eastern Studies in Honor of William W. Hallo*, ed. Mark R. Cohen (Bethesda: CDL Press, 1993), 116-19.

[20] The use of the d.-l. in these contexts allows for two possibilities, that the slaughter occurred "on" the altar, ḫuwaši- and hearth, or simply "at" them. A single example of "altar" (ZAG.GAR.RA) with šer "upon" confirms that the sacrifice took place on the altar (KBo 22.216:11' [CTH 670, NS]). For the ḫuwaši-, on the other hand, when a d.-l. is not used, the texts consistently give ANA "to, at" rather than INA "on," and although Hittite scribes did not always differentiate between INA and ANA, the consistent use of ANA in these contexts suggests the slaughter took place near the ḫuwaši-s. This notion is supported by a number of texts that mention ḫuwaši-s being used in conjunction with altars, with the slaughter taking place on the latter. For more on ḫuwaši-s see Itamar Singer, "The ḫuwaši of the Storm-God in Ḫattuša," *IX. Türk Tarih Kongresi (Ankara, 21-25 Eylül 1981). Kongreye Sunulan Bildiriler I* (Türk Tarih Kurumu Yayınları, IX/9; Ankara: Türk Tarih Kurumu Basımevi, 1986), 245-53.

[21] "[They] present one sheep behind the temple. He kills (it) at the hearth in the temple for Telipinu." KUB 53.12 iii 21'-22' (CTH 638), ed. Volkert Haas and Liane Jakob-Rost, "Das Festritual des Gottes Telipinu in Ḫanḫana und in Kašḫa: Ein Beitrag zum hethitischen Festkalendar," *AoF* 11 (1984): 50-52.

[22] "They kill one sheep at the ḫuwaši- of Telipinu. They kill another sheep at the ḫuwaši- of the Stormgod." KUB 53.4 i 14'-15' and etc., w. dupls. Bo 3478(+)368/v iv 13'-14', KUB 53.8 rev.!? 12-13 (CTH 638), ed. V. Haas and L. Jakob-Rost, *AoF* 11 (1984): 73, 77.

The master of the estate presents them (the ram and bull) to the Stormgod of Kuliwišna. The cooks elevate (the heads of) the ram and the bull and they give the bronze knives to the master of the estate. The master of the estate places the hand with the bronze knife on the jugular vein of the ram and of the bull. The cooks kill (*ḫuek-*) them on the altar. They give those knives to the cook who accomplishes the killing. As soon as he cuts off a portion of the slaughter (lit. "he cuts off the slaughter of a portion") for the pyre of the deity, and if the master of the estate has vowed something to the deity—whether some utensil or an ox and sheep,—(they do the following:) They place the utensil on the loaves of soldier-bread. The cook consecrates the ox and sheep with *tuḫḫueššar*. They drive them in and the master of the estate bows behind them. He speaks, himself, before the deity: "With this word I vowed this and that. Now, I have just brought it to the deity, and before the deity [I have consecrated (?)] it."[23]

At the point of the slaughter, some texts tell us, ritual performers make noise, a practice that in Greek cult has been interpreted as an attempt to cover the death cries of the animal, or, by Jameson, as a means of summoning the god:[24] "On the third day when it is light, the queen bathes for the praised ZABABA. Further, she goes into the forest and presents one sheep and one goat for the praised ZABABA. The singer cries "*aha*" and they kill them at the *ḫuwaši*. The singer shouts."[25] Musical instruments might also be used: "He presents one sheep to the god Ḫilašši. They kill the *annalli*-(sheep) on the altar. The men of the thunderhorn blow. The shouter shouts. They set (out) the meat."[26]

An apparent alternative to noise-making was to provide entertainment for the deity, as in the following cult inventory text:

They provide cups, while the *ḫazgara*-women entertain the god. They divide the young men in half and name them. They call one half the "men of Ḫatti" and they call the other half the "men of Maša." The men of Ḫatti have weapons of bronze while the "men of Maša" have weapons of reed. And they do battle. The "men of Ḫatti" prevail over them and take a prisoner and give (*ḫink-*) him to the god. They pick up the god and

---

[23] KBo 15.33 iii 9-22 (CTH 330, MH/MS), ed. G. C Moore, B.A. thesis (1975), 77, 85f.

[24] Michael H. Jameson, *Civilization of the Ancient Mediterranean: Greece and Rome* (1988), 970.

[25] KBo 20.72 ii 14'-18' (CTH 694, OH/MS?).

[26] IBoT 2.103 iv 11-14 (CTH 530, NH).

carry him into the temple and set (him) on the altar. They break one loaf of a handful, libate beer and set down the lamps.[27]

The body parts of the victim are treated in a standard fashion. The shoulder, breast, head, forelegs, hindlegs, thigh bone and fat are either set before the deity raw or made into a stew. The purpose of the stew may have been to create a greater volume of food to go around. The liver and heart are generally cooked over a flame prior to being set in front of the deity.[28] Other body parts could on rare occasions be cooked in this way .[29] Often the ritual will take a short cut in describing the use of the body parts by stating simply that the meat "both raw and cooked" is set before the deity (raw referring to the shoulder, breast, head, feet, etc., and cooked referring to the liver, heart and occasionally the fat).[30] These raw cuts of meat are usually placed on or beside loaves of several types of bread (often broken) that have been set on the offering table before the deity along with various alcoholic beverages. A ritual performed at Nerik provides a rare example of the animals (a lamb and kid) cooked and served to the god unbutchered.[31]

---

[27] KUB 17.35 iii 8-17 (CTH 525.2, NH), ed. C. Carter, Ph.D. diss. (1962), 129f., 143.

[28] The free exchange of *happinit zanu-* and IZI-*it zanu-* suggests that they are synonymous in these contexts. Cf. J. Puhvel, *HED Ḫ* (1991), 121-22, who interprets *happena* as a solid object where roasting is done, hence, "baking kiln, fire-pit, broiler (oven)," in contrast to IZI-*it* (Hittite reading *paḫḫuenit*) *zanu-* "to cook over a flame."

[29] For example KUB 24.9 iv 2'-3' w. dupl. KUB 41.1 iv 12'-13' (UZU*kudur*), KUB 24.9 iv 13' (*manninkuwanda* UZUTI "short ribs") (CTH 402, both MH/NS), ed. Liane Jakob-Rost, *Das Ritual der Malli aus Arzawa gegen Behexung (KUB XXIV 9+)*, THeth 2 (Heidelberg: Winter, 1972), 50-53 (=ll. 14-15); KUB 27.67 ii 48-49 (shoulder of a ewe) (CTH 391, MH/NS), trans. A. Goetze, *ANET* (1969): 348; KBo 15.10 iii 69'-70' (shoulder of a rodent) (CTH 443, MH/MS), ed. Gabriella Szabó, *Ein hethitisches Entsühnungsritual für das Königspaar Tuthaliia und Nikalmati*, THeth 1 (Heidelberg: Winter, 1971), 46-47; KBo 11.10 iii 2 (MH/NS) w. dupl. KBo 11.72 ii 41-42 (MH?/NS) (kidney) (CTH 447); VBoT 24 ii 36-37 (ear), 39-40 (breast) (CTH 393, MH/NS), ed. E. H. Surtevant and G. Bechtel, *Chrest.* (1935), 110f.; KBo 20.64 obv. 11 (head and breast) (CTH 631).

[30] KUB 7.24 obv. 7 (CTH 506, NH), KUB 25.23 left edge 4-5 (CTH 525, NH). Raw meat only: KBo 12.96 iv 15-16 (CTH 433, MH/NS), KUB 53.20 rev. 20' (CTH 323), KUB 7.1 i 9-10 (CTH 390, pre-NH/NS). With the formulation "the meat, namely x, is set out": KUB 17.28 iii 4-5 (CTH 456.2, MH/NS). Not specifying whether the meat is raw and/or cooked: KUB 55.15 iii (?) 9 (CTH 530), KBo 20.92 iv 16 (CTH 447, MH?/NS).

[31] "They skin ? them whole, cook them, and place them before the god." KUB 38.25 i 13'-15' (CTH 524, NH), ed. V. Haas, *KN* (1970): 276f.

On rare occasions, a text might provide a more detailed list of
the body parts. Those parts that are less often referred to include
the kidney (UZUELLÁG.GÙN), the shoulder blade (UZUNAGLABU),
the testicle (UZUarki), the "hand (i.e., foreleg)" (UZUQĀTU), the
hind leg (UZUwallaš ḫaštai), the unidentified UZUkudu and
UZUmūḫ(ḫa)rai-, which are also cooked in a stew, and UZUkatta-
pala-, which is set out for the god.

The hide and bones of the animal are treated differently from
the other parts. In a ritual for the Protective Deity, the hides are
given to the leatherworkers, presumably to be processed and used
elsewhere.[32] Like the other animal parts, however, the hide could
sometimes be set before the deity.[33] Occasionally, the skin and/or
bones are burned: "As soon as the bones and lambskin are set in
each place, they burn [them] up right there;"[34] and elsewhere:
"They gather up the bones and put them down on the hearth.
They finish and they burn the bones."[35]

None of the texts that describe the ritual meal specifically refer
to the blood of the animal. However, other descriptions of sacrifice do refer to it. In these rituals the blood is either caught in a
vessel (ḫuppar "bowl", zeri-/GAL "cup"), or allowed to flow into a
pit (ESAG "grain storage pit," wappu- "clay pit"), or onto flour or
bread (ZÍD.DA, NINDA.GUR₄.RA, resp.). In one ritual, the blood
and fat of the animal are mixed with porridge.[36] The text breaks
off before telling us whether this porridge is served to the deity.
Either way, the blood of the victim seems to have little importance in the context of the ritual feast itself.

After all these preparations, the food is set before the deity so
that he may eat it "with his eyes."[37] Libations might be poured at

---

[32] "[They give (?)] the pelts to the leatherworkers." KBo 13.179 ii 14'-15'
(CTH 683.2).

[33] "They gut the sheep. Then they take the raw meat and set the hide, breast
and shoulder before the deity." KUB 7.1 i 9-10 (CTH 332, pre-NH/NS).

[34] KBo 13.164 iv 1-2 (CTH 670, OH/NS).

[35] KBo 15.25 rev. 18-19 (CTH 396, MH/NS), ed. Onofrio Carruba, Das
Beschwörungsritual für die Göttin Wišurijanza, StBoT 2 (Wiesbaden: Harrassowitz, 1966), 6f. The restorations follow Carruba (see his commentary).

[36] "They mix the blood and fat of the goat (dupl. and the sheep fat) with a
handful of porridge. They make two iduri-loaves." KBo 15.49 i 9'-11' w. dupl.
KUB 32.128 ii 21'-24' (CTH 628, both MH/NS).

[37] A. L. Oppenheim, Ancient Mesopotamia: Portrait of a Dead Civilization,
rev. ed. (Chicago: University of Chicago Press, 1977), 183-98, esp. 191f., discusses the "Care and Feeding of the Gods."

this point in the proceedings, that is, just prior to the feasting.[38] Often libations are poured in conjunction with the breaking of bread.[39] Libations could also occur after the feast, although seemingly with less frequency.[40] In one instance, a libation is poured while the statue of the deity is *en route* back to the temple.[41]

Those who are designated to eat (this does not always include everyone present) may now seat themselves before the deity. The feasting is generally initiated by the phrase "then they eat and drink."

The final act in any sacrificial celebration is the drinking ceremony, in which the participants "drink the god." The god in question is always the one(s) to whom the ritual is directed. The procedure may be illustrated by the following examples: "Then he (the client) drinks the Sungod of Heaven, the Stormgod, and all the gods three times. They eat. Then they come away."[42] "They give to the client for drinking and he drinks the Stormgod. The singer sings in Hurrian. But the exorcist recites from the tent in Hurrian as follows."[43] "They (the augurs) make goat stew and they eat (it). Then they drink the Protective Deity of the Hunting Bag, standing, three times. But afterward, what gods are valuable for them, those gods they continue to drink."[44] "He (the palace servant) asks to drink. The chief palace servant con[tinues] to libate. The first time, he drinks (to) the Sungod of Heaven. Afterward he drinks t[o] the Stormgod. Afterward he drinks t[o] the Protective Deity. But we continue to drink, seated [. . .]."[45]

---

[38] KUB 12.58 iv 1, 5 (CTH 409, NH), ed. Albrecht Goetze, *The Hittite Ritual of Tunnawi* (New Haven: American Oriental Society, 1938), 20f.; KBo 12.96 iv 17 (CTH 433, MH/NS); KUB 57.79 iv 21-22 (NS); IBoT 1.29 rev. 45 (CTH 633, OH/MS?); KBo 20.72 iii 24'-25' (CTH 694, OH/MS?), KUB 27.67 ii 53, 57 (CTH 391, MH/NS), KUB 17.28 iii 12 (CTH 458, MH/NS).

[39] KUB 24.9 iv 10'-11' (CTH 402, MH/NS), ed. L. Jakob-Rost, THeth 2 (1972), 52f.; KUB 53.20 rev. 17'-18', w. dupl. VBoT 58 iv 42-43 (OH/NS) (CTH 323); KBo 15.25 rev. 8 (CTH 396, MH/NS), ed. O. Carruba, StBoT 2 (1966), 4f.

[40] KUB 4.1 iii 7'-9' (CTH 422, MH/NS), ed. E. von Schuler, *Kaškäer* (1965), 172f.; KBo 12.96 iv 17 (CTH 433, MH/NS).

[41] KBo 15.25 rev. 23-24, see n. 50.

[42] KUB 9.32 rev. 30-32 (CTH 394, NH), ed. Ali M. Dinçol, "Ašḫella Rituali (CTH 394) ve Hititlerde Salgın Hastalıklara Karsı Yapılan Majik islemlere Toplu Bir Bakıs," *Belleten* 49/193 (1985): 22-23.

[43] KUB 12.11 iv 17-20 (CTH 628, MH/NS).

[44] VBoT 24 iv 27-31 w. dupl. KBo 12.104 iv 2'-7' (CTH 393, NH), ed. E. H. Surtevant and G. Bechtel, *Chrest.* (1935), 116f.

[45] KBo 15.25 rev. 14-17 (CTH 396, MH/NS), ed. O. Carruba, StBoT 2 (1966), 4-7.

The meaning of the phrase "to drink the god" continues to be in dispute.[46] The problem centers on the use of an accusative rather than a dative for the object,[47] forcing a translation "drink the god" rather than the more easily explained "drink to the god," or, as has been proposed, "give to the god to drink," with the verb taking on an uncharacteristic causative sense. Melchert has summarized previous discussion in his article on the subject, in which he reasserts the meaning "drink to (the honor of) the god x."[48] Güterbock disagrees with all these proposals and asserts instead that the god being "drunk" is the liquid contained in the cup.[49] For the sake of caution, the phrase is translated literally in this essay.

Finally, the participants remove themselves from the place of the ritual and the deity is also removed (unless the ritual occurs in the temple), as the following examples illustrate: "They eat and drink. Then they come away" (see note 69); "The deity [goes back] into the temple and as soon as the deity arrives at the threshold, the client bows [to the deity] and libates beer. Then I [br]ing the deity into the [temple]."[50]

*   *   *

Those attending the ritual include members of the temple personnel, members of the royal family when required, and professional ritual practitioners who officiate when the feast occurs in the context of a purification. In such cases, a client (a.k.a., the patient, offerant, sacrificer) is also present. The agent of the

---

[46] To Frantz-Szabó's extensive bibliography on the subject in *RlA* 7 (1987-90): 5, add the following references: Jaan Puhvel, "On an Alleged Eucharistic Expression in Hittite Rituals," *MIO* 5 (1957): 31-33; *idem, Hittite Etymological Dictionary A, E/I* (Berlin: de Gruyter, 1984), 261-68, esp. 266f.; A. Kammenhuber, *HW²* II (Heidelberg: Winter, 1988), 30-31; *ead.* "Nochmals: der hethitische König trinkt Gott NN," *Text, Methode und Grammatik: Wolfgang Richter zum 65. Geburtstag*, ed. W. Gross, H. Irsigler and T. Seidl (St. Ottilien: Eos Verlag, 1991), 221-26. For a possible parallel from the Greek world see William Brashear, "Ein Berliner Zauberpapyrus," *ZPE* 33 (1979): 261-78, esp. 271; and Robert W. Daniel and Franco Maltomini, *Supplementum Magicum II*, (Opladen: Westdeutscher Verlag, 1992), no. 72, pp. 109f., 117-19.

[47] Examples of this construction using the dative can be found, albeit infrequently. See the last example above, with n. 44.

[48] "'God-Drinking': A Syntactic Transformation in Hittite," *JIES* 9 (1981): 245-54.

[49] Hans G. Güterbock, "To Drink a God," *Proceedings of the 34th Rencontre Assyriologique Internationale, Istanbul, Turkey, 1988* (Ankara, forthcoming).

[50] KBo 15.25 rev. 22-25 (CTH 396, MH/NS), ed. O. Carruba, StBoT 2 (1966), 6f.

slaughter is the primary officiant, whether an old woman, augur, exorcist, priest, cook, or some other official.

Not everyone present is expected to participate in every ritual feast. Such exclusionary practices are sometimes indicated in the ritual with the injunction "no one else may eat."[51] Participants who are specifically enjoined to eat of the meat include, from the royal family, the king, the prince and possibly the queen; from the temple personnel, the priests, the cooks, the augurs, the exorcists, the singers, the so-called "guardians of the hearth," the "men of the courtyard," the "lion-men," the *hazgara*-women, the staff-men, the "sister of the deity" priestesses, the "mother of the deity" priestesses, *asusala*-men, and female attendants; outsiders include the men of the city called "Deaf Man's Tell," a man from the city of Isdahara, and children.[52] The *hassumas* Festival provides an extensive and specific list of feasters:

> Wherever in the kitchen the Prince requests to eat, twelve priests are seated in front (of him): the priest of the Stormgod, the man of the Stormgod, the pri[est of . . .], the priest of Katahha, the priest of the Grain(-goddess [?]), the priest of *ZABABA*, the priest of Tasmidu, [. . .] the

[51] KBo 23.67 iii 12 (CTH 704, MH/NS); KUB 45.47 iv 35 (CTH 494, MS?).
[52] King KUB 12.12 v 22-23 (CTH 628, MH/NS), ed. Ilse Wegner and Mirjo Salvini, *Die hethitisch-hurritischen Ritualtafeln des (h)issuwa-Festes*, Corpus der Hurritischen Sprachdenkmäler I.4 (Roma: Multigrafica Editrice, 1991), 149, 151; KBo 13.194:8' (CTH 670), KUB 17.28 iv 39-41 (CTH 458, MH/NS); prince KUB 53.4 rev. 19' (CTH 638.2), IBoT 1.29 rev. 41-43 (CTH 633, OH/MS?); queen possibly in KBo 20.92 iv¹ 13-17 (CTH 447, MH/NS), KUB 45.47 iv 34-35 (CTH 494, MH/MS?); priests KBo 17.33 iv 1'-4' w. dupl. KBo 17.36 iii 9'-12' (CTH 661, OS), KUB 58.30 ii 7'-9' (CTH 638, OH/NS), ed. V. Haas and L. Jakob-Rost, *AoF* 11 (1984): 67f.; cooks KUB 54.65 iii¹ 13'-14' (CTH 425.2, NH); augurs KBo 12.96 iv 4-19 (CTH 433, MH/NS), VBoT 24 ii 42-43 (CTH 393, NH), ed. E. H. Sturtevant and G. Bechtel, *Chrest.* (1935), 112f.; exorcist and singer KUB 12.11 iv 11-12 (CTH 628, MH/NS); guardians of the hearth KBo 10.45 iv 16-17 w. dupl. KUB 41.8 iv 15-16 (CTH 446, both MH/NS), ed. H. Otten, *ZA* 54 (1961): 136f.; "men of the courtyard" KBo 20.51 i 16'-18' (CTH 694); "lion-men" and *hazgara*-women KUB 55.15 iii (?) 7-11 (CTH 530); staff-men KUB 54.65 iii¹ 13'-14' (CTH 425.2, NH); "sister of the deity" priestesses Bo 6594 iii (?) 3-4 (CTH 738, OH), translit. Erich Neu, *Althethitische Ritual-texte in Umschrift*, StBoT 25 (Wiesbaden: Harrassowitz, 1980), 99; "mother of the deity" priestesses KUB 25.24 ii 15 (CTH 524, NH), ed. V. Haas, *KN* (1970): 244f.; *asusala*-men KBo 17.36 iv 12'-13' (CTH 661, OS); female attendants KUB 54.65 iii¹ 13'-14' (CTH 425.2, NH), KUB 17.28 i 23 (CTH 730.1, MH/NS); men of the city called "Deaf Man's Tell" KUB 25.23 left edge a1-b3 (CTH 525, NH); a man from *Isdahara* KUB 60.147 iv (?) 12-13 (CTH 670); children Bo 7937 left column 4 (CTH 648), ed. Sedat Alp, *Beiträge zur Erforschung des hethitischen Tempels*, TTKY VI/2 (Ankara, 1983), 234f., KUB 9.31 ii 13-14 (CTH 757, MH/NS).

priest of Ḫalmaššuitti, two priests of Anzili [...], the priest of Ḫašammili, one Staff-Man, one Spear-Man, one [...]-man, [N] fore-court-sweepers, two *šarmieš*-men, one cupbearer, one table-man, one baker, one crier, one smith of the deity, three temple servants, three farmers—these [sit down] to eat.[53]

On at least one occasion the text specifies that the entire congregation (*panku-*) may eat. However, most often it is the unspecified "they" who are enjoined to sit and eat. We must assume that "they" include all persons present and that the scribes are not simply neglecting to mention to which group the word "they" refers. The texts do not provide any indication of why particular officials or individuals were singled out for the feast.

One of the more enigmatic groups of participants is a poorly attested people called the *dampupi-*, which means "untaught" or "uneducated," and refers to attendees who were not trained in religious observances.[54] In one unique case of a purification, these persons consume a puppy that has been ritually killed.[55] Puppies and dogs are not eaten in Hittite texts outside of this instance. On one other occasion the *dampupi-* are given bread to eat, but are prohibited from eating the meat of the goat that has just been killed.[56]

There is evidence that the persons who partook of the feast had to be consecrated, or at least clean, prior to the meal. In one text we read, "The consecrated [priests e]at cheese (and) rennet. But

---

[53] IBoT 1.29 obv. 18-24 (OH/MS?) w. dupls. KUB 51.57 obv. 21-29 (OH?), Bo 3228:7'ff. (restorations are from this frag.) (CTH 633), cf. V. G. Ardzinba, "The Birth of the Hittite King and the New Year," *Oikumene* 5 (1986): 91-101.

[54] In the lexical text KBo 1.30 obv. 8', 9' ([CTH 305], ed. Hans G. Güterbock, in *Materials for the Sumerian Lexikon* XII [Rome: Pontificium Institutum Biblicum, 1969], 214f. ["uncivilized," the Sumerian column gives the equivalent lú aš-ḫab]), *dampupi* is twice paired with Akk. *nuʾu. Nuʾu/nuwaʾum* was the term used by the Old Assyrian merchants to refer to the native Anatolian population. For a discussion, see D. O. Edzard, "Altassyrisch nuwaʾum," *Anatolia and the Ancient Near East: Studies in Honor of Tahsin Özgüç*, ed. Kutlu Emre et al. (Ankara, 1989), 107-09.

[55] KUB 9.7 obv. 3-4 (CTH 763, NH).

[56] "They kill a billy goat and they burn it with [...]. Offering loave[s ...] the uninitiated eat up [...]. But the meat they do not give (out). But the dead [...] they kill it, and they come away [...]." KBo 3.63 ii 3'-8' (CTH 655, pre-NH/NS). The goat is burnt whole rather than cooked, and this may be the reason for the prohibition on its consumption.

[57] KUB 45.49 iv 8-10 (CTH 790, NH), translit. H. Otten, *Materialien zum hethitischen Lexikon*, StBoT 15 (Wiesbaden: Harrassowitz, 1971), 29.

the impure ones (*šaknuwanteš*) do not eat. It is inappropriate."[57] Another passage states that the "men of the courtyard" (LU.MES*ḫilammieš*), whichever of them have bathed, may eat the meat and drink the cup of wine that has been provided.[58]

The "leftovers" from the ritual are sometimes distributed to various parties. In one Hattian ritual the bones of the sacrificed piglet are taken to the kitchen and sold. The skin of another victim is given to the leatherworkers in a ritual for the Protective Deity (see note 32). In a ritual to be performed prior to a campaign against the Kaškaeans, the "master of the deity" is given the sheepskins and the model implements used in the feast.[59] In these sparse examples, I do not perceive anything akin to the distribution of the animal parts as salary to the temple personnel that we see in later periods in Mesopotamia.[60]

* * *

The animal of choice for the ritual meal, and indeed for all offerings, was the sheep. This was more an economic than a religious decision. Goats are almost as common as sheep in meat offerings. Lambs and kids are also offered, but with much less frequency than adult animals. Calves are the rarest of all animals to be offered. Cattle in any form are relatively rare in comparison to sheep because of their high cost and the larger the quantity of meat they provide per animal. Bulls (GU$_4$.MAḪ) are most frequently offered to the Stormgod, with whom they are identified in myth and who stands very high in the pantheon.[61] Unspecified forms of cattle (GU$_4$) and other kinds of animals—such as plow oxen—could be offered to other deities.

---

[58] KBo 20.51 i 16'-18' (CTH 694).

[59] "You (gods) eat and [drink]! Re[turn] (to the army) and bat[tle] the enemy! When he (the practitioner) has finished, he goes again before the gods of Ḫatti and they consume the fat and the bread. He offers libations to the gods of Ḫatti, the Stormgod of the Army and ZABABA. They drink however many times it seems good to them. The master of the deity takes the model implements and the sheepskins. They return to the army and go to battle thus." KUB 4.1 iii 2'-14' (CTH 422, MH/NS), ed. E. von Schuler, *Kaškäer* (1965), 172f., tr. A. Goetze, *ANET* (1969), 355.

[60] Cf. Gilbert J. P. McEwan, "Distribution of Meat in Eanna," *Iraq* 45 (1983): 187-98.

[61] KBo 13.93 rev. 10'-11' (CTH 500); KUB 9.32 rev. 21-24 (CTH 394, NH), ed. A. Dinçol, *Belleten* 49/193 (1985): 21, 26; uncertain, 1238/v:10'-12' (CTH 638), ed. V. Haas and L. Jakob-Rost, *AoF* 11 (1984): 67f.

The animal allotted for sacrifice had to be of high quality.[62] The offering of a lesser animal was a matter of some concern to the officiants as we are told in a text of Instructions to the Temple Personnel: "If any cowherd or shepherd perpetrates a deception on the road and turns aside a fattened ox or fattened sheep, and (either) he sells (the fattened one), or he kills it and they consume it and substitute a thin one in its place, and it becomes known, that is a capital crime for them. They have taken the fine(st) food of the gods' choice."[63]

Multiple animals, multiple species of animals and animals of varying ages and sexes might be offered in a single ritual or festival. Each might also be sacrificed following a different formula.

What Jameson refers to as the "principle of appropriateness" applies to Hittite cult as well as Greek.[64] Male animals will be offered to male gods and female animals to female gods. But this practice appears not to be strictly enforced—at least, more often than not, the sex of the animal is not specified. More frequently there is a color requirement.[65]

$$*\qquad*\qquad*$$

Most of the rituals discussed herein are "occasional" rituals— that is, they were performed when there was a need for them. In these rituals, in exchange for the meal, the officiants seek the favor of the god in question on behalf of the client. More than simply a communion with the god, the ritual feast was a chance to sway a god or goddess to benevolence. In these cases, the sacrifice serves to reinforce the prayer:[66] "Then (the augurs) kill the sheep

---

[62] Cf. CHD L-N (1989) 298, sub mišriwant- b.

[63] KUB 13.17 rev. 21-25 (NH) w. dupl. KUB 13.4 iv 61-67 (pre-NH/NS) (CTH 264), ed. Aygül Süel, Hitit Kaynaklarında Tapınak Görevlileri ile ilgili Bir Direktif Metni (Ankara: A.Ü. dil ve Tarih-Coğrafya Fakültesi Basımevi, 1985), 86f., CHD L-N (1989) sub maršatar, maklant-.

[64] The Ritual of Ašhella against a plague in the army specifies that the ewe chosen for the sacrifice must be virgin: "They bring one bull, one ewe, and one wether. But (it must be) a ewe to which a ram has not yet gone." KUB 9.32 rev. 21-22 (CTH 394, NH), ed. A. Dinçol, Belleten 49/193 (1985): 21, 26.

[65] For example, Bo 3752 ii 3' (CTH 470, OS?), translit. E. Neu, StBoT 25 (1980), 179; KBo 17.15 rev. 6' (CTH 645, OS), translit. E. Neu, StBoT 25 (1980), 73; KUB 30.32 iv 15'-16' (CTH 304, MS?); KUB 7.53 i 11-12 (CTH 409, NH), ed. A. Goetze, Tunn. (1938), 4f.; KUB 54.64 rev. 2 (CTH 678, NS), ed. V. Haas, KN (1970), 304f.; KUB 55.39 i 3' (CTH 591, OH).

[66] For a discussion of sacrifice reinforcing prayer see Michael H. Jameson, in Civilization of the Ancient Mediterranean: Greece and Rome (1988), 963-64.

for the god and say as follows: 'Now the client is giving you an offering. Take the offering, O god, and turn in favor to him. What he keeps saying to you turn your ear to him.'"[67] In another text the officiant cries, "Who(ever) is hungry, who(ever) is thirsty (among) the gods, come, eat and drink, and join with me. From the house and city may you cleanse the evil impurity, bloodshed, perjury, sin, and curse. He bound them, (each evil's) feet and hands, so let the dark earth keep them in."[68] Finally, a ritual against plague in the army—compare Richard Beal's essay above—includes a sacrifice with a very specific purpose in mind: "They present the billy goat, the sheep and the pig to that very deity who made this plague in the army, (saying), 'Let that deity eat and drink, let him be friendly to the land of Ḫatti and to the army of the land of Ḫatti. Let him turn in favor (to the army).' They eat and drink. Then they come away."[69]

Ritual meals were also an important part of the state cult, but festival texts tend toward brevity in the description of shared ritual meals. The AN.TAḪ.ŠUM Festival describes very briefly preparations for a meal in the temple of *ZABABA*, but omits the meal itself.[70] The "Great Assembly" that takes place during the KI.LAM Festival may provide a model of a state-level cultic meal involving sacrifice, but while many of the usual activities are described, including an extensive drinking ceremony, a description of the sacrifice itself is omitted, as are any incantations or prayers. Without such invocations, we cannot deduce the nature of the Hittites' communications with the gods in these circumstances. That is, we cannot know, based on the festival texts alone, what "give and take" the participants in the feast at the state cultic level expected to initiate by sharing a meal with the gods.

We are, however, offered a glimpse into the reciprocity symbolized by the shared cultic meals by the prayer of Arnuwanda I and Ašmunikal with which this essay began. Implicit in the king and queen's lament is that the gods, by not protecting the interests of their worshippers, have contributed to the downfall of the religious system that kept them in offerings. The sentiment of reciprocity is more explicitly stated in the Hurrian mythological

---

[67] KBo 12.96 iv 9-14 (CTH 433, MH/NS).

[68] KBo 10.45 iv 11-15 w. dupl. KUB 41.8 iv 10-14 (CTH 446, both MH/NS), ed. Heinrich Otten, "Eine Beschwörung der Unterirdischen aus Boğazköy," *ZA* 54 (1961): 134-37.

[69] KUB 9.32 rev. 14-19 w. dupls. KUB 9.31 iv 19-27, HT 1 iv 23-30 (CTH 394, all NH), ed. A. Dinçol, *Belleten* 49/193 (1985): 19f., 25.

[70] KBo 4.9 i 11-24 (CTH 612), ed. S. Alp, *Tempel* (1983): 156f.

text, the Song of Hedammu: "[Ea], King of Wisdom, spoke among
the gods. [The god Ea] began to say, 'Why are y[ou] destroying
[humankind]? They will not give sacrifices to the gods. They will
not burn cedar as incense to you. [If] you destroy humankind, they
will no longer [worship] the gods. No one will offer [bread] or
libations to you any longer. . . . Why are you, O Kumarbi, seeking
to harm humankind? Does [not] the mortal take a grain heap and
do they not promptly offer (it) to you, Kumarbi? Does he make
offering to you alone, Kumarbi, Father of the gods, joyfully in the
midst of the temple? Do they not (also) offer to Teššub, the Canal
Inspector of humankind? And don't they call me, Ea, by name as
King?'"[71]

---

[71] KUB 33.103 ii 1-5, 9-14 (NS), w. dupls. KUB 33.100 + KUB 36.16 iii 8-
13, 17-23 (MH?/NS), KUB 33.116 ii 1'-6' (MH?/NS) (CTH 348). The translation
is that of H. A. Hoffner, Jr., *Hittite Myths* (Atlanta: Scholars Press, 1990), 49; cf.
p. 73 for bibliography.

CHAPTER SIX

MAGICAL USES OF ANCIENT MESOPOTAMIAN FESTIVALS OF THE DEAD

J. A. Scurlock

In ancient Mesopotamia, the happiness of the dead in the Netherworld was dependent upon a continuous series of funerary offerings provided by their surviving relatives.[1] Moreover, ghosts periodically left their homes in the world below to come back for visits during the course of which they expected to receive entertainment from the living. What interests us here about these festivals is that they also provided an occasion for private rituals in which opportunistic use was made of the fact that the ghosts had to return to the Netherworld at the end of their formal visits. The roads between the worlds being opened to receive the returning dead, what better opportunity could one find to rid oneself of one's illnesses or other personal problems?

The month of Abu (roughly August in our calendar) was the occasion for one such general return of the dead,[2] and it provided an appropriate setting for the following ritual designed to cure an unspecified ghost-induced illness. "If the ghost of a man's father or mother keeps seizing him, on the 27th of Abu, you take clay from a potter's pit. You make a figurine of a man and a woman. You put a reed (made) of gold on the male figurine. You put a [st]aff (var. ears) (made) of gold on the female figurine. You thread carnelian (var. lapis) on red wool. You put it on her (the female figurine's) neck. You abundantly fit them (the figurines) out. You honor them; you treat them with care. You seat those figurines at the head of the patient for three days. You pour out hot broth for them. On the third day, the 29th, when the ghosts are (customarily) provided with food offerings, you make a sailboat. You assign (them) their travel provisions. You present them to

---

[1] For more details on this subject, see A. Tsukimoto, *Untersuchungen zur Totenpflege (kispum) im alten Mesopotamien,* Alter Orient und Altes Testament 216 (Neukirchen-Vluyn: Neukirchener Verlag, 1985).

[2] See Tzvi Abusch, "Mesopotamian Anti-Witchcraft Literature: Texts and Studies. Part I: The Nature of *Maqlû*: Its Character, Divisions, and Calendrical Setting," *JNES* 33 (1974): 261 with n. 34.

Šamaš. You make them face downstream and you say as follows: 'From the body of NN, son of NN, be 3,600 double-hours distant, be far away, be distant, be distant. You are made to swear (this) by the great gods.'"[3]

The manufacture of both male and female figurines is a relatively common feature of ancient Mesopotamian magic, the object being to ensure results in cases where the real perpetrator of the offense (sometimes a ghost but more usually a sorcerer) was unknown to the victim.[4] Placing the figurines at the head of the patient for three days drew away the illness which was being combated so that it could be sent, along with the figurines, down river to the Netherworld. The presentation to the sun-god Šamaš was more than a simple exposure of the figurines to sunlight. By virtue of his journey through the heavens, the sun-god was the divine judge of the upper and lower worlds in whose court were adjudicated cases which arose between living persons and their dead relatives over the performance of funerary offerings.[5] By involving Šamaš in such offerings, the living ensured that the ghostly recipients could not later complain to the god about being neglected (a legitimate grounds for ghost-induced illness). The final oath administered to the ghosts is another common element in ancient Mesopotamian magical rites, the object being to establish a sort of quasi-contract between the patient and the afflicting spirit. The acceptance of a conditional offering by a ghost or demon obligated him to go away and leave the patient alone in the same way that the

---

[3] *BAM* 323:79-88//*BID* p. 210ff:1-13 (= J. A. Scurlock, "Magical Means of Dealing with Ghosts in Ancient Mesopotamia" [Ph.D. diss., University of Chicago, 1988] [= MMDG], prescription no. 58).

[4] For references to "unknown" assailants in ghost-expelling texts, see, for example: "Šamaš, the evil ghost whom you know but (whom) I do not know shall not approach me; he shall not come near me, he shall not come close to me; keep him from coming" (*CT* 23.15-22+ i 53'-54'//*KAR* 21:r. 2-4//K 3576:9-10 [= Scurlock, MMDG no. 16]); "I, NN, son of NN, whose personal god is NN (and) whose personal goddess is NN, who is sick with illness; and you, O god, know (what it is) but I do not know (it) and nobody (else) knows (it)" (*KAR* 32:37-39//K 9175:9'-11' [= Scurlock, MMDG no. 67]).

[5] Note, for example: "He whom an *utukku* has seized (or) a ghost has seized, etc. . . . to save him from (them) (lies) with Šamaš. For the ghost to . . . to assemble the [family] ghost(s) from the Netherworld, to have a true judgement taken in order for the dead not to oppress the living, to calm the angry ghost, to separate the dead from the living, to return [him to the Netherworld (?)], to loosen his wrath, to keep away his ghost (lies) with Šamaš" (E. von Weiher, *Spätbabylonische Texte aus Uruk* 3, Ausgrabungen der Deutschen Forschungsgemeinschaft in Uruk-Warka 12 [Berlin: Gebr. Mann, 1988], no. 67 ii 27-28, 37-46).

oath formulae on actual contracts bound the swearing party to fulfill his side of the bargain.[6]

Also involving the use of boats to send returning ghosts to the Netherworld is an anti-slander ritual accompanying an unfortunately fragmentary incantation. "You take clay from both banks of a river. You make a sailboat. You make seven and seven (i.e., seven to the right and seven to the left, or a total of fourteen) model tongues of clay. You make a sorcerer and sorceress figurine of clay." (Notice here again the doubling of surrogates; seven tongues to the right and a sorcerer figurine to combat unknown male slanderers and seven tongues to the left and a sorceress figurine to combat unknown female slanderers). "You put the tongues and the figurines on the sailboat (along with) seven and seven breads. You envelop the sailboat with clay. You seal the gate of the sailboat with a seal made from *šubû*-stone and hematite and you fasten its prow on it. You recite the incantation seven and seven times over it. You take it and you . . . Afterwards, you recite the incantation 'Demon, (off) to your desert' as far as the outer gate and then you draw [a magic cir]cle in the gate. [If] this ritual is per[formed] on the 28th of Abu, he (the patient) will be all right."[7]

Another ritual involving the manufacture of a ghost figurine can only be described as baroque. "Ditto (i.e., assuming that something ill-omened happens on the 26th of Abu), you make a figurine of the ghost of your father. You make a lamentation to your (personal) god and goddess. When you lament, you envelop the head of the figurine of your father in women's clothing. You say as follows: '(My) god (and) goddess, my father has brought my sin hither; let him (also) take its punishment away (with him).' You say this (and) at the same time you uncover its head. You dress it in clean clothing. You pour fine oil on the head of the figurine. You fill seven and seven *burzigallu*-vessels with a decoction of dates. You put three *burzigallu*-vessels of fired clay, (and) three each of unfired clay, into a potstand and then you put (it) before Samaš. You say as follows: 'Samaš, my sin belongs to my relatives. My negligence, my curse, my . . . belong to . . . Let the corpse receive the crime (and) the (broken) oath. Samaš, you know what I

---

[6] For a discussion of the general principles involved, see E. Westermarck, *Ritual and Belief in Morocco* (London: Macmillan, 1926), 1.518-69.

[7] O. R. Gurney, "A Tablet of Incantations Against Slander," *Iraq* 22 (1960): 224:21-27 (on the reading of the date, see Abusch, *JNES* 33 [1974]: 260 with n. 33).

do not know; let it cross the river Ḫubur with the figurine of my
father; let it all turn out for the best.'"8

What is essentially happening here is that the ghost is being
taken through a supplication rite designed to enlist the sympathy
and soothe the heart of an angry god. Rites normally associated
with mourning the dead (such as wailing and covering one's head
with one's garments) were frequently used by ancient Mesopotamian penitents in hopes of divine forgiveness.[9] Upon successful
completion of his penitence, the ex-sinner cleansed himself of any
residue of his sin in the same way that one customarily marked the
end of formal mourning, i.e., by such actions as dressing in a clean
garment and anointing himself with oil.[10] By taking the figurine
through this ritual, the patient ensured that his father's ghost
would not later be punished for the sin which he was being asked to
take with him to the Netherworld.

The ghost festival in Abu was not the sole opportunity for
ghosts to pay a visit to living relatives; at the end of the legend of
Ištar's descent to the Netherworld it is mentioned that not only
does the god Dumuzi return every year, but also that the dead are
to "come up and smell the incense"[11] during Dumuzi's festivities
(that is, from the 27th to the 29th of the month of Duʾuzu or
roughly July in our calendar). This association of ghosts with the
shepherd-god Dumuzi is quite natural when it is realized that the
well-known annual "wailing for Tammuz" had nothing to do with

---

8 *KAR* 178 vii 35-52 (= Scurlock, MMDG no. 84).

9 Note, for example, the actions taken to counteract an eclipse: "Until the
eclipse brightens, the people of the land remove their head wrappings; their
heads are covered with their garments . . . . They add their voices to the lament;
they keep shouting until the eclipse clears up . . . . When the eclipse begins, the
lamentation-priests are dressed in linen garments; their heads are covered with
their torn garments. During the eclipse, they offer lamentation, grief, and wailing
to Sîn" (*BRM* 4.6 [= E. Ebeling, *Tod und Leben nach den Vorstellungen der
Babylonier* (Leipzig: Walter de Gruyter, 1931), no. 24]), 21, 23, 27-28, 41, 43-
45.

10 Compare: "On the seventh day, (the people mourning the king's mother)
shaved off their head h[air] and [changed] their garments . . . he (the king) poured
sweet oil over [their] heads; he made them rejoice and br[ightened] their faces. He
sent them on [their] way and they retur[ned] home" (C. J. Gadd, "The Harran
Inscriptions of Nabonidus," *Anatolian Studies* 8 [1958]: 52 iii 29-32, 38-43 [as
restored in W. L. Moran, "The Creation of Man in Atrahasis I 192-248," *BASOR*
200 (1970): 137]) with "[Let (your suppliant) re]move (his) dirty rags; let him
don his (usual) clothing" (W. G. Lambert, "The Gula Hymn of Bulluṭsa-rabi," *Or,*
n.s. 36 [1967]: 128:194).

11 *CT* 15.47:58 (W. R. Sladek, "Inanna's Descent to the Netherworld" [Ph.D.
diss., Johns Hopkins, 1974 (University Microfilms no. 74-27, 928)], 250:138).

"fertility" but was a Passover-type rite designed to ward off the deleterious effects of the summer dying season. As the grim myth "The Descent of Ištar" makes abundantly clear, the hope held out to those who properly performed the annual mourning rites for Dumuzi was that they would thereby be spared the attentions of Inanna/Ištar and her ghostly crew of merciless demons, with the result that the shepherd-god Dumuzi would have to go to the Netherworld in their stead.[12]

A ritual to be used "if a ghost or an 'assistant-of-evil' demon or anything evil has seized a man and pursues him"[13] gives the following instructions. "In the month of Du'uzu when Ištar makes the people of the land wail for Dumuzi, her spouse—a man's relatives are gathered together there—Ištar takes a stand and chooses out men's concerns; she takes away illness (or) she puts illness on. The 28th, the day of the sheepfold, you give a miniature vulva (made of) lapis lazuli (and) a golden star to Ištar. You invoke the patient's name. You say, 'Cause the patient to escape!' and you take twelve breads (and some) mihhu-beer to the temple of Ištar and you give a dyeing vat (and) a cord to Ištar-reṣua, Dumuzi's herd boy. (Herdsmen need vats to prepare wool for rug manufacturing.) You say, 'Ištar-reṣua, intercede for NN, the patient, with Dumuzi.' You do (all) this on the day of the sheepfold

---

[12] "Inanna was about to ascend from the Netherworld, but as she was going up, the Anunnaki-gods seized her (saying), 'Who has ever risen from the Netherworld? Who has ever risen from the Netherworld alive? If Inanna wants to ascend from the Netherworld, let her give a substitute as substitute for herself.' . . . Upon Inanna's ascending from the Netherworld, Ninšubur threw herself at her feet; clothed in dirty rags, she wallowed in the dust. The demons cried out to pure Inanna, 'O Inanna, go home to your city; let us take this one back.' The pure Inanna answered the demons, 'This is my messenger of consoling words, my mounted messenger of true words, who did not forget my directions, did not neglect the orders which I gave her. She set up a lament for me in my ruin(ed temple)s. She beat the drum for me in the temple throne room. She went in a circle round the temples of the gods for me. She scratched her face; she scratched her nose; she scratched her thighs, a place (women) do not speak of with men. She dressed in a single garment like a poor man. . . . How could I ever turn her over to you?' . . . And there was Dumuzi clothed in a magnificent garment, sitting on a magnificent throne. The demons seized him by the thighs; the seven of them poured the milk out of his churns; the seven of them shook their heads like . . . The shepherd did not play his flute and pipe before her. She (Inanna) looked at him with the look of death, spoke to him with the speech of wrath, shouted at him with the cry of 'guilty!' (She said to the demons): 'Take this one away!' And thus pure Inanna gave the shepherd Dumuzi into their hands" (Sladek, *Inanna's Descent*, 138ff.:284-89, 306-321, 327, 349-58).

[13] W. Farber, *Beschwörungsrituale an Ištar und Dumuzi*, Akademie der Wissenschaften und der Literatur 30 (Wiesbaden: Franz Steiner, 1977), 127ff.:1-2.

in/for the temple of Ištar. § On the 29th, the day when the bed is laid down for Dumuzi, you take a *qû*-measureful of flour which a man has ground and you ignite ashes at the head of his (Dumuzi's) bed. You bake an ash cake in the ashes. You moisten it with good milk. You put it at the head of the bed. (The grain is specifically ground by a man, baked in ashes, and moistened with milk because this is the characteristic food of shepherds and nomads, not the normal, woman-ground, oven-baked, oil-moistened, bread of sedentary agriculturalists). You set out *laḫannu*-vessels (full) of water and first-quality beer. You give a *šappu*-bowl, a wooden box, a flute, a *ṣinnatu*-instrument encrusted with gold, a donkey saddle, and a waterskin to Dumuzi. (The latter two gifts were intended to facilitate the journey; the musical instruments were appropriate because shepherds then, as now, used them to while away long hours guarding the flocks). You set up an offering arrangement for Dumuzi. You put a censer (burning) *ballukku*-resin at his head and a censer (burning) juniper at his feet. You set up an offering arrangement for Ištar. You put out a censer (burning) juniper. You pour out a libation of first quality beer. You sprinkle a sprinkling. You put down magic heaps of flour. You make funerary offerings to the family ghosts to the right of the bed and to the left of the bed to the Anunnaki. You pour out a libation of cold water and beer (flavored with) roasted grain. You put out *mersu*-halvah for Dumuzi's herd boys. You put out seven food portions for the male and female *zabbu*-ecstatics (and) the male and female *maḫḫu*-ecstatics. . . . You have the patient enter (the space) beneath the bed and you have him lie flat on his face. You put his face at the foot end (of the bed). (If one imagines Dumuzi as lying on the bed on his back, the patient is thus doubly disassociated from the god and his dreadful fate.) You touch him (the patient) seven times with a seven-knotted reed stalk. When you have touched him he turns himself over. (The evil is thus literally turned over onto Dumuzi who is lying above on top of the bed.) You also say as follows: 'Ištar, may your beloved go at your side.' He (the patient) comes out from under the bed and dresses in sackcloth and strikes his sides. He circles round seven times to the right and seven times to the left and squats down in the place for mourning. He also says as follows: 'Ištar, I have squatted down in your place for mourning, I have beaten my breast with your people; on this day, remove from my body the evil spy, "assistant of evil," which has come to be in my body, my flesh (and) my sinews, which is fastened to me and pursues me for evil purposes, and give him to your angry heart.' He says this seven times and you pluck out hair from his head and (wool from) the hem of his garment. You throw (them) into the river (along with) twelve breads and some *mashatu*-flour and it will be good for the . . . [mood?] of Ištar."[14]

These ritual actions were accompanied by prayers addressed to Ištar, Dumuzi, the Anunnaki, and the family ghosts in which Dumuzi and the family ghosts were asked (with the assistance or permission of Ištar and the Anunnaki)[15] to take the evils which have been plaguing the patient down with them when they returned to the Netherworld. "(Ištar), intercede with Dumuzi, your lover. May Dumuzi, your lover, carry away my pain . . . I, NN, son of NN, whose (personal) god is NN (and) whose (personal) goddess is NN, have turned to you (Dumuzi and) sought you out; entrust the evil spy, etc. . . . to the mighty Ḥumbaba, the unforgiving *gallû*-demon . . . remove him from my body and take him with you. . . . On this day, stand forth, [great (Anunnaki) gods,] and ju[dge] my case, [make a decision about me]. [Remove the evil s]p[y], etc. . . . from my body; s[eize him and] take [him] down to the 'land of no re[turn].' Entrust [him into the care of] the fate deity, Namtar, vizier of the 'broad earth.' May Ningizzida, chair bearer of the 'broad earth,' strength[en] the watch over him. May Bidu, great doorkeeper of the Netherworld, lock (the gate) in their faces. . . . You are my family ghosts, creators of ev[erything], my father, my father's father, my mother, m[y] mother's mother, my brother, my [sis]ter, my kith, m[y] kin and my relations, as many as sle[ep] in the earth, I have [ma]de for you a funerary offering; I have poured yo[u] (a libation of) water. I have honored [y]ou; I have made yo[u] proud; I have shown [y]ou [respect]. On this day, stand forth before [Ištar and D]umuzi and [judge my] case, [make a] de[cision about me]. [Seize the evil s]py, etc. . . . [and take] him [down] to the grave. [May he not approach, may he not come near, may he not g]et close, may he not blow upon me and spy on me. [May I, you]r [servant], live; may I get well. [On account of magical] practices (which have been performed against me), I want to invoke you]r [names]. Let me pour [c]old water [via] you[r] wate[r p]ipe. (The reference is to liquid offerings to the dead which were literally poured down a tube laid into the earth above the grave.) [Keep] me [al]ive so that I may [pr]aise you. . . . When you (Dumuzi) have set your face towards the Netherworld, may (the evil) not set his face towards NN, son of NN. When you (Dumuzi) go on your road, turn the evil about and let him go

---

[14] Farber, *Beschwörungsrituale an Ištar und Dumuzi*, 127ff.:3-32, 190-205.
[15] Farber, *Beschwörungsrituale an Ištar und Dumuzi*, 127ff.:32-189.

before you. When you (Dumuzi) cross the river Ḫubur, administer to him an oath by Ea (god of sweet waters) that he never return. When you (Dumuzi) go across the steppe, administer to him an oath by the pasture land that he never come round again. When you chase away the beasts, may they take him away (across) the entire pasture land. Cause the patient to escape so that he may exalt your godhead, so that he may sing your praises to the widespread peoples."[16]

A second ritual which seems also to have been linked to the annual wailing for Dumuzi provided a cure for a sick prince.[17] "They put down a bed. They make a (funerary) display.[18] They wash the feet. (They put out) a torch of sweet reed and a *saplu*-bowl of sweet oil. The daughter-in-law (i.e., the patient's wife playing the part of Ištar) washes the feet (with the oil). She goes three times in a circle around the bed (carrying the torch of sweet reed). She kisses the feet; she goes and sits down. She burns cedar; she quenches it with wine. She lays a sheep heart in *tappinu*-flour. She lays (it) on the hips of the figurine. They pour wine onto the ground from a stone *anzagullu*-vessel. They crush the stone *anzagullu*-vessel on the top of the sideboard of the bed. They mix (wine with water) in two sprinkling-vessels. They pour (it) out before Šamaš. She throws herself at the feet. (All this is done) on the day they put down his bed. On the day that they burn the burnt offering (they do the following). They bring water, oil, and thickbread near (to the bed). They take out the equipment. He (the patient) makes a (funerary) display. They wash the feet. She (the daughter-in-law) lifts a torch of sweet reed; she goes three times in a circle around the bed. She kisses the feet. She burns cedar; she quenches it with wine. She lays a sheep heart in *tappinu*-flour; she lays (it) on the hips of the figurine. They pour wine onto the ground from a stone *anzagullu*-vessel. They crush the stone *anzagullu*-vessel on the top of the sideboard of the bed. They go three times in a circle around the animal-paddock. The daughter (i.e., the patient's sister playing the part of Geštinanna) strews

---

[16] Farber, *Beschwörungsrituale an Ištar und Dumuzi*, 127ff.:119-20, 127-32, 138-46, 154-69, 177-88.

[17] For this interpretation of K 164, see J. A. Scurlock, "Wailing for Dumuzi?: A New Interpretation of K 164 (*BA* 2:635)," *RA* 86 (1992): 91-105.

[18] See J. A. Scurlock, "*Taklimtu*: A display of grave goods?," *Nouvelles Assyriologiques Brèves et Utilitaires* (1991) no. 3, correcting M. Stol, "Greek ΔEIKΘΗΡΙΟΝ: the Lying-in-State of Adonis," in *Funerary Symbols and Religion. Essays dedicated to Professor M. S. H. G. Heerma van Voss*, J. H. Kamstra, H. Milde, and K. Wagtendonk, eds. (Kampen: J. H. Kok, 1988), 127-28.

parched grain. They prepare a *qabūtu*-bowl of apples. (After) they
have made (her) go [three times] in a circle around the animal-
paddock, they crush (the bowl). They place salt on the equipment
before Šamaš. They invoke her name; they set (it) on fire. When
they have stamped out the fire, (they put out) a rib cut (and) a
shoulder cut, nine and a half *qû* of *sēpu* ("yellow")-bread (and) a
cake (baked in ashes) made with emmer, a *kallu*-bowl of flour (and)
a *kallu*-bowl of parched grain in the middle of which they have
drawn a river (and) a boat made of [wh]eat flour. They make a
hole in the ground; [t]hey pour oil and honey into the hole. The
palace women cry ou[t, saying], 'Come; [y]ou (f. pl.) [should b]ury
the palace woman, your (f. pl.) daughter.' They seal everything
with blood from the nose of the person for whom [the ceremony
was performed]. They prepare a table before great Antu (i.e.,
Ereškigal, queen of the Netherworld), a table before Gilgameš
(hero-king who after his death became a judge of the Netherworld),
(and) a table before the boatmen. They bring water (and) oil near
(to the table). They place a drinking-vessel of beer (and) a drinking-vessel of wine before great Antu (and) before Gilgameš; they
make (the contents) flow out of them. When he (the patient)
kneels before Šamaš, he says, 'She (the daughter) was girdled; (now)
she is ungirdled.' They say, 'Why was she girdled (and now)
ungirdled?' He says, '(It is because) her gods are reverenced.' They
say (to the daughter), 'Pronounce blessings (f.) on the king (and)
his seed.'"[19]

Our somewhat scanty information on the celebrations at the
end of Du'uzu, drawn from these and other texts, allows for the
following reconstruction.[20] A (funerary) display was made on four
days near the end of the month. Dumuzi was released from his
Netherworld prison on the 27th, accompanied by the family
ghosts; to assist him in his journey, a bed was set up, and mourning
rites were carried out under the supervision of Dumuzi's wife Ištar
accompanied by the burning of incense and offerings to Šamaš
("lord of ghosts") and Dumuzi. By laying the floured sheep heart
on the hips of the figurine, the women playing Ištar granted him a
return to life. By sunrise on the 28th, Dumuzi had reached the
upper world with the assistance of women playing his sister
Geštinanna whose job it was to parch and scatter grain over him
and to soak a figurine of him in beer to ensure his safe arrival (he

---

[19] W. von Soden, "Aus einem Ersatzopferritual für den assyrischen Hof," *ZA*
45 (1939): 42-61:1-51.

[20] See Scurlock, *RA* 86 (1992): 91-105.

was to rise up like the smoke from the grain and to float up like
the figurine in the beer). The 28th was thus Dumuzi's day, the day
when the sheepfold was circumambulated; the mourning rites,
burning of incense, the laying of hearts on figurines, and the offerings to Dumuzi of the previous day were repeated, accompanied
this time by offerings to Ištar (the apples) and to Netherworld
deities (Antu and Gilgameš) and by a burnt offering. This last was
necessitated by the fact that, in order to bring up Dumuzi (and the
accompanying ghosts), Geštinanna had herself to go to the Netherworld as his surrogate, i.e., the women playing her had to be
symbolically buried. Geštinanna was not, however, destined to
remain permanently in the lower regions; that is to say, the
"girdling" (i.e., the captivity of Geštinanna in the Netherworld as
surrogate for her brother) was immediately followed by an
"ungirdling" (i.e., the release of Geštinanna with the return of
Dumuzi to the Netherworld). The 29th was the day of the bed
when Dumuzi was prepared for his journey home to the Netherworld. This was consequently also "the day of the captivity of
Dumuzi" which marked the end of the festival. On this day, the bed
was again set up and offerings were made on various sides of this
bed to Dumuzi, Ištar, the family ghosts, and the Anunnaki.

What is unique to this particular performance of the mourning
rites for Dumuzi is the fact that the patient was asked to seal the
offerings to be sent to the Netherworld with blood from his nose.
We have already seen an example of the use of hair and wool from
the hem of a patient's garment as a means of getting rid of ills (by
throwing them into the river). It is interesting to note in this
connection that the offerings which are being sealed with the blood
consist of three pairs of objects separated by a river of flour. One
component of each of these pairs (the rib cut, the cake, and the
parched grain) was an appropriate offering to the dead or to Dumuzi or both. The other three (the shoulder cut, the sēpu-bread,
and the flour) were appropriate offerings to living gods. By laying
out the rib cut, the cake, and the parched grain on one side of the
flour river and the shoulder cut, the sēpu-bread, and the flour on
the other, the officiant signaled that it was a separation from death
that was desired. The presence of a boat which, in view of the fact
that its boatmen receive offerings alongside Ereškigal and Gilgameš, was presumably intended to carry the offerings to the
Netherworld, is also suggestive of a controlled transfer or exchange
(on the divine scale between the living Geštinanna and the dead
Dumuzi and on the human scale perhaps between the patient's
illness which accompanied the offerings to the Netherworld and

the blessings brought back for the patient and his sponsoring father by Geŝtinanna from the realm of the dead).[21]

Also a good candidate for an opportunistic ritual of this type is a text which includes, alongside prayers to Ŝamaŝ and Gilgameŝ,[22] the following addresses to the Anunnaki and ghosts. "'Stand forth, great [(Anunnaki) gods], and judge my case; [make a decision] about me. [Make] me [l]ive and remove him from [my] body. May my [fa]mily [ghosts] seize them; may they not let th[em] go. . . . the male and female sorcerer—may they rec[eive them]. . . . Take [anything] evil which was set on me (and) the male and female sorcerer down to the "land [of no return]." Entrust them into the care of Namtar, the *sukkallu*-official of the "broad earth." May Ningizzida, chair bearer of the "broad earth," strengthen the watch over them. May Nedu, great door keeper of the "broad earth," lock their gate.'[23] . . . When you have recited this (the preceding incantation) before the Anunnaki, you say as follows before the [family] gho[sts]: 'You are my family ghosts, creators of every-thing, my father, my father's father, my mother, my mother's mother, my brother, my sister, my kith, my kin and my relations, as many as sleep in the earth. I have made for you a funerary offering; I have poured you (a libation of) water. I have honored you; I have made you proud; I have shown you respect. On this day, stand forth before Ŝamaŝ (and) Gilgameŝ and judge my case, make a decision about me. Entrust the evil which is in my body, my flesh (and) my sinews into the care of Namtar, the *sukkallu*-official of the Netherworld. [Ma]y Ningizzida, chair bearer of the "broad earth," strengthen the watch over them. [May] Nedu, great door keeper of the Netherworld, [lock] (the gate) in their faces (var. behind th[em]). Seize it and take it down to the "land of no return." May I, your servant, live; may I get well. Yet, on account of magical practices, I want to be cleared in your name. Let me give (you) cold water to drink via your water pipe. Keep me alive so that I may praise you.' § When you have recited this (three times) before the ghost(s) of relatives, you say as follows before a skull: 'You are the ghost of nobody, you who have no one to bury

---

[21] Compare: "When a mourner returns from her *ponos* (pain) with or without consolation, she will signal her return by asking the dead to give blessings to those left behind, or she will include her own greetings or blessings to the attending mourners" (C. N. Seremetakis, *The Last Word: Women, Death, and Divination in Inner Mani* [Chicago: University of Chicago Press, 1991], 119).

[22] *KAR* 227 and duplicates (= Ebeling, *Tod und Leben* no. 30) i 47-ii 6, ii 7-iii 10.

[23] Tsukimoto, *kispum*, 191 B:17-26.

(you) or to invoke (your name), (whose) name nobody knows, (but whose) name Šamaš, who takes care of (you), knows. Whether you be a man who is like a (living) man or whether you be a woman who is like a (living) person, you have received a gift before Šamaš, Gilgameš, the Anunnaki (and) the fami[ly] ghosts; you have been treated kindly (with) a present. Listen to m[e], to whatever I say. Whether he be an [evil] *utukku*-demon, or an evil *alû*-demon or an evil ghost, or Lamaštu or Labāṣu or Aḫ[ḫāzu], or a *lilû*-demon or a *lilītu*-demon or an *ardat li[lî]*-demon,[24] or any nameless evil which continually seizes me and pu[rsues me], (which) is fastened to my body, my flesh (and) my sinews and cannot be loosed—I have made a figurine of the male and female witch who . . . to me with Šamaš as witness (and) a figurine of the evil which has seized me. I have entrusted th[em] (to you) before Šamaš, Gilgameš, (and) the Anunnaki. Seize them and do not release them; take them so that they may not retu[rn]. You are made to swear (to do this) by the oath of Šamaš, who takes care of you. Yo[u] are made to swear by the oath of the great gods of heaven and earth. You are made to swear by the oath of the Igigi, the gods above. You are made to swear by the oath of the Anunnaki, the gods below. You are made to swear by the oath of Lugalgirra, Ninazu (and) Ningizzida. You are made to swear by the oath of Ereškigal, queen of the Netherworld. If you let them go (you will be punished)."[25]

In view of the striking similarity between the prayers addressed to the Anunnaki and ghosts in this text with those to be found in the Ištar and Dumuzi rituals which we have already examined, it seems likely that this ritual, too, was timed to coincide with one of the periodic returns of the dead, but a more generalized visit in which not only the family ghosts but also strange and uncared-for ghosts were allowed to come up to the upper world. If so, then the obvious suggestion is that this ritual was meant to be performed at the end of Abu, both because that is the only other known festival of the dead and because it contains prayers to Gilgameš, whose connection with the "festival of the ghosts" in Abu is explicitly mentioned in the Sumerian composition, "The Death of Gilgameš."[26] The emphasis on sorcery in the latter ritual is perhaps

---

[24] For a discussion of these demons, see J. A. Scurlock, "Baby-Snatching Demons, Restless Souls and the Dangers of Childbirth: Medico-Magical Means of Dealing with Some of the Perils of Motherhood in Ancient Mesopotamia," *Incognita* 2 (1991): 153-59, with previous literature.

[25] *KAR* 227 iii 6-50//*LKA* 89+90:1-43//Si. 747:1-12 (= Scurlock, MMDG nos. 85, 87).

[26] "Without (Gilgameš), the daylight is not put before their eyes (in) Abu, at

also significant in view of the possibility that *Maqlû* and/or other anti-sorcery incantations may also have been timed to coincide with this period at the end of Abu.[27]

A very similar address to a ghost appears in another anti-sorcery text which also mentions sorcerous dedications to Gilgameš and the nefarious manufacture of figurines of the patient at the beginning of Abu[28] and which includes separate prayers to Šamaš.[29] "[Before] Šamaš, the judge, [you have] re[ceived a gift; yo]u [have been treated kindly] (and) [a pre]sent has been give[n] to you. . . . appropriate to the Netherworld . . . [I have made a figurine of] my [m]ale and femal[e] sorcerer . . . I have entrusted th[em] to you. [Remove hi]m(?); take [him] away with you. [Do not rel]ease them. You are made to swear by [the oath of Šamaš, who tak]es care of you. [By the oath of the Igigi], the gods above, etc. [By the oath of the Anunnak]i, the gods below, etc. [By the oath of Lugalgirra], Ninazu (and) Ningizzida, etc. [By the oath of Ereškigal], que[en of the Netherwor]ld, etc. [If you let them] go (you will be punished)."[30]

A final candidate for inclusion in this category of opportunistic rituals is an unfortunately broken anti-witchcraft ritual in which the family ghosts play an unusually prominent part: "If a man is chosen as a mate for a dead person and, as a result, a ghost has seized him [. . .] You purify the clay pit. You put *mašhatu*-flour into it. In the morning, you say, 'I will buy clay from the potter's pit for a representation of anything evil, the male and [female] sorcerer.' You pinc[h] off clay. [. . .] You make [x] figurines of the male and female sorcerer. You make [them] hold . . . You dress them in makeshift garments. You an[oint them] with fine oil. [Befo]re Šamaš, you sweep the ground. You sprinkle pure water (on it). [You put down] a pure seat for [Šamaš]. You stretch out a *mišhu*-cloth on it. [You set up] a reed altar before [Šamaš]. In three groups you p[ut out] food portions before Šamaš, Ea, and Asalluhi. You scatter dates and *sasqû*-flour. [You set up] three a[*dagurru*]-vessels. You set up three censers (burning) aromatics.

---

the festival of the ghosts" (S. N. Kramer, "The Death of Gilgamesh," *BASOR* 94 [1944]: 7:31-32).

[27] See Abusch, *JNES* 33 (1974): 259-61.

[28] "[Th]at [man] is bewitched; the waters of 'cutting the brea[th]' have been broken [ove]r him; [they gave] his [. . .] to Gilgam[eš]; they manu[factured] his figurines at the coming in of Abu" (*BAM* 231 i 15-17//*BAM* 332 i 1').

[29] *BAM* 231 i 19-27//*BAM* 332 i 3'-18'.

[30] *BAM* 332 iv 5'-17' (= Scurlock, MMDG no. 88).

You scat[ter] all manner of grain. You put down a seat to the left of the offering arrangement for his (the patient's) family ghosts. (That is to say,) you put down a seat for his family ghosts to the left of the (other) ghosts to the left (of the offering arrangement). You make funerary offerings to (his) family ghosts. You give them gifts. [You] made them proud; you show them respect. Secondly, you lay out hot br[oth] [for] (his) family [gho]sts. You give them a gift. You make them proud; you show them respect. You pour out a libation of [water] for them. You make a pure sacrifice before Šamaš. You bring the [shoulder], caul fat (and) roasted meat near (to the offering table). You pour out a libation of [first quality beer]. You pu[t] aside a rib section for his family ghosts. You recite [the incantation: '. . .] anything evil' three times . . . you/he raise(s) . . . and then . . ."[31]

We have so far only spoken of ghosts as convenient vehicles for getting rid of evils. However, there was in ancient Mesopotamia also a strong tradition of consultations of the dead for the purpose of divining the future.[32] We have a number of manuals for the performance of necromancy, or as the ancient Mesopotamians called such procedures, "Incantation (to be used when you wish) to see a ghost in order to make a decision."[33] Instructions accompanying necromantic incantations indicate that the favored method was to prepare an ointment which was smeared on the practitioner's face or on a figurine or skull which housed the ghost.[34] There is also a somewhat broken lexical reference to digging (?) a ditch,[35] presumably as a prelude to filling it with offerings to the dead. There was even a professional raiser of ghosts.[36]

One might, then, expect that the periodic returns of the dead would provide a prime opportunity for such activities and, indeed, one of the necromantic instructions makes it explicit that it should be performed on the 29th of Abu: "You crush rue (?) in water and (cedar) oil. You recite the incantation three times over it. (If) you

---

[31] *BBR* 2 no. 52:1-23 (= Scurlock, MMDG no. 68).

[32] Note, for example, "Here, we have been questioning the dream-interpretesses, female diviners and the ghosts (and the result is) that the god Aššur continually gives you a warning" (TCL 4.5:4-7 [see J. Tropper, *Nekromantie: Totenbefragung im Alten Orient und im Alten Testament*, AOAT 223 (Neukirchen-Vluyn: Neukirchener Verlag, 1989), 71 with n. 115]).

[33] *BAM* 215:59//*SpTU* 2 no. 20 r. 22 (= Scurlock, MMDG no. 82).

[34] For details, see Scurlock, MMDG, chap. 6.

[35] Hg. B IV 149 (see *CAD* M/2 265a s.v. *mušēlû* B lexical section).

[36] Lu II iii 27'; Lu Excerpt I 183; OB Lu A 357, C₄ 4; Hg. B IV 149; OB Lu C₄ 6; Lu Excerpt II 19 (see *CAD* M/2 265a s.v. *mušēlû* B lexical section).

rub (it) on your face on the 29th of Abu, the Anunnaki will talk with you. Let it (the ghost) make a decision for you."[37]

In sum, the annual festivals of the dead were, on one level, celebrations reaffirming the ongoing relationship between the living and their dead ancestors. Since, however, the visiting ghosts had to return to the Netherworld at the end of these celebrations, and since the Netherworld was a convenient dumping ground (one might almost say, the natural habitat) of evils, these annual festivals of the dead could also be made to serve a secondary purpose. That is, they provided favorable opportunities for appending to the rites normally performed in the course of their celebration, private rituals designed to rid people of their ills. In addition, the temporary presence in the upper world of friendly ghosts gave those anxious for unbiased and hopefully prescient advice a chance to engage in consultations.

---

[37] *BAM* 215:60-63//*SpTU* 2 no. 20 r. 23-26 (= Scurlock, MMDG no. 82).

PART THREE

MAGIC AND RITUAL POWER
IN JUDAISM AND EARLY CHRISTIANITY

CHAPTER SEVEN

THE "WITCH" OF EN-DOR,
1 SAMUEL 28, AND ANCIENT NEAR EASTERN
NECROMANCY

Brian B. Schmidt

Through the centuries, Saul's ominous encounter with the prophet Samuel *post mortem* has engendered a wide range of response from Jewish and Christian interpreters alike.[1] Nevertheless, two interpretative details of the "Witch" of En-Dor account in 1 Samuel 28 have withstood the test of time, namely the second-millennium Canaanite origins of Israelite necromancy and the divine status of the early Israelite dead.[2] To be sure, both find particulars in the text that warrant their plausibility. The narrative's chronological framework (the settlement of Canaan) and its geographical setting (the Canaanite city of En-Dor) serve to characterize necromancy as an ancient and distinctly Canaanite practice.[3] Interpreters also classify the apparition(s) conjured up

---

[1] For examples from the history of interpretation, cf. A. F. Kirkpatrick, *The First Book of Samuel* (Cambridge: Cambridge University Press, 1888), 244-45 (a survey of nineteenth-century scholarship), and K. A. D. Smelik, "The Witch of Endor: I Samuel 28 in Rabbinic and Christian Exegesis Till 800 A. D.," *VC* 33 (1977): 160-78.

[2] Cf. the definition of necromancy offered by E. Bourguignon, "Necromancy," *Encyclopedia of Religion,* ed. M. Eliade (New York: MacMillan, 1987), 345, "the art or practice of magically conjuring up the souls of the dead ... to obtain information from them, generally regarding the revelation of unknown causes or the future course of events." In the end, Bourguignon implemented a more inclusive definition, one useful for analyzing traditions of non-Western cultures (347). The narrower definition is more appropriate for the present investigation, for it has as its close analogue (and probably its basis) in a tradition like 1 Sam 28:3-25. J. Tropper, *Nekromantie: Totenbefragung im Alten Orient und Alten Testament,* AOAT 223 (Neukirchen-Vluyn: Neukirchener Verlag, 1989), 13-23, and M. S. Moore, *The Balaam Traditions: Their Character and Development* (Atlanta: Scholars Press, 1990), 53-55, employ a broad definition which allows them to incorporate a variety of practices involving contact with the dead, many of which do not record the ghost's benevolent capacity to reveal esoteric knowledge concerning the future of the living.

[3] Josh 17:11 lists the city of En-Dor and its dependencies among those Canaanite enclaves Israel failed to dispossess. According to this tradition, Israel was only able to force the inhabitants of En-Dor to pay tribute (v. 13). J. Van

from below as both god or ʾĕlōhîm and man, and commentators
typically assume a single referent for these two terms, namely the
dead prophet Samuel.[4] In other words, at death Samuel became
both god and ghost. What follows is an evaluation of this consensus as well as some alternative proposals for not only the origins,
but also the character, of Israelite necromancy and for the affiliation of ghost and god in early Israelite religious tradition.

*   *   *

Did the Israelites adopt a late second-millennium version of Canaanite necromancy? Our compositional analysis favors the view
that 1 Sam 28:3-25 is a literary construct of the mid-first millennium. As a unified text, these verses form a sequel to 1 Sam 15.[5]
Therefore, whatever can be reconstructed in terms of a compositional history for ch. 15, that for 28:3-25 should follow. Contex-
tual features indicate that 1 Sam 15 comprises a late addition to
the Deuteronomistic History.[6] Both the style and the language of

---

Seters, *In Search of History: Historiography in the Ancient World and the
Origins of Biblical History* (New Haven: Yale University Press, 1983), 335 and
339, argues that Josh 14-17 reflects P's typical penchant for delineating the
inheritance of individual tribes and families.

[4] Cf. 28:13-14. In v. 14, Samuel is "an old man" or *ʾîš zāqēn* in the MT and
"an erect man" or *anēr orthios* in the LXX.

[5] Vv. 17-18, which clearly presuppose 1 Sam 15, are often viewed as a secondary addition to ch. 28. If so, then the remainder of 28:3-25 need not be taken as
dependent upon 1 Sam 15. But the isolated redactional character of vv. 17-18 is
doubtful. Together with vv. 16-19, vv. 17-18 comprise a unified prophetic
speech: an accusation (as question, v. 16), a rehearsal of past obedience (vv. 17-
18a), an announcement of judgement (*ʿal-kēn*, v. 18b) and a judgement speech (v.
19). V. 15 anticipates vv. 16 and 20 presupposes v. 19, cf. Van Seters, *In Search
of History*, 262 and n. 55. F. Foresti, *The Rejection of Saul in the Perspective of
the Deuteronomistic School: A Study of 1 Sm. 15 and Related Texts,* ST 5 (Rome:
Edizioni del Teresianum, 1984), 130-31, points out that the remark in 15:35,
"Samuel did not see Saul again until the day of his death," anticipates 28:3-25,
esp. v. 3. Lastly, 28:17-18 presuppose the account in ch.15 concerning the
destruction of the Amalekites.

[6] Cf. Van Seters, *In Search of History*, 254-58. The redactor never fully resolved the tension between 15:35 and 19:18-24. For 19:24, the LXX has Saul
speak in ecstasy "before them," *enōpion autōn*, i.e., before the other prophets,
rather than "before Samuel" with the MT *lipnê šĕmûʾēl*, in an attempt to harmo-
nize 19:24 with 15:35, 25:1, and 28:3. The non-historicity of the Amalekite
engagement in ch. 15 is confirmed by 1 Sam 16:14 - 2 Sam 5:12, which does not
recognize Saul's control of Judah as in ch.15. The annihilation of the Amalekites
in ch.15 does not account for David's campaigns against them in ch. 30. Further-

1 Sam 15 point to a deuteronomistic orientation.[7] The chapter's character is also borne out by its form, the prophetic didactic legenda which has definite deuteronomistic associations.[8] One would expect, then, that 28:3-25 would have a similar deuteronomistic (or perhaps post-deuteronomistic) viewpoint. The same can be said for its alignment with deuteronomistic language and ideology.[9] To be sure, there are also independent arguments for the redactional status of 28:3-25.[10] Furthermore, an analysis of the related text, Deut 18:11, confirms the above observations. Deut

---

more, early stories about Saul (1 Sam 9:1-10:16, 11:1-15, 13:2-14:46) reveal that Samuel had no role in Saul's monarchy. That he did belongs to a later hand.

[7] The phrases "hearken to the voice of Yahweh" (vv. 1b, 19, 20, 22) and "thus says Yahweh of hosts" (v. 2) are deuteronomistic. The following are as well: "show loving kindness" (v. 6), "the word of Yahweh came to . . . " (v. 10), "he did not confirm my word" (v. 11), "do that which is evil in the eyes of Yahweh" (v. 19), "devoted to God" (v. 21a), and "violate Yahweh's command" (v. 24); cf. also K.-D. Schunck, *Benjamin, Untersuchungen zur Enstehung und Geschichte eines israelitschen Stammes,* BZAW 86 (Berlin: Walter de Gruyter, 1963), 82-85; M. Weinfeld, *Deuteronomy and the Deuteronomistic School* (Oxford: Clarendon Press, 1972), 337 and 339; Foresti, *The Rejection of Saul,* 89; and Van Seters, *In Search of History,* 260.

[8] Following A. Rofé, "Classes in the Prophetic Stories: Didactic Legenda and Parable," *Studies on Prophecy,* SVT 26 (Leiden: E. J. Brill, 1974), 145-64, esp. 145-53. This form in which the prophet is depicted as the medium of the divine word is characteristic of the Deuteronomistic History in Kings and of the post-classical period more generally, cf. 1 Kgs 17:8-24, 2 Kgs 5, 2 Kgs 20:1-11.

[9] 28:3a, "now Samuel was dead," depends on deuteronomistic 25:1 as it presupposes the death of Samuel as already known. 28:3a, "and all Israel mourned and buried him in his own town of Ramah," is a revision of 25:1a. The fact that 28:3 repeats 25:1 increases the unlikelihood that the same author would repeat the same fact twice. If the story was deuteronomistic, it is surprising that Saul was not commended (cf. Van Seters, *In Search of History,* 262). The language and style point to its dependency upon such deuteronomistic passages as Deut 18:10-11, 2 Kgs 21:6 and 23:24, and to those elements it shares with the post-deuteronomistic Isa 8:19, 91:3, and 29:4, for which cf. Foresti, *The Rejection of Saul,* 133 n.142.

[10] 28:3-25 creates a distinct disturbance in the geographical and chronological progression of the battle against the Philistines. 28:2 has its direct continuation in 29:1. In 28:4-5, the Philistines are at Shunem north of the Jezreel while the Israelites are stationed on Mt. Gilboa, whereas in 29:1 the Philistines are at Aphek some distance away and Israel is encamped in the plain. The Philistines arrive at Jezreel only in 29:11. Thus, 28:3-25 comprises a secondary addition to the Deuteronomistic History: 28:1-2 + 29:1-11 (cf. Van Seters, *In Search of History,* 262). Schunck, *Benjamin,* 95, and Foresti, *The Rejection of Saul,* 133-34, note the linkage 28:3-25 has with accounts in 1 Sam 7-14 and the story of David's rise or *Aufstiegsgeschichte,* 1 Sam 16:14 - 2 Sam 5:12, which could only presuppose the synthesis offered by the Deuteronomistic History.

18:11 not only assumes the Canaanite origins of the necromancy which it condemns (cf. v.9), it is positioned within a narrative chronological framework that predates that of 1 Sam 28, namely the eve of the conquest of Canaan. Nevertheless, Deut 18:11 is clearly deuteronomistic in orientation as its style and language indicate.[11] It is a redactional addition as well, comprising part of the *Ämtergesetze*, or laws of the officials, that span 16:18-18:22.[12] The cumulative effect of the preceding points establishes the mid-first millennium, (post)-deuteronomistic redactional status of 1 Sam 28:3-25.[13]

Be that as it may, while it is often possible to delineate the compositional history of a biblical text, it might be altogether a different matter to ascertain the antiquity of its underlying tradition. Having so said, it should nevertheless come as somewhat of a surprise that necromancy remains unattested in second to mid-first millennium BCE texts from the Levant (Ugaritic, Hebrew, Phoenician, and Aramaic).[14] Necromancy's protracted absence in these

---

[11] Lohfink has argued that 18:9-22 belongs to an exilic deuteronomistic sketch of a constitution for the nation's restoration on the basis of the extensive deuteronomistic language present throughout; cf. now N. Lohfink, "The Cult Reform of Josiah of Judah: 2 Kings 22-23 as a Source for the History of Israelite Religion," *Ancient Israelite Religion: Essays in Honor of Frank Moore Cross*, ed. P. D. Miller, P. D. Hanson, and S. D. McBride (Philadelphia: Fortress Press, 1987), 459-75, and "Review of *Von der politischen Gemeinschaft zur Gemeinde*, 1987 by U. Rüterswörden," *TLZ* 113 (1988): cols. 425-30. Lohfink is followed by P. E. Dion, "Quelques aspects de l'interaction entre religion et politique dans le Deutéronome," *ScEs* 30 (1978): 47-51; *idem*, "Deuteronomy and the Gentile World: A Study in Biblical Theology," *Toronto Journal of Theology* 1 (1985): 200-21.

[12] Cf. H. D. Preuss, *Deuteronomium* (Darmstadt: Wissenschaftliche Buchgesellschaft, 1982), 136-38; F. García López, "Un profeta como Moisés. Estudio crítico de Dt 18,9-22," *Simposio Bíblico Español*, ed. N. F. Marcos (Madrid: Universidad Complutense, 1984), 289-308; U. Rüterswörden, *Von der politischen Gemeinschaft zur Gemeinde*, BBB 65 (Frankfurt am Main: Athenaum, 1987); and G. Braulik, "Zur Abfolge der Gesetze in Deuteronomium 16,18 - 21,23," *Bib* 69 (1988): 63-92.

[13] The post-deuteronomistic status of 28:3-25 is confirmed by v. 3b where Saul's reform is mentioned. As noted previously, if this pericope were deuteronomistic, it would have been exceptional for Saul not to have been commended for it.

[14] The Ugaritic texts *KTU* 1.161 and 124 have been cited as examples of necromancy; cf. most recently Tropper, *Nekromantie*, 144-56, and M. Dietrich and O. Loretz, *Mantik in Ugarit, Keil- alphabetische Texte der Opferschau - Omensammlungen - Nekromantie* (Münster: UGARIT-Verlag, 1990), 205-40. But *KTU* 1.161 more likely preserves a coronation rite with occasional funerary rites included. As for 1.124, the reading *w yʿny nn dtn tʿny* in lines 4-5 might be translated with the *'adn* or "lord" instructing *dtn* in the vocative case, "then he

traditions favors an alternative socio-historical stimulus to its widely assumed early "Canaanite" origins as the explanation for necromancy's appearance in ancient Israelite tradition.

Likewise, Egyptian sources are of no help as necromancy is not attested in these traditions prior to the mid-first millennium.[15] Although ghosts of the dead in Egypt were on occasion considered benevolent numina, matters complicate when it comes to the practice of necromancy per se.[16] For example, the letters to the dead are frequently cited in support of an Egyptian version of necromancy.[17] However, the prominent aspect of the dead portrayed in these letters is their manipulated hostility or confrontational posture.[18] In any case, the rites depicted in the letters played no direct role in the adoption of necromancy in Israelite tradition, for the letters lack close congruities with the conceptual and ritual elements found in 1 Sam 28:3-25. The Egyptian dead are not summoned above to the immediate presence of the living nor do they dispense special knowledge concerning the fate of the living.[19] Rather, they are petitioned to cease haunting the living, to

---

('*adn*) answered him, 'O Ditanu, you shall reply ... '." In other words, a major deity is consulted by a mythic hero named Ditanu or *dtn* who then is given directions rather than vice versa, but cf. D. Pardee, *Les textes paramythologiques de la 24e campagne,* Ras Shamra-Ougarit 4 (Paris: Editions Recherches sur les civilisations, 1988). The Aramaic Hadad inscription, *KAI* 214, records the phrase, "and (he) invokes the name of Panammū," *wyzkr 'sm pnmw,* which is not a summons of the dead, but a rite in which the deceased are commemorated (see 2 Sam 18:18 and Ruth 4:10), cf. H. Donner and W. Röllig, *Kanaanäische und Aramäische Inschriften,* 3 vols. (Wiesbaden: Otto Harrassowitz, 1971-73), 38-39, 214-23.

[15] Moreover, necromancy per se does not appear in early Anatolian sources, cf. I. Finkel, "Necromancy in Ancient Mesopotamia," *AfO* 29-30 (1983-84): 15 and n. 65, and J. Tropper, *Nekromantie,* 110-22.

[16] Cf. R. J. Demarée, *The 3h ikr n R^c-Stelae: On Ancestor Worship in Ancient Egypt* (Leiden: Nederlands Instituut Voor Het Nabije Oosten, 1983), the review by A. L. Schulman, "Some Observations on the *3h ikr n R^c-Stelae,*" *BO* 43 (1986): 302-48, and J. Baines, "Society, Morality, and Religious Practice," *Religion in Ancient Egypt: Gods, Myths, and Personal Practice,* ed. B. E. Schafer (Ithaca: Cornell University Press, 1991), 123-200, esp. 150-61.

[17] Cf. e.g., Tropper, *Nekromantie,* 27-46.

[18] Cf. E. Wente, *Letters From Ancient Egypt,* SBL Writings from the Ancient World Series (Altanta: Scholars Press, 1990), 210-19; Baines, "Society," 153-55. R. K. Ritner, *The Mechanics of Ancient Egyptian Magical Practice,* Studies in Ancient Oriental Civilization 54 (Chicago: The Oriental Institute, 1993), 180-83, also highlights this negative or malevolent aspect of the dead in the letters.

[19] Contra Tropper, *Nekromantie,* 27-46. In Book of the Dead spells 148 and 190, the ghost reveals the fate of those in the underworld including its own, not

initiate a haunt against another, to take legal proceedings against a malevolent ghost, or to dispense knowledge about the underworld.[20]

While Demarée assumed that the "able ancestor" *3ḥ iqr* intervened beneficently in the birth of a healthy child in one such letter, the Chicago jar stand, the context makes clear that the ghost was to banish any numina which might attack the mother-to-be.[21] In other words, although advantageous side effects might on occasion accrue to a letter's sender, the action performed by the dead is characteristically hostile, or at times couched in legal terminology and depicted as merely confrontational.[22] In the final analysis, what underlies the letters is the malevolence or hostility of the ghost, and while communication with the ghost might be sought, necromancy—and in particular, compelling analogues to that rendition preserved in 1 Sam 28:3-25—are lacking in Egyptian sources. In fact, where close congruities with late Egyptian

---

the fate of the living, cf. T. G. Allen, *The Book of the Dead or Going Forth by Day*, Studies in Ancient Oriental Civilization 37 (Chicago: The Oriental Institute, 1974), 141, 214. (For the following references, I am indebted to Gary S. Greig, private communication 12/6/88.) The same applies in the case of the late stories of Setne Khaemwas, in M. Lichtheim, *Ancient Egyptian Literature* (Berkeley: University of California Press, 1980), 127-51, which might evince Greek influence. The Teaching of King Amenemhat I, in W. K. Simpson, R. O. Faulkner, and E. F. Wente, *Literature of Ancient Egypt: An Anthology of Stories, Instructions, and Poetry* (New Haven: Yale University Press, 1973), 193-97, is a wise admonition placed in the mouth of a dead king, not a prediction or disclosure of special knowledge. The Late Egyptian story of Khonsuemhab, in Simpson, Faulkner, and Wente, *Literature*, 137-41, mentions favors for the dead, not vice versa. Add to the texts cited by Borghouts in Finkel, "Necromancy," 15 and n. 64, J. F. Borghouts, *Ancient Egyptian Magical Texts* (Leiden, E. J. Brill, 1978), 11-12 (no. 12), 24 (no. 33), 29-30 (no. 41) as other examples of contact with the dead.

[20] Cf. Wente, *Letters*, 210-19, and Baines, "Society," 150-61.

[21] Demarée, *Ancestor Cult*, 213-18, and cf. A. H. Gardiner, "A New Letter to the Dead," *JEA* 16 (1930): 19-22.

[22] As acknowledged even by Demarée, *Ancestor Cult*, 215 and n. 105, the *iqr* or "able" ghost in the Louvre bowl might be hostile as indicated by the use of a tick differentiating between the determinatives *mwt* and *mwtt.i;* and cf. W. K. Simpson, "A Late Old Kingdom Letter to the Dead from Nagʿ Ed-Deir N 3500," *JEA* 56 (1970): 60 note h. These observations do not contradict the fact that the *3ḥ iqr* was the recipient of ritual in the mortuary cult as intermediary between its descendants and the underworld tribunal. Howeever, the purpose of such a ritual was to exact vengeance from the gods, on which cf. Demarée, *Ancestor Cult*, 1983; Schulman, "Observations," 302-48, esp. 316, 346; and Ritner, *Mechanics*, 180-83.

sources can be detected, a Levantine tradition like that underlying 1 Sam 28 might have provided the socio-historical stimulus for its appearance in Egypt.

Matters are otherwise in contemporary Mesopotamian religious traditions. For example, the reigns of the seventh century Assyrian kings, Esarhaddon and Ashurbanipal, comprised a period of intense interest in various forms of divination. Texts from this period and later provide the earliest unequivocal examples of ancient Near Eastern necromancy. Two aspects of these phenomena are particularly relevant. First, in numerous extispicies dated to Ashurbanipal's reign, diviners are depicted as inquiring about the success of planned military strategies and the eventual outcome of armed battle.[23] Second, in a letter dated to the reign of king Esarhaddon (672 BCE) wherein the topic of his son's suitability for the position of crown prince is addressed, the answer given is in the affirmative and its medium is the consulted ghost or $etemmu$ of Esarhaddon's recently deceased wife, Esharra-khamat (lines 1-11):[24]

[1] [The crown [2] prince] explained [3] [it as follows]: "The gods Ashur (and) Shamash ordained me [4] to be the crown prince of Assyria [5] because of her (= the dead queen's) truthfulness." (And) her ghost [6] blesses him to the same degree as [7] he revered the ghost: [8] "May his descendants rule over Assyria! (As it is said), [9] fear of the gods creates kindness, [10] fear of the infernal gods returns life. [11] Let the [king, my] lord give order."

In 1 Sam 28, King Saul likewise seeks supernatural assistance in order to devise a military strategy against the Philistines and to ascertain the outcome of the battle. After failing to obtain such assistance and information using conventional methods (dreams, Urim and Thummim, and prophecy, cf. vv. 6,15), Saul seeks the aid of a surreptitious necromancer in order to contact the ghost of the deceased prophet Samuel (vv. 4-7,15b). Once conjured up,

---

[23] Cf. J. Pečírková, "Divination and Politics in the Late Assyrian Empire," *ArOr* 53 (1985): 155-68; *idem*, "The Administrative Methods of Assyrian Imperialism," *ArOr* 55 (1987): 162-75; and I. Starr, *Queries to the Sungod: Divination and Politics in Sargonid Assyria*, State Archives of Assyria 4 (Helsinki: Helsinki University Press, 1990), XXX-XXXV and 262-70.

[24] Cf. S. Parpola, *Letters from Assyrian Scholars to the King to Esarhaddon and Assurbanipal*, AOAT 5/1-2 (Neukirchen-Vluyn: Neukirchener Verlag, 1970), 107 and 1983:120 [*LAS* 132]; also M. Bayliss, "The Cult of the Dead Kin in Assyria and Babylonia," *Iraq* 35 (1973): 124; Finkel, "Necromancy," 1, 3; A. Tsukimoto, *Untersuchungen zur Totenpflege (kispum) im alten Mesopotamien*, AOAT 216 (Neukirchen-Vluyn: Neukirchener Verlag, 1985), 159; and Tropper, *Nekromantie*, 76-83.

Samuel's ghost conveys an unfavorable outcome for the impending battle (cf. v. 19). Not only does Samuel's raised ghost predict the Israelites' defeat, it also announces the cessation of the Saulide dynasty, for Saul *and his sons* meet their death on the morrow (vv. 17-19 and cf. 13:13-14). Thus, the biblical writer demonstrates an acquaintance with rites and functions characteristic of not only Mesopotamian divination more generally, but with Mesopotamian necromancy in particular (for additional parallels in specific details, see below). In other words, the author of 1 Sam 28 might display an awareness of techniques similar to those attested in first millennium Mesopotamian sources employed for the purpose of predicting the outcome of war as well as the destiny of a royal house.

Necromancy's absence in Levantine, Anatolian, and Egyptian magical traditions before the mid-first millennium BCE, its appearance in Mesopotamian texts during that same general time period, and the close correspondences between the Mesopotamian and Israelite versions of necromancy favor an eastern origin for the tradition reflected in 1 Sam 28. The fact that it is attested, or at best only rarely present, in Mesopotamia prior to the mid-first millennium adds further support for the late compositional history of 1 Sam 28:3-25.[25] Nevertheless, it would be premature to assume that an eastern origin of Israelite necromancy authenticates those other biblical traditions that point to an extensive Mesopotamian religious influence on Israelite culture of the first millennium BCE (cf. e.g., 2 Kgs 16:10-18 and 17:24-41). The tendentious character of those traditions precludes any such overly simplistic solution.

---

[25] Evidence for necromancy in earlier periods of Mesopotamia depends on how one interprets lines 238-43 of the Sumerian Gilgamesh (Enkidu and the Netherworld), lines 4-7 of the Old Assyrian letter from Kültepe (*TC* 1,5) and the lexical entry *mušēlû eṭemmi* = lú sag-bulug-ga in second-millennium Lu professions lists, cf. Finkel, "Necromancy," 1-2, and Tropper, *Nekromantie*, 47-76. The š causative of *elû* might signify "to remove," cf. *CAD* 4 (1958): 134, #11c, in which case the *mušēlû eṭemmi* = lú sag-bulug-ga would be an exorcist, not a necromancer. The same applies in the case of *šūlû ša eṭemmi* = bur₂ in the Lu excerpt II. On bur₂, cf. Å. Sjöberg, ed., *The Sumerian Dictionary*, vol. 2, "B" (Philadelphia: The University Museum, 1984), 195 which is commonly listed with Akkadian *pašāru* "to loosen, to free". So, the question arises, is the meaning "to free from a ghost" or "to free a ghost"? The presumed references in Gilgamesh and Kültepe are controvertible. The first is a mythical context perhaps depicting an exceptional phenomenon, not a known mantic practice. In any case, Enkidu is not explicitly identified as a ghost or *eṭemmu*, but as "servant" subur-a-ni or "demon" *utukku* in the Akkadian. The second might be the strongest evidence for necromancy in earlier periods, but the context makes clear neither the means nor ends of that inquiry.

Such traditions are highly rhetorical and polemical in their own right as is highlighted further by the scant artifactual and textual evidence suggestive of the underlying historical processes attached to these traditions.[26]

Whether the Mesopotamian religious influence on a tradition like that preserved in 1 Sam 28 was the result of forced imposition by Israel's eastern overlords or the outgrowth of voluntary syncretism on the part of Israel is irrelevant to the present investigation. What is worthy of note is the familiarity exemplified by Israel's scribal elite *vis-à-vis* selected aspects of Mesopotamian divination. Such familiarity is also borne out for example, by biblical references to the funerary custom of burning a fire for a dead king or *śarap śᵉrēpāh* (Jer 34:5; 2 Chr 16:14 and 21:19). The funerary fires were attributed to Israelite kings like Asa and Zedekiah (but not Jehoram). At least at the literary level, if not the historical, this rite is modelled on the Assyrian practice of burning a funerary fire attested in royal letters from the reign of Esarhaddon, Manasseh's contemporary. As apotropaic rituals of the Assyrian royalty, they were appropriated by late Israelite writers and projected into traditions about earlier kings.[27] Examples such as these strengthen the case for a Mesopotamian stimulus underlying the adaptation by biblical writers of other foreign mortuary rites such

---

[26] E.g., Esarhaddon might have regulated sacrifices to Assyrian gods in Egypt, so the same might apply in Israel. For differing views on the degree and type of Assyrian influence on the Judahite temple cult of the mid-first millennium, cf. J. McKay, *Religion in Judah under the Assyrians 732-609 B.C.*, SBT 26 (London: SCM Press, 1973); M. Cogan, *Imperialism and Religion: Assyria, Judah and Israel in the Eighth and Seventh Centuries B.C.E.*, SBLMS 19 (Missoula: Scholars Press, 1974); H. Spieckermann, *Juda unter Assur in der Sargonidenzeit*, FRLANT 129 (Göttingen: Vandenhoeck & Ruprecht, 1982); R. H. Lowery, *The Reforming Kings: Cult and Society in First Temple Judah* (Sheffield: Sheffield University Press, 1991); S. Holloway, "The Case of Assyrian Religious Influence in Israel and Judah: Inference and Evidence" (Ph.D. diss., University of Chicago, 1992); and G. W. Ahlström, *The History of Ancient Palestine from the Paleolithic Period to Alexander's Conquest* (Sheffield: Sheffield Academic Press, 1993), 677-79, 684-90. All recognize such influence regardless of how such influence took place or its extent.

[27] The Akkadian cognate phrase is *šuruptu šarpat*, cf. Parpola, *Letters*, 2.6-8 [*LAS* #4], 190-92 [*LAS* #195], 270-72 [*LAS* #280] for a treatment of the pertinent Assyrian letters, and W. Zwickel, "Über das angebliche Verbrennen von Räucherwerk bei der Bestattung eines Königs," *ZAW* 101 (1989): 267-77. That the funerary fires were designed to appease or drive away malevolent ghosts might be suggested by their close association with *namburbi, āšipūtu*, and related rites in *LAS* 280: 16-21. Of course, demons other than ghosts might be in view.

as necromancy, and if that stimulus was not historical, then at least it was literary.[28]

*   *   *

We come now to the second issue we set out to investigate, namely the deification of the dead in ancient Israelite tradition. The *crux interpretum* in 1 Sam 28 is the term ʾĕlōhîm or "god(s)" in v. 13. It is typically understood to refer to the dead Samuel in spite of the several syntactic complexities such a view creates. The woman's response to Saul's query in v.13—that she saw "gods ascending"—comprises a plural noun coupled with a plural participle: ʾĕlōhîm . . . ʿōlîm. But Saul's immediate response in v. 14, "what is his/its appearance?" or *mah-to'ŏrô*, employs a singular pronominal suffix.[29] Now the same term ʾĕlōhîm shows up in v. 15, but there it is followed by a singular finite verbal form *sār* and given a singular force: "God (= Yahweh) has turned away from me," ʾĕlōhîm sār mēʿālāy. In Exod 32:1 the same form occurs with a plural finite verb denoting multiple gods: ʾĕlōhîm ʾašer yēlĕkû lĕpānênû, "the gods who will go before us." Thus, the immediate morpho-syntactic distinctions indicated by the two occurrences of ʾĕlōhîm in 1 Sam 28 might be a deliberate attempt to convey the respective numbers intended: in the first instance more than one god is in view, in the second case, clearly a single god. This might also help to resolve the potential discrepancy involving the singular suffix (*to'ŏrô* v. 14) and its plural antecedent (ʾĕlōhîm v. 13). In any case, the explicit mention of Samuel in v. 12 can provide the appropriate antecedent for the singular masculine suffix on *to'ŏrô* in v. 14.[30] As for the question posed in v. 14,

---

[28] As to why certain appropriated Mesopotamian mortuary practices were polemicized against while others were not is addressed in the conclusion to this study. The lack of polemic in the instance of the funerary fire might indicate the writers' ignorance of the origins of the rite or an attempt to enhance the status of the Israelite kings by depicting their funerals as on par with those of Assyrian kings while suppressing any "magical" elements possibly associated with the fear of the dead.

[29] The term *to'ŏrô* is derivative of *t-'-r*, "to regard intently" (Qal) or "to form (a shape)" (Piel).

[30] Less concerned with the woman's mention of gods in v. 13, Saul sought foremost information regarding the appearance of the apparition first mentioned in v. 12, for its appearance led the woman to identify Saul. That Saul, although present, did not have direct access to the woman's vision is confirmed by the fact that in the first-millennium Mesopotamian necromancy incantations, procedures involving recitations and smearing preparations on the face must be followed in

the LXX reads *ti egnōs*, "what have you perceived?" not "what is his/its appearance?" Its underlying Hebrew *Vorlage* probably read *mh t'rt*, "what did you make out" (< *t- '-r*).[31] In other words, in the Greek text and its underlying Hebrew tradition, the need to identify an antecedent in v. 13 for the question posed in v. 14 does not arise.[32]

Admittedly, both of the preceding scenarios leave the "gods" or *ʾĕlōhîm* in v. 13 unidentified, but before we offer our interpretation of the term *ʾĕlōhîm* or "gods" in v. 13, the comparative evidence often advanced in support of the deification of the Israelite dead demands evaluation. Literary data from Mesopotamia, Syria, and elsewhere have been cited as indicative of the divine status of the Israelite dead. Often mentioned are the Akkadian *Ersatznamen*, the association of the *ilānu* with the *eṭemmū* in Akkadian texts from Assyria and Nuzi, the parallels between *ilānu* and *mētū* in the Emar texts, the Ugaritic king list (*KTU* 1.113) wherein the form *'il* is followed by a personal royal name (i.e., "Divine So-and-So"), and the *'ilm* or "gods" which parallel the *mtm* or "dead" in the Shapash hymn of the Baal-Mot myth from Ugarit (*KTU* 1.6.VI:45-49).[33]

Interpreters repeatedly affirm that the dead in Mesopotamia are designated by the lexeme *ilu* or its plural form *ilānu*. But the cited data are sparse and highly controvertible. The *ilu* element in the so-called *Ersatznamen* more likely refers to "good fortune," "luck," or a "personal god" (often an unnamed member of the pantheon), rather than to a ghost of the dead.[34] Second, while the

---

order for the necromancer to see the ghost, cf. Finkel, "Necromancy," 5, 10, and J. Scurlock, "Magical Means of Dealing with Ghosts in Ancient Mesopotamia," 2 vols. (Ph.D. diss., University of Chicago, 1988), 324-26 (and n. 201), 337-42. In other words, it was the necromancer's sole prerogative to see a ghost.

[31] P. K. McCarter, *1 Samuel*, AB 8 (Garden City: Doubleday, 1980), 419, preferred the LXX and proposed *mh ydʿt* as its Hebrew *Vorlage*. T. J. Lewis, *Cults of the Dead in Ancient Israel and Ugarit*, HSM 39 (Atlanta: Scholars Press, 1989), 109, favored the MT and offered *mh tr'y* (< *r-'-h*), but see n. 29 above. Both presumed the equation of god and ghost.

[32] Moreover, the criterion of *lectio difficilior* is not *a priori* to be preferred; cf. now E. Tov, *Textual Criticism of the Hebrew Bible* (Minneapolis: Fortress Press, 1992), 302-05.

[33] Cf. K. Spronk, *Beatific Afterlife in Ancient Israel and in the Ancient Near East*, AOAT 219 (Neukirchen-Vluyn: Neukirchener Verlag, 1986), 163, who also mentions Egypt; and Lewis, *Cults*, 49-51, 115.

[34] Following *CAD* 7 (1960): 102, contra Lewis, *Cults*, 49-50. For a list of the names, cf. J. J. Stamm, *Die akkadische Namengebung* (MVÄG 44; Leipzig: Hinrichs, 1939), 278-306. A name like *Ilum-ḫabil*, "the god is taken

ghosts of the dead are associated on occasion with the "gods" or *ilānu*, their supposed equation is another matter altogether. The bilingual incantation text from Assyria, *CT* 17,37 "Y", 1-10 is often cited in this regard: "the captive gods come forth from the grave, the *zaqīqu* come forth from the grave, for the offering of the *kispū*, for the water libation, they come forth from the grave."[35] But the fact that the captive gods are located in the netherworld merely confirms what was already known, namely that the Mesopotamian underworld was inhabited by sundry forms of numina. Furthermore, in addition to comprising grave goods to be included in a burial (*Totenbeigabe*), the *kispu* frequently comprised a gift offered to the gods of the underworld or a form of enticement to the infernal deities—particularly the Anunnaki—for protection from tormenting ghosts.[36] In fact, mid-first millennium necromancy incantation texts record offerings to be made to various deities such as Shamash, the Anunnaki, Pabilsag, and the primordial deities of the netherworld for their aid in raising a ghost from the grave (more on this below).[37]

That the captive gods come up from their graves in the netherworld might be expressive of the Mesopotamian belief reflected in Enuma Elish. These gods, having been slain for their rebellion against the established pantheon (and perhaps imprisoned in their sepulchers), could be released from the netherworld only by the appropriate means, whether it be the requisite incantational procedure or the decree of Marduk at creation as in Enuma Elish.[38] It appears that there were many groups of such gods who comprised the defeated and slain divine enemies, not all of which had appar-

---

away/wronged," might refer to the perceived abandonment of the personal god (often a major deity) during childbirth as expressed in the resultant impairment, near-death, or death of the mother and/or the impairment or near-death of her child. A name like *Itūr-ilum*, "the god has returned," might refer to a similar situation, but one in which the personal god, having temporarily abandoned its human protégé, unexpectedly intervened and preempted disaster.

[35] The text reads *ilānu ka-mu-ti iš-tu qab-rì it-ta-ṣu-ni za-qí-qu lim-nu-ti iš-tu qab-rì it-ta-ṣu-ni a-na ka-sa-ap ki-is-pi ú na-aq mé-e iš-tu qab-rì* KIMIN, cf. *CAD* 21 (1961): 59, and most recently Tsukimoto, *Totenpflege*, 148. Usage reveals that the term *zaqīqu* cannot be simply equated with *eṭemmu* "ghost of the dead"; cf. *CAD* 21 (1961): 58-59, and *AHw* 3 (1981): 1530a.

[36] Cf. Tsukimoto, *Totenpflege*, 140-45, 184-200.

[37] For references, cf. Finkel, "Necromancy," 1-17; E. von Weiher, *Spätbabylonische Texte aus Uruk 2*, ADFU 10 (Berlin: Gebr. Mann, 1983), 100-03; and J. Scurlock, "Ghosts," 5-8, 103-12, 318-42.

[38] Cf. Enuma Elish IV:93-120 (esp. line 120), VI:11-34, VII:26-32.

ently rebelled, been captured, and released at the creation of man. For example, many Asakku demons and Tammuzes show up after the death of the Asakku demon in Lugale and the death of Tammuz.[39] These slain divine enemies are given various titles: "the conquered Enlils," "the dead gods," or simply "the battered" *abtūtu* or *šulputūtu*.[40]

In any case, one cannot appeal to Enuma Elish VII:26-27 to buttress a simplistic equation of the captive gods and the ghosts of the dead.[41] The relevant lines read as follows: "Lord of the holy incantation who raises the dead to life, who has compassion on the captive gods."[42] While the captive gods are described as dead, the significance is not that the captive gods are to be equated with the ghosts of deceased mortals, for humankind had yet to be created. Rather, the following lines 28-29 make clear that not only are the dead of line 26 the captive gods of line 27, but that both refer to those gods who were slain for their rebellion against the great gods. These lines also point out that it is by means of creating humankind, whose lot it is to relieve the captive gods of their service, that these dead gods can be restored to their former positions in the pantheon.

Among the few remaining texts, the Neo-Assyrian version of the Legend of Etana mentions "the gods" or *ilānu* and "the ghosts of the dead" or *eṭemmū* as parallel members of a poetic bicolon. But parallelism alone cannot insure the equation of the *ilānu* with the ghosts of the dead. A complementary force of the poetic parallelism might equally apply. The text reads, "I honored the gods, served the ghosts of the dead."[43] Now the term *ilānu* most frequently designates the gods of the pantheon and quite often the personal protective gods. Thus, in the Legend of Etana, one would expect that the term *ilānu* refers to the personal gods, that is, if

---

[39] W. G. Lambert, "The Theology of Death," in *Death in Mesopotamia*, RAI 26, ed. B. Alster (Copenhagen: Akademisk Forlag, 1980), 65.

[40] Cf. Enuma Elish IV:119-20 and VI:151-54; and Lambert, "Theology," 65. In a Seleucid-period bilingual incantation, *UVB* 15.36:5, 9-10, Shamash is said to be in charge of "the dead gods"; cf. A. Falkenstein, "Zwei Rituale aus seleukidischer Zeit," *Vorläufiger Bericht über die von dem Deutschen Archaeologischen Institut . . . Uruk-Warka* 15 (1959): 36-40.

[41] Cf. e.g., Tsukimoto, *Totenpflege*, 148 and n. 490.

[42] The phraseology employed is *be-el šip-tu* KÙ-*tì mu-bal-liṭ mi-i-ti šá an* DINGIR.DINGIR *ka-mu-ti ir-šu-ú ta-a-a-ru*; cf. Tsukimoto, *Totenpflege*, 148 n. 490.

[43] The phraseology employed is *ilī ú-kab-bit e-tém-me ap-làḫ*, cf. J. Greenfield, "Un rite religieux araméen et ses paralläles," *RB* 80 (1973): 52, and now J. V. Kinnier-Wilson, *The Legend of Etana: A New Edition* (Chicago: Bolchazy-Canducci, 1985), 100 (lines 134-36).

familial obligations are in view, but if not, then to the gods of the
pantheon more generally. In other words, the text simply seeks to
convey the widely embraced virtue of performing the respective
services for both the gods as well as the ghosts of the dead, two
distinct groups of supranatural beings.

That the *ilānu* delineate the same group as that signified by the
dead may be actually contradicted in the few instances where the
ilānu are mentioned alongside the *eṭemmū* at Nuzi and the *mētū* at
Emar. In view of the general usage of *ilānu* outlined above and the
non-poetic contexts of the Nuzi and Emar texts, a distinction was
probably intended. Some distinction is recognized even by those
who seek to identify the gods with the ghosts of the dead.[44] One is
otherwise forced to make the unwarranted assumption that the
ancient writers in this case were guilty of blatant redundancy.

At Nuzi, both "the gods" or *ilānu* and "the ghosts of the dead"
or *eṭemmū* are depicted as deserving of service (*palāḫu*). As in the
case of the Legend of Etana, "the gods" or *ilānu* might just as
conceivably refer to the family personal gods, which is what we
would expect in the context of inheritance. The same can be said
for the references to "the gods" or *ilānu* alongside "the dead" or
mētū in the Emar texts. In the genre of testament at Emar, the
gods and the dead are "honored" (*kunnû*) and "called
upon/commemorated by name" (*nabû* A).[45] Again, the explicit
mention of the gods together with the dead in a non-poetic context lends credence to the view that the former designate a group
of supranatural beings distinct from the dead. Within the context
of inheritance, we might expect the *ilānu* to represent personal
gods who the evidence reveals were often none other than the
major deities.

The phrase *'il* + personal royal name in the Ugaritic king list
KTU 1.113 (and cf. the Eblaite king list) most likely refers to a
dynasty's personal god to whom ritual is directed for purposes of
legitimation. The god is repeatedly referred to in a listing of deceased kings. The *'il* element precedes each royal name and proba-

---

[44] Tsukimoto, *Totenpflege*, 104-05 and H. Rouillard and J. Tropper, "*Trpym*,
rituels de guérison et culte des ancêtres d'après 1 Samuel XIX 11-17 et les
parallèles d'Assur et de Nuzi," *VT* 37 (1987): 354-56, recognized the redundancy of merely equating these terms at Nuzi. They labelled the *eṭemmū* as the
recent identifiable ancestors and the *ilānu* as the remote unidentifiable ancestors.
For a list of most of the relevent Emar texts, cf. J.-M. Durand, "Tombes familiales et
culte des Ancêtres à Emar," *NABU* 3 (1989): 85-88.

[45] Perhaps they are "lamented" (*nabû* B). Even so, this rendition alone cannot secure the status of the *ilānu* as ghosts of the dead.

bly designates the order of offerings and the associated public recitation of each name as offerings were made to "the god of so-and-so". Moreover, the terms "gods" or *'ilm* and the *mtm* or "men" (rather than "dead") in the Shapash hymn in the closing section of the Baal-Mot myth (*KTU* 1.6.VI:45ff.) stand in antithetical rather than synonymous parallelism. Nowhere in the myth proper are the dead mentioned. Humanity is threatened with death, but Shapash stays Mot's hand and spares humanity. In other words, the closing hymn highlights the point that Shapash dictates the fates of those living in the divine and earthly realms.

The preceding analysis renders suspect the position that the dead in early Syria-Palestine obtained the status of "god" in any sense of the term. Furthermore, the internal and external data render highly unlikely the widely accepted view that *ʾĕlōhîm* in 1 Sam 28:13 is Samuel's ghost. Besides, if by "god" a ghost of the dead was intended, why was the term *'ôḇ* or *yiddeʿōnî* not mentioned instead in v. 13, for these two are the deuteronomistic technical terms for ghosts participating in necromancy?[46] Lastly, if it were granted that the dead were deified, the woman's reference to the ghost of the dead by the use of the term *ʾĕlōhîm* would have been superfluous for her and for Saul.

Who then are the intended referents designated *ʾĕlōhîm* in 1 Sam 28:13? One viable alternative to understanding the phrase *ʾĕlōhîm . . . ʿōlîm* reflects a striking resemblance to elements attested in Mesopotamian necromancy. In the first-millennium necromantic incantation texts referred to previously, various deities including Shamash and the primordial deities of the netherworld are called upon in order to insure the appearance of the ghost of the dead.[47] In one such incantation, Shamash is depicted as follows: "Shamash, O Judge, you bring those from above down below, those from below up above."[48] This role of the solar deity is also underscored in another incantation text:[49]

---

[46] The *'ôḇōṯ* and the *yiddeʿōnîm* of vv. 3,7-9 refer neither to a class of professional mantics nor to ancestral images, but to the ghosts of the dead, "the ones-who-return" (< Arabic *'āba*, "to return") and "the knowers." The decisive passage is Lev 20:27 where it is reported that a man or woman might have "in them" (*bāhem*) the *'ôḇ* or the *yiddeʿōnî*. This surely eliminates the practitioner and the image as interpretive options.

[47] On this role of the gods, cf. esp. Scurlock, "Ghosts," 106-10. M. Hutter, "Religionsgeschichtliche Erwägungen zu *'lhym* in 1 Sam 28,13," *Biblische Notizen* 21 (1983): 32-36, concluded that "gods coming out of the earth" did not refer to Samuel's supernatural character. However, he wrongly based his argument on Hittite evidence and on an early date for the 1 Sam 28 text and tradition.

[48] Cf. Finkel, "Necromancy," 11, and Scurlock, "Ghosts,' 327-28 (lines 13b-

¹ [. . . ² . . .] dust of the netherworld [. . .]. ³ May he (Shamash) bring up a ghost from the darkness for me! May he (put life back) into the dead man's limbs. ⁴ I call (upon you), O skull of skulls: ⁵ May he who is within the skull answer [me]! ⁶ O Shamash, who opens the darkne[ss. Incantation. . .].

In view of the likelihood that the Syro-Palestinian dead were not equated with the gods, that the gods were active participants in the Mesopotamian necromancy rituals, that the text of 1 Sam 28:13-14 manifests considerable complexity in transmission, and that the biblical traditions show some acquaintance with Mesopotamian necromancy, it is our conclusion that the term *ʾĕlōhîm* in 1 Sam 28:13 designates those gods known to be summoned—many from the world below—to assist the necromancer in the retrieval of a ghost. Our interpretive rendition of vv. 11-14 follows:

> ¹¹ At that, the woman said, "Whom shall I bring up for you?" He answered, "Bring up Samuel for me." ¹² When the woman saw Samuel, she shrieked loudly, and the woman said to Saul, "Why have you deceived me? You are Saul!" ¹³ The king said to her, "Do not be afraid. What do you see?" And the woman said to Saul, "I see (chthonic) gods coming up from the earth."¹⁴ Then he said to her, "(Now) what have you perceived (cf. LXX)?" And she said to him, "An old/upright man coming up from the earth, and he is wrapped in a robe."

*   *   *

The affinities that 1 Sam 28:3-25 shares with the mid-first millennium divination and (in particular) necromantic traditions from Mesopotamia are remarkable. These include the role of divination in dictating military strategy and in predicting the outcome of armed engagement, necromancy's role in determining the fate of the royal dynasty, and the assistance of the gods in the retrieval of a ghost. These similarities which 1 Sam 28:3-25 shares with Mesopotamian divination and necromancy, its compositional history, the absence of necromancy in Levantine, Egyptian, and Anatolian religions pre-dating the mid-first millennium, all point to a late Mesopotamian stimulus underlying not only the text of the

---

14a). The verb *abālu* with the ventive can signify "to bring" rather than "to carry"; cf. *CAD* 1 (1964): 14.

⁴⁹ For the text, cf. Finkel, "Necromancy," 5, 9 and Scurlock, "Ghosts," 322-23.

"Witch" of En-Dor account, but also its tradition. Therefore, the Canaanite origin of Israelite necromancy is best viewed as a retrospective ideological construct of the biblical writers.[50] We would propose that the (post)-deuteronomistic writer's rhetorical strategy involved projecting necromancy into a narrative about more ancient times, attributing to it ancient Canaanite origins, and having it condemned by a venerable hero of the past: the prophet Samuel.[51]

A comparison of 1 Sam 28:3-25 with other texts in the Deuteronomistic History—the list of Manasseh's sins in 2 Kgs 21:6, the cultic reform of Josiah in 2 Kgs 23:24 and the deuteronomistic passage in the Mosaic law, Deut 18:10-11—indicates that our author drew from the stock deuteronomistic language of "necromancy as taboo." With its inclusion in the episode involving the woman of En-Dor, necromancy's performance and proscription was relocated in the formative stage of the nation's history. The proscription of necromancy could no longer be viewed as an issue of concern only for late-comers such as the deuteronomistic ideologists. Now it was an age-old problem. Whereas the deuteronomistic ideology polemicized against necromancy by attaching it to Manasseh's apostasy during the last days of the Davidic dynasty (2 Kgs 21:6), the hand responsible for 1 Sam 28:3-25 established a much earlier precedent by associating necromancy with Israel's first monarchy, the Saulide dynasty. Saul, Israel's first king, violated the law of Moses as set forth in Deut 18:11—itself a deuteronomistic text set in a context about much earlier times.

---

[50] Like the terms Amorite and Hittite, the biblical Canaanite functioned primarily as an ideological term denoting the pre-Israelite inhabitants of Palestine, later foreign occupiers, and ultimately all groups, including those who embraced competing forms of Yahwism, who were perceived as a threat to Israel's claim to the land and its blessings; cf. J. Van Seters, "The Terms 'Amorite' and 'Hittite' in the Old Testament," *VT* 22 (1972): 64-81; J. Levenson, "Is There a Counterpart in the Hebrew Bible to New Testament Anti-Semitism?" *JES* 22 (1985): 242-60; and now N. P. Lemche, *The Canaanites and Their Land* (Sheffield: Sheffield Academic Press, 1991). Isa 19:3 preserves a rhetorical expansion on the Canaanite origins of necromancy in its depiction of the Egyptian as observer of necromancy. Besides the absence of necromancy in early Egyptian sources, the use of typical Akkadian terminology in 19:3 like the term *eṭemmu(m)* or "ghost"—the Hebrew equivalent of which is *'iṭṭîm*— and the presence of technical Hebrew terminology for the ghost such as *'ôḇ* and *yiddeʿōnî* provide further clues to the rhetorical nature of necromancy's Egyptian associations in Isa 19.

[51] Elsewhere it is condemned by the prophets Moses (Deut 18:11) and Isaiah (Isa 8:19) and the good king, Josiah (2 Kgs 23:24).

Crucial to deuteronomistic ideology was the general premise that the land and its blessings were dependent upon complete separation from foreign religious practices. Viewed in this light, the legend of Saul demonstrates that when the leaders of the nation embrace religious beliefs of the foreigner—like Saul in his rendez-vous with the Canaanite woman of En-Dor—the nation's rights to the land and its blessings are jeopardized. Be that as it may, we have yet to address the question of why the deuteronomistic and associated traditions selected necromancy as the straw that broke the back of both dynasties.

Necromancy is unique among rituals preserved in the Hebrew Bible, mortuary or otherwise, in that it precipitated direct contact with the world of the gods as well as with the world of the dead (although not of the deified dead!). In necromancy, both the dead and the gods "bodily" invade the world of the living; therefore it is the quintessence of liminality. Its (con)fusion of three worlds—those of the gods, the living, and the dead—explains why necro-mancy—among the many magical and mortuary rites mentioned in the biblical traditions—became a distinctly anomalous rite within the rigid classification systems of both the deuteronomistic and priestly traditions (cf. Deut 18:11, 2 Kgs 21:6 and 23:24 and Lev 19:31, 20:6,27 respectively). It epitomized both Israel's prostitu-tion and pollution.[52] As the archetype for the abnormal and as the esteemed rite of her Mesopotamian overlords, necromancy was pressed into service as the Achilles heel of Israel's two royal houses, the house of Saul and the house of David, for it is Saul and Manasseh who are to blame for the destruction of their respective dynasties (and cf. 2 Kgs 21:10-15). In the final analysis, for the deuteronomistic tradition, necromancy—more than any other

---

[52] I. Morris, "Attitudes Toward Death in Archaic Greece," *Classical Antiq-uity* 8 (1989): 296-320 has proposed that, coincident with the rise of the Greek polis, humankind's central place in the cosmos as a citizen in the new social order led to the spatial separation of the gods, the living, and the dead into three discrete areas within the polis. Their confusion was rationalized as pollution. In biblical traditions, the special status of the dead's polluting power is reflected in the unique performance outside the sanctuary and camp of priestly rituals aimed at compensating for contact with a corpse (other forms of purification required performance at the sanctuary; Num 19), the prohibition against priests engaging in funerary rites (though the family could; Lev 21), and especially the blanket prohibitions against self-mutilation and necromancy. The last two entailed the most explicit (con)fusion of worlds: the former presupposed the presence of the dead through imitation; and the latter, their very presence in the form of a ghost along with the involvement of other gods.

rite—epitomized *the* abomination of the Canaanite in the history of Israelite kingship.

CHAPTER EIGHT

THE MAGICIAN AS OUTSIDER
IN THE HEBREW BIBLE AND THE NEW TESTAMENT

Stephen D. Ricks

Several recent studies on magic in antiquity, including essays published in this volume, have stressed its continuity, rather than cleavage, with religion.[1] According to these studies, magic in antiquity was not regarded as a separate institution with a structure distinct from that of religion, but was rather a set of beliefs and practices that deviated sharply from the norms of the dominant social group, and was thus considered antisocial, illegal, or unacceptable.[2] The evidence of the Hebrew Bible corresponds to this view of magic. There it is not the nature of the action itself, but the conformity of the action (or actor) to, or deviation from, the

---

[1] This essay represents a revision and expansion of my earlier essay "The Magician as Outsider: The Evidence of the Hebrew Bible," in Paul V. M. Flesher, *New Perspectives on Ancient Judaism* V (Lanham: University Press of America, 1990), 125-34.

[2] David E. Aune, "Magic; Magician," in Geoffrey W. Bromiley, ed., *The International Standard Bible Encyclopedia* (Grand Rapids: W.B. Eerdmans, 1986), 3.213. Cf. Aune, "Magic in Early Christianity," in *ANRW*, ed. Wolfgand Haase, (Berlin: Walter de Gruyter, 1980), 2.23.2:1515. In a similar vein, see Haralds Biezais, *Von der Wesensidentität der Magie und Religion,* in *Acta Academiae Aboensis, Series A: Humaniora* 55:3 (1978); note the comment of Jorunn Jacobsen Buckley in *Abstracts: American Academy of Religion/Society of Biblical Literature Annual Meeting 1986* (Decatur: Scholars Press, 1986), 53, concerning a Mandaean document that "lends itself well to defend the thesis that there is no difference between 'religion' and 'magic'—this distinction is a scholarly evaluative fiction." Among the more recent literature that maintains a solely or primarily structural distinction between "religion" and "magic," see Stephen Benko, "Magic," in *Harper's Bible Dictionary*, Paul J. Achtemeier, ed. (San Francisco: Harper and Row, 1985), 594-96; Piera Arata Mantovani, "La magia nei testi preesilici dell' Antico Testamento," *Henoch 3* (1981): 1-21; J. B. Segal, "Popular Religion in Ancient Israel," *Journal of Jewish Studies* 27 (1976): 6-7. Among the older works, see, e.g., Arvid Kapelrud, "The Interrelationship between Religion and Magic in Hittite Religion," *Numen* 6 (1959): 32-50; A. Lods, "Le rôle des idées magiques dans la mentalité israélite," in *Old Testament Essays: Papers Read Before the Society for Old Testament Study* (London: Charles Griffin and Co., 1927), 55-76; and A. Lods, "Magie hébraïque et magie cananéenne," *Revue d'Histoire et de Philosophie Religieuses* 7 (1927): 1-16.

values of Israelite society—as these values are reflected in the
canonical text of the Bible—that determines whether it is characterized as magical. Further, "magic" (as this and related words have
been understood in Hebrew and Greek and rendered in versions
from the Septuagint to the most recent English translations)[3] is
quintessentially the activity of the "outsider" in the Bible. The
matter of the translation and subsequent interpretation of words
traditionally rendered as "magic" is an important one that should
not be overlooked in investigations of magic, since the choice of
words used in a translation reflects a whole host of *a priori* assumptions made by the writer or translator, not only in a target language, such as English, but also in intermediate languages, such as
the Greek of the Septuagint or the Latin of the Vulgate.

As I am using the term, "outsider" includes both the non-
Israelite as well as the native Israelite whose practices deviated
sharply from the Israelite norm, particularly because these acts
were perceived as being performed through a power other than
Israel's God. In this essay I discuss the traditional distinction between magic and religion that has prevailed in Western scholarship
since the Reformation and contrast it with the view of magic and
religion in antiquity. These methodological reflections, though
they take us somewhat afield from antiquity, are not inappropriate
for such a discussion, since questions of definition should be resolved at the outset of any study of magic. Thus, for instance, the
value of Valerie I. J. Flint's otherwise admirable study, *The Rise of
Magic in Early Medieval Europe*, and Keith Thomas' *Religion and
the Decline of Magic*, is somewhat undermined by rather debatable
definitions of magic.[4] Further, I consider accounts from the Bible

---

[3] The matter of the translation and subsequent interpretation of words traditionally rendered as "magic" is an important one that should not be overlooked
in investigations of magic, since the choice of words used in a translation reflects
a whole host of *a priori* assumptions made by the writer or translator. For a
convenient list of biblical Hebrew terms related to sorcery and their Septuagint
equivalents, see G. André, "*kāšap*," in *Theologisches Wörterbuch zum Alten
Testament*, G. Johannes Botterweck, Helmer Ringgren, and Heinz-Joseph Fabry,
eds. (Stuttgart: W. Kohlhammer Verlag, 1984), 4.376-77.

[4] Consider Flint's definition, in *The Rise of Magic in Early Medieval Europe*
(Princeton: Princeton University Press, 1991), 3: "Magic may be said to be the
exercise of a preternatural control over nature by human beings, with the assistance of forces more powerful than they. This combination of human and superhuman power will sometimes employ strange instruments and is always liable to
produce remarkable and unaccustomed results. Thus we may expect an element of
the irrational, and of the mysterious too, in a process that deserves to be called
magical." But does not nearly every religious tradition have some elements that

as examples of the magician as "outsider," and show that the characterization of activities in ancient Israel and in the New Testament as "magical" is based upon the norms of those societies.

The traditional view of the structural cleavage between magic and religion that has prevailed in Western scholarship in recent centuries is the result, in part at least, of the sharp Protestant reaction to certain Roman Catholic sacraments and other practices. This position was represented at least as early as 1395 by the Lollards in their "Twelve Conclusions":

> That exorcisms and hallowings, made in the Church, of wine, bread, and wax, water, salt and oil and incense, the stone of the altar, upon vestments, mitre, cross, and pilgrims' staves, be the very practice of necromancy, rather than of the holy theology. This conclusion is proved thus. For by such exorcisms creatures be charged to be of higher virtue than their own kind, and we see nothing of change in no such creature that is so charmed, but by false belief, the which is the devil's craft.[5]

According to the Lollard Walter Brute, the very procedures of the priests were modelled on those of the magician. Both priest and magician thought their spells were more effective when pronounced in one place and at one time rather than another; both turned to the east to say them; and both thought that mere words could possess a magic virtue.[6] But if the Protestants criticized holy water and the consecration of church bells, they launched a veritable frontal assault against the central Catholic doctrine of the Mass. In the view of one Reformer, transubstantiation differs in no significant way from conjurations, "the pretense of a power, plainly magical, of changing the elements in such a sort as all the magicians of Pharaoh could never do, nor had the face to attempt the like, it being so beyond all credibility." John Calvin wrote that the Roman Catholics "pretend there is a magical force in the

could be described in this way, at least to an outsider? Certainly the biblical tradition does. For whom are the "instruments," of which Flint speaks, "strange"? To whom are its results "remarkable and unaccustomed"? To the practitioners themselves? I doubt it. And how are such magical acts to be distinguished from ritual ones? Flint's definition says at least as much about the speaker or writer as it does about those acts thus described.

[5] Cited by H. S. Cronin in "The Twelve Conclusions of the Lollards," *English Historical Review* 22 (1907): 298.

[6] John Foxe, *The Acts and Monuments of Matters Most Special and Memorable* (London: Adam Islip, Foelix Kingston and Robert Young, 1632), 3.179-80, cited in Keith Thomas, *Religion and the Decline of Magic* (New York: Charles Scribner's Sons, 1971), 52.

sacraments, independent of efficacious faith." According to Bishop
Hooper, the rite of the Roman Mass was "nothing better to be
esteemed than the verses of the sorcerer or enchanter ... holy
words murmured and spoken in secret."[7] The essential features of
magic thus came to be understood as consisting of the automatic
efficacy of ritual words (incantations) and ritual procedures
(magical operations). Based on this view of the automatic and
immediate efficacy of ritual words and procedures, a different
relationship to deity (or deities) was posited: magic was said to be
manipulative and coercive, while religion (based on the Reformers'
views of efficacious faith) was perceived as supplicative.

In contrast to this view of magic that developed during the period of the Reformation, magic in antiquity was viewed, according
to David Aune, as "that form of religious deviance whereby individual or social goals are sought by means alternate to those normally sanctioned by the dominant religious institution."[8] As both
Jonathan Z. Smith[9] and Morton Smith[10] have shown in the case of
the Greco-Roman world, magic and magical practices are *par
excellence* the activities of the outsider. According to J. Z. Smith,
in the Greco-Roman world, "magic was not different in essence
from religion, but rather different with regard to social position
.... The one universal characteristic of magic" is that "it is illegal, ... and it carried the penalty of death or deportation."[11] In
the same vein, Morton Smith notes, "in the Roman Empire, the
practice of magic was a criminal offense (Paulus, *Sententiae*
5:23.14-18), and the 'magician' was therefore a term of abuse. It
still is, but the connotation has changed: now it is primarily fraud;
then it was social subversion."[12] As in the Greco-Roman world,
magic in the Bible was a practice of the outsider. It was also perceived as a form of subversion and was consequently severely
punished, since it was viewed as undermining Israel's religious
foundations.

---

[7] Thomas, *Religion and the Decline of Magic*, 53.

[8] Aune, "Magic in Early Christianity," 1515.

[9] J. Z. Smith, "Good News Is No News: Aretalogy and Gospel," in *Map Is
Not Territory* (Leiden: Brill, 1978), 163.

[10] Morton Smith, *Clement of Alexandria and a Secret Gospel of Mark*
(Cambridge: Harvard University Press, 1973), 221.

[11] J. Z. Smith, "Good News Is No News," 163; cf. Jules Maurice, "La terreur
de la magie au IV. siècle," *Comptes rendus de l' Académie des Inscriptions et
Belles-Lettres* (1926): 88.

[12] M. Smith, *Clement of Alexandria*, 221. In the light of this statement, it is
significant—and telling—that one of Smith's subsequent books is entitled *Jesus
the Magician*.

The biblical accounts that most lucidly show magicians as outsiders and refute a simple definition of magic as the employment of words and actions that function *ex opere operato* (i.e., have their desired effect merely by being performed or spoken) are the stories of Moses and Aaron and Pharaoh's wise men and magicians, Joseph and the wise men and magicians of Pharaoh, and Daniel and the Babylonian astrologers and wizards. According to the account in Exodus 7-9, the Lord said to Moses and Aaron, "When Pharaoh speaks to you and says, 'Produce your marvel' (Heb. *môpēt*), you shall say to Aaron, 'Take your rod and cast it down before Pharaoh.' It shall turn into a serpent" (Ex 7:8-9). They came before the Pharaoh and did precisely that: Aaron cast down his rod in the presence of Pharaoh, and it turned into a serpent. The Pharaoh then summoned his own wise men (*ḥăkāmîm*) and sorcerers (*mĕkaśśĕpîm*), and the Egyptian magicians did the same thing with their spells (*wayyaʿaśû gam-hēm ḥarṭummê miṣrayim bĕlahăṭêhem kēn*) (Ex 7:11). Though the rods of the Egyptian magicians were able to become serpents, Aaron's rod swallowed all of their rods. The Egyptian wise men and sorcerers were further able to imitate Moses and Aaron in the turning of the bodies of water in Egypt into blood and in bringing frogs upon the land by their spells (*bĕlahăṭêhem*), but they failed in their efforts to produce lice (*kinnîm*); they were fully discomfited when the boils affected them as they did the other Egyptians, so that they were not even able to stand before Pharaoh.

In Genesis 41, Pharaoh had dreams that left him troubled. He sent for his magicians (*ḥarṭummê miṣrayim*) and for his wise men (*ḥăkāmêhā*) to interpret his dreams for him. After Pharaoh had told them his dreams, the magicians and wise men said that they were not able to interpret them for him. At this point the chief cupbearer remembered Joseph, who was then called before Pharaoh and was able, through the gift of God (Gen 41:16), to interpret Pharaoh's dreams to his satisfaction.

In Daniel 2, Nebuchadnezzar, like Pharaoh, had dreams that left his spirit agitated, whereupon he called his magicians (*ḥarṭummîm*), exorcists (*aśśāpîm*), sorcerers (*mĕkaśśĕpîm*), and Chaldaeans (*kaśdîm*) to tell him what he had dreamed. They were threatened with death if they failed to produce for him both his dream and its interpretation, but they claimed that such a demand as the king was making of them had never been made of a magician, exorcist, or Chaldaean before: "The thing asked by the king is difficult; there is no one who can tell it to the king except the gods whose abodes are not among mortals" (Dan 2:11). Thereupon the king flew into a violent rage, and gave an order to kill all of the wise men of Babylon. However, Daniel, who would also have fallen under this death order, was able to interpret the dream through the power of the "God of heaven," thereby saving himself and the others from death.

Several significant features in these stories that are relevant to our subject are worth noting: In each of these three instances, Israelites are pitted against practitioners of the religion of non-Israelite "outsiders," and in each instance the superior power of God is shown. When the magicians and wise men of Pharaoh are not able to produce lice by their own spells, they exclaim to Pharaoh, "This is the finger of God" (ʾeṣbaʿ ʾĕlōhîm hîʾ) (Ex 8:14). Daniel similarly emphasizes Israel's God as the source of his power and its superiority to the power of the wise men and magicians: "The mystery about which the king has inquired—wise men, exorcists, magicians, and diviners cannot tell to the king. But there is a God in heaven who reveals mysteries, and he has made known to King Nebuchadnezzar what is to be at the end of days" (Dan 2:27-8). Further, in the instances of Joseph and Daniel, there is no clear indication given of the specific manner in which they show themselves superior to the Egyptian and Babylonian magicians, except through prayer and the power of God. However, in the case of Moses and Aaron in Pharaoh's court, the action by which the effect was achieved was the same (wayyaʿăśū gam-hēm ḥarṭummê miṣrayim bĕlahăṭêhem kēn). In addition, the very word used here in the text for the Egyptian magicians—ḥarṭom (in the phrase "ḥarṭummê miṣrayim")—is borrowed from the Egyptian ḥr tp, "lector priest," one who, in Egyptian materials at least, is not generally associated with magic (but see the essay by Robert K. Ritner, above).[13] This suggests an implicit polemic in the text against all practitioners of Egyptian religion, with the hint that they are all magicians (because they are non-Yahwists).

Jacob Milgrom has pointed out that Moses is silent before the performance of each miracle; Pharaoh's magicians, on the other hand, are only able to copy Aaron's actions "by their spells" (bĕlahăṭêhem—if we follow the new Jewish Publication Society translation—rather than the more traditional translation "by their secret arts").[14] By acting alone, and not speaking, Moses behaves

---

[13] Adolf Erman and Hermann Grapow, eds., Ägyptisch-Deutsches Wörterbuch, 6 vols. (Leipzig: J. Hinrichs, 1929), 3.177.

[14] Jacob Milgrom, "Magic, Monotheism, and the Sin of Moses," in The Quest for the Kingdom of God: Studies in Honor of George E. Mendenhall, H. B.

in a manner that is distinct from that of the Egyptians (which is, by implication, "magical"). I find this position somewhat unsatisfying. As Milgrom himself notes, later Israelite prophets do not refrain from speaking while performing their wonders. Thus, Elijah said to King Ahab, "As the Lord, the God of Israel lives, whom I serve, there will be no dew nor rain in the next few years except at my word" (1 Kings 17:1). During his contest with the priest of Baal on Mount Carmel, Elijah both speaks and acts (1 Kings 18:16-46). Similarly, Elisha speaks and acts when miraculously providing oil for the widow (2 Kings 4:2-7). If the essence of magic is acting and speaking together when performing wonders, why are these prophets never referred to as "magicians" or "sorcerers" in the text of the Bible, despite its rich vocabulary for describing practitioners of such arts? Departing for a moment from Israelite religion, it should be noted that practitioners of numerous normative religious traditions, both ancient and modern, include both words and actions in their rites. By the definition of magic that Milgrom uses, do these traditions also become "magical"? That definition, based as it is upon notions that only gained wide currency during the Reformation and that are extrinsic to the Hebrew Bible itself, must be reassessed.[15] The decisive element in all of these accounts—of Elijah and Elisha, as well as Moses—is the Israelite, Yahwist context.[16]

Probably the best-known list of prohibited practices in the Pentateuch is found in Deut 18:10-11: "Let no one be found among you who consigns his son or daughter to the fire, or who is an augur (qōsēm qĕsāmîm), a soothsayer (mĕʿōrēn), a diviner (mĕnaḥḥēš), a sorcerer (mĕkaššēp), one who casts spells (ḥōbēr ḥāber), one who consults ghosts or familiar spirits (šōʾēl ôb wĕyidʿōnî), or one who makes inquiries of the dead (dōrēš el-hammētîm)." These activities are typically the practices of the outsider, as the context of the list makes clear: they are not merely considered abhorrent practices (tôʿabōt) when performed by Israelites, but their abhorrent nature is at least in part the result of their being observed by

---

Huffmon, F. A. Spina, A. R. W. Green, eds. (Winona Lake: Eisenbrauns, 1983), 251-65.

[15] Aune, "Magic," 213.

[16] I readily concede that Moses may be shown as refraining from speaking in order to distinguish him from the "magicians" and "sorcerers" in Pharaoh's court, but I question whether these Egyptians are thus described because they speak when performing their acts, rather than because they are non-Israelites and non-Yahwists.

Israel's neighbors, as the wider context of the pericope shows. The verse immediately preceding the list of prohibited practices begins: "When you enter the land that the Lord your God is giving you, you shall not learn to imitate the abhorrent practices of those nations." Further, these practices of the people of the land form one of the grounds for their being dispossessed, as the passage following the list indicates: "For anyone who does such things is abhorrent to the Lord, and it is because of these abhorrent things that the Lord your God is dispossessing them before you. You must be wholehearted with the Lord your God. Those nations that you are about to dispossess do indeed resort to soothsayers and augurs; to you, however, the Lord your God has not assigned the like" (Deut 18:12-14).

There are numerous words in the Hebrew Bible that refer to practices or practitioners of magic (as it is generally understood), falling roughly into the categories of magic in general or sorcery, divination, and astrology (these categories, it should be pointed out, are not explicit in the Bible itself: in none of these lists are these types of magical practices expressly divided).[17] Roughly three-quarters of the occurrences of the words refer, explicitly or not, to non-Israelite practitioners or activities. Indeed, some of the words are used exclusively of non-Israelites. At least three of these words (ôb "familiar spirit, sorcerer," aššāp, ḥarṭōm) are most likely of foreign origin: ḥarṭōm is Egyptian in origin, aššāp derives from Akkadian, while ôb apears to be a non-Semitic migratory word that is found in Sumerian, Akkadian, Hurrian, Hittite, and Ugaritic.[18]

The remaining quarter of the occurrences of the terms for magicians and magical practices refers to prohibited Israelite practices or to Israelites engaged in these forbidden practices. In no case have I found any of these terms used favorably of an Israelite practice. For example, in Isaiah 3:2, the "augur" (qôsēm) is mentioned together with warrior, priest, and king; in Micah 3:6, 7, 11, the "augur" (qôsēm) is mentioned together with the prophet. If there is no explicit disapproval of the diviner in either of these passages, neither is there any approval: both passages occur in oracles of doom prophesied against all of these persons.

---

[17] These categorical distinctions are to be found in G. André, "kāšap," 379.

[18] Harry A. Hoffner, "ôbh," in Theological Dictionary of the Old Testament, G. Johannes Botterweck and Helmer Ringgren, eds., tr. John T. Willis (Grand Rapids: Eerdmans, 1974), 1.131.

Even in those instances where there is no strongly negative value to magic, magician, and related words, they refer either to non-Israelites or to Israelites in a non-Israelite setting.[19] Thus, Laban says to Jacob at one point, "If you will indulge me, I have learned by divination that the Lord has blessed me on your account" (Gen 30:27). Similarly, Joseph tells his servant to follow after Joseph's brothers and to accuse them of having wilfully taken his cup: "Up, go after the men! And when you overtake them, say to them, 'Why did you repay good with evil? It is the very one which my master drinks and which he uses for divination'" (Gen 44:5).

The three divinatory instruments regularly associated with the Israelite cultus—lots (gôrāl),[20] Urim and Thummim,[21] and ephod[22]—have a distinct vocabulary associated with them. Unlike any of the words mentioned above, these terms are used primarily in connection with Israelites, only occasionally with non-Israelites,[23] and invariably in a favorable, or neutral, context. Nowhere in the Hebrew Bible is there a detailed description of the method by which these divinatory instruments are used. Because of this, there is no way to compare the divinatory methods used in connection with the lot, ephod, and Urim and Thummim with the techniques used by the ôb, ḥōbēr, yidʿōnî, měnaḥḥēš, měʿōnēn, and qōsēm, all of whom were viewed as magicians by the writers of the Hebrew Bible. The decisive difference between the two groups is their association with, or estrangement from, Israel's religion and cultus: the ephod, Urim and Thummim, and lots are acceptable because they are Israelite, while the others are rejected because they are not.

*   *   *

In the New Testament "magic," "magician," and related terms are ascribed to persons based upon their perceived standing vis-a-vis Israelite religion and the putative power by which their works

---

[19] E.g., Gen 30:27, 44:5, 15; 1 Kings 20:33.

[20] Lev 16:8; Num 26:55; Josh 7:14; 14:2; 1 Sam 10:16-26, 14:42; Dan 12:13; Joel 1:3; Ps 22:18; Prov 18:18; 1 Chron 24:5, 25:8, 26:13. The pûr, explicitly identified with the gôrāl in Esther 3:7, was used by Haman to determine the month and day on which to carry out the pogrom against the Jews.

[21] Ex 28:30; Lev 8:8; Num 27:21; Deut 33:8; 1 Sam 14:41, 28:6; Ez 2:63, Neh 7:65.

[22] 1 Sam 23:9-12; 30:7-8.

[23] E.g., Jonah 1:7; Obad 11; Nahum 3:10.

and wonders were performed: outsiders, who used demonic powers to perform their wonders, might have such terms applied to them, while those within the tradition would not. Such accusations that Jesus was a magician are implicit in the New Testament and explicit in the writings of the early church fathers. This seems to be clearly reflected in the "Beelzubub" passage recorded in Mark 3:20-26:

> Then Jesus entered a house, and again a crowd gathered, so that he and his disciples were not even able to eat. When his family heard about this, they went to take charge of him, for they said, "He is out of his mind."

> And the teachers of the law who came down from Jerusalem said, "He is possessed by Beelzebub! By the prince of demons he is driving out demons." So Jesus called them and spoke to them in parables: "How can Satan drive out Satan? If a kingdom is divided against itself, that house cannot stand. And if Satan opposes himself and is divided, he cannot stand; his end has come."

The phrase "by the prince of demons" mentioned here probably refers to the charge of the use of demonic powers in order to achieve miracles.[24] According to P. Samain, such an accusation of using demonic powers to achieve miracles is tantamount to a charge of "magic" since, in a Jewish context, prophets and other holy people were thought to validate their missions by the performance of miracles, while the outsider—those thought to be in league with Satan (including "magicians" and "sorcerers")—were also believed capable of performing wonders.[25] This passage serves as a response to such a charge by claiming that one is hardly likely to use "magic" (that is, the agency of demonic powers) in order to drive out demons.

The gospel accounts of the temptation of Jesus may also be understood as showing Jesus rejecting conventional magical means to attain his goals. In this account, which is recorded in detail in Matthew and Luke, Jesus, following his forty-day fast, is tempted by the devil to turn a stone into bread, to leap from the pinnacle of the temple, and to worship him in return for all the kingdoms of the earth.[26] The temptation story is commonly interpreted as relating to the question of religious versus political messianism.

---

[24] Matt 12:24; Mk 3:22; Lk 11:15.
[25] P. Samain, "L'accusation de magie contre le Christ dans les Évangiles," *Ephemerides Theologicae Lovanienses* 15 (1938): 455.
[26] Matt 4:1-11; Luke 4:1-13.

However, since the power to turn stones into bread and to fly through the air is commonly claimed by wonder-workers and magicians, Samain suggests that the account of the temptations should also be understood as implying the refusal of Jesus to use magical powers to accomplish his goals.[27]

The charge that Jesus was a magician has been preserved outside the New Testament in both Jewish[28] and pagan traditions.[29] In the tractate *Shabbat* of the Babylonian Talmud, the following note is recorded in the midst of a discussion on impurities: "Did not Ben Stada (i.e., Jesus) bring forth sorcery from Egypt by means of scratches on his flesh?"[30] The church fathers, among them Irenaeus, Arnobius, Justin Martyr, Lactantius, and Origen, were keenly aware of the charge—made by Jew and Gentile alike—that Jesus was a magician.[31] In reply to this assertion, these early Christian writers made no effort to distinguish Jesus' actions from those of a wonder-worker. Rather, they affirmed the divine source of his power and the prophetic predictions of his life and activities. It was a question not of the form of the wonders, but of the relationship of the purported doer to the person speaking or writing. Thus,

---

[27] *Ibid.*, 489; cf. Aune, "Magic in Early Christianity," 1540-41.

[28] T. B. Sandhedrin 43a; J. Klausner, *Jesus of Nazareth* (New York: Macmillan, 1925), 18-47; H. L. Strack, *Jesus, die Häretiker und die Christen nach den ältesten jüdischen Angaben* (Leipzig: Hinrichs, 1910); H. L. Strack and P. Billerbeck, *Kommentar zum Neuen Testament aus Talmud und Midrasch* (Munich: Beck, 1926), 1.38, 84, 631. H. van der Loos, *The Miracles of Jesus* (Leiden: Brill, 1965), 156-75; Samuel Krauss, "Jesus," in *The Jewish Encyclopedia*, I. Singer, ed., 12 vols. (New York: Funk and Wagnalls, 1904), 7.170-73.

[29] These accusations are clearly preserved in Origen's *Contra Celsum*, a tract written in response to a variety of charges against Jesus and the Christians by the pagan Celsus.

[30] T. B. Sabbath 104b. H. Freedman, who translated and annotated the tractate *Sabbath* in *The Babylonian Talmud*, I. Epstein, ed., (London: Soncino, 1938), 2.1:504 n. 2, adds the following passage from the unexpurgated version of T. B. Sabbath: "Was he then the son of Stada—surely he was the son of Pandira?— Said R. Hisda: the husband was Stada, the paramour was Pandira. But the husband was Pappos b. Judah?—His mother was Stada. But his mother was Miriam the hairdresser?—It is as we say in Pumbeditha: This one has been unfaithful to (lit. "turned away from"—*satah da*) her husband." It is generally agreed that this passage refers to Jesus; thus R. Travers Herford, *Christianity in Talmud and Midrash* (Clifton: Reference Book Publishers, 1966), 35-41, 54-56; Smith, *Jesus the Magician*, 47, 178.

[31] Jewish charges that Jesus was a magician: Arnobius, *Against the Heathen* 1.44; Irenaeus, *Against Heresies* 32:3; Justin Martyr, *First Apology* 30; Lactantius, *Divine Institutions* 4.15.1, 5.3; Origen, *Contra Celsum* 1.28. Pagan charges that Jesus was a magician: Origen, *Contra Celsum* 1.6, 38, 68; 2.9, 14, 16, 48, 49; 6.77.

members of the Christian community saw Jesus as God-inspired, and therefore not a magician. Jews and pagans, on the other hand, who viewed the Christians as the "outsiders," viewed Jesus' miraculous acts as either fraudulent or demon-inspired, but in either case "magical." In effect, whether Jesus was viewed as a magician or not was almost solely dependent upon whether he was seen as an "insider" or an "outsider."

No one has more thoroughly documented the parallels between the activities of the wonder-worker of the Hellenistic world and Jesus' activities than Morton Smith in *Jesus the Magician*. Based solely on superficial similarities between the acts of these (generally Gentile) wonder-workers and Jesus, an impartial observer might be compelled to apply, or withhold, the designation "magician" from both. But by his own definition, noted above, a subjective judgment is decisive in designating an individual as magician: magic, according to Smith, is a term of abuse, and is used of an "outsider" who is viewed as being particularly subversive.[32] Similarly, for the Jewish contemporaries of Jesus who believed both genuine prophets as well as God's enemies were capable of working miracles, it is less the nature of the act as its source that determines whether or not it is miraculous in a positive sense. Colin Brown touches the crux of the issue when he notes, in his review of *Jesus the Magician*, "Morton Smith's argument is an elaborate statement of the charge that, according to the Gospels, was brought against Jesus from the start, namely that his actions were evil, that he was demon-possessed and even in league with Satan. . . . Perhaps the greatest service that Smith's book can perform is to state forcibly the question, 'By what power did Jesus act?'"[33] Geza Vermes in his book, *Jesus the Jew*, is even more to the point. He observes that "the representation of Jesus in the Gospels as a man whose supernatural abilities derived, not from secret powers, but from immediate contact with God, proves him to be a genuine charismatic, the true heir of an age-old prophetic religious line."[34]

*   *   *

---

[32] See n. 5.

[33] Colin Brown, *Miracles and the Critical Mind* (Grand Rapids: Eerdmans, 1983), 276.

[34] Geza Vermes, *Jesus the Jew: A Historian's Reading of the Gospels* (London: Collins, 1973), 69, cited in Brown, *Miracles*, 276-77.

Haralds Biezais, in his study on the relationship between religion and magic, denies any formal distinction between the two, claiming that all such presumed differences are ideologically motivated.[35] Although starkly formulated,[36] I think that Biezais' observation contains a fundamentally important insight: where religion ends and magic begins on the religion-magic continuum depends upon the stance of the person speaking or writing, since it is not possible to divide religion and magic on the basis of any objective set of criteria. In the case of the Bible, the major factor dividing acts that might be termed "magical" from those that might be termed "religious" is the perceived power by which the action is performed. Acts performed by the power of Israel's God are, in the view of the writers of the Bible, by that very fact nonmagical, even where they may be formally indistinguishable from those that are depicted as magical. "Magic," "magician," and related terms describing practices mentioned in the Bible remain useful designations in discussions of the life of ancient Israel as long as one takes into consideration the internal categories of the writers of the Bible itself, retains a sensitivity to the subjective nature and potentially pejorative connotations of these terms, and remains aware of his or her own presuppositions in applying them.

---

[35] Biezais, *Wesensidentität*, 30.

[36] Based on empirical differences reported by field workers among modern nonliterate peoples, the anthropologist William J. Goode, in three studies— "Magic and Religion: A Continuum," *Ethnos* 14 (1949): 172-82; *Religion Among the Primitives* (Glencoe: Free Press, 1951), 50-55; and, most recently, in "Comment on: 'Malinowski's Magic: The Riddle of the Empty Cell,'" *Current Anthropology* 17:4 (December, 1976): 677—has suggested a more reticulated model of "nondichotomous empirical differences" between magic and religion than that proposed by Biezais. However, in Goode's model, too, the element of group and individual perspective remains a dominant feature, and his view of the continuity between magic and religion underscores the subjective nature of the distinction between the two.

CHAPTER NINE

CHARMING CRIMINALS:
CLASSIFICATION OF MAGIC IN THE
BABYLONIAN TALMUD

Jonathan Seidel

We read in a passage in the Babylonian Talmud that in order to
sit as a judge on the Sanhedrin one needs to be a person of stature,
wisdom and indeed a "master of magic" (*Ba'al Keshafim*).[1] While
medieval commentators may have felt that knowing "magic" was
important in order to refute those who believed in it, earlier Talmudic rabbis considered it vital in order to understand praxis. It is
best to go beyond a "scientific" investigation of what the Talmudic
rabbis thought of "magic" and instead utilize new paradigms for
looking at rabbinic constructions of biblical figures and practitioners. In this essay I intend to examine the Rabbinic typologies and
definitions of magic within the Babylonian Talmud from a cultural
and literary point of view. I propose to ask new questions of these
texts, i.e., what function does the label "magic" serve in Rabbinic
sources? If we move beyond the "magic"/"religion" dichotomy,
what can the jurisprudential discourse tell us about the nature of
power in this culture? What sort of magic might be permitted and

---

[1] BT Menakhot 65a: "We don't seat any one on the Sanhedrin unless they are
wise men, men of vision, men of stature, elders, masters of magic, and knowledgeable in seventy languages." Rabbi Isaac ben Yedaiah of Provence, in his Commentary on the Aggadot of the Talmud (MSS Escorial G.IV.3 26b-27a), claims
that *keshafim* in this passage means knowledge of science and the true nature of
the universe. Compare the discussion of magian practice and teaching magic in
the following selection from BT Shabbat 75a: "As for magian practice: Rav and
Shmuel (disagree about what it is). One believes it should be considered sorcery,
the other that it should be considered blasphemy. It can be proven that it was Rav
who maintained (that magic should be considered blasphemy) since R. Zutra b.
Tuviah said in Rav's name, 'He who learns a single thing from a magician deserves the death penalty.' Should you suppose that (*m'gushta*) refers to sorcery,
scripture reads, 'When you come into the land which the Lord your God is
giving to you, you shall not learn to do (JPS: imitate) the abhorrent practices of
those nations,' meaning that you do not learn it in order to practice but in order
to understand and teach. It is proven!"

who might practice it? What can the category of superstition tell
us about illicit magic?

In the last decade of the last century the great Hungarian rabbi
and scholar Ludwig Blau published the first cross-cultural and intra-
Talmudic study of Jewish magic, *Das altjüdische Zauberwesen*.
Blau's study was not the first German monograph on the subject[2]
but it certainly has proven the most durable, for two reasons: it
contains an outstanding philological investigation of the terminology of Rabbinic texts concerning magic, and it poses many excellent questions in comparative magic and ritual. Blau's knowledge of
diverse documents which illuminated Rabbinic magic was impres-
sive. The first to apply social scientific methods and move beyond
the methodology of an intellectual historian, he anticipated the
work of Joshua Trachtenberg's cultural history of Jewish folk
magic and religion[3] and Morton Smith's various historical studies
of Jewish magic.[4]

Despite his enormous erudition and the critical questions he
asked, Blau clearly adopted the Rabbinic explanation of magic
ritual and practice and accepted the delineation of the subject set
forth in the sources. This position was itself dependent on the
biblical rhetoric found in Deuteronomy and the prophets. Rabbinic
sources amplify upon the topic and condemn certain magical
practice as a vestigial and superstitious remnant of earlier dominant cultures, chiefly those of the Babylonians and Egyptians as
well as other "foreigners" who inhabited the land.[5] Blau took such
claims at face value.[6] While we cannot *a priori* reject Rabbinic
definition and classification of magic, we must not automatically

---

[2] See G. Brecher, *Das Transcendentale, Magie, und magische Heilarten im
Talmud* (Vienna, 1850). Cf. Trachtenberg, *Jewish Magic and Superstition* (New
York: Behrman House, 1939) for an extensive bibliography of early scholarship
on Jewish magic, as well as the more recent Hebrew bibliography by M. D. Herr,
"Halakhic Issues in Israel in the 6th and 7th Centuries (CE)," *Tarbiz* 49 (1980):
62-80 n. 20.

[3] Trachtenberg, *Jewish Magic and Superstition* (New York: Behrman House,
1939 [1972]).

[4] The most comprehensive treatment is found in his *Jesus the Magician* (San
Francisco: Harper and Row, 1977).

[5] This attitude is recalled in a famous Rabbinic maxim: "Ten measures of magic
have come into the world. Egypt received nine of these, the rest of the world but
one measure" (BT Qidushin 49b).

[6] Biblical writers were already designating magicians as "outsiders," members of the hated outgroup. See Stephen Ricks' essay in this volume. My claim is
that while the terminology connotes "foreignness," the actual behaviors are more
likely deviant Israelite practices which are internally problematic.

view "magic" as it is characterized by "native" definitions. There is more evidence now that many of the "vestiges" of magical practice are not extrinsic to Judaism but essential to the core of Rabbinic religion and culture in general. It is in the Second Temple period, especially in the wake of the rhetoric of monotheism and diatribes against paganism, that sorcery and magic become part of a constellation of "foreign" or polluting influences.[7] As Saul Lieberman, Morton Smith, Jacob Neusner and others have argued, the rabbis were people of their day and in their own literature describe practices by all sorts of Jews that might be considered "magic" by their own definitions of the term.[8] In my view, there are many rituals and beliefs that surface in the Rabbinic period.

Equipped with a solid historical/philological method, Blau examined the "realia" behind the Rabbinic statements and descriptions. His knowledge of Rabbinic sources was exemplary, and his comparative effort noteworthy. Despite his bold venture into what was considered embarrassing, superstitious or arcane behavior in his day (and for that matter in ours as well), he remained a rather condescending rationalist, and his scholarship was colored by his internal Rabbinic perspective. While he was indeed ahead of his time in construing magic as a subject of historical inquiry when it was condemned as unworthy of scholarly attention in *fin de siècle* Budapest, Blau chose not to investigate a host of related performative rituals practiced by Rabbinic Jews, notably divination. Blau adopts the same condescending attitudes toward the "primitive" or the "magical" as post-Talmudic rationalists and his peers in *Wissenschaftliche* circles.

While Blau initiated a "cultural history" of magic in the last decade of the nineteenth century and Lieberman demonstrated the Greco-Roman legal and philological basis of certain magical motifs, Jacob Neusner reshaped the discourse on the use of magic by Rabbinic holy men. Here I would like to concentrate on taxonomy. The theoretical statements which lie behind the taxonomies are compelling because they show us a serious engagement with the

---

[7] E.g., Wisdom of Solomon 12:3-5: "Those who lived long ago in your holy land, you hated for their detestable practices, their works of sorcery and unholy rites, their merciless slaughter of children, and their sacrificial feasting on human flesh and blood." These charges are also grouped together in the Enoch literature and in Rabbinic sources.

[8] Most recently a solid critique of Blau and other scholars of Jewish magic has been published by Lawrence Schiffman and Michael Swartz, *Hebrew and Aramaic Incantation Texts from the Cairo Geniza* (Sheffield: JSOT Press, 1992). They have also called for a re-evaluation of Blau's survey of biblical magic.

implications of magic and offer a glimpse into the Rabbinic consideration of marginal behaviors that are not fully idolatrous.

*   *   *

The first text for our consideration is Babylonian Talmud Sanhedrin 67b ff., easily the most sustained discourse in Rabbinic literature concerning illicit practitioners and their activities. The Rabbinic reaction is catalyzed by the pronouncement in Deut 18:10-11: "There shall not be found among you (JPS: Let no one be found among you) one who consigns his son or daughter to the fire, or who is an augur, a soothsayer, a diviner, a magician, or one who binds spells, or one who consults ghosts or familiars, or one who inquires of the dead."[9] Any discussion of the development of Rabbinic attitudes towards a classification of magic must take into account the Rabbinic interpretation of this key prohibition. It is this Deuteronomic classification which externalizes "magic" and all its ritual varieties as a foreign implant. In Babylonian Talmud Tractate Sanhedrin, the discussion of magic and magicians does not simply evolve from quandaries found in the biblical proscriptions but takes on a hermeneutic life of its own.[10]

In this particular section (BT Sanhedrin 65a-67b) Rabbis Yohanan, Aibu bar Nagri, and Abaye offer terse but packed definitions of magicians and magic. We cannot assume, however, that we know what they are talking about. The first question, then, is not what is the historically attested "magic" they are referring to, but what sort of cultural demarcations are being made by the use of this term. The former question must be addressed but only after we are careful in defining our own use of such language. In Bavli Sanhedrin, the rabbis are committed to defining and criminalizing the "other"—and legitimatizing the subjects of society. This Rabbinic "other" is shown to be a social deviant who is fenced out while

---

[9] לא ימצה בך מעביר בנו ובתו באיש קוסם קסמים מעונן ומנחש ומכשף /11/ וחובר חבר ושאל אוב וידעני ודורש אל המתים. See Carmichael, *The Laws of Deuteronomy* (1974), 46, and Daube, "To be Found Doing Wrong," *Studi in onore di Volterra II* (Rome, 1969), for a rhetorical study of the Deuteronomic phrase לא ימצא בך. Carmichael, quite correctly I think, has shown it to be indicative of a "shame" culture. The prohibited figures are closely associated with false prophecy as well. On the meaning of "abomination" in Deuteronomy, see Weinfeld, *Deuteronomy and the Deuteronomic School* (Oxford: Clarendon Press, 1972), 268-69.

[10] My Ph.D. dissertation examines a variety of related topics that cannot be treated here, including the early exegesis of Deut 18:10, the Hellenization of the concept of magic in Rabbinic culture, witchcraft and gender, and the problem of folklore and magic.

legitimate ritualists are fenced in. The text constructs for the reader that which is not "other"; its rhetoric works to persuade the as-yet unconverted observer, but this observer is already a knowledgeable listener who follows Rabbinic reasoning and rhetoric both legal and literary.

Babylonian Talmud Sanhedrin, built ostensibly on Tannaitic precedent, is chiefly concerned with criminal law that must be decided by the most important tribunal of the land. It is very hard to determine whether the cases reflect "reality" in history or whether the discourse reflects hermeneutical development in and of itself, without interest in actual precedent and attested legal cases. One gets the sense upon reading the dialectic on magic that the rabbis might have commissioned performances of magic, especially if membership on the Sanhedrin required mastery of its mechanics or techniques. Justice Potter Stewart's comment about obscenity ("I know it when I see it"), quoted as an epigram by C. Robert Phillips, does not seem to fit here. Idolatry, a more serious charge, needs definition and clarification as well.[11] "Magic" might be that suspicious activity which leads to idolatry, the first step in a lifestyle that eventually leads one to something worse. The legal statements are complemented by representations of magical activities; these pictures of magic are drawn in colorful strokes in the folktales and accounts of praxis by Rabbinic heroes and their enemies.[12]

The Mishnah (Sanhedrin 7:11) offers an apparently simple definition of who is really a *mechashef*:

The מכשף if he actually performs an act (*ma'aseh*) is liable to punishment while the one who merely creates illusions is not liable.

The key word here is *ma'aseh*, best rendered "act" or "action." Creating "illusion" might be understood, of course, as a type of action.[13] The context of this statement within Mishnah Sanhedrin

---

[11] See the recent study of idolatry in Jewish thought by Halbertal and Margalit, *Idolatry* (Cambridge: Harvard University Press, 1992).

[12] The brevity of the Mishnah's legal locution often demands exegesis and detailed explanation. As a case in point, the legal status of magicians is mentioned only briefly in Deuteronomy, and the nature of magical practice is described in fractured, incomplete fashion in other parts of scripture. The rabbis would need more scripture text to establish law. It is in the filling of gaps that we are given contemporary data about magic and magical practice.

[13] The Talmud (BT Sanhedrin 65a ff.) offers several humorous tales of trickery and deceptive "stage" magic that are apparently guilt-free activities—indeed, humorous and entertaining ones.

is crucial to understanding the larger cultural concerns that produce
such a distinction. The criminals enumerated throughout chapter
seven of this section of the Mishnah are uniquely dangerous anti-
social types, including sexual deviants, misleaders, and idolators
considered worthy of ultimate retribution. Mishnah Sanhedrin,
then, is deliberately concerned with establishing the exact nature of
an act; if the act is not illusionary, what is it that must have taken
place? A fraudulent showman, like the curser who does not use
God's name, does not qualify as a threat to Rabbinic society. The
illusionist may manipulate, but he does not "act" per se. In fact, in
direct contrast to Greco-Roman legal literature, magicians are
considered guilty not because of trickery but because of transformation of that which should not be tampered with. Magical action
utilizes natural laws in unnatural ways. *Kishuf* implies an abuse of
divine/human boundaries; the rabbis felt that only rabbis, and only
a select few, could tamper with divine forces.[14]

The Amoraim were left to wonder aloud about the nature of this
distinction and the criteria for "action." The Gemara in the Talmud provides further clues about the nature and the motivations of
these crimes, and it continues with a discussion of the gender of the
magician.[15] Are these actions crimes against society, against person (i.e., against a person's body or will or both), against God and
his heavenly host? Is magic essentially a crime of illlicit language,
like the crime of blasphemy? The actions of a *mekhashef* do not
offend in the same way that unauthorized approach or use of
divine *sancta* offend (the crime of Nadav and Abihu), and yet they

---

[14] This has been cogently argued by Neusner in his original article on the
"Phenomenon of the Rabbi," *Numen* 16/1 (1969): 1-20: "... it follows that
Torah was held to be a source of supernatural power. The rabbis controlled the
power of Torah because of their mastery of Torah quite independently of heavenly
action. They could issue blessings and curses, create men and animals. They were
masters of witchcraft, incantations, and amulets. They could communicate with
heaven. Their Torah was sufficiently effective to thwart the action of demons.
However they disapproved of magic, they were expected to do the things magicians do."

[15] The term used in the prohibition against witchcraft in Exodus 22:17 is in
the feminine. Surely the Sanhedrin cannot condemn only women! The discussion
leads to the opinion of inclusivity: it applies to both men and women, however
"(most) women engage in witchcraft" (BT Sanhedrin 67a). Cf. PT Sanhedrin 7:13
(Leiden MSS) on the same verse: "But (in mentioning sorceress) scripture
teaches you about the way of the world in which the majority of women are
witches." See now the articles by Simcha Fishbane, "Most Women Engage in
Sorcery," and Meir Bar-Ilan, "Witches in Bible and Talmud," in *Approaches to
Ancient Judaism* (New Series 5), eds. Herbert Basser and Simcha Fishbane
(Atlanta: Scholars Press, 1993).

are viewed in the Talmudic *sugya* as having larger reverberations than violating someone's person. In my view it is best to see the offense as part of a conglomerate of ritual obscenity and disruption acted out by violators of the norms of Rabbinic power relationships. Halbertal and Margalit,[16] in their study of idolatry in Jewish law and society, have emphasized the danger of alternative magic ritual as a "lifestyle" problem, one that borders on the overtly pagan. Practicing magic is but one step along the way to full-blown *avodah zarah*. Propitiation of demons, claim certain Rabbinic voices, might be construed as false ritual. Gender-typing of magicians is an important component of the borderline status of magical practice within Rabbinic circles. Jewish as well as non-Jewish women are more likely to be suspected of practicing witchcraft than are men.[17] In my reading of the witchcraft stories, Rabbinic exercise of apotropaic magic protects the male individual and corporate body from extrinsic powers that threaten the cultural agenda. Catherine Bell has described the ability of ritualization to create "social bodies" in the image of relationships of power.[18] The Rabbinic "social body" is created by the textual community which must confront Jewish society without a traditional cult and sacred center. The boundaries of this corporality must be determined through confrontation with the written and oral Torah. In Mishnah Sanhedrin and in the Bavli's amplification of the Mishnah, the rabbis are concerned with the matrix of cosmic and social deviancy. Like the deeds described by the Greek term *asebeia*, often rendered "impious," these crimes have serious social ramifications. In the Rabbinic discourse they are treated as a violation of divine law—a violation which is so heinous as to deserve capital punishment.[19] The criminality of malevolent sorcerers is given

---

[16] *Idolatry* (Cambridge: Harvard University Press, 1992).

[17] E.g., the story of Jannai and the witch who attempts to transform him through a magical brew (BT Sanhedrin 67). The only legitimate use of *keshafim* by women occurs in BT Gittin 45a, in which the daughters of Rabbi Nahman stir a cauldron with their bare hands.

[18] *Ritual Theory, Ritual Practice* (New York: Oxford University Press, 1992).

[19] Sorcery as a capital crime is particularly sensitive because, in one text, an anonymous Rabbinic source justifies Jesus' execution on the grounds of sorcery (BT Sanhedrin 43a). Historical opinions about the scope of jurisdiction of Rabbinic courts in capital cases have often differed significantly. Gedalia Alon ("On Philo's Halacha," in *Jews, Judaism and the Classical World* [Jerusalem: Hebrew University Press, 1977], 111-24) compares Philonic criminal "halacha" with Rabbinic law and claims that the jurisdiction of these cases was exclusively in Jerusalem. This claim is countered by Urbach, *The Halakha* (Jerusalem: Yad

more attention in later Amoraic times. Earlier traditions indicate
that proto-Rabbinic leaders executed sorcerers summarily without
due process; such punishment is very problematic for the
Amoraim.[20]

The powers of malevolent sorcery are themselves very real for
the rabbis. They have direct consequences in many spheres, as is
made clear from the next "definition" which follows in BT Sanhedrin:

> Why are they called *keshafim* (magicians)? Because they injure the divine
> family (*KikheSH Familia shel Ma'ala*) (BT Sanhedrin 67b).[21]

This brief but loaded explanation points to a classic Rabbinic
rhetorical style in which terms are decoded with homiletic intention. In typical midrashic *notarikon* fashion, which requires creating a series of new meanings from key letters in the original
phrase, the text supplies new meaning. כשפים *keshafim* is broken
down, as is noted above, in order to make an important point.
Kishuf signifies not only perverted and deviant behavior in an
earthly context but a disruption of the cosmic "family" as well.[22]

LaTalmud, 1986), 59-71; 374 n. 17 who provides a thorough overview of scholarship in this arena.

[20] Alon speculates that Philo (*de Spec. Leg.* 94-102) knew a Rabbinic ha-
lachic tradition supporting the lynching of sorcerers without trial, since for
Philo sorcerers are suspect of using lethal potions and are tantamount to the
Greek φαρμακεύς ("poisoner"). Philo follows the Septuagint's tradition of
interpreting *makhshefa* in Exodus as malevolent herbologists or pharmacolo-
gists. It is difficult to say whether there was summary execution of sorcerers in
early Second Temple "proto-Rabbinic" law. Such a claim here is tenuous and is
based on shaky ground in Rabbinic sources—the story of Shimon ben Shetach
and the execution of the 80 witches in Ashkelon. I cannot find any text which
explicitly equates the crime of magic with poisoning but this is not to deny the
representation of witches as lethal and the imminent danger one faces in confronting their powers. Peretz Segal ("The 'Divine Death Penalty' in the Hatra
Inscriptions and the Mishnah," *Journal of Jewish Studies* 39 [1989]: 46-52)
discusses the phrase *mittah b'dei shamayim*, "death at the hands of heaven" or
"divine death penalty," as it occurs in the Hatra inscription. He claims (*contra*
Cohan in the *Encyclopedia Judaica*, 6.120-22) that this penalty was exacted
immediately and not at an unspecified future time. It applied to one who steals a
kisvah (Temple vessel), one who curses by magic (*kosem*) or one who cohabits
with a Gentile woman (m. Sanhedrin 9:6). Might it also apply to a witch?

[21] Soncino: "because they lessen the power of the Divine agencies." Neusner,
The Talmud of Babylonia Tractate Sanhedrin, chs. 4-8, esp. p. 216: "because
they deny the power of the family above."

[22] This Talmudic phrase resonates strongly with language in the Talmud and
in the extra-Talmudic Hekhalot corpus, where we find the "cosmic family"

In this locution we do not find a dispassionate phenomenology of magical action apart from its impact on divine and human society. In other sections of the *sugya*, however, it seems that the editors are interested only in mechanics and not cosmic theology or theosophy. Taken as a whole, however, we see that this particular homological reading demonstrates the Rabbinic philosophy of power: *makhhishin* implies a weakening, perhaps a wounding of the power of the angelic hosts (cf. Jastrow, *Dictionary* s.v. כחש p. 629),[23] who in turn can become angry when summoned by practitioners. Misdirected "words of power" might result in some frightening angels appearing to the practitioner.[24] This reading of *kishuf* serves a different but clearly strategic rhetorical purpose. The rabbis' homiletic etymology in this case shows little concern with the essence of sorcery but much more with its consequences. Through his spells or paraphernalia the magician wounds and weakens. The malevolent magician might be seen as a perverted or subversive theurgist who is jealous of Rabbinic power, as an envious outsider whose powers can indeed humiliate or injure the Rabbinic elite.[25]

For the medieval commentator Rashi this clause "injures the divine family" signifies that magicians "kill that which was decreed to live" (BT Sanhedrin *ad loc.*). Nachmanides' reading of this passage is even more relevant to our interpretation. The secret of all sorcery is the power of contradiction of the "simple powers," Nachmanides claims, and is similar to violating the prohibition of *kilayim*.[26] It is the *mixing* of cosmic forces that is so problematic

---

terminology in numerous visionary texts. *Familia*, a Latin loan-word, is found in a Midrashic parable where it refers to a group or retinue who would accompany a king or distinguished person on a journey (Gen. Rabbah 39:10).

[23] The verb כחש can be used to describe something much more mundane as well. מכחיש מצוה "lessening a mitzvah" in BT Shabbat 22a implies that one must perform the mitzvah of lighting the Hannukah lamp exactly as the rabbis specify it or else the light is diminished.

[24] On the dynamics of performative speech in the Hekhalot incantations, see the essay in this volume by Rebecca Lesses. On attaining instant wisdom through magic, see the essay by Michael Swartz.

[25] In Rabbinic exegesis Balaam is often portrayed as such a malevolent sorcerer whose speech is powerful but can be countered by more potent priestly amulets and gestures. See Ginzberg, *Legends of the Jews*, 3.352, 354, 357, 362, 380; 6.123, 124, 133.

[26] הפך הכוחות הפשוטים והם הכחשה לפמלייא בצד מהצדדים (Ramban *ad loc.*). Nahmanides is thought by many scholars to be the author of several works of Kabbalistic theurgic magic, and we find extensive interest in pneumatic magic and the operations of the heavens in his commentary on Deuteronomy 18:10-11,

and threatening. The Divine Body—here illustrated as a familiar collective—is indeed subject to alien power. One might take this a step further. The Divine "male" Body can become impotent when witchcraft infects or afflicts the supernal or terrestrial agents of this Body—that is, the angels and the rabbis. The rabbis are front-line defenders who are expert articulators in defining the real enemy. The implication of this reading remains problematic: is there another opposite "power"? Do God's designated representatives on earth and perpetuators of his revelation develop apotropaic rites and words that have cosmic significance? A proper reading of this section of the Talmud acknowledges the cosmic aspect of the struggle for power in its earthly manifestation; we have here a strategy for consolidation of Rabbinic power and its literary legitimation.[27]

* * *

A comparison between Rabbinic magic and other synchronic discourse on magic, witchcraft and sorcery is vital, although I cannot pursue such a comparison at length here.[28] It is particularly important to look at Rabbinic notions of magic and the demonic in comparison with other Jewish or contiguous societies of the first few centuries and especially at notions of the demonic and the magical in the New Testament.[29] One might also successfully

---

the essential biblical verses on magical practice.

[27] See Alan Segal, *Two Powers in Heaven* (Leiden: E. J. Brill, 1977), on the Rabbinic responses to the charges of "Two Powers in Heaven." Do we have here a precursory notion of the *Sitra Ahra,* the "side of the Other," before it is developed in medieval Kabbalah? It is no historical accident that numerous exorcistic and incantational texts have been discovered in the Dead Sea Scrolls, some of which were produced by writers who pictured the world as both internally and externally polarized.

[28] Saul Lieberman's small but weighty chapters on magic and charms in his *Greek in Jewish Palestine* (New York: Feldheim,1965), 109-13, must still be consulted; Daniel Sperber has just published an important work on magical motifs in Rabbinic Judaism in relationship to folklore in the Greco-Roman world, *Magic and Folklore in Rabbinical Literature* (Tel Aviv: Bar Ilan University Press, 1994).

[29] Rabbinic conceptions of a realm under the grip of an evil, demonic agent are not as developed as in Luke and Acts. Susan Garrett (*The Demise of the Devil* [Minneapolis: Fortress Press, 1989], 102) has written about the conception of the demonic magicians in the New Testament in general and in Luke in particular. Garrett seems quite uncomfortable with any of the charges against Jesus highlighted by Morton Smith, and to my mind has gone too far in her hermeneutics of

compare (with attention to materials in BT Gittin and Pesachim) Rabbinic demonological beliefs with other Hellenistic handbooks of demonology such as the *Testament of Solomon*—one of the most extensive descriptions of the actions of demons available.[30] Demonological beliefs in Bavli are more prevalent than in the Palestinian Talmud.[31] Certain demonological legends, especially the encounter of King Solomon and Asmodeus, are clearly Palestinian in origin but gain new life in a Babylonian setting. While the text does not detail the techniques of mastering demons as do the Hellenistic Greek handbooks, Solomon does demonstrate mastery of the famous Ashmedai in BT Gittin 68b. The Mesopotamian background of the Jewish versions of the Asmodeus tale (in Tobit and the Talmud) also points to a stronger Rabbinic connection to contemporary Iranian demonology.[32]

Rabbinic notions of illegitimate specialists preserved in the Palestinian and Babylonian Talmuds can be compared successfully

---

suspicion of the recent secondary literature which emphasize Jesus' magical behavior.

[30] The *Testament of Solomon* remains the best example of Hellenistic appropriation of earlier Mesopotamian medical/magical guides. See the excellent translation in Charlesworth, *Old Testament Pseudepigrapha*, 2 vols. (New York: Doubleday, 1983), 1.960-987 and the discussion of magic and exorcism in this work by Dennis Duling, "The Eleazar Miracle and Solomon's magical wisdom in Flavius Josephus' *Antiquitates Judaicae* 8:42-49," *Harvard Theological Review* 78/1-2 (1985): 1-25. The characteristics of the demons mentioned there are expanded in the Talmudim, where they develop more "character" and "personality" and even play quasi-human roles in narrative.

[31] This was noted first by Ludwig Blau and mentioned in the works of both Lieberman and Morton Smith. Neusner devotes most of his study of the Rabbinic magicians to the texts in the Bavli. My survey of demonological traditions supports this hypothesis, but we cannot establish with historical certainty the "causes" for a greater number of demon tales or citations in the Babylonian tradition. Might representations of witches, demons and tales of magic depend on the relationship to the hegemonic powers of the culture and the nature of political power within the Jewish community?

[32] Ashmedai/Asmodeus clearly develops from the figure mentioned in the Gathas, *aēšma-daeuua*, a demon of rushing fury who has bloody attributes. See Kohut, *Über die jüdische Angelologie und Daemonologie in ihrer Abhängigkeit von Parsimus* (Leipzig: Brockhaus, 1866), 72-80, on this demon, as well as *Jewish Encyclopedia*, s.v. "Asmodeus." The earliest Talmudic manifestations of the Solomon/Ashomodai legend is found in PT Sanhedrin 2:2 and BT Gittin 68a-68b; cf. BT Pesahim 110a. On the relationship of Jewish magic to Iranian demonology see Shaul Shaked, "Bagdana: King of the Demons," in *Acta Iranica Monumentum Mary Boyce* (Leiden: E. J. Brill, 1985), 511-35, as well as the chapter on the subject in Isaiah Gafni *The Jews of Babylonia in the Period of the Talmud* (Jerusalem: Merkaz Zalman Shazar, 1990).

with Paul's discourse on opponents exercising witchcraft or magic.
Paul's writings constitute the only inner view of a (once) Phari-
see's notion of the operations of bewitching in the Jewish polity of
the mid first-century diaspora. One might view his writings as one
literary component of the nexus of early Jewish views of the
dynamics of spells in local societies.[33] The Rabbinic method of
accusation is less uncompromisingly dualistic than Paul's, but the
legal discourse betrays the same type of conceptualization about
competing powers.

A Mediterranean model, however, of competition between
charismatic magicians must be distinguished from a Mesopotamian
model, a task that is made difficult by the nature of the Rabbinic
sources.[34] Competition of this sort may reflect specific social
configurations, political concerns, and relationships to colonizing,
oppressive powers. Neusner [35] has aptly noted that it is the locus
of the power that differs in contrasting "us" and "them"—not the
actual magic itself but the source of the magic. I would refine the
description of such a generator of cosmic magic by arguing that the
"other" practitioner also derives his power from God but perverts
that power. The threatening deviant practitioner is labelled
"magician," but what the cultural definers mean by that term shifts
even among individual interpreters. Consequently, legitimate
counter-magic may or may not be labelled *kishuf*. This dissonance
of opinions and perspectives, so characteristic of much of rabbinic
discussion, does not prevent us from seeing the representation of
kishuf as mostly negative.

The encounter with actual non-Jewish magicians raises other
questions for the rabbis. In Babylonian Rabbinic society of the
Parthian and Sassanian periods the rabbis came into contact with
historical "magi" and sought to classify them in light of biblical
categories. In one key pericope in the Bavli we see the differing
views of the crime of the *magus*: "One who learns just one thing
from a *magus* deserves death" (הלומד דבר אחד מן המגוש חייב מיתה
[BT Shabbat 75a]). The context of this statement is a dispute
between Rav and Shmuel over the classification of "magianism,"

---

[33] Jerome Neyrey, *Paul in Other Words* (Louisville: Westminster/John Knox
Press, 1990), 181-224, has convincingly shown that the matrix of accusations in
Paul's letters demonstrates the operations of Mary Douglas' "witchcraft culture." Might the rhetoric that accompanies such classification be seen as a type of
accusation at a local level?

[34] Compare my dissertation.

[35] In his introductory remarks in *Magic, Science and Religion,* eds. Neusner,
Frerichs, and Flesher (New York: Oxford University Press, 1989).

i.e., the religion of the Iranian priests. Classifying this *magushta* as sorcery (Shmuel's opinion) would allow it to be taught within the curriculum of privileged rabbis, while classifying it as blasphemy (Rav's opinion) places even greater social boundaries around it.[36] Neusner[37] studied the functional parallels between rabbi and *magus* and found their roles to be quite similar. One of his most important points is that while the Zoroastrians may have seen the rabbis as Judaized *magi*, the Rabbinical stereotype is that the *magus* is a malicious grave-robber and mumbler. While this is correct, I would go further to suggest that the use of the term *magus* preserves an interest in the "outgroup" practitioner, who, in this case, might be classified as a blasphemer or a sorcerer. While the Talmud does not preserve very much about the religious rituals of the *magi*, it mentions Zoroastrian priests in a negative light.[38] Babylonian Jewish sources, which preserve more extensive halakhic and folk traditions about magic than do Palestinian sources, more frequently associate impurity with demonic force. Indeed, in my survey of witchcraft stories and discussions I have found that impurity and demonology are more closely associated, and that witches are increasingly demonized as well. Chaos and disorder assume demonic character in these tales, perhaps reflecting Zoroastrian demonological traditions.[39]

---

[36] See Kohut, *Aruch Completum*, 1.113 for further discussion of the terminology of אמגושא *amgusha* and מגוש[ת]א *magush[t]a* in the Babylonian Talmud.

[37] "Rabbi and Magus in Third Century Babylonia," *History of Religions* 6/2 (1966).

[38] Gittin 16b preserves the story of one Zoroastrian חברא who forcibly trespasses in the home of Rabba bar Hanna and seizes a candelabrum. On this and other related stories see the recent study of Rabbinic Judaism and Sassanian religious coexistence by Robert Brody, "Judaism in the Sassanian Empire," in *Irano-Judaica II*, eds. Shaul Shaked and Amnon Netzer (Jerusalem: Ben Tzvi Institute, 1990), 52-62, and the study of Rabbinic society in general by Gafni, *The Jews of Babylonia in the Period of the Talmud* (Jerusalem: Shazar Institute).

[39] See, most recently, the important work on women and demonology by Jacob Lassner, *Demonizing the Queen of Sheba* (Chicago: University of Chicago Press, 1993). On Zoroastrian demonology see M. Schwartz, "The Religion of Achaemenian Iran," in *Cambridge History of Iran*, 1.681-83, as well as Mary Boyce, *History of Zoroastrianism* (Leiden: E. J. Brill, 1990), vol. 3, and Shaul Shaked, "Iranian Influence on Judaism," in *The Cambridge History of Judaism*, 2 vols. (Cambridge University Press, 1984), 1.317. These traditions must be studied along with the Lilith legends and the magical bowls and amulets which frequently contain spells against the child-stealing witches called "Liliths." In the magical bowls and incantations of the 4th-7th centuries, it should be noted, there are still male "Liliths" (*lillin*).

In the following terse statement concerning the nature of magic, R. Aibu b. Nagri quotes a tradition in the name of R. Hiyya b. Abba, who is commenting on the discrepancy in terminology used to describe the actions of Pharoah's magicians in Exodus 7:

בלטהם *belatehem* refers to magic through the agency of demons; בלהטהם *belehatehem* refers to magic without outside help (BT Sanhedrin 67b).

In this statement we find an example of what I. Heineman terms "creative philology"—an explanation of a variant spelling which allows the rabbis to import distinctions where the biblical authors may have intended none at all. Since nothing is superfluous in scripture and there are no real discrepancies in meaning, the additional "h" in the word used to describe the technique of Pharoah's magicians in Exodus 7:11 evokes automatic magic. *B'lahatehem* is compared to "the sword that turns on its own" (להט החרב המתהפכת [Gen 3:24]).[40] This variant provides a convenient locus for Rabbinic "reading in." In the distinction drawn here between magical action with and without demonic agency we find an early "native" taxonomy of ritual. One cannot but be struck by the similarity to so-called "primitive" locutions about witches and magicians in contemporary ethnographies. This distinction is clearly reminiscent of some social scientific observations of African notions of witches and witchcraft/sorcery. For Evans-Pritchard's Azande tribesmen[41] the sorcerer uses paraphernalia to effect his power and can invoke agents with that equipment. The witch emits psychic, mental, malevolent energy either consciously or unconsciously. We need not, however, read Evans-Pritchards' theoretical discourse into the typology of Talmudic discourse about praxis.

This Rabbinic association of demonic sorcery with magical technology also resonates strongly with contemporary Greco-Roman literary representations of magical practice and with recipes for ritual magic in the papyri.[42]

---

[40]The Hebrew here denotes constant turning, i.e., perpetual motion apparently needing no help.

[41]Edward Evans-Pritchard, *Witchcraft, Oracles and Magic among the Azande* (Oxford: Clarendon Press, 1976), 56-64.

[42]The papyri give us a way to look at ritual prescriptions which involve both methods carefully delineated by a presumed expert in these operations. The rabbis might indeed have had in mind the secretive writer of Greek, Latin, Aramaic, or Mandaic curse tablets (*defixiones*) as a bona fide *mekhashef*. But the rabbis do not tell us with any specificity about any historical cases of sorcery or trials that included such charges.

The next definitional statement about *kishuf* delves further into the techniques of the sorcerer, his intentionality and sphere of operation:

> Abaye said, "He who insists on exact paraphernalia (דקפיד אמנא)[43] is practicing demonic ritual while he who does not insist is simply engaging in (non-demonic) magical practice (כשפים)."

Here is yet a more refined typology of magic which illuminates the character of demonic praxis and its relation to *keshafim*. As in our previous theoretical statement, Abaye associates demonic magic with the accoutrements of spell-casting and bewitching. The language here is worth noting: a catch-all term with a plural suffix is used. The singular *kishuf* is used only in the later strata of the Talmud and in medieval sources.[44]

Like the statement attributed to R. Hiyya quoted above, Abaye's clarification distinguishes between demonic and non-demonic ritual. If practicing magic constitutes a criminal act, what exactly constitutes the deviancy of demonic operations? Demonological magic requires specific technique and "know-how." When demons serve as agents of magical spells or rituals, the nature of the crime changes. Are the practitioner *and* his non-human accomplice to be held accountable? Is the demon a willful, cognisant entity who collaborates in mischief? In the Greek Magical Papyri we find several texts in which the magician employs an assistant or *paredros*.[45] This tradition, I would claim, may have influenced the literary representation of the master-demon relationship in Talmudic literature.[46] In both the Talmud and the

---

[43] The sense here I take to mean "requires specific tools of the craft" or "specific technique."

[44] See *Aruch Completum* s.v. כשף.

[45] See the essay in this volume by Leda Ciraolo on this subject.

[46] I do not mean to say that a linear literary borrowing took place. Rather, I would contend that these hierarchical relationships reflect domination and slavery in contemporary Egyptian and later Mesopotamian society. A demon, it seems, functioned as the least expensive slave on the market. The comparable compulsions of slaves and demons in Arabic folklore is a worthwhile comparison here. In the words of Hajji Khalifah, "When the conditions are brought together and the incantations pronounced, God makes the latter like a mighty devastating fire, encircling the demons and the *jinn* until the corners of the world close in around them and there is no place left for them to hide, nor any other choice than to come out and resign themselves to do as they are commanded. What is more, if the performer is skillful, being of good conduct, and praiseworthy morals, God will dispatch powerful, rough, and strong angels to the demons to inspire them and lead them to obey and serve him" (*Kashf al-zunun*, 8 vols., ed. O. Flügel, London, 1955-58; translation into French by T. Fahd and into English by David

magical papyri, the boundary between demonic magic and "human" magic is not clearly marked.[47] Paraphernalia might be included in the nexus of other types of illicit objects of worship and suggest an improper connection with the divine. The use of ritual paraphernalia that suggest compulsion and binding are clearly problematic. And while the tools are taken into consideration in the legal discourse, it is intention that is weighed most significantly. In a related *sugya* (BT Sanhedrin 65a) the rabbis compare the propitiation of demons with idolatrous worship.[48] One of the questions that emerge from a reading of this section is, under what circumstances might relationships with demons be considered acceptable aside from a magical operation? The Amoraic rabbis seem comfortable with specific interactions with certain demons, albeit quasi-personal ones.[49] Making legal decisions about the status of a magical action requires, it seems, research into the theory and mechanics of ritual relationships. We do not find such hair-splitting discussion, however, in the consideration of folk customs which also might come under the rubric of magic.

*   *   *

Like the Greeks and Romans, early Rabbinic Jews reveal a need to classify some actions as reprehensible but not quite so seriously anti-social as magic. In the following text from Tosefta Shabbat ch. 7 [Lieberman, TK *Moed* 25-29], BT Shabbat 67a (פרק אמרי), we encounter a taxonomy of practices which are not to be consid-

---

Weeks, "Magic in Islam" in the *Encyclopedia of Religion* [Chicago: MacMillan, 1989]).

[47] Vajda, "Israel et le Judaisme," in *Le Monde du Sorcier* (Paris, 1966), 137, notes the following in his essay on Israelite and Jewish sorcery: "En fait, la ligne de démarcation entre influence démoniaque et magie humaine n'est pas nette puisque aussi bien l'on reconnaît au sorcier le pouvoir de faire agir les démons."

[48] Since the *mekhashef* and the *hover hever* are contiguous figures in Deuteronomy, it is natural for the rabbis to conflate the two in several passages. In wrestling with the description of the *hover hever,* the text compares its essential crime—charming—with idolatrous propitiation of demons. "Charming" might involve illicit use of spices and fire: 'Ulla describes a particular type of *Baal Ov* as one who burns incense to propitiate a demon. The text continues, "Raba asked him, But shouldn't burning incense to a demon be considered idolatry? Raba said, The *Baal Ov* in Keritot refers to one who burns incense in order to charm (לחבר). Abaye said to him, Burning incense as a charm is to act as a charmer, which is merely prohibited by a negative precept. While that is the case the Torah suggests stoning the charmer."

[49] E.g., the stories in BT Pesachim 110b and following.

ered full-blown magic but which are nevertheless prohibited because they are vestigial native or "Amorite" customs (or, in conventional English, "superstitions"):

> Abaye and Rabba both claim that whatever is used for healing cannot be forbidden as an Amorite practice. If it is not a remedy, is it (automatically) forbidden as an Amorite custom? No doubt that it was taught: If a tree is shedding its fruit, one paints it with sikra[50] and suspends stones from it. Loading it with stones clearly diminishes its vitality, but painting it with sikra, how is that remedial? It was taught, "And he will cry, 'Tameh, Tameh' (impure)," making his condition public so that people will pray for him. Following whose opinion do we suspend a bunch of dates on a (sterile) date tree? In accordance with this Tanna (who teaches the custom described above?).

The subsequent discussion in the Talmud includes one startling tradition which is not to be considered of the "ways of the Amorites"—incantations for alleviating choking on a bone. This list of condemned practices[51] seems to be part of a section of marginal behaviors collected together because of their popular persistence and legal questionability. That they are *ipso facto* pagan is not necessarily the case.[52] The meaning of the term "Amorite" is unclear to scholars. The use of the phrase might indicate that it was appropriated and reinvested with new meaning in the Rabbinic period to describe "in-group" practices that needed to be pushed outside the boundaries of society. It may also have evolved as a clever pun on the Hebrew term for "Roman" (*emori/romi*). Contemporary Roman customs, well known to the Rabbinic writers, may have become assimilated to indigenous

---

[50] A type of red paint which presumably was believed to cure or work apotropaically.

[51] I.e., husband and wife exchanging names, chanting "idolatrous" incantations, breaking eggs before a wall in front of chickens, dancing for *kutah*, cooking with silence or sound, urinating before a cooking pot, crying so that beans will cook more quickly. The parallel section in the *Tosefta Shabbat* (chs. 7-8) is perhaps the more comprehensive list of these barely acceptable customs. Lieberman, *Tosefta Kifshuta Moed* (New York: Jewish Theological Seminary, 1962), 25-29, remains an essential commentary. See also the analysis of these customs in the article by Mireille Hadas-Lebel, "Le Paganisme à travers les sources rabbiniques," *ANRW*, 2.19.2: 397-485.

[52] Contrary to the classification of them by Hadas-Lebel, "Le Paganisme à travers les sources rabbiniques." The first important historical/philological study of these customs was accomplished by Heinrich Lewy, "Morgenländischer Aberglaube in der römischen Kaiserzeit," *Zeitschrift des Vereins für Volkskunde* 3:24-40, 130-43.

Palestinian practices in the minds of the editors. The *Darche Emori* chapter presents a category of vestigial practices and practitioners—some of whom match the list of Deuteronomy 18:10-11—but most of whom are not mentioned in the Bible; these are obscure and marginal practices, and the editors have a difficult time establishing rigorous criteria for delimiting the category. While they are not considered *toevot* (abominations), neither are they to be tolerated, and one is warned not to practice them. The cultural context of these practices has been studied only in part.[53] As Judah Goldin has noted in his study of Jewish magic, the lines between magic and superstition are not sharp and the criteria which establish something as "Amorite" are somewhat arbitrary. One is reminded here of Pliny the Elder's fulminations against magic and his recommendations for remedies, materials, and techniques that look to us very much like magic . The principle "that which heals cannot be considered an Amorite custom" (and hence is permitted)[54] is itself arbitrarily applied. "Healing" remedies can be considered magical in some cases and not in others. "Healing" is a socially constructed concept, and in Rabbinic texts this aphorism remains more of a slogan than an applicable guideline for halacha.[55] For the rabbis, a cure which utilizes improper, politically/socially incorrect language is not a cure at all. In the Yerushalmi (Shabbat 14d; Avodah Zarah 2:2) a story is told to substantiate the argument that it is improper to be healed by a *min*—a heretic.[56] One should not expect Rabbinic culture to evolve

---

[53] Most of the studies seek exact parallels in superstitions of the Greco-Roman world. See Heinrich Lewy, "Morgenländischer Aberglaube"; Blau, *Zauberwesen,* 65-66; and Lieberman, *Tosefta K'fshuta* (on Shabbat ch. 7); Judah Goldin, "The Magic of Magic and Superstition"; and the overview by Mireille Hadas-Lebel, "Le Paganisme." The last essay offers a fine topical analysis of each of the "customs" in Greco-Roman context.

[54] ‏.כל דבר שיש בו משום רפואה אין בו משום דרכי אמורי‎

[55] The work of Michael Herzfeld is helpful in this regard. In a recent article ("Closure as Cure: Tropes in the Exploration of Bodily and Social Disorder," *Current Anthropology* 27/2 [1986]: 107) he writes about the social significance of sickness.

[56] "The grandson of (R. Joshua b. Levi) had a choking fit. A man came and pronounced a charm (*lachash*) over him in the name of Jesus Pandira and he recovered. When the healer went out he (R. Joshua) said to him, 'What charm did you say to him?' (The healer) said to him, 'Such and such a word.' He (i.e., R. Joshua) said to him, 'It would have been better for him if he had died and not been healed like this.'" The name of Jesus can heal but that ritual is illegitimate and *ipso facto* outside the boundaries of the oral and textual culture that transmits such stories. On the use of Jesus' name in the incantation bowls see M. Geller, "Jesus's Theurgic Powers: Parallels in the Talmud and Incantation Bowls,"

a systematic application of this rule in any case. A good study of the criteria used in establishing a category of superstition (in diachronic and synchronic perspective) would be very helpful for future scholarship.[57]

As I have noted above, one important Talmudic reference (BT Menahot 65a) lists the criteria for sitting on the Sanhedrin, and includes among the requirements that of *ba'alei keshafim,* "master of magicians" or "master of magic." What is meant here is most likely the ability to understand magical praxis in order to judge cases in which the criminality of magicians must be established. Other sources emphasize the possibility of teaching but not practicing magic (cf. BT Sanhedrin 67a-b).[58] Were there collections of magical traditions available to rabbis or learned male Jews? Did magic belong to the curriculum of well-schooled Pharisees or rabbis? In the following statement attributed to Abaye, the laws of magic are divided into three categories, much like the "laws of Sabbath":

Abaye said, The laws of magicians are similar to those of the Sabbath. Certain activities are punished by stoning, some are not liable to punishment, yet forbidden *a priori*, and others are entirely permitted. Therefore if one actually performs magic he is stoned; if he creates an illusion he is exempt but the action is still forbidden; and what is entirely permitted? Such deeds as were performed by R. Hanina and R. Oshia, who spent every Sabbath evening studying the "Laws of Creation" (*Hilchot Yezira*) by means of which they created a one-third size calf and ate it (BT Sanhedrin 67b).

We cannot be sure that this "entirely permitted" type of magic may have emerged from a specifically Greco-Roman tradition of *voces magicae.* Specialists in many cultures have used unintelligible syllables and sounds to communicate with spirits. The text is frustrating in its brevity: can this type of activity actually be considered *kishuf*—since *kishuf* carries overwhelmingly negative connotations in every other text? That certainly seems to be the

---

Journal of Jewish Studies 28 (1977): 2.

[57]Judah Goldin ("The Magic of Magic and Superstition") has called attention to this rather arbitrary distinction of healing and magic in his classic essay on the *Darchei Emori.* On the development of the concept of superstition see Dieter Harmening, *Superstitio* (Berlin: E. Schmidt, 1979), 33-42.

[58]See Rashi and Tosofot on both passages. In my reading, this distinction is tenuous at best but flows from a careful reading of Deut 18:12: "For anyone who does such things is abhorrent to the Lord ...."

implication of the three-fold taxonomy. The linguistic special-
ist/rabbi who is knowledgeable about cosmic semiotics can emulate
the deity. Creation *ex nihilo* can be performed by legitimate and
legitimized magicians. Ultimately, however, these linguistically
talented rabbis create very imperfect humanoids in addition to
calfs. They may be able to animate anthropoids, as in this prototype of the Golem myth, but lack the finishing touches of the
ultimate, divine magician. Whether the Hekhalot texts are actual
handbooks for these magician/linguists is a difficult historical
problem and an appropriate subject for another occasion.[59]

One can surely gain insight into the theoretical discussion of
magic by examining "realia" that embody the textual history of
praxis. The Aramaic incantation bowls and amulets, perhaps the
chief examples of the *materia magica* of the Jewish world, provide
a contemporary vantage point from which to examine Talmudic
classification.[60] I can only make some general remarks about this
relationship here. In numerous bowls the magician promises protection against the generic *keshafim* and its Aramaic equivalent
harshin, and these terms are usually accompanied by *ruchin
bishin*—evil spirits. In the magical amulets, for example, the scribe
calls for the release of the afflicted from all sorts of witchcraft and
sorcery, all malevolent writing, all evil spells and the evil eye.[61]
What strikes the reader in reading the incantational materials is
their all-inclusive nature, and the connection of evil writings with

---

[59] See the relevant studies of G. Scholem, J. Dan, P. Schäfer, D. Halperin, S.
Wasserstrom, as well as various essays in *Jerusalem Studies in Jewish Thought*
(1986) on early Jewish mysticism; also the papers in this volume by Rebecca
Lesses and Michael Swartz.

[60] Baruch Levine's seminal analysis of the language of the bowl texts, "The
Language of the Magical Bowls," in Neusner, *History of the Jews of Babylonia,*
Vol. 5 (Leiden: E. J. Brill, 1970), must be consulted, as well as the careful study of
Schiffman and Swartz, *Hebrew and Aramaic Incantations from the Cairo Geniza*
(Sheffield: JSOT, 1992), and the new collection edited by Shaked and Naveh,
Magic Spells and Formulae (Jerusalem: Magnes Press,1993).

[61] E.g., שרין כן ישתרון כל מיני כשפים וכל מיני חרשין וכל כתבין בישין (Geniza amulet
formulae). See the index of Montgomery (1913), s.v. כשף.חרש. The incantation
bowls from Mesopotamia and the amulets from various Middle Eastern sites
evidence lists of malevolent *mazikin, shedim*, and *ruhin bishin*. As has been
shown by Baruch Levine ("The Language of the Bowls"), Mark Geller ("Taboo
in Mesopotamia," *Journal of Cuneiform Studies* 42 [1990]: 1), and other linguists, there is an Akkadian incantational background to these lists and their
style. The bowl texts preserve a performative taxonomy: the practitioner must be
inclusive, lest the incantation fail; and the generic phrasing helps the practitioner to complete the ritual cursing/exorcism.

long-distance curses.[62] In their second volume of Aramaic incantation texts, Shaked and Naveh have noted the large number of
quasi-medical texts which do *not* involve incantations.[63] The
amulets and bowl incantations never describe the spell as effective
kishuf but as a "successful" or "effective" spell, amulet or writing.

*   *   *

Like the Deuteronomic writers, the rabbis seek to distance
themselves and Jewry from what are clearly indigenous Jewish
magical practices. Yet even more is at stake. Early Rabbinic discussion breaks down the biblical list of Deuteronomy 18:10-11, and
BT Sanhedrin presents the most significant theoretical discussion
of "magic" *per se*. Going into remarkable depth, this discourse
dissects magic considered from the perspective of criminology and
penology, including rather sophisticated discussion of the intentionality of magical ritual and ritualists in the context of other
related practices and practitioners. The "laws of magic" include
magic which is prohibited *a priori*, magic which is prohibited only
ex posteriori, and magic which, while permitted, can be performed
only by special holy men who have knowledge of esoteric linguistic
cosmology.

In later non-Rabbinic ritual texts the term "magician" or
"sorcerer" becomes depersonalized and is included in lists of demonic agents; it becomes harder to distinguish between personal-
ized demons and demonized persons.[64] Demons and sorcerers are
more highly gendered than before; there is a greater emphasis on
the Lilith threat as well.

The Rabbinic discourse on magic and its nature demonstrates the
particularly Rabbinic tendency towards dissection of a behavior,
action, or ritual, albeit with a decidedly Greco-Roman disposition.
While Rabbinic literature is surely more dissonant and uneven than
a treatise on magic or theurgy in Latin and Greek sources, it is
concerned with classification nevertheless. Working with the
biblical data and much more, these pages in Tractate Sanhedrin

---

[62] See John Gager's recent work (*Curse Tablets and Binding Spells*) on
curses and *defixiones* in the Greco-Roman world.

[63] Joseph Naveh and Shaul Shaked, *Magic Spells and Formulae*, (Jerusalem:
Magnes Press, 1993).

[64] See the introductory discussion in Shaked and Naveh's second volume of
incantation texts, as well as the general discussion of the rationality of early
medieval magic by Richard Kieckhefer, "The Specific Rationality of Medieval
Magic," *American Historical Review* 99/3 (1994): 813-36.

help to carry on the Western critique of magic, and the taxonomic mode we find there anticipates later scholastic consideration of the problem. The discourse is at once as fascinating and complex as the magic it seeks to understand.

CHAPTER TEN

MAGICAL PIETY
IN
ANCIENT AND MEDIEVAL JUDAISM

Michael D. Swartz

In recent years, there has been increased interest in the role of
tradition in mysticism. One of the best-known examples of this
change is the work of Steven Katz, who has edited important
volumes emphasizing what he calls "the conservative character of
mysticism" and the role of convention and culture in shaping
mystical literatures and practices.[1] In the study of Jewish mysticism, scholars have shown the extent to which the development of
Kabbalah was meant to be a stabilizing influence in relation to
Jewish tradition.[2] These essays build on Gershom Scholem's in-
sights into the tension between conservative and anarchic trends in
Jewish mysticism.[3]

The issue of the function of tradition and society also plays an
important part in the study of magic. The magician can be seen as
functioning primarily as an individual, who has, in Emile Durkheim's formulation, "a clientele and not a church."[4] As Durkheim
puts it, W. Robertson Smith saw magic as "opposed to religion as
society is to the individual."[5] More recently, scholars of ancient

---

[1] See the essays in Steven Katz, ed., *Mysticism and Religious Traditions*
(New York: Oxford University Press, 1983), especially Katz, "The
'Conservative' Character of Mysticism," 3-60.

[2] For example, Daniel C. Matt, "The Mystic and the *Miẓwot*," in Arthur Green,
ed., *Jewish Spirituality from the Bible to the Middle Ages* (New York: Crossroad, 1987), 367-404, emphasizes the extent to which the author of the Zohar and
other early Kabbalists saw themselves as guardians of the tradition by explaining
the inner purposes of the commandments (*ta'ame ha-miṣvot*).

[3] See Gershom Scholem, "Religious Authority and Mysticism," in *On the
Kabbalah and Its Symbolism* (New York: Schocken, 1969), 1-31. In pointing up
this tension, Scholem emphasized the anarchic dimension of mysticism in history;
see David Biale, *Gershom Scholem: Kabbalah and Counter-History*
(Cambridge: Harvard University Press, 1979).

[4] Emile Durkheim, *The Elementary Forms of the Religious Life* (New York:
Free Press, 1965), 60.

[5] Durkheim, *Elementary Forms*, 61 n. 62, summarizing W. Robertson Smith,
Lectures on the Religion of the Semites (3rd ed., 1927; repr. New York: Ktav,

Greco-Roman magic have emphasized its subversive nature. For example, Ramsay MacMullen listed magicians, along with philosophers, astrologers and soothsayers, among the "enemies of the Roman order."[6] Moreover, those theories of social analysis that see magic primarily as an expression of accusation against objects of a community's social disapproval can also be related to the notion that magic is a subversive phenomenon.[7] In these more purely social definitions of magic, it is identified not with the characteristics of a particular set of practices, but with its anti-normative status.[8] According to this approach, it is not merely that magic is by definition subversive, but that subversive religious practices are by definition magic.[9]

However, there have been others, such as Bronislaw Malinowski, who have stressed the role of tradition in the validation of magical

---

1969), 264-65. Durkheim cites the second edition. As Durkheim's note implies, we need not posit a dichotomy between magic and religion to see magic as subversive both of a religious society's social order and its traditional values.

[6] Ramsay MacMullen, *Enemies of the Roman Order: Treason, Unrest, and Alienation in the Empire* (Cambridge: Harvard University Press, 1966), 95-127. See now John Gager, "Moses the Magician: Hero of an Ancient Jewish Counter-Culture?" *Helios* 21 (1994): 179-88; cf. David E. Aune, "Magic in Early Christianity," in *ANRW*, 2.23.2: 1507-57; cf. p. 1519 on the opinion that Greco-Roman magic, because of its international character acted as a kind of "intellectual fifth column."

[7] It can be said that E. E. Evans-Pritchard, *Witchcraft, Oracles and Magic Among the Azande* (Oxford: Clarendon, 1937), led the way to this approach by focusing not on the practice of witchcraft but on how accusations of witchcraft functioned in the society. The implications of this approach are drawn out in Mary Douglas, ed., *Witchcraft Confessions and Accusations* (London: Tavistock, 1970); for its application to the Greco-Roman environment see Peter Brown, "Sorcery, Demons and the Rise of Christianity from Late Antiquity into the Middle Ages," 17-45 in that volume.

[8] For an early formulation of such a social definition see Marcel Mauss, *A General Theory of Magic*, trans. Robert Brain (London and Boston: Routledge & Kegan Paul, 1972), 24. For the application of this idea to Greco-Roman religions see in particular Jonathan Z. Smith, "Good News Is No News: Aretalogy and Gospel," in Jacob Neusner, ed., *Christianity, Judaism and Other Greco-Roman Cults: Studies for Morton Smith at Sixty* (Leiden: Brill, 1975), 21-38; cf. David D. Aune, "Magic in Early Christianity," *ANRW*, 2.23.2: 1507-57, who identifies magic with deviant religious practices. For a summary and discussion of this argument see H. S. Versnel, "Some Reflections on the Relationship Magic-Religion," *Numen* 38 (1991): 182-84.

[9] This theory thus cannot by definition center on a body of evidence for practices alleged to be magical themselves. Nor, as Versnel observes ("Reflections," 183), does such analysis "preclude the existence of more concrete 'substantive' implications of the term."

practices.[10] In an important essay, Hans Dieter Betz also emphasizes this element of the rhetoric and self-conception of Greco-Roman magicians.[11] This argument modulates the characterization of magic as individualistic or anti-social. The appeal to tradition would seem to indicate a magician conscious of social norms and shared myths. Moreover, historians in Judaism have observed that the Rabbinic leadership in late antiquity cultivated practices that could conventionally be considered magical.[12]

We can therefore delineate the polarity in this way: Can we who study magic speak, like Katz, of its "conservative character"? Do magicians reinforce the traditional values of their society? Or are they somehow subversive of them, appropriating divine and human power? Current research on Jewish magic suggests a deep ambivalence along these lines. This ambivalence is manifest in what can be called magical piety. This essay concerns two literary motifs and magical phenomena brought together under this rubric: the use of tradition, authority, and ideal figures in magical texts; and the use of magical practices to gain memory, wisdom and Torah.[13] The evidence for these phenomena is selected from magical handbooks and amulets from late antiquity and the early Middle Ages, which are preserved in manuscripts from the Cairo Genizah and other collections, and from passages in the literatures of Rabbinic Juda-

---

[10] Bronislaw Malinowski, *Magic, Science and Religion* (Garden City: Doubleday Anchor, 1954), 74-75. Cf. Max Weber, *The Sociology of Religion* (Boston: Beacon, 1964), 20-31 and elsewhere, who relates magic closely to priestcraft and thus to old aristocratic elements in religious society.

[11] "The Formation of Authoritative Tradition in the Greek Magical Papyri," in Ben F. Meyer and E. P. Sanders, eds., *Jewish and Christian Self-Definition* (Philadelphia: Fortress Press, 1983), 3.161-70.

[12] For magical practices among the Babylonian Rabbis see Jacob Neusner, *A History of the Jews in Babylonia* (Leiden: Brill, 1965-70), vols. 4 and 5, several chapters of which are collected in Jacob Neusner, *The Wonder Working Lawyers of Babylonia* (Lanham: University Press of America, 1987). The medieval German pietists known as the *Ḥaside Ashkenaz* collected and annotated many earlier magical texts such as the *Havdalah de-Rabbi Akiba* and *Sefer ha-Razim*; however, this does not necessarily mean that these texts themselves derived from circles of the ancient Jewish elite.

[13] These discussions are based on research undertaken for my forthcoming study *Scholastic Magic: Ritual and Revelation in Early Jewish Mysticism* (Princeton: Princeton University Press, in press). For a more extensive discussion of the comparison of the role of tradition in Jewish magical texts to its place in Rabbinic Judaism and early Jewish mysticism, see Michael D. Swartz, "Book and Tradition in Hekhalot and Magical Literatures," *Journal of Jewish Thought and Philosophy* 3 (1994): 189-229; for memory practices, see *Scholastic Magic*, chap. 2.

ism and early Jewish mysticism, which preserve many examples of ancient and medieval Jewish magic.[14]

A discussion such as this one, which seeks to compare magical forms with other spheres of religious activity, raises questions about definition and comparison. Much of the controversy surrounding the term magic has focused on how the notion of magic is applied to traditional, non-Western societies. Bound up with this issue is the question, raised throughout this volume, of whether there is something intrinsic called "magic" that can be separated from "religion," and whether this dichotomy presupposes an evolutionary view that sees those societies that employ "magic" as inferior. Yet our use of this term need not imply this dichotomy. Indeed, to separate or rank magic in opposition to religion not only misstates their relationship, but limits the sphere of religion, which can encompass the use of ritual power for the individual's needs.[15]

Furthermore, for the history of religions in Greco-Roman antiquity and medieval Europe and the Mediterranean, the term magic has served a practical function. This volume is the result of a gathering of scholars who have recognized something of what they study in the term magic—even if some might think that term

---

[14] The standard introduction to Jewish magic is Joshua Trachtenberg, *Jewish Magic and Superstition* (New York: Atheneum, 1982); see also Ludwig Blau, *Das Altjüdische Zauberwesen* (Budapest, 1897-98; Berlin: Louis Lamm, 1914). For a survey of Jewish magical literature see P. S. Alexander, "Incantation and Books of Magic," in Emil Schürer, *The History of the Jewish People in the Age of Jesus Christ*, rev. and ed. Geza Vermes, Fergus Millar, and Martin Goodman, 3 vols. (Edinburgh: Clark, 1986), 3.1.42-79; and Peter Schäfer, "Jewish Magic Literature in Late Antiquity and the Early Middle Ages," *JSJ* 41 (1990): 75-91. An example of the magical handbooks of late antiquity and the Middle Ages can be found in Mordechai Margalioth, *Sefer Ha-Razim: Hu' Sefer Keshafim mi-Tequfat ha-Talmud* (Jerusalem: American Academy for Jewish Research, 1966), translated in Michael Morgan, *Sepher Ha-Razim: The Book of the Mysteries* (Chico: Scholars Press, 1983). For amulets from late antiquity and the early Middle Ages see Joseph Naveh and Shaul Shaked, *Amulets and Magical Bowls: Aramaic Incantations of Late Antiquity*, 2nd ed. (Jerusalem: Magnes, 1987), and Lawrence H. Schiffman and Michael D. Swartz, *Hebrew and Aramaic Incantation Texts from the Cairo Genizah* (Sheffield: Sheffield Academic Press, 1992); see also the more extensive bibliographies in these works. The major texts of early Jewish mysticism, known as Hekhalot literature, are published in Peter Schäfer, *Synopse zur Hekhalot-Literatur* (Tübingen: Mohr, 1981), and *idem, Genizah-Fragmente zur Hekhalot-Literatur* (Tübingen: Mohr, 1984). On magical elements in this literature see Gershom Scholem, *Jewish Gnosticism, Merkavah Mysticism, and Talmudic Tradition* (2nd ed., New York, 1965), and Schäfer, "Jewish Magic Literature."

[15] On this point see especially Versnel, "Reflections."

should be abandoned entirely. In part, this is because there are specific literary forms in these cultures that have been identified as magical since the inception of modern historical studies. These literatures usually concern the use of rituals techniques, esoteric names and words for what are generally considered practical purposes.

In this essay the term magic will thus be used within a particular heuristic frame of reference, as the applicability of the notion of magic to each cultural context must be decided on a case-by-case basis. In the case of Judaism, it is possible to use the term to describe identifiable textual corpora having distinct literary traits. It is those literary characteristics, and not any preconceptions of the inherent properties of magic, that can guide us to a description of the contours of the phenomena described in this essay.

In paying close attention to literary features of magical texts, we have the opportunity to listen to the voices of the magicians themselves, concentrating on their distinctive rhetoric and logic. Based on recent studies of Jewish magical texts in late antiquity and the earlier Middle Ages,[16] we can identify three prevailing elements of Jewish magical texts: (1) the emphasis on the power of the name of God; (2) the intermediacy of the angels in negotiating between divine providence and human needs; and (3) the application of divine names and ritual practices for the needs of specific individuals.[17]

This characterization has the advantage of describing a type of activity that can exist *within* the framework of religious behavior, as each of its components can be found in other areas of ancient Judaism.[18] Yet these elements come together in a fairly coherent way in what are conventionally called magical texts—especially amulets, handbooks containing incantation texts and ritual prescriptions. We therefore have a way of designating them that, like all heuristic terms, allows us to proceed in an economical manner.

*   *   *

In magical piety, magicians express their desires through some of the most deeply held values and priorities of the society and its

---

[16] See the studies cited in n. 14 above.

[17] See Swartz, "Scribal Magic and Its Rhetoric: Formal Patterns in Hebrew and Aramaic Incantation Texts from the Cairo Genizah," *HTR* 83 (1990): 179; Schiffman and Swartz, *Incantation Texts*, 12-15.

[18] Cf. Aune, "Magic in Early Christianity," 1516: "Magic is not religion only in the sense that the species is not the genus."

religious leadership. These can be expressed in the way myth and history are used in magical texts, their rhetoric, or the goals of magical activity. The magicians' approach to their tradition and social framework can be seen most clearly in those literary genres that make magical use of tradition and mythic history.

One of the most telling of these is the "chain of tradition" motif.[19] In this form, the magical practice, book, or name is said to have been transmitted from the biblical heroes through a succession of ideal figures, who used it to perform their miracles and who owe their success as historical figures to its secrets. This motif echoes the famous Rabbinic "chain of tradition" that opens the Mishnah tractate 'Avot, which describes the transmission of Torah from Moses at Sinai:

> Moses received Torah from Sinai and handed it down to Joshua, and Joshua to the Elders, and the Elders to the Prophets, and the Prophets to the Men of the Great Assembly. (m. 'Avot 1:1)

The chain of tradition continues to a series of Pharisaic and Rabbinic sages. As Henry Fischel and others have shown, this passage follows a prevalent Greco-Roman *topos* of scholastic succession.[20] But the magical version of the chain of tradition deviates from the Rabbinic pattern in a significant way. A key example is the introduction to the magical manual *Sefer ha-Razim*. This introduction represents the book as "one of the books of the mysteries that was given to Noah," and from Noah it passed

> to Abraham and from Abraham to Isaac and from Isaac to Jacob and from Jacob to Levi and from Levi to Kohath and from Kohath to Amram and from Amram to Moses and from Moses to Joshua and from Joshua to the Elders and from the Elders to the Prophets and from the Prophets to the Sages and so to every generation until Solomon arose to be enlightened by many books of wisdom . . . for many books were handed down to

---

[19] For a detailed description of this motif and its historical implications, see Swartz, "Book and Tradition."

[20] See, for example, Henry A. Fischel, "The Uses of Sorites (*Climax, Gradatio*) in the Tannaitic Period," *HUCA* 44 (1973): 119-51; Elie Bickerman, "La chaîne de la tradition pharisienne," *RB* 59 (1952): 44-54, repr. in Henry A. Fischel, ed., *Essays in Greco-Roman and Related Talmudic Literature* (New York: Ktav, 1977), 127-37; and Anthony Saldarini, *Scholastic Rabbinism: A Literary Study of the Fathers According to Rabbi Nathan* (Chico: Scholars Press, 1982); cf. also Steven D. Fraade, *From Tradition to Commentary: Torah and its Interpretation in the Midrash Sifre to Deuteronomy* (Albany: State University of New York Press, 1991), 69-70.

him, but he found this most precious and honored and enduring (*qasheh*) of all.[21]

The introduction emphasizes that this book was used by Noah to fashion the ark, and to perform countless other historical miracles. That same powerful book thus now rests in the hands of the contemporary magician. The mishnaic chain of tradition validates the authority of the Rabbinic process of accumulated wisdom of Torah, passed down from teacher to disciple. The magical rendering of this form, on the other hand, serves to lend power to a physical text, and to all who can get their hands on it.

This motif, variants of which can be found in the *Sefer ha-Malbush* section of *Sefer Raziel* and other texts,[22] is not confined to magical books. We also find it in an early Jewish magical manual, known as the Book of Medicines of Asaph the physician.[23] The Book of Asaph also advertises itself as the product of divine wisdom given to Noah by the angel Raphael, and on to Solomon, and to Asaph the physician by way of the wise man *'Asqlepianos*.[24] The affinities of the introduction to magical books to that of the medical manual point up both the instrumental nature of the both texts, which are said to be effective for anyone who learns their contents, and the need for both to validate their techniques.

Related to this model is a form called the magical *historiola*, also known as the "epic motif" or "magical antecedent."[25] The

---

[21] Margalioth, *Sefer ha-Razim*, 66.

[22] See, for example, *Sefer Raziel* (Amsterdam, 1701), fol. 2b.

[23] This medical text, which is deserving of renewed attention from scholars of Judaism in Late Antiquity, is probably of Byzantine origin. See Elinor Lieber, "Asaf's *Book of Medicines*: A Hebrew Encyclopedia of Greek and Jewish Medicine, Possibly Compiled in Byzantium on an Indian Model," in John Scarborough, ed., *Dumbarton Oaks Papers* 38 (1984): 233-49, and the earlier studies cited there. The introduction to this book contrasts somewhat with the rather technical medical manual that follows; because of its textual affinities with the Book of Jubilees, it was printed independently by Aaron Jellinek as *Sefer Noaḥ* (Aaron Jellinek, *Bet Ha-Midrash* [Leipzig, 1878, repr. Jerusalem: Wahrman, 1967], 1.155-56), and has often been treated as a late apocryphon by scholars unaware of its origins in the medical book.

[24] See the Hebrew text in Suessman Muntner, *Mavo' le-Sefer 'Asaf ha-Rofe'* (Jerusalem: Genizah, 1967); Aviv Melzer, "Asaph the Physician—the Man and His Book: A Historical-Philological Study of the Medical Treatise, The Book of Drugs" (Ph.D. diss., University of Wisconsin, 1972), and in Jellinek, *Bet ha-Midrash,* 1.155.

[25] On the *historiola* in Greco-Roman magic see especially David Frankfurter, "Narrating Power: The Theory and Practice of the Magical *Historiola* in Ritual Spells," in this volume. For an early definition of the *historiola* see F. Ohrt,

historiola is a figure in which the magician uses a "historical" event to validate the magic at hand, or to call the divine powers to the aid of the client. In its simplest form, the incantation employs an analogy, as in this amulet from the Cairo Genizah for "grace and favor"—that is, social acceptance:

> "Noah found favor in the eyes of the Lord" of Hosts. So may Menashe ben Shamsi find favor in the eyes of all children of Adam and Eve.[26]

The reasoning of this clause is obvious. The same favor shown Noah is asked for Menashe. This idea is a form of "magical analogy" like that often applied to ritual actions.[27] However, it can also be said that the rhetoric underlying this passage is related to that of *zekhut 'avot*, the Rabbinic doctrine of the merit of the fathers that informs talmudic stories and liturgical prayers.[28] According to this idea, the present-day community is deserving of preservation only because of its ancestors' deeds. One particularly striking expression of such an idea among many is a petitionary litany recited on Day of Atonement:

> He who answered our father at Mt. Moriah,
> May he answer us;
> He who answered Isaac his son as he was bound on the altar,
> May he answer us;
> He who answered Jacob at Bethel,
> May he answer us;[29]

and so on, down through history.

"Segen," *Handwörterbuch des deutschen Aberglaubens* (Berlin/Leipzig: De Gruyter, 1935-36), 7.1590-91. On the term "magical antecedent" see G. Van der Leeuw, *Religion in Essence and Manifestation*, trans. J. E. Turner; 1938 (repr. Gloucester: Peter Smith, 1967), 2:423-24.

[26] TS K1.6, lines 14-16. The text was published in Schiffman and Swartz, *Incantation Texts*, 64-68.

[27] On the use of analogy in ritual and magic see Stanley J. Tambiah, "Form and Meaning of Magical Acts," in *Culture, Thought, and Social Action: An Anthropological Perspective* (Cambridge: Harvard University Press, 1985), 64-77.

[28] The classic discussions of this idea are A. Marmorstein, *The Doctrine of Merits in Old Rabbinic Literature* (1920; repr. New York: Ktav, 1968), and Solomon Schechter, "The Zachuth of the Fathers," in *Some Aspects of Rabbinic Theology* (New York: Macmillan, 1923), 170-98.

[29] For the entire prayer and commentary see Daniel Goldschmidt, ed., *Maḥazor le-Yamim Nora'im* (Ashkenaz) (Jerusalem: Mosad Bialik, 1970), 2.55-56; cf. m. *Ta'an.* 2:4.

In several cases, however, the *historiola* manifests a subtler variation. Another Genizah amulet, MS. TS K1.168, employs a well-known talmudic story that Gabriel taught Joseph the seventy languages and added a letter of the divine name to his name.[30] The midrash, as James Kugel has pointed out, is based on a textual anomaly.[31] Joseph's name has an extra *heh* in Ps 81:6: "He made a decree on Yehosef, when he went out over the land of Egypt; I heard a language that I did not know." The midrash thus speculates that Gabriel gave him both the extra letter and the "unknown language" mentioned in the Psalm. Our magician's innovation, however, is to put that fact to practical use by making that same name available to him and his client. Examples of this kind of extension of exegetical midrash to magical application can be multiplied in Jewish magic.[32]

This is a critical feature of the magical use of history, midrash, and textual exegesis. Unlike the canonical Rabbinic texts, the magical texts vividly make the historical case part of the mechanism by which the client receives the benefits of divine providence. These forms are notable as examples of a pattern of magical midrash or practical exegesis. They can be added to Steven Katz's description of esoteric uses of ideal figures in his essay, "Models, Modeling, and Mystical Training."[33] According to Katz, mystical experiences provide not radical exegesis of scripture but experiential confirmation of it:

> . . . this very use of allegory and symbolism, as well as other varied hermeneutical devices, functions to *maintain* the authority of the canonical sources under interpretation rather than to destroy or transcend them, as is usually assumed. That is to say, the presupposition on which the mystical use of allegory and symbolic modes of exegesis depends is that the canonical books of one's tradition do in fact possess *truth* and *authority* claimed for them.[34]

And, it can be added, power. Magical writers' use of ideal figures serves at once to maintain their forebears' sanctity and to marshall

---

[30] MS. TS K1.168 lines 25-30; cf. b. *Soṭah* 36. See Schiffman and Swartz, *Incantation Texts*, 145; see p. 156 on the Rabbinic sources.

[31] James L. Kugel, "Two Introductions to Midrash," in Geoffrey H. Hartman and Sanford Budick, *Midrash and Literature* (New Haven: Yale University Press, 1986), 95-100.

[32] See further Swartz, "Book and Tradition," and Schiffman and Swartz, *Incantation Texts*, 40-42.

[33] *Religion* 12 (1982): 247-75.

[34] Katz, "Models," 30 (Katz's italics).

the power of their holiness to perform the necessary tasks. This is nevertheless a variation from the scholastic process of Rabbinic exegesis that produced the canonical midrash on which the magical midrash is based. So too, the magical chain of tradition substitutes the concrete, instrumentally potent book or magical name for the dialectical process of Torah. The magicians thus manage to circumvent the sanctioned channels of tradition and authority even as they invoke them.

* * *

In the previous examples, we have seen the terms and symbols of the traditional culture put to use for the purposes of magic. In the following description, we see the purposes of magic put to use for a central value of Rabbinic scholasticism—the pattern of traditional learning that is a central characteristic of classical Rabbinic Judaism, expressed as Torah.

In Rabbinic theology, Torah constitutes both the substance of revelation and its content. To apply terms articulated for the study of ancient Judaism by Michael Fishbane, the idea of Torah embraces both *traditio*—the way in which a sacred culture is transmitted—and *traditium*—the message of that culture.[35] The study of Torah was both a ritual act and the sign of a great man. The authors of these genres, particularly the texts known as the *Sar-Torah* literature, sought to achieve this greatness through magical means.

These texts range from brief formulae for improving memory to full-fledged myths of how the magical secrets for learning Torah were acquired by the elders in the Jerusalem Temple. The former texts are rituals and incantations for the "opening of the heart"; the latter are those texts within the literature of early Jewish mysticism, or Merkavah mysticism, known as the *Sar-Torah* literature. (See the following essay by Rebecca Lesses.) These concern the cultivation of an angel or "prince" who will grant the individual prodigious skill and—as is particularly significant—a spectacular memory.[36] In order to understand this type of magic, it

---

[35] Michael Fishbane, *Biblical Interpretation in Ancient Israel*, 6-19. In using these terms Fishbane followed Douglas A. Knight, *Rediscovering the Traditions of Israel* (Missoula: Scholars Press, 1975); see Fishbane, *Biblical Interpretation*, 6, n. 17.

[36] See Swartz, *Scholastic Magic*, which explores this literature in detail and the relationship of its authors to the sources of holiness and authority of their society. Cf. David J. Halperin, *The Faces of the Chariot: Early Jewish Responses*

is important to recall a few things about the scholastic praxis and ethos in which they grew.

The practice of memory in premodern civilizations has only recently been given concentrated attention. In recent decades historians such as Francis Yates and Mary Carruthers have demonstrated the importance of memory both as an activity and as a value and psychological concept in classical and medieval scholastic civilizations.[37] In traditional Rabbinic education, the basic texts were to be memorized before they were understood and discussed.[38] In its emphasis on memorization and oral recitation of sources, Rabbinic society was consonant with its Greco-Roman cultural surroundings.[39] While there appear to have been no true equiva-

---

to *Ezekiel's Vision* (Tübingen: Mohr, 1988), which also discusses the *Sar-Torah* traditions at length. The main texts of the corpus are translated into German in Peter Schäfer, *Übersetzung der Hekhalot-Literatur* (3 vols. published so far; Mohr: Tübingen, 1987-91). English translations of *Sar-Torah* texts appear throughout Halperin, *Faces of the Chariot*, and in Sections II and III of *Ma'aseh Merkavah*, translated in Michael D. Swartz, *Mystical Prayer in Ancient Judaism: An Analysis of Ma'aseh Merkavah* (Tübingen: Mohr, 1992), 235-47; cf. Naomi Janowitz, *The Poetics of Ascent: Theories of Language in a Rabbinic Ascent Text* (Albany: State University of New York Press, 1989).

[37] Francis A. Yates, *The Art of Memory* (Chicago: University of Chicago Press, 1966); Mary J. Carruthers, *The Book of Memory: A Study of Memory in Medieval Culture* (Cambridge: Cambridge University Press, 1992). See also Helga Hadju, *Das Mnemotechnische Schriften des Mittelalters* (Vienna: Franz Leo, 1936). For non-Western cultures see Frits Staal, *The Fidelity of Oral Tradition and the Origins of Science* (Amsterdam/Oxford/New York: North-Holland Publishing Co., 1986); cf. also Jan Vansina, *Oral Tradition as History* (Madison: University of Wisconsin Press, 1985), 42-48. On memory in Buddhist practice and thought see now Janet Gyatso, ed., *In the Mirror of Memory: Reflections on Mindfulness and Memory in Indian and Tibetan Buddhism* (Albany: SUNY Press, 1992); and Thomas Blenman Hare, "Reading Writing and Cooking: Kūkai's Interpretive Strategies," *Journal of Asian Studies* 49 (1990): 253-73.

[38] For discussions of the role of memorization in Rabbinic learning see Birger Gerhardsson, *Memory and Manuscript: Oral Tradition and Written Transmission in Rabbinic Judaism and Early Christianity* (Lund: C. W. K. Gleerup and Copenhagen: Ejnar Munksgaard, 1961), 122-70; Dov Zlotnick, "Memory and the Integrity of the Oral Tradition," *JANES* 16-17 (1984-85): 229-41; and Swartz, *Scholastic Magic*.

[39] The standard account of the role of memorization in the Greco-Roman educational system is H. I. Marrou, *A History of Education in Antiquity*, trans. George Lamb (New York: Sheed and Ward, 1956); see also Stanley F. Bonner, *Education in Ancient Rome* (Berkeley and Los Angeles: University of California Press, 1977); and William V. Harris, *Ancient Literacy* (Cambridge and London: Harvard University Press, 1989), 30-33 and elsewhere.

lents to the elaborate mnemonic systems of the Roman orators
and their scholastic successors, other common means of improving
memory do find their counterparts in ancient and medieval Judaism.

In late antiquity, magic was called upon to assist the individual
in every conceivable aspect of daily life.[40] Considering the importance of memory in both the value system and the social structure
of ancient Jewish society, we should not be surprised to see magical
practices designed for the acquisition of memory. These are not
restricted to Jewish magic; there are at least four memory spells in
the corpus of the Greek Magical Papyri.[41] Moreover, Ignaz
Goldziher has documented extensively that ritual memory practices were widespread in medieval Islamic and Jewish popular beliefs.[42]

Dietary recommendations for the improvement of memory occur in the Babylonian Talmud.[43] Jewish magical manuals also
contain recipes and ritual formulae for improving memory. This
process is known as *petiḥat lev,* or "opening the heart." Like their
Greek and Islamic counterparts, these procedures usually involve a
ritual of ingestion—of a particular substance, such as an egg, as in
the talmudic text—or of a substance containing magical names or
letters. In many such texts the letters are to be engraved into a
cake and eaten; in others the letters are to be dissolved in a cup or
bowl of wine and drunk. Following a notion attested for many
cultures, both Eastern and Western, the ingestion of the letters
prefigures the expected ingestion of knowledge.[44] A magical text
from the Cairo Genizah contains the following instructions:

---

[40] For the range and distribution of purposes of amulets in the Genizah, see
Schiffman and Swartz, *Incantation Texts*, 46-48.

[41] *PGM* I:232-47, III:410-23, III:467-78; III:424-66 is for "foreknowledge
and memory."

[42] I. Goldziher, "Muhammedanischer Aberglaube über Gedächtnisskraft und
Vergesslichkeit; mit Parallelen aus der jüdischen Litteratur," in A. Freimann and
M. Hildesheimer, eds., *Festschrift zum siebzigsten Geburtstage A. Berliner's*
(Frankfurt: J. Kaufmann, 1903), 131-55.

[43] See especially the collection of traditions about memory in b. *Hor.* 13b, on
which see Martin Jaffee, *The Talmud of Babylonia: An American Translation:
XXVI. Tractate Horayot* (Atlanta: Scholars Press, 1987), 206-07, and Goldziher,
"Muhammedanischer Aberglaube"; cf. b. *Pes.* 111a.

[44] Betz, *The Greek Magical Papyri in Translation* (Chicago: University of
Chicago Press, 1986), 9 n. 45, cites *Handwörterbuch des deutschen Aberglaubens* 8.1156-57 on examples of this practice. For an example in Japanese
esoteric Buddhism and its interpretation see Hare, "Reading Writing and Cooking."

If you want to perform the opening of the heart, purify yourself and take a cup of wine and say the psalm over the cup seven times and drink. Thus one shall do three times in the morning and drink, and one's heart shall be opened. And this is reliable and tested. "My God, my God, why are you . . ."[45]

The following text, also from the Genizah, occurs alongside a malevolent incantation for sending a harmful fire into someone:[46]

Opening the heart: Say over the *havdalah* cup three times and drink it: 'DRNWS 'BRYNWS ḤQQ'L PTḤY'L, whom God engraved (*de-ḥaqqaq 'El*) in Torah; Pethaiel, may you open (*de-tiftaḥ*) words of Torah: Open my heart, I, NN son of NN, to Torah, to wisdom, and to understanding, and may I learn all that I hear speedily; and all that I learn may I not forget forever. "Blessed are you, Lord, teach me your statutes."[47]

The cup of wine used for the traditional *havdalah* ceremony, which separates the Sabbath from the rest of the week, is employed in this ritual.[48] Moreover, this is an incantation directed at angels, whose names reflect their function: the name of ḤQQ'L was engraved (*ḥqq*) by God in Torah, and PTḤY'L opens (*ptḥ*) the heart of the supplicant.

Two similar rituals are found in a fragmentary handbook, TS K1 132. One instructs the practitioner to write three names in water, dissolve them, and drink the water. Another advises taking the water in which the names have been dissolved and kneading it into cakes. As Peter Schäfer points out, this procedure also appears in magical texts for wisdom and memory set into the Hekhalot literature.[49] In one text, an Aramaic ritual text inserted into *Ma'aseh Merkavah* in one manuscript, the practitioner is to write magical

---

[45] MS. TS K1.28 fol. 3a. Here the writer seems to have conflated Ps 63, אשחרך אלי אתה, with Ps 22, אלי אלי למה עזבתני, which appears a few lines down. For a similar example of conflation of verses in an amulet see Schiffman and Swartz, *Incantation Texts*, 117-18.

[46] TS K1.117.

[47] Ps 119:12, which is a popular verse in these incantations.

[48] Cf. the geonic Babylonian magical text *Havdalah de-Rabbi 'Akiba*, which opens with a ritual for "invalidating sorcerers and for one who is harmed by an evil spirit, and one who is banished from (the presence of) his wife, and for opening the heart": Gershom Scholem, "*Havdalah de-Rabbi 'Aqivah: Maqor le-Masoret ha-Magiah ha-Yehudit bi-Tequfat ha-Ge'onim*," *Tarbiṣ* 50 (1980-81): 243-81. Some medieval manuscripts of the ninth-century liturgical manual *Seder Rav 'Amram Gaon* include an incantation directed at the "Prince of Forgetfulness" to be recited over the wine of Havdalah. See Daniel Goldschmidt, ed., *Seder Rav 'Amram Gaon* (Jerusalem: Mosad ha-Rav Kook, 1971), p. פג.

[49] Schäfer, "Jewish Magic Literature," 90.

names on a series of substances or objects and consume them, including a cup of wine, fig and olive leaves, and an egg.[50]

The distinctive *Sar-Torah* texts in the Hekhalot corpus, however, do not correspond to this ritual pattern. In these texts, a narrative pattern takes prominence. They concern the success of the *Sar-Torah* practice in turning a poor student into a great one.[51] Rituals prescribed in these narratives, in contrast to those for *petihat lev*, are rituals of abstention and ablution, involving fasts, ritual immersions, and the avoidance of all contact with impurity.[52] Moreover, their goal, unlike most of the *petihat lev* rituals, is to bring a potent angel, the Prince of the Torah, to the practitioner. It is this angel, adjured by the divine names held by the Rabbi-magician and acting under God's authority, who bestows upon the human being extraordinary skill and cosmic secrets. In these, more sophisticated narrative texts, the scholastic nature of the enterprise is emphasized. In the Chapter of Rabbi Nehunia Version A, Rabbi Ishmael relates his distress because of his trouble in learning:

> A scriptural passage that I was reading one day I would forget the next, and a Mishnaic passage that I was repeating one day I would forget the next.[53]

When he performs the *Sar-Torah* ritual correctly,

> immediately my heart was enlightened like the gates of the east, and my eyes gazed into the depths and paths of Torah, and never again did I forget anything my ears heard from my teacher, of study; nor would I ever again forget anything of the paths of Torah in which I engaged for their truth.[54]

Rabbi Ishmael's "enlightenment" consists not only of spiritual or intellectual insight, or encompassing wisdom.[55] Rather, he has been

---

[50] Schäfer, *Synopse*, §571-78.

[51] Although these texts, which are sometimes considered to be mystical, do not always contain the specific adjuration formulae characteristic of incantation texts, they still place emphasis on the power of divine names to oblige the angels to act on behalf of individuals and thus fall well within the scope of this study.

[52] On rituals in Hekhalot literature, see Ithamar Gruenwald, *Apocalyptic and Merkavah Mysticism* (Leiden: Brill, 1980), 99-102; *idem, From Apocalypticism to Gnosticism* (Frankfurt: Peter Lang, 1988), 262-71; and Michael D. Swartz, "'Like the Ministering Angels:' Ritual and Purity in Early Jewish Mysticism and Magic," *AJS Review* 19 (1994): 135-67.

[53] Schäfer, *Synopse*, §278.

[54] *ibid.*, §279.

[55] It must be remembered that the heart was the seat of the intellect for ancient

blessed by the angel with an exceptional memory. Thanks to the magic of the *Sar-Torah*, Rabbi Ishmael will now be able to remember not only the Bible and Mishnah of his curriculum, but every statement and analytical discussion (*talmud*) he hears.

The agency of the angels in the *Sar-Torah* texts also has a magical model in the conjuration of divinitory figures who will answer any questions the practitioner asks. Ascetic rituals and incantations for these figures, who sometimes descend in dreams, are found in Jewish and non-Jewish magical texts. They also appear in the Hekhalot corpus, and are often identified with the *Sar ha-Panim*, the Prince of the Presence. An unusual incantation for the Great Name promises a "man" who will visit the individual— perhaps like the "man of dreams" referred to in several Rabbinic sources, himself the ancestor, as it were, of the angelic *Maggid* who visited Joseph Karo and other pre-modern Jewish intellectuals.[56] This idea has numerous parallels in Mediterranean magic, most notably the *paredroi* of the Greek Magical Papyri, the supernatural "assistants" who will perform any task the conjurer commands.[57]

The *Sar-Torah* and related magical literature maintain the scholastic virtues of Torah study, reverence for authority and respect of protocol. But unlike the Babylonian Rabbis, whose magical power was said to be derived from their mastery of Torah,[58] these practitioners sought to acquire Torah—as well as its tangible social benefits—through their magic. Like the examples of

---

Jews. See Fred Rosner, ed. and trans., *Julius Preuss' Biblical and Talmudic Medicine* (New York: Hebrew Publishing Company, 1983), 104-05; Preuss notes Rabbinic expressions (for example, b. *Menaḥ*. 80b and *Yeb*. 9a: "He doesn't have a brain in his skull") that also ascribe intellectual function to the brain. That idea, however, is not found in our corpus.

[56] For the Great Name incantation, see Schäfer, *Synopse*, §§489-495. On the "man of dreams" see, for example, t. *Ma'as. Sheni* 5:9; cf. y. *Ma'as. Sheni* 55b; cf. b. *Sanh*. 30a. On Joseph Karo's *Maggid* and its precedents see R. J. Zwi Werblowsky, *Joseph Karo: Lawyer and Mystic* (London: Oxford University Press, 1962), 38-50; see especially pp. 46-48 on angelic figures and dream divination.

[57] On this phenomenon see Leda Jean Ciraolo, "Conjuring and Assistant: *Paredroi* in the Greek Magical Papyri" (Ph.D. thesis, University of California at Berkeley, 1992), and *idem*, "Supernatural Assistants in the Greek Magical Papyri" in this volume.

[58] See the sources cited in n. 12 above.

magical midrash described above, these texts at once reinforce the
Rabbinic sources of authority and appropriate their power for the
practitioners' purposes.

*   *   *

The phenomena described here can tell us about the relationship
between the central values of ancient and medieval Judaic society
and the subculture of magical practitioners. In the first case, we
have seen how Rabbinic notions of tradition and scholastic succession serve the cause of the magical text or ritual. In the second, we
have seen how techniques drawn from the literature of Jewish and
Mediterranean magic are deployed for the purposes of increasing
the individual's prowess in what Rabbinic Jews considered to be the
greatest form of piety—the study of Torah. In each case, the
phenomenon's indebtedness to the central values of the society is
offset by a tendency at odds with those values. The magical text
not only uses the ideal figures and chains of tradition for purposes
not intended by the originators of those patterns of succession, but
circumvents the scholastic process by which only a dialectical
system of learning and discipleship can reveal God's word to the
individual. The same is true for the *Sar-Torah* and memory rituals.
They seek to bypass the Rabbinic academic process by offering a
kind of magical shortcut to the success and prestige of a sage.
These factors have subtle social ramifications. By seeking media-
tion between the priorities of the elite and the needs of the individual, our practitioners both acknowledge their dependence on the
larger society and create an avenue for their own power.

Is the magician a subversive? If we consider it subversive to employ a system's values for purposes not necessarily advocated by
that system, then the Jewish magician may be one. Jewish magicians seem to have functioned in Jewish societies neither as out-
casts nor as those who held the reigns of power. The proliferation
of magic among all classes of late-antique and medieval Jewish
societies suggests that magicians were tolerated, if suspiciously, by
official society.[59] Yet their attitude to human authority was one of
ambivalence. They appropriated the image and charisma of the
Rabbis and biblical sages for their praxis, thus siphoning off, as it
were, a bit of their power but not seizing it entirely.

---

[59] On the social standing of the Genizah magicians and their clients, see
Schiffman and Swartz, *Incantation Texts*, 49-52.

With regard to divine authority, Jewish magic is clear. The authors of Jewish amulets and other magical texts are in continual need to validate their practices by showing that their power derives from God and is sanctioned by those most in communication with him. Magical names serve as tokens of divine authorization and permit the practitioner to marshall the deity's power for the needs of their clients. We might therefore say that our magicians are addressing, in their own way, the problem of providence. How does the divine providential power arrive at the level of the individual? Our practitioners are in the business of working out the mechanics of that process. They do so in confidence of the approval of God and the sages.

CHAPTER ELEVEN

THE ADJURATION OF THE PRINCE OF THE PRESENCE: PERFORMATIVE UTTERANCE IN A JEWISH RITUAL

Rebecca Lesses

The adjuration of the Sar ha-Panim, the Prince of the Presence,[1] is found in the early Jewish mystical texts known as the Hekhalot literature.[2] This adjuration calls on ꜢOzhayꜢa, the Prince of the Presence, to come down to earth and reveal wisdom to

---

[1] My thanks to Bernadette Brooten and Adele Reinharz for their help in revising this article. I also acknowledge the support of a Fulbright-Hays Doctoral Dissertation Research Abroad Grant for the period of October 1992 - August 1993; for part of the time of the grant I was revising this article.

[2] The adjuration of the Sar ha-Panim is found in four large medieval European manuscripts of the Hekhalot literature: MS New York JTS 8128, MS Oxford 1531 (Michael 9), MS Munich 40, and MS Dropsie 436. The first three manuscripts are Ashkenazic, and the last one is Sephardic. None is earlier than the 14th century (Peter Schäfer, ed., *Synopse zur Hekhalot-Literatur* [Tübingen: Mohr, 1981], IX). The Hekhalot material contained in these four manuscripts has been published in the *Synopse* in paragraphs §623 to §639. Part of paragraph §623 is also represented in one of the Geniza fragments of the Hekhalot literature, T.-S. K 21.95.S. This fragment has been dated to before the 9th century (Peter Schäfer, ed., *Geniza-Fragmente zur Hekhalot-Literatur* [Tübingen: Mohr, 1984], 10).

The adjuration of the Sar ha-Panim appears to be self-contained; it does not obviously belong to any of the other larger groupings of Hekhalot material (Peter Schäfer, "Die Beschwörung des *sar ha-panim*: Edition und Übersetzung," in *idem, Hekhalot-Studien* [Tübingen: Mohr, 1988], 120). There appear to be two recensions of the adjuration: one represented by the European manuscripts, and one by the Geniza fragment. Within the European manuscripts, MSS Munich 40 and Dropsie frequently give the same readings, and seem to be closer to MS Oxford than to MS New York. As Schäfer remarks, MS New York has many special readings (Schäfer, "Die Beschwörung des *Sar ha-Panim*," 122). The Geniza fragment of §623 is significantly different from the other manuscripts, but clearly comprises the same introductory paragraph of instructions.

The Hekhalot literature has been dated anywhere from the 3rd to the 9th century CE, originating in Palestine or Babylon. Recently, Michael Swartz has traced a process of development of one Hekhalot text from 4th century Palestine through to Babylon in the 9th-10th century (*Mystical Prayer in Ancient Judaism* [Tübingen: Mohr, 1992], 216-20). In my discussion, I will assume that a similar process of development is true for many of the Hekhalot texts. For the adjuration of the Sar ha-Panim I assume a later Babylonian dating and provenance.

human beings, "like a man who speaks to his friend."[3] The Prince
of the Presence is the greatest angel in heaven, second only to God
in power and control. The adjuration is introduced by ascetic
preparations, goes on to a four-fold adjuration of the angel by
divine and angelic Names, and ends with the dismissal of the angel
from the presence of the adept.

The adjuration begins with an initial pseudepigraphic framing
paragraph in which Rabbi Aqiba asks Rabbi Eliezer the Great how
one can "adjure the Prince of the Presence to descend to earth to
reveal to man secrets of above and below . . . secrets of wisdom and
subtlety of knowledge."[4] It continues with Rabbi Eliezer's account
of how he once caused the Prince of the Presence to descend in
such a way that he sought to destroy the world. The narrative then
moves from a dialogue between Rabbi Eliezer and Rabbi Aqiba to
the narrator's instructions addressed to the implied reader of the
incantation.[5] The narrator gives instructions on how to bring down
the Prince of the Presence in a safe manner:

> The one who binds himself to make theurgic use of him (*lě-hištammeš*
> *bô*) should sit in fast one day, and before that day he should sanctify him-
> self seven days from seminal emission *(kerî)*, dip himself in the water-
> canal, and not have conversation with his wife.[6] At the end of the days of
> his fasting and purification, on the day of his fast, he should go down and
> sit in water up to his neck, and say before he adjures . . . .[7]

The words "The one who binds himself to make theurgic use of
him" could refer back to Rabbi Aqiba but also potentially to the
implied reader of the passage—or even both at the same time,
justifying the reader's (possibly) engaging in the adjuration by
reference to the authority of Rabbi Eliezer and Rabbi Aqiba. Following the instructions come an adjuration to defend the adjurer
against the dangerous angels who injure those who are not worthy,
a mention of the 42-letter Name of God by which the adjurer seals

---

[3] §634.

[4] §623.

[5] The shift from dialogue to address of the implied reader is clearer in the version of the text found in the Geniza fragment (see note 37, which gives a translation of the entire Geniza text). For an initial discussion of reader-response
criticism, from which the term "implied reader" is taken, see Steven Mailloux,
"Learning to Read: Interpretation and Reader-Response Criticism," in *Studies in
the Literary Imagination* 12 (1979): 93-108.

[6] Only MS New York has the words *ʾim ʾishto* ("with his wife"); the other
European manuscripts merely say, "should not have conversation."

[7] This translation follows the New York manuscript.

himself for strength and protection,[8] and finally a rendition of the adjuration itself by which ᵓOzhayᵓa, the Prince of the Presence, can be brought down to earth.[9] The initial paragraph provides a Rabbinic framework for the adjuration and instructions for purification, while the subsequent sections of the text include an adjuration against harm as well as the actual adjuration of the Prince of the Presence. Rabbi Eliezer's words to Rabbi Aqiba seem intended to provide a Rabbinic testimony for the authenticity, effectiveness, and licit nature of the practice which the text describes.

In this essay I use J. L. Austin's theory of the performative use of language to analyze the adjuration as a ritual.[10] Austin's theory of language is appropriate for the analysis of adjurations and other ritual speech, because it accounts both for the active force of words and for the ritual setting within which they have their force. Thus, my analysis considers both the preparations that the adjurer must undergo and the words of adjuration that he speaks to the angels. I will first outline Austin's theory, and then show how it can be applied to the initial paragraph of instructions and to the words of the adjuration itself. However, before I begin, I will briefly discuss some of the problems caused by the literary nature of the evidence for the adjuration, which might stand in the way of analyzing it as a ritual.

As I have described above, the adjuration is placed within the framework of a pseudepigraphic dialogue between Rabbi Eliezer and Rabbi Aqiba. All that is available is a literary presentation of the ritual.[11] We cannot observe it to see how someone might actually have performed it, ask the participant what it means to him and what his experience of it is, or even know if the ritual was ever actually performed.[12] However, although the text of this particular

---

[8] §§624-25. I refer to the adjurer in the masculine because the text instructs the adept to purify himself from seminal emission.

[9] §§626-38.

[10] The discussion will be based on Austin's *How to Do Things with Words*, eds. J. O. Urmson and Marina Sbisa, 2nd ed. (Cambridge: Harvard University Press, 1975). For a definition of ritual, see Stanley Tambiah, "A Performative Approach to Ritual," in *idem, Culture, Thought and Social Action: An Anthropological Perspective* (Cambridge: Harvard University Press, 1985), 128.

[11] One of the signal disadvantages to working with historical texts rather than observing present-day rituals is, of course, the fact that only the literary mention of the ritual remains. This is a particular problem in the Hekhalot texts, which present almost all of the rituals of adjuration in the framework of pseudepigraphic dialogues between Tannaitic rabbis, and do not in any case provide a first-person account.

[12] For a later period there is evidence for actual use of invocation rituals.

adjuration does not provide enough evidence to decide if anyone
ever recited it, there is ample evidence both from the land of Israel
and from Babylon in the late Byzantine/early Arab period that
both Jews and non-Jews made use of incantations and amulets for
many different purposes.[13] My analysis of the ritual only seeks to
understand the directions and the adjuration itself within the literary Hekhalot setting of the text, rather than in an actual performance. In any case, the instructions for the adjuration of the Prince
of the Presence do not give many details on what the adjurer
should experience, except to say that the angel should speak to
him as a man speaks to his friend; it does not contain a report of
his experience. An additional limitation on the scope of what it is
possible to learn from the text is imposed by its presentation as
ritual. Ritual is conventionalized action; rituals are not meant to
express the intentions, emotions, and states of mind of individuals
in a direct, spontaneous, and natural way.[14] For this reason, and

---

Keith Thomas says about the "notory art" practised in 17th century England:
"There is no doubt whatsoever that these rituals were extensively practiced, both
by contemporary intellectuals and by less educated would-be magicians. The so-
called 'Books of Magic' often found in manuscript collections of the period
contain quite explicit formulae for invoking spirits, and there is no shortage of
evidence for such *séances* in the manuscript 'Books of Experiments' which have
survived" (*Religion and the Decline of Magic* [New York: Scribner's, 1971],
230). At least some of these invocations drew on earlier Jewish adjurations
(Thomas refers to the *Key of Solomon*, which includes invocations based on
Jewish traditions).

[13] See many of the incantation bowls from Babylonia; the bowl-texts refer to
the expulsion of demons from all parts of a person's house (Charles Isbell, *Corpus
of the Aramaic Incantation Bowls* [Missoula: Scholars Press, 1975]). Both the
incantation bowls and the Aramaic amulets from the land of Israel call on angels
to help the person named in the amulet. See, for example, amulet 7 in Joseph Naveh
and Shaul Shaked, *Amulets and Magic Bowls: Aramaic Incantations of Late
Antiquity*, 2nd ed. (Jerusalem: Magnes Press, 1987), 68-69: "Put mercy from
heaven on SLWNH. In the name of Michael, Raphael, ʿAzael, ʿAzriel, ʾAriel ...
you holy angels who stand in front of the throne of the great God." There is also
evidence for the use of other adjurations that are related to the adjuration of the
Sar ha-Panim. See, for example, the series of prayers/adjurations known as *Sheva
Zutarti*, which is built on the framework of the prayer of the ʿAmidah recited on
the Sabbath. There are several Geniza fragments of this text (published in P.
Schäfer, *Geniza-Fragmente*, 135-158), and MS Oxford 1531 (Michael 9) also
preserves a version. The Geniza fragments present the adjurations as a formulary,
without the name of a specific person, while the scribe of the Oxford manuscript
(Yedidyah b. Yitzhak ha-Levi) has filled in his name at appropriate points (fol.
115a-116b).

[14] Stanley Tambiah, "A Performative Approach to Ritual," 132.

because of the literary nature of the evidence, the experience or feelings of the person who might have enacted the ritual of the adjuration of the Prince of the Presence will not become clear in an analysis of the adjuration. It will only be possible to determine what this person should experience, not what he actually does experience.

*   *   *

The English philosopher of language, J. L. Austin, developed a theory of verbal utterances as performers of action, not only as descriptive of action. The term *performative utterance* "indicates that the issuing of the utterance is the performing of an action—it is not normally thought of as just saying something."[15] Austin initially opposed the "performative" to the "constative" (which describes or reports), but then came to see them as existing on the same continuum. The quintessential example of the performative utterance is the marriage ceremony: "When I say, before the registrar or altar, &c., 'I do,' I am not reporting on a marriage: I am indulging in it."[16] According to Austin, the most obvious and easily defined performative utterance is phrased in the first person singular present indicative active.[17]

An explicit performative utterance, in order to work, must be spoken in certain defined circumstances. This is where Austin's theory seems to be most useful for the analysis of ritual, since many rituals (particularly a carefully constructed one like the adjuration of the Prince of the Presence) must take place in certain circumstances in order to work.[18] John Searle, who built on Austin's speech-act theory, also notes the importance of what he calls the "institutional facts." As he says, "It is only given the institution of marriage that certain forms of behavior constitute Mr. Smith's marrying Miss Jones." A "system of constitutive rules" undergirds an institution; in fact, this system creates the institution, and it is only by acting according to the rules of the institution that one can felicitiously act.[19] I will discuss these

---

[15] Austin, *How to Do Things with Words*, 6-7.

[16] *Ibid.*, 6.

[17] *Ibid.*, 56.

[18] See Austin's references to the utility of his conditions with reference to discussion of rituals, 19 and 25.

[19] John Searle, *Speech Acts: An Essay in the Philosophy of Language* (Cambridge: Cambridge University Press, 1969), 51-52.

circumstances (or "constitutive rules") first, and then go into a discussion of the varieties of the performative utterance itself.

Austin describes six conditions which govern the successful operation of a "highly developed explicit performative," and he calls the possibilities of what can go wrong the doctrine of the "Infelicities." The Infelicities can apply to any ritual or ceremonial act, even one which contains no words at all.[20] In contrast to a constative utterance, a performative utterance can be "happy" or "unhappy," rather than right or wrong. His six conditions are as follows:

(A. 1)　There must exist an accepted conventional procedure having a certain conventional effect, that procedure to include the uttering of certain words by certain persons in certain circumstances, and further,

(A. 2)　the particular persons and circumstances in a given case must be appropriate for the invocation of the particular procedure invoked.

(B. 1)　The procedure must be executed by all participants both correctly and

(B. 2)　completely.

(C. 1)　Where, as often, the procedure is designed for use by persons having certain thoughts or feelings, or for the inauguration of certain consequential conduct on the part of any participant, then a person participating in and so invoking the procedure must in fact have those thoughts or feelings, and the participants must intend so to conduct themselves, and further

(C. 2)　must actually so conduct themselves subsequently.[21]

While Austin concentrated on the social circumstances which allowed an utterance to have force, many of those who followed him in developing speech-act theory focused instead on the intentions of the individual who is speaking. For example, Searle "uses 'promising,'—in place of Austin's oath of marriage . . . —to serve

---

[20] Austin, *How to Do Things with Words*, 25.
[21] *Ibid.*, 14-15.

as paradigmatic of our ways of 'doing things with words.'"[22] In doing so, he concentrated on the "good intentions" of the one doing the promising, rather than emphasizing the social rules that make it possible to promise.[23] In my analysis, however, I will be following Austin's initial impulse to focus on the norms governing a given ritual, rather than on the intentions of the one participating in the ritual, because the adjuration of the Prince of the Presence (including the introductory dialogue section) provides no information about the expected or real state of mind of the adjurer. It only gives information on the state of purity that the adjurer must attain, where he must recite the adjuration, and the words of the adjuration itself.

What exactly is a *performative utterance*? Austin developed a three-fold distinction between locutionary acts, illocutionary acts, and perlocutionary acts. A *locutionary act* is the act of saying something: making noises, which are words in a certain grammatical construction, which have a meaning. Thus any speech act "does something," in this sense.[24] The question is whether it does more than that. An *illocutionary act* is the performance of an act *in* saying something.[25] It is a conventional act, done as conforming to a convention.[26] "Something happens" when one performs an illocutionary act because one acts within an already established framework in which one's words have an effect (i.e., the "felicitious conditions" outlined above are met). If one's words meet with failure it is because one of the conditions has not been met. A *perlocutionary act* is one which produces certain consequential effects upon the feelings, thoughts, or actions of the audience, or of the speaker, or of other persons, and it may be done with the design, intention, or purpose of producing them.[27] It is not a conventional act. To give a brief example which may make these distinctions clearer: A locution is: "He said that . . ." An illocution is: "He argued that . . ." A perlocution is: "He convinced me that . . ."[28] There is a difference of emphasis between illocutionary and perlocutionary acts: an illocutionary act focuses

---

[22] Michelle Z. Rosaldo, "The things we do with words: Ilongot speech acts and speech act theory in philosophy," *Lang. Soc.* 11 (1982): 211.

[23] *Ibid.*, Rosaldo's article is a cogent critique of Searle's emphasis on intention in his development of speech-act theory.

[24] Austin, *How to Do Things with Words*, 94.

[25] *Ibid.*, 100.

[26] *Ibid.*, 105.

[27] *Ibid.*, 101.

[28] *Ibid.*, 102.

on my action, and a perlocutionary act focuses on how my action
has an effect on others, for example, the difference between: "I
argue that X is true" and "I persuaded them that X was true." My
argument does not necessarily convince them, but in arguing I did,
in fact, perform an act.

Austin describes five general classes of "illocutionary forces of
an utterance," which were subsequently revised by Searle.[29] His five
illocutionary forces consist of verdictives (the giving of a verdict
or a reckoning), exercitives (exercising power), commissives
(promising or undertaking to do something), behabitives (relating
to attitudes and social behavior), and expositives (making plain
how people use words in the course of an argument or conversation).[30] The second and third categories, exercitives and commissives, are most commonly found in the adjuration. Austin defines
exercitives as the "exercising of powers, rights, or influence . . .
[Their] consequences may be that others are 'compelled' or
'allowed' or 'not allowed' to do certain acts."[31] Examples that he
gives are: appoint, dismiss, name, order, choose, command.[32]
About commissives Austin says, "The whole point of a commissive is to commit the speaker to a certain course of action." Examples which he gives are: bind myself, give my word, vow.[33] To
sum up these two categories, "the exercitive is an assertion of

---

[29] *Ibid.*, 150-51. At this point Austin changes his terminology from
"illocutionary act" to "illocutionary forces" to refer to the general type of force of
a verb in a particular category. See John Searle, "A Taxonomy of Illocutionary
Acts" in *Expression and Meaning: Studies in the Theory of Speech Acts*
(Cambridge: Cambridge University Press, 1979): 12-20.

[30] Austin, 151-152. Searle's taxonomy includes assertives, directives, commissives, expressives, and declarations. Although I follow Austin's categories
here, I think that his categorization would be more complete if Searle's category
of "declarations" was added. "Declarations bring about some alteration in the
status or condition of the referred to object or objects solely in virtue of the fact
that the declaration has been successfully performed" (Searle, 17). Examples
would be "I resign," "You're fired," "War is declared," etc. Austin puts these
into the category of "exercitives," but it seems to me that there is a sufficient
difference between these types of declarations and other exercises of power to
justify an additional category. This is an area where more research is needed with
specific reference to the types of illocutionary forces found in the Hekhalot
adjurations (as M. Rosaldo did in the classification of illocutionary forces in
Ilongot speech).

[31] *Ibid.*, 151. This is close to Searle's category of "directives."

[32] *Ibid.*, 155-56.

[33] *Ibid.*, 157-58.

influence or exercising of power, the commissive is an assuming of an obligation or declaring of an intention."[34]

*   *   *

Austin's theory accounts both for the conditions in which speech must be uttered in order to be effective as well as the specific force of various utterances. In the analysis that follows I consider first the conditions or circumstances that govern the adjuration of the Prince of the Presence, going through Austin's conditions of "Felicity" in order, and then I go on to analyze the specific utterances that the adjurer speaks in order to bring down the angel, showing particularly how the verbs of adjuration work together with the Names of God to produce the illocutionary effect. Before beginning the analysis itself, I provide at this point a translation of the introductory paragraph of instructions (§623), and an overview of the contents of the adjuration.

Overview of the Adjuration of the Prince of the Presence
(Synopse §623-639)

1. [§623, according to MS New York]
  Rabbi Aqiba asked Rabbi Eliezer the Great, "How do they adjure the Prince of the Presence to descend to earth, to reveal to man secrets of above and below, depths of foundations of above and below, secrets of wisdom and subtlety of knowledge?"
  He said to me, "My son, one time I caused him to descend, and he sought to destroy the entire world, for he is the mightiest prince among all the heavenly retinue, and stands always and serves before the king of the world, in cleanness, separation (perishut), purity, fear and awe, for the glory of his creator, for the Shekhinah is with him in every place."
  I said to him, "Rabbi, behold, I bind him sevenfold,[35] according to the instruction which you taught me,[36] at the time that I bind myself to make theurgic use of him (le-hištammeš bô)."

---

[34] Ibid., 163.

[35] The notes to the German translation of this passage suggest that the word translated here "sevenfold" (ŠBʿH) could be a mistake for "oath" (ŠBWʿH). See Peter Schäfer, ed., Übersetzung der Hekhalot-Literatur IV, §§598-985 (Tübingen: Mohr, 1991), 19.

[36] This is an emendation, based on a combination of MS New York and MS Dropsie. Schäfer's translation in his edition of the text is "mittels der Lehre, die

He said to me, "The one who binds himself to make theurgic
use of him should sit in fast one day, and before that day he
should sanctify himself seven days from seminal emission (kerî),
dip himself in the water-canal, and not have conversation with
his wife. At the end of the days of his fasting and purification,
on the day of his fast, he should go down and sit in water up to
his neck, and say before he adjures."[37]

2. Adjurations against the dangerous angels who threaten the
person who is not fit to "make theurgic use of the servants of
the Most High." One of the Names employed is that of the
"Prince who injures and burns up all of the destroying angels."
(§624-625)

3. First "Call" of ʾOzhayʾa, the Prince of the Presence (this is
the only time his Name is mentioned) "by this Name and by
this language." (§626)

4. First "Adjuration" of the Prince of the Presence, using verbs
such as "adjure, decree, be bound to me, accept my oath and decree, perform my request, fulfill my desire," combined with
verbs telling him not to injure the adjurer. The strength of the
adjurer is emphasized. (§627)

5. Second "Call" of the Prince of the Presence, "by your four-
teen Names," which are revealed to prophets and seers. This
"Call" gives fourteen pērush (explicit) and kinnuy (substitute)
Names. (§628)

6. Second "Adjuration" by fourteen Names (probably of God).
Four are engraved on the heads of the holy creatures (ḥayyôt),
four are engraved on the four sides of God's throne, four are engraved on the crowns of the ʾôfānnim (a class of angels), and
two are engraved on God's crown. These Names are not the
same as the fourteen Names in the second "Call." (§629-633).

---

du mich gelehrt hast" (P. Schäfer, "Die Beschwörung des śar ha-panim," 124).

[37] The Geniza fragment of this passage is as follows: "Rabbi Aqiba asked
Rabbi Eliezer the Great, he said to him, 'How do they adjure the Prince of
Princes of Princes to descend to earth?' He said to him, 'One time I caused him to
descend, and he sought to destroy the entire world, for he is the mightiest prince
among all the heavenly retinue, and stands always and serves before the king of
the world, because the Shekhinah is with him in every place.' He said to him,
'The one who binds himself to make theurgic use of him should sit in fast one
day, and before that day he should sanctify himself for seven days, and on the
eighth day, the day of his purification . . .'" (the fragment breaks off at this point).
The Hebrew text is from T.-S. K21.95.S, F/22-33, published by Schäfer, Geniza-
Fragmente, 16-17.

This adjuration orders the Prince of the Presence to descend to the adjurer and reveal mysteries to him. (§634)

7. Third "Call" of the angel, by his five Names. (§635)

8. Third "Adjuration" of the angel, again by five Names, to descend and do the will of the adjurer. These Names are not the same as in #7, and appear to be Names of God. (§636)

9. Fourth "Call" of the angel, by the greatest of his Names. This Name is given in two forms, one comprising a combination of permutations of the Tetragrammaton plus other Hebrew letters, and the other its form in the "language of purity," permutations of the letters of the Tetragrammaton. (§637)

10. Fourth "Adjuration" of the angel by the Name of God (probably—it is not the same as the Name in the fourth "Call"). The second part of this Adjuration orders the angel not to prevent the adjurer's words from operating and not to change his decree. (§638)

11. Dismissal of the Prince of the Presence—"Ascend in peace," followed by a protective charm in Aramaic against demons.

(A.1.) Austin's first condition calls for an "accepted conventional procedure having a certain conventional effect." The framers of the Hekhalot adjuration believed that certain letters, the letters of God's Name, were used by God in creating the world.[38] The adjuration asserts that God himself set up the conventional procedure in which the Names have power if they are spoken by human beings: "about them you were ordered and warned from the mouth of the Highest that if you heard an oath by these Names, do honor to your Name, and hurry and descend and do the will of your adjurer" (§636). God himself warned the angels that if they heard these Names they must obey the one who speaks them. This is not a procedure originated by human beings; it has divine authority behind it. Human utterance of the divine Names has divine power behind it.

According to Austin's analysis, performative utterances have an effect because they act within the institutions of human society. The particular culture within which this adjuration was composed and used saw the human and divine realms as intimately connected.[39] Society extended beyond the human to include angels,

---

[38] See §§16, 57-60, 634.

[39] For an overview of the larger framework of Hekhalot texts of which the adjuration is a part, see Peter Schäfer, *The Hidden and Manifest God* (Albany:

demons (who do not play an important role in the Hekhalot
texts), and God, and thus performative utterances could have an
effect in extra-human institutions, particularly within the ordered
divine/angelic hierarchy. To put it another way, the social world of
the adjurer did not consist wholly of (possible) mystical circles, the
larger Jewish community, and then the larger non-Jewish community; it included as well close links with the angelic/divine and
demonic realms.[40] The world was inhabited by more than just
humans; it was filled as well by a multitude of angels and demons.
This view of the world made plausible both ascents to the
Merkabah and adjurations of angels to descend from heaven.

In the Hekhalot texts the divine/angelic hierarchy contains several elements: (1) God, the creator of heaven, earth, angels, and
humans; (2) the divine Names, by which God created everything,
including the angels and the divine Throne;[41] (3) the highest angels, including the Prince of the Presence, and their Names; (4)
angels on a lower level, like the "princes of fear," who are appointed to attack those who are not worthy of "making theurgic
use" of the angels (§624); and (5) the pure human being, who can
make use of the Names of creation to force the Prince of the
Presence to do his will (§§636-637). Acts which people can perform verbally if they possess sufficient power in a particular human institution (e.g., a king ordering a subject to come into his
presence) provide an analogy for the types of acts which people
with sufficient power can order angels to do. Extra-human society
is built on a model similar to (but not necessarily identical with)
human society; laws and modes of operation which work in human
society also work in that society. Thus humans can interact with
the denizens of the extra-human world as they might act with
other humans. An example from related texts shows this analogy
even more clearly. In the incantation bowls from Babylonia, which
have some formulae in common with the Hekhalot texts, the
relationships between people served as an exact analogy for the
relationships between humans and demons, and words which had
power in human interaction also worked with regard to the demons. In one formula used by the authors of the bowl-texts, the

---

SUNY Press, 1992).

[40] See, for example, *b. Ber.* 6b, on how to see the demons.

[41] §634, 637, 59. These names include both the Tetragrammaton and names
which combine letters of the Tetragrammaton with other letters of the Hebrew
alphabet.

words of the Jewish divorce document (*get*) served to exorcise the demons.[42] Just as humans marry and divorce, so do demons, and the unwanted attentions of the demons (both male and female) are conceived of as a marriage which the human partner (either male or female) can dissolve by pronouncing the words of the *get* against them.

An important part of the procedure of the adjuration is the "uttering of certain words." When human beings know "certain words," then they can effect the descent of the Prince of the Presence from heaven. The words which the adjurer uses are both words used in ordinary speech, verbs such as "I decree," "I ordain," and special words: the Names of the Prince of the Presence and the Names of God. Uttering these words is part of the "accepted conventional procedure" of bringing down the Prince of the Presence, and knowledge of these special words is part of what singles out the adjurer as one fit to bring him down. The adjuration of the Prince of the Presence spells out the accepted procedure (with divine authorization) for calling the angel down and learning wisdom from him. This important matter is not left to the individual imagination of the person who wishes to speak to the angel. The framers of the adjuration carefully worked out a procedure to draw him down. They accepted it as legitimate, and they tried to indicate (and advocate for) its acceptance, by putting the words of the instructions in the mouths of Rabbi Aqiba and Rabbi Eliezer the Great.

(A.2.) Austin says that "the particular persons and circumstances in a given case must be appropriate for the invocation of the particular procedure invoked." The person who says this adjuration must be in a specific relation to the powers which constitute his world in order for his words to be effective in the ritual. As I said, the Hekhalot texts assume a system of power leading from God as the most powerful, to the Prince of the Presence and the other angels, and finally to human beings. Certain people, by virtue of their ascetic practices, are able to gain power in the system, say the words of the adjuration effectively, and bring down the Prince of the Presence. Knowledge of the divine or angelic Names is also crucial to placing the adept in a position of power. (Other parts of the Hekhalot literature spell out other moral or purity requirements to descend to the Merkabah.) According to the directions

---

[42] See for example, James Montgomery, *Aramaic Incantation Texts from Nippur* (Philadelphia: University of Pennsylvania, The Museum, 1913), bowl texts 8 and 17.

spelled out in section §623, the adept must purify himself from any seminal emission for seven days (so we know that the adept must be male), immerse himself in a river, not converse with others (particularly women, according to MS New York), and on the eighth day, fast, immerse himself, and speak the words of the adjuration. He should be sitting in a river in water up to his neck as he is speaking the adjuration. By following these directions, the adept isolates himself from other people and ordinary human life. He comes to approach the angelic state of purity, which in other parts of the Hekhalot literature is contrasted with the human state of impurity (§181-182). In this condition he is fit to say the words of adjuration. §624 spells out the dangers for the person who has not reached the appropriate state of purity; if he dares to say the adjuration, "the princes of fear" will attack him.

(B.1. & 2.) Rabbi Eliezer's words, "one time I caused him to descend and he sought to destroy the entire world," imply that it is possible to execute the procedure incorrectly. The Prince of the Presence is not only a powerful angel who can reveal secrets to human beings; he is also dangerous, as is made clear at several points in the adjuration. The adjurer must be very careful to say the correct words in order to control the angel. At a number of points in the adjuration, the adjurer orders the angel not to injure him. The danger is not merely that one could fail to bring the angel down; in fact, the adjuration does not mention this possibility. Failure to follow the correct procedure could result in the destruction of the world, or in injury to the adjurer. Because this is the real danger in the incorrect or incomplete execution of the procedure, the adjurer must continually order the angel not to hurt him and not to distort his speech.

(C.1. & 2.) The text of the adjuration provides no information on the state of mind or intention of the participants. However, one might be able to learn from the requirements for fasting and purification that the human participant needs to have a serious and solemn attitude towards the utterance of the adjuration and the goal of bringing the angel down to earth.[43]

My analysis of the first part of the adjuration has made clear the circumstances in which the adjuration must be uttered and the

---

[43] For a similar formulation, see Sam D. Gill, "Prayer as Person: The Performative Force in Navajo Prayer Acts," *History of Religions* 17 (1977): 155: "The participants ... must have proper and serious intentions. They must demonstrate these intentions by observing specific dietary and social restrictions before, during, and after the performance of the ceremonial."

qualifications that the adjurer must possess. In the analysis that follows I will discuss the two elements of illocutionary force in the adjuration: verbs that fit the category of "performative utterances," and the Names of God and the angel which provide further power for the illocutionary force of the verbs.

The second part of the adjuration (§§624-639) offers many examples of verbs or verbal phrases that fit the category of "performative utterances" very closely, particularly those phrased in the first person, singular, participle form. Examples are: "I adjure," usually in conjunction with the words, "by the Name . . ."; "I decree," "I call to you by X Name," "I establish." These words are not descriptive of other actions, they are actions in their own right. The emphasis is on what the adjurer is doing, not on the consequences of his act; these are illocutionary acts, not perlocutionary acts. The words do not need any concomitant physical action to take effect; they need only to be spoken, usually in conjunction with a series of divine or angelic Names. They belong in the category of "exercitives," because they consist of the exercising of power. The adjuration interweaves "calling" on the angel by his many Names, and adjuring him by the many Names of God to follow the orders of the adjurer. In the first paragraph of the adjuration there is an example of a commissive, when it says, "at the time that I bind myself to make theurgic use of him." This use of the verb indicates that he is committing himself to do something, in this case to make theurgic use of the angel, while the use of the same word to apply to the angel, "I bind him sevenfold (or, by an oath)," is an example of an exercitive, because it is an exercise of his power over the angel.

The adjuration also contains two other classes of verbs which are performative utterances, but it is a little trickier to figure exactly how they act. The second class consists of positive imperatives issued by the adjurer to the angel or angels: (§627): perform my request! fulfill my plea! (§636): descend quickly! do the will of your adjurer! act for his Name! (§639): ascend in peace! These are direct orders, calling on the angel to do specific acts. With these verbs the focus of the action shifts from the adjurer to the angel, from the act of adjuration to the acts which the angel should perform. The third class of verbs is that of negative imperatives directed to the angel or angels, in which the adjurer tells them, in a variety of ways, not to hurt him. (§624): do not injure me, do not trouble me, do not frighten me! (§638): do not pervert my lips, do not change my decree! These verbs describe all of the actions which the angel could perform against the will of the adjurer.

An example from §627 may provide a way to understand how these verbs operate as performative utterances: "I adjure you, and I order you further to be bound to my will; you shall accept the oath of my decree; perform my request, fulfill my desire, and do not confuse me ..." The verb "to be bound to my will" depends upon the verb "I order." Although the other verbs do not formally depend upon this verb, it seems to me that they imply such a connection between the will of the adjurer and the angel. These two classes of verbs refer to possible actions of the angel, but they are not actions voluntarily initiated by him; they are ordered by the adjurer. They could be put into the form: "(I order you) to ascend, not to hurt me," etc., so that just as in the first case, the action flows from the adjurer to the angel, and never in the other direction. It might be possible to classify these as perlocutionary acts, since the focus is on what the angel will do as a consequence of the adjurer's order, not on the order itself. Otherwise, one might see the angel's action as part of the illocutionary act in the sense of section C.1. & 2 of Austin's six conditions of felicity: the consequential conduct called for and engaged in is the following of the adjurer's order. It depends on how closely one sees the angel's action as being bound to the adjurer's order; it seems to me that the adjuration tries to tie these two actions very closely together.

There is also another class of verbs which do not directly order or prohibit action of the angel. These verbs either describe the angel, God, other human beings, or most frequently, the Names by which the adjurer swears. Although the various verbs of the adjuration do not seem to need them, in many cases they provide the force for the adjurational verbs. They point out how powerful the divine Names are that the adjurer uses and show how the adjurer can use them to command the angel. Following Austin's scheme, they would seem to fit more closely into the category of "locutions" rather than "illocutions," since they are descriptions and not performatives. However, they are locutions in the service of illocutions, and are not present for their own sake.

*   *   *

An important part of the illocutionary force of the verbs in the adjuration are the angelic and divine Names by which the angel is summoned and by which he is adjured. The "locutionary" phrases that I quoted above strengthen the illocutionary force of the

Names. For example, the incantation in section §625 reads, "Afterwards, he should begin and adjure, because he has strengthened himself, and sealed himself by the Name of 42 letters, which is called QHTY WH HH SNṬQQ RWTT HWR HYH PPNN HYH WH WH ʾG QS YHYH, mighty over all the letters, for those who hear, all the host of heaven, they are agitated and afraid and tremble." Section §624 gives the text of the adjuration of the "princes of fear" by the 42-letter Name, while this section emphasizes the power of this Name. The 42-letter Name frightens and intimidates "all the host of heaven"; it is thus appropriate that the adjurer should use such a Name as a protective seal. This Name is one of the Names of God and as such has inherent power. The locutionary verbs do not themselves act against the angels, but they make clear the power of the Name against the angels.

There are other examples of the importance of locutionary phrases. In paragraph §628 the adjurer calls to the angel by his own Names: "Again I call to you by your fourteen Names, by which you are revealed to prophets and seers, to sweeten words of prophecy in their mouths and to make pleasant words of pleasantness." "Prophets and seers" can make use of these Names in order to reveal the angel and to "sweeten words of prophecy." This section specifies that these Names are powerful for bringing a revelation of the angel. In the same way, they will bring a revelation of the angel to the person who is currently uttering the words of the adjuration.

The fourteen divine Names of sections §§629-634 are powerful in another way because they are "the fourteen Names by which all the hidden secrets, and letters, and seals are made, and in them are the foundations of heaven and earth" (§629). These may be the Names which maintain heaven and earth, or the Names by which heaven and earth were created. In any case, these Names are intimately bound up with the structure of the entire universe. These fourteen Names are engraved on various parts of the structure of heaven: four Names "on the heads of the ḥayyôt," four on the four sides of the divine Throne, four on the crowns of the "ʾōfānnim of power," and two on the crown of God. The Names receive divine titles, such as "Lord of powers," or "Master of wonders." While the previous list of fourteen Names referred to Names of the angel, these particular Names are clearly the powerful Names of God. It is unclear in the context of the adjuration whether the titles refer to God himself or to his Names, although this distinction may be lost on the authors of the adjuration. In another Hekhalot text, Maʿaseh Merkabah, the text reads,

Be sanctified, God of heaven and earth, Lord of lords, mighty of mighty ones, God of the *kerûbim,* who rides on the *kerûbim,* God of hosts whose dominion is over the hosts, God of the servants (=angels), whose Name is sanctified over the servants. He is his Name, and his Name is he, he is in him and his Name is in his Name, song is his Name and his Name is song. (§588, MS Oxford)[44]

A similar passage is found at §557: "his Name is in his strength, and his strength is in his Name, he is his power, and his power is he, and his Name is like his Name" (MS New York). Section §588 uses some of the same titles of God as the adjuration of the Prince of the Presence, and identifies God with his Name: "He is his Name and his Name is he." From the point of view of the adjurer, God and his Name are so close that by calling on God's Name, one is calling on God's own power.

These same fourteen Names are those by which the angel is adjured in section §634 to come down to the adjurer. They are the Names "by which were established the throne of glory and the seat of the highest, a precious instrument by which were made wondrous things of old, before you were formed and before all the host of heaven was refined, before he made earth and fields, and dwellers of earth and creatures of praise." These very Names are those by which God's Throne was made before the creation of both humans and angels, and which thus have power over the angels. In this description of the Names the angel is reminded that he too is created by God, and that there is something higher than him that humans can make use of: the Names of God. Section §636 provides a further example of the reification of the Names and of their power vis-à-vis the angels: "I adjure you by five Names, corresponding to the five of your Names whose letters are written in fire and hover above the throne of glory. One rises and one descends so that the Princes of the Presence will not gaze at them." A similar picture of the "Explicit Names" appears in 3 Enoch: "When the ministering angels utter the 'Holy,' all of the Explicit Names (*šemôt hammefōrašôt*), which are engraved with a flaming pen on the Throne of Glory, fly like eagles with sixteen wings, and surround and go around the Holy One on the four sides of the place of glory of his Shekhinah." The other orders of angels fall on their

---

[44] My translation is based on Michael Swartz, *Mystical Prayer in Judaism,* 244. Schäfer, however, understands this passage differently: "In an almost philosophical manner, the personal pronoun *hû*' ("he [is]") is composed as the name of God: 'He [is]' is his name, and his name is 'he [is]'; 'he [is]' in 'he [is],' and his name in his name" (*The Hidden and Manifest God,* 80).

faces three times and say, "Blessed is the Name of his glorious kingdom for ever and ever" (§57). By these Names everything was created, including all the angels, and the Throne of Glory itself; they sustain and maintain the world (§59). 3 Enoch also points to various heavenly phenomena which exist or are sustained by virtue of specific divine Names. For example, Meṭaṭron showed R. Ishmael "water suspended in the height of ʿarābôt rāqîaʿ by the Name Yāh Ehyeh Ašer Ehyeh ('I am who I am' [Ex 3:14])" (§60). The five Names have power even over the Princes of the Presence, of which the object of this adjuration, ʾOzhayʾa, is one. God ordered the angels to descend to earth when the adjurer uttered these five Names (see discussion above about the "conventional procedure" of the adjuration).

The locutionary phrases that are associated with the Names and make clear their illocutionary force in association with the verbs of adjuration are comprehensible, yet the Names themselves are literally incomprehensible, at least to a modern reader. See, for example, the Names cited in paragraphs §§637-38, which are given in two forms, a series of consonants of the Hebrew alphabet and permutations of the letters of the divine Name ("the language of purity"):

> And thus is its explanation, their blinding light,[45] their power and their adornment: ʾŠŠ MṢQTT MG MSṢYY MPQYY PYPG HWGYY HSS PṢSYH HʾMṢTNYH QSN HWḤP and its explanation in the language of purity, with yûd hē, how it is said: YHWH YW YHWH WW YHWH HW HW YHWH YH HYH YHWH HY WHYY HYW HYH YH YH HHW <YH> YYH HWH YH YHWH YW HY.[46]

How can these Names be understood? I suggest that they were meant to be understood by someone, even if not by the human writers or readers or users of these texts. In contrast to the "demon language" of exorcism, which the demons understand when humans speak to expel them,[47] I suggest that these are the words

---

[45] Following Schäfer's translation, "blendendes Leuchten" (Schäfer, "Die Beschwörung des śar ha-panim," 134).

[46] §637 (MS New York).

[47] The phrase was used by Stanley Tambiah in his discussion of a Sinhalese healing ritual to refer to the type of language by which the exorcist addresses the demons: "When demons are directly addressed and commanded, the words are a polyglot mixture and therefore unintelligible, being compounded of Sinhalese, Tamil, Pali, Sanskrit, Malayalam, Telegu, Bengali, and even Persian. This exotic and powerful mixture is the 'demon language.' ... The 'demon language' is consciously constructed to connote power, and though largely unintelligible is

of the "divine" or "angelic language." Terms like these are found
in 1 Corinthians 13 and T. Job 49-50, referring to the "tongues of
angels" and the specific dialects of the various kinds of angels. One
might even say that there are two "implied readers" for this adjuration: human and angelic. The intended reader or user of the adjuration is the human adept who engages in ascetic preparations and
then utters the adjuration, but his intended audience is the angel.
The angel possesses knowledge beyond that known to the human
adjurer (in this case knowledge of the "language of purity," as the
adjuration puts it) and thus the human being may in fact utter
words in the adjuration that he does not understand. In the context
of the adjuration it is not important that he comprehend them.
What is important is that the angel understands and obeys the
words.

The adjuration of the Prince of the Presence works by the combination of three main elements, two of which act independently.
The Names of God and the angel and verbs with illocutionary force
each independently possess the power to compel the angel to act
in the way that the adjurer desires. The third factor, locutionary
phrases referring to the power of the Names, joins the Names and
the illocutionary verbs together to give the adjurer still more
power to compel the angel. The different sections of this adjuration weave these three elements together, sometimes emphasizing
one element more strongly and sometimes another (e.g., section
§627 almost exclusively uses verbs of the class of exercitives, in
contrast to section §628, which is taken up almost entirely by the
fourteen Names of the Prince of the Presence). At other points all
three elements are present. For example, section §636 begins with
an exercitive, "I adjure you by five Names," brings in a locutionary
phrase in support of the verb ("corresponding to the five of your
Names, whose letters are written in fire and hover above the
Throne of Glory. One rises and one descends so that the Princes of
the Presence will not gaze at them"), and then sets out the five
Names by which the angel is adjured. Following this are several
locutionary phrases linked together in praise of the Names. One of
them claims that the angels were ordered by God to obey anyone
who utters the Names:

---

nevertheless based on the theory of language that the demons can understand"
("The Magical Power of Words," in *Culture, Thought, and Social Action: An
Anthropological Perspective* [Cambridge: Harvard, 1985], 20-21).

You have been commanded and warned from the mouth of the Highest: "If you hear an adjuration by these names, do honor to your name, and hasten and descend and do the will of the one who adjures you. If you hesitate I will push you into the *Rigyôn*[48] of pursuing fire, and make another stand instead of you and instead of your authority."

At this point the adjurer commands the angel by the use of several verbs which act as exercitives that are again backed up by the power of God's Name. This section mentions God's Names twice and spells out the Name once:

Do honor to his name, and hurry and descend to me NN son of NN (f.), not in anger and not in terror and not in flashes of fire and hailstones and walls of anger and storehouses of snow, not in stormwinds and not in powerful whirlwinds which come from you. And perform my demand and uphold my request and fulfill my will for all is in your hand, by the authority of ʾNDDW RDSW HYH my God and your God, the Lord of all and your Lord. By his names I have adjured you, that you be bound to me, and hurry and descend and do my will and do not hesitate.

The adjurer commands the angel both positively ("do honor to his name, and hurry and descend") and negatively ("not in anger and not in terror"). The locutionary phrase that comes after the divine Name emphasizes that the Name refers to the God of both angels and humans, thus telling the angel again that he must obey the one who utters this Name. This section ends with a series of exercitive verbs in which the action flows from the adjurer to the angel, which can be viewed either as verbs of illocutionary force ("I have adjured you that you be bound to me") followed by perlocutionary verbs ("hurry and descend and do my will and do not hesitate") or as one illocutionary act of commanding, in which the necessary consequence of the adjurer's words is the obedience of the angel.

*   *   *

In this essay I have begun to apply the theories of performative language, pioneered by J. L. Austin and further used by anthropologists in the analysis of present-day rituals, to an ancient Jewish ritual text, the adjuration of the Prince of the Presence. Austin's theory has illuminated both the particular circumstances in which the adjuration must take place, and the power of the words that are

---

[48] See §154 and *Pesiq. R.* 97a/b. *Pesiq. R.* 97a/b reads: "*Rigyon*, river of fire [whose coals] burn up angels and humans" (Schäfer, "Beschwörung des *śar ha-panim*," 133, n. 91).

spoken. I hope that this analysis has shed light on how such a series of performative utterances might have worked within the framework of the worldview found in the Hekhalot literature, in particular how the illocutionary verbs work in concert with the powerful divine Names. Although it is impossible to go back and enter into the consciousness of those who wrote, edited, and used this literature, such an analysis can give an idea of a ritual they may have performed and how it may have worked for them.

PART FOUR

MAGIC AND RITUAL POWER
IN GREEK ANTIQUITY

CHAPTER TWELVE

NEW GREEK MAGICAL AND DIVINATORY TEXTS IN BERLIN

William M. Brashear

The ongoing cataloguing of Greek texts in the Ägyptisches Museum und Papyrussammlung der Staatlichen Museen zu Berlin—Preussischer Kulturbesitz has resulted in the following recent accretions. The texts are all written on papyrus in the centuries CE. The provenances unless otherwise indicated are unknown. Vertical measurements precede the horizontal ones: → designates the side with horizontal fibers, ↓ the side with vertical fibers. I thank Donata Baccani (DB), Roy Kotansky (RK), Robert Daniel and Richard Gordon (RG) for reading earlier versions and offering helpful advice; and Joan Christman for proofreading.

Photographs of these texts (used with the permission of the Museum) are presented below, near the end of the present volume.

1. Wartetext

   P. Berol. 21300, 9.2 x 6 cm., fourth century

The papyrus is broken off on all sides except for the upper one. Both surfaces are covered with writing by the same hand. The text on the horizontal fibers is extremely faded and difficult to read, whereas that on the vertical fibers presents no deciphering problems. On the side with vertical fibers is an upper margin of 0.5 cm.

The writing is somewhat similar to that of H. Harrauer and P. Sijpesteijn, *Medizinische Rezepte und Verwandtes* (Vienna: Brüder Hollinek, 1981), no. 6, and may be dated to the fourth century CE or later.

The text so far defies all attempts at explanation—either it is a banal account or a list of prognostic calculations—and must remain for the time being a *Wartetext*. I present it here in hopes that someone will be able to take up where I have left off.

↓

  ]κατοτερε   ζ() α + β δ [
  ]πετε.η.   ζ() γ η η η[
  ]ηικτορδιακ   ζ() δ η α ζ[
  ]ηελεπηρη   ζ() η α η η[
5]πλωσαμαϊ   ζ() η η η γ[
  ]ισαπολου   ζ() η η η . .[
  ]κουϊλομι   ζ() η η η η η[
  ]φιαλζφιη   ζ() - η η γ .[
  ] .   ζ() ε η ε η[

  ————   ————

→

  ]παμ ⟦ζ ιε = .. κδ .⟧ [
  ] ⟦σω ζ ιε - v.⟧ [
  ]   N -   [
  ] traces - N [
5]   H -   [
  ]---.   [
  ]---N   [

  ————

When I first showed this text to the late Otto Neugebauer in 1987, he said he was confident that the *zeta* preceding the figures in ↓ column II was an abbreviation for ζωή. He suggested dividing the words in the left column into syllables, computing their numerical values and comparing these numbers with those in other ancient prognostic calculations.[1] A disconcerting discrepancy (which Neugebauer was unable to explain) was the fact that the numbers following *zeta* in P. Berol. 21300 all belong to the section of θάνατος in the ancient prognostic tables[2] (taking the usual numerical equivalents: α - θ = 1-9, ι - ϙ = 10-90, ρ - ϡ = 100-900).

κατο	391	τερε	510
ικτορ	510	διακ	35
ηελε	48	πηρη	196
πλωσ	1110	αμια	52
ισαπ	291	ολου	570
κουι	500	λομι	150

Neugebauer said some of the numbers in Berthelot could be explained as relevant to the moon and to a shift from syzygies to the Trine aspect. He felt this text might belong to the same genre.

Pursuing, however, the investigation along the lines suggested by Neugebauer resulted in nothing definite, and so I neglected any further work on the papyrus for several years. Recently, Herwig Maehler, going on the basis of κουϊλομι (Coptic "little man"), suggested the entries in the first column might be names. In fact, most of the entries can be identified as names, and parallels are easily located in Friedrich Preisigke, *Namenbuch* (Heidelberg: Preisigke, 1922):

1 Κατοτ: Cf. Preisigke, 168: Κατῦτις = ⲕⲁ̇ⲍⲱⲍ
3 <B>ίκτωρ διάκ(ων): Cf. Preisigke, 76: Βίκτωρ.
5 Πλῶς: Cf. Preisigke, 332. Ἀμᾶϊς: Cf. Preisigke, 22.
6 ισαπολου: Cf. Preisigke, 96: Εἰσαπόλλων = Ἰσαπόλλων.
7 κουϊλομι: Cf. Preisigke, 183: Κοῦι, as well as G. Heuser, "Die koptischen Personennamen ägyptischen Ursprungs" (diss., Heidelberg, *ca.* 1928), 21: ⲕⲟ̇ⲧⲓ.

Is this list just a banal account with names and tallies of goods or money sums? What then does the *zeta* stand for, and what are the series of numbers after it? Accounts never display an entire series of numbers succeeding the names but only a single number indicating either goods or money owed or paid. Hence, I am inclined to catalogue this text among the *magica* and not among run-of-the-mill, pedestrian accounts and tallies.

Are the numbers in the righthand column maybe onomatomantic calculations?[3] So far any attempts to force this text into any system described by the ancients have met with ultimate defeat. Nothing in all of ancient prognostic or divinatory literature seems even remotely to begin to compare to this particularly enigmatic text. *De his rebus videant peritiores.*

2. Apotelesmatikon

P. Berol. 21198, 12.5 x 8 cm., second to third century

The fragment is broken off on all sides except the upper one where there is a margin of 2.5 cm. The present text is written on the horizontal fibers in an elegant, rapid, documentary cursive of the 2nd-3rd centuries, characterized by florid ascenders and descenders. In line 8 there is a semi-high dot. Criteria for determining the original line lengths are non-existent. The astrological text on the vertical fibers of the same fragment (probably originally comprising many columns) was published by G. Ioannidou, *ZPE* 72 (1988): 261f. Ioannidou was able to reconstruct the missing portions of the text on the other side, where only 3-5 letters are lacking from the right of that particular column of writing.

In all likelihood the present text on the horizontal fibers was the first to be written on the roll which undoubtedly contained many columns of writing in its entirety. The roll was probably later turned over for writing the second (astrological) text on the vertical fibers.

The text under consideration is, on the one hand, reminiscent of an *Amtstagebuch* describing the various activities of a government official.[4] Especially the phrase δίκην λέγει ἕνεκα δημοσίω[ν in lines 7 and 9 (?) as well as the verb ἐσπροσωπήσεται lend credence to this interpretation. However, the language is couched in verbs not of the past, recording what has already taken place, but verbs of the future tense, describing what *will* happen. (The two clauses already quoted from lines 7 and 9 which contain present-tense verbs are the only exceptions.) Hence, it might rather be an official's agenda, prescribing his future activities. On the other hand, the phrase τῆς ἰδίας γυνα[ικός (l. 3) smacks more of private than of public affairs.

There are, however, several indications that the text more likely belongs to the corpus of ἀποτελεσματικά, describing the effects which planetary conjunctions and astral positions have on human destinies and mortal affairs. Two such texts are P. Merton 56 (= Pack 2042) and P. Oxy. 465 (= Pack 2056)[5] which share the following striking features with the work under discussion:

1) Both P. Merton 56 and P. Oxy. 465 are couched in verbs of the present and future tenses—a point which bothered the editor of P. Merton 56. P. Berol. 21198 likewise contains present and future tense verbs.

2) Even more remarkable is the fact that the curious idiom τόπον ἐκ τόπου occurs in all three papyri—coincidence or characteristic of such texts?

The unusual compound of προσωπέω here in line 8 (ἐσπροσωπήσεται) may be compared with such other unusual προσωπέω-compound words as ἰδιοπροσωπέω and ἀλλοιοπροσωπέω which appear in astrological texts (cf. *LSJ*, pp. 69 and 818; Gundel, *Dekane*, 32ff.). Μετεωρίζω (l. 5) is likewise attested in the astrological works of Vettius Valens. Tenuous criteria though they may be, they nonetheless indicate that the Berlin text is probably apotelesmatic instead of documentary.[6]

The total period involved in the text on this papyrus covers *ca.* 3 months. The transcript is based on one made by Herwig Maehler.

→ ἀ]πὸ Χοιὰκ λ- ἕως Μεχ[εὶρ ῑα
   ]ρεως πόλλα λήμψεται ε[
   ]γκενικὸν τῆς ἰδίας γυνα[ικὸς
   ]σεται ἀπὸ τόπον ἐκ τόπου .[
5]γησει καὶ μετεορισθήσεται [
   ἀπ]ὸ Μεχεὶρ ῑβ ἕως Φαρμοῦθι [
   δί]κην λέγει ἕνεκα δημοσίω[ν
   ]γήσει· καὶ ἐσπροσοπήσεται [
   ]σει καὶ δίκην λέγει ἕνεκα [

───────────────────────

1   Μεχ[εὶρ ῑα: Restored on the basis of l. 6, where Μεχεὶρ ῑβ is the day initiating the next period in question.

2   ˝Α]ρεως πόλλα λήμψεται Ἑ[ρμοῦ? Cf. Hephaestio, *Apotelesmatica* I,1 138f. (Pingree I, p. 19.4f.): ὃ εἰς τὸ αἰδοῖον παραλαμβάνεται, ἔστι οἶκος ˝Αρεως. For the juxtapostion of Ares and Hermes cf. Hephaestio, *Apoteles. Epitome* IV 42 (256.24-25 Pingree): ἐν δὲ ˝Αρεως τόποις ... ἐν δὲ Ἑρμοῦ τόποις. (RK)

3   ]γκενικόν: There is no such word as κενικόν in Greek; only such a compound word as συγγενικόν or ἐγγενικόν can once have stood here. *L.* συγγενικῶν, τῆς ἰδίας γυνα[ικός in a list? Cf. Vettius Valens IV 12,1 (Pingree 170.5): δόξα, πατήρ, τέκνα, γυνὴ ἰδία, κτλ. (in the fourth position of the dodekatropos); under the 10th position is a list in the genitive, as here: πράξεως, δόξης, προκοπῆς, τέκνων, γυναικός, κτλ. (RK)
    Pap. ἴδιας
    Cf. P. Merton II 56.9f.: [καὶ κακ]οστοματισθήσε[ται χάρ]ιν γυναικὸς ὑπ[ὸ φθονερ]ῶν ἀνθρώπων [καὶ πλαν]ήσεται τόπον ἐκ [τόπου ..] καὶ ἐπιστρέφουσι [πρὸς τὴν] ἰδίαν.

4   πορεύ]σεται, πλανή]σεται?, the idea being that the person will be in constant flux, having no home.
    {ἀπὸ} τόπον ἐκ τόπου: For the idioms τόπον ἐκ τόπου, πόλιν ἐκ πόλεως cf. T. Skeat, P. Lond. VII 2049.8-9n., 2193.18-19n., who cites further examples. Add to those:

P. Merton II 56.12-13 (quoted above in line 3n.); P. Oxy. 465.7 (both occurrences in *apotelesmata*); Hephaestio, *Apotelesmatica* 2, 33.9 (Pingree I 214.4f.): ἐν δὲ Σελήνης τόποις χαλεπὸς καὶ ἄπρακτος ἔσται, τόπους ἐκ τόπων μετα– λαμβάνων; *id.*, *Epit.* IV 41.9 (Pingree II 253.31f.): τόπους ἐκ τόπων μεταβάλλων; and compare the Latin expression in *CIL* 14.2112 = C. Bruns, *Fontes Iuris Romani Antiqui* (Tübingen: Mohr-Siebeck, 1907, repr. Aalen: Scientia Antiquariat, 1958), 175.25: *item placuit, ut quisquis seditionis causa de loco in alium locum transierit, ei multa esto HS IIII n.* (Lanuvium, 136 CE). Apparently such expressions are common in, though obviously not restricted to, *Vereinssatzungen* and *apotelesmata*.

The expression recalls such phrases in Greek and Coptic magical texts as *SM* I 46.4-5: ἐνιαυτοὺς [ἐξ ἐ]νιαυτῶν, μῆνας ἐκ μηνῶν, ἡμέρας ἐξ ἡμερῶν, νύκτας ἐκ νυκτῶν, ὥρας ἐξ ὡρῶν; *ibid.*, 47.4-5, 48.5, 49.13; SM II 73.3-4 ἐκ παντὸς τόπ[ου ... εἰς πάντα] τόπον; P.C. Smither, *JEA* 25 (1939): 173-74 (Coptic): "let him seek me from village to village, from city to city, from field to field, from country to country." Cf. *SM* II 73.3-4n. and D. Martinez, *P. Mich. XIV: A Greek Love Charm from Egypt*, 49-50, citing numerous parallels.

5 κι]γήσει (?) καὶ *l.* μετεωρισθήσεται: These verbs refer to the mental agitation of the person under the influence of this particular astronomical conjunction. Cf. Vettius Valens, *Anthol.* 194.24: Ζεὺς Κρόνῳ μετεώρους κινήσεις καὶ ἐξοδιασμοὺς ποιεῖ καὶ οἰκείων ἀπειθείας, τινῶν δὲ καὶ θανάτους. (RK)

7 δί]κην λέγει ἕνεκα δημοσίῳ[ν: The clause is similar to Hephaestion I, p. 178: Κρόνος μὲν <τὸν γάμον> διαφέρει ἕνεκα ἀρχαίων ἢ πατέρων, ὁ δὲ Ζεὺς ἕνεκα δημοσίων. Here the verb λέγει must be translated "means, signifies, indicates," equivalent to δηλοῖ in P. Oxy. 465.20. (RK)

8 *l.* ε<ἰ>σπροσωπήσεται? This would be the most logical reading of the ink marks on the papyrus, except that the first *sigma* in the word is like no other *sigma* on the whole papyrus, and the word is, furthermore, nowhere attested.

l. ἐκπροσωπήσεται? The putative *kappa*—if it is a *kappa*—is improperly written, lacking the vertical *hasta* on the left. This word, however, has the advantage of at least being attested, although it appears in neither *LSJ* nor F. Preisigke, *Wörterbuch der griechischen Papyrusurkunde*

(Berlin, 1925). Both Sophocles, *s.v.* ἐκπροσωπέω, -ήσω "to stand in the place of, to be the representative of" and Du Cange, *Glossarium* . . . *Graecitatis* (Lyon, 1688, repr. Graz: Akademische Druck- u. Verlagsanstalt, 1958) *s.v.* ἐκπροσωποῦν "*personam representare, legati officio fungi*," document its existence in later antiquity. It continued to be used by Hellenophones throughout the ages, surviving into modern times with the same meaning in present-day Katharevusa as it had before.

However, provided that the present text is in fact apotelesmatic, then even this attested προσοπέω-compound might have an entirely different, and probably astrological, import here. Based on the root word πρόσωπον, ἐκπροσωποῦν would probably mean (in the alleged apotelesmatic context) something like "pass out of a decan (πρόσωπον)." Conversely, εἰσπροσωπήσεται would mean "pass into a decan (πρόσωπον)."

9]σει καὶ δίκην λέγει ἕνεκα [: Cf. Pingree I, p. 206.17f.: ἀπραγίας καὶ διαβολὰς ποιήσει, καὶ κρισεὶς καὶ φθόνους καὶ μερίμνας ἕνεκεν δημοσίων. (RK)

Translation

. . . from Choiak 30 until Mecheir (11) . . . (in the house of) Ares. He will receive many things . . . of kinship matters, of his own wife . . . he will wander from place to place . . . he will be agitated and become unsettled . . . from Mecheir 12 until Pharmuthi . . . betokens a lawsuit in regards to the public . . . he will . . . and will enter into the planet's domain . . . it will create . . . and indicates a lawsuit in regards to . . .

3. Magical Formulary

   P. Berol. 21336, 8 x 3.5 cm., fourth century

The papyrus is broken off on at least three sides. It is impossible to say whether or not the space above the first line on either side of the papyrus represents the respective upper margin or simply an interlinear space between two different sections of text.

This fragment preserves portions of a magical handbook. Given the scant amount of intelligible text preserved, the possible lines of interpretation are multifarious: directions for preparing a silver amulet perhaps for attaining favor or inducing dreams.

→]ησιωνθαυ[
]ναργυρουνγρ[
]σωνοματιν[
]ερινησαπο.[

5]αβλαναθα[ναλβα
]οιθεοιαβρ[α

1   [ἐπὶ χαριτ]ησίων θαυ[μαστῶν?: Cf. *PGM* IV 2227: ἐπὶ χαριτησίων καὶ φίλτρων· ἐν χρυσῇ λεπίδι γράψον κτλ. (in a recipe heading). *L.* χαριτ]ήσιον θαυ[μαστόν? (RK). Also possible is ὀνειρωτ]ησιῶν (RG).

2   [εἰς πέταλο]ν ἀργυροῦν γρ[άψον . . .], or [εἰς λάμνα]ν ἀργυροῦν *aut sim.*: Cf. *PGM* IV 2705: φυλακτήριον εἰς πέταλον ἀργυροῦν.

3   ]σων ὄμμασιν,]ς ὧν ὀμμάτιον,]ς ὀνόματι ν[,]ς ὀνόματ' ἵν[α, -οι]ς ὀνόμασιν are some of the possible emendations that come to mind.

4   ἐπὶ λεπίδος κασσιτ]ερινῆς ? (RK)

4ff.   Bibliography on these "ring symbols" is cited in Wm. Brashear, *CdE* 58 (1983): 2.2. Add: A. Barb, *Folklore* 77 (1966): 302-03 (positing a Jewish origin) and M. Pieper, *MDAIK* 5 (1934): 125-26 (positing an Egyptian one).

5   αβλαναθα[ναλβα: Cf. Wm. Brashear, *APF* 38 (1992): 21, summarizing suggested etymologies and discussions: *inter alia*, Ginsburger *ap.* P. Perdrizet, *REG* 41 (1928): 78, an acronym of the Hebrew: <u>atta barouch leolam adonai</u> + Nathan + alba "*du bist ewig gesegnet, O Herr; Nathan*"; C. Bonner, *Studies in Magical Amulets* (Ann Arbor: Univ. of Michigan Press, 1950), 202; F. Maltomini, *SCO* 29 (1979): 85; D. Robinson, "A Magical Text from Beroea in Macedonia," *Classical and Mediaeval Studies in honor of Edward Kennard Rand,* ed., L. Jones (1938; repr. New York: Books for Libr. Pr., 1968), 250f.; H. Leclercq, *DACL* I, 1, col. 152f. In Demotic: F. Griffith, H. Thompson, *The Demotic Magical Papyrus of London and Leiden* (London: H. Grevel and Co., 1904): vso. 22.13:

n'th'n'lb'; and Aramaic: Joseph Naveh, Shaul Shaked, *Amulets and Magic Bowls* (Jerusalem: Magnes Press, Leiden: Brill, 1985), 57, l. 25: *'blnh'lblh.*

6   μεγάλ]οι θεοὶ 'Αβρα[σαξ?: Cf. Wm. Brashear, *APF* 38 (1992): 20 (P. Berol. 9873, line 19): 'Αβρασαξ θεοῦ [μ]εγίστου. Otherwise, κύρι]οι θεοὶ 'Αβρα[ωθ ? Cf. R. Kotansky, C. Faraone, *ZPE* 75 (1988): 263 (RK).

(*m. altera*)

↓]λετε...ε.[

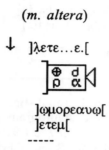

]ωμορεαυω[
]ετεμ[

So far the text on the vertical fibers has obstinately resisted all attempts at interpretation.

On the *tabula ansata* (which also appears in the fever amulet *SM* I 10), see R. Kotansky, *J. Paul Getty Mus. Jnl.* 11 (1983): 175-76. On the circle with cross see Wm. Brashear, *Magica Varia* (Brussels: Fondation égyptologique Reine Elisabeth, 1991), 59-60; Wm. F. Albright, *Archeology and the Religion of Israel* (Baltimore: Johns Hopkins Univ. Press, 1946), 72; E. Neumann, *Ursprungsgeschichte des Bewusstseins* (Zurich: Rascher, 1949), 50-51; J. Rykwert, *The Idea of a Town* (London: Faber and Faber, 1976), 192; M. Lurker, *Der Kreis als Symbol* (Tübingen: Wunderlich, 1981), 57-66, 83.

4.   Christian Amulet (?)

P. Berol. 21337, 3.3 x 3 cm., sixth century

This minuscule fragment is broken off from all sides except for the upper one where there is an upper margin of negligible dimension. The writing is that of an experienced hand, the ciphers in the second line practically calligraphic in their quadratic proportions. The vertical fibers are devoid of writing.

Preserved on the horizontal fibers are two staurograms heading the text (the sole survivors of the presumable original seven?)

succeeded by names of archangels, the number 3663 and *voces magicae*. Although the purpose for which this text was written can no longer be ascertained, one can theorize it was probably a protective amulet.

→   ] ☧   ☧ [
      ]ιηλ ΓΞ ΧΓ[
      ]ωχ Μιχαηλ ϊα[
      Γα]βριηλ ιᾱ ιᾱ [

5   ]   [

1   Cf. P. van der Laan, P. Lugd.-Bat. XIX, p. 100, on the differences between the staurogram (as here) and the christogram; P. Sijpesteijn, *ZPE* 5 (1970): 58 (bibliography); M. Black, "The Chi-Rho Sign—Christogram and/or Staurogram," *Apostolic History and the Gospel. Biblical and Historical Essays pres. to F.F. Bruce,* eds. W. W. Gasque and R. P. Marti, (Exeter, 1970), 319-27; A. Lukaszewicz, "A Travesty of Signum Crucis," *Nubia et Oriens Christianus. Fs. C.D.G. Müller,* eds. P. Scholz, R. Stempel (Cologne: Dinter, 1988), 29-32; E. Dinkler and E. Dinkler-von Schubert, "Kreuz," *Reallexikon f. byzantinische Kunst* 5 (1991): 1-219, esp. 34f.
2   ΓΞ ΧΓ: Supralinear strokes cap the numbers.
      In *ZPE* 78 (1989): 123-24, hoping to exorcise the ghost of the pseudo-palindromic number 3663 (the isopsephistic value of Βαινχωωωχ) which has led a phantom-like existence, haunting the writings of various papyrologists, ever since Theodor Hopfner conjured it up early in this century, I argued that in Greek ciphers (which are, after all, the mode of expression used in the texts under discussion) 'Γχξγ is by no means palindromic. The fact that in modern Arabic ciphers 3663 happens to be a palindrome is a mere coincidence and completely irrelevant to ancient isopsephistic magical calculations.
      As it stands here the Greek number is mathematically incorrect, the ciphers having been written in reverse order with presumably the unit cipher (the first γ = 3) preceding the tens cipher (ξ = 60) which precedes the hundreds cipher (χ = 600), the final *gamma* presumably representing the

thousands cipher (Γ = 3000). Provided that the order of
ciphers as they stand was intentional (and not inadvertent
and mistaken), it must have had significance for the person
responsible for writing this text. Otherwise, he would have
written them in the arithmetically correct order. Does this
mean that for him χ = 600 and ξ = 60 were interchangeable? Must I sing a palinode on the matter of this putative
palindrome?

As Roy Kotansky pointed out to me, my argumentation
in the *ZPE*-article overlooks one important aspect of
numbers, both in ancient and modern times, namely, their
pronunciation; otherwise, one would not find such numbers
as 9999 (C. Bonner, *JEA* 16 [1930]: 6-9); 2662 (R. Kotansky, C. Faraone, *ZPE* 75 [1988]: 262); or 3663 (Wm.
Brashear, *ZPE* 78 [1989]: 123-24) in magical and religious
(e.g. 666 in the *Apoc. Ioh.*) contexts. Whereas the corresponding Greek ciphers of these numbers—'Θϡϙθ, Τχξγ
and χξϛ—do not produce visually convincing palindromes,
these numbers were not simply there for the eyes. These
numerical configurations were not pronounced as letters
(e.g., *gamma-chi-xi-gamma*) but read aloud as numerals.
Hence, pronounced—ἐννέα χίλια ἐνακόσια ἐνήκοντα ἐννέα,
τρισχίλια ἑξακόσια ἑξήκοντα τρία, ἑξακόσια ἑξήκοντα ἕξ—
they must have had a pleasantly alliterative, sing-song
character similar to the English "nine thousand nine hundred and ninety-nine" or German "*neuntausendneun-
hundertneunundneunzig.*" [7]

Palindromicity, however, is a phenomenon appreciable
only in script, and palindromes exist for the sake of their
congruent reversibility. Τχξγ thus is not a palindrome; it is
not reversible. (RG)

However, from an arithmological point of view, the
present number allows interesting speculation. By reducing
higher numbers (= later letters in the alphabet) to
"monads," a procedure Hippolytus, *Ref. omn. haer.* IV.14
(see n. 3) describes as a common technique of charlatans
and impostors, it is possible to interpret Γχξγ as γϛϛγ
(3663) which is an authentic palindrome. (RG)

In the final analysis, no palinode on my part is necessary, as Richard Gordon demonstrates, for the following
reasons: the present erroneous order of at least the middle
two digits may be due to simple scribal negligence and error. (Proving that the first and fourth have been trans-

posed is more difficult, if not impossible. There is no apparent difference between the *gamma* as it is used for the thousands and as it is used for the unit cipher.) The source of error may also have been the "resurgence of the alphabetic value," alphabetic value taking priority over numerical value, since *xi* precedes *chi* in the alphabet. Finally, the symbols might be employed here as *characteres*, the transposition of the middle two symbols being intentional only in the sense that the origin of the *characteres* in the numerical scheme was to be disguised.

3 Ἰαβ]ωχ: Cf. *PGM* IV 2204. Another possibility is Βαινχωω]ωχ. Cf. *PGM* LXXIX 3: ανοκ πε Βαινχωωωχ Ἀβρασάξ εριντ Μιχαήλ and LXXX 2, two parallel *thymokatocha*, wherein Bainchoooch, Abrasax and Michael are all invoked in one breath. Given the isopsephistic value of the name Bainchoooch (=3663), albeit in garbled form, in the previous line, this restoration is attractive.

Μιχαηλ: Cf. W. Lueken, *Michael. Eine Darstellung und Vergleichung der jüdischen und der morgenländisch-christlichen Tradition vom Erzengel Michael* (Göttingen, 1898) *non vidi*; J. P. Rohland, *Der Erzengel Michael. Arzt und Feldherr. Zwei Aspekte des vor- und frühbyzantinischen Michaelkultes* (Leiden: Brill, 1977), esp. 75f., 106f.; D. Wortmann, *Bonner Jahrbücher* 166 (1966): 101; Müller, 8-35; A. Hermann, *JbAC* 2 (1959): 43f.; Michl 199f.; H. Leclercq, *DACL* I,2, 2085, 2088, 2144f.; A. Kropp, *Der Lobpreis des Erzengels Michael* (Brussels: Fondation égyptologique Reine Elisabeth, 1966).

4 Γα]βριηλ: See Müller, 36-47.

On archangels in general see: M. Schwab, *Vocabulaire de l'angélologie d' après les manuscrits hébreux de la Bibliothèque nationale. Mémoires présentés par divers sav. à l'Acad. des Inscr. et Belles Lettres*, sér. I, tome X.2 (Paris: Klincksieck, 1897); Michl; Müller; Y. Yadin, *The Scroll of the War of the Sons of Light against the Sons of Darkness* (London: Oxford Univ. Press, 1962), 237-40 (discussing the order of their names in apocryphal, pseudepigraphical and rabbinic literature); V. Stegemann, *Die koptischen Zaubertexte der Slg. Papyrus Erzherzog Rainer in Wien* (SB Heidelberger Akad. d. Wissens., phil.-hist. Kl. 1933-34), 37 (on the varying order in Coptic magical texts); A. Kropp, *Ausgewählte koptische Zaubertexte* III (Brussels: Fondation égyptologique Reine

Elisabeth, 1930), §128; Hopfner, *OZ* I §141; G. Viaud, *BSAC* 23 (1976-78): 106 (in Arabic magic); E. Peterson, "Engel- u. Dämonennamen. Nomina Barbara," *Rhein. Mus.* 75 (1926): 393-421; Reuben Margulies, *Mala'ke Elyon* (Jerusalem, 1962) (in Hebrew; *non vidi*); S. Eitrem, P. Oslo. I, 78-80; F. Maltomini, *ZPE* 48 (1982): 166-67; G. Davidson, *A Dictionary of Angels* (New York-London: Free Press, 1967); J.-H. Niggemeyer, *Beschwörungsformel aus dem "Buch der Geheimnisse (Sefer ha Razim)": zur Topologie der magischen Rede,* Judaistische Texte u. Studien 3 (Hildesheim-New York: Olms, 1975), 225-38; and on individual ones in particular: E. Peterson, "L' archange Ouriel," *Seminarium Kondakovianum* 2 (1928): 246f.; S. Grébaut, "Les miracles de l' archange Ragou'el," *ROC* 18 (1913): 113-20, 277-82; H. Polotsky, "Suriel der Trompeter," *Le Muséon* 49 (1936): 231-43.

ια ια: Above the first ια is a half-circle, above the second ια a horizontal bar. A variant of Iao; cf. P. Moraux, *Une défixion judiciaire au musée d' Istanbul* (Mémoires. Acad. Royale de Belgique. Cl. des Lettres et des sciences morales et politiques) 54.2 (1960), 29; D. Jordan, *Hesperia* 54 (1985): 245; S. Sciacca, "Phylakterion," *Kokalos* 28-29 (1982-83): 97; A. Jacoby, *ARW* 28 (1930): 273.8; R. Daniel, *ZPE* 50 (1989): 151. According to L. Vischer, *RHR* 139 (1951): 19.3, Astorre Pellegrini, *D' una Abraxa inedita* (Bergamo, 1874) was the first to suggest a connection between the Coptic ⲓⲁ and the Semitic Iao. Cf. C. Harrauer, *Meliouchos* (Wiener Studien. Beih. 11; Vienna: Verlag der Österreichischen Akademie der Wissenschaften, 1987), 24.19, 66.67.

5   Visible on the lower edge of the papyrus is a long horizontal stroke, all that remains of the *vox magica* originally written in this line.

5.   Sortes Astrampsychi

P. Berol. 21341, 27 x 16.5 cm., third century

Single sheet of papyrus with writing in a fluid documentary cursive script of the third century on both sides. Since the one answer (↓19) mentions the *dekaprotos*, the text on this papyrus was probably written before 302 CE, when the *dekaproteia* was abolished. Similar hands are those of the *Sortes Astrampsychi* papyri, P. Oxy. 2833 (Browne, *Papyri*, plate I) and P. Gent inv. 85 (*CdE* 63 [1988]: 313, pl. 1).

Papyri of the *Sortes Astrampsychi*: P. Oxy. 1477 = *PGM* XXVI = G. Björck, "Heidnische und christliche Orakel mit fertigen Antworten," *SO* 19 (1929): 97f. (= A.S. Hunt, C.C. Edgar, *Select Papyri* I [London: Heinemann; Cambridge: Harvard Univ. Press, 1959], no. 195 = J. Hengstl, *Griechische Papyri aus Ägypten* [Darmstadt: Wissenschaftliche Buchgesellschaft, 1978], no. 65); Browne; Gerald Browne, "A New Papyrus Codex of the Sortes Astrampsychi," in *Arktouros: Hellenic Studies . . . Bernard M.W. Knox*, (Glen Bowersock *et al.*, edd., Berlin: de Gruyter, 1979), 434-39; *id.*, *Papyri* (= P. Oxy. 1477, 2832, 2833—see the review by Revel Coles, *BASP* 13 (1976): 85-87); Randall Stewart, *Sortes Astrampsychi* II: Ecdosis altera (Stuttgart: Teubner—forthcoming); G. H. R. Horsley, *NDIEC* 2, 37-44. More recently the following papyri have come to light: P. Iand. V 71, P. Rain. I 33 (Jean Lenaerts, *CdE* 58 (1983): 187ff.); P. Lugd.-Bat. XXV 8; P. Oxy. 3330; P. Gent inv. 85 (Willy Clarysse, Randall Stewart, *CdE* 63 [1988]: 309-14).

Translations: N. Lewis, *Life in Egypt under Roman Rule* (Oxford: Clarendon Press, 1983), 99 (English); F.J. Presedo Velo in: *Religion, Superstición y Magia en el Mundo Romano* (Cadiz: Departamento de historia antigua, Univ. de Cadiz, 1985), 94 (Spanish); S. Donadoni, *La religione dell' antico Egitto* (Bari: Editori Laterza, 1959), 593-94 (Italian); A. Bülow-Jacobsen, "Orakler i det graesk-romersk Aegypten," *Dagligliv blandt guder og mennesker. Den naere orient i oldtiden* (eds. Bendt Alster and Paul J. Frandsen; Copenhagen: Museum Tusculanums Forlag, 1986), 189-94 (Danish); Hengstl, *op. cit.* (German).

Discussions and literature: G. Browne, *opp. citt.*; *id.*, "The Composition of the Sortes Astrampsychi," *BICS* 17 (1970): 95-100; *id.*, "The Origin and Date of the Sortes Astrampsychi," *ICS* 1 (1974): 53-58; R. Stewart, *ZPE* 69 (1987): 237-42; *id.*, "The Textual Transmission of the Sortes Astrampsychi," *ICS* (forthcoming); W. Clarysse, F. Hoogendijk, "De Sortes van Astrampsychus. Een orakelboek uit de oudheid bewerkt voor het middelbaar onderwijs," *Kleio (Driemaandelijks tijdschrift)* n. r. 11 (1981): 53-99; H. Versnel, *Faith, Hope and Worship* (Leiden: Brill, 1981), 6; W. Hübner, *Zodiacus Christianus: jüdisch-christliche Adaptationen des Tierkreises von der Antike bis zur Gegenwart* (Beitr. z. kl. Phil. 144; Königstein, Czech.: Hain 1983), 49; Franz Hennevetter, "Würfel- und Buchstabenorakel in Griechenland und

Kleinasien" (diss., Breslau, 1912), 52.2, cites more modern parallels to the *Sortes Astrampsychi.*

Cf. the somewhat similar *Tabula Aristobuli,* described by Gundel, *Dekane* 285, 314, 406-08.

→ margins: left 3 cm., lower 3.5 cm., upper 1.8, right variable, up to a maximum of 5.5 cm.

→

	α' ου προκοπτ[εις ο] επ[ιβ]αλλη[	
	β' ο επιβαλλη[..] αμελη[	
	γ' πλεε ου ναυγαγις	12
	δ' ουκ εχις γενων απαλλ[	90
5	ε' νυν μη ...ς ου συνφ[ερει	
	ς' γεινη βουλευτης αμεριμ[νως	88
	ζ' ου 〚β〛 πρεσβευεις μακραν [	87
	η' φυγαδοντα .λ[..] . εχις [	86
	[θ' .] ..[..] .θηκ.[. α]γοραζη [	84
10	ι' πωλις και καλ[ως	83
	αμεριμνια	
	α' ουχ ευρισκις ο ζη[τεις	40
	β' κληρονομ.[..]ριαν[	33
	γ' ελευθερουσι δικ[	32
15	δ' υβριζη ο‵υ′χ απρο[σδοκ-	31
	[ε]' το γεννωμ<ε>γογ [	30
	ς' τεκτης τη[ς κατ]ηγο[ριας	29
	ζ' μηδως ην[....]υς ν[	28
	η' βραδιον ελευσεται ο [αποδημο]ς	27
20	θ' αποδιδως α[με]ριμγ[ως	26
	[ι'] ου πιστευε τον δανι[ζοντος	25
	υπνος	
	α' υβρισθησ. [	31
	β' ουκ αναλημψη .ησι[	
25	γ' ουκ εση δεκαπροτος [	95
	δ' τη γυναικι α.[.] .....εχη.....[....] ...	
	ε' εχις την πατριδα ειδιν [	94
	ς' καθαρτηθι μεμαγευσαι [	91
	ζ' ευλυτ<ρ>ωσης ο επιβαλληται [	93
30	η' εαν μητε γαγαγησης λυπη[....] .ις	12

→

1   One expects the name of a deity heading this section such as in lines 11 and 22.

3   *l.* πλεῖ. οὐ ναυάγεις. On the epenthetic *gamma* in ναυγαγις see F. Gignac, *A Grammar of the Greek Papyri of the Roman and Byzantine Periods* I (Milan: Cisalpino-Goliardica, 1976), 72-73.

    Cf. Browne 8.9, 84.7, 92.2, 97.2: ἐὰν πλεύσῃς (ἄρτι), ναυαγήσεις, 19.5, 79.7: πλέεις μετὰ ἐγκοπῆς, 20.1: οὐ πλέεις καλῶς καὶ ἀβλαβῶς, 35.8: ἐὰν ἄρτι πλεύσῃς, ναυαγήσεις, 44.3: πλέεις ἐξαίφνης μετὰ φόβου, 46.10: πλέεις μετὰ κόπου, 93.6: οὐ πλέεις. οὐ συμφέρει σοι, 98.4: πλέεις ἐξαίφνης μόνος.

4   *l.* οὐκ ἔχεις γαμῶν ἀπαλλ[άσσεσθαι ? Cf. Browne, p. 3: εἰ ἀπαλλάσσομαι τῆς γυναικός, 12.2, 29.4, 54.8, 57.3, 65.9, 77.7, 89.6: οὐ καταλλάσῃ τῇ γυναικί, 25.5, 81.1: ἀπαλλάσσῃ τῆς γυναικός, P. Iand. V 71.1: [ἀπαλλάσ]σῃ τῆς [γυναικός], P. Oxy. 2832. 13: οὐκ ἀπ[αλλάσσῃ τῆς γυναικός.

5   νῦν μὴ πλῇς οὐ συνφ[ερει might be an attractive reading of these traces (cf. Browne 93.6: οὐ πλέεις. οὐ συμφέρει σοι), except for the fact that a similar answer already appears just two lines above this entry in line 3.

6   *l.* γίνῃ. Cf. Browne 12.4: γίνῃ βουλευτής, ἄρτι δὲ οὔ, 13.2, 29.6, P. Oxy. 2833 II 14: γίνῃ βουλευτής, 25.7, 81.3: βουλευτὴς γίνῃ καὶ ἄρχων, 54.10: οὐ γίνῃ βουλευτὴς νῦν, 57.5, 72.1, 77.9: οὐ γίνῃ βουλευτὴς ἄρτι, 89.8: μὴ γίνου βουλευτὴς καὶ ὠφεληθήσῃ.

7   Cf. Browne 9.1: οὐ πρεσβεύεις, οὐχ ἁμαρτών, 12.5: οὐ πρεσβεύεις μόνος, 13.3, 29.7, 57.6, 77.10, 81.4, 89.9, P. Oxy. 2833 II 15: πρεσβεύεις, οὐ μόνος (δέ), 25.8: πρεσβεύεις καὶ εὐημερεῖς, 72.2: πρεσβεύεις. ἑτοιμάζου, 92.1, 97.5: πρεσβεύεις καὶ κινδυνεύεις.

8   *l.* φυγαδεύοντα ... ἔχεις or <τὸν> φυγαδεύοντα εὑρίσκεις ? Cf. Browne 9.20: οὐ φυγαδεύῃ, ὑβρίζῃ δέ, 12.6, 25.9, 57.7, 72.3, 81.5: οὐ φυγαδεύῃ. μὴ φοβοῦ, 13.4: φυγαδεύῃ πρὸς χρόνον ὀλίγον, 29.8: οὐ φυγαδεύῃ. μὴ ἀγωνία, 63.3, 82.2: (οὐ) φυγαδεύῃ δι' αἰῶνος, 67.1: φυγαδεύθητι πρὸς ὀλίγον, 89.10: φυγαδεύῃ καὶ φιλανθρωπευθήσῃ, P. Oxy. 2832.21: [φυ]γαδεύῃ πρὸς ὀλίγον χρόν[ον].

9   Cf. Browne 9.4, 26.1, 29.10, 57.9, 67.3: ἀγοράζεις ὃ ἐνθυμεῖσαι, 12.8: οὐκ ἀγοράζεις ἄρτι ὃ ἐνθυμεῖσαι, 66.2: οὐκ

ἀγ. ὃ ἐνθ., 72.5: ἀγοράζεις ὃ ἐνθυμηθῇς, 81.7: ἀγοράζεις ὃ
ἐνθυμῇ; P. Oxy. 2832.24: ἀγοράζεις τὸ ἐνθυμῇ.

10 *l*. πωλεῖς καὶ καλ[ῶς: Cf. Browne 9.5: ἐὰν ἄρτι πωλήσῃς,
βλάπτῃ, 12.9: εὑρήσεις πωλῆσαι, 26.2, 57.10: οὐχ εὑρήσεις
ἄρτι πωλῆσαι, 66.3: εὑρίσκεις πωλῆσαι μετὰ κέρδους, 67.4:
εὑρίσκεις πωλῆσαι βραδέως, 72.6: εὑρίσκεις πωλῆσαι
καλῶς, 81.8: εὑρίσκεις πωλῆσαι ταχέως, 87.1: εὑρίσκεις
πωλῆσαι τὸ φορτίον, P. Oxy. 2832.25: πωλεῖς, βραδέως δέ.

11 ἀμεριμνία: According to the heading introducing the list of
such similar personifications and deities in P. Lugd.-Bat.
XXV 9.1, ἀμεριμνία is a θεὸς χρηματιστὴς καὶ σημάντωρ.
However, neither ἀμεριμνία nor ὕπνος (l. 22) are themselves preserved in that list. In general on the personification of abstract nouns see E. Kantorowicz, "Σύνθρονος
Δίκη," *AJA* 57 (1953): 65-70; G. Downey, "Personifi-
cation of Abstract Ideas in the Antioch Mosaics," *TAPA* 69
(1938): 349-63; *id*., "Representations of Abstract Ideas in
the Antioch Mosaics," *Jnl. of the History of Ideas* 1
(1940): 122ff.; D. Levi, *Antioch Mosaic Pavements* I
(Princeton: Univ. Press, 1947), 253ff.; K. R. Haworth,
*Deified Virtues, Demonic Vices and Descriptive Allegory in
Prudentius' Psychomachia* (Amsterdam: Hakkert, 1980);
H. A. Shapiro, "Personification of Abstract Concepts in
Greek Art and Literature to the End of the 5th c. B.C."
(diss., Princeton, 1977); T. B. L. Webster,
"Personification as a Mode of Thought," *JWCI* 17 (1954):
10-21; Β. Παπαδάκη-'Αγγελίδου, Αἱ προσωποποιήσεις εἰς
τὴν ἀρχαίαν ἑλληνικὴν τέχνην (Athens, 1960) *non vidi*;
M. Nilsson, "Kultische Personifikationen," *Eranos* 50
(1952): 31-40; Leiva Petersen, *Zur Geschichte der Per-
sonifikation in griechischer Dichtung und bildender Kunst*
(Würzburg-Aumühle: K. Triltsch Vlg., 1939); *ANRW* II
17.2, 827-948.

12 εὑρίσκεις: Cf. Browne 5.8, 21.1: οὐχ εὑρήσεις τὸ
ἀπολόμενον, 20.8, 23.2: τὸ ἀπολόμενον εὑρεθήσεται, 31.6,
33.7, 99.4: οὐχ εὑρίσκεις τὸ ἀπολόμενον, 45.9, 62.5, 70.3:
εὑρίσκεις τὸ ἀπολόμενον, 100.10: τὸ ἀπολόμενον εὑ-
ρίσκεται, P. Gent inv. 85.7: οὐκ εὑρίσκις τὸ ἀπολωλε-
μέν[ον].

13]ριαν[,]ριαν[: *non liquet*; cf. Browne 4.5, 21.8, 23.9, 40.7,
50.3, 53.4, 68.1, 70.10, 76.2, 96.6, P. Oxy. 3330.25, P.
Gent inv. 85.14, P. Rain. I 33: (οὐ) κληρονομεῖς τὸν
πατέρα, Browne 68.1: ... οὐ μόνος.

14 Cf. Browne 3.1, 4.6, 23.10, 50.4, 68.2: οὐκ ἐλευθεροῦσαι ἄρτι, 21.9, 76.3, 96.7: ἐλευθεροῦσαι βραδέως, 40.8: ἐλευθεροῦσαι μετὰ ληγάτου, 53.5: ἐλευθεροῦσαι τὸ ἀργύριον διδούς, P. Oxy. 3330.26: ἐλευθ[εροῖ δ]οῦς ἀργύριον, P. Gent inv. 85.15: ἐλευθε[ροῦ]σαι, ἄρτι δὲ οὔ.

15 Cf. Browne 3.2: ὑβρίζῃ, οὐ λίαν δέ, 4.7: ἄχρι λόγων ὑβρισθήσῃ, 21.10: ὑβρισθήσῃ ταχέως, 34.1: ὑβρισθήσῃ δεινῶς (= P. Oxy. 3330.27), 40.9: ὑβρίζῃ καὶ ζημιοῦσαι, 50.5, 76.4, 95.8, 96.8: οὐχ ὑβρίζῃ. μὴ ἀγωνία, 53.6: ὑβρίζῃ δεινῶς, 68.3: οὐχ ὑβρίζῃ. μὴ φοβοῦ, 91.1: ἔχεις ὑβρισθῆναι μεγάλως, P. Gent inv. 85.16: ὑβρ]ισθή[σῃ ... δε]ινῶς.

16 Cf. Browne 3.3, 40.10, 68.4, 91.3: σώζεται τὸ γεννηθέν, 4.8, 96.9: ζῇ τὸ γεννηθὲν καὶ τρέφεται, 34.2: τὸ γεννηθὲν θρέψεις, 38.1: τὸ γεννηθὲν οὐ σώζεται, 50.6: τὸ γεννώμενον σώζεται, 53.7: οὐ ζῇ τὸ γεννηθέν, 76.5: τὸ γεννηθὲν οὐ τρέφεται, P. Oxy. 3330.28: τὸ γεν[νώμεν]ο[ν] μὴ τρέφε.

17 Cf. Browne 3.4, 4.9, 34.3, 38.2, 47.1, 50.7, 53.8, 68.5, 93.8, 96.10: (οὐ) σώζῃ τῆς κατηγορίας, 76.6: κινδυνεύσεις κατηγορούμενος, P. Oxy. 3330.28: οὐ σώζει τῆς κατηγορίας.

18 This entry so far defies all attempts at deciphering. The corresponding entries in Browne are 3.5, 38.3, 53.9: οὐ δίδεις ἄρτι τοὺς λόγους, 4.10: δίδεις τοὺς λόγους μετὰ ἀγνωσίας, 34.4, 50.8: δίδεις τοὺς λόγους. μὴ ἀγωνία, 47.2: δίδεις τοὺς λόγους βραδέως, 56.1, 68.6, 76.7: δίδεις τοὺς λόγους μεθ' ὕβρεως, 88.5: δίδεις τοὺς λόγους καὶ ζημιοῦσαι, P. Oxy. 2833 II 1: δίδ[ως] τοὺς λόγου[ς μ]εθ' ὕβρεως, P. Oxy. 3330.30: οὐ δίδοις ἄρτι τοὺς λόγους.

19 Cf. Browne 3.6, 47.3, 50.9: ἔρχεται ὁ ἀπόδημος ἐξαίφνης, 34.5, 38.4, 53.10, 56.2, 82.3: οὐκ ἔρχεται ὁ ἀπόδημος (ἄρτι/νῦν), 37.1: βραδύνει ὁ ἀπόδημος, ἀλλ' ἔρχεται, 68.7: ἔρχεται ὁ ἀπόδημος βραδέως, P. Oxy. 2833 II 2, P. Oxy. 3330.31: οὐκ ἔρχεται ἄρτι ὁ ἀπόδημος.

20 Cf. Browne 3.7: ἀποδίδεις ὃ ὀφείλεις καλῶς, 34.6: οὐκ ἀποδίδεις ὃ ὀφείλεις, 37.2: ἀποδίδεις ὃ ὀφείλεις, βραδέως δέ, 38.5, 50.10: ἀποδίδεις ὃ ὀφείλεις, 47.4: ἀποδίδεις ἐκ μέρους ὃ ὀφείλεις, 56.3: ἀποδίδεις ὃ ὀφείλεις ἐξ ἀλλοτρίων, 68.8: οὐκ ἀποδίδεις νῦν ὃ ὀφείλεις, 76.9: ἀποδίδεις ὃ ὀφείλεις ἐκ κόπου, P. Oxy. 2833 II 3: ἀποδίδις ἃ ὀφίλις ἐκ κόπων, P. Oxy. 3330.1: [οὐκ ἀποδίδοι]ς ἃ ὀφείλεις.

21 *l.* μὴ πίστευε τῷ δανείζοντι: Cf. Browne 3.8: οὐχ εὑρίσκεις
ἄρτι δανείσασθαι, 18.1: οὐχ εὑρίσκεις δανείσασθαι, 31.7:
δανείζῃ καὶ εὐθέως δαπανᾷς αὐτά, 34.7: δανείζῃ καὶ εὐθέως δαπανᾷς αὐτά, 37.3: δανείζῃ καὶ βλάπτῃ μεγάλως,
38.6: οὐ δανείζῃ. οὐδείς σοι δίδει, 47.5: δανείζῃ ἐπὶ
ὑποθήκῃ, 56.4: οὐ δύνη νῦν δανείσασθαι. σιώπα, 68.9:
δανείζῃ βραδέως εὑρών, 76.10: οὐ δύνη ἄρτι δανείσασθαι,
P. Oxy. 2833 II 4: οὐ δύνη δανίσασθαι ἄρτι.
22 See l. 11 n.
23 See l. 15 n.
24 *Non liquet.*
25 *l.* δεκάπρωτος. Cf. Browne 2.8: δεκάπρωτος ἔσῃ ἐξάπινα,
28.10, 32.6, 65.4, 77.2, 80.9, 89.1, P. Oxy. 2833 II 7:
(οὐ) γίνῃ δεκάπρωτος, 54.3: δεκαπρωτεύσεις καὶ βλάψῃ,
63.2, P. Oxy. 3330.34: δεκαπρωτεύεις καὶ βλάπτῃ, 73.5:
γίνῃ δεκάπρωτος ἐξαίφνης, P. Gent inv. 85.6: γείνῃ
δεκάπρωτος βραδέως.
26 Cf. l. 4 n. Perhaps something similar once stood here.
27 *l.* ἔχεις, ἰδεῖν. Cf. Browne 2.9, 54.4, 65.5, 73.6, 77.3,
80.10, 89.2, P. Oxy. 2833 II 8: ἔχεις τὴν πατρίδα θεωρῆσαι, 25.1, 32.7: οὐ θεωρεῖς τὴν πατρίδα, P. Oxy. 2832.
9: οὐκ ἔχεις τὴν πατρίδα θεωρῆσαι.
28 *l.* καθάρθητι μεμάγευσαι: Cf. Browne 12.1, 65.8: πεφαρμάκευσαι. βοήθησον ἑαυτῷ (ἑαυτῷ βοήθησον), 25.4, 54.7,
77.6: οὐ πεφαρμάκευσαι. μὴ φοβοῦ, 29.3: οὐ πεφαρμάκευσαι, 32.10, 57.2: πεφαρμάκευσαι. ἑαυτῷ βοήθει,
89.5: πεφαρμάκευσαι ἀκριβῶς, P. Oxy. 2832.12:
πεφ[αρμάκωσαι.
29 Cf. Browne 2.10, 25.2, 29.1, 32.8, 54.5, 65.6, 77.4, 89.3,
97.4, P. Oxy. 2832.10, P. Oxy. 2833 II 9: (οὐκ) ἀπαρτίζεις ὃ ἐπιβάλλῃ, 73.7: ἀπαρτίζεις ὃ ἐπιβάλλῃ βραδέως.
30 *l.* ἐὰν <πλεύσῃς>, μήτε ναυαγήσῃς. λυπῇ[ς μό]γις? Cf. line
3 n.

↓ : margins: upper 1.5 cm., right 3 - 6.7 cm., lower 2.5 cm.,
left 3.5 cm. So far it has not been possible to identify more
than two of the answers here with any certainty.

↓   μ]η απα[λλ-]
                               ] ...ιγου[
    [
    [   ]ελπη
5   [   ]ωφιλ{ .}τησι

[   ] . μη αγωνια
[   ] ...ημενε ου [σ]υμφερει
[.]' λημψει ην θελις γυναικα αμεριμ[νως   55
[.'] ου συμφερι νυν μη λεγε
10 [.'] των πλαστων αλλ[..] .[..]ινη εν αλληγ[ματι
[.'] σ]υκοφα[ντ
[   ] .[
] .πασχον[.] ..κο[πτεις
                    ]ης ου λαμβανις νυν [
15 κληρονο]μησης μητρυχου
                    ]ασιλια
                ] ...[.]αλησον
                          ]ση
                    ] .νον αμερ<ι>μν.[
20   ] .[ ] εχθρους
                ] ..[ ] .. επιτευξας
                      ] .ος
                ] .τω φερομενω
                  ] ..[..]ηζη
25   ] .[
                ] ..αμος αρτι
              ] αγτισε
              ] .λυσα
              π]ροκοπτι
30 γ['   ] ....[..].
δ' [..] ..[   ]απο...εξις
ε' εργαση αμ[ελ]ης νυν
ς' πλις μεν ... βραδεως
ζ' εκι ουδεν .[...] . σοι
35 η' κεραν ολιγον [....]ν
[θ' .] .χαι ευτυχ...εισα
[ι'] ..ρις θανατον   64

↓
8   *l.* θέλεις. Cf. Browne 6.8, 42.9, 49.1, 52.7, 61.5, 75.6,
     78.10, 83.2, 86.4, 94.3: (οὐ) γίνη μοναχός, P. Oxy. 1477 I
     16: [νε· εἰ λαμβάνω ἢν γυν]αῖκα θέλω, P. Oxy. 2833 II 26:
     οὐ λαμβάνεις ἢν θέλεις γυνεκα, P. Oxy. 3330.18:
     [λαμβάνεις ἢ]ν θέλεις γυναῖκα.
9   *l.* συμφέρει.
14   *l.* λαμβάνεις.
15   *l.* μητρούχου?: *addendum lexicis.* Cf. Sophocles, *s.v.*
     μητρόχος (Joh. Lyd. 71.17), who emends this word to μι–

τροῦχος, deriving it from μίτρα and ἔχειν, but in the context of the *Sortes Astrampsychi* this neologism would be irrelevant. The heretofore unattested word on the Berlin papyrus would be a congener of πατροῦχος "heiress," a word which appears only in some codices of Herodotus 6.57. More likely, however, is simply μὴ τρύχου. (RK)

17 μὴ λάλησον ?

20 ἐχθρούς: *Theta* corrected from *rho*.

26 γάμος ἄρτι ? (RK) The speck of ink preceding *alpha* is too minuscule for deciding what letter it could belong to. Furthermore, answers whch include ἄρτι are always in the second person singular. However, one could imagine an answer like the following: [οὐκ ἔσται] γάμος ἄρτι—which, although it is not attested, would nicely fill out the lacuna.

29 *l.* π]ροκόπτει: See R. Stewart, *ZPE* 69 (1987): 241, on this verb and the difficulties involved in placing it in a proper context in the *Sortes Astrampsychi*.

33 *l.* πλεῖς.

34 *l.* ἐκεῖ.

35 *l.* κερδάνεις ?

36 *l.* θεωρεῖς θάνατον. Cf. Browne 1.5: θεωρεῖς θάνατον τοῦ ἰδίου σου, 7.4: οὐκ ἔχεις ἰδεῖν θάνατον, 17.8, 51.10: ὄψει θάνατον ἐπικερδῆ, 22.9: θεωρεῖς θανάτους, 48.2: οὐκ ἔχεις θάνατον ἰδεῖν νῦν, 59.3: θεωρεῖς θάνατον πρὸ καιροῦ, 78.1: ὄψει θάνατον μὴ θέλων, 90.7: ὄψει θάνατον ταχέως, 95.6: οὐ θεωρεῖς θάνατον νῦν, P. Oxy. 2833 II 16: ὄψι θάνατον <ὃν> οὐ θέλις.

6. Sortes Astrampsychi

P. Berol. 21358, Oxyrhynchos, 9 x 3.7 cm., third century

→ upper margin: 1.8 cm. ↓ upper margin: 1.4 cm.; variable right margin. The present fragment was found in a box of papyrus fragments evidently deriving from Oxyrhynchos, bought in Luxor on October 16, 1908. Comparing its writing with those on published photos of other *Sortes Astrampsychi* papyri from Oxyrhynchos, however, produced no join.

→] πωλη ταχ[εως ελευ-	74
] θερουσα [	
] οπου εαν α[πελθης, ου	73

```
          ] μενις
     5    ] πς ερμην[
          ] μη δαν[ειζε. μη                           58
          ] διδου  [
          ] πωλις το φο[ρτιον ευτυ-                   57
          ] χως [
    10    ] . ουκ α[πολυη της συνοχης                 56
          ------

  ↓       ] ο δρομος                                  89
          ]ως
          ]
          ]
          ] ..
          ]ς
             ]ν
          ------
```

→

1-2 Above the first word is a decorative stroke. Cf. Browne
     [14.4], [30.6], 36.2, 55.5, 64.7, 98.6: οὐ πωλῇ (ἄρτι). οὐ
     συμφέρει σοι; 43.3: ἐὰν πραθῇς, μετανοήσεις; 58.8, 93.9:
     (οὐ) πωλῇ ἐπὶ τὸ συμφέρον; 60.1: πωλῇ, ἄρτι δὲ οὐκέτι,
     84.6: πιπράσκῃ καὶ φεύγεις, 85.9: πιπράσκῃ καὶ ὠφελεῖσαι
     ἐξαίφνης, 87.10: οὐ πιπράσκῃ. ἐλευθεροῦσαι, P. Oxy.
     2832.1: οὐ πωλη[θ]ή[ση.] οὐ συμφέρε[ι.

4   l. μένεις. Cf. Browne [14.5], [30.7], 36.3, 43.4, 51.1, 58.9,
     P. Oxy. 2322.2.: ὅπου ὑπάγεις (οὐ) μένεις, Browne 55.6:
     μένεις ὀλίγον χρόνον ὅπου ὑπάγεις, 60.2: μένεις ὀλοχρονεὶ
     ὅπου ὑπάγεις, 64.8: ὅπου πορεύῃ, οὐ μένεις ἐκεῖ, 85.10:
     ὅπου ἐὰν ἀπέλθῃς, οὐ μένεις, 98.10: μένεις ὀλίγον χρόνον
     καὶ ἀναχωρεῖς.

5   ] πς ἑρμην[εία ?: Undoubtedly another θεὸς χρηματιστὴς
     καὶ σημάντωρ. V. supra ad P. Berol. 21341, lines 11 and
     22 n. and P. Lugd.-Bat. XXV 9. As the maleficent κακο-
     δαίμων of papyrologists would have it, that list of gods
     breaks off precisely at 85—just one short of number 86,
     the number of the deity here!
        ] πς ἑρμην[εύεται ?: "(Decade) 86 means: do not lend
     money," etc. (RK)

6   Cf. Browne 6.5, 86.1: μὴ δάνειζε, μὴ δίδου, 7.10: ἐὰν
     δανείσῃς, ἐπὶ ὑποθήκῃ δάνεισον, 42.6, 75.3: δανείσας,
     βραδέως ἀπολήψῃ, 48.8: δανείζεις ἐπὶ ὑποθήκῃ, 52.4:

δανείσας, βραδύ ἀπολήψῃ, 59.9: μὴ δάνειζε καὶ βλαβήσῃ, 61.2, 78.7: δάνεισον ἐπὶ ὑποθήκη, P. Oxy. 2833 II 23: δάνισον ἐπὶ ὑποθήκη, P. Oxy. 3330.15: [δανείσας βρα]δέως ἀ[πολήμψει.

8   l. πωλεῖς. Cf. Browne 6.6, 75.4, 78.8, 94.1: οὐ πωλεῖς τὸ φορτίον (ἄρτι), 42.7: πωλεῖς τὸ φορτίον ἐπὶ κέρδει, 48.9, 52.5, 61.3: πωλεῖς τὸ φορτίον (καλῶς), 59.10: οὐ πωλεῖς τὸ φορτίον καὶ βλάπτῃ, 86.2: πωλεῖς τὸ φορτίον εὐτυχῶς, P. Oxy. 2833 II 24: οὐ πωλεῖς ἄρτι τὸ φορτίον, P. Oxy. 3330.16: [πωλεῖς τὸ φ]ορτίο[ν].

10   ἀ[πολύεσαι ? Cf. Browne 6.7, 48.10, 61.4, 75.5, 78.9, P. Oxy. 2833 II 25: (οὐκ) ἀπολύῃ τῆς συνοχῆς, 42.8, 52.6, 83.1, 86.3, 88.6, 91.7, 94.2: (οὐκ) ἀπολύεσαι τῆς συνοχῆς, 92.8: κινδυνεύεις συνεχόμενος, P. Oxy. 3330.17: [οὐκ ἀπολύῃ] τῆς συνοχῆς ἄρτι.

↓ 1   l. δρασμός. Cf. Browne 12.3, 13.1, 25.6, 29.5, 54.9, 57.4, 65.10, 77.8, 79.10, 81.2, 89.7, P. Oxy. 2832.14, P. Oxy. 2833 II 13, P. Iand. V 71: (οὐ) λανθάνει σου ὁ δρασμός.

7.   Horoscope

P. Berol. 21316, 30 x 9.5 cm., Dime, May 15, 141 CE

On the horizontal fibers are a few traces in two columns of what appears to be an official register. Heading the right-hand column is a deleted line then σημ‹ε›ίωσις / [τ]οῦ κυρίου [.]λ.[/ ‹ε›ὶς Φαμενὼθ .[/ succeeded by a few names.

The vertical fibers bear a horoscope, a hyleg recording the astrological position of planets at the hour of someone's birth, written in a fluid, cursive, documentary style script of the second century CE.

In general on Greek horoscopes see K. Maresch, P. Köln V 236 introd.; G. Ioannidou, *ZPE* 72 (1988): 261-63; Parker 28; D. Baccani, *ZPE* 76 (1989): 98-100; *ead.*, *Analecta Papyrologica* 1 (1989): 67-77; *ead.*, *Oroscopi*; Brashear, *Papyri*; G. Bastianini, C. Gallazzi, *Tyche* 5 (1990): 5-7; H. Gundel, A. Kehl, "Horoskop," *RAC* 16 (1992): 597f. On Demotic horoscopes: R. Parker, "A Horoscopic Text in Triplicate," *Grammata Demotika. Fs. für Erich Lüddeckens*, eds. H. Thissen, K.-Th. Zauzich (Würzburg: G. Zauzich Verlag, 1984), 141-43; GH, p. 161.3; O. Neugebauer, "Demotic Horoscopes," *JAOS* 63 (1943): 115-27; O. Neugebauer and R. Parker, *Egyptian Astronomical Texts III: Decans, Planets,*

Constellations and Zodiacs (Providence: Brown Univ. Press; London: Lund, Humphries and Co., 1969), *passim*; Jürgen Osing, "Horoskop," *LdÄ* III 11-13; Baccani, *Oroscopi*, 25-26, 30, 50-52.

↓ margins: upper: 2.7 cm., lower: 19.8 cm., right: variable.

↓   ἔτους δ   Α]ἰλείου 'Αντω[νε]ίνου
       Παχὼν ιθ εἰς]κ̄ καθ' Ἑλλ[η]νας
          κατὰ δ]ὲ τοὺς ἀρχαίου[ς Α]ἰγυπτίους
          ]ς ὥρᾳ ι   νυκτὸς
5   Ἥλιο]ς ['Ε]ρμῆς Ταύρ[ῳ]
       Σελ]ή[ν]η [.] Ἄρης Ὑδρ[ηχό]ῳ
       Κρόνο]ς 'Αφροδείτη ['Ω]ρ[οσ]κόπος
       ἀρχὰ]ς Ἰχθύσι
       Ζεὺς] Καρκίνῳ

1-4 These formulaic opening lines contained (according to both Greek and Egyptian calendrical systems) the year, month, day and hour of the person's birth. Likewise, his or her name would have stood in the lacuna.

2   Παχὼν ιθ εἰς]κ̄: DB, citing *GH* 167.

3-4 Cf. BGU 957.2 (= *GH*, p. 16, no. 9): κα[τ' ἀρχαίους ὥ]ρᾳ γ̄ νυκτό(ς); P. Oxy. 235 (= *GH*, p. 18, no. 15/22): κατ[ὰ δὲ τοὺς] ἀρχαίους χρόνους; P. Hamb. 96 (= *GH*, p. 47, no. 145): κατ' ἀρχαίους; P. Aberd. 13 (= *GH*, p. 51, no. 187): κα[θ'] Ἑλλήνων κατὰ δὲ [Α]ἰγυπτί[ω]ν; G. Ioannidou, *ZPE* 72 (1988): 262-63. For such double datings see *GH* 166-68; *ZPE* 104 (1994): 243-55.

4   ὥρᾳ: See K. Maresch in: P. Köln V 236.2n., on the various ways of expressing the day and hour in horoscopes. On precise references to hours in documentary papyri see H. Harrauer, *Analecta Papyrologica* 2 (1990): 132-37; on methods of time-telling by night in antiquity, Wm. Brashear, *APF* 36 (1989): 67.20 and *APF* 38 (1992): 30: "Anm. 20"; A.J. Turner, *Of Time and Measurement* (Aldershot: Variorum, 1993) *non vidi*.

8   Restoring Kronos here has the drawback that all the possible entries are filled and one is still left with additional writing at the beginning of l. 7. Probably Kronos is to be restored in l. 7, and the traces in l. 8 belong to some such word as ἀρχάς or ἔσχατα such as in P. Oxy. 585.8 or P. Oxy. 2565.8. (DB)

Donata Baccani kindly prepared the following astronomical computations, noting that the calculations are all
correct, apart from those for Venus, for whose completely
erroneous position it is difficult to give a satisfactory explanation.

The positions of Helios and Taurus are confirmed by
the fact that the Ascendant is in Pisces, indicating a birth
taken place around 2 or 3 A.M. The system underlying the
layout of this horoscope is that common to horoscopes
written before 150 CE (cf. *GH*, p. 164), where the arrangement is Helios, Luna, Saturn, etc., Venus, Mercury.
This arrangement is somewhat disturbed by the fact that
several planets lie within one zodiacal sign.

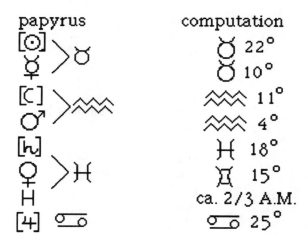

8.   Astrological Text: Zodiac?

P. Berol. 21347, second century

The papyrus has been pieced together from numerous small
fragments so that at present there are three more or less contiguous larger fragments (10 x 8.5, 5.3 x 1.8, 4.7 x 1.5 cm.) and three
smaller fragments (all *ca.* 1.5 x 1.5 cm.).

For a discussion of the unusual rulings on this papyrus see U.
Horak, *Illuminierte Papyri, Pergamente und Papiere* II (Vienna,
forthcoming).

The writing is strikingly similar to that of the Berlin astronomical table in *BASP* 7 (1970): 38, and somewhat similar to that of P.

Lund inv. 35 a, reproduced in Neugebauer, *Sciences*, pl. 2. The
scribe of the Berlin papyrus sought a somewhat more elegant style
than either of those responsible for the two aforementioned papyri. However, his serif-adorned letters are not always uniform in
size or appearance: cf. the two highly discrepant *rhos* in line 3 and
12, the two *alphas* in line 2, the two *xis* in lines 1 and 16.

```
         οἴαξ π[ά]σης γενέσε[ως
         ἀναφορ[ὰ] τῶν κανον[ικῶν
         σασεερο.[        ]διω[
         λε' λ̄ οικ[
    5    τι Κρονο.[
         ου ζῳδια[
         μερινωτρ[
         μουσ[.]οι[
         ριασε[....].[
   10    ανετι[
         ρα τοῦ ζ[
         κα ἀριθμ[
         ]————[
         break of uncertain length
         κα.
         —————
         spatium
   15    μεσω[
         ξινε[
         οικο[
         τεπε[
         .[
         [
         [
         ———
         [
         [
         ἐν μέσ[ῳ?
         [...]ωρα[
```

One loose fragment:]κα
                      ]
                      ]..

Another loose fragment showing a *kollesis*. Two pale red horizontal rulings and traces of writing which might be either a numeral
with supralinear stroke or else the symbol for 200.

1   Cf. P. Lond. 130.165 = *GH* no. 81 (pp. 21-28): ὁ δ' οἴαξ τῶν ὅλων ὡροσκόπος κτλ. (briefly discussed in *AG* 258.4); P. Berol.ined. 21225, col. II, 2: ὅλης γενέσεως (Fayum, late II CE).

4   Pap. λε' λ¯= λε(πτὰ) 30 "thirty degrees." Cf. PSI 23a = *GH* no. 338.7,16,18, for similar entries.

4-5 Λεόν]τι ?, Φαίνον]τι ?

7   καθη]μερινῷ, (μεθ)η]μερινῷ, χει]μερινῷ τρ[όπῳ are just some of the restorations that come to mind.

7-8 Διδύ]μους?

Pittakos and the Millstone: *ad* SM II 56

Pittakos, the 7th-century BCE Lesbian politician, was fond of taking his exercise by grinding grain with a millstone. This curious habit, which is recorded for posterity by Diogenes Laertius I 81 and Aelian, *var. hist.* VII 4, undoubtedly inspired the folksong reported almost a thousand years later in the work attributed to Plutarch, *Septem sapientum convivium* 14: ἄλει μύλα ἄλει· καὶ γὰρ Πιτ–τακὸς ἄλει μεγάλας Μυτιλήνας βασιλεύων (*PMG* 869 [43 B., 30 D.]).

In 1976, Eric Turner published a Greek magical text on a papyrus sheet from Oxyrhynchos dating to the third or fourth century CE. Despite the papyrus' relatively small size (8 x 8 cm.) and short text (a mere 29 words distributed over a paltry eight lines), in the ensuing 19 years it has generated conjecture and discussion all out of proportion to its size—much more than that ordinarily accorded such a minute and mundane magical text. For although Turner and others after him regarded the incantation as amatory, according to its latest editor, Robert Daniel in *SM* II 56, the charm is coercive. It is presumably directed against a female slave, either already fugitive and on the lam or else suspected of entertaining plans of escape.

The text on the papyrus begins: ὥσπερ στρέφεται ὁ ἑρμῆς τοῦ μυλαίου καὶ ἀλήθεται τοῦτο τὸ πιττάκιον ... ("as the Hermes-stone [?] of the mill turns and as this chit is ground ..."). In other words, the magician sets up a simile: as the mill turns, and as the slip of papyrus is pulverized beneath the millstone, so too should a certain woman change her mind and desist from thoughts of escape. Daniel, citing parallel "*Mühlenzauber*" from both antiquity and more modern European folkloric traditions, brings conducive evidence for the use of the mill with coercive magical intent in similar contexts.

Ἄλει μύλα ἄλει· καὶ γὰρ Πιττακὸς ἄλει in the ancient Greek folksong and ἀλήθεται τοῦτο τὸ πιττάκιον in the incantation from Roman Egypt—happenstance or deliberate design? The similarity—Πιττακὸς ἄλει and ἀλήθεται . . . τὸ πιττάκιον—any way one looks at it—is striking.

The gamut of possible explanations for this Pittakion[8] reminiscence on the *pittakion* ranges from a purely coincidental similarity on the one hand to deliberate punning on the other. One thing, however, seems certain: it is highly unlikely that a folksong popular on 7th-century Lesbos was still *en vogue* and being sung to the cadence of the grinding millstone a millennium later in the backwater town of Roman Oxyrhynchos. If the similarity is not entirely happenstance, then either a subconscious recollection of the Lesbian milling song as related by Plutarch (?) or else a deliberate and conscientiously premeditated allusion to it is at play here—unless Pittakos' legendary calisthenic and political millings were so well known as to have become paroemiac.

To posit a possible scenario or two: It is conceivable that the person responsible for composing this charm could have picked up the Pittakion milling song while reading his/her copy of the *Septem sapientum convivium*. This work, as we now know since the publication of P. Oxy. 3685, was indeed copied and read in 3rd-century Oxyrhynchos—the very place and time the magical charm was also committed to papyrus. The song, lingering in the circuitous recesses of the Oxyrhynchite magician's cerebrum, thus exerted its subliminal, subconscious influence as the unwitting, unsuspecting sorcerer considered the set-up—"*Mühlenzauber*" and *pittakion*—and penned the text on the papyrus chit.

Otherwise the set-up triggered the Plutarchan (?) association, the ancient Greek song leapt into recall, prompting a deliberate *jeu d' esprit*, and the Oxyrhynchite recondite was able to give full rein to his/her ingenuity. Making a punning play on the name Pittakos, he/she cleverly converted/bent the elements of a time and a situation long past into an arcane allusion suited for his/her own immediate and nefarious purposes—appropriate grist for this provincial magician's preternatural, coercive mill—even if the final product was intended for his/her eyes only.[9]

Provided that the highly speculative, house-of-cards theory proposed here should hold true, then this vestigial *carmen popularium* from 7th-century BCE Lesbos, recorded by Plutarch (?) in the 2nd century CE, and punningly revamped for use in a magical charm of the 3rd-4th centuries, would be the latest example of this humble literary genre to come to light.[10]

Supposing that the Mytilenian reminiscence in Roman Egypt was in fact premeditated makes one wonder what the underlying impulses could be for such a *recherché* display of erudition in this profane, quotidian and transitory context. In all probability it was nothing more than a case of whimsical, self-indulgent *l'art pour l'art*. To paraphrase that classic of papyrological sleuthing, H.C. Youtie's "Callimachus in the Tax Rolls":[11] The trivial display for no eyes but his own, the light and barely sarcastic touch—they are all there. What could be more satisfying to a small-time magician with pretensions to learning than a borrowing from Plutarch furtively copied onto a minuscule papyrus chit, where no one would ever notice it?

Notes

[1] For example, Marcelin Berthelot, *Introduction à l' étude de la chimie des anciens et du moyen-âge* (Paris: Librairie de sciences et des arts, 1938), 86ff., whose illustrations are incompletely and inaccurately reproduced in AG 539-40.

[2] The only somewhat parallel text among the Greek and Latin papyri from Egypt is the so-called "Sphere of Democritus" in *PGM* XIII 351f., which spawned a long line of long-lived progeny, for example, Ign. Hardt, *Catalogus codicum manuscriptorum bibliothecae regiae Bavaricae* I,3: *Codices graeci* (Munich, 1806), 205-06; M. Förster, "Beiträge zur mittelalterlichen Volkskunde VIII," *Archiv f. d. Studium der neueren Sprachen und Literaturen* n.S. 29 (1912): 16-49, esp. 45-49; Valerie J. Flint, *The Rise of Magic in Early Medieval Europe* (Oxford, 1991): 134, 141, 279-80, 314, 317-18; L.E. Voigts, "The Latin Verse and ... the Sphere of Life and Death in Harley 3719," *Chaucer Review* 21 (1986): 291-305; K. Gillert, *Neues Archiv der Gesellschaft für ältere deutsche Geschichtskunde* 5 (1880): 254; Gundel, *Dekane,* 405-06; Viktor Stegemann, "Prognostikum," *HDA* 7, 335-38; Marie-Louise von Franz, *Zahl und Zeit* (Stuttgart: Klett, 1970), 174 f.; Lynn Thorndike, *A History of Magic and Experimental Science* (Columbia Univ. Press, 1947), 1.682f.; Vittorio Enzo Alfieri, *Gli atomisti. Frammenti e testimonianze* (Bari, 1936) 305-6.801. Such computations are known in other cultures: M.-L. von Franz, *op. cit.,* 177.5, quotes a Chinese example.

[3] On the subject of onomatomancy see: Paul Tannery, "Notice sur des fragments d'onomatomancie arithmétique," *Notices et extraits des manuscrits de la Bibliothèque nationale* 31 (Paris, 1986), 231-60 (translating and discussing a passage from Hippolytus, *Refutatio omnium haeresium* IV 14ff.); W. Kroll, "Onomatomanteia," *RE* XVIII,1 (1939): 517-20; R. Böker, "Die Schiksalshoroskopie und ihre ältesten Hilfsmittel," *Hermes* 86 (1958): 220-320; Gundel, *Dekane,* 70; Marcelin Berthelot, *Introduction à l' étude de la chimie* (Paris: Librairie de science et des arts, 1938), 86-92; E.A. Wallis Budge, *Egyptian Magic* (repr. Evanston-New York: University Books, 1958), 228-30; Udo Becker, "Decumbitur-Horoskop," *Lexikon der Astrologie, Astronomie, Kosmogonie* (Freiburg-Basel-Vienna: Herder, 1981); F. Dornseiff, *Das Alphabet in Mystik und Magie,*

Stoicheia 7 (Leipzig-Berlin, 1925), 113-14; Eduard Sachau, *Verzeichnis der syrischen Handschriften* (*Berlin*) (Berlin: A. Asher, 1899), 619; Iona and Peter Opie, *The Lore and Language of Schoolchildren* (Oxford Univ. Press, 1959), 337 (for contemporary examples of "onomancy" [sic]).

See on M. Berthelot: Arion Rosu, "Marcelin Berthelot, historien des sciences," *Sudhoffs Archiv* 74 (1990): 186-209.

[4] For literature on *Amtstagebücher* see Klaus Maresch in: P. Köln 230 introd.

[5] For a German translation of P. Oxy. 465 see Gundel, *Dekane,* 413.

[6] For hemerological or menological prognostications in Greek see *PGM* III 275, 424, IV 26, 2221, 3146, V 243, VII 155-67, 272-84, 285-300, XII 308, 378, XXXVI 330, LXXXVI; P Heid. V,1, pp. 247-49; P. Oxy. 3831 (Homeric oracle); Hopfner, *OZ* I §§ 827ff., *id.*, *RE* XIV 356f.; M. L. West, *Hesiod, Works and Days* (Oxford Univ. Press, 1980), 346ff.; R. MacMullen, *Anc. Soc.* 2 (1971): 105-16. In Aramaic: J. Greenfield, M. Sokoloff, *JNES* 48 (1989): 201-14. In Egyptian: W. Wreszinski, "Tagewählerei im alten Ägypten," *ARW* 16 (1913): 86-100; W.R. Dawson, "Some Observations on the Egyptian Calendars of Lucky and Unlucky days," *JEA* 12 (1926): 260-64. In Demotic: Parker. For Babylonian practices: S. Langdon, *Babylonian Menologies and the Semitic Calendars* (Schweich Lecture, 1933; London: Oxford Univ. Press, 1935); G. Furlani, "Interdetti assiri", *SMSR* 16 (1940): 34-82; Neugebauer, *Sciences* 188. For modern Egyptian examples: C.G. Seligmann, "Ancient Egyptian Beliefs in Modern Egypt," in: *Essays and Studies pres. to Wm. Ridgeway,* ed. E. Quiggin (Cambridge: Univ. Press, 1913), 455-57. In ancient Persia: L. A. Campbell, *Mithraic Iconography and Ideology,* EPRO 11 (Leiden: Brill, 1968), 144.68. In ancient China: D. Harper, "A Chinese Demonography of the Third Century B.C.," *Harvard Journal of Asiatic Studies* 45 (1985): 468-69 (RK). In medieval and later Europe: Flint, *op. cit.*, and Förster, *op. cit.*, and his "Vom Fortleben antiker Samellunare im Englischen und in anderen Sprachen," *Anglia* 67 (1944): 1-171; *HDA s.v.* "Ägyptische Tage"; W. Gundel, *Jahrb. d. Charakterologie* 4 (1927): 135-93; J. Bidez, "Le nom et les origines de nos almanachs," *Mélanges Boisacq. Annuaire de l'Institut de Philologie et d'Histoire Orientales et Slaves* 5 (1937): 77-85.

Demotic and Coptic *apotelesmata*: G. R. Hughes, "An Astrologer's Handbook in Demotic Egyptian," *Egyptological*

Studies in Honor of Richard A. Parker, ed. L. H. Lesko (Hanover and London: University Press of New England, 1986), 53-69; J. Cerny, P. E. Kahle and R. A. Parker, "The Old Coptic Horoscope," *JEA* 43 (1957): 86-100.

[7] See on the universal practice of reading aloud in antiquity: J. Balogh, "Voces Paginarum. Beitrag zur Geschichte des lauten Lesens und Schreibens," *Philologus* (1927): 84-108, 201-40; T. Skeat, "The Use of Dictation in Ancient Book Production," *Proc. Brit. Acad.* 42 (1957): 179-208, esp. 186-87; J. Svenbro, *Phrasikleia. Anthropologie de la lecture en Grèce ancienne* (Paris: La Découverte, 1988), 178-206. RK: Cf. P. J. Achtemeier, "Omne verbum sonat," *JBL* 109.1 (1990): esp. 16f.; M. Slusser, "Reading Silently in Antiquity," *JBL* 111.3 (1992): 499.

[8] Cf. *LSJ s.v.* Πιττάκειος and W. Pape, *Wörterbuch der griechischen Eigennamen* II (Braunschweig: Friedrich Bieweg und Sohn, 1884), 1203.

[9] However, as Daniel, *SM* II, p. 32, notes, "surely it has not passed through the works of a mill. It may be an exemplar of a text that was to be recopied and then used."

[10] Popular songs are often found lurking in magical (con)texts, and their use is hallowed by a long-standing tradition. For examples of metrical incantations deriving from folk charms and other poetry see R. Heim, "Incantamenta magica graeca latina," *Jahrbücher f. classische Philologie,* 19. Supplementband (Leipzig, 1893), 544-50; L. W. Daly, *AJPh* 103 (1982): 95-97; A. A. Barb, "Animula Vagula Blandula," *Folklore* 61 (1950): 15-30; and most recently David Jordan, "Choliambs for Mary in a Papyrus Phylactery," *HTR* 84 (1991): 343-46. The literature on relics and holdovers from more ancient civilizations and languages in magical contexts in later periods is vast. See Brashear, *Papyri* ("Relics").

[11] *Proc. of the Twelfth International Congress of Papyrology* (Toronto: Hakkert, 1970), 551.

ABBREVIATIONS

Editions of papyri are abbreviated according to J. Oates, Roger Bagnall, W. Willis, Klaas Worp, *Checklist of Editions of Greek Papyri and Ostraca.* 3rd ed. Scholars Press, 1985.

AG = A. Bouché-Leclercq, *L' astrologie grecque.* Paris, 1899. Reprint. Brussels: Culture et Civilisation, 1963.

Baccani, *Oroscopi* = Donata Baccani, *Oroscopi greci: documentazione papyrologica.* Messina: Editrice Sicania, 1992.

Brashear, *Papyri* = William Brashear, "The Greek Magical Papyri: An Introduction and Survey," *Aufstieg u. Niedergang der römischen Welt,* II 18.5. Berlin-New York: de Gruyter, 1995, 3380-684.

Browne = Gerald Browne, *Sortes Astrampsychi* I. Leipzig: Teubner, 1983.

Browne, *Papyri* = Gerald Browne, *The Papyri of the Sortes Astrampsychi.* Beitr. z. kl. Phil. 58. Meisenheim am Glan: Anton Hain, 1974.

DACL = *Dictionnaire d' archéologie chrétienne.* Paris: Letouzey et Ané, 1907-53.

Gundel, *Dekane* = Wilhelm Gundel, *Dekane und Dekansternbilder.* Glückstadt-Hamburg: J. J. Augustin, 1936.

GH = Otto Neugebauer and H.B. van Hoesen, *Greek Horoscopes.* Philadelphia: American Philosophical Society, 1959.

HDA = *Handwörterbuch des deutschen Aberglaubens.* Berlin-Leipzig, 1927-42. Reprint. Berlin: de Gruyter, 1987.

Hopfner, OZ = Theodor Hopfner, *Griechisch-ägyptischer Offenbarungszauber* I. Studien zur Palaeographie u. Papyruskunde 21. Leipzig, 1921. Reprint. Amsterdam: Hakkert, 1974.

LdÄ = *Lexikon der Ägyptologie.* Wiesbaden: Harrassowitz, 1975-86.

LSJ = H. Liddell, R. Scott, H. Jones, *A Greek-English Lexicon.* Oxford: Univ. Press, 1940.

Michl = J. Michl, "Engel V (Engelnamen)." *RAC* 5 (1962): 200-39.

Müller = C. D. G. Müller, *Die Engellehre der koptischen Kirche.* Wiesbaden: Harrassowitz, 1959.

Neugebauer, *Sciences* = Otto Neugebauer, *Exact Sciences in Antiquity.* 2nd ed. Providence: Brown Univ. Press, 1957.

Pack = Roger Pack, *The Greek and Latin Literary Texts from Greco-Roman Egypt.* Ann Arbor: Univ. of Michigan Press, 1965.

Parker = Richard Parker, *A Vienna Demotic Papyrus on Eclipse- and Lunar-Omina.* Providence: Brown Univ. Press, 1959.

PGM = Karl Preisendanz-A. Henrichs, *Papyri Graecae Magicae* I-II (2. verb. Ausg.). Stuttgart: Teubner, 1973-74.

RAC = *Reallexikon für Antike und Christentum*. Stuttgart: Anton Hiersemann, 1950f.

SM = Robert Daniel, Franco Maltomini, *Supplementum Magicum*, I-II. Opladen: Westdeutscher Verlag, 1990-92.

Sophocles = E. Sophocles, *Greek Lexicon of the Roman and Byzantine Periods*. Cambridge: Harvard Univ. Press; London: Humphrey Milford, 1914.

CHAPTER THIRTEEN

GREEK EXORCISTIC AMULETS

Roy Kotansky

Acts 19:13-17 provides an absorbing anecdote of roving Jewish exorcists who try their hand at an innovative style of expunging demons: "But certain of the wandering Jewish 'exorcists' (ἐξορκισταί) even endeavored to name the name of the Lord Jesus over those who had evil spirits, saying, 'I adjure you (ὁρκίζω ὑμᾶς) by the Jesus whom Paul preaches'" (v. 13). According to the account, the Ephesian exorcists—named in the following verse as the seven sons of Sceva—fizzle miserably in their endeavor: the demon fails to recognize these otherwise experienced clerics and crashes upon them with so sound a joggling that they are forced to flee naked and injured.[1]

Nothing in the report of the sons of Sceva tells of the exorcistic use of amulets, engraved or otherwise, nor of attendant rituals in the exorcistic act; apparently the adjuration of Jesus' name was thought sufficient.[2] This stands in marked contrast, on the other

---

[1] For literature and discussion of this passage, see G. H. Twelftree, *Jesus the Exorcist*, WUzNT 2. Reihe 54 (Tübingen: Mohr [Siebeck], 1993), 30-34, whose views on this passage and interpretation of ὁρκίζω, are not, however, to be recommended. The MSS traditions of the magical papyri are roughly contemporary with those of the NT; however, much of the magical material antedates the NT considerably (note 5 below).

[2] There are some clues, however, that the episode may have entailed more than our writer is letting on to. For one, only in the end do we read that the whole exorcism took place in a house (19:16). The itinerancy of the exorcists suggests that this house would have been that of the afflicted. But failing this otherwise casual reference, readers would have been led to believe that the attempted exorcism took place out-of-doors, as was the apparent case with the handkerchief episode (19:11-12). Furthermore, the fact that the exorcists performed their ceremonies as a group of seven, perhaps to enhance their abilities magically, suggests somewhat elaborate rituals. There may have been a ritual word-play on "seven": as discussed below, the Semitic equivalent for "adjure," or "exorcise" (ἐξορκίζω), is שבע, *sbᶜ*, "to adjure"; but the word also means "seven." Or was there a possible misunderstanding of an Aramaic source that described "adjuring" sons (שבע = ἐξορκίζειν) rather than "seven" sons (שבע = 7)? There are also some conflicts in the manuscript tradition: did one, two groups (ἀμφότεροι), or a college of seven perform the adjuration? On some of the problems of this

hand, to the brief story aforementioned in vv. 11-12, a story advertising small face-cloths and bandaging strips (σουδάρια ἢ σιμικίνθια) that, when touched to Paul's skin, could heal the sick and exorcise demons (ἀπαλλάσσεσθαι ἀπ' αὐτῶν τὰς νόσους, τά τε πνεύματα τὰ πονηρὰ ἐκπορεύεσθαι).[3] Such cloths were indeed amulets (φυλακτήρια), and though not engraved with magic words, there is little to detract from the prospect that the cloths, once used effectively, would have been deployed again and again.[4] These magically-charged reliquaries would have no doubt been reapplied with the necessary prayers or incantations: the young Christian community at Ephesus, it seems, adhered tenaciously to their magical beliefs, in some cases for up to two years after conversion (Acts 19:10). Only with the failure of the Jewish exorcists do the "many of those who had believed" burn their magic books (Acts 19:18-19); some will never burn theirs.[5]

---

passage, see recently, W. A. Strange, "The Sons of Sceva and the Texts of Acts 19:14," *JTS* 38 (1987): 97-106 (with literature).

[3] ἀπαλλάσσειν is, by the way, one of the most common verbs for healing in the magical literature; see *Suppl. Mag.*—note 5 below—I. 7, 13; 9, 8; 12, 5; 18, 5; 29, 8; II. 74, 17; 84, [1?]. The verb is found only here in all of the NT for healing disease (elsewhere, cf. Luke 12:58; Heb 2:15 for entirely different usages).

[4] On the mechanism of applying uninscribed materials accompanied by verbal incantations, see Roy Kotansky, "Incantations and Prayers for Salvation on Inscribed Greek Amulets," in C. A. Faraone and D. Obbink, eds., *Magika Hiera. Greek Magic and Religion* (Oxford: Oxford University Press, 1991), 107-37, esp. 108-10; on σουδάρια used in magic ritual, cf. *PGM* VII. 826; XXXVI.269; note also σινδών, σινδόνιον; σινδονιάζειν in *PGM* II.162 III.294, 706; IV.88, 171, 175, 429, 1861, 3095; V.217; XIII.98; 653. The word σινδών is used of the linen burial-cloth of Jesus (Mt 27:59; Mk 15:46 [cf. 14:51,52!]; Lk 23:53), but only the Gospel of John lays emphasis on a separate *facial* burial-kerchief: καὶ τὸ σουδάριον, ὃ ἦν ἐπὶ τῆς κεφαλῆς αὐτοῦ, οὐ μετὰ τῶν ὀθονίων κείμενον ἀλλὰ χωρὶς ἐντετυλιγμένον εἰς ἕνα τόπον (John 20:7; cf. 11:44). On *othonia* in magic, note *PGM* IV. 1073, 3003; VII. 338; XII. 122; XIII.1011. It is difficult not to imagine that this non-synoptic reference to an otherwise commonplace face-cloth betrays a special interest in a powerful amuletic reliquary within Johannine circles. Do Acts 19:12 and John 20:7 echo a common historical tradition of the use or veneration of powerful σουδάρια of Jesus and the apostles for exorcistic rituals?

[5] See R. Kotansky, *Greek Magical Amulets. The Inscribed Gold, Silver, Copper, and Bronze* Lamellae, Part I: *Published Texts of Known Provenance*, Papyrologica Coloniensia XXII/1 (Opladen: Westdeutscher Verlag, 1994), 202-05, no. 37, for an example of a Christian gold magic *lamella* from Ephesus, dated 2nd-3rd century CE (or possibly earlier). For Greek magical books prior to or contemporary with the writing of the New Testament, see R. Daniel and F. Maltomini, *Supplementum Magicum I-II*, Papyrologica Coloniensia XVI.1-2 (Opladen: Westdeutscher Verlag, 1990, 1992)—hereafter, *Suppl. Mag.*—nos. 70 (II-I BCE); 71 (I BCE); 72 (Augustan Age); 52,73 (I CE); 67 (I/II CE); Kotansky, *Greek*

Although the Ephesus episode does not mention the use of inscribed amulets, the specific reference to the burning of the magical books in the immediate context of Acts 19:18-19 implies a close kinship between the ritual acts of the itinerant Jews and the Pauline amuletic kerchiefs, on the one hand, and the sorts of exorcisms and magic acts (πράξεις) recorded in the magic literature, on the other. Indeed, the wording preserved in the Lukan account says much about what sort of formulae were used in the performance of exorcism, and surprisingly these very formulae are the ones encountered on amulets preserved in the papyri and on magic *lamellae,* our best contemporary records of such practices.

It should come as no surprise, then, to find that the exorcistic formula of the sons of Sceva comes close to actual examples found in extant magic books and amulets. This attests to the accuracy of the formulation preserved in Acts 19:13 and implies an historical recollection of real incantations that the Jews must have used.[6] Either the writer of Acts has recorded often-heard and well-known exorcistic sayings of the 1st-to-2nd century CE, or he has actually copied the formulae directly from the sorts of books named and burned in Acts 19:19.

In this study, we shall turn to an assessment of the actual exorcisms in Greek as preserved on inscribed magical amulets, paying close attention to the sorts of formulae they employ and from where they may have derived. Before this, however, it will be necessary to furnish the following material: (1) a general overview of exorcism in its cultural-historical milieu; (2) a look at the derivation of the term "to exorcise"; and (3) some representative examples of exorcism from Jewish and Greek literature. Finally,

---

Magical Amulets, xvi; William Brashear, "Magical Papyri: Magic in Bookform," Peter Ganz, ed., *Das Buch als magisches und als Repräsentationsobjekt* (Wiesbaden: Harrassowitz, 1992), 25-57.

[6] In one remarkable instance, the name of Jesus—in an otherwise non-Christian context—attests to the general historicity of Jewish exorcists using the name of Jesus to cast out demons: Justin Martyr, *Dialog. c. Tryph.* §85 (22) *et passim,* who gives a lengthy exposé on demonology; see F. C. Conybeare, "The Demonology of the New Testament," *JQR* 8 (1896): 576-608, esp. 597-99; cf. *idem,* "Christian Demonology," *JQR* 9 (1897): 59-114; 444-70; 581-603—a substantial monograph on demonology that covers most everything; A. Harnack, *The Mission and Expansion of Christianity in the First Three Centuries,* trans. J. Moffatt, vol. I (New York: Putnam's Sons, 1908), chap. III: "The Conflict with Demons," 125-46, esp. 134; cf. H. A. Kelly, *The Devil, Demonology, and Witchcraft. The Development of Christian Beliefs in Evil Spirits* (Garden City: Doubleday, 1968): "The Demonology of Justin," 23-26.

when we do turn to the exorcistic amulets themselves, we shall analyze common features rather than provide long, philological commentary. Throughout our discussion, the language of these amulets will provide much to support the long-standing position that Greek exorcism represents a phenomenon largely indebted to traditional Jewish practice, a practice that, among other things, must have gained much impetus from healing rites performed by groups attached to synagogues of a more mystical orientation. Though a full study of the relationship between magic and the synagogue, in general, and liturgical prayer and incantation, in particular, is not attempted here, we shall discover some comparative material with which to pursue a subsequent inquiry into the matter.

*   *   *

Scholars have long recognized that the concept of an unfamiliar spirit possessing a human being by somehow infiltrating the body and securing control over the faculties is Semitic; it is largely foreign to Greek thought in classical and Hellenistic times.[7]

---

[7] See Wesley D. Smith, "So-called Possession in Pre-Christian Greece," *TAPA* 96 (1965): 403-26, esp. 409: "there is no description of exorcism in pagan literature before Lucian, who in the *Philopseudes* describes a Syrian exorcist from Palestine" (chap. 16)—see further, below; S. Vernon McCasland, "Religious Healing in First-Century Palestine," in J. T. McNeill, M. Spinka, and H. R. Willoughby, eds., *Environmental Factors in Christian History* (Chicago: University of Chicago, 1939), 18-34: "... but true possession, in the Mediterranean world, may not be much older than the first century" (22); F. E. Brink, "In the Light of the Moon: Demonology in the Early Imperial Period," *ANRW*, 2.16.3: 2081: "It (sc. the 'Greek' demon) was never in a human body ... nor is it embarrassed by an exorcist. It is limited to a number of psychic functions: thoughts, dreams, a feeling of supernatural strength and purpose. It is vaguely responsible for misfortune, and guides things through difficult places for good or evil .... It has only the faintest association with disease, though this it sends. *There is not a hint that it could ever enter a body*, and only the slightest that it could perform any physical action" (italics mine). See also M. J. Edwards, "Three Exorcisms and the New Testament World," *Eranos* 87 (1989): 117-26, who covers the same ground as Smith (supra). A resourceful collection of demonological texts can be found in J. Tambornino, *De antiquorum daemonismo*, RGVV 7/3 (Giessen: Töpelmann, 1909), which however, should still be supplemented by J. J. Semler's three studies: *Umständliche Untersuchung der dämonischen Leute oder sogenannten Besessenen* (Halle, 1762); *Versuch einer biblißchen Dämonologie* (Halle, 1776); and *Commentatio de daemoniacis quorum in novo testamento fit mentio* (Halle, 1777). See also K. Thraede, "Exorzismus," *RAC* 7 (1969): cols. 44-117, with much material.

Though a notion of dangerous spirits occurs widely in Hellenic guise, even this belief may owe something to Near Eastern demonological categories. The Greek sources, at least in this early stage, usually depict evil δαίμονες as ghosts (εἴδωλα, ψυχαί) and apparitions (φάσματα, φαντάσματα) that frazzle careless wayfarers caught in unsafe environments;[8] they are not "indwelling." At other times, spirits are represented as avenging Erinyes and Alastors ('Ερινύες, ἀλάστορες, etc.) bent on punishing offenders for various social crimes.[9] In the case of the former category, simple protective measures ensure safety against their attacks; in the latter, more complex cathartic rituals are often required.[10] In either case, the unwanted entities confront their victims by ap-

---

Of course during the archaic and classical Greek periods the concept of a malicious δαίμων must have undergone considerable change under the influence of the ancient Near East, so such of the categorization that we attempt here, to some extent, must be artificial. Recently, W. Burkert, *The Orientalizing Revolution. Near Eastern Influence on Greek Culture in the Early Archaic Age*, trans. M. E. Pinder and W. Burkert (Cambridge and London: Harvard University Press, 1992) has contributed enormously to our understanding of cultural contacts between the ancient Near East and Greece, particularly in the 8th cent. BCE.

[8] That is, generally in the countryside and at dangerous crossroads, grottos, graveyards, fields and streams; see Brink, "Light of the Moon," 2070, 2091. Such "Greek" demons—whether confronting specters or avenging spirits—are also judged responsible for outbreaks of pestilence and war in the larger life of the community; in the more private domain, they bring selective afflictions, mishaps, disease, and especially μανία. Though—like their ancient Near Eastern and levantine counterparts—"Greek" demons appear in animal-form, the most common portrayal is an apparition of Hekate; see Sarah Iles Johnston, *Hekate Soteira*, APA American Classical Studies 21 (Atlanta: Scholars Press, 1990), esp. chap. VIII: "The Epiphany of Hekate," 110-33 *et passim*; cf. Smith, "So-called Possession," 406.

[9] See the literature and discussion pertinent to the new *lex sacra* from Selinous (ca. 460 BCE): M. H. Jameson, D. R. Jordan, and R. D. Kotansky, *A Lex Sacra from Selinous*, GRBM 11 (Durham: Duke University, 1994), 53-58; 79-80; 117-20; B. C. Dietrich, *Death, Fate, and the Gods* (London: The Athlone Press, 1965), 91-156; Hugh Lloyd-Jones, "Erinyes, Semnai Theai, Eumenides," *'Owls to Athens.' Essays on Classical Subjects Presented to Sir Kenneth Dover* (Oxford: Clarendon Press, 1990), 203-11; Sarah Iles Johnston, "Xanthus, Hera, and the Erinyes (Il. 19.400-18)," *TAPA* 122 (1992): 85-98.

[10] Jameson, Jordan, Kotansky, *Lex Sacra*, esp. Col. B (pp. 16-17, with commentary), gives the fullest account of such rituals with purification involving washing with water, hosting the offending ghost with meal and salt, aspersion, and sacrifice. See also Smith, "So-called Possession," 409.

pearing in visible form.[11] There is no perceived danger of the demons insinuating themselves into the body as unseen entities.

On the other hand, by the time of the composition of the New Testament, belief in an indwelling spirit that could be ceremonially exorcised is attested throughout the eastern Empire and seems specifically local to the Syro-Palestinian world. In addition to what can be gleaned of Jewish practices from primary sources (e.g., Pseudo-Philo, Josephus, Christian pseudepigraphic writings, and some Church Fathers), we know that sectarian groups at Qumran also engaged in complex exorcistic rituals.[12] Their compositions, however, are preserved largely in Hebrew and Aramaic, even though the contemporary Gospel accounts picture Jesus as an exorcist in a sort of Semitic-Greek garb. So too, the late antique depictions of Greek exorcism—the accounts of Apollonius of Tyana, Lucian of Samosata, and others—seem to pattern their accounts after a prevailing "Semitic" model: the notion of a malicious demon taking possession of an individual must be viewed as a largely Near Eastern doctrine.[13]

---

[11] In the Selinuntine *Lex Sacra*, B7f. (previous notes), for example, the offending ghost, called an *elasteros*, is described as one that is "foreign or ancestral; or heard, or seen"; see M. H. Jameson, D. R. Jordan, and R. D. Kotansky, *Lex Sacra*, 44 with refs. to Assyrian ghosts.

[12] This is plain at least from the non-canonical psalms they wrote, especially the variant recension of Ps 91 (90 LXX), a psalm called the "Song for the Stricken"; see J. A. Sanders, *The Psalms Scroll of Qumran Cave 11 (11QPsa)*, DJD 4 (Oxford: Clarendon, 1965), 91-93. But a study of the Qumran exorcisms takes us too far afield from this study. The most recent treatment of this exorcistic psalm is that of Emile Puech, "Les deux derniers Psaumes davidiques du rituel d'exorcisme, 11QPsAp[a] IV 4-V 14," in D. Dimant and U. Rappaport, eds., *The Dead Sea Scrolls. Forty Years of Research*, STDJ 10 (Leiden: Brill & Jerusalem: Magnes Press, 1992), 64-89 (with lit. and full discussion); see, *idem*, "11QPsAp[a]: un rituel d'exorcisme. Essai de reconstruction," *RQ* 14 (1990): 377-408; and J. P. M. van der Ploeg, "Un petit rouleau de psaumes apocryphes (11QPsAp[a])," in *Tradition und Glaube. Festschrift für Karl Georg Kuhn* (Göttingen: Vandenhoek & Ruprecht, 1971), 128-39; cf. Lawrence H. Schiffman, "Merkavah Speculation at Qumran: The *4Q Serekh Shirot 'Olat ha-Shabbat*," in J. Reinharz and D. Swetschinski, eds., *Mystics, Philosophers, and Politicians. Essays in Jewish Intellectual History in Honor of Alexander Altmann* (Durham: Duke University Press, 1982), 15-47, esp. 22-34; note, further, Dennis C. Duling, "The Eleazar Miracle and Solomon's Magical Wisdom in Flavius Josephus's *Antiquitates Judaicae* 8.42-49," *HTR* 78 (1985): 1-25, esp. 14f. Verses from Ps 90 (LXX) become famous in exorcistic and healing formulae on amulets of later date: H. Gitler, "Four Magical and Christian Amulets," *Liber Annuus* 40 (1990): 365-74, esp. no. 3, 371-73.

[13] If represented in the Greek language, it always appears to be dependent upon "oriental" analogies and chronologically late. "Indwelling" of a semi-

How can we reconcile these two seemingly diverse and competing notions of ancient demonological practice? To what extent has
a Semitic or Jewish concept of ritual exorcism come to influence
an older model of a "Greek" demonology? Can one discern in the
later Greek accounts a dependence upon a particularly Jewish
procedure in casting out demons? To answer these questions we
have first to examine the actual accounts that document ancient
exorcistic procedures. In so doing, we also attempt to determine
what marks these texts as primarily "exorcistic."

*   *   *

The account in Acts 19 targets Jewish ἐξορκισταί as the victims
of the back-fired demonological attack. An ἐξορκιστής—a term
not found before the second century CE[14]—is simply the name
given to what the "exorcists" do: they "adjure" (ἐξορκίζειν) the
demons, or "place them under oath," usually with the aim of
driving them out. Certain details provided by the relatively early
NT papyrus, P. Mich. 138 (P[38], ca. 300 CE) and by Codex D also
add to this "oath" the fact that the demons are exhorted "to come
out of" (ἐξελθεῖν) the possessed person(s). This command, com-

---

divine deity in classical Greece is restricted to "divine possession" such as that
encountered with the Pythian oracle, for which see the ample study of Smith,
"So-called Possession," 413-25: *Enthousiasmos*. The idea of a prophetic spirit
indwelling a seer, or of an inner δαιμόνιον guiding a sage, such as Socrates,
represent different matters altogether.

[14] Apart from Acts (whose date is unsure), the noun occurs first in second century CE writers: the *Anth. Pal.* 11.427 in an epigram attributed to Lucian; in
Ptolemy, *Apotelesmatica* IV. 4,10, who also uses the synonym ἐπορκιστής
(*Tetrabiblos* 182); and in Justin Martyr (also using ἐπορκιστής). Both forms of the
noun then become fairly popular with 4th-century church fathers. The noun is
never used of Jesus in the Gospels, nor of Solomon, the Jewish exorcist par
excellence, who in Josephus (1st cent. CE), is described as a writer of τρόποι
ἐξορκώσεων (*Antiq.* VIII.45), not of ἐξορκισμοί (see note 63 below). Evidently the
word (and the cognate ἐξορκιστής) was not yet coined. The fact that no securely
dated writer of the 1st century CE (or earlier) uses the term in contexts where it
would have been most expected provides a strong argument for the dating of
ἐξορκιστής *after* the 1st century. Its occurrence in Acts may well argue for the
book's 2nd-century composition, a date for which there are compelling arguments; cf. J. C. O'Neill, *The Theology of Acts in its Historical Setting* (London,
1961), and others. A *desideratum* would be a thorough study of the vocabulary
peculiar to Acts with the use of the Duke databanks. If such a study were to yield
otherwise 2nd-century words repeatedly occurring for the "first" time in Acts (as,
e.g., ἐξορκιστής), this would certainly call into question the traditional dating of
the book.

bined with the socio-historical nuances that the term "exorcist" has come to bear on the narrative, shows that we are dealing with a belief-system that imagines the presence of a harmful unclean spirit thought to indwell body and soul physically.

Although the verb ὁρκίζω is at least as old as Xenophon (*Symp.* 4.10; 5th cent. BCE)—with the form (ἐξ)ορκόω attested earlier in inscriptions—it is not used early on in adjuratory formulae spoken to demons, but in the context of oaths sworn between contracting parties.[15] The use of ὁρκίζω especially to adjure *demons* is a comparatively recent development and seems to be attested no earlier than the 1st century BCE.[16] In the erotic and related curses on papyri and leaden tablets it is the normal term of compelling a *nekydaimon* to perform a task on behalf of the practitioner. The adjured demon acts as a kind of malign servant or ally. In contexts of a more healing sort, on the other hand, ἐξορκίζω is used rather differently. The demons (or the diseases they cause) are actually adjured to depart from an afflicted patient; the sense of the verb becomes truly "exorcistic."[17] Though perhaps the difference is perfunctory, it is not unimportant, for this "amuletic" use of ἐξορκίζω is, with few exceptions, both distinctly Jewish and exorcistic. It is what gives rise, in the history of magic, to the special category of healing amulet that will have important ramifications for the development of later Christian ritual. In the examples discussed below, however, we shall also find that ἐξορκίζω in the adjurations of the *defixiones* points to a particularly Jewish use of the verb. Here a curious cross-over from the Jewish exorcisms of benevolent magic to the more malicious adjurations of the aggres-

---

[15] See R. Hirzel, *Der Eid: Ein Beitrag zu seiner Geschichte* (Leipzig: S. Hirzel, 1902); J. Prescia, *The Oath and Perjury in Ancient Greece* (Tallahassee, 1970). The social context of early oaths in magic ritual is most recently discussed in C. A. Faraone, "Molten Wax, Spilt Wine, and Mutilated Animals: Sympathetic Magic in Near Eastern and Early Greek Oath Ceremonies," *JHS* 113 (1993): 60-80. The noun ὅρκος is cognate with Greek ἕρκος, "enclosure; fence." Particularly attractive is the possibility that the Greek word-group is akin to Semitic ערך, *ʿRK* (**to connect; join*), though it might be difficult to explain ʿayin > *h-. In Aramaic and Hebrew, ʿRK means *to place side by side; arrange; set in order*, precisely how a fence might be made.

[16] Cf. *PGM* XVI: see note 18 (I^P love spell); *Suppl. Mag.* II 52,2: ἐξορκίζω σε τοὺς / θεοὺς τοὺς ἐνδά/{α}θι σαρα/φάκους (r. σαρκοφάγους), "I adjure you by the gods who are here and those that eat flesh . . ." (I^a grave curse); *Suppl. Mag.* II 71 (fr. 14, 2f.): ἐξορ[κίζω / τ]οὺς ἐν ̔Αδη θεοὺς . . ., "I adjure the gods in Hades" (I^a formulary).

[17] As in the variant tradition in Acts 19:14. Our modern verb "exorcise" comes from the Greek (cf. n. 43 below).

sive-sexual spells can be detected. The serial adjurations of the Jewish god and of his saving acts found in the early Judeo-Greek exorcisms reappear in the context of the curses and *defixiones*.[18] Linguistically, as well, there can be little doubt that the use of ἐξορκίζω to adjure demons—whether those who fetch and serve or those that are expelled—mirrors an originally Semitic שבע, "to adjure"—a verb used in the Dead Sea Scrolls for exorcism, as well as in later Aramaic amulets.[19]

Before examining the individual examples of this special category of adjuration, the exorcism, it would prove worthwhile to present two possible "ancestors" of our more fully developed exorcistic texts: the one, a Hellenistic Greek amulet on lead; the other, a roughly contemporary Hellenistic Jewish exorcism from the apocrypha. We will apply these two examples to construct a "trajectory" of exorcistic theory in order to facilitate our understanding of how later exorcistic texts developed into a fixed form of sorts.

*　　*　　*

The classical and Hellenistic Greek worlds have left us with surprisingly few ancient texts that could be described as amulets, even fewer that speak of warding off demons. Prophetic healers and ἰατρομάντεις,[20] the most famous of whom was perhaps Orpheus,

---

[18] The ἐξορκίζω-type adjurations, whatever their contexts, are often distinctively Jewish in their formulae and magic names. Cf., e.g., *PGM* XVI. 9f.: ὁρκίζω σε, νεκυδαίμονα, κατὰ τοῦ Ἀδωναίου Σαβ[αὼθ] αμιαραχθει αξιαωθ, κτλ. The adjuration formula occurs *in seriatim*, as in the more standard exorcistic examples discussed below.

[19] Forms of שבע are common on the magic *lamellae* of gold, silver, copper, and bronze. The now standard corpora of these amulets are those of Naveh and Shaked: J. Naveh and S. Shaked, *Amulets and Magic Bowls. Aramaic Incantations of Late Antiquity* (Jerusalem: Magnes Press and Leiden: E. J. Brill, 1985), nos. 1-15 (amulets); idem, *Magic Bowls and Formulae. Aramaic Incantations of Late Antiquity* (Jerusalem: Magnes Press, 1993), nos. 16-32 (amulets). Additional examples: R. Kotansky, "Two Inscribed Jewish Aramaic Amulets from Syria," *IEJ* 41 (1991): 267-81; R. Kotansky, J. Naveh, and S. Shaked, "A Greek-Aramaic Silver Amulet from Egypt in the Ashmolean Museum," *Le Muséon* 105 (1992): 5-24. The verb שבע occurs at least 15 times in ten amulets in the Naveh-Shaked corpora, almost exclusively in formulae that adjure the demons directly (A 1:21; A 4:28, 31; A 8:3; A 9:4; A 12:9; A 18:1; A 26:1,9,14; A 27:14). Only in A 19:10,30 do we find an exception: the writer adjures in the name of Abrasax and in the name of ʾbhy to uproot a fever-demon.

[20] See P. Laín Entralgo, *The Therapy of the Word in Classical Antiquity*, trans. L. J. Rather and J. M. Sharp (New Haven: Yale University Press, 1970), 42-

were acclaimed for their preternatural healing powers, and one can
hardly imagine that purifying unsafe habitats from noxious influences would have been excluded from their repertoire of sacerdotal
activities.[21] But of their authored works, none of historical count
has survived, though we have an occasional alluring reference, like
that of the chorus in Euripides' *Alcestis* [965-72]:

> Nothing mightier than Necessity ('Ανάγκας)
> have I found: Not any remedy (φάρμακον)
> on Thracian tablets (Θρήσσαις ἐν σανίσιν) that
> a voice of Orpheus engraved,
> nor as many such remedies Phoebus (Apollo) gave to
> the sons of Asklepios
> as an antidote for the many pains of mortal men.

As for the possible contents of such "magic tablets" of either
Orpheus or Apollo, we can only guess.[22] Are we to envision

44; 55, and esp. Burkert, *Orientalizing Revolution*, ch. 2: "A Seer or a Healer,"
41-87.

[21] This study will deal mostly with tracing the development of a Jewish form
of exorcism and how this came to be preserved on amulets inscribed in Greek.
Hence, a broader enquiry into the whole process of exorcising ghosts from sacred
places and other environments in both the ancient Near East and in classical
Greece cannot be addressed here. One of the best most recent works to get at all
this "ghost-banning" material can be found in C. A. Faraone, *Talismans and
Trojan Horses. Guardian Statues in Ancient Greek Myth and Ritual* (New York
and Oxford: Oxford University Press, 1992), esp. 79-84. The broader category of
ritual exorcism is also brilliantly analyzed in Burkert, *Orientalizing Revolution*,
55-72. On such healing figures, the following earlier works should also be
consulted: E. R. Dodds, *The Greeks and the Irrational* (Berkeley: University of
California Press, 1951), 135-78; Laín Entralgo, *Therapy of the Word*, 42, 74-86;
G. E. R. Lloyd, *Magic, Reason, and Experience: Studies in the Origin and
Development of Greek Science* (Cambridge: Cambridge University, 1979), 37-49;
W. Burkert, *Lore and Science in Ancient Pythagoreanism*, trans. E. L. Minar, Jr.
(Cambridge, Mass.: 1972), 162-65; *idem*, "Γόης. Zum griechischen Schamanis-
mus," *RhM* 105 (1962): 36-55; M. Eliade, *Shamanism: Archaic Techniques of
Ecstasy*, trans. W. R. Trask (New York, 1964); see also John Pollard, *Seers,
Shrines, and Sirens* (New York, 1965); M. L. West, *The Orphic Poems* (Oxford:
Oxford University Press, 1983), chap. II: "Some Mythical Poets other than
Orpheus," 39-67, and 20 n. 47.

[22] Linforth suggests that the lost work contained charms and incantations
with liturgical instructions for their use; see I. M. Linforth, *The Arts of Orpheus*
(Berkeley and Los Angeles: University of California Press, 1941), 137: "Of the
contents of Orphic books Euripides tells us nothing except that they included
pharmaka for use in extreme need. We may guess that these pharmaka consisted of

"purification rites" (καθαρμοί) that were read from house to house as Epicurus did with his mother, or as Plato describes of the "vagabonds and diviners" who, at the doors of the wealthy, offer healing sacrifices and incantations for iniquities past and present?[23]

A folded and inscribed lead tablet from Phalasarna in Crete, dated to the 4th or early 3rd century BCE, comes close to what we might imagine as a magic incantation for banishing unwanted demons. The inscription had evidently been doubled over several times into a compact square to be worn as an amulet.[24]

Much of the text is clearly difficult; however, there is enough preserved to demonstrate that we have an incantation written against noxious spirits described variously as Epaphos, a she-wolf (λύκαινα), a dog (κύων)—or pair of dogs (κύνε)—and the like.[25] In

---

charms and incantations with liturgical directions for their use." See also Laín Entralgo, *Therapy of the Word*, 48-49; G. Lanata, *Medicina, magica, e religione popolare in Graecia fino all' età di Ippocrate* (Filologia e critica 3; Rome, 1967), 48; P. Boyancé, *Le culte des Muses chez les philosophes grecs* (Paris, 1937), 39. On the ultimate Near-Eastern origin of such writing materials, see Burkert, *Orientalizing Revolution*, 30-33.

[23] For Epicurus, see the description of his accompanying his mother in reading purificatory rites from house to house: Diog. Laert. X. 4, καὶ γὰρ σὺν τῇ μητρὶ περιιόντα αὐτὸν ἐς τὰ οἰκίδια καθαρμοὺς ἀναγινώσκειν. The "purificatory" exorcists of Acts 19 also "go about" (οἱ περιερχόμενοι), perform their rites at homes (i.e., they flee the οἶκος), and are accompanied by apprenticing parents, by implication. Plato's wandering priests also read from books and used binding spells to work harm (Plato, *Rep* II. 364B-E); see Burkert, *Orientalizing Revolution*, 42, 125 (on Plato), and 41-87 (on all such purifiers being of Near Eastern importation).

[24] A new reading, with a tracing from the original, is given in D. R. Jordan, "The Inscribed Lead Tablet from Phalasarna," *ZPE* 94 (1992): 191-94, with prev. lit. A different, independent reading can be found in the excellent study of William D. Furley, "Zur Form und Funktion von ΕΠΩΙΔΑΙ in der griechischen Zaubermedizin," in Glenn W. Most, Hubert Petersmann, and Adolf Martin Ritter, eds., *Philanthropia kai Eusebeia. Festschrift für Albrecht Dihle zum 70. Geburtstag* (Göttingen: Vandenhoeck and Ruprecht, 1993), 80-104, esp. 96-99.

[25] The thrice-named Epaphos—a son of Zeus and Io, according to Aeschylus (so LSJ)—may represent nothing other than a personified plague, a thing that touches someone by contact or contagion, as the etymology implies. The noun ἐπαφή means "touching" or "handling; contact," sometimes in a punitive or severe manner. LSJ, s.v. Ἔπαφος, directs the reader as well to ἀφή, which in addition to the meanings "grip; touch," "contact," signifies an infection, especially leprosy, or, more generally, a plague (s.v., def. II.8). Here we contend that Epaphos is a contagious plague-demon. For Epaphos within the larger Near-Eastern context of healing, note Burkert, *Orientalizing Revolution*, 125, with p. 216, n. 8. See also Faraone, *Talismans and Trojan Horses*, 45-53:

a section that seems to mention magic ingredients targeted to
injure the bearer of the verses, we find further allusions to composite, mythic beings: the tongue of a *lion-serpent*, something
from a *Chimaera*, a hawk's feather, and the claw of a lion. Despite
some *lacunae*, these seem to describe the "wicked things" (κακά)
that some sorcerer had apparently concocted in an ointment or
potion; the hexameters work as a counter-charm against ghosts
and demons sent against the holder of the amulet.[26]

This text shows at an early stage two crucial procedures for the
expelling of demons: the use of the "flee"-formula and the application of an oath (ὅρκος). Though the demonology of this relatively
early Greek charm does not contain a notion of a possessing demon, the tablet's rich folklore shows animal-plagues being van-
quished by invocations that become standard in the later, true
exorcistic texts. The method is rather straightforward: alongside
the summoning of Greek healing gods, the incantation wards off
the demons by commanding them to flee (φεῦγε). This stratagem
of expulsion is widely found in late antique magic spells, particularly in exorcisms, but can also be used of banishing diseases and
ailments in general—themselves the manifestation of demonic
activity. The φεῦγε-formula is used several times in the Phalasarna
piece in commanding the animal-demons with the aim of driving
them back mad to their own domains (μαινόμενοι δ<ρ>άντων πρὸς
δώματα αὐτοῦ ἕκαστος).[27]

"Theriomorphic Demons and House Amulets," with many very insightful arguments on this and kindred texts.

[26] I hope to argue elsewhere that the Phalasarna tablet was written against
Erinyes-like avenging ghosts that had been sent against the holder of the charm,
much in the same way as the regulations drafted against such ghosts at 4th
century BCE Kyrene (Burkert, *Orientalizing Revolution,* 68-73) or at 5th
century BCE Selinous (note 9 above).

[27] Another early Greek papyrus spell, the famous chant of Philinna from Thessaly (*PGM* XX), dated to the 1st century BCE, also preserves fragmentary hexameters commanding a headache, described alongside animal-demons, to flee (the text
is studied further by Faraone in this volume); see also Furley, "Form und Funktion," 93-95. The representation of demons in various animal forms is, of course,
originally Near Eastern, and there is no reason not to acknowledge that the
Greeks of the archaic period borrowed extensively from their Mesopotamian
neighbors; see E. Langton, *Essentials of Demonology: A Study of Jewish and
Christian Doctrine, Its Origin and Development* (London, 1949). Theriomorphic demons were also described in the Hebrew Bible, but this particular demonology seems to have had little influence on the later anthropology of first-century
Syro-Palestinian demonology.

As for the Phalasarna tablet's use of the oath for the ridding of plagues and demons, we have a little less to go on. The context of line 9 yields little sense; only the verbal form ὁρκῶμεν, "we adjure" (or "let us adjure"), seems certain,[28] followed by the letters πομ–παι [..] ϝτωι—letters that, fractured as they are, certainly summon to mind Hermes Pompaios, the "conductor of souls." This could further pursuade one to deduce that the twin "dogs" at the end of the same line refer to avenging spirits, such as the Erinyes mentioned above, or to escorts of Hekate, or Kerberos-like watchhounds of Hades. In any event, in ancient Greece oath-takers routinely consecrated their solemn vows by summoning the god of the Underworld. There is hardly reason not to assume that such an oath by Hades is here envisioned and that the string of *Ephesia Grammata* in line 10 also represents additional names by which the chthonian oath was made. The adjuration, then, can best be understood as the administration of a magic oath by both the power of the Netherworld and by the authority of the famous "Ephesian letters." ὁρκῶμεν surely operates as a supernaturally binding formula, which in tandem with φεύγειν aims to banish the harrassing demons represented as theriomorphic.

But there are also other compelling phrases found on the tablet for banishing noxious influences. In lines 10-11 a list of magic names seems to be cryptically ordered to "drive away" (ἐλαύνετε), by force (βίᾳ), a she-goat from a garden. Though the lines may have originally come from an older, independent context in the Mysteries, in their present setting the words "drive away from the garden" probably have in mind protection and purification of the owner's actual estate; the she-goat will then be a kind of goat-demon like those of Near Eastern heritage.[29] This would parallel

---

[28] While this essay was already in press, I noticed that Jordan (n. 24, above) prints ὁρκῶμεμ, which is seemingly inconsistent with his actual tracing (APKOMEM = ἀρκῶμεν, "let us ward off" / "we are warding off"). But his printed reading (and our interpretation), ὁρκῶμεν, may still be defensible. In several places on the tablet A is mistaken for O (e.g., πατωι for ποτωι in line 20). Also the 1st person plural (ἀρκῶμεν) might perhaps be inconsistent with other verbs of driving away (as in line 11, ἐλαύνετε) that invoke the *deities* to act.

[29] Cf. the Hebrew male *śĕʿîrîm*, a kind of hairy demon in the form of a he-goat (Lev 17:7; Isa 13:21; 34:14; 2 Chron 11:15). The female counterpart, the *śĕʿîrāh*, "she-goat" (Lev 4:28; 5:6), would match our tablet's αἴξ (line 11); cf. the *śēdîm* (demons) of Deut 32:17; Psalm 106:37. In Isa 13:21; 34:14 *śĕʿîrîm* (cf. Aramaic *śĕʿîrîn*) is rendered σειρῆνες in LXX. Greek σειρ-ήν, ῆνος, ἡ, is morphologically identical to Semitic *śĕʿîr* and must be a loan-word. The Greek sirens, who generally play a destructive rôle, also live in Hades, according to Plato (*Crat.* 403D), and can still the wind (Hesiod, Fr. 69 [Rzach]) with their song (see *OCD*, s.v.). It

line 2 of the spell, where the wild beasts are bidden to "flee from these houses of ours." They are to go back to their own domains (δώματα), a description, incidentally, often used of the dark quarters of Hades. The banishing motif thus represents one of spatial relationships and boundaries. The demons do not belong in the realm of the living but of the dead.

The use of ἐλαύνειν in the Phalasarna text for driving out demons is common as an exorcistic verb in later texts, especially in the context of making oaths. One may cite, by way of example, Lucian, who in his *Lover of Lies* (16) tells of an exorcist using "oaths and threats to drive out a demon" (ὁ δὲ ὅρκους ἐπάγων ... καὶ ἀπειλῶν ἐξελαύνει τὸν δαίμονα). And a text on a gold tablet, also from Thessaly like the Philinna papyrus, similarly describes an unusual δαιμόνων ἐλάτης, "a driver of demons," on a house amulet—the epithet is cognate with our verb ἐλαύνειν.[30]

The Phalasarna tablet works its protective magic by also summoning one of the more famous of the so-called "Ephesian Letters," the powerful Damnameneus, who is to "tame (or subdue) by force those wickedly constraining." The imperative "tame" (δάμασον) as well as the adverbial ἀνάγκᾳ ("by force") provide twin etymological *aitia* of the god's name: Damnameneus is the one who "subdues, tames, or conquers" by constraint.[31] The powerful name of Damnameneus is one encountered often in later magical texts. "Necessity" or "Constraint" (*Anankē*) is also the focus of the Thracian tablets in the *Alcestis* named above.

The example of the Phalasarna tablet, though far removed from the later demonology of spontaneous possession, provides us with the earliest formulaic vocabulary of "exorcism," both in its par-

---

is no accident that line 12 of the Phalasarna tablet also mentions a mysterious "windy promontory" (ἀνεμώλιος ἀκτή), the very place from which the sirens could control the winds and lure (Cretan) sailors to their deaths. All these traits can be explained as cultural translations of the goat-like Semitic *śĕʿîrîm/-în*, and *śĕʿîrôt*—"sirens"—that the Phalasarna spell has rendered as male and female goats (τράγος/αἴξ). Is ἕλκει in line 5, then, a reference to the sirens' luring of ships to destruction (accepting Furley's ἀί(αι) ἐτ' ὥδ' ἕλκει)?

[30] Kotansky, *Greek Magical Amulets,* no. 41,18.

[31] Pseudo-Dioscorides 4.131 tells us so much when he defines the form δαμ-ναμένη as κατανάγκη, "a means of constraint"; "a spell." Damnameneus is one of the so-called Idaean Dactyls: Bengt Hemberg, "Die Idaiischen Daktylen," *Eranos* 50 (1952): 41-59, esp. 50: δαμνᾶν = δαμάζειν. Additional literature and discussion in R. Kotansky and C. A. Faraone, "An Inscribed Gold Phylactery in Stamford, Connecticut," *ZPE* 75 (1988): 257-66, esp. 264; C. C. McCown, "The Ephesia Grammata in Popular Belief," *TAPA* 54 (1923): 23.

ticular use of the adjuration and "flee"-formula, and in the accompanying banishment motifs, just described. These and other elements of this Greek form of "exorcism," so to speak, shall come up again in many of the exorcistic amulets of later antiquity. First, though, before examining these in some detail, we must direct our focus to the particular notion of Jewish expulsion of demons and exorcism.

*   *   *

We find little in the Jewish scriptures that speaks of exorcism of demons, though the story of the evil spirit that afflicts Saul in the Book of Kings provides the classical identification of David as an exorcist par excellence in the tradition of Solomon.[32] From this account, and no doubt additional influences, the Qumran Community of the Dead Sea Scrolls seems to have developed its own liturgical system of exorcism, as mentioned above; however, since these texts are largely in Aramaic and lie outside the scope of this study, we turn rather to the apocryphal Book of Tobit, whose well-known account of exorcism is given in Greek.

The Book of Tobit, known from two main Greek recensions of the Septuagint, was probably originally composed around the 3rd century BCE, though perhaps in Aramaic;[33] it thus represents a

---

[32] Although an ἐξορκίζω-formula similar to that of Acts 19 is attested several times in more civil or mundane contexts where other human beings, and not spirits, are adjured by oath. The evil spirit that afflicts Saul in the Book of Kings (1 Kings 16:14-16, 23; 19:9) is in fact a "wicked spirit" (LXX πνεῦμα πονηρόν), though this is one that is sent by the Lord himself, as a form of punishment or trial. David, as an early Jewish exorcist himself anticipating Solomon of later lore, is able to ward off the spirit by singing and playing the *kinnor* (1 Kings 16:23 LXX: ἀφίστατο ἀπ' αὐτοῦ τὸ πνεῦμα τὸ πονηρόν).

[33] That of Codex Sinaiticus (S = R^S) and that of Vaticanus and Alexandrinus (BA = R^V). A third, textually mixed recension (= R^c) contains only 6:9-12:22; see D. C. Simpson, "The Chief Recensions of the Book of Tobit," *JTS* 14 (1912-13): 516-30. The recent publication of some fragmentary Aramaic portions from Qumran may antiquate earlier reconstructions. On Tobit, see Carey A. Moore, "Scholarly Issues in the Book of Tobit Before Qumran and After: An Assessment," *JSP* 5 (1989): 65-81, and *idem*, art. "Tobit, Book of," in D. N. Freedman, ed., *ABD* (1992), 6.588-94, who presents among other things, die-hard views of those who maintain that Tobit was originally composed in Greek. A still very useful text, translation, and commentary is that of F. Zimmermann, *The Book of Tobit. An English Translation with Introduction and Commentary,* Dropsie College Edition (Jewish Apocryphal Literature; New York: Harper and Brothers, 1958).

text roughly contemporary with the Phalasarna tablet.[34] A remarkable vignette of this engaging romance tells of the use of the
intestines of a fish for certain healing remedies, including the
expulsion of the demon Asmodeus. Tobias, Tobit's son, while
embarking on a journey to Ecbatana in Media, with Raphael the
archangel,[35] encounters the magical fish at the banks of the Tigris
River. The angel exhorts the lad to capture the fish, for its heart,
liver, and bile carry certain magical properties; when fumigated,
they expel demons. Also, the bile rubbed on the eyes cures the
blinding leukoma from which the elderly Tobit suffers.[36]

After the fumigation, so verse 6:8 insures the reader, every assault of a demon shall *flee* his presence. Although here recension
BA does not agree in giving the exorcistic expulsion with this
"flee"-formula, later in 7:17 and elsewhere it does: "the demon
shall smell it and flee and will not return forever." Again, at 8:3
when the actual exorcism is performed, recension BA tells how the
demon "fled" (ἔφυγεν) to the uppermost parts of Egypt, where
Gabriel "bound" (ἔδησεν) him. The same verse in recension S,
however, uses somewhat different wording: "And the aroma of the
fish prevented it, and the demon ran away up to the parts of
Egypt, and Raphael went and fettered him there and bound him
immediately."

Of some interest is the fact that recension BA of the exorcism
evidently reflects in its ritual instructions and overall diction a
dependence upon magico-medical handbooks, much like those

---

[34] It has been argued that the exorcistic sources that lie behind Tobit may be
based largely on the Egyptian Bentresh-stele, a propagandistic text that tells of
an exorcism of a princess. This so-called tractate of Khons is of perhaps Persian or
Ptolemaic date; see, most recently, Scott N. Morschauser, "Using History:
Reflections on the Bentresh Stela," *Studien zur Altägyptischen Kultur* 15
(1988): 203-23 (with extensive lit.); cf. Moore, "Book of Tobit," 74; P. Tresson,
"Un curieux cas d'exorcisme dan l'antiquité: La stéle égyptienne de Bakhtan,"
RB 42 (1933): 57-78; cf. T. K. Oesterreich, *Possession. Demoniacal & Other
among Primitive Races, in Antiquity, the Middle Ages, and Modern Times,*
trans. D. Ibberson, (New Hyde Park: University Books, 1966), 148-51 (for a
translation). Our study does not allow a more detailed examination of this
valuable document.

[35] That is, *incognito* as his cousin Azarias. See P.-E. Dion, "Raphaël,
l'Exorciste," *Biblica* 57 (1976): 399-413; cf. Brenk, "Light of the Moon," 2093f.,
esp. on the comparison between Tobit and Plutarch.

[36] The instructions, of course, are central to the narrative, for both medica-
ments are indeed used by Tobias: the demon, Asmodeus, has been slaying the
suitors of his bride-to-be, Sarah—the demon is enamored of her—and on their
wedding night, Tobias is to expel the demon from their presence with the fish
ingredients. Later, Tobias applies the bile to cure his father's affliction.

preserved in the later magical papyri; hence the story itself probably used as its source an early form of written magic which contained rituals for exorcism.[37]

Like the Phalasarna tablet of our "Greek" model, the ceremonial exorcism in Tobit describes the demon's expulsion in terms of flight (the φεῦγε-formula). Because our example is preserved in its final edited, literary form, and does not come from an actual amulet, some differences can be expected. Thus, for example, no adjuration formulae, nor any form of a spoken exorcism at all, are given. The method of casting out is achieved through fumigation; however, it is not unimportant that Raphael instructs Tobias to remember in the bridal-chamber to pray for God's mercy and deliverance.[38] The prayer, then, serves as a kind of protective measure—a blessing—against the demon's renewed assault. We shall encounter the same motif again in the exorcisms of the Great Magical Papyrus of Paris, where it assumes the form of a protective amulet that the bearer is actually to wear.

---

[37] That recension gives, for instance, in 6:4, the instructions "Take the heart and the liver and the bile and set it aside carefully" (λαβὼν τὴν καρδίαν καὶ τὸ ἧπαρ καὶ τὴν χολὴν θὲς ἀσφαλῶς). The aorist participle λαβών preserves the common manner of providing ritual in magical texts. It is, in fact, the very form used in the ritual exorcism of Pibechis, discussed in this essay. Even the adverb ἀσφαλῶς is used in magical instruction-books in this manner. The Sinaitican recension, on the other hand, seems to avoid such ritual language altogether. The explicit references to the demonic possession that the fish-remedies cure also differ in the two recensions. The first (BA) refers to the attack of the demon with the verb ὀχλέω, "to disturb, annoy." Both the noun ὄχλησις and the verb are commonly used of demon possession in the papyri and literature. One possessed of a demon is explicitly so called in Luke 6:18 and in Acts 5:16: ὁ ὀχλούμενον, "the one tormented." Other exorcistic texts also occasionally use the term. For example, in the exorcistic interpolations of MS. L of the *Testament of Solomon*, such a tormented demoniac is to be treated by the very ritual described here in the Book of Tobit: καὶ λαβὼν ὁ ἀναγινώσκων τὴν ἁγίαν διαθήκην ταύτην· ἰχθύος χολὴν καπνίσας τὸν ὀχλούμενον λέγ<ε>· διώκει σε Ῥαφαὴλ ὁ παρεστικὸς (sic) ἐνώπιον τοῦ θεοῦ, "And the lector—taking this holy Testament (of Solomon)—after fumigating the fish's gall-bladder over the tormented person, says, 'Raphael who stands before God is chasing you.'" See H. M. Jackson, "Notes on the Testament of Solomon," *JSJ* 19 (1988): 19-60. Here, too, it should be observed, we find the ritual use of λαβών. Recension S, on the other hand, calls the demonic attack an ἀπάντημα. This term, we shall see, is also widely represented in Greek exorcistic amulets and probably derives from Hebrew/Aramaic פגע, "assault; affliction"—the very translation given it in the Hebrew version of Tobit; note Zimmermann, *Book of Tobit*, 81 n. 8.

[38] The ritual prayer, now well-worked into the story's narrative, is made to God after the expulsion of the demon: "Cry to the mercy of God, and he shall save you and show mercy" [BA] (or: "Pray and beseech the Lord of heaven that there might be mercy and salvation upon you" [S]).

The occurrence of an oath-formula on a Greek apotropaic amulet of Hellenistic date introduced us to the early use of the adjuration. In the apocryphal Book of Tobit we read of no adjuration, but simply of an attack of an evil spirit sent to flight (φεύξεται) by the fumigated heart and liver of a fish. The rite contains no mention of an engraved amulet, nor of the use of divine names; however, the language of the account does use terminology occurring often on engraved amulets,[39] and a belief in a demon who seizes possession of a person begins to take shape.[40]

We also observed above that the formalized expression ἐξορκίζω σε κατά, "I adjure you, by the . . .," has its most frequent attestation in aggressive sexual spells and curses (defixiones) that routinely summon a νεκυδαίμων ("ghost") to act on the caller's behalf. Such netherworld spirits serve the magicians by targeting their intended victims in a vengeful and treacherous manner. Similarly, the formula can occur in divinatory spells, which summon oracle-giving deities to grant some sort of esoteric knowledge.

But less common is the use of ἐξορκίζω on general amulets and protective charms for healing named afflictions.[41] When the afflictions are demonic assaults, as is almost always the case, the formulaic ἐξορκίζω σε seems invariably to describe the *exorcism* of the evil spirit. The procedure—even the religious disposition—

---

[39] One benefit that can be derived from such a literary account is that ritual instructions, which might otherwise be lost to the amulets, provide us with what sort of attendant gestures and acts accompanied the exorcistic pronouncement found on the amulets themselves. Even if our account is cast in the form of a literary romance, its vocabulary of exorcism can easily draw us back to the sort of performative utterances found commonly preserved on extant amulets and *phylaktēria*.

[40] Recension S reads, "And they shall never more find an abode with him" (καὶ οὐ μὴ μείνωσιν μετ᾽ αὐτοῦ εἰς τὸν αἰῶνα).

[41] When we do find these, they can be shown to represent "composite" texts that have conflated the formula from coercive spells with other, more "benign," expressions of healing or deliverance; the result is an often bewildering mixing of stereotypical formulae; cf., for example, PGM XVIIIb: Γοργωφωνας (in wing-formation), ἐξορκίζω ὑμᾶς κατὰ ἁγίου ὀνόματος, θεραπεῦσαι Διονύσιον ἤτοι ᾽Ανυς, ὃν ἔτεκεν Ἡρακλία, ἀπὸ πα[ν]τὸς ῥίγου<ς> καὶ πυρετοῦ ἢ το[ῦ] κα<θ>ημερινοῦ ἢ μίαν παρὰ μίαν νυκτερινοῦ τε καὶ ἡμερι<νοῦ> ἢ τετρ<α>δ<ι>ο<υ>, <ἢ>δη ἤδη, ταχύ, ταχύ, "Gorgophonas, I adjure you (pl.) by the holy name, to heal Dionysius alias Anys, whom Heracleia bore, from all ague and fever, daily or quartan, now, now, quickly, quickly." XXXVI 257-60: ᾽Ασστάηλος, Χράηλος, λύσατε πᾶν φάρμακον γενόμενον κατ᾽ ἐμοῦ τοῦ δεῖνα, ὅτι ὁρκίζω ὑμᾶς κατὰ τῶν μεγάλων καὶ φικτρῶν ὀνομάτων, κτλ., "Asstaelos, Chraelos, lose every enchantment occurring against me, so-and-so, because I adjure you [pl.] by the great and frightful names."

of such exorcisms differs considerably from the adjurations that evoke netherworld demons to serve a purpose on the practitioner's behalf, and these shall be the spotlight of the remainder of our discussion.

* * *

The study of exorcistic amulets must begin with the first of two much-discussed adjurations of the Great Magical Papyrus of Paris (*PGM* IV). The text (lines 1227-64), of which only the exorcism formula proper is discussed here, shows by its title (Πρᾶξις γενναία ἐκβάλλουσα δαίμονας, "Excellent Method for Casting out Demons") that it is intended to expel indwelling demons.[42] The first lines give a unique ritual in Greek involving the crowning of the demoniac's head with olive branches and then, in Coptic, an invocation of the "god of Abraham, Isaac, and Jacob." A widely acknowledged interpolation, "Jesus Christ, the Holy Spirit, the son of the Father," then follows (among other things). The Coptic section concludes by describing the driving away of "the unclean demon Satan who is in him (sc. the patient)."

The hallmark of this exorcism is its use of ἐξορκίζω with specific verbs of expulsion: "I adjure you (ἐξορκίζω σε) ... *to come out of* (ἐξελθεῖν) ... and *stand away from* (ἀπόστηθι) so-and-so." These attendant imperatives, in effect, turn the adjuration itself into a true exorcism, for the imperatives represent the resultant action of the adjuration. The adjuration formula specifically aims at expelling the demon: "I adjure you *out*" (ἐξ-ορκίζω ... ἐξ-ελθεῖν); hence, "I *exorcise* you" (i.e., "I compel you under oath to come out").[43] Beginning with the Western text of Acts, preserved in manuscripts contemporary with our *PGM* IV, such a combination of phrasing becomes the standard method of expressing exorcism on amulets and texts of the period.[44]

---

[42] See R. Merkelbach, "Astrologie, Mechanik, Alchimie und Magie im griechisch-römischen Ägypten," *Riggisberger Berichte* 1 (1993): 49-62, esp. 60-61: "Ein christlicher Exorzismus." ἐκβάλλειν of casting out demons is also used in the Gospels for exorcism: Mk 1:34,39; 3:15,22,23; 6:13; 7:26; 16:9, 17 (par.).

[43] This is the force of ἐκ- admitted by Webster's *Third New International Dictionary. Unabridged*, s.v. "exorcise," 798. In Greek, ἐκ- in compounds can mean both "removal; out, away from," as well as be used to express "completion: utterly" (so LSJ, s.v. C). The latter must have been implied in the earliest Greek uses of the verb (i.e., ἐξ-ορκόω), whereas the former is made explicit by the later, demonological uses (ἐξ-ορκίζω).

[44] Though the verb ἐξελθεῖν is used of exorcism already in the earliest strata of the Gospel tradition (in Q and Mark), it is only here in Codex Bezae

Our rite concludes with instructions for the writing of an amulet
aimed at the patient's continued protection during convalescence:
"Having cast out (the demon), tie around NN a protective charm,
which the patient is to put on after the demon is cast out: (write)
these things on a leaf of tinfoil" (magic names + "protect so-and-
so"). The text of the *lamella* itself, however, says surprising little
of exorcism.[45]

The second exorcism of the long Paris papyrus manual also adjures the demons "to come out of" the sufferer and further recommends the manufacture of a tin *lamella* as an amulet. It also
executes its oaths by adjuring the demon by the name of the Jewish
god. The so-called "Tested Charm of Pibechis for those possessed
of demons" (= *PGM* IV. 3007-3086) promotes a series of magical
words that ends again in the formula "come out of" (ἔξελθε).[46] The
spell then addresses the requisite amulet: "On a tin *lamella* write,
IAEO ABRAOTH IOCH PHTHA MESENPSIN IAO PHEOCH
IAEO CHARSOK, and hang it on the patient. It is terrifying to
every demon, a thing he fears." The rubric guarantees that the
phylactery of tin, containing again only magic names, will prove

---

Cantabrigiensis and p[38] in all of the New Testament that the verb is used *together* with ἐξορκίζω. It seems that the vernacular of D (and p[38]) is simply mirror-
ing an exorcistic parlance contemporary with the 3rd or 4th century date of the
manuscript itself (or possibly contemporary with the 2nd-century date of Acts, as
argued above). The most recent, thorough study of the document, that of D. C.
Parker, *Codex Bezae. An Early Christian Manuscript and its Text* (Cambridge:
Cambridge University, 1992), 30 *et passim*, dates it to ca. 400.

[45] The words to be written on the leaf are permutations of the magic name
PHORBA, PHORPHOR, and BOPHOR, a formulaic name found rather on the
more compulsive curses of the aggressive-coercive kind. Is the expelled demon,
then, being cursed and bound? The presence of the phrase δαῖμον, ὅστις ποτ' οὖν
ᾖ also shows the language of a *defixio*. But appended to this coercive formula,
however, is a more tell-tale prophylactic formula, φύλαξον τὸν δεῖνα, "protect so-
and-so."

[46] For this spell, cf. S. Eitrem, *Some Notes on the Demonology of the New Testament*, Symbolae Osloenses Suppl. 20, 2nd ed. (Oslo: Universitetsforlaget,
1966), 15-30—a brilliant study that deserves more scrutiny than the strictures of
this paper permit; A. Deissmann, *Light from the Ancient East*, trans. L. R. M.
Strachan (New York and London: Hodder and Stoughton, 1910; 1911[2]), 250-60
(with photograph of the relevant leaf, text, translation, and commentary); A.
Dieterich, *Abraxas* (Leipzig, 1891), may well be right in dating the earliest form
of this spell to the 2nd century BCE; cf. Conybeare, "Christian Demonology,"
91f.; W. L. Knox, "Jewish Liturgical Exorcism," *HTR* 31 (1938): 191-203;
Daniel Sperber, "Some Rabbinic Themes in Magical Papyri," *JSJ* 16 (1985): 93-
103, esp. 95-99; cf. C. K. Barrett, *The New Testament Background: Selected
Documents* (London: SPCK, 1956; repr. New York: Harper, 1961), no. 27.

disquieting to demons. "Fear" complements the notion of "flight" found in the Phalasarna tablet and the Book of Tobit and often communicates a particular demonic response to invoked magic names. The potency of putting the demon to flight *in fear* is double-edged, but the motif of banishment remains single. It is the exorcist's great psychological weapon against unseen powers. If it is not the demon's flight that is mentioned, it will be his fear; the net result is the same, once the patient is seen as relieved of demons and healed.

The bulk of the Paris spell comprises a long series of short, independent ὁρκισμοί, adjurations-become-"exorcisms." The series in effect contains a repetition *in seriatim* of the formulaic ἐξορκίζω σε, with the demon pounded by a relentless series of divine, "biblical" adjurations invoking the mighty character and deeds of the Jewish god; the later Christian adaptations of these exorcisms will name the deeds of Christ.[47] W. L. Knox qualifies this sort of biblical adjuration as "a series of exorcisms following a general type of a kerygma of Judaism, with special reference to those aspects of the action of God which are calculated to impress demons."[48] The "redemptive" typology is based largely on the biblical accounts of Genesis and Exodus (Ex 7:8-11:10; 13:21f.), though smatterings of other Septuagintal excerpts are spread throughout the text. Such allusions from holy writ contain the sort of narrative themes found again and again in these and later liturgical exorcisms; they ultimately derive, no doubt, from the Hellenistic Jewish synagogue.[49] In this sense such exorcisms are truly

---

[47] Conybeare, "Demonology of NT," 598-99, on Justin's (*Dial.* 247C; *Dial.* 311B; *Apol.* II. 45A) mention of Christians using credal formulas to cast out demons; *idem*, "Christian Demonology," 63-64, on Origen's (*Contra Cels.* I, 6) naming Christians who also use kerygmatic stories to exorcise (... ἀλλὰ τῷ ὀνόματι 'Ιησοῦ μετὰ τῆς ἀπαγγελίας τῶν περὶ αὐτὸν ἱστοριῶν, ed. Borret). Conybeare, "Christian Demonology," 590, is the first, to my knowledge, to have noted the importance of the use of creed-like formulations in connection with both exorcisms and healing rites: "I believe, therefore, that one reason at least for the formation of the earliest creeds was the want of a short and effective formula for the exorcism of demons. Jesus had indeed enjoined the mere use of his name; but his followers soon found that this was not enough; and so Origen informs us that to the name was added ... an announcement of the history of Jesus"—an announcement, we may add, that was rendered more effective by being enchanted over the afflicted. These credal exorcisms are surely formed on the earlier Jewish model of reciting the *historia* of the god of Israel; cf. also Eitrem, *Notes*, 21-24.

[48] W. L. Knox, "Jewish Liturgical Exorcism," 202.

[49] The study of credal and liturgical exorcism within the Jewish synagogue and how this may have come to influence the practice within formative Christianity cannot be addressed here. For some introductory comments along these lines,

liturgical. The Pibechian exorcism itself even claims its essentially Jewish nature: "For the formula is Hebraic and continually guarded by pure men" (lines 3085f.).

The first of the serial adjurations exorcises the demon by the Jewish god, an adjuration to which again has been appended a reference to Jesus: "I adjure you by the god of the Hebrews, *Jesus*, Iaba, iaê, abraoth," etc. (ὁρκίζω σε κατὰ τοῦ θεοῦ τῶν Ἑβραίων / Ἰησοῦ· Ιαβα; ιαη· αβραωθ, κτλ., lines 3019f.). The name "Jesus" might be a late Christian interpolation, for the god of the Hebrews would normally refer only to Iaba (= יהוה). Is the use of Jesus' name a mere addition by Jewish exorcists to empower their spell, as in Acts 19? The exorcisms then continue with only Jewish—not Christian—kerygmatic themes: "I adjure you (ὁρκίζω σε) by the one who appeared to Israel in the fiery pillar and a cloud by day and who rescued his people from Pharaoh and brought upon Pharaoh the ten plagues because of his disobedience . . . I adjure you by (ὁρκίζω σε κατά) the Seal that Solomon placed upon the tongue of Jeremiah and spoke," and so on. A litany of biblical accounts of God's redemptive acts are enumerated one after another.

The "Hebraic" adjurations of the spell as a whole look heavenward in their exorcistic method: the scene is consistently one of splendor, radiance, and angelology. The adjurations exorcise the demons, as it were, by a sort of fiery onslaught of divine, celestial incandescence: the god by whom the demon is adjured "appears in fire" and "in a shining pillar;" is called the "phosphorescent" (or "light-bearing") god (lines 3045f.); it is he who "burned up the stubborn giants with lightning" (lines 3048-60), and he is the one whom "heavenly powers of angels and archangels praise." The heavy emphasis on light certainly looks like the esoterica of a more mystical synagogal Judaism and probably reflects the widespread solar worship of Yahweh.

But the radiance of fire can prove both infernal as well as sublimely celestial. Precisely because magical texts draw so often upon incongruous ancient sources, Pibechis' exorcism also gives glimpses of a vestigial Greek netherworld demonology—that of the coercive and binding spells of the chthonian world. Juxtaposed to the description of the "light-bearing" god comes a seemingly antithetical *Beiname*, the god who is ἀδάμαστος, "unsubdued, inflexible." It is an epithet that not only reminds us of our old Greek "subduer,"

see R. Kotansky (rev. of Lee I. Levine, ed., *The Synagogue in Late Antiquity* [Philadelphia: ASOR, 1987]) in *Hebrew Studies* 20 (1988): 167-74.

Damnameneus, it also represents a title entirely uninfluenced by biblical ideologies of God: *Adámastos* is none other than Hades himself; his particular title here is modelled upon an epithet familiar from Homer (*Iliad* IX.158: δμηθήτω—'Αΐδης τοι ἀμείλιχος ἠδ' ἀδάμαστος, "Let him yield—*Hades, I ween, is not to be soothed, neither overcome*," tr. Murray). In a word, there is no compromise to be made with death.

Netherworld and heavenly juxtapositions continue in the text as if to combine a concept of the Jewish creator god with a Greek nether deity. The Jewish god is not only "the one who formed of dust the race of humans" (3047f.), he is also the god who "packs the clouds together and waters the earth and blesses its fruit" (3050f.). But the same god appears to be he who also τὸν ἐξαγαγόντα ἐξ ἀδήλων (lit. "leads out from the unseen," line 3048). The reference is cryptic; it does not refer to creation *ex nihilo*—for this is given later in the spell—nor does it refer to God's formation of clouds. Rather, it names one who evokes spirits from the underworld: ἐξάγειν ἐξ ἀδήλων means "to lead out from unseen places" and draws upon the mythology of the evocation of souls from the dead, the land of Hades. The phrasing is again based on Homer and mirrored in a fragment of Empedocles that describes the famed wonder-worker's magic abilities, one of which was to "lead from Hades the spirit of a dead man," ἄξεις δ' ἐξ 'Αΐδαο καταφθιμένου μένος ἀνδρός (Fr. 101 Wright). The expression is immediately recollective of the Psychopomp of Souls described briefly in the Phalasarna lead tablet (above).

In another adjuration of the spell (lines 3062-64), the nether realms are again mentioned alongside creative activity, though the precise meaning of the passage is difficult to fathom: "I adjure you by the one who set the mountain around the sea—a wall of sand—and ordered them not to overflow; and the Abyss heeded—so you also heed, every spirit, demon, because I am adjuring you . . . ." As the text stands, the Abyss or primordial Sea obeys this injunction, and so accordingly should the demons acquiesce, demons who, by the inherently magic power of the words contained in this subtle "like-by-like" formulation, are to recognize their own limitative status and to observe boundaries: their home is the Abyss, and that is where they belong. It is as if the surly demons had signed an unwritten clause in some unseen cosmological contract, the public reading of which—through the performance of the exorcism—has bound them to their legal obligation. This setting of boundaries between the demonic and human realms again recalls the Phalasarna tablet with its command that the demons flee to their rightful domains.

The exorcism of *PGM* IV. 1227-1264, the first of the two Paris spells (discussed above), echoes essentially the same views in its threat to bind up the demon with unbreakable chains and to cast it back to Hades. The exorcised demon is fastened with adamantine chains (ἐπεί σε δεσμεύω δεσμοῖς ἀδαμαντίνοις ἀλύτοις)—the adjective derives again from the same root as the name of our "inflexible" subduer, *Adámastos*—and is again returned to his dark chaos (καὶ παραδίδωμί σε εἰς τὸ μέλαν χάος ἐν ταῖς ἀπ-ωλείαις).[50] The very *daimones* of the coercive spells, *daimones* who are routinely summoned from graves and infernal regions to work havoc, are now "revoked." This revocation reverses the mechanism by which the writers of curses (κατάδεσμοι) evoke their νεκυδαίμονες and fetter them in dutiful service.

* * *

These motifs—adjurations by the Jewish creator god combined with more chthonian, Greek elements—recur on other exorcistic texts and amulets contemporary with the Great Magical Papyrus of Paris. It is no coincidence that in the majority of cases, the adjurations are to be written onto thin sheets of gold, silver, bronze, or tin. Many such exorcistic *lamellae* have survived from antiquity.[51] Regularly, as well, these exorcisms choose and select one or more of the thematic ingredients accentuated above—the demon as a wild beast, the "flee"-motif, the command to the spirit to depart, the mention of Solomon and his Seal, and most importantly, the development of ἐξορκίζειν as "to exorcise." In the remaining survey of magical texts, we concentrate on limited aspects of these motifs rather than provide extensive commentary. In so doing, we may be able to discern a certain internal consistency within the particular spells in question, a consistency that may well point to a common origin or cultural milieu.

PGM VII. 260-271 provides an excellent example of an exorcistic formula written on a tin *lamella*. Here, unlike the exorcisms of the Paris papyrus, an important development occurs: whereas in

---

[50] A knowledge of Greek binding spells is certainly presupposed in the choice of language, such as, "I bind you" (δεσμεύω σε), and "I hand you over" (παραδίδωμί σε)—technical verbs in the *defixiones* of binding human opponents.

[51] Kotansky, *Greek Magical Amulets,* Part I, gives 68 examples in Greek (and Latin). A second volume of such texts (in preparation) will increase the figure considerably. See also Kotansky, "Incantations," 107-37.

both the Pibechian exorcism and the shorter Coptic-Greek example, the tin phylacteries contained no texts that in themselves described exorcism, the whole text of *PGM* VII gives an adjuration formula to be engraved onto the tablet itself.[52] What was formerly a spoken adjuration has now become a written one.

Another noted difference in the text of *PGM* VII, in fact an adjuration of an unstable, wandering uterus, is that the "exorcism" is intended merely to check the malicious activity of the offending creature, not to expel it. It was a widespread, folkloric belief that the uterus represented an uncontrollable entity that could meander arbitrarily throughout the body, wrecking torment and generally tribulating the female patient.[53] It had to be controlled, and in this manner is the demon of the womb quietly "exorcised" by being admonished to abide in its proper domain.

The spell contains all the elements of a typical Jewish exorcism, adjuring the womb by the one established over the primordial Abyss before creation, and by the one over the Cherubim. And just as the demon in the exorcism of Pibechis was adjured not to violate (μὴ ὑπερβῆναι) the boundaries of the Abyss, so also is the womb-demon, likened to a gnawing beast, made to remain in the "Abyss" of its own dark uterus: she is to be returned and restored (ἀποκατασταθῆναι ἐν τῇ ἕδρα) to the place from whence she came, "to remain in her own lands (χῶροι)."[54] A second "exorcism" in the spell further adjures the womb by the Jewish god "who in the beginning made heaven and earth, and all things in them"—a reference to Exod 20:11 (LXX). Distinctively Jewish, too, is the closing exclamations, "Hallelujah!" and "Amen!"

The same "liturgical" citation of Exodus 20:11 occurs in an exorcism written on an actual *lamella*, though this time one of silver,

---

[52] The exorcisms of the Paris magical text gave somewhat detailed instructions, including the exorcistic adjurations to be spoken (not written) during various stages of the exorcistic operation. The British Museum's spell gives none.

[53] Jean-Jacques Aubert, "Threatened Wombs: Aspects of Ancient Uterine Magic," *GRBS* 30 (1989): 421-49; A. A. Barb, "Diva Matrix," *JWCI* 16 (1953): 193-238. An actual gold *lamella* from Beirut (cited in translation in Aubert, "Threatened Wombs") provides an excellent match to the text of *PGM* VII. 260-71. Published since 1853, but misread, a new edition of the text is now available in Kotansky, *Greek Magical Amulets*, Part I, no. 51, 265-69 (the text dates to the 1st cent. BCE/1st cent. CE, or slightly later).

[54] The verb ἀποκατασταθῆναι is a compound of the normal exorcistic term ἀποστῆναι, "to depart, stand away," and the reference to the beast as a biting dog compares the rebellious entity to a rustic, savage beast who rages against passersby in the manner of less citified demons.

not of tin.[55] This Jewish text is genuinely exorcistic: "I ad-
jure/exorcise every evil and wicked spirit, by the great highest god
who created the heaven and the earth and the seas and all things in
them, *to come out of* (ἐξελθεῖν) Allous whom Annis bore—she who
has the Seal of Solomon, on this very day, in this very hour, now,
now, quickly, quickly." The exorcistic formula compares closely to
that of the Western reading of Acts 19. Further, the naming of the
famous Seal of Solomon, with a drawing of the seal on the *lamella*
enclosing יהוה written in palaeo-Hebrew letters, places this amulet
in a special category of itself, a category to which we shall turn
again, briefly.

A Hebrew-Greek copper bilingual *lamella* from 'Evron in western Galilee[56] draws on biblical references to adjure a fever to be
banished from the body of its client, Casius. The relevant portions
of the spell command "the great and the small fever *to (be) extinguished*" (ἀποσβῆναι), or "*to stand away from*" (reading
ἀποσθῆναι), the owner of the amulet, followed by a second adjuration of "the one who made the heavens and founded earth and
established sea, who made all things, Iao Sabaoth." The formula,
naming again the god of the Jewish scriptures, prosecutes the fever,
characterized as a demon, by commanding it to "stand away from"
the afflicted, much as we find in the account of the evil spirit of
King Saul, discussed above. But the charm, as a whole, except for
its use of the "mystic" names of the holy god in the opening
Hebrew vocables, is altogether "orthodox." In its being addressed
primarily to God and not the disease itself (as in standard exorcisms), the text of the *lamella* truly preserves a prayer whose
focus is upon the divine. The Greek begins with a petition reminiscent of the "salvific" prayer in Tobias' exorcism of the demon,
Asmodeus: it reads, "Holy is the Lord! The god who by his word
created all things shall give health and salvation for the whole body
of Casius whom Metradotion bore" (Ἅγιος κύριος· αὐτὸς ὁ θεὸς ὁ
ἐν τῷ α[ὐ]/τοῦ λόγῳ κτίσας τὰ πάντα, ἐν αὐτῷ τῷ λό/γῳ δωρήσε
ὑγίαν, σωτηρίαν παντὸς τοῦ σώματος Κασίου οὗ ἔτεκεν Μητραδ-
ώτιον). Only with the concluding adjuration does the language of
the text move from God to the affliction itself.

---

[55] Cologne, *Institut für Altertumskunde, Universität zu Köln*, Papyrus
Sammlung, T. 33, silver *lamella*, 4th cent. CE. Text: D. R. Jordan and R. D. Kotansky, *ZPE* (in preparation).

[56] Kibbutz 'Evron, Galilee. Jerusalem, Israel Antiquities Authority, IAA No.
88-193, copper *lamella*, 4th-5th cent. CE. Text: R. D. Kotansky, *'Atiqot* 20
(1991): 81-87; *idem, Greek Magical Amulets*, Part I, no. 56, 312-25.

A short exorcism on a lead (or silver) *lamella*, now lost, was apparently uncovered in 1897 from a child's grave in the Crimean peninsula.[57] The tablet again adjures evil spirits (pl.) to "stand away" (ἀποστῆναι) from the wearer. This simple adjuration—made by (κατά) the living God—describes the offending demon as an apparition or wild beast (φάντασμα, θηρίον). But such potential beasts, at least, are "metaphorical"—they are only ghostly phantoms that can possess the soul: the spirits are commanded to stand away from the woman's soul (ψυχή)!

Adjuring demons directly by the name of the affliction they cause is keenly illustrated on a now lost exorcism inscribed on a lead tablet found at Arkesine on the island of Amorgos.[58] Composed largely of a repeating series of ἐξορκίζω σε-formulations similar to the liturgical exorcisms of Pibechis, the spell directly adjures a φῦμα ἄγριον—literally a "rustic," "wild," or "ravaging" tumor—to "come out of" (ἔξελθε) the demoniac: "I adjure (or exorcise) you, ravaging tumor, [by the Father ?. . .] by the one who shines over Jerusalem with a lantern, and by the one who slew the twelve-headed serpent, and by Michael and Gabriel, his holy archangels: come out of (ἔξελθε), and do not harm either the one exorcising or the one who is being exorcised! I exorcise you, ravaging tumor, by the one who has '*measured the heaven by the span of his hand and the earth by his hand*' (cf. Is 40:12, LXX), by the one who '*holds the world as a vault*' (cf. Is 40:22, LXX)."[59]

---

[57] Text: Kotansky, *Greek Magical Amulets*, Part I, no. 67, 383-86.

[58] 5th-6th (?) cent. CE lead tablet. Text: Th. Homolle, *BCH* 25 (1901): 430-56.

[59] We have already read of the shining god of Jerusalem in another exorcistic text, but the reference to the god who slew the twelve-headed serpent (= Hydra) is reminiscent of some cosmological battle not readily known to us, though compounds referring to serpents are named in the old Greek incantation from Phalasarna. The command to "come out of" is the technical term of the exorcisms underscored above. The repeated reference to the demon not harming the adjurer is found in the early Phalasarna lead tablet, where the oath-taker of ὀρκῶμεν adjures that he not be harmed by such things as the tongue of a λεωδράκων. But here the distinction between the exorcist, ὁ ὁρκίζων, and the one being exorcised, ὁ ὁρκιζόμενος, indicates something new: it must presuppose the use of a text, like those of the "case-histories" of the Paris magical exorcisms, that gave instructions to the adjurer on how precisely to heal his patient. In those texts the patient was referred to separately as ὁ κάμνων, "the patient," and ὁ πάσχων, "the sufferer," respectively—the exorcists, as the "one who adjures." Of note for the text of the Amorgos tablet is the fact that an exorcism engraved onto a tablet (intended to be worn) gives between its very lines a sort of memento of the performative relationship between the client and the acting officiant.

In the adjuration of the "womb-demon," and even more so in the Coptic-Greek exorcism of *PGM* IV, we have observed the notion of handing over the demon to the Abyss—a sort of reversal of magic control. Lines 54-60 of the Amorgos text, though sadly broken, give now the truly Christian adaptation of this netherworld motif: Christ's *descensus ad infernos*. The text reads, "I adjure you, ravaging tumor, by the one who descended to the nether places [and] on the third [day rose up]." Unfortunately, three whole lines of the following text are missing. Nonetheless, Christ, likened to the Escorter of the Phalasarna piece, to Pibechis's god who "leads out of unseen places," and to Empedocles who draws out the souls from Hades, descends as well into the netherworld of the Abyss to redeem souls ensnared by the unclean devils. Those possessed of demons, though living on earth, are enchained in their own private, abyssmal existence, and though in a body they must continue to dwell among the dead like the Gerasene demoniac of the Gospels who makes his habitat among the stoney tombs.

* * *

A remaining group of texts takes up again specific exorcisms that invoke the power of the Seal of Solomon, a motif seen (above) in the markedly Jewish charm of Pibechis and on the Cologne silver *lamella*. Solomon, acknowledged as the premier exorcist by at least the 1st century CE, needs little by way of introduction: he is attested in numerous sources, Jewish, Christian, and Arabic, and is known primarily from the *Testament of Solomon* as the great king who compelled an army of demons, one by one, to complete the construction of the Great Temple.

A late papyrus in the Vienna National Library (*PGM P* 10) follows in the tradition of the Exorcism of Pibechis by repeating in liturgical fashion an adjuration (ὁρκίζω ὑμᾶς) directed against "unclean spirits" (ἀκάθαρτα πνεύματα). Like the Kibbutz 'Evron tablet, this spell begins with an exorcism of various types of fever. But in line 9, a single fearful spirit is named and described as having the feet of a wolf and the head of a frog—a bizarre theriomorphic depiction recalling the earlier Phalasarna tablet and other Semitic models. Adjurations are made by the god of Israel—in company with celestial angels—and by the minerals and elements of the "seven thrones of heaven" (reading [θρόνους] for Preisendanz's [κύκλους] on the papyrus at line 14). The spirits are adjured, as in the Amorgos tablet, not to "harm" the bearer of the ὁρκισμοί. They are told to depart (ἀναχωρήσατε)—a technical term derived from the *Testament of Solomon*.[60] The text also gives a sort of catalogue of places where the demons shall not hide.

Lines 29-36 provide the powerful Solomonic material: "I adjure you, those who made an oath (ὠμόσατε) before Solomon, not to injure a man, neither harming (μὴ κακὸν ποιήσητε) in fire, nor [in water], since by the oath you fear (τῷ ὅρκῳ φοβηθέντα) the Amen, the Hallelujah, and the Gospel of the Lord, who suffered on account of us humans."[61] Besides the several motifs already encountered—harming, fear, and the Amen and Hallelujah of the "wandering-uterus" exorcism—that of the demon working mischief "by fire or water" recalls the earlier devices "with potion or ointment" found in the Phalasarna tablet.[62]

The famous *P. Ianda* 14 (*PGM P* 17), a confusing pastiche of scrambled verses that mix in the Lord's Prayer with a previously unknown Solomonic exorcism, is noteworthy for its title: "An Exorcism of Solomon for every unclean spirit" ('Εξορκισμὸ<ς> Σαλομῶνος πρὸς πᾶν ἀκάθαρτον πν(εῦμ)α). It is a genre of Solomonic composition already known to Josephus.[63] The two motifs worthy of comment are the likening of the afflicting demon to a cobra, viper, lion, and *drakon*—again the theriomorphic depictions—and the reference to a demonic attack as a πονηρὸν συνάν–τημα, the special term first occurring in the Book of Tobit, in the form ἀπάντημα.[64]

---

[60] Cf. Kotansky, *Greek Magical Amulets*, Part I, no. 35,1-6 (p. 170, Christian): Πρὸς πν/εύμαθα (-ματα)· Φοαθφρο, / ἀναχώρη/σον ἀπὸ Βα/σελείου, κτλ. (3rd-4th cent. CE silver amulet from Antiochia Caesarea in Pisidia), with commentary and excursus, "Liturgical Exorcism, Solomon, and Magic *Lamellae*," 174-80, *ad loc*.

[61] Cf. also the short though rather fragmentary 5th-cent.-Solomonic exorcism on papyrus in Daniel-Maltomini, *Suppl. Mag.* I. 24, fr. A, line 1: ὁρκίζω σε, πνεῦμα [. . .] + fr. B, 3-4: ἔθετο ὅρκον κατὰ τοῦ θ(εο)ῦ τοῦ π[. . .]/ καὶ Σολομῶνα τὸν βασιλέα, κτλ.

[62] Closer yet is the parallel in Mark 9:22, where a malicious demon seeks to destroy the patient by casting him into fire or water: καὶ πολλάκις καὶ εἰς πῦρ αὐτὸν ἔβαλεν καὶ εἰς ὕδατα ἵνα ἀπολέσῃ αὐτόν.

[63] Josephus, *Antiq.* VIII, 2.5 describes Solomon composing (συνταξάμενος) incantations for disease and *leaving behind* (κατέλιπεν) "types of exorcisms" (τρόποι ἐξορκώσεων) to expel demons. See Dennis C. Duling, "The Eleazar Miracle and Solomon's Magical Wisdom in Flavius Josephus's *Antiquitates Judaicae* 8.42-49," *HTR* 78 (1985): 1-25, and note 14 above.

[64] See also the long exorcistic gemstone discussed below (note 66), and R. Kotansky, J. Naveh, and S. Shaked, "A Greek-Aramaic Silver Amulet from Egypt in the Ashmolean Museum," *Le Muséon* 105 (1992): 21 (commentary, line 32).

Finally, a particularly interesting gold tablet, formerly in the Louvre Museum but long lost,[65] adjures demons along with a litany of additional supernatural woes. Special reference is given to the oath that the demons made in Solomon's presence. Here not only do we appear to find a reference to the *Testament of Solomon* (ἡ διαθήκη ἧς ἔθεντο ἐπὶ μεγ<άλου> Σολομῶνος) itself, but a verbatim account of the oath (ὅρκος) the demons were made to swear. Closer study of this tablet should influence the question of the genre of the pseudepigraphic *Testament of Solomon*, as well as its date and origin, but such an inquiry is not attempted here. Of special note for our line of argument is the fact that, among one of the "great and holy names of the living Lord God," we find again our old friend Damnamaneus, "the Subduer." Hence we have come full circle with the early charm from Phalasarna, whose god, Damnameneus, was invoked to tame (δάμασον) the "unwilling ones" and hence protect the charm's bearer from harmful magic.

* * *

Further texts give representative examples of fragmentary exorcisms found on gemstones. Like the serial exorcisms on papyrus and *lamellae*, one longish text[66] seems to preserve as much of an adjuration of the "Jewish kerygmatic" type as the tiny size of the gem's surface would allow. The text begins with the phrase, "I adjure you (ἐξορκίζω σε) (sc. demon) by the great god Barbathiêaôth, by the Sabaôth god (= "god of hosts") who sits above Mt. Palamnaios," and continues with a hierarchical inventory of

---

[65] Provenance unknown. Formerly Musée du Louvre (now lost). Text: Vatican Library, Unpublished papers of J. Amati (fol. 9767 30R & 9768 6R); cf. also W. Froehner, *Sur une amulette basilidienne inédite du Musée Napoléon III* (Caen, 1867), 3-17 (=*Bulletin de la Société des Antiquaires de Normandie* 4 [1866-67]: 217ff.); F. X. Kraus, "Ueber ein angeblich basilidianisches Amulet," *Annalen des Vereins für Nassauische Altertumskunde* 9 (1868): 123-31; G. Pelliccioni, "Communicazioni sopra una scoperta paleografica dell' Abate Girolamo Amati ed illustrazione di un filatterio Esorcistico," *Atti e memorie delle RR. deputazione de storia patria per le provincie dell' Emilia* 5 (1880): 177-201, etc.

[66] Text: A. Delatte & Ph. Derchain, *Les intailles magiques gréco-égyptiennes* (Paris: Bibliothèque nationale, 1964), 316-17, no. 460; cf. L. Robert, "Amulettes grecques," *Journal des Savants* (1981): 6-27. For two other gemstones see P. Zazoff, V. Scherf, & P. Gercke, *Antike Gemmen in deutschen Sammlungen, III: Braunschweig, Göttingen Kassel* (= Die Gemmensammlung der Staatlichen Kunstsammlung Kassel [Wiesbaden: F. Steiner, 1970], 249-50, nos. 200 and 201).

attributes of the Hebrew God, ending with a reference to the one "who sits upon the Cherubim."[67] Following the acclamation "He is Pantokrator," a jumbled line appears to contain the noun συνάν-τημα, a reference to the kind of demonic encounter discussed above. Apparent fragments of a rubric or subtitle are also found, the most curious of which reads, "This is an exorcism (ὀρκισμός) of the Lord God of Hosts (Σαβαὼθ 'Αδωναί) that it (sc. the demon) not draw near, because it is (an exorcism) of the Lord God (κυρίου θεοῦ) of Israel." Ὀρκισμός ("adjuration" / "exorcism") is the designation found in each of the Solomonic exorcisms described above. It also occurs in the Pibechean exorcism. A final adjuration on the gem is written to insure that the demon not "disobey the name of God," a reference recalling the obedience of the Abyss and its devils in the spell of Pibechis, discussed above. Robert's excellent study on this gem in *Journal des Savants* (1981) will serve as the reader's guide, should one wish to learn more of this fascinating piece.

*   *   *

At first glance, the appearance of serial Jewish exorcisms on long curse tablets—our final category of texts—might seem surprising. After all, nearly all cases of the "Greco-Jewish" exorcisms we have been studying were written to expel demons, not to summon them up from the grave; they are therapeutic amulets, not malicious curses. Did the writers of these particular *defixiones* simply take over amuletic ἐξορκισμοί from the spells of the Greek-speaking Jews and adapt them for their own purposes? Possibly so. But a more likely solution is to be found in a closer scrutiny of the actual provenance of the lead tablets themselves.

---

[67] The text is here close to the incipit of a long Beirut silver *lamella* that combines adjurations of the ὀρκίζω σε-type with a long series of invocations of the kind, "I call upon the one who sits ... " (ἐπικαλοῦμαι τὸν καθήμενον ...); see D. R. Jordan, "A New Reading of a Phylactery from Beirut, *ZPE* 88 (1991): 61-69. The text is clearly exorcistic, but also treats other magical operations and is thus too complex to be treated further in this study; see Kotansky, *Greek Magical Amulets*, Part I, no. 52, 270-300 for lengthy commentary. Another text not dealt with here is a bilingual exorcism composed of about 38 lines of Aramaic and Greek. It treats a whole host of exorcistic themes, including expelling demons that appear in the "form of a reptile, bird and cattle, or in the form of a human being" (line 15), and addressing both David and Solomon as exorcistic figures. It is also clearly liturgical, at least in the Greek portions, and deserves further study as to its complex demonology. See the *editio princeps* in Kotansky, Naveh, Shaked, "A Greek-Aramaic Silver Amulet," 5-25.

Two of these *defixiones* come from North Africa, where Jews were known to have populated the larger communities of Africa, Tunisia, and Cyrenaica.[68] It is no coincidence that the adjurations of both *defixiones* (one from Carthage and one from Hadrumetum) contain distinctly Jewish formulations, much of which seem liturgical in nature. The metropolitan areas from which the texts stemmed must have supported numerous local synagogues, and we suggest that it is Gentile contact with these synagogues that would have contributed to the writing up of these adjurations. It is also entirely possible, however, that Jewish practitioners themselves were responsible for the composition of the curses found on these tablets. There is little in them that militates against the literary integrity of the spells themselves, and the text from Hadrumetum is entirely Jewish.[69]

The fact that a synagogue at Antioch was built over the graves of the Maccabaean martyrs should alert us to the prospects that some form of necromancy or magic ritual was performed at synagogues elsewhere.[70] Christians flocked to the synagogues for healing and "because they were sure that the Jews would make them

---

[68] Curse against charioteers in the circus, from Carthage. Musée St. Louis, 3rd cent. CE. Text: R. Wünsch, *Antike Fluchtafeln*. Kleine Texte für Lesungen und Übungen 20 (Bonn: Marcus & Weber, 1912), 13-21, no. 4. Aggressive-coercive love-spell, from Hadrumetum. Musée Alaoui, Tunisia, 3rd cent. CE. Text: R. Wünsch, *Antike Fluchtafeln*, 21-26, no. 5

[69] Interesting in this regard is a statement of Posidonius (Fr. 279 *ap*. Strabo) to the effect that Jews were known to employ incantations: "But according to Posidonius the (Jewish) people are sorcerers and pretend to use incantations" (trans. H. L. Jones, *LCL*). Posidonius (ca. 135-50 BCE) devoted several years of research in North Africa. Other magical texts (both gems and *defixiones*) from Carthage and Hadrumetum support the view that the regional practice was heavily influenced by the Jews; cf. the texts of the lead pieces in D. R. Jordan, "New Defixiones from Carthage," in J. H. Humphrey, ed., *The Circus and the Byzantine Cemetery at Carthage* (Ann Arbor: Univ. of Michigan, 1988), 1.117-34; *idem*, "Magica Graeca Parvula," *ZPE* 100 (1994): 321-35, esp. "3. The Fruit of Sodom and Gomorrah," 323-25; Y. Le Bohec, "Inscriptions juives et judaïsantes de l'Afrique romaine," *Antiquités africaines* 17 (1981): 165-207 (with extensive literature), esp. 196-201 (on other Judaistic gems and tablets).

[70] The most recent assessment of the evidence (with previous literature) is that of Shaye J. D. Cohen, "Pagan and Christian Evidence on the Ancient Synagogue," in *The Synagogue in Late Antiquity*, ASOR (Philadelphia, 1987), 159-81, esp. 168-69, with special reference to Chrysostom's *Against the Jews*. Further support for such practice is found in the text of an Aramaic bronze *lamella* written by Yose son of Zenobia to curse an entire town (ancient Meroth?): Naveh and Shaked, *Magic Spells and Formulae*, no. 16, 43-50. The tablet had been found, folded and rolled up, within the northern wall of the synagogue.

well by using incantations and amulets."[71] What sort of *praxeis* would have been performed in synagogal contexts, in general, is not entirely clear, but given the reputation of Jewish practitioners for magic ritual, the calling up of the dead cannot have been excluded, along with other exorcistic rites.[72] It seems that oaths taken in the synagogue were judged particularly fearful.[73] Jewish liturgical synagogal prayers appear regularly in the amulets, both Jewish and Greek.[74] For our purposes, suffice it to say that long strings of formulations such as the ἐξορκίζω σε of the lead *defixiones* indicate that the calling up of ghosts from the grave must have derived from Jewish practice itself. A curse (dated 1st-2nd century CE) from Megara[75] describes a series of fragmentary anathemas as "sacred Jewish adjurations" (ὑπὸ τῶν ὀνομάτων ἀβραϊκῶν τε ὀρκισμάτων and ὀρκίσμ[ασί] τε ἀβραϊκοῖς). Clearly such "exorcisms" were at least borrowed from the Jews, if not entirely the products of Jewish practitioners.

*   *   *

Through the archaeological and literary record we have traced and attempted to differentiate between what can be viewed as a Semitic (Jewish) versus Hellenistic (Greek) paradigm for ancient exorcism. Commencing with the tale of Jewish priests in the Book of Acts—juxtaposed to the apostolic use of (uninscribed) exorcistic handkerchiefs—we have found that the rite of expelling a demon follows a set pattern and uses stereotyped formulae (ἐξορκίζω, ἐξελθεῖν, φεύγειν, etc.). At a remarkably early stage, as well, we

---

[71] Cohen, "Evidence," 168, on Chrysostom, *Against the Jews* VIII. 5,6 (= Migne, *PG* 48.935); and VIII. 8,7-9 (= Migne, *PG* 48.940-41). See also his remarks, "Evidence," 167: "According to the book of Acts, Gentiles crowded into the synagogues of Asia Minor in the first century. If the synagogue attracted Gentiles, we may presume that its language was Greek."

[72] Cohen, "Evidence," writes specifically: "Here the dead served not as sources of impurity but as *intermediaries* between earthly and heavenly realms" (p. 169, italics mine). The matter would benefit from further inquiry.

[73] Cohen, "Evidence," 168, and passim; citing R. Wilken, *John Chrysostom and the Jews* (Berkeley: University of California Press, 1983), 79-83. This emphasis on oaths provides the historical nexus for the adaptation of the magical formula ἐξορκίζω σε from Jewish synagogal practice.

[74] Kotansky, *Greek Magical Amulets*, Part I, nos. 2, 56; cf. also nos. 32, 33, 52; Naveh and Shaked, *Magic Spells and Formulae*, 22-31; 47, 83, 285 (index, s.v. "prayer").

[75] Berlin Museum, 1st-2nd cent. CE. Text: R. Wünsch, *Antike Fluchtafeln*, 4-7, no. 1.

have discovered the use of inscribed tablets (of wood, lead, tin, silver, and gold) in preserving exorcistic formulae and healing spells, in general. This development of a sort of "literary" magic, though used at first in tandem with the verbal exorcism found in the papyri, shows a need to preserve the texts of the actual exorcisms themselves. By examining the language of these texts (found on *lamellae*, papyrus, and gems), we have discovered a remarkable constancy in the conservation of age-old exorcistic motifs.

We have further noted that the language of adjuration tends to divide down the middle, in terms of "Greek" versus "Jewish" application and utilization. What distinguishes the adjurations of the Jewish "exorcistic" type from the "Greek" evocation-type depends upon each's own characteristic understanding of the numinous: the Semitic πνεῦμα ἀκάθαρτον is an entity to be expelled from the sufferer (the demon-possessed); the Greek δαίμων is a genie awakened from the dead to render service. Further, the coercive Greek netherworld adjurations (written on lead and papyrus *defixiones*) regularly set oaths upon the ghosts of the dead, compelling them of bitter Necessity (πικρᾷ Ἀνάγκῃ). The Jewish exorcisms, on the other hand, adjure the demons by the great God of Israel, the Lord of Hosts (Iao Sabaoth), a Lord made splendid and alive in the recounting of his mighty deeds of history.

But we have also perceived a bewildering crisscrossing of the leitmotivs in our hypothetical scale-models. Certain older Greek ideas of warding off demons—particularly the "flee"-motif—persist into the Hellenistic Jewish examples of exorcism (e.g., the Book of Tobit). The image of manacling a demon to a nether domain, or otherwise fencing it within a proper boundary, also overlaps in both our Jewish and Greek constructs. Further, the presentation of demons in theriomorphic form is common to both paradigms. Primarily, however, we have concluded that the "Greek" adjurations conjure up the underworld dead to serve. True "Jewish" adjurations, on the other hand, cast out (i.e., "exorcise") the demons represented as actually indwelling the afflicted.

Such a theoretical distinction, however, can become quickly dismantled, once we examine the whole spectrum of magical texts containing adjurations. Exceptions will always force us to reevaluate the broader context in which such "exorcisms" might have arisen. Jews, as much as Greeks, would have been inclined to curse their enemies as to heal their friends. When dealing with highly individual matters of personal gain or the preservation of health and well-being, synthetic reconstructions of cultural models prove insensitive to racial and ethnic boundaries. The enactment of the oath (ὅρκος) is common to most ancient societies, and there is an intrinsic risk in assuming that its use in magic would have been particularly, or exclusively, Jewish rather than Greek. Nonetheless, at least in the context of the phenomenology of spontaneous demon-possession and subsequential expulsion, the epigraphic and papyrological records repeatedly point to a practice tightly influenced by Jewish exorcists. It has also been shown that ancient practitioners may have advised the use of the serial "Jewish" oath (ἐξορκισμός) for the evocation of the dead, as well as for the healing of the aggrieved.

CHAPTER FOURTEEN

SUPERNATURAL ASSISTANTS IN THE GREEK MAGICAL PAPYRI

Leda Jean Ciraolo

There are ten texts within the Greek magical papyri which use the term πάρεδρος or one of its cognate forms. Πάρεδρος is an adjective meaning "sitting beside or near" from the verb παρε-δρεύω, "to wait or attend upon." In classical times the adjective was used as a substantive to designate a variety of governmental and military officials.[1] In the Greek magical papyri πάρεδρος most commonly refers to a supernatural assistant who serves the practitioner of magic.[2] In this essay I examine the descriptions of the πάρεδροι found in the papyri, offering a taxonomy and discussion of the interrelationship of their various manifestations.[3]

A number of terms are used in the Greek magical papyri to describe the πάρεδροι. Unlike other supernatural beings, who may be designated θεοί, δαίμονες, or ἄγγελοι, and nothing else, the πάρεδροι are never identified simply as πάρεδροι. In each text more than one nature or name is ascribed to them.[4]

---

[1] See the entries under πάρεδρος and παρεδρεύω in *LSJ*.

[2] The term πάρεδρος or one of its cognate forms appears in the following texts: *PGM* I.1-42; I.42-195; IV.1331-89; IV.1716-1870; IV.1928-2005; IV.2006-2125; IV.2145-2240; VII.862-918; XI a.1-40; and XII.14-95.

[3] I would like to thank the conference participants for their interest in this topic and Chris Faraone in particular for his careful reading of an earlier version of this paper.

[4] Anywhere from one to four different natures are ascribed to each individual πάρεδρος. There are two examples in which the assistants have only one identity in addition to that of πάρεδρος: *PGM* IV.1331-89, in which the πάρεδροι are δαίμονες, and *PGM* VII.862-918, in which the πάρεδρος is an ἄγγελος. In the majority of instances, the πάρεδρος is described as having two different aspects. The πάρεδρος has two aspects in *PGM* IV.1716-1870, IV.1928-2005, IV.2006-2125, IV.2145-2240, XIa.1-40, and XII.14-95. In two unusual texts, *PGM* I.1-42 and *PGM* I.42-195, the πάρεδρος is given four different identities. It is worth noting that the two texts which ascribe the greatest number of aspects to the πάρεδρος' identity both come from the same papyrus and one of them, *PGM* I.42-195, offers by far the most extensive elaboration found in any of the documents of the πάρεδρος' abilities.

In order to understand the different aspects of the πάρεδροι, it is helpful to separate the various characteristics of each πάρεδρος, for instance as deity and physical object, and to compare the portrayal of each of these aspects to that which is found in the other πάρε–δρος texts. The forms which the πάρεδροι assume may be divided into four broad categories: the divine, the celestial, the spiritual, and the material.[5]

In the overwhelming majority of instances the πάρεδρος may be considered a divine being. In all but three of the texts, the πάρεδρος is identified at least once as a divinity, a divine being of human form, an ἄγγελος or a δαίμων of non-specific character.[6] The term denoting a divine being which is used most commonly to refer to the πάρεδρος is θεός, meaning a god or a goddess.

Sometimes the πάρεδρος is identified directly with a well known deity, and called by his name. So, for example, the πάρεδρος is addressed as Eros in PGM IV.1716-1870 and XII.14-95. In some instances what was originally a descriptive title is used as one of the assistant's names. In PGM I.26 the πάρεδρος is called Ἀγαθὸς Δ[αί]μων, the "Good Daimon," who in classical times and later was the protective spirit of a family, household, or individual.[7] Similarly in PGM I.164-65, the πάρεδρος is called Aion, a name which appears frequently in the magical papyri as an epithet or title of a god and as an abstraction meaning "eternity." [8] On other occasions the allusion is less direct, as when the assistant is invoked as ἀγαθὲ

---

[5] It is impossible, given the paucity of our evidence, to reproduce entirely the original structure of beliefs regarding the πάρεδροι. I present this analysis primarily as a means of facilitating our understanding of the material, acknowledging the uncertainty of whether or not the categories I discern accurately replicate ancient belief.

[6] The exceptions are PGM IV.1928-2005, PGM IV.2006-2125, and PGM IV.2145-2240. It is difficult to know whether the ἄγγελοι and δαίμονες who are not the spirits of dead people should be considered divine or spirit-beings. In the absence of precise information concerning their status, I classify them under the general category of divine being.

[7] The Ἀγαθὸς Δαίμων appears elsewhere in the magical papyri, for example in PGM XII.244; PGM IV.1609 and 1712, where the variant Αγαθὸν Δαιμόνιον occurs. For bibliographic references see the entries under ἀγαθὸς δαίμων in LSJ, 366; "Agathodaimon" in RE; and "Agathos Daimon" in the glossary of GMPT.

[8] For example PGM I.201-02; PGM I.311; PGM IV.521-22 and 596; PGM IV.1163; PGM IV.1171; PGM IV.1207; PGM IV.2198; PGM VII.511; PGM XIII.983 and 995-96. For a discussion of the concept and worship of Aion see A. D. Nock, "A Vision of Mandulis Aion," HTR 27 (1934): 78-99, and Raffaele Pettazzoni, Essays on the History of Religions. Studies in the History of Religions (Supplements to Numen), I (Leiden: E. J. Brill, 1954), 171-79.

γεωργέ, "Good Farmer," in *PGM* I.26. This title is similar to one given to Anubis.[9]

The most precise and powerful method which can be used to refer to the πάρεδρος is his individual magical name. This individual name is, as the practitioner in *PGM* I.36 proudly announces, the genuine name of the πάρεδρος, his *real* name: [το]ῦ[το] αὐ–θεν[τικόν] σου ὄνομα· αρβαθ ᾽Αβαὼθ βακχαβρη. In a more extended interchange in *PGM* I.160-63, the practitioner requests that the πάρεδρος reveal his name: τί ἐστιν τὸ ἔνθεόν σου ὄν[ομ]α; μήνυσόν μοι ἀφθόνως, ἵνα ἐπικαλέσωμαι α[ὐτό]. The name of the πάρεδρος is then given: σουεσολυρ φθη μωθ. These individualized names would have been of the utmost value and importance to the practitioner. They are valuable because they provide the practitioner with direct access to the assistant. Knowledge of the name of the πάρεδρος enables the practitioner to summon and control him. The practitioner need only utter the assistant's name and he appears, ready to obey.[10]

These individualized magical names may be divided into two categories for the sake of convenience: names which are relatively short and memorable such as αρβαθ ᾽Αβαὼθ βακχαβρη and σουεσολυρ φθη μωθ, and the much longer, more conventionalized names which are commonly termed *voces magicae*.[11] The *voces magicae* contain many different elements, such as recognizable names of deities, strings of vowels and syllables, as well as names and words which are usually meaningless in Greek but do sometimes have a meaning in one of the other languages from the cultural milieu of the magical papyri. Both the shorter and the longer magical names are used for summoning and addressing the divine being. In addition to these functions they also display the practitioner's knowledge and power.[12] In attempting to determine the identity of the πάρεδροι, I exclude the *voces magicae* from my consideration. I do this not because they are unimportant but rather because they are largely incomprehensible to us, as indeed they may have been to the ancient practitioners of magic.[13]

---

[9] For this epithet of Anubis see *PDM* xiv. 17, 35, 400 and 422.

[10] As in *PGM* I.89-91 and I.182-83.

[11] For an excellent brief introduction to the *voces magicae* see Fritz Graf, "Prayer in Magical and Religious Ritual," in C. A. Faraone and Dirk Obbink, eds., *Magika Hiera: Ancient Greek Magic and Religion* (New York and Oxford: Oxford University Press, 1991), 191-92 and 210 n. 27 for references to the literature.

[12] On this issue see Graf, 191-92.

[13] On this point see Iamblichus, *Myst.* 7.4 , quoted by Graf, 210 n. 27.

When the individualized name of a πάρεδρος is given, it is in no instance used repeatedly. The πάρεδρος in *PGM* I.42-195, for example, is not referred to as σουεσολυρ φθη μωθ throughout the entire text. Instead, the most common and general term for a divine being, θεός, is frequently substituted for the proper name of the πάρεδρος.[14]

When the πάρεδρος is identified with a well known deity such as Eros, the god's name is used without hesitation. This is because the deity's name is not endowed with the same power as a less familiar magical name. In *PGM* IV.1716-1870 and XII.14-95, for instance, the author frequently uses "Eros" or "the Eros" to refer both to the deity and the statuette of the god. This may be contrasted to texts such as *PGM* I.42-195 in which the deity has an individualized magical name, rather than a more familiar one.

In one unique text, the πάρεδρος is a being of human form. In *PGM* XIa.1-40 the practitioner summons a goddess who is called "mistress of the house," ή θεὸς ή καλουμένη οἰκουρός, and compels her to serve him.[15] Reluctant to endure this servitude in person, the goddess transforms herself into an old woman, sheds the decrepit body like a snake's discarded skin, and then reconstitutes herself as goddess, leaving the old woman in existence as well. This old woman is the πάρεδρος forced to serve the practitioner. Although the πάρεδρος assumes a fully human appearance, her physical reality is tenuous. The maintenance of her human shape depends upon a magical device: the goddess gives the practitioner two teeth, one from her donkey and one from the old woman. The practitioner is to set the teeth in gold and silver and wear them always. As long as he preserves them, the πάρεδρος maintains her form. If he should ever throw the teeth into a fire, the πάρεδρος will immediately vanish.[16] The old woman is not herself a goddess,

---

[14] *PGM* I.78, 83-84, 87, 90, 91, 93, 94, 95, 96, 155, 187, 192.

[15] This is a literal translation into Greek of the Egyptian name of the goddess Nephthys. See Jan Bergman and Robert Ritner's note 3, *GMPT*, 150.

[16] This magical device is similar to motifs found in many folk tales. In the story of Althaia and Meleagros, the Fates appeared to Althaia when Meleagros was born and told her that her newborn son Meleagros would live until the piece of wood which was on the fire burned to ashes. Althaia immediately snatched the wood off the fire and kept it safe, until one day after Meleagros had killed his mother's brothers, she threw it back on the fire and caused her son to die (Apollod. I. VIII; Ovid, Met. 8. 451-525). Compare Stith Thompson's motif F321.1.4.3: a changeling is thrown on the fire and thus banished; and the general category D712.2.1: disenchantment by throwing into fire. D1741.8 also offers an interesting comparison: a sorcerer's power is lost when his teeth are knocked out (*Motif-Index of Folk-Literature: A Classification of Narrative Elements in*

but she is presented as being the product of divine artifice. As such she may be considered a divine being.

After the gods, the πάρεδροι are most frequently identified as ἄγγελοι and δαίμονες of an unspecified character. These two types of beings occur frequently in the Greek magical papyri.[17] The πάρεδρος is called an ἄγγελος in just two texts, each of which presents a different characterization of the ἄγγελος. In the first, *PGM* I.42-195, the term ἄγγελος is used interchangeably with θεός, essentially as a synonym, and the word does not appear to have any special connotations. The situation is far different in the second instance, *PGM* VII.862-918. Here the ἄγγελος is a subordinate being who obeys the commands of the goddess Selene. The practitioner is not even sure which ἄγγελος the goddess will send: he gives a lengthy catalogue of the names of her ἄγγελοι and the hours of the night to which they are appointed, but he is uncertain which one will perform the task for him. He may expect the ἄγγελος appointed to the hour during which he is performing his ritual, but this is not clear. Despite the fact that their names are given, these ἄγγελοι lack individuality and are completely devoid of personality. The contrast between the dutiful ἄγγελος of *PGM* VII.862-918 and the vivacious activity of σουεσολυρ φθη μωθ in *PGM* I.42-195 could not be more striking. Σουεσολυρ φθη μωθ is a "mighty angel,"[18] a "mighty assistant,"[19] "god of gods,"[20] apparently subject to no divine power. This is emphasized by lines 130-31: καὶ συνφων[ή]σουσι πάντα οἱ θεοί· δίχα γὰρ τούτου οὐδέν ἐστιν, "and the gods will agree with him in all matters, for apart from him there is nothing." Although the practitioner addresses his πάρεδρος-spell to Helios and Selene, there is no intimation that the πάρεδρος is subject to their control. The difference in the status of

---

Folktales, Ballads, Myths, Fables, Mediaeval Romances, Exempla, Fabliaux, Jest-Books and Local Legends, rev. ed. [Bloomington: Indiana University Press, 1955-58]).

[17] A thorough examination of the ἄγγελοι and the δαίμονες as types of beings apart from the πάρεδροι is beyond the scope of my present discussion. The forthcoming concordance to the Greek magical papyri, currently being prepared by Edward O' Neil, will be the starting point for any examination of the ἄγγελοι and δαίμονες within the magical papyri. I appreciate Professor O'Neil's kindness in giving me the opportunity to see the entries for these two words in advance of publication and regret that I cannot adequately consider the ἄγγελοι and δαίμονες here.

[18] *PGM* I.173.
[19] *PGM* I.181.
[20] *PGM* I.164.

the two ἄγγελοι is further emphasized by the fact that the ἄγγελος in *PGM* VII.862-918 is never called θεός, or god, as the πάρεδρος in *PGM* I.42-195 is repeatedly. A comparison of these two texts reveals that what appears to be a simple term designating a class of divine beings can have divergent meanings.

The πάρεδροι are frequently identified as δαίμονες, generally the δαίμονες of dead people. There are, however, two texts, *PGM* I.1-42 and IV.1331-89, in which the πάρεδρος is called a δαίμων, and the δαίμων is clearly something different from the ordinary spirit of a dead person. As in the case of the two ἄγγελος texts discussed above, the same term, δαίμων, is used to denote beings of different status.[21] In *PGM* IV. 1331-89, the divine beings are παρέδρους τοῦ μεγάλου θεοῦ, τοὺς κραταιοὺς ἀρχιδαίμονας, "assistants of the great god, the mighty chief-δαίμονες."[22] The author goes on to present a lengthy catalogue of their descriptive epithets before asking them to perform a task. As in the case of *PGM* VII.862-918, the practitioner in *PGM* IV.1331-89 has no idea which δαίμων will actually perform his will. He wants to get one of the deity's lackeys to perform his task; any one of them will do. These δαίμονες are, like Selene's ἄγγελοι, faceless, subordinate beings, controlled by a more powerful divinity.

In *PGM* I.1-42 it is no subordinate δαίμων who is invoked: it is the 'Αγαθὸς Δαίμων, the Good Daimon. The term is used here as a title or proper name for the πάρεδρος, who is equated with Anubis and Orion, although his individual magical name, αρβαθ 'Αβαὼθ βακχαβρη, is also given in line 36. He is a powerful being, as the text proclaims: " . . . you who cause the currents of the Nile to roll down upon and mingle with the sea . . . you who have established the world on an unshakeable . . . foundation . . . you who travel through the pole under the earth and rise, breathing fire . . . "[23] The multitude of titles and references confuses the identity of the πάρεδρος, but his authority is unequivocal.

These four texts referring to the assistant as an ἄγγελος or a δαίμων not of a deceased person reveal some characteristics of the πάρεδροι. The term πάρεδρος is used to designate beings of diverse rank in the divine hierarchy. Some of them are powerful beings: these deserve the appellation θεός. Others are subordinate to deities: these πάρεδροι of lower rank may be termed ἄγγελοι or δαίμονες, but they are not called θεοί.

---

[21] *PGM* I.1-42 and IV.1331-89.

[22] *PGM* IV.1349-50.

[23] *PGM* 1.30-35.

In two of the texts from the same papyrus, *PGM* I.1-42 and I.42-195, the πάρεδρος is identified with a celestial phenomenon. In *PGM* I.30 the πάρεδρος is addressed as ὁ ἅγιος Ὡρίω[ν, ὁ ἀνακ]είμενος ἐν τῷ βορείῳ, "Holy Orion, lying in the north." The reference is to the constellation of Orion, which is seen as shaping and influencing life on many levels. The Orion presented in this text can be described in general terms as a deified and personified constellation.[24]

The πάρεδρος in *PGM* I.42-195 is also identified as a celestial phenomenon, but in this text he is a star rather than a constellation. Instead of being a specific, named constellation, he is an unknown, unnamed star.[25] It is not until he materializes as an angel and a god that he reveals his divine name, σουεσολυρ φθη μωθ.[26] The identification of the πάρεδρος in *PGM* I.1-42 with Orion serves to establish the cosmic nature and extent of his power. There are no other references to the celestial aspect of the πάρεδρος outside of this context. The situation is very different in *PGM* I.42-195. Here the nature of the πάρεδρος as a star is not used to emphasize his powers. His abilities are amply described in another context, after the ritual for producing him has been explained. Rather, the references to the nature of the πάρεδρος as a star emphasize that the heavens are his home. The πάρεδρος originates from the heavens, descending to the earth as a star.[27] While on earth, σουεσολυρ φθη μωθ is impatient to return home.[28] His permanent dwelling place is the air: when the practitioner speaks his name into the air, he hears,[29] and when the practitioner dies, the πάρεδρος takes his spirit and carries it into the air with him.[30] His nature as a celestial being is developed to an extent not seen in any other text. The image is one of a highly individual being, far different from the stately but stiff portrayal of the πάρεδρος as Orion in *PGM* I.1-42.

---

[24] The deification and personification of Orion in this text reflect a variety of Egyptian and Greco-Roman beliefs (Erik Hornung, *Conceptions of God in Ancient Egypt. The One and the Many*, trans. John Baines [Ithaca: Cornell University Press, 1982], 80-81; Franz Cumont, *After Life in Roman Paganism* [New Haven: Yale University Press, 1922], 126 and 208-13).

[25] *PGM* I.76, 155.

[26] *PGM* I.162.

[27] *PGM* I.75-77.

[28] *PGM* I.186.

[29] *PGM* I.182-83.

[30] *PGM* I.178-79. There are numerous parallels between the portrayal of the πάρεδρος in this text and conceptions of the soul in Neoplatonic thought. For an overview of some of these ideas see Cumont, 91-109 and 38-40.

In four of the πάρεδρος texts the assistant is identified as what may best be termed a spirit-being. Most of these spirit-beings are the disembodied former inhabitants of bodies. They seem to be primarily, though not exclusively, incorporeal entities. Most commonly these disembodied beings are the δαίμονες of the deceased.[31] The πάρεδρος is identified with a rarer sort of being in *PGM* I.42-195. Here he is called an ἀέριον πνεῦμα, an "aerial spirit."[32] The practitioner is accordingly addressed as φίλε ἀερίων πνευμάτων, "friend of aerial spirits."[33] It will be recalled that the same πάρεδρος is elsewhere called a star, and that during his sojourns on earth he is anxious to return to the heavens, his dwelling place. In addition to being called an aerial spirit, he is also called ὁ μόνος κύριος τοῦ ἀέρος, "the only lord of the air."[34] The term ἀέριον πνεῦμα occurs again in lines 180-81, where it refers not to the πάρεδρος, but to the practitioner after his death: εἰς γὰρ "Αιδην οὐ χ[ω]ρήσει ἀέριον πνεῦμα συσταθέν κραταιῷ παρέδρῳ, "for no aerial spirit which is joined with a mighty assistant will go into Hades." From this passage it is clear that the practitioner entertained hopes of becoming an ἀέριον πνεῦμα following his death.

In six of the texts the πάρεδρος is identified not only as a type of divine or spirit-being but also as a physical object. The material objects which are πάρεδροι take a variety of forms: two are skulls, one is a mummified falcon, two are statuettes of the god Eros, one of which operates in conjunction with an engraved stone, and one is an inscribed metal *lamella*.[35]

A distinction is made in these texts between the manufacture, the initial preparatory procedures, the magical activation of the object, and the actual use of the πάρεδρος for a specific purpose.[36]

---

[31] This is the case in three of the texts. In *PGM* IV.1928-2005 the πάρεδρος is the δαίμων of a person who died a violent death and in *PGM* IV.2145-2240, the δαίμων of a person who died a violent or an untimely death. In *PGM* IV.2006-2125 the πάρεδρος is the δαίμων of a person whose manner and time of death are not specified. It is noteworthy that all of these texts come from the same papyrus, and that the πάρεδροι are not identified with δαίμονες of the dead in any other papyri we have.

[32] *PGM* I.98.

[33] Lines 51-52.

[34] Lines 129-30.

[35] Skulls: *PGM* IV.1928-2005 and 2006-2125. Mummified falcon: I.1-42. Statuettes of the god Eros: IV.1716-1870 and XII.14-95. Eros operating in conjunction with an engraved stone: IV.1716-1870. Inscribed metal lamella: IV.2145-2240.

[36] More than one word is used to describe the phase of a ritual procedure in which the object becomes magically powerful or activated. Three of the nouns

An examination of the actions required prior to employing the physical object-πάρεδροι illuminates the manner in which they were regarded.

In *PGM* IV.1928-2995, one of two skull texts, the practitioner is required to utter magical phrases and burn fragrant substances before using his πάρεδρος. As part of the main procedure, which in this instance is an inquiry, he is to write a magical phrase and to wreathe the skull, an action which I would call in general terms manipulation or handling of the object. In *PGM* IV.2006-2125, the second skull text, the reader is instructed to perform three actions prior to using his πάρεδρος: utter magical phrases, write magical words, and handle the skull. *PGM* I.1-42, the text in which the πάρεδρος is a mummified falcon, prescribes a more detailed preparation than either *PGM* IV.1928-2005 or IV.2006-2125. The practitioner must first prepare the falcon by killing and mummifying it. Then he writes and speaks magical phrases, and makes an offering of non-animal foods and wine. He engages in ritual eating and drinking and walks backwards. All three of these texts describe preparatory procedures which involve uttering magical phrases, writing magical words and physical handling or manipulation of the object. Although *PGM* I.1-42 involves offering non-animal foods and wine, none of these texts involves animal sacrifice.

In *PGM* IV.2145-2240,[37] a text in which the πάρεδρος is a thin sheet of metal or *lamella* inscribed with Homeric verses, two preliminary ritual activities are required: one entails immersing the *lamella*, ὅταν βάψῃς τὴν λάμιναν, and the second involves activating the *lamella*, καθιέρωσις τῆς πλακός.[38] Neither procedure is described in detail. The temporal relationship of these actions to one another is not mentioned. The arrangement of the text suggests that the "baptism" comes first, but this is not clearly stated.

---

employed are ἀφιέρωσις, καθιέρωσις and τελετή. ἀφιέρωσις: *PGM* XII.16; καθιέρωσις: *PGM* IV.2189-90; τελετή: *PGM* IV.1598; *PGM* V.231. Verbal expressions are common as well, with both ἀφιερόω and τελέω occurring; ἀφιερόω: *PGM* IV.2194 and *PGM* XII.20; τελέω: *PGM* IV.1655-56 and 1746.

[37] There are many texts within the Greek magical papyri in which verses from Homer are used. These include *PGM* IV. 467-74; IV.821-24; IV.830-34; VII.1-148; and XXIIa.

[38] ὅταν βάψῃς τὴν λάμιναν: *PGM* IV.2181; καθιέρωσις τῆς πλακός: *PGM* IV.2189-94.

The procedure for the activation of the *lamella* appears to be fairly straightforward. It is described in *PGM* IV.2189-94 as follows:

καθιερωσις τῆς πλακός· ἐλθὼν οὖν εἰς οἶκον καθαρὸν θήσεις τράπεζαν, ἐν ᾗ ἤτω σινδὼν καθαρὰ καὶ ἄνθη τὰ τοῦ καιροῦ, καὶ θύσεις ἀλέκτορα λευκόν. παρακείσθω δὲ αὐτῷ πόπανα ζ, πλακοῦντες ζ, λύχνοι ζ. σπένδε γάλα, μέλι, οἶνον, ἔλαιον.

Activation of the plaque: having gone into a pure room, set up a table, on which let there be a clean linen cloth and flowers of the season. Then sacrifice a white cock and place beside it seven cakes, seven wafers and seven lamps. Pour a libation of milk, honey, wine, and olive oil.

An object similar to the *lamella*, a πέταλον χρυσοῦν, an inscribed gold leaf, is described in *PGM* IV.1716-1870. This text is more complicated than *PGM* IV.2145-2240 because it involves three different objects: the gold leaf, an inscribed magnetic stone, and a statuette of Eros. These three objects act in conjunction with one another. Although separate procedures are mentioned or described for each item, the text forms a coherent unit. In lines 1745-47 the practitioner is told, γλυφέντι δὲ τῷ λίθῳ καὶ τελεσθέντι χρῶ οὕτως, "use the stone, when it has been engraved and endowed with power, as follows . . . ." No details are given. However, the preparatory procedure for the gold leaf is described. The procedure entails writing a magical phrase, giving the leaf to a partridge to swallow, and killing the bird. The gold leaf is then ready for use in conjunction with the stone and the Eros.

The second Eros text, *PGM* XII.14-95, contains the most detailed instructions for activation of a physical object πάρεδρος found in any of the documents. Here the practitioner must speak magical phrases, engage in ritual eating, provide non-animal offerings and arrange a table, handle the object, make a burnt offering and an animal sacrifice of birds.

The sacrifice is described as follows:

καὶ λαβὼν τῇ πρώτῃ ἡμέρᾳ ἀπόπνιξον ζῷα ζ· ἕνα ἀλε[κτ]ρυόνα, ὄρτυγα, βασίλισκον, περιστεράν, τρυγόνα καὶ τὰ ἐνπεσόντα σοι [νε]οσσὰ δύο. ταῦτα δὲ πάντα μὴ θύε, ἀλλὰ κατέχων εἰς τὴν χεῖραν ἀποπ[νίξ]εις ἅμα προσφέρων τῷ Ἔρωτι, μέ[χ]ρις οὗ ἕκαστον τῶν ζῴων ἀποπνιγῇ καὶ τ[ὸ] πν[εῦ]μα αὐτῶν εἰς α[ὐ]τὸν ἔλθῃ, καὶ τότε ἐπιτίθει εἰς τὸν βωμὸν τὰ ἀπο[πνι]γ[έν]τα [σ]ὺν ἀρώμασιν πα[ν]τοίοις.

Take also on the first day seven living creatures and strangle them: one rooster, a partridge, a wren, a pigeon, a turtledove, and any two nestlings that you can find. Do not make a burnt offering of any of these; instead, taking them in your hand, strangle them while holding them up to your Eros, until each of the creatures is suffocated and their breath enters him. After that, place the strangled creatures on the altar together with aromatic plants of every variety.

τῇ δὲ δευτέρᾳ ἡμέρᾳ νοσσάκιον ἀρρενικὸν π[ρὸ]ς τὸν ῎Ερωτα ἀπόπνιγε καὶ ὁλοκα[ύσ]τει.

On the second day, strangle a male chick before your Eros and burn it as a whole offering.

τῇ δὲ γ ἡμέρᾳ ἕτερον νοσσάκιον βω[μ]ῷ εἰσ[θές]. ποιῶν τὴν τελετὴν κατάφαγε τὸν νεοσσὸν μόνος, ἄλλος δὲ μηδεὶς συν[έστω]. ταῦ]τ' οὖν ποιήσας ἁγνῶς καὶ καθαρῶς, ἁπάντων ἐπιτεύξῃ.

On the third day, place another chick on the altar; while doing this ritual, eat the chick by yourself, with no one else present. If you perform the above actions in a holy and pure manner, you will have complete success.[39]

While the speaking and writing of magical words or phrases, the making of non-animal offerings and the physical handling of the object are elements common to the preliminary procedures for all of these πάρεδροι, the three objects which are the remains of living beings, the two skulls and the mummified falcon, do not require an animal sacrifice. Only the πάρεδροι which are man-made objects with no connection to a formerly living being call for an animal sacrifice, which in each case consists of one or more birds.

The presence or absence of an animal sacrifice may point to an underlying difference in conception between πάρεδροι which are man-made objects and those which are the partial remains of a formerly living being.

I would suggest that when a magical object has its origin in what was once a human being or animal, it is regarded as intrinsically

---

[39] Porphry's *Vita Plotini*, chapter 10, offers an interesting comparison to this text, although in this instance strangulation of chickens causes the spirit to depart. Recent evidence from animal burials in Egypt suggests that many animals, such as kittens, were sacrificed by strangulation (Alain Charron, "Massacres d'animaux à la Basse Epoque," *REg* 41 [1990]: 209-13). I am grateful to Robert K. Ritner for this reference.

possessing magical power. The purpose of preliminary rituals and spells in such a case is to harness this supernatural power, rather than to endow the object with a power it did not previously possess. Man-made objects such as the metal *lamella*, the two statuettes of the god Eros, and the engraved magnetic stone and gold leaf which act in conjunction with the image of the god, lack this inherent connection to a source of supernatural power. The function of the ritual is to establish a bond between the object and a source of magical power.

An elaborate ritual of animal sacrifice is the means which provides this connection. The ritual is most fully described in *PGM* IV.1716-1870, XII.14-95 and XII.270-350. The animal sacrifice endows the magic object with senses, intelligence and mobility. Once it has been animated through the accomplishment of prescribed ritual actions, the man-made object is viewed as magically potent. It is now ready as a πάρεδρος to receive and carry out the practitioner's instructions.

Although it is possible to distinguish the various facets of each πάρεδρος as divine or spirit-being, celestial phenomenon, and physical object, the aspects are related and complementary. In two instances, *PGM* IV.1716-1870 and XII.14-95, the πάρεδρος is both the god Eros and a physical object. The object to be manufactured is in both instances an image of Eros, a wooden statuette in *PGM* IV.1716-1870 which is to be employed in conjunction with a stone engraved with figures of Eros, Aphrodite and Psyche, and an image made out of wax and aromatic plants in XII. 14-95. The two texts *PGM* IV. 1716-1870 and XII.14-95 form a pair in which the aspects of the πάρεδρος described in each correspond.

The πάρεδροι in *PGM* IV.1928-2005 and IV.2006-2125 also have two aspects, but in these texts they are a skull and a δαίμων of a dead person, rather than a god and a statuette. In one text, *PGM* IV.1928-2005, the πάρεδρος is the δαίμων of a person who died a violent death. In the other text, *PGM* IV.2006-2125, this detail is not specified. The similarities between these two texts must be considered in light of their textual relation to one another: they occur consecutively in the same papyrus, and thus appear to reflect two different versions of a similar procedure.

Two texts are interposed between *PGM* IV.2006-2125 and the next πάρεδρος text, IV.2145-2240. Their character is worth noting: *PGM* IV.2125-39 contains instructions for restraining unsuitable skulls and preventing them from talking or doing anything similar, and IV.2140-44 contains instructions for interrogating corpses. As with the two preceding and one subsequent πάρεδρος texts, these documents give instructions for practices involving human remains.

In *PGM* IV.2145-2240 the πάρεδρος again has two aspects: the δαίμων of a dead person and a material object. As in *PGM* IV.1928-2005, the δαίμων can be that of a person who died a violent death, but in this case another option is also given: the δαίμων of a person who died an untimely death may also be used. The object employed is also different from that in the previous two texts: instead of skulls Homeric verses inscribed on *lamellae* are used. The two objects have few apparent similarities, although the text does seem to reflect the same beliefs about the πάρεδρος observed in *PGM* IV.1928-2005 and IV.2006-2125.

The two texts in which the πάρεδρος is the most complex, *PGM* I.1-42 and I.42-195, also present a number of similarities to one another. It should be noted that, as with *PGM* IV. 1928-2005, IV.2006-2125, and IV.2145-2240, these texts occur on the same papyrus. Their physical proximity makes their structural parallels more noticeable and suggests that they too may have a common origin or be variants of one another.

In both of the texts the πάρεδρος is called a θεός and is identified with a celestial phenomenon: in *PGM* I.1-42 the constellation Orion and in I.42-195 an unspecified star. The two aspects of the πάρεδρος as god and as celestial phenomenon are closely parallel in these texts. The πάρεδρος in each instance is also identified with other divine beings, but the identifications are not directly comparable. In I.1-42 the πάρεδρος is addressed as Ἀγαθὸς Δαίμων and in I.42-195 as both an ἄγγελος and an aerial spirit. Although the exact nature of these beings is not specified, they clearly may be considered divine or spirit beings of one sort or another. I would suggest that the elaborations upon the nature of the πάρεδρος as a divine or spirit-being in the two texts are structural equivalents.[40]

Parallelism is more difficult to detect in the fourth aspect of the πάρεδρος in *PGM* I.1-42, that of a mummified falcon. As noted before, the dead falcon may be considered an object which was once an animate being. There is no apparent parallel for a physical object as one of the aspects of the πάρεδρος in *PGM* I.42-195. It may be that it is not the falcon's aspect as a physical object which is important here, but rather his nature as a formerly living being. This provides us with a basis of comparison to *PGM* I.42-195. As I

---

[40] The additional category of being found in *PGM* I.42-195 appears to be related to the length and elaboration of the description of the πάρεδρος; *PGM* I.1-42 is quite abbreviated in comparison.

mentioned when discussing aerial spirits, the texts suggest that the
aerial spirit may in some cases be the spirit of a deceased person. If
this is accurate, *PGM* I.1-42 and I.42-195 would both describe a
πάρεδρος who is identified with a formerly living creature, although
in one case it is an animal and in the other a human being. This is,
however, speculative. What can be said for certain is that both of
these texts describe a πάρεδρος who has four aspects, and that two
of them, as god and as celestial phenomenon, are the same.[41]

Consideration of the superficial similarities in the aspects of the
identities of the πάρεδροι suggests that there are deeper categorical
parallels beneath the surface. These categorical parallels form
recognizable patterns. These patterns include the πάρεδρος as a god
and as a physical representation of a god; the πάρεδρος as the
partial physical remains of a dead person and as δαίμων of a dead
person; and the πάρεδρος as a god, celestial phenomenon and
physical object. The pattern may be seen in Table 1.

A series of formulae determining the traits of the πάρεδρος appears to lie behind the texts as we have them. It is apparent that
there are different types of πάρεδροι, and that each type is regarded
as possessing certain requisite parts. We might think of the different types of πάρεδροι as the various declensions of nouns in a
language. We can figure out the case endings, in this case the
broader categories which encompass the various aspects of each
πάρεδρος, for some of the declensions. But we do not know how
many declensions, or different basic types of πάρεδροι, there were.
It is probable that if we possessed more πάρεδρος texts, the other
basic types of πάρεδροι would become clear, and then the texts
which currently seem to present an anomalous πάρεδρος, such as
PGM XIa.1-40, would be seen to be variations of a consistent
formula.

The Greek magical papyri display an internal consistency and
formulaic character. This has often been observed in the use of
fixed expressions, both in instructions to the practitioner and in
the spells themselves. My consideration of the nature of the
πάρεδροι confirms this impression. The variations between similar
πάρεδρος texts seem to be different versions of the same tale,
rather than completely different stories. An encompassing struc-

---

[41] The πάρεδροι in each of the three remaining texts are not directly comparable
to those in any other documents. In *PGM* VII.862-918, the πάρεδρος is the ἄγγελος
of the moon goddess Selene, in *PGM* XI a.1-40 an old serving woman, and in
PGM IV.1331-89 the term παρέδρους is used simply as one of many epithets of the
δαίμονες the practitioner invokes.

tural regularity which reflects the beliefs held about πάρεδροι in antiquity appears to lie behind the individual descriptions.

Table 1
Categorical Parallels of πάρεδρος

πάρεδρος texts	PGM I.1-42	PGM I.42-195	PGM IV.1331-89	PGM IV.1716-1870	PGM IV.1928-2005	PGM IV.2006-2125	PGM IV.2145-2240	PGM VII.862-918	PGM XIa.1-40	PGM XII.14-95
divine being	θεός, Ἀγαθὸς Δαίμων	θεός, ἄγγελος	ἀρχιδαίμονες	Eros				ἄγγελος of Selene	divine being of human form	Eros
celestial phenomena	constellation Orion	unnamed star								
spirit-being		ἀέριον πνεῦμα			δαίμων of a person who died a violent death	δαίμων of a dead person	δαίμων of a person who died a violent or an untimely death			
physical object	mummified falcon			statuette of the god Eros, stone engraved with images of Eros, Aphrodite and Psyche	skull	skull	metal sheet engraved with Homeric verses			statuette of the god Eros

ABBREVIATIONS

Abbreviations used for classical authors and texts are those of N. G. L. Hammond and H. H. Scullard, eds., *The Oxford Classical Dictionary*. 2nd ed. Oxford: Clarendon Press, 1970. I follow the abbreviations of standard reference works approved by the *American Journal of Archaeology* 95 (1991): 1-16 unless otherwise indicated.

GMPT = Betz, Hans Dieter, ed., *The Greek Magical Papyri in Translation, Including the Demotic Spells*. Vol. 1, *Texts*. Chicago and London: University of Chicago Press, 1986.

PDM=*Papyri Demoticae Magicae,* as cited in *GMPT*.

PGM=Preisendanz, Karl, *Papyri Graecae Magicae. Die griechischen Zauberpapyri*. 2 vols. Leipzig: Teubner, 1928 and 1931. 2nd ed. rev. A. Henrichs, ed. Stuttgart: Teubner, 1973-74.

CHAPTER FIFTEEN

THE MYSTODOKOS AND THE DARK-EYED MAIDENS:
MULTICULTURAL INFLUENCES ON A LATE-HELLENISTIC
INCANTATION

Christopher A. Faraone

The so-called "Philinna Papyrus" dates to the first century BCE
and appears to be a fragment of a collection of hexametrical
incantations, the second of which is the focus of this paper (PGM²
XX 4-10):[1]

[　6-8　]ας Σύρας <Γ>αδαρηνῆς
[　6-8　] πρὸς πᾶν κατάκαυμ[α]
[　6-8　μ]υστοδόκος κατεκα[ύθη]
[ὑψ]ọτάτῳ δ' ἐν ὄρει κατεκαύθ[η]
ἑπτὰ λύ[κ]ων κρήνας, ἑπτ' ἄρ[κτων],
ἑπτὰ λεόντων. ἑπτὰ δὲ παρθενικαὶ κυ[α]νώπιδες ἤρ<υ>σαν [ὕ]-
δωρ κάλπ[ι]σι κυανέαις καὶ ἔσβεσαν ἀκ[άμ]ατον πῦρ.[2]

_____

[1] P. Maas, "The Philinna Papyrus," _JHS_ 62 (1942): 33-38, reconstructed the
text by joining together _P. Berol._ 7504 and _P. Amherst_ ii, Col.II(A) with guid-
ance from a fragmentary fourth-century CE papyrus that preserves a truncated
version of the same spell (see n. 2 for text). The "Philinna Papyrus" gets its
nickname from the third and final spell on the papyrus, which has the rubric:
"The incantation of Philinna the Thessalian woman for headache." For more
recent commentary and discussion of textual problems, see R. Merkelbach,
"Literarische Texte unter Ausschluss der christlichen," _APF_ 16 (1958): 85-86
no. 1046; L. Koenen, "Der brennende Horosknabe: Zu einem Zauberspruch des
Philinna-Papyrus," _Chr. d'E._ 37 (1962): 167-74; A. Henrichs, "Zum Text einiger
Zauberpapyri," _ZPE_ 6 (1970): 204-09; _PGM²_ XX; E. N. O'Neil in H. D. Betz, ed.,
The Greek Magical Papyri in Translation (Chicago, 1986), 258; H. Lloyd-Jones
and P. Parsons, eds., _Supplementum Hellenisticum_ (Berlin, 1983), no. 900; and
R. W. Daniel, "A Note on the Philinna Papyrus," _ZPE_ 73 (1989): 306. I give the
text as it appears in _PGM²_.

[2] A late-antique version of this spell, that Maas and subsequent editors refer
to as _P. Oxy.ined._ (= Pack² 1872), has only recently been fully edited; see R. W.
Daniel and F. Maltomini, eds., _Supplementum Magicum_ 2, Papyrologica Coloniensia 26.2 (Opladen, 1992), 191-93 no. 88, lines 6-9:

The rubric and the hexameters have been supplemented and re-stored as follows:[3]

[6-8]ας Σύρας <Γ>αδαρηνῆς [ἐπαοιδὴ] πρὸς πᾶν κατάκαυμ[α]

[<σεμνοτάτης δὲ> θεᾶς παῖς μ]υστοδόκος κατεκαύθη,
ἀκρ]οτάτῳ δ' ἐν ὄρει κατεκαύθη· <πῦρ δ' ἐλάφυξεν>
ἑπτὰ λύκων κρήνας, ἐπτ' ἄρκτων, ἑπτὰ λεόντων·
ἑπτὰ δὲ παρθενικαὶ κυανώπιδες ἤρυσαν ὕδωρ
κάλπισι κυανέαις καὶ ἐκοίμισαν ἀκάματον πῦρ.

The [incantation] of [   ]a, the Syrian woman from Gadara for every inflammation:

[The son of the <most august> goddess,] the initiate was scorched.[4] On the highest mountain[5] he was scorched. <The fire

---

πρ(ὸς) ἐρυθρὸν λόγος· ἑπτὰ [λύκων, ἐπτ' ἄρκτων],
ἑπτὰ λεόντων, ἑπτὰ [δὲ παρθενικαὶ κατε-]
κοίμισαν αἰθέριον πῦρ.
λέγε.

The restorations were suggested by Merkelbach (n. 1) 86, using the "Philinna Papyrus" as his guide. If we insert an anapaestic- or spondee-shaped word after λύκων (i.e., where κρήνας appears in the *mystodokos* spell) the charm comprises two full hexameters without, however, any syntactical link between them (see n. 105, for a similar problem in the *mystodokos* spell). Lines 1-5 of *Supp. Mag.* no. 88 preserve yet another healing charm that seems at first glance to echo the same theme; a *logos* designed to combat erysipelas (yet another febrile skin disease) begins with the same words ἑπτὰ λύκων, ἑ[πτὰ ...], but then veers off to speak of "great bones" and the goddess Earth.

[3] I give the text as it appears on p. 265 of the second volume of *PGM²*. The restorations and additions are the combined work of Maas, Preisendanz, and Koenen. In the final hexameter Maas (n. 1) replaced ἔσβεσαν with ἐκοίμισαν from the late-antique version of the spell (*Supp. Mag.* no. 88. line 8; see n. 2) because it seemed "more poetical" and produced a nice alliteration of *kappa* in the final line. Koenen (n. 1), using parallels from Egyptian myths (discussed in detail below), supplied the additions at the beginning of line 1 and the end of line 2 to fill out the hexameters. For his restoration of ἀκρ]οτάτῳ see n. 98.

[4] *PGM²* and O'Neil (n. 1) translate the verb κατακάω as "geriet in Brand/ was set aflame" and πῦρ as "Feuer/ fire," but both words have secondary meanings in Greek medical discourse, such as "to be thirsty or feverish" and "fever." The rubric recommends the incantation πρὸς πᾶν κατάκαυμ[α, an expression that can refer to a fever or a reddish, burning eruption or rash on the skin, such as shingles. The late-antique version of the spell (see n. 2) has the rubric πρὸς ἐρυθρὰν, a word that probably also refers (like τὰ ἐρυθρά, *LSJ* s.v.) to reddish eruptions on the skin.

[5] This is the usual translation of the Greek word ὄρος. It must be noted, how-

gulped down> seven springs of wolves, seven of bears, seven of lions, but seven maidens with dark-blue eyes drew water with jugs of lapis lazuli and quieted the untiring fire.

This text is a type of mythological narrative known to students of magic as a *historiola*;[6] here we find an initiate, probably (if the restorations are correct) assimilated to a divine or semi-divine child, who is either immolated on a mountaintop, or (as the parallels cited below will suggest) in danger of dying of thirst or fever precipitated by scorpion-sting or snake-bite. Salvation is equated with the quenching of the fire, fever or thirst.

The date of the hexametric incantation itself has been debated. The original editor suspected that the final couplet had a "true Hellenic ring" to it, but he could not find any Greek source for the activity of the seven waterbearers.[7] The mention of the *mystodokos* ("initiate")[8] and close similarities to a popular Egyptian *historiola* about Isis and the child Horus have led most scholars to conclude that these verses were borrowed from a hymn or liturgy associated with some late-Hellenistic, syncretistic cult like

---

ever, that in Greek texts from Egypt (i.e., like the "Philinna Papyrus") the word ὅρος can sometimes mean "desert." See W. Bauer, W. F. Arndt and F. W. Gingrich, *A Greek-English Lexicon of the New Testament* (Chicago, 1979) s.v.

[6] In Greek magical texts, *historiolae* supply a mythical paradigm for the desired magical action, e.g., Theocritus 2.45-46, *PGM*[2] IV 1471-79; VII 199-201; LXI 45. For discussion and further examples, see R. Heim, *Incantamenta Magica Graeca Latina*, Jahrbücher für classische Philologie Suppl. 19 (Leipzig, 1892), 495-507; A. A. Barb, "Antaura the Mermaid and the Devil's Grandmother," *JWCI* 29 (1966): 1-23; an appendix to the second volume of *PGM*[2] (pp. 264-66); and R. Kotansky, "Incantations and Prayers for Salvation on inscribed Greek Amulets" in C. A. Faraone and D. Obbink, eds., *Magika Hiera: Ancient Greek Magic and Religion* (New York, 1991), 112-13 and 121-22.

[7] Maas (n. 1) 38: ". . . the two soft-flowing hexameters about the seven maidens have a true Hellenic ring; ἐπῳδαί of this kind may have been those which appealed to Aeschylus, Pindar and Plato."

[8] The adjective literally means "receiving the mysteries" or "receiving the initiates" and only appears in one other place in extant Greek (Arist. *Clouds* 303), where it apparently refers to Eleusis. S. Eitrem, "Varia," *SO* 29 (1952): 130, suggested that the Aristophanic passage actually referred to Socrates' *phrontistêrion*, which is destroyed by fire at the end of the play, and argued unconvincingly that if we restore δόμος or οἶκος in line one of the spell, we can understand a reference to Aristophanes' play. Although there are instances—in the worship of Apollo in Greece and Baal in Syria—of the immolation of sacred buildings (see N. Robertson, "The Ritual Background to the Dying God in Cyprus and Syro-Palestine," *HTR* 75 [1982]: 335-38), it is difficult to comprehend how the destruction of a building (without any eleventh-hour rescue) can provide an *aition* for the salvation of the patient in a practical healing charm.

the mysteries of Isis.[9] The arguments for a simple Egyptian
provenance, however, overlook the Syrian authorship attested in
the rubric of the spell itself[10] and fail to consider other indications
that the incantation is either of Semitic origin or that it has been
significantly altered by contact with Semitic culture. In this essay I
first review the arguments for Egyptian influence, and then move
on to discuss very similar (and even earlier) Mesopotamian myths
that also appear in the context of practical healing rites. Instead of
simply replacing one "single-source theory" (Egypt) with another
(Mesopotamia), I argue for the early synthesis of both traditions in
the Levant and the eastern Mediterranean world in general, pointing out that such myths probably reached the Aegean at least as
early as the classical period, in connection with healing and mystery cults. I conclude by arguing that this short charm about the
mystodokos might very well be precisely what it claims to be: an
incantation composed by a Syrian woman living in the thoroughly
Hellenized city of Gadara—an incantation that not only synthe-
sizes two diverse versions of a traditional eastern Mediterranean
healing incantation, but also combines Greek and Semitic poetic
forms. In short, this brief and unassuming incantation will provide
a small window into the rich and vibrant multicultural world of the
eastern Mediterranean basin, where from the Bronze Age onward

---

[9] The groundbreaking study is by Koenen (n. 1), whose additions and restorations of the original hexameters are used in both the German (*PGM²* XX) and
English (O'Neil [n. 1]) translations. In essential agreement are, e.g.: Henrichs (n.
1) and W. Burkert, *Ancient Mystery Cults* (Cambridge, 1987), 20-21.

[10] It is usually assumed that this attribution of eastern origin, like so many
others found in Greek magical texts, is simply an invention designed to increase
the market-value of a spell by claiming some mysterious eastern antecedent; so
Maas (n. 1) 38: "Syrian origin is just what a forger would be likely to invent for
the author of a charm." H. D. Betz, "The Formation of Authoritative Tradition in
the Greek Magical Papyri" in B. F. Meyer and E. P. Sanders, eds., *Self-Definition
in the Greco-Roman World* (Philadelphia, 1982), 61-70, explains the frequent
false claims to Near Eastern magical knowledge as a way of gaining authority for
what are in fact homemade Greek recipes. There are, however, examples of very
ancient Mesopotamian magical lore surviving in Greco-Roman handbooks, see,
e.g., A. A. Barb, "Birds and Medical Magic," *JWCI* 13 (1950): 316-18, and C. A.
Faraone, "Aphrodite's ΚΕΣΤΟΣ and Apples for Atalanta: Aphrodisiacs in Early
Greek Myth and Ritual," *Phoenix* 44 (1990): 224 n. 9 (magic rings), 224-25 n. 10
(magic ointments) and 233-36 (erotic spells spoken over apples). Nor should we
dismiss out of hand the possibility that a Syrian woman from Gadara might have
limited renown for her expertise in healing the sick; see P. Brown, *Society and
the Holy in Late Antiquity* (Berkeley, 1982), 151, for references to "wise women"
in late antique Syria and Palestine who provide traditional amulets and healing
charms to the sick.

unceasing trade, military conquest and large scale migrations con-
spire to produce an astounding mixture of peoples, rituals and
ideas, a result that in some ways is not dissimilar to the last century
or so of American cultural history.

*   *   *

Several parallels to the activity of the seven dark-eyed maidens
have been discovered in Egyptian hieratic papyri (i.e., written in
the Egyptian language) of Ptolemaic date which preserve spells
designed to heal burns by evoking the dramatic salvation of Horus
in the desert:[11]

P. *British Museum* 10059 [no. 47] 14.14-15.2:[12]

Another conjuration for a burn on the first day:
"Your son Horus is burnt in a place where there is no water."
[Isis replies]: "Water is in my mouth, an inundation is between my
thighs. It is to extinguish the fire that I have come. Flow out, O
burn!" The spell is to be said over the milk of a woman who has
given birth to a male child, gum and hair of a cat. To be placed on
the burn.

P. *Ebers* 69.6-8:[13]

"Your son Horus is burnt in the desert. There is no water there."
"I am not there. May you (woman) bring water from the banks of
the stream in order to extinguish the fire." Words to be said over
the milk of a woman who has given birth to a male child.

P. *Leiden* 1.348 Spell no. 37 (= Rev. 3.1):[14]

---

[11] These parallels are collected and discussed by Koenen (n. 1).

[12] This is the translation of J. F. Borghouts, *Ancient Egyptian Magical Texts*,
Nisaba: Religious Texts in Translation Series 9 (Leiden, 1978), no. 35, with
substantial revision by Prof. R. K. Ritner *per litteras*. This spell is nearly identical to *P. Ebers* 69.3-5 (which substitutes the hair "of a ram" for those of a cat in
the final line). Prof. Ritner kindly provided me *per litteras* with a translation of
yet another parallel, spell no. 48.(col. 15.2-3) of the London Medical Papyrus
(see n. 33 below): "My son Horus is burnt in the desert." Isis comes into [..]
alone. "There is no water there. My mouth is as water; my lips are as the banks of
the stream. It is in order to extinguish the fire that I have come. Go out, O fire!"

[13] This is the translation of B. Ebbell, *The Papyrus Ebers* (Copenhagen,
1937), 82, with substantial revision by Prof. Ritner *per litteras*.

[14] This is the translation of J. F. Borghouts, *The Magical Texts of Papyrus
Leiden I 348* (Leiden, 1971), 33-34.

Beginning of the spells for burns: "Now look, let your face not tremble, my son Horus! My son, have you seen the flame of the Great One? (But) my mouth has water from the border of a stream! I have come to extinguish the fire!" This spell is to be recited over honey which has been applied to it.

In these Egyptian spells Horus' life is saved either by water carried by an unnamed woman at Isis' direction or by Isis' own bodily fluids[15]—fluids which are clearly assimilated to the waters of the flooding Nile.[16] In all of these texts, the incantation is recited over an ointment which is then applied directly to the patient's burn, a common enough combination of *logos* (verbal action) and *praxis* (coincident ritual action).[17] Similar spells for curing scorpion-sting or snake-bite are found on the bases of the so-called "statues guérisseuses" or "Horus cippi" first attested in Egypt in the New

---

[15] The fluid is assimilated to both the saliva and the urine of Isis. For the curative effect of the former in Egyptian rituals, see R. K. Ritner, *The Mechanics of Ancient Egyptian Magical Practice*, Studies in Ancient Oriental Civilization 54 (Chicago, 1993), 74-91, and n. 63 below for Greek parallels. The reference to the water (probably urine) from between Isis' legs is odd, but not unparalleled. For the Greek world, see, e.g., A. B. Cook, *Zeus* (Cambridge, 1933), 3.333-35, and G. Nagy, *Studies in Comparative Greek and Indic Meters* (Cambridge, 1974), 231-37, for discussions of a similar Greek belief that beneficial rain was the urine of the sky god passed through a sieve.

[16] It is curious that these native Egyptian texts never allude to the celebrated fact, at least among the Greeks and Romans, that the Nile river had seven mouths. Such an allusion would offer considerable help in corroborating the Egyptian origin of the seven dark-eyed maidens in the "Philinna Papyrus." The earliest (and as far as I know the only) use of the number seven in an Egyptian mythological narrative of this type is in two much later Coptic spells (A. M. Kropp, *Ausgewählte koptische Zaubertexte* [Brussels, 1931], 2.3-9, discussed by Koenen [n. 1] 169-70) designed to assuage another kind of burning—the burning of *eros*. In both texts Horus complains that he is sleepless and suffering greatly on account of his desire for the "seven maidens," and it is clear that the fulfillment of Horus' desire for water in the form of the seven maidens is to be equated with the operator's successful conquest of his female target. In the first spell, Isis rebukes her son for not calling on *her* for help (*P. Hs. Schmidt* 1.14-17): "You have seized a cup of little water, because you have not found me, because you have not found my name." Isis seems to imply that the maidens would be an inferior thirst-quencher ("cup of *little* water"), when compared with his mother Isis, who is assimilated to the Nile flood. In the second text, the seven maidens are in fact connected with a non-Nilotic water source, for Horus seems to tell how he first caught sight of these maidens "sitting near a spring" (*P. Hs. Schmidt* 2. 5).

[17] J. Scarborough, "On Medications for Burns in Antiquity," *Clinics in Plastic Surgery* 10 (1983): 603-04, discusses the Egyptian tradition of burn ointments, some of which contain pharmaceutically active ingredients.

Kingdom; they, too, contain mythological narratives, in which the sacred child (usually dying from fever or venom) is saved by his mother Isis who rushes to the scene with water.[18] Several of these inscribed bases have depressions or basins in their upper surfaces in which water collected after it had been poured over the statue or its inscriptions. This water seems to have been given to sick patients to drink or anoint themselves, in the latter case much like the ointments prescribed in the papyrus spells quoted above.[19] This use of Nile water to "save" living patients from disease and discomfort has also been connected with the use of Nile water in the mysteries of Isis, where water apparently played an important role in protecting an individual from the fires of the underworld.[20]

---

[18] K. C. Seele, "Horus on the Crocodiles," *JNES* 6 (1947): 43-52; N. E. Scott, "The Metternich Stela," *BMMA* 9 (1951): 201-04; A. Klasens, *A Magical Statue Base (Socle Behague) in the Museum of Antiquities at Leiden* (Leiden, 1952); E. Jelínkova-Reymond, *Les inscriptions de la statue guérisseuse de Djed-Her-Le-Sauveur* (Cairo, 1956); L. Kákosy, "Horusstele," *LÄ* 3 (1980): 60-62; H. Sternberg-el-Hotabi, "Die Göttersdarstellungen der Metternichstele," *Göttinger Miszellen* 97 (1987): 25-70, esp. 26-28; and R. K. Ritner, "Horus on the Crocodiles: A Juncture of Religion and Magic in Late Dynastic Egypt" in W. K. Simpson, ed., *Religion and Philosophy in Ancient Egypt*, Yale Egyptological Studies 3 (New Haven, 1989), 103-16. See Klasens *loc. cit.* 5-7 and Scott *loc. cit.* 203-04 for agreement among scholars that there must have been a recognized body of texts and illustrations from which the designers of the pedestals of magical statues could pick and choose in order to create their particular set of spells. This explains why although no two statue bases are exactly alike, the same favorite passages appear again and again in different order and in various truncated forms. The language and orthography of the individual spells also suggest that they originated (or at least were codified) at different points in time. In fact, individual healing spells involving stories about the infant Horus appear in the magical papyri and on the bases of statues in the New Kingdom, e.g., see Borghouts (above n. 14) for a translation and discussion of *P. Leiden* I 348, a recipe book dominated by such spells, which dates somewhere between 1580-1085 BCE. The more recent studies of Kákosy (p. 60), Sternberg-el-Hotabi (p. 27) and Ritner (p. 105) all stress the continuity from the Bronze Age down until Roman times.

[19] A statue base in the Louvre (E 10777) refers to the patient as "this man who drinks the water." Another in Cairo requires that the spell "be recited over cool water" which is subsequently laid over the heart of the patient. See Klasens (n. 18) 5-6 and Ritner (n. 18) 106-07 for discussion. Ritner, *ibid.* 108-09, suggests that some of the smaller copies of these statues were probably immersed in water and then worn about the neck as amulets.

[20] Koenen (n. 1) 170-71, cites *inter alia* the sprinkling of Nile water in the Isis temple at Rome (Juvenal 6. 526-28) and Apuleius' allegorical tale of Psyche and Eros. After Eros (= Horus) is accidently burned and in danger of dying (5. 28 *dubium salutis*), he is healed by Psyche (= Isis), who brings water up from the Styx and Kokytus (6.13) to cure him. There was, of course, a very old Egyptian eschatological tradition about the salvific effect of cool water in the underworld;

The fact that this Egyptian interpretation of the *mystodokos* spell has remained unchallanged for thirty years is testimony to its coherence and persuasiveness. There are, however, parallels in healing rituals from another Near Eastern culture that help explain three puzzling details in the Greek spell that find no corollary in the mother-and-child stories discussed above: the use of the number seven, the young age and unmarried status of the maidens, and the peculiar blue color of their water-jugs. In a series of second-millennium Mesopotamian medical incantations the daughters of Ea or Anu are asked to bring water to cure the patient:[21]

Old Assyrian Spell for uncertain purpose[22] (Farber no. 1):

---

see G. Zuntz, *Persephone: Three Essays on Religion and Thought in Magna Graecia* (Oxford, 1971), 370-76 for a brief overview. Several spells of the *Book of the Dead* are concerned with the acquisition of water including, for example, Spell 63A, which is entitled "Spell for drinking water and not being burnt by fire" and illustrated in the fourteenth-century BCE funerary papyrus of the nobleman Nakht (BM 10471) by a picture of a female deity in a tall tree pouring water for Nakht. See R. O. Faulkner and C. Andrews, *The Ancient Egyptian Book of the Dead* (New York, 1972), 68-70. The so-called "Cool Water" funerary inscriptions from late imperial Rome and Roman Egypt contain a similar plea on behalf of the dead with similar eschatological expectations (δοίη σοι ὁ Ὄσιρις τὸ ψυχρὸν ὕδωρ) and suggest that the tradition continued (in somewhat altered form) for centuries in Greco-Roman Egypt. See W. M. Brashear, "Ein neues Zauberensemble in München," *SÄK* 19 (1992): 95-96, and D. Delia, "The Refreshing Water of Osiris," *JARCE* 29 (1992): 181-90, for the most recent discussions and bibliography. This tradition survived well into late antiquity; see, e.g., the threats addressed to the dead in a fifth-century CE lead *defixio* from Egypt, a text recently re-edited by R. W. Daniel and F. Maltomini, *Supplementum Magicum* 1, Papyrologica Coloniensia 16.1 (1991), no. 45.12-15.

[21] These and similar texts are collected and discussed by A. Goetze, "An Incantation against Diseases," *Journal of Cuneiform Studies* 9 (1955): 8-18; B. Landsberger and Th. Jacobsen, "An Old Babylonian Charm against *MERHU*," *JNES* 14 (1955): 14-21, with additions and corrections in *JNES* 17 (1958): 56-58; and W. Farber, "MANNAM LUSHPUR ANA ENKIDU: Some New Thoughts About an Old Motif," *JNES* 49 (1990): 299-320. I give Farber's translations and follow his interpretation. The generally accepted dates for the historical-linguistic terms used to describe the dialects of these texts is as follows: Old Babylonian or Assyrian (1950-1530 BCE); Middle Babylonian or Assyrian (1530-1000 BCE); Standard Babylonian, the literary language of the Neo-Assyrian Period (1000-625 BCE); and Late-Babylonian (from 625 BCE sporadically down through the Seleucid and Parthian periods); see W. von Soden, *Grundriss der Akkadischen Grammatik*, Analecta Orientalia 33/47 (Rome, 1969), 2-4. I also wish to thank Prof. J. Scurlock for her kind assistance with regard to the bibliography and interpretation of these texts.

[22] Goetze (n. 21) suggested that the spell cured dog bite, but Farber is agnostic on the point. In any event, the dog seems to be the source of the trouble, either as a real dog, a caniform demon or as an evil omen which portends disaster. For a similar ambiguity in Greek and Phoenician beliefs, see C. A. Faraone, *Talismans*

A black dog is lying on the hill; he waits for the scattered pack. His eyes are fixed on a good-looking young man.

Whom should I send the daughters of Ea, (saying)
[. . . . . .], and take your [pots] of carnelian and your potstands of *khulâlu*-stone; then come, and [cle]anse (them) in the river with [pure (?)] water!

Old Babylonian Spell for curing a sty (Farber no. 2.2):

Earth, they say, was (just) earth. It (then) bore morass, morass bore stalk, stalk bore ergot. In, they say, the square field of Enlil, Sin reaped 70 acres of field, had Shamash gather the yield. Into, they say, the eye of the young man the ergot entered.

Whom should I send with orders to the seven (+) seven daughter(s) of Anun? May they take the *egubbû*-vessel of carnelian, the pot of *khulâlu*-stone. May they draw pure sea water. May they remove the sty from the eye of the young man!

Middle Babylonian Spell for uncertain purpose (Farber no. 3.2):

The heart is strong, the heart is a hero. The strong heart's [eyes] are long, it ho[lds] a bowlful of blood . . . .

Whom should I send to the heavenly daughters of [Anu], whose potstands are of g[old], whose pots [are of pure lapis lazuli (?)]? May they lift (them) up, may they draw [pure] water from the Ajabba, the [wide] sea (?).

Like their Egyptian counterparts, these Mesopotamian[23] incantations aim at curing specific medical problems, the great majority of which are manifested by a burning sensation (e.g., skin-diseases, eye-problems or fevers).[24] They generally begin with a short

---

and Trojan Horses: Guardian Statues in Ancient Greek Myth and Ritual (Oxford, 1992), 39-54.

[23] It is important to note, however, that there is evidence that this type of spell was (as early as the late second millennium) known outside of the boundaries of Mesopotamia proper; the third text quoted above was found at Alalakh, a Syrian city situated on the Orontes River within forty kilometers of the Mediterranean coast.

[24] Farber (n. 21) 302. The complete list is as follows (following Farber's numeration of the texts): 1 (attack or omen of a black dog?); 2.2 (sty in the eye); 2.3 (list of 17 diseases that cause fever); 2.4 (list of 19 diseases that cause fever); 2.5 (list of 9 diseases); 2.6 (difficult birth); 2.8 (crying baby); 4.1 (list of skin-diseases); 4.2 and 4.3 (list of eye-diseases); 4.4 (mouth disease); 4.5 (list of skin-

description of the cause of the malady, which is often expressed in universal or mythological terms, for example, the genealogical poem about the ergot/sty in the Old Babylonian incantation quoted above. This introductory statement is almost always followed immediately by the rhetorical question "Whom shall I send . . ." and then an exhortation (in the third or second person) that the named deities come and extinguish or cool the burning discomfort.

The second-millennium tradition represented above seems to arise from formulaic folk poetry composed orally and exhibits a great deal of flexibility and variety, especially in the first section of the incantations which are often unique, as the examples quoted above reveal. In the first millennium, however, although these types of spells appear to be even more popular, they are being produced by a more "bookish" process, whereby scribes manipulated a somewhat limited number of standardized lines or groups of lines in order to adapt the spell to an increasing variety of diseases.[25] As a result, the later versions usually are "omnibus spells" designed to combat a large number of diseases, and they generally take the following form:

Standard Babylonian spell for skin diseases (Farber no. 4.1):

(spell begins with a list of skin diseases) descended [from the stars (?) of heav]en and made feverish the young men all day long, made feverish [the baby on the sh]oulder (?) of the nursemaid.

Whom should I send to the heavenly daughter(s) of Anu? May they lift up [their potstands] of *khulâlu*-stone and their pots of pure lapis lazuli. May they draw water from the Ayabba, the wide sea (var. A inserts: water from the Tigris, water from the Euphrates), over which an unclean woman has not bent down, [in whi]ch a tabooed woman has [not washed herself].

---

diseases); 4.6 and 4.7 (toothache) 4.8 (intestinal trouble) and 4.9 (sorcery). In several of the more fragmentary texts the name and even the nature of the ailment is lost (2.1, 2.7, and 3.1-3.3).

[25] The earlier process (as Farber describes it) is not unlike the oral composition familiar to us from Homeric poetry, where interchangeable formulaic phrases are the basic building block. In the later tradition, however, whole sentences or groups of sentences are quoted nearly verbatim, a technique that Farber (n. 21) 302-04 aptly compares to the use of "boilerplates" in legal and other formulaic documents. Both processes allow for some degree of flexibility, but it is clear that these licenses diminish over time. This two-stage development is also observable in other Mesopotamian incantation series, see, e.g., W. Farber, "Magic at the Cradle," *Anthropos* 85 (1990): 139-48.

May they extinguish and may then go away (the list of skin diseases is repeated here).

Like the Egyptian spells discussed above, this scribal tradition survives into the Hellenistic period; a spell of very similar type, for instance, is extant in six copies, the last of which was found at Uruk and probably dates to Seleucid times.[26] Like the earlier versions, these first-millennium spells begin by describing the cause of the disease in mythic or cosmic terms ("it descended from the stars . . . and made feverish the baby on the shoulder of the nurse-maid"), and they then go on to exhort the water-carrying maidens to intervene.

These Mesopotamian spells offer some obvious parallels to the vignette narrated in the second half of the *mystodokos* spell. The daughters of Anu[27] are expected to draw "pure" water from a sea or a river,[28] and bring it to the patient in order to "extinguish" or "cool"[29] his or her disease. Their jugs, moreover, are most often

---

[26] Farber (n. 21) no. 4.4, which is designed to cure a mouth disease.

[27] Farber (n. 21) 303 states that the first-millennium spells "give clear preference to just one version of the motif, the one referring to the daughters of Anu." Of the twenty-one versions of this type of MANNAM LUSHPUR formula (named after the incipit: "Whom shall/should I send . . .") collected by Farber, eleven call on the daughters of Anu (nos. 2.2-2.6, 3.2, 4.1-4.5). Of the remaining ten, three are too fragmentary to know who is invoked (nos. 2.1, 3.1, 3.3) and the rest seem to be individual variations: "the daughters of Ea" (no. 1); "the dweller in great Apsû" (2.7); "Enkidu" (2.8); "Asalluhi, the son of Ea" (4.6); "Marduk" (4.7); "the canal inspector(s) of your insides" (4.8) and "Bêlet-sêri" (4.9).

[28] The water is more frequently (7x) described as "sea water" or "water from the sea" (nos. 2.2-2.4) or "water from the Ayabba (var. Eulaios), the wide sea" (3.2, 4.1, 4.2, 4.4), but there are variants: "[cle]anse (them) in the river with [pure (?)] water" (no. 1); "the plant of life, a waterskin [with cold water (?)]" (4.6) and "water from the Tigris, water from the Euphrates" (variant A of 4.1). Nos. 2.5, 4.3 and 4.5 mention water, without designating a particuliar type or source, nos. 2.1, 2.6, 3.1 and 3.3 are too lacunose to know the source of water and nos. 2.7, 2.8, 4.7-4.9 are designed for discomforts that do not produce a burning sensation (e.g., crying babies or intestinal problems) and consequently make no mention of water.

[29] Of the sixteen spells that speak of water (see n. 28), the action is usually described as follows: "may they draw water, may they sprinkle (it), may they extinguish (the disease)" (nos. 2.3-2.5, 4.1, 4.3, 4.5) or "may they sprinkle and cool of the fever, the burning of the eyes" (4.2). Other variants focus on the cleansing action of the water: "[cle]anse them in the river with [pure (?)] water!" (no. 1); "may they draw water . . . and remove (i.e., wash out?) the sty from the eye" (2.2); and "may they let (the water) flow into his mouth, so that there be removed (list of mouth diseases)" (4.4). Only one spell refers to drinking the water: "[may they draw pure] water, may they give (it) to drink" (2.1). Nos. 2.6, 3.2 and 4.6 mention water but do not specify its use, and nos. 2.7, 3.1 and 3.3 are

described as of lapis lazuli,[30] a likely source for the peculiar κάλπιδες κυάνεαι (lit., "water-jugs of lapis lazuli") in the *mystodokos* incantation, while their number ("seven [+] seven")[31] and unmarried status recalls the ἑπτὰ παρθενικαί. We should, of course, imagine for all of these Mesopotamian incantations some accompanying *praxis* which involved multiple sprinklings with or immersions in water actually drawn from the rivers or seas mentioned in the spell.[32]

*   *   *

If one were to insist upon a single eastern source for the *mystodokos* spell, Mesopotamia would perhaps seem to be a better candidate, as the Babylonian and Assyrian texts quoted above

---

too fragmentary to reveal how the water was thought to heal the patient.

[30] Of the twelve spells which mention the containers that hold the water, seven designate vessels of lapis lazuli: "their golden potstands, their pots of pure lapis lazuli"(2.3, 2.4, and 3.2 [restored]); "their potstands of *khulâlu*-stone, their pots of pure lapis lazuli" (4.1, 4.3 and 4.5); and "their flasks of *khulâlu*-stone, their pots of pure lapis lazuli" (4.2). Variants are: "[pots] of carnelian and potstands of *khulâlu*-stone" (no. 1); "the *egubbû*-vessel of carnelian, the pot of *khulâlu*-stone" (2.2); "their flasks of silver and their phials of gold" (4.4); " a waterskin" (4.6). In one text (2.6) the material of the pot is lost in a lacuna.

[31] Of the eleven versions that name the daughters of Anu as the agents of the cure (see n. 27) the five Old Babylonian versions specify their number as "seven (+) seven" (2.2-2.6). The later (Middle and Standard Babylonian) versions simply refer to them as the '"heavenly daughters of Anu." Farber's text no. 1 gives the water-carrying role to the "two daughters of Ea."

[32] The Hebrew Bible provides a possible example of just such a rite: at the instruction of Elisha, Naaman the Syrian immerses himself *seven* times in the Jordan River to cure his "leprosy," as a result of which his flesh becomes clean once more "like the flesh of a little child" (2 Kgs 5:1-14). The Hebrew word here traditionally translated as "leprosy" can refer to a wide variety of skin diseases, but probably does not indicate modern leprosy (known as "Hansen's disease"). See M. Cogan and H. Tadmor, *II Kings: A New Translation* (Garden City, 1988), *ad loc.*, who point out that Naaman's condition was probably some minor skin disease, since he never loses his access to the king's court at Aram-Damascus. See G. Grottanelli, "Healers and Saviors of the Eastern Mediterranean in Pre-Classical Times" in U. Bianchi and M. J. Vermaseren, eds., *La soteriologia dei culti orientali nell' impero Romano* (Leiden, 1982), 651-54, for a full discussion of Elisha as a charismatic healer. Prof. J. Scurlock brings to my attention a centuries-old Tibetan "Bathing Festival," for which the following *aition* is given: During a serious epidemic the people prayed to a goddess, who sent seven fairy maidens, who poured into the rivers and lakes of Tibet seven bottles of holy water from the jade vase of the goddess. The next day, directed by a dream, the people of Tibet immersed themselves in the water and were all cured. See Q. Xing, *Folk Customs at Traditional Chinese Festivities* (Beijing, 1988), 78-79.

provide immediate explanations for several puzzling details in the Greek incantation. There is, moreover, at least one example of this type of Mesopotamian spell surviving into the Hellenistic period (the Seleucid-age spell from Uruk), providing the opportunity of direct influence. There are, however, several other factors which counsel restraint and suggest that the whole concept of a single, uncontaminated source (in this part of the world at least) may be itself extremely problematic. First of all, there is good evidence that magical spells, especially healing spells, moved quite easily between Egypt and the Levant. The earliest examples are found in a fourteenth-century BCE Egyptian medical papyrus, which contains a number of curative incantations that appear to be in a dialect of Northwest Semitic and another said to be in the language of the Keftiu, nowadays presumed to be the Minoans of Crete; in each case, the foreign incantations are spelled out phonetically in Egyptian hierogylphic script.[33] Influence was moving in the other direction as well, for the Egyptian Horus cippi, which contain numerous healing spells including variants of the burning Horus spells (discussed above), have been found outside of Egypt in Byblos, Hama and Nippur, although here the extant evidence can only be traced to the Persian period at the earliest.[34]

There is, however, early evidence that the Egyptian mother-saves-the-child myth was borrowed in the Levant in the context of a healing incantation, and thus may have been combined with the Mesopotamian motifs discussed above. A twelfth-century BCE snake-bite incantation from Ugarit contains a mythological vi-

---

[33] London Medical Papyrus spells nos. 27-31 and 33 (the Semitic spells) and no. 32 (the Keftiu spell). See R. C. Steiner, "Northwest Semitic Incantations in an Egyptian Medical Papyrus of the Fourteenth Century BCE," *JNES* 51 (1992): 191-200, for discussion; for a recent translation and interpretation of the Keftiu spell, see H. Goedicke, "The Canaanite Illness" in H. Altenmüller and D. Wildung, eds., *Festschrift für W. Helck*, Studien zur Altägyptischen Kultur 11 (Hamburg, 1984), 91-105, esp. 101-03, who gives earlier bibliography.

[34] The small fragment from Byblos, which quotes spells very similar to those on the Metternich Stele, is without any archeological context, and thus cannot be securely dated, see P. Montet, *Byblos et l'Egypte*, Bibliothèque Archaeologique et Historique 11 (Paris, 1928), 249-32 no. 948. The example from the Syrian city of Hama is dated securely between 161-64 BCE, see H. Ingholt, *Rapport préliminaire sur sept compagnes de fouilles à Hama en Syrie 1932-38* (Copenhagen, 1940), 132, pl. 40.1. J. H. Johnson, "Appendix B: A Hieroglyphic Text" in M. Gibson, ed., *Excavations at Nippur, Eleventh Season* (Chicago, 1975), 143-50, publishes the example from Nippur which dates to the Persian or early Hellenistic period. Sternberg-el-Hotabi (n. 18) 28 argues that they were made for export, but Ritner (n. 18) 106 is more cautious, suggesting that they were carried out of Egypt by travelers concerned about their health.

gnette in which a hitherto unknown individual named "Shrgzz" is apparently bitten by a snake and cries out:[35]

9   The venom [   ]ed him,
       and the "destruction" made him powerless:
10   Shrgzz [fell in a seizu]re,
       he wept like a boy,
11   and shed tears li]ke a child.
       Shapash cried from the heaven:
12   "[   ] didst thou fall, O my off[spring (?)]?
       Why didst thou fall in a seizure,
13   [Shrg]zz, and dost weep li[ke] a boy,
       shedst tears like
14   [a chil]d?"
       Weepingly [Shrgzz] answered,
       in his [p]ain (?)
15   [he moan]ed . . . .   (trans. M. Astour)

The remainder of the text is hopelessly fragmentary after this point, but it is clear that the goddess Shapash (known from other texts) does respond to Shrgzz again. There is, moreover, agreement among most commentators that this episode must have had a happy ending, in which the goddess intervenes and saves the child from death—otherwise the mythological exemplum would be of no use as part of a curative incantation.[36] There are clear signs of Egyptian influence in other parts of this text (not quoted here),[37]

---

[35] For translations and commentaries, see C. Virolleaud, "Les Nouveaux Textes Mythologiques et Liturgiques de Ras Shamra (XXIVᵉ Campagne, 1961)" in C. F. A. Schaeffer, ed., *Ugaritica* vol. 5 (Paris, 1968), 545-606; M. C. Astour, "Two Ugaritic Serpent Charms," *JNES* 27 (1968): 28-36; A. Caquot, "Nouveaux Documents Ougaritiens," *Syria* 46 (1969): 241-65; S. G. Brown, "The Serpent Charms of Ugarit," (diss., Brandeis University, 1973), 18-25 and 66-71; and W. Farber, *Texte aus der Umwelt des Alten Testaments* 2 (1987): 345-50. For a complete bibliography, see B. A. Levine and J.-M. de Tarragon, "Shapshu Cries Out in Heaven: Dealing with Snake-bites in Ugarit (*KTU* 1.100, 1.117)," *Revue Biblique* 95 (1988): 481-518. D. Pardee, *Les textes para-mythologiques de la 24ᵉ campagne (1961)*, Ras Shamra-Ougarit 4 (Paris, 1988), 227-56, provides a full, authoritative text and commentary. He places the lines quoted here at the beginning instead of the end of the incantation.

[36] E.g., Astour (n. 35) 35. To my knowledge, Brown (n. 35) 73 is unique in insisting that Shrgzz dies at the end of the *historiola*.

[37] Brown (n. 35) 81-82 notes, for example, that the defeat of the snake by the sun-god Shapash and her seventeen companions is an adaptation of the well known Egyptian myth in which Re, accompanied by seventeen other gods, confronts and destroys his arch-enemy, the serpent Apophis. Brown also sug-

and I suggest that the scenario at the end of this incantation is also indebted to an Egyptian source—namely the spells discussed above which narrate the salvation of Horus in the desert. In both, the victim is described as a weeping child[38] suffering from thirst or venom-induced fever, to whom a female deity responds by asking what is the matter or by simply bringing help. Furthermore, if we accept Astour's restoration at line 12 ("O my off[spring (?)]!"), the goddess is also (like Isis) the mother of the sufferer.[39]

Some similar myth also seems to be reflected at Genesis 21:14-19, part of the so-called "E" narrative, which is usually dated somewhere between the tenth and eighth centuries BCE.[40] After Hagar, Abraham's Egyptian concubine, is expelled from the house at his wife Sarah's insistence, she carries her son Ishmael on her shoulder and wanders the Negev desert. After her waterskin runs

---

gests (ibid., 83-98) that the Canaanite god Horon, who plays such an important role in UT 607 (the much longer serpent charm found with UT 608), may have been assimilated to the Egyptian god Horus, whose name he would like to restore in the lacuna at UT 608.12 (below, n. 39).

[38] That the child Horus is thought to weep in the Egyptian incantation can be inferred from Isis' description of the child in the spell from the Metternich Stele (trans. Klasens [n. 18] 54 line M-170): "... the innocent, fatherless child *has moistened the banks with the liquid of his eye*...." At line e-1 of the so-called "Socle Behague" (an inscribed statue base) a similar spell reads: "The innocent child wept in distress" (trans. Klasens [n. 18] 55).

[39] Astour (n. 35), *ad loc.*, suggests further that the very name of the victim "Shrgzz," which is attested nowhere else in Ugaritic literature, is a pet name of sorts for Shapash's son Ql-bl, and that it means "chosen child" or "favorite child." The two alternate restorations suggested by Brown (n. 35) *ad loc.* either involve a mother-and-son relationship (*yhd*, "only son") or another direct reflection of Egyptian influence (*yhr*, "O Hor!" i.e., the vocative of the Egyptian god Horus).

[40] Scholars of the Hebrew Bible use "E" to refer to the documentary source of *Genesis* that regularly refers to god as "Elohim" and not "Yahweh" as is the habit of the "J" source. "J," which is dated to about a century earlier, preserves (as often happens) a very different version of the story of Hagar in the desert (Gen 16:7-15): Hagar runs away into the desert by herself and sits by a different well, Beerlahairoi ("The Well of the One Who Sees Me [i.e., Yahweh] and Lives"), which lies between Kadesh and Bered; Yahweh appears and persuades her to return. See B. Vawter, *On Genesis: A New Reading* (Garden City, 1977), 15-24, and E. A. Speiser, *Genesis*[2] (Garden City, 1978), xxii-xxxvi, for a general discussion of "E" and "J", and his specific comments (*ad loc.*) on chapters 16 and 21. For a history of source criticism and a detailed analysis of the Elohist tradition, see A. W. Jenks, *The Elohist and North Israelite Traditions,* SBL Monograph Series 22 (Missoula, 1977), *passim*, who places Gen 21:14-19 squarely in the Elohist tradition (p. 23).

dry, Hagar places the child[41] under a shrub and sits down some distance away, unable to witness his death:[42]

> God heard the cry of the boy, and the angel of God called to Hagar from heaven and said to her, "What troubles you, Hagar? Fear not, for God has heeded the cry of the boy, where he is. Come lift up the boy and hold him by the hand, for I will make a great nation of him." Then God opened her eyes and she saw a well of water. She went and filled the skin with water, and let the boy drink.

The well revealed to Hagar is called Beersheba, a name which originally meant "Well of Seven" or "The Seven Wells."[43] The kinship between this narrative and the Egyptian and Ugaritic *historiolae* discussed above is clear enough; in all three narratives a divinity hears or becomes aware of an injured or dying child, and subsequently intercedes first by questioning and encouraging the victim directly and then by providing the needed water.[44] Even

---

[41] The Hebrew verb used to indicate Hagar's action is sometimes rendered literally as "she flung the child down." M. Cogan, "A Technical Term for Exposure," *JNES* 27 (1968): 133, points out that it is in fact a technical usage for the exposure of unwanted children, usually newborn. Plutarch (*de Is. et Os.* 14 = *Mor.* 356f) relates a much rarer variant of the myth of Isis and her child, in which Anubis is the child. He tells us how Isis, fearful of Typhon (= Seth) after the death of Osiris, *exposed* Anubis, her newborn child by Osiris (the aorist infinitive ἐκθεῖναι, proposed by Xylander instead of the non-sensical ἐκεῖνο, has been universally adopted by editors). Later on, she uses dogs to find and rescue the child. For other attestations of this tale, see Th. Hopfner, *Plutarch: Über Isis und Osiris*, vol. 1 (rpt. Darmstadt, 1967), 47-49, and J. G. Griffiths, *Plutarch: De Iside et Osiride* (Cambridge, 1970), 313-19.

[42] The translation quoted below is that of the Jewish Publication Society, *Tanakh: A New Translation of the Holy Scriptures* (New York, 1985).

[43] Speiser (n. 40) 159-60, argues that the "original and appropriate 'Seven-Wells' was later replaced by a popular etymology 'Well of the Oath' on account of the homophone 'sheba' which can mean both 'seven' and 'oath'." Both etymologies are hopelessly intertwined in the story that follows (Gen 21:23-32), in which a dispute over the water-rights to the well is resolved by an oath solemnized by a gift of seven ewes. For the use of a plural to designate a single well, see the Enneakrounos ("Nine-Springs") in Athens, a special, sacred spring for woman to wash in (Thuc. 2.15, with Gomme's commentary *ad loc.*) and the "seven rivers flowing from one spring" at Rhegium in which Orestes allegedly purified himself (n. 59).

[44] In *P. Leiden* 1.348, Spell no. 37 (quoted in full above), for example, Isis directly encourages and questions her son (". . . let your face not tremble, my son Horus! My son have you seen the flame of the Great One?") and then tells him, " I have come to extinguish the fire." The Ugaritic spell is lacunose, but we find a similar sort of direct questioning of the child (". . . didst thou fall, O my off[spring (?)]? Why didst thou fall into a seizure . . . and shedst tears like a child?"), and we presume that here, too, there is a positive outcome from her intervention (see

more telling, however, is the fact that the author of the Genesis passage seems almost self-conciously to point to the original provenance of the myth when he informs us that Hagar is an Egyptian, and that Ishmael will marry an Egyptian and become the founder of the nomadic tribes which inhabit the Negev and the Sinai, traditionally areas of Egyptian political and cultural influence. If, as it seems, "E" has tampered with a local Negev legend about the miraculous salvation of a famous ancestor by his divine mother, it would certainly not occasion any great surprise to discover that such a local myth would betray strong Egyptian influence.[45] Here, too, however, the Egyptian parallels do not explain the whole story; two details recall motifs present in the Mesopotamian spells discussed above. The most obvious is the name of the well that supplies the saving waters: Beersheba, "The Seven Wells" which might faintly recall another version of the story in which the seven streams appeared to the child, much like the seven water-carrying maidens in the Greek spell.[46] The other puzzling feature is the fact that Hagar carries the dying Ishmael "on her shoulder," a detail that has stymied biblical commentators since it destroys the chronology of events in this stretch of narrative.[47] Could this, too, be a faint memory of the Standard Babylonian spells, which in their formulaic introductions recount how

---

above n. 36). In the biblical narrative, there is a peculiar splitting of the scene, caused no doubt by inserting Elohim and his angel into the divine machinery of the traditional scene and by demoting the mother from divine to human status. The result is that Elohim hears the baby crying and sends his angel who addresses Hagar in the manner that the children are addressed in the Egyptian and Ugaritic examples, i.e., both questioning and encouraging her ("What troubles you, Hagar? Fear not for Elohim has heeded the cry of the boy, where he is"). Elohim reveals the water, but even in this reworked version of the story it is still the mother who draws the water and gives it to the suffering child to drink.

[45] Similar historicizing of Canaanite, Assyrian or Egyptian myths is not unknown in the books of Genesis and Exodus (see, e.g., Yahweh's appearance to Abraham and his promise of progeny in Genesis 15 or the "Potiphar's Wife" motif). For discussion see, e.g., the pioneering work of F. M. Cross, *Canaanite Myth and Old Testament Epic: Essays in the History of the Religion of Israel* (Cambridge, 1973).

[46] This equation between *hydria*-carrying nymphs and actual streams of underground water is extremely common in Greek thought; see below for a full discussion.

[47] According to the established chronology of events, Ishmael should be about fifteen years old; see Vawter (n. 40) *ad loc.* and Cogan (n. 41). All the MSS, both Hebrew and the LXX, agree in their report that Hagar carried Ishmael "on her shoulder," suggesting a much smaller child.

diseases fell from the stars and made feverish "the baby on the shoulder (?) of the nursemaid"?[48]

It is, I think, rather easy to explain how Egyptian healing magic for burns and scorpion-stings finds its way into an Ugaritic incantation for snake-bite.[49] But how do we understand such influence on the Hagar story, which was apparently an etiological legend designed to explain both the ancestry of the nomadic tribes of the Negev and the creation of the "Seven Wells" at Beersheba? I would begin to answer this question by pointing out that there is typically a political dimension to the myths about the infant Horus as well. In the Pyramid Texts, for instance, the pharaohs as early as the Sixth Dynasty assimilated themselves to the infant Horus who tramples on snakes and scorpions (e.g., "Tety is Horus, the little child with finger in his mouth, he can trample on you") and who if injured can rely on the help of his mother.[50] There are also local variants of the myth, in which the god Horus is replaced by the infant son of a king or a high ranking nobleman, who is similarly saved by Isis. Thus according to yet another *historiola* preserved in the Metternich Stele, Isis is said to travel incognito with a bodyguard of seven scorpions to a town on the Nile delta. When a "noblewoman" sees her approaching, she closes her door in the goddess' face, an action that prompts one of the scorpions to sting the woman's infant son. The resulting anguish of the child is described in terms of fire: "Fire broke out in the house of the lady, there was no water there to extinguish it." In the end Isis takes pity and saves the child with an incantatory exorcism.[51] Plutarch

---

[48] As the question mark in the translation of the Assyrian spell indicates, however, the word for "shoulder" here is not secure.

[49] C. Gordon, "Ugaritic Guilds and Homeric *DEMIOERGOI"* in S. Weinberg, ed., *The Aegean and the Near East: Studies Presented to Hetty Goldman* (Locust Valley, 1956), Grottanelli (n. 32) 649-70, and W. Burkert, *The Orientalizing Revolution: Near Eastern Influence on Greek Culture in the Early Archaic Age* (Cambridge, 1992), 41-87, argue persuasively for the existence of wandering professionals such as artisans, purifiers, prophets and healers, who moved easily about the eastern Mediterranean basin carrying practical "technologies" with them, including forms of sacrifice, divination and other rituals.

[50] See Scott (n. 18) 204. Prof. Ritner informs me *per litteras* that the Pharaoh was regularly assimilated to Horus from the very beginnings of Egyptian history.

[51] The longest and most detailed version can be reconstructed by combining the beginning of a long spell in the Metternich Stele, and what appears to be the end of the same spell on the "Socle Behague." For translations and discussions, see Borghouts (n. 12) no. 90 and Klasens (n. 18) 52-53 spell no. I. Scott (n. 18) 210-11, gives a synopsis and discussion of the version preserved by the Metternich Stele.

preserves a similar tale about Isis in Byblos,[52] and there are obvious parallels between this story and that of the disguised Demeter in the Homeric *Hymn to Demeter*. Scholars have usually assumed that Plutarch is giving a late version of the Isis story which has been contaminated by the Demeter myth,[53] but more recently Burkert has emphasized the importance of the story in the Metternich Stele and has argued for the reverse process: the *historiola* was originally an Egyptian one which was borrowed by the Greeks in the sixth century.[54] In her Homeric *Hymn*, Demeter, like Isis in Byblos, disguises herself as a mournful old woman and sits by a well in the Greek town of Eleusis. She, too, becomes the nurse of the infant son of a wealthy noble and subjects it to the same alternation of nocturnal burning and then diurnal ambrosia. In the Homeric *Hymn*, as in the story of Hagar, this treatment is part of an etiological myth explaining and justifying the political prominence of the descendants of the child. The idea is a simple one: the goddess shows favor by nursing and imparts a certain degree of immortality as well.[55]

---

[52] *De Is. et Os.* 15-16 (= *Mor.* 357a-d). Isis disguises herself and travels to Byblos in search of Osiris' body. When she arrives in the city, she sits dejectedly by a spring and weeps until she is befriended by the servants of the king, who arrange for her to become the wet nurse for the king's infant. Isis burns this child in the fire by night, and then feeds him ambrosia by day. Burkert (n. 9) 20-21 points out the parallels between this story and the one on the Metternich Stele. There is some evidence that texts like the Metternich stele were known in Byblos; Montet (n. 34) 249-52, no. 948, published a small undated fragment of an inscribed Egyptian magical stele found at Byblos, which contains spells very similar to lines 35-37 and 56-57 of the texts found on the Metternich Stele. The fragment was, unfortunately, not found in its original archeological context and is therefore undatable. For the massive Egyptian influence on the city in the second and first millennia BCE, see nn. 56 and 57 below.

[53] See S. Hermann, "Isis in Byblos," *ZÄS* 82 (1957): 48-55; Griffiths (n. 41) 319-22 and N. J. Richardson, *The Homeric Hymn to Demeter* (Oxford, 1974), 238. Griffiths (*loc. cit.* 321-22) suggests that Isis and Osiris were worshipped at Byblos as early as the sixth century BCE and that the influence of the Homeric *Hymn* could have occurred anytime from the Hellenistic period onward.

[54] Burkert (n. 9) 20-21; he accepts, however, that Plutarch's story of Isis at Byblos is due to Greek influence (142 n. 42), i.e., it is presumably some kind of mythic "back formation."

[55] Indeed, it has recently been argued that the seventh-century BCE cult of the Samian Hera celebrated the goddess' suckling of Herakles, a motif that probably originated in Egypt and spread in the second millennium into the Levant and Anatolia, adapting itself to local beliefs and practices as it went. B. M. Fridh-Haneson, "Hera's Wedding on Samos: A Change of Paradigms" in R. Hägg, N. Marinatos, and G. C. Nordquist, eds., *Early Greek Cult Practices*, Skrifter Utgivna av Svenska Institutet i Athene 38 (Stockholm, 1989), 205-13.

In the abbreviated versions of the myths about Isis saving or nursing the babies of a noblewoman of the delta and the king of Byblos, there is unfortunately no explicit evidence that they served as foundation myths of this same sort, designed to legitimate or sanction the rule of the individual or family so treated. There is, however, much archeological evidence of extraordinary Egyptian influence on Byblos for most of the second millennium BCE,[56] and despite the breakdown of Egyptian hegemony in the first millennium, her cultural influence remained profound.[57] It is not, then, out of the realm of possibility that at some point during the long history of their close relations an Egyptian myth was adopted and adapted by its close Phoenician ally to legitimize the relationship and the power of the ruling dynasty. Such an implicit political connection would be quite similar to that stated explicitly in the story of Hagar and Ishmael in the desert, where the angel promises to "make a great nation" of the child. If we assume that the Elohist narrator has borrowed some local Negev tradition here about the origin of their founder Ishmael, it would make sense that here, too (in an area subject to intense Egyptian political and cultural influence), the rule of Ishmael's line would be legitimized by a myth which identifies him with the infant Horus and narrates his salvation at the hands of the disguised Isis, who like Demeter at Eleusis and Hagar, appears as a beggar woman or a slave.

*   *   *

Some of the folkloric motifs of these early eastern-Mediterranean myths are also reflected in traditional myths and lustral rites performed in the Greek world. If we recall the traditional assimilation of fresh-water springs to water nymphs in Greek thought, there appears to be a number of instances in which

---

[56] Montet (n. 34) catalogues hundreds of Egyptian and Egyptianizing objects found in Byblos; see S. Bondi, "Origins in the East" in S. Moscati, ed., *The Phoenicians* (Milan, 1988), 28-34, for a general discussion. During the Egyptian Middle Kingdom (16th-11th centuries BCE) the rulers of Byblos were the only ones in the East to whom the Egyptians referred as *haty-a*, "Prince" or "Count," a title of great respect that was conferred by the pharaoh alone (*ANET* p. 229; see Bondi *ibid.* 30 for discussion).

[57] Royal inscriptions from Byblos suggest, for example, that the supreme goddess and royal patroness Baalath ("Mistress" or "Sovereign") was equated with the Egyptian Goddess Hathor-Isis. Vehimik, the fifth-century BCE king of Byblos, declares that he owes his throne to her and he begs her for protection, long life and vengeance against his enemies. See S. Ribichini, "Beliefs and Religious Life" in Moscati (n. 56) 107-08.

water drawn from seven springs is used for purification or healing. There are also several myths in which a person threatened with a fiery death is saved by the timely arrival of fresh water, usually by the miraculous appearance of a spring or stream as in the Ishmael story. In general these tales seem to be connected with a long lived Greek belief in the special efficacy of moving water, especially if it could be drawn from several streams or springs.[58] In a few instances we hear of water being drawn from seven different streams for lustration. Medea, before preparing the charm to protect Jason from the fire-breathing bulls, bathes "in seven ever-flowing streams" (A. R. 3. 860), and there is a tradition preserved by a scholiast to Theocritus that Orestes was ordered by an oracle to be purified by bathing himself "in seven rivers flowing from one spring" (ἐν ἑπτὰ ποταμοῖς ἐκ μιᾶς πηγῆς ῥέουσιν).[59] A third example is a second-century CE oracle response of the Clarian Apollo which prescribes an elaborate lustration rite for the Lydian city of Caesarea Troketta,[60] during which water drawn from seven fountains (ἀπὸ μὲν λιβάδων ἑπτά) is sprinkled in the houses of the city, either to cure an existing plague or to prevent further outbreak. In each of these instances it must be stressed that the polluted houses or sick people are probably washed or sprinkled with the water and

---

[58] The earliest reference is in a fragment of Empedocles (B 143 D-K) that speaks of drawing water from five springs; compare also Sophocles *OC* 479 (although the phrase τρισσάς γε πηγάς can also be understood as three lustrations from the same fountain; see the scholia *ad loc.*); Menander, *Plasma* 54-56 (Körte); and Theophrastus, *Char.* 16.2 (with the sensible emendation proposed by Borthwick [see below] *ad loc.*). For full discussion see: E. Rohde, *Psyche: The Cult of the Soul and the Belief in Immortality among the Greeks* (London, 1925), 588-89; M. Teufel, "Brauch und Ritus bei Apollonios Rhodios," (diss., Tübingen, 1939), 29-32; and E. K. Borthwick, "Notes on the Superstitious Man of Theophrastus," *Eranos* 64 (1966): 106-08.

[59] This story is corroborated by Varro, see G. Hermann, *Opuscula* vol. 2 (1827), 71-75, who quotes all the relevant passages and gives a detailed discussion. Borthwick (n. 58) 107 n. 3, suggests that Euripides may be alluding to this tradition when he uses of the plural λουτροῖσι καθαροῖς to describe Orestes' purification on another occasion (*El.* 794).

[60] See K. Buresch, *Klaros* (Leipzig, 1889), 10-24, O. Weinreich, *Antike Heilungswunder* (Giessen, 1909), 150-51, and H. W. Parke, *The Oracles of Apollo in Asia Minor* (London, 1985), 149-59, for text and discussion of the oracle which they all date to the devastating plague of 166 CE. J. Keil and A. V. Premerstein, *Bericht über eine Reise in Lydien und der südlichen Aiolis*, Denks. Akad. Wien 53.2 (1908): 8-12, and J. Gilliam, "The Plague under Marcus Aurelius," *AJP* 82 (1961): 225-51, esp. 234-37, adopt a more cautious view about the date, arguing that since plague and famine were regular events in the ancient world it is impossible to say to which plague the oracle refers.

thereby cleansed of their afflictions.[61] The idea that plagues or the fevers they caused had to be "extinguished" magically is also attested in the Greek tradition.[62] Pliny the Elder reports a cure for abscesses that involves a naked and fasting maiden, who touches the patient, spits[63] three times on the ground and then says, "Apollo denies that the plague can increase in a patient, if a naked maiden extinguishes it."[64]

The Clarian oracle mentioned above describes the lustration of Caesarea Troketta as follows: "draw it (i.e., the water) off eagerly and sprinkle the houses immediately with nymphs who have become pleasant"—a somewhat strained expression of an equation that was quite common throughout the Greek world: the personification (as water nymphs) of springs and other underground sources of fresh water. It comes as no surprise, I think, that such nymphs also figure in a number of Greek myths about salvation from fiery death by the timely arrival of water (i.e., much like that of the *mystodokos*). In fifth-century Attic vase-paintings of Herakles' apotheosis, artists depict two or three maidens dousing the fire with water-jars (*hydriai*) as Herakles mounts a chariot for heaven.[65] The painter of a late fifth-century BCE pelike in Munich

---

[61] Burkert (n. 49) 55-64, stresses the fact that both Greek and Near Eastern purification rites were thought to provide cures for a wide variety of mental and physical illnesses.

[62] See D. Wortmann, "Neue magische Texte: Nr. 6: Fieberamulett," *BJ* 168 (1968): 104-05 and Daniel and Maltomini (n. 20) 7-10 no. 2, for a silver amulet which contains the phrase: "If fever catches hold of him, extinguish (κατασβένοις = κατασβεν<νύ>οις) it once and for all." Cf. R. Kotansky, "An Inscribed Copper Amulet from 'Evron," *'Atiqot* 20 (1991): 81-87, for a text from the western Galilee which asks that fever "be extinguished" (ἀποσβῆναι) from the person carrying the amulet. All of the editors cited above provide parallels from Greek medical literature.

[63] The spittle of the naked maiden may indicate a lustration like that at Caesarea or may recall the water from the lips of Isis discussed above (n. 15); given, however, the widespread belief in the magical efficacy of saliva, neither point can be stressed. For a general discussion, see R. W. Nicolson, "The Saliva Superstition in Classical Literature," *HSCP* 8 (1897): 23-40, esp. 27-35.

[64] Pliny, *NH* 26.60.93: *negat Apollo pestem posse crescere cui nuda virgo restinguat*. The anonymous source for this spell is either quoting an oracle (*Apollo negat ...*) originally aimed at curing some kind of plague (*pestem*), or (more likely) it is simply translating a popular Greek formula of the type "The god X commands ..." found on magical amulets and gemstones; e.g., C. Bonner, *Studies in Magical Amulets* (Ann Arbor, 1950), no. 77 (an inscribed bronze prism in the Antioch Museum): Φοῖβος κελεύι μὴ κύ<ε>ιν πόνον πόδας.

[65] J. D. Beazley, *Etruscan Vase Painting* (Oxford, 1947), 103-05, reviews all the known examples in his discussion of two Faliscan vases in the Villa Giulia. Maas (n. 1) 38 n. 25, was aware of these paintings, but dismissed their signifi-

labels two of these figures as the water-nymphs Arethousa and
Premnousa, both attested as natural springs in Attica.[66] Herodotus
reports that according to a Boeotian etiological legend,[67] the river
Dyras that flows above Thermopylae sprang miraculously from the
ground to help the hero when he was immolated (7.198: τὸν βο—
ηθέοντα τῷ Ἡρακλέϊ καιομένῳ).[68] As in the Hagar story, one
purpose of these myths seems to have been to explain how local
wells (e.g., Beersheba) or springs (e.g., Premnousa) came into
existence.

There is another Greek tradition that places this type of timely
"salvation" from fire at the beginning of life, not near the end.
Euripides reports the two births of the child Dionysus, the first
prematurely from Semele's womb under a lightning blast, and the
second from Zeus' thigh (*Bacchae* 88-98). Later in the same play,
however, the chorus adds a significant detail when they invoke the
river Dirke: "... for it was you who once seized the infant of Zeus
in your springs, at the time when Zeus snatched him from the

cance because of the discrepancy in the numbers, i.e., there are seven maidens in
the *mystodokos* incantation but only two or three on the vase paintings. Beazley
(*loc. cit.*) suggests, however, that the small number of nymphs in the vase-
paintings may simply reflect an artistic convention for depicting the larger
number of nymphs who appear in the original myth. For the most recent assessment of these paintings, see: H. Shapiro, "Heros Theos: The Death and Apotheosis of Heracles," *CW* 77 (1983): 7-18; J. Boardman, "Heracles in Extremis" in
Studien zür Mythologie und Vasenmalerei: Festschrift für K. Schauenburg
(Mainz am Rhein, 1988), 127-32; and *LIMC* s.v. "Heracles" nos. 2909 and 2916-
20.

[66] Cook (n. 15) 515; Beazley (n. 65); and E. Diehl, *Die Hydria: For-
mgeschichte und Verwendung im Kult des Altertums* (Mainz am Rhein, 1964),
206.

[67] H. Stein in his 1889 commentary on Herodotus suggests *ad loc.* that the
story was perhaps originally an etiology for the hot baths at nearby Thermopylae.
There is evidence that in Euboea and Attica hot baths were regularly connected
with Heracles; see especially Ar. *Clouds* 1050 and the scholia.

[68] The hot springs at Himera on Sicily were similarly thought to have appeared (in the form of water nymphs) to refresh Heracles when he was weary from
his labors in the West (Diod. Sic. 4. 23), a story apparently known elsewhere in
the ancient world, judging by the connection of Heracles and water-nymphs at
curative springs. See M. Bieber, "Archaeological Contributions to Roman
Religion," *Hesperia* 14 (1945): 272-77, who discusses a type of fountain relief
depicting Heracles reclining on rocks that have been covered with his lionskin;
in each case, nymphs or satyrs fill his raised cup, or the water-spout of the fountain emerges from a water-skin tucked under his arm. Bieber suggests that this
type of sculpture, attested only in the Imperial period, is related to fourth-century
BCE coins of Himera that depict Heracles reclining near the springs mentioned
by Diodorus; for the most recent discussion, see *LIMC* s.v. "Heracles" nos. 1322-
28.

immortal fire (πυρὸς ἐξ ἀθανάτου) . . ." (lines 519-25).[69] Plutarch, a native Boeotian, associates this story with the spring Kissoussa near Haliartus in which the "Nurses of Dionysus" washed the newborn god (Lys. 28.7); according to another early tradition (one preserved by Hesiod, Hippias of Elis and Pherecydes) five or seven nymphs, known either as the Nysai, the "Nurses of Dionysus" or the Hyades, were involved.[70] There is, moreover, an early version of this story that places the rescue on Mt. Nysa, "the highest mountain ... of far-off Phoenicia, near the streams of the Nile."[71] In most of these accounts, we need perhaps only assume that the nurses swaddled and comforted the infant god. There is, however, one later Greek text that suggests the nymphs actually extinguished the fire. In a somewhat frivolous epigram about diluting wine (= Bacchus) with water (= nymphs), the Hellenistic poet Meleager, another Syrian from Gadara, seems to allude to this very myth (Pal. Anth. 9.331):[72]

---

[69] Aeschylus' lost Semele or Hydrophoroi (frags. 219-24 Radt) and Sophocles' lost Hydrophoroi (frags. 670-74 Radt) both apparently dealt with the death of Semele and the miraculous birth of Dionysus. In both plays the chorus consisted of women who probably arrive at the palace carrying water in hydriai, with which (presumably) they wash the newborn Dionysus. See Diehl (n. 66) 193-94 for the most recent discussion.

[70] For the Nysai, see Nilsson (n. 82) 111-12. As for the Hyades, Hesiod frag. 291 (West) names five, while Pherecydes FGrHist 3 F90 and Hippias FGrHist 6 F9 say there were seven and identify them closely with the stars in the head of the bull in the Pleiades constellation, whose heliacal rising was traditionally thought to signal the start of the rainy season in Greece. See RE s.v. "Hyaden" and LIMC s.v. "Hyades" for a full survey of the later literary sources, especially in the astronomical writings. The action of these nurses is not (to my knowledge) actually depicted in early Greek art, although they occasionally appear as bystanders in scenes where Hermes presents the child to Zeus (LIMC s.v. "Dionysus" nos. 696-705). For later depictions of two or more nymphs pouring water from a hydria into a basin over the head or feet of the infant Dionysus, see R. Merkelbach, Die Hirten des Dionysos: Die Dionysos-Mysterien der römischen Kaiserzeit und der bukolische Roman des Longus (Stuttgart, 1988), plates 30 (4th cent. CE mosaic), 43 (1st or 2nd cent. CE relief from Perge), 56 (2nd cent. CE Roman sarcophagus), 58 (2nd cent. CE Roman sarcophagus), and 83 (undated Roman sarcophagus). Nonnus claims they are "the daughters of Lamus," a Boeotian river-god (e.g., Dion. 9.28 and 14.146); see RE s.v. "Hyaden" 2621-22.

[71] Homeric Hymn 1. 8-9 (the lines are quoted thrice by Diod. Sic. 1.15.7, 3.66.3. and 4.2.40): ἔστι δέ τις Νύση ὕπατον ὄρος ἀνθέον ὕλῃ / τηλοῦ Φοινίκης σχεδὸν Αἰγύπτοιο ῥοάων. The fragment is generally thought to be from an "early" hymn; see T. W. Allen, W. R. Halliday and E. E. Sikes, The Homeric Hymns² (Oxford, 1936), lxvii-xix, who argue that Diodorus—a first-century BCE contemporary of the scribe that penned the mystodokos charm—is quoting older antiquarians.

[72] I give the text of A. S. F. Gow and D. L. Page, eds., The Greek Anthology:

αἱ νύμφαι τὸν Βάκχον, ὅτ' ἐκ πυρὸς ἦλαθ' ὁ κοῦρος,
   νίψαν ὑπὲρ τέφρης ἄρτι κυλιόμενον·
τοὔνεκα σὺν νύμφαις Βρόμιος φίλος· ἢν δέ νιν εἴργῃς
   μίσγεσθαι, δέξῃ πῦρ ἔτι καιόμενον.

The Nymphs washed Bacchus when the lord leapt from the fire
   and upon the ashes was just then turning.
Therefore when Bromios is with the Nymphs he is friendly,[73]
   but if you prevent their union, you will receive the fire still burning.

One must conclude that if it were not for the timely intervention of the nymphs, Dionysus would have continued to burn. Despite the confusion over the names and numbers of the nymphs, the one consistent feature of these stories is that Dionysus is immersed in some kind of water or washed by nymphs immediately after he is removed from the fire.

If it now seems less certain that the infant Horus was the *mystodokos* mentioned in the charm, who is he or she? Demophon has been mentioned as a possibility,[74] but his burning takes place indoors, he is (to my knowledge) never referred to as an "initiate," and he is not the "son of a goddess."[75] If, however, we restore, e.g., [<αἰγιόχου δὲ> Διὸς παῖς μ]υστοδόκος κατεκαύθη to the first line of the incantation instead of Koenen's [<σεμνοτάτης δὲ> θεᾶς παῖς μ]υστοδόκος, two possible candidates emerge: Dionysus and Heracles.[76] Heracles was said to have been initiated into the Lesser

---

Hellenistic Epigrams (Cambridge, 1965), 252 no. 127. For Meleager's Syrian heritage and Gadarene birthplace, see *ibid.*, pp. xiv-xvii. Gadara was fully Hellenized in this period—"an Attica among the Syrians" (*Pal. Anth.* 7. 417), as Meleager himself describes it—and was remarked upon as the birthplace of several famous men of letters, including Meleager, the philosopher-poet Philodemus and the satirist Menippus (Strabo 16.759). For discussion, see M. Hadas, "Gadarenes in Pagan Literature," *CW* 25 (1931): 25-30.

[73] I.e., "friendly to humankind" following Gow and Page (n. 72) *ad loc.*

[74] Burkert (n. 9) 141-42 n. 40.

[75] Except perhaps indirectly by "adoption" on account of Demeter's nursing; see *Hymn to Dem.* 237 (χρίεσκ' ἀμβροσίῃ ὡσεὶ θεοῦ ἐκγεγαῶτα) with the comments of Richardson (n. 53) *ad loc;* on the concept of divine adoption, an idea that seems to underlie some Byblian depictions of Isis nursing the king, see above notes 55 and 57.

[76] The phrases Διὸς παῖς and Διὸς τέκος are found in Homeric hexameters (e.g. *Il.* 1. 202; 13.825 or *Od.* 6.488); the latter is more common. Euripides has Dionysus identify himself as Διὸς παῖς in the first line of the *Bacchae* and he employs altered forms of this phrase twice in the *Ion* (lines 200 and 1144) to refer to Heracles. He also uses Διὸς γόνος of Dionysus in one of the chorus's prayers to the god at *Bacchae* 603. See the comments of E. R. Dodds, *Euripides: Bacchae*² (Oxford,

Eleusinian mysteries just prior to his descent into the underworld, and therefore he qualifies as a *mystodokos*.[77] As discussed above, while burning on a mountain in Boeotia he, too, was "saved" by the sudden appearance of a river or (in a competing version) by a group of hydria-bearing nymphs in Attica. Given the apparent Semitic influences on this text and its alleged Gadarean provenance, the regular assimilation of Heracles to Melqart at Tyre and to Sandon (or Sandes) at Tarsus may be significant; both were apparently thought to be immolated and reborn each year in a celebration that is strikingly similar to the myth and ritual associated with Heracles' immolation and apotheosis on Mt. Oeta.[78] Given the connection between Heracles and hot-springs it may be significant that Gadara, too, was renowned for the curative effects of its hot springs.[79]

1964), on line 1, for the importance of this claim throughout the play.

[77] The tradition can be traced at least as early as the end of the fifth century BCE, and it probably goes back even earlier to a lost sixth-century epic *katabasis* of Heracles; see H. Lloyd-Jones, "Heracles at Eleusis: *P. Oxy.* 2622 and *P.S.I.* 1391," *Maia* 19 (1967): 206-29, F. Graf, *Eleusis und die orphische Dichtung Athens in vorhellenisticher Zeit*, RGVV 33 (Berlin, 1974), 142-50, and N. Robertson, "Heracles' 'Catabasis,'" *Hermes* 108 (1980): 274-99, esp. 295-99.

[78] J. G. Frazer, *Adonis, Attis, Osiris: Studies in the History of Oriental Religion*[3], The Golden Bough 5 (Cambridge, 1914), 110-16 and 172-79, was the first to gather the scattered evidence (mainly from late Greek authors) for the worship of Sandon/Sandes at Tarsus and Melqart at Tyre, Carthage and Gades, and for the legendary self-immolation of Hamilcar (after the defeat at Himera), Croesus (in Bacchylides' version) and other Near Eastern kings. He provocatively traced a pattern whereby human leaders (usually kings) imitate the immolation of the chief god of their city (e.g., Melqart at Tyre, Sandon at Tarsus, and Heracles at Sardis), who is himself believed to have been immolated and then reborn at an annual celebration. Although the larger theoretical framework of Frazer's approach (especially his solar gods and the Year Daimon) have been completely discredited, his arguments about this pattern of Near Eastern and Anatolian myth and Heracles' connection with it have persisted, although no one agrees how the Greek and Near Eastern similarities came to be. G. R. Levy, "The Oriental Origin of Heracles," *JHS* 54 (1934): 47-49, argued for a Near Eastern source for the legend about the pyre on Mt. Oeta. H. Goldman, "Sandon and Heracles" in *Commemorative Studies in Honor of T. L. Shear*, Hesperia Suppl. 8 (Athens, 1949): 164-74, esp. 167-68, following the lead of Nilsson, argued for a reverse process: the myths about Heracles, a hero surviving from Mycenean times, gradually moved eastward, where they were assimilated to indigenous cults. On the difficulties in assessing these close parallels, see esp. Burkert (n. 90).

[79] Public baths were built there in the Hellenistic and Roman periods and the waters were famed for their curative powers, especially with regard to leprosy, scabs and swellings. See E. L. Sukenik, "The Ancient Synagogue of El-Hammeh," *JPOS* 15 (1935): 108-14, for lengthy quotations of Greek, Roman and rabbinic testimonia.

Another equally good candidate can be found, however, for the *mystodokos* in the Philinna papyrus: that other famous son of Zeus, Dionysus. According to early Greek legend he, too, was initiated into a mystery cult—the mysteries of Rhea.[80] He was threatened as a newborn child by the fire that resulted from Zeus' thunderbolt and was then saved by a special spring (Dirke) or by the Hyades who also seem to have been depicted in art as *hydro-phoroi*.[81] Most important, however, is the fact that child initiation was a regular practice at his mysteries in Hellenistic and Roman times, and uniquely so, as far as the rest of the Greek world was concerned.[82] Thus in the later periods there is increasing interest in his childhood, and the child Dionysus becomes a prototype of the child initiate.[83] If Dionysus is indeed the *mystodokos* mentioned in the Philinna papyrus, this may help explain a significant variation in the late-antique copy of the spell, which reads ἐκοίμισαν αἰ–θέριον πῦρ in the final line—apparently a reference to the fire of a lightning bolt.[84] As seems to be the case with Heracles, there

[80] Eumelus *Europia* frag. 1 (Davies) and Apollod. 3.5.1. For the most recent discussion of this incident, see T. H. Carpenter, "On the Beardless Dionysus" in T. H. Carpenter and C. A. Faraone, eds., *Masks of Dionysus* (Ithaca, 1993): 197-98, and W. Burkert, "Bacchic *Teletai* in the Hellenistic Age," *ibid.*, 272-73. Later authors (reflecting the popular child initiations of the Hellenistic and later periods) describe how the infant Dionysus was initiated into his own mysteries; see Nilsson (n. 82) 110 for discussion.

[81] *LIMC* s.v. "Hyades."

[82] M. P. Nilsson, *The Dionysiac Mysteries of the Hellenistic and Roman Age*, Skrifter Utgivna av Svenska Institutet i Athen 8 (Lund, 1957), 106-15 and Merkelbach (n. 70) 88-95.

[83] Depictions of the childhood of Dionysus multiply in the Roman period; see n. 70 above and the discussion in Nilsson, *ibid.*, 110-12.

[84] Maas (n. 1) suggested that αἰθέριον πῦρ in the late-antique version of the *mystodokos* spell (see n. 2) refers to a lightning bolt, a motif which also appears in Euripides' *Bacchae* (line 288: ἐκ πυρὸς κεραυνίου) and in one family of the so-called "Orphic" *lamellae*, where the phrase εἴτε με μοῖρ' ἐδάμασσ' εἴτε ἀστεροπῆτι κεραυνῶι appears; for text see Zuntz (n. 20) 314-16. There is still no agreement as to the exact description of the beliefs expressed in the gold tablets. The traditional label "Orphic" (given to the tablets at the turn of the century) has been called into question in more recent times. Zuntz, *ibid.*, 277-86 calls them "Pythagorean" while S. G. Cole, "New Evidence for the Mysteries of Dionysus," *GRBS* 21 (1980): 223-38, and Burkert (n. 9) prefer the adjective "Bacchic" in light of the mention of *bacchoi* in line 16 of the Hipponion tablet. The presence of *Bacchios* on the recently discovered ivy-shaped tablets from Trikka, seems to confirm their suspicions; see F. Graf, "Dionysian and Orphic Eschatology: New Texts and Old Questions" in Carpenter and Faraone (n. 80) 239-58. For further connections between lightning blasts and ancient Greek eschatological beliefs, see W. Burkert, "Elysion," *Glotta* 34 (1961): 208-11, who argues that Elysion, the home of the blessed in the underworld, is derived from ἐνηλύσιος, "struck by

appears to have existed an epichoric Levantine version of
Dionysus' birth "on Mt. Nysa, the highest mountain of far off
Phoenicia";[85] it would not be surprising to find out that this story
stressed or elevated the role of the nymphs from mere servants
(who swaddle the child) to saviors (who douse him with water while
he is "still burning"), very much, in fact, like the playful version of
the myth composed by the poet Meleager (quoted above) who may
have learned of it as a youth in Gadara or Tyre.[86]

I should hasten to point out here that the appearance of the
term *mystodokos* in the Philinna papyrus is no guarantee that the
hexameters were originally part of a poem used in rituals connected with initiation. In fact, since the story narrated in the
charm stands at the end (not the beginning) of a long tradition of
eastern Mediterranean incantations aimed solely at curing bodily
discomforts, I can see no reason in this instance to insist that the
author or her source pillaged a liturgy of a mystery cult and then
"retooled" it for more concrete medical problems—a traditional
type of analysis which employs a theoretical model of "magic" as
a later degeneration of "religion."[87] Indeed, even if the story did
figure prominently in the liturgy of a mystery cult, there is no
need to label its use in a practical, curative charm as a degeneration
of some original, purer sentiment. Recent research points out that

---

lightning," an etymology approved by Chaintraine, s.v.

[85] *Hom. Hymn* 1.8-9, see n. 71 above. M. Smith, "On the Wine God in Palestine" in S. Lieberman, ed., *Salo Wittmayer Baron: Jubilee Volume on the Occasion of his Eightieth Birthday.* (New York, 1974), 815-29, gives a good general
discussion of the assimilation of Dionysus to local Levantine gods in the late-
Classical and Hellenistic periods.

[86] S. J. D. Cohen, "The Beauty of Flora and the Beauty of Sarai," *Helios* 8
(1981): 41-53, documents another, very similar instance of North Semitic-Greek
syncretism in his discussion of the famous epigram in praise of Flora, *Pal. Anth.* 5.
132, written by a first-century BCE Greek poet, Philodemus of Gadara, and the
similar Hebrew description of the beauty of Sarai in the first-century BCE Dead
Sea Scrolls text called the *Genesis Apocryphon.* H. Jacobson, "Demo and the
Sabbath," *Mnemosyne* 30 (1977): 71-72, similarly comments on a Jewish concept
that shows up in a poem of Meleager of Gadara (*Pal. Anth.* 5.160). Note that both
instances involve Greek poets raised in Gadara at a time roughly contemporary
with the papyrus under discussion. For other instances of direct Near Eastern
influence on the Greek literature of this period, see the general survey in M. L.
West, "Near Eastern Material in Hellenistic and Roman Literature," *HSCP* 73
(1969): 113-34.

[87] This approach is illustrated, for example, by A. A. Barb, "The Survival of
the Magic Arts" in A. Momigliano, ed., *The Conflict between Paganism and
Christianity in the Fourth Century* (Oxford, 1963), 100-25, and *idem*, "Mystery,
Myth and Magic" in J. R. Harris, ed., *The Legacy of Egypt*[2] (Oxford, 1971), 138-
69.

Greek mystery cults from the archaic period onward seem to be very much concerned with the initiates' welfare while they were alive, as well as after they were dead; for example, Samothracian initiates apparently believed that they had special protection against shipwreck and drowning or Mithraic initiates were thought to be safer in battle,[88] suggesting that the ancients did not regularly and clearly distinguish between the two kinds of salvation, one for this world and another for the next.

*   *   *

There appears, then, to be a rich and complicated melange of traditions reflected in the short magical charm quoted at the beginning of this essay. I shall begin my summation of the data by presenting a rough chronology of the different Greek and non-Greek texts discussed above:

SECOND MILLENNIUM BCE

Place	Document	Discomfort	Victim (infant) (patient)	Savior (female)
Mesopotamia (18th -11th cent.)	incantation	eye and skin problems	(patient)	14 daughters of Anu
Egypt (16th-11th cent.)	individual spells on statue-bases	burns and bites	Horus	Isis
Ugarit (12th cent.)	incantation	snake-bite	Shrgzz	Shamash

FIRST MILLENNIUM BCE

Place	Document	Discomfort	Victim (infant) (patient)	Savior (female)
Mesopotamia (10th -7th cent.)	incantation	eye and skin problems	(patient)	daughters of Anu

---

[88] Z. Stewart, "L'ascesa delle religioni soteriologiche" in R. B. Bandinelli, ed., *La società ellenistica: Economia, diritto, religione*, Storia e civiltà dei greci 8 (Milan, 1977), 530-61, and Burkert (n. 9) 12-29. For a similar crossover of purposes in Greek magical incantations, see M. Smith, "Salvation in the Gospels, Paul, and the Magical Papyri," *Helios* 13 (1986): 63-74; and R. Kotansky (n. 6) 114-16 and 121-22.

Negev (10th -8th cent.)	narrative	thirst in desert	Ishmael	Hagar
Boeotia (5th cent.)	narrative	immolation	Heracles	river Dyras*
Boeotia (5th cent.)	narrative	lightning blast	Dionysus	Kissuossa (a spring)
Attica (5th cent.)	narrative	immolation	Heracles	Arethousa and Premnousa (springs)
Uruk (3rd cent.)	incantation	mouth disease	(patient)	daughters of Anu
Egypt (3rd cent.)	medical papyri	burns	Horus	Isis w/ Nile water
Egypt (5th-3rd cent.)	Horus cippi	scorpion-bite	Horus	Isis w/ Nile water
Gadara (?) (1st cent.)	incantation	inflammation	"initiate"	7 dark-eyed maidens
Rome (1st cent.)	incantation (Apolline oracle?)	abscesses (plague?)	(patient)	naked maiden spits thrice

FIRST MILLENNIUM CE

Place	Document	Discomfort	Victim (infant)	Savior (female)
Caesarea Troketta (2nd cent.)	Apolline oracle	plague	(city)	seven nymphs (= seven springs)

*The river Dyras is the only masculine source of water in this column.

As is probably clear by now, one cannot, either in the case of the mythological narratives or in the case of the rituals themselves, establish any tidy pattern of dissemination from a single source. The model of a single point of invention and then an orderly ripple-effect of successive borrowings from one neighboring people to the next is far too neat and rigid to reflect the continual cultural give-and-take that has always been typical of the eastern Mediterranean basin, an area (we must remember) of relatively small compass. This situation is, in fact, typical when one tries to grasp the relationship between Greek myths or rituals and their Near Eastern counterparts.[89] Indeed, recent work on the migration of eastern myths to Greece argues vigorously (and to my mind correctly) against such a "philological" approach, pointing out that myths are not inscribed documents like medieval manuscripts that were physically carried from one monastery to another and that can be arranged centuries later by scholars in a rational stemma.[90] If one recalls the close commercial contacts between Egypt, the Levant and the Aegean from at least the Greek Bronze Age onward, it seems much more likely that certain popular myths (especially those linked with practical healing or purificatory rituals) would move quite easily among all three cultures, producing an utterly confusing situation, where different versions of the same myth were combined and recombined in a dizzying variety of forms—a state of affairs that a textual critic might call widespread "contamination" if it occurred in a manuscript tradition.

It would seem, then, that a Syrian woman living in Gadara could have been influenced by a bewildering array of texts and traditions. There are, however, some readily identifiable patterns in these different traditions which allow us to distinguish (as is often the case of Phoenician art, for example[91]) two different and competing strands of influence, one Egyptian and the other Mesopotamian—both at work from early on.[92] The Egyptian or Egyptianizing stories involve a small child dying of thirst in the desert or suffering from the venom of a scorpion or snake; the actual narratives usually quote (in first-person speech) the words of the mother Isis, by which we learn that she is rushing to her son's side with a

---

[89] See Zuntz (n. 20) for a careful discussion of the mixture of Egyptian and Mesopotamian influences in the texts of the so-called "Orphic" gold tablets.

[90] For studies which stress the difficulty and impropriety of applying a philologically-based model of the transmission of manuscripts to the vastly more complicated movement of myths and rituals from the east to Greece, see W. Burkert, "Oriental and Greek Mythology: The Meeting of Parallels" in J. N. Bremmer, ed., *Interpretations of Greek Mythology* (London, 1987), 10-40; R. Mondi, "Greek and Near Eastern Mythology" in L. Edmunds, ed., *Approaches to Greek Myth* (Baltimore, 1990), 142-99; Faraone (n. 22) 26-29; and *idem* (n. 10) 219-43.

[91] See, e.g., G. Markoe, *Phoenician Bronze and Silver Bowls from Cyprus and the Mediterranean* (Berkeley, 1985), 34-71.

[92] This approach to the material is admittedly a simplistic one, which obscures the robust syncretism that went on at all points in the eastern Mediterranean. It, does, however, have a certain heuristic value, as it broadly mirrors the continual struggle between Assyria and Egypt for political and cultural hegemony in the area.

liquid that is frequently assimilated to the waters of the Nile, to her
bodily fluids, or to both.[93] The Mesopotamian tradition of healing
spells frequently has a similar curative focus on "cooling" fever,
skin eruptions, or burning eyes with sprinkled water, but the incantation itself only involves the exhortation of the daughters of
Anu, who are encouraged to bring water in blue jugs and extinguish
the discomfort or cool the affected part of the body. The Greek
myths and rituals predictably reflect both traditions. The mythological narratives of the salvation of Heracles (at the end of his
earthly life) and Dionysus (at the beginning of his) present a situation that is dramatically like the Egyptian stories—the son of a
deity is threatened by fire—, but whose resolution (the arrival of
an anonymous group of young females who carry water-jugs and
who are sometimes connected with the sky god[94]) is much closer to
the Mesopotamian tradition. In the Greek tradition these water-
carrying maidens are closely associated in etiological myth with
sources of underground water (e.g., the salvation of Heracles or
Dionysus) as in the Hagar story. The Greek spell attributed to the
Gadarene woman is, given its late-Hellenistic date and the language

---

[93] The twelfth-century serpent charm from Ugarit is closest in structure to the
Egyptian incantations; a female goddess, probably the victim's mother, questions the victim who is said to act like a child after he is bitten by the snake. As
discussed above, we can only assume that the mythological vignette ended with
the cure of the snakebite. There is only one small indication, however, that the
effect of the snakebite was related to "burning", a consistent component of the
Egyptian and Greek incantations; Astour (n. 35) 34-35, defends his translation
of *npl b sr* in line 10 as "fell into a seizure" on the grounds of context and
"because of the availability of a fitting Arabic cognate *sawrat, sawar*, 'force, fire,
violence (of an intoxicating drink, fever, etc.),'" indicating perhaps that burning
or fever may in fact be an important element of Shrgzz' suffering. Brown (n. 35)
translates the phrase as "falls in agony." My colleague Prof. D. Pardee also
points out *per litteras* that the North Semitic word for "venom" used in this text
(*hmt*) is derived from a root meaning "to be hot."

[94] Zeus is the agent behind the rescue of the baby Dionysus, but he seems to
have been assisted by water nymphs; the chorus in Euripides' *Bacchae* invoke
Dirke as the goddess who received the infant Dionysus in her streams, *after* Zeus
had plucked him from the fire (lines 519-25). Some vague parallels between the
daughters of Anu and the Greek Hyades ("Rain Nymphs") are perhaps worth
noting. R. D. Biggs, *SA.ZI.GA: Ancient Mesopotamian Potency Incantations,*
Texts from Cuneiform Sources 2 (Locust Valley, 1967), 18-19, discusses a potency spell that refers to the "*nalshu* of the daughters of Anu," which appears to
be some sort of liquid falling from the sky; Biggs translates it as "dew." T.
Jacobsen, in his review of Biggs in the *Bulletin of the History of Medicine* 43
(1969): 384-85, goes even further, suggesting that the daughters of Anu were
personified clouds. Landsberger and Farber (both in n. 21) refrain from speculation on the matter.

in which it is preserved, understandably eclectic: an "initiate" suffering from thirst or a burn is cured or saved by seven maidens who carry water to him in dark-blue containers. As mentioned earlier, the color blue, the number seven, and the unmarried status of the young women all suggest that a Mesopotamian spell has probably influenced the local tradition reflected in this incantation, since none of these details appear in the pre-Coptic Egyptian texts.

The persistent bipartite form of the Mesopotamian spells provides, I think, the best clue to explaining the peculiar combination of Near Eastern motifs that presents itself in the *mystodokos* incantation. Each spell begins with a description of the malady, often in historic tenses and poetic language, for example: "(the diseases) descended from the stars of heaven" or "the ergot entered into the eye of the young man." It is in this first section, moreover, that the composer of the incantation had the greatest freedom to choose materials from popular concepts or myths that were not otherwise intrinsic to this particular type of spell, motifs ranging from a traditional description of the onslaught of disease as an animal[95] to imaginative descriptions of the patient's unseen body parts[96] or (more importantly for this inquiry) to mythological narratives of otherwise unknown exploits of the gods.[97] The second half of this type of Mesopotamian spell, however, is much more predictable: it invariably begins with the MANNUM LUSH-PUR formula ("Whom shall I send . . . ?") and then usually goes on to request or describe the arrival of the daughters of Anu with their jugs of soothing water. It is not, I think, difficult to imagine how a

---

[95] Farber (n. 21) nos. 1 ("A black dog is lying on the hill; he waits for the scattered pack. His eyes are fixed on a good-looking young man.") and 4.4: ("The *bu shânu*-disease gives the impression of a lion; not quite like that of a lion, the *bu shânu*-disease's grip is strong. Like a wolf, it takes hold of the mouth, like a tiger it takes hold of the gums").

[96] Farber, *ibid.*, nos. 3.2 ("The heart is strong, the heart is a hero. The strong heart's [eyes] are long, it ho[lds] a bowlful of blood.") and 4.6 ("The door is the flesh, the bolt is the bone," apparently a description of a tooth and the surrounding gum).

[97] Farber, *ibid.*, nos.2.2 ("In, they say, the square field of Enlil, Sin reaped 70 acres of field, had Shamash gather the yield"), 2.6 ("The cow is pregnant, the cow is going to give birth. In the courtyard of Shamash, in the corral of Shakkan, Shamash saw her and could not help weeping, Ellammê [= Sîn] saw her with tears in her eyes ...."), and 4.3 ("They are two, the daughters of Anû; between them stands a [clay] wall. One sister cannot visit [her] other sister"). Farber suggests (p. 304) that this last description (in a cure for eye disease) of two other, unknown daughters of Anu serves as an imaginative description of the patient's two eyes separated by the ridge of the nose.

Syrian woman living in Gadara, and wishing to compose a traditional type of spell for burns or skin ailments inserted a popular
mother-and-child story (probably, at some point, of Egyptian
origin) into the first and most variable part of this traditional type
of Mesopotamian incantation, which itself had at some point been
rendered in delightful Greek hexameters and stripped of its formulaic question ("Whom shall I . . .?"), but nevertheless retained the
still recognizable daughters of Anu and their jugs of lapis lazuli.

Recognition of an independent source of the first two lines of
the spell leads us to one further observation: If we remove the
supplements of previous editors (based on the premise of a single
source of direct Egyptian influence and designed to restore them to
full hexameters), the first two lines contain little traditional Greek
poetic diction[98] and seem to exhibit a formal parallelism that is
strikingly similar to that found in the poetry of the Hebrew Bible
and other ancient Near Eastern poetry:

[6-8 μ]υστοδόκος κατεκα[ύθη]
[ὑψ]ροτάτῳ δ' ἐν ὄρει κατεκαύθ[η]

The repetition of the main verb, although unattractive to the
Greek ear, is one of several types of parallelistic technique that
mark the highest form of Semitic poetry.[99] In this form we get a
relatively short sentence consisting of two brief clauses A and B, in

---

[98] Despite the dactylic cadence, none of the vocabulary in the first two lines
of the *mystodokos* spell appears in Homer or the Homeric *Hymns*. The phrase
ἀκρ]ροτάτῳ δ ἐν ὄρει (if it is the beginning of a hexameter as argued by Koenen
and others) may be a combination of Hes. *Th.* 7 and 484. It should be noted,
however, that Henrichs (arguing that the space is too small for Koenen's restoration) prints ὑψ]ροτάτῳ in *PGM²*, a word that appears neither in Homer nor in
Hesiod.

[99] Most of the full-scale studies concern poetry in the Hebrew Bible, but they
draw on comparative materials from Ugaritic and other Semitic languages: S. A.
Geller, *Parallelism in Early Biblical Poetry*, Harvard Semitic Monographs 20
(Missoula, 1979); M. O' Connor, *Hebrew Verse Structure* (Winona Lake, 1980),
88-132; and J. L. Kugel, *The Idea of Biblical Poetry: Parallelism and its
History* (Yale, 1981). Levine and de Tarragon (n. 35) 516-18 point out similar
instances of parallelistic technique in the Ugaritic snake-bite spell discussed
above, e.g. "[   ] *didst thou fall*, O my off[spring (?)]? Why *didst thou fall* in a
seizure?"(italics mine). For parallelism in Sumerian poetry, see A. Berlin, *En-
merkar and Ensuhkesdanna: A Sumerian Narrative Poem*, Occasional Publications of the Babylonian Fund 2 (Philadelphia, 1979), 19-28. A similar phenomenon has sometimes been noted in Egyptian verse, see, e.g., J. L. Foster, "Thought
Couplets in Khety's 'Hymn to the Inundation,'" *JNES* 34 (1975): 1-29, esp. 8-
10.

which B often repeats the sense of A, but nonetheless completes the thought or adds some new emphasis to it. Of the dozen or so techniques employed in these parallelistic verses, a common one involves exact repetitions of words or whole phrases in a way very similar to the opening line of the spell under discussion here:[100]

πρὸ προσώπου κυρίου ὅτι ἔρχεται
ὅτι ἔρχεται κρῖναι τὴν γῆν.
(Psalm 94 [95]:13-4)

καὶ ἀπώλοντο παρὰ τὸ μὴ ἔχειν φρόνησιν
ἀπώλοντο διὰ τὴν ἀβουλίαν αὐτῶν
("Wisdom Poem" in Baruch 3:28)

In both of these examples, as in the opening couplet of the *mystodokos* spell, the second clause repeats the main verb (ἀπώλοντο and ἔρχεται) and then adds extra emphasis or information.[101]

Although this type of technique is best known as a feature of very ancient Semitic poetry, we need not assume that the alleged Syrian author of the Greek spell (or her source) has translated some ancient text, since parallelism of this sort appears in Hebrew poetry continually into the late-antique period[102] and seems to have been used in the native Phoenician text (dated in all likelihood to the Hellenistic period) which Philo of Byblos translated in the Hadrianic era.[103] Indeed, it would be rash even to suppose that the first two lines of the *mystodokos* spell is a word-for-word translation at all; the first five books of the apocryphal *Wisdom of*

---

[100] Geller (n. 99) 297-98 and Kugel (n. 99) 35-40. I give examples from the LXX and the Greek Apocrypha to illustrate how such forms are translated into or composed in Greek in the period roughly contemporaneous with the production of the "Philinna Papyrus." Exact repetition of this type is generally avoided in the Hebrew Bible; the reverse is true for Sumerian poetry, see Berlin (n. 99) 15 n. 23. I provide one Sumerian example: "My king has sent me to you; The lord of Aratta, Ensuhkesdanna, has sent me to you" (trans. Berlin, *ibid.*, 14).

[101] It is tempting to suggest that the actual layout of the first sentence of the spell on the papyrus in two short clauses ending with κατεκαύθη indicates that the scribe was trying to preserve its parallelistic form, but this is probably only a coincidence of column width and syntactic sense.

[102] Kugel (n. 99) 304-14.

[103] A.I. Baumgarten, *The Phoenician History of Philo of Byblos*, EPRO 89 (Leiden, 1981), 100-04, corrects the notion of previous editors that the parallelism in the cosmogony is proof of an early date (10th - 8th centuries BCE) of the Phoenician original.

Solomon were apparently composed in Greek during Caligula's reign (37-41 BCE) by an Alexandrian Jew who employed traditional parallelistic techniques.[104] Since the meter of the last three lines of the *mystodokos* spell is relatively uncorrupted,[105] it seems imprudent to suppose that the same scribe (or his source) mangled the first two as badly as the proposed restorations imply. I suggest therefore that the first two lines of the spell may not have been meant to be hexameters at all, but were perhaps written in parallelistic form albeit with some attempt at keeping a dactylic cadence.

The fourfold variation of the *mystodokos* spell in form and content is, I think, extraordinary, and well worth examining in schematic form:

	Mystodokos Section	Seven-maidens Section
Content	Egyptian motif	Mesopotamian motif
Poetic Form	Semitic parallelism	Greek hexameter

The thoroughly hybrid nature of this spell gives us stronger grounds, I think, for taking the Syrian provenance of the spell seriously. Given the local Levantine tradition reflected in the Ugaritic snake-charm and the Hagar story in Genesis 21, it does not seem farfetched to suppose that a local Syrian poet had at some previous point recast an Egyptian myth in Semitic poetic form. More difficult, I think, is to understand how the Mesopotamian motif of the daughters of Anu came to be expressed in such beautifully rendered Greek hexameters. It is tempting to suggest

---

[104] D. Winston, *The Wisdom of Solomon*, Anchor Bible 43 (Garden City, 1979), 12-25.

[105] The third line of the *mystodokos* incantation (ἑπτὰ λύ[κ]ων κρήνας, ἐπ' ὄρ[κτων], ἑπτὰ λεόντων), although it is a fine adaption of some epic model—as its parallel in the Homeric *Hymn to Hermes* 223 suggests: οὔτε λύκων πολιῶν, οὔτ' ἄρκτων, οὔτε λεόντων—makes extremely poor syntactical sense as it appears in the papyrus. There are two problems: the noun κρήνας has no verb to govern it and the entire line has no apparent syntactical construction with the preceding line. The proposed restorations are unsatisfactory, because they fail to explain what the poet means by "seven springs of wolves etc."; e.g., Koenen's addition of <πῦρ δ ἐλάφυξεν> at the end of the second hexameter. Merkelbach (n. 1) 86 offers the following reconstruction without comment: ἑπτὰ λύκων <κεφαλαί>, ἐπ' ἄρκτων, ἑπτὰ λεόντων / <- - - -κρήνας ἐφύλαξαν>; he seems to have envisaged a building or architectural facade over the spring which has animal-head protomes looming over it. I think Merkelbach is on the right track in suspecting that the word κρήνας is corrupt or misplaced, but unfortunately no obvious emendation springs to mind. It is interesting to note that the truncated late-antique version of the spell (see n. 2 for text) omits κρήνας, but does so to the detriment of the meter.

that some archaic Greek poem—perhaps even a lost hymn narrating Dionysus' birth on Mt. Nysa in Phoenicia or an epic composition about Heracles' salvation on the pyre—lies behind these words, but this approach does not do justice to the great poetic skill of contemporary Gadarene poets like Meleager or Philodemus. It seems to me far more likely that the final couplet of the spell is the work of some well trained local poet—perhaps even the mysterious Syrian woman mentioned in the rubric—writing in Greek during the Hellenistic period, but steeped in local mythological traditions, perhaps even connected with the creation of the curative springs for which Gadara had become famous. In any event, the content of the *mystodokos* spell and even its peculiar form can, I think, be appreciated in a much richer and fuller sense if we see it as a reflection of a multicultural tradition whose constituent parts can never be completely separated and analyzed.[106]

---

[106] Earlier portions of this paper were presented at the Annual Meeting of the Society of Biblical Literature in November 1989. I am also indebted to S. Ackerman, W. Brashear, J. Collins, J. H. Johnson, R. Kotansky, D. Obbink, D. Pardee, R. K. Ritner, J. Scurlock and Z. Stewart, who kindly commented on earlier drafts of the written version. Much of the final draft was completed while I was a junior fellow at the Center for Hellenic Studies in Washington D. C. during the academic year of 1991-92. I owe many thanks to my hosts Z. and D. Stewart, the other junior fellows, and the staff for making my stay a particularly enjoyable and productive one.

CHAPTER SIXTEEN

"MAY SHE NEITHER EAT NOR DRINK": LOVE MAGIC AND VOWS OF ABSTINENCE

David Martinez

Writing sometime in the eighth century BCE, Homer describes Achilleus' vow not to eat or drink until he kills Hektor (*Iliad* 19.205-10).[1] In the first century CE, according to the Acts of the Apostles 23:12, a band of Jewish conspirators swear that they will neither eat nor drink until they kill Paul. In a magical lead tablet of the fourth century CE a party named Ailourion commands the infernal spirits that his beloved Kopria neither eat nor drink until she comes to him and fulfills his desires.[2] My contention is that these three texts and many others like them, culturally and chronologically diverse as they are, all represent a similar tradition of cursing. The last mentioned is an erotic κατάδεσμος, "binding spell," in which the central focus is to capture and constrain a lover.[3] As a convienient term for the type represented by the first

---

[1] This article is dedicated to Ludwig Koenen on his sixty-fifth birthday. I wish to thank C. A. Faraone, who helped me improve this paper considerably by reading a preliminary draft and offering advice. I am also grateful to J. A. Dearman and D. Key for their help on a number of points, especially with regard to biblical and ancient Near Eastern materials. The translations of Greek and Latin texts are my own unless otherwise specified. The translations of the Hebrew Bible are those of the Revised Standard Version. Translations of Semitic and Egyptian texts are indicated *ad loc.* Abbreviations of papyrus editions (usually beginning with *P.*) are those used in J. F. Oats, R. S. Bagnall, W. W. Willis, K. A. Worp, *Checklist of Editions of Greek Papyri and Ostraca*, BASP Supplements 4, 3rd ed. (Scholars Press, 1985). Papyrus vols. published after 1985 are footnoted.

[2] D. G. Martinez, *P. Mich. 757: A Greek Love Charm From Egypt*, American Studies in Papyrology 30 (Atlanta: Scholars Press, 1991). The text with a brief commentary also appeared in R. W. Daniel, F. Maltomini, *Supplementum Magicum*, vol. I, Papyrologica Coloniensia XVI.1 (Opladen: Westdeutscher Verlag GmbH, 1990), 184-92 (# 48).

[3] For various types of κατάδεσμοι, see C. A. Faraone, "The Agonistic Context of Early Greek Binding Spells," *Magika Hiera*, ed. C. A. Faraone and D. Obbink (New York and Oxford: Oxford University Press, 1991), 3-32, esp. 21 n. 3 on the word itself. For specifically erotic κατάδεσμοι, see *ibid.*, 13-15, and in the same volume, J. J. Winkler, "The Constraints of Eros," 214-43, esp. 231; cf. also Martinez, *P. Mich. 757*, 2 n. 7.

two texts I have chosen the Hebrew word *issar* (אסר).[4] The *issar* has a varied and complex history in biblical and post-biblical Hebrew usage. Similar to κατάδεσμος, the root meaning of the word group is "binding" or "constricting." That basic significance has diverse applications, one being the binding of oneself under a solemn obligation—a vow.[5] As such it is related to, and sometimes synonymous with, the more common word for vow, *neder* (נדר). When the two are distinguished, especially in the post-biblical language, *neder* means a vow to do, *issar* a vow not to do, that is, a vow of renunciation or abstinence.[6] This is not the place to engage in a lengthy discussion of the various forms of the *issar* in biblical and rabbinic literature. The form which will concern us is "I will not . . . (e.g., eat or drink) until . . ." In the following discussion I will first examine such abstention vows as they occur in two distinctive types, which I call "self-actualizing" and "agonistic." I will then analyze and compare similar cursing or "binding" formulae in Greek erotic magic of the Roman and Byzantine periods.[7] I begin with the Homeric passage to which I have already alluded.

---

[4] For אסר in general, see M. Jastrow, *A Dictionary of the Targumim, the Talmud Babli and Yerushalmi, and the Midrashic Literature* (New York: Pardes, 1950), s.v.; J. Jeremias, *Die Abendmahlsworte Jesu*, 4th ed. (Göttingen: Vandenhoeck und Ruprecht, 1967), 204-07 (Eng. trans., *The Eucharistic Words of Jesus* [Philadelphia: Fortress Press, 1977], based on the third German ed. 1960, 212-16). For parallels from other Semitic languages, see R. S. Tomback, *A Comparative Semitic Lexicon of the Phoenician and Punic Languages*, SBLDS 32 (Missoula: Scholars Press, 1978), 27.

[5] For bibliography and analyses of vows in the Hebrew scriptures and Jewish tradition, see W. Kaiser, "נדר," *TWAT*, 5.261-74. For ancient Greek vows which center on the votive gift, see W. H. D. Rouse, *Greek Votive Offerings* (Cambridge: Cambridge University Press, 1902); more recently, W. Burkert, *Greek Religion* (Cambridge: Harvard University Press, 1985), 68-70; F. T. van Straten, "Gifts for the Gods," *Faith, Hope, and Worship*, ed. H. S. Versnel (Leiden: Brill, 1981), 65-151.

[6] Already in Num 30:2 (v. 3 Heb.) the words are distinguished: "When a man vows a vow or swears an oath *to bind himself by a pledge* (לאסר אסר), he shall not break his word." נזר is of course the root connected with abstention vows of the Nazarites; cf. Kaiser, "נדר," 274.

[7] Besides the magical "cursing" aspects about to be argued for the vow, the אסר word group is used in specifically magical contexts. The verb means "bind by spell or charm" in Targ. Ps. 17:4 and elsewhere (Jastrow, *A Dictionary of the Targumim, the Talmud Babli and Yerushalmi, and the Midrashic Literature*, s.v., 2) and 3)) and is also frequent in Aramaic magic (C. D. Isbell, *Corpus of the Aramaic Incantation Bowls*, SBLDS 17 [Missoula: Scholars Press, 1975], 1.12; 5.1, 3, 4; 7.12 *et passim*). Erotic binding is suggested by Song of Songs 7:6, "Your head crowns you like Carmel, and your flowing locks are like purple; a king is held captive (אסור, LXX δεδεμένος) in the tresses."

* * *

The lengthy preoccupation with Achilleus' refusal to eat and drink in *Iliad* 19.145-237 and his desire to impose his abstinence on the entire army has long disturbed interpreters. The comment of D. Page, who holds this passage in low esteem, exemplifies scholarly bewilderment: "More than 180 lines have now passed since luncheon stole the limelight and nothing has been achieved."[8] The most obvious reason for Achilleus' fasting is mourning Patroklos, as he himself states (306ff., 312ff., *et al.*).[9] But the grounds of his abstinence center as much in the future as the past. His grief over the death of his *hetairos* erupts in rage and headlong determination to gain revenge, a determination which is sealed and consecrated by a pledge not to eat or drink until vengeance is accomplished. It is this forward-focusing aspect of the fast to which he summons the entire army:

ἦ τ' ἂν ἔγωγε
νῦν μὲν ἀνώγοιμι πτολεμίζειν υἷας 'Αχαιῶν
νήστιας ἀκμήνους, ἅμα δ' ἠελίῳ καταδύντι
τεύξεσθαι μέγα δόρπον, ἐπὴν τεισαίμεθα λώβην.
πρὶν δ' οὔ πως ἂν ἔμοιγε φίλον κατὰ λαιμὸν ἰείη

---

[8] *History and the Homeric Iliad* (Berkeley and Los Angeles: University of California Press, 1966), 314. On his view and others, see M. W. Edwards, *The Iliad: A Commentary*, vol. 5, bks. 17-20 (Cambridge: Cambridge University Press, 1991), 253. Edwards himself seeks to understand the passage on the basis of J. B. Hainsworth's observation that in some cases in the *Iliad* (e.g., 2.399, 8.53f.) the meal consitituted part of the ritual of joining battle. Achilleus' refusal to dine therefore stresses the theme of his differentiation from the rest of the Greeks.

[9] Cf. Priam for Hektor, *Il.* 24.601-20, cf. 641-42. The practice appears in numerous cultures (E. Westermarck, "The Principles of Fasting," *Folklore* 18 [1907]: 397-409) but does not appear to be a regular feature of Greek and Roman mourning rites (L. Ziehen, "νηστεία," *RE,* 17.1.95). To the extent that it does occur, however, the mourning fast may have a strong apotropaic component, since in Greek religious conception, as long as the soul of a dead person is near (which would be the case with one as yet unburied), there is danger from demonic infestation through eating and drinking; cf. Luc. *de luctu* 24, Apul. *met.* 2.24, and other material cited by J. Behm, "νῆστις κτλ.," *TDNT,* 4.926; cf. also F. Pfister, "Daimonismos," *RE Supp.,* 7.113; Westermarck, "The Principles of Fasting," 403-07. P. R. Arbesmann (*Das Fasten bei den Griechen und Römern*, RGVV XXI 1 [Giessen: Töpelmann, 1929], 28) wishes to understand the present case of Achilleus in this light (see also *idem*, "Fasten," *RAC,* 7.464-65).

οὐ πόσις οὐδὲ βρῶσις, ἑταίρου τεθνηῶτος.[10] (205-10)

"No, but I would now enjoin the sons of the Achaians to go into battle fasting and without food, but at sunset to prepare a great feast, once we have avenged the outrage. But until then, for my part, drink or food will by no means pass down my throat, seeing that my friend is dead."

Achilleus' obsessive behavior and his wish that the army follow his lead annoy Odysseus as much as modern commentators; his response is vintage Odyssean reasoning (155ff.; 216ff.). He asserts that, were it advisable to mourn the dead with abstinence, the Greeks would never eat, and soldiers need their nourishment to fight. Achilleus, however, is not operating in terms of reason. We will best understand him at this juncture if we see as the basis of his actions the belief that renouncing food and drink until a goal is attained solemnizes one's commitment to that goal and sanctifies its accomplishment within the supernatural realm. In other words, the abstinence and emptiness generates a kind of "power made perfect in weakness," to borrow a phrase from the apostle Paul (2 Cor 12:9), a force which both binds and energizes the resolve to complete the stated task. Recognition that Achilleus is operating within a well-established tradition of vow-taking provides adequate rationale for his actions and should relieve some scholarly anxiety over all the talk of food. Luncheon has stolen the limelight for good reason.

The persuasive power of Odysseus, however, prevails as it so often does in the *Iliad*, and Achilleus stands alone in his resolve. Yet Athene, at Zeus' behest, by distilling nectar and ambrosia within him (19.347-54), vindicates his action against the victorious Odysseus. In forsaking human sustenance, he has received the food of the gods, which advances his stature beyond that of the other heroes.[11] It enhances his might on the one hand and his isolation on the other, two qualities which also characterize another great hero and general of antiquity.

The account of Saul's engagement of Israel's sworn enemies the Philistines in 1 Samuel 13-14 belongs to what some scholars have called "the Saul cycle," perhaps compiled around the latter part of

---

[10] ἂν ... ἀνάγοιμι is a "wünschendes Potential"; cf. E. Schwyzer, *Griechische Grammatik*, 2 vols. (München: C. H. Beck, 1939, 1950), 2.330; and F. Slotty, *Der Gebrauch des Konjunktivs und Optativs in den griechen Dialekten*, I Der Hauptsatz, Forschungen zur griechischen und lateinischen Grammatik 3 (Göttingen: Vandenhoeck und Ruprecht, 1915), 99f., 133f. (§315). οὔ πως ἂν ... ἰείη is a "voluntive" optative of emphatic denial (see below n. 59).

[11] M. W. Edwards, *Iliad*, 253.

the ninth century BCE.[12] In 1 Sam 14:24 we read, "And the men of Israel were distressed that day,[13] for Saul laid an oath on the people (or, "put the people under a curse"),[14] saying, 'Cursed be the man who eats food until it is evening and I am avenged on my enemies.'" Since the word "people" here means "army,"[15] the parallels between this passage and the Homeric text are striking. First, the empowering force of the abstinence is focused upon military victory and vengeance,[16] which will occur by sundown.[17]

---

[12] Cf. P. K. McCarter, *I Samuel*, Anchor Bible 8 (Garden City: Doubleday, 1980), 26-27; W. Brueggemann, "Samuel, Books of 1-2," *ABD*, 5.963.

[13] The translation of the clause reflects the MT. LXX: καὶ Σαουλ ἠγνόησεν ἄγνοιαν μεγάλην ἐν τῇ ἡμέρᾳ ἐκείνῃ, "And Saul committed a grave error on that day," which puts a different complexion on the entire passage, indicating that Saul's binding of the soldiers by the vow was misguided. McCarter (*I Samuel*, 245) accepts the Septuagintal reading as more congruent with the context and rejects the MT as corrupt. I concur with the earlier judgment of S. R. Driver (*Notes on the Hebrew Text and the Topography of the Books of Samuel*, 2nd ed. [Oxford: Oxford University Press, 1913], 112), that the LXX does not in fact agree with the bigger picture. Indeed the Israelites routed the Philistines convincingly that day (v. 31), and Yahweh's displeasure at the breaking of the oath is obvious from the failure of the divination because of sin in the camp (v. 37) and the condemning lot falling upon Jonathan as the guilty party (v. 42); see H. C. Brichto, *The Problem of "Curse" in the Hebrew Bible*, JBL Monograph Series 13 (Philadelphia: Society of Biblical Literature, 1963), 80.

[14] The Hebrew אלה can have either sense. Cf. J. Scharbert, "אלה," *TDOT*, 1.263. Brichto (*The Problem of "Curse"*, 45ff.) argues for the latter meaning and understands that Saul merely pronounces a curse upon or "adjures" the army, as if he were standing outside the process and inflicting it on others. In the context of the parallels adduced in this paper, however, Scharbert is surely right when he says "ויאל = er liess das Volk eine Selbstverfluchung sprechen" (*Biblica* 39 [1958]: 4 n. 6). This may have taken the form of Saul articulating the curse for the entire community (including himself) and the rest responded with "Amen," a common way of communal acceptance of an oath with its self-imprecation; see S. H. Blank, "The Curse, Blasphemy, the Spell, and the Oath," *HUCA* 23.1 (1950-51): 89 nn. 53 and 54.

[15] Hebrew עם like Greek λαός can bear that sense, which is certainly the meaning here. The Hebrew word is so used both for the various armies of the gentiles (Ex 14:6, 17:13; Num 21:33-35, etc.) and, as in our passage, for the hosts of Israel (Josh 10:7; I Chron 11:13, 19:11, etc.). With regard to the latter, N. Lohfink examines the phrase עם יהוה as "army of Yahweh" (*Probleme biblischer Theologie*, ed. H. W. Wolff [München: Kaiser, 1971], 275-303 *passim*, esp. 281ff.). In general see Lipínski, "עם," *TWAT*, 6.192; H. Strathmann, "λαός," *TDNT*, 4.34. Similarly the early epic usage of Greek λαός (M. Schmidt, "λαός," *Lexikon des Frühgriechischen Epos*, 14. Lieferung (Göttingen: Vandenhoeck und Ruprecht, 1991), 1638-42; Strathmann, "λαός," 30f.).

[16] This is also the focus in certain vows which involve refusing to cut one's hair. E.g., Suet. *Jul.* 67.2; Tac. *Hist.* 4.61; *Germ.* 31; and cf. (although not in a

Second, Saul, like Achilleus, is concerned with imposing the abstention vow on the entire community which, unlike the Achaian hero,
he can mandate as king and commander of the troops. Jonathan in
the biblical narrative corresponds to Odysseus as the voice of
reason; both question the wisdom of renouncing food and drink in
the case of soldiers who fight more effectively with nourishment
(cf. vv. 29-30 with *Il.* 19.160-72).[18]

The communal abstinence is not simply "a grandiose gesture of
self-denial" to secure the favor of Yahweh, as P. K. McCarter
says.[19] Neither the Greek nor the Hebrew warrior undertake the
fast in the context of prayer to a deity, or asking a deity's favor.
Rather, they both engage in an act of self-cursing or communal
self-cursing in which divine names are not mentioned. This will be
discussed in greater detail below. Suffice it for now to say that
Saul's vow, as Achilleus', effects a solemnizing and empowering of
a stated goal by declaring oneself bound to abstinence, an accursed
state, until that goal is accomplished. The biblical account differs
from the Homeric in the aspect of an impending curse if the vow is
not fulfilled, an idea not explicit in Homer, but which appears in a
New Testament example of the *issar*, to which we now turn.

Acts 23:12 reads as follows: οἱ Ἰουδαῖοι ἀνεθεμάτισαν ἑαυτοὺς
λέγοντες μήτε φαγεῖν μήτε πιεῖν ἕως οὗ ἀποκτείνωσιν τὸν Παῦλον,
"The Jews put themselves under a curse, saying that they would
neither eat nor drink until they killed Paul."[20] The verb which I
translate "put themselves under a curse," ἀναθεματίζειν, is rare in
pagan magical texts; I find it only in Audollent 41a.5, 8 (*defixio*

---

military context) Acts 18:18, with Jeremias, *Die Abendmahlsworte Jesu*, 205
(Engl. trans., 214).

[17] On the topos of sundown as the time of breaking the fast, cf. Arbesmann,
Das Fasten, 78f.; Westermarck, "The Principles of Fasting," 399.

[18] The Achilleus-Saul and the Odysseus-Jonathan correspondence in these
two passages (and in some respects in general) is fascinating from a number of
angles. The former pair have in common a brooding demeanor which is unpleasing
and causes them to pale in comparison with the reasonableness and likableness of
the latter two. Achilleus and Saul both experience vindication through divine
acts and signs, which does not, however, mitigate the frustration and ill destiny
which hovers over them and all of their accomplishments.

[19] *I Samuel*, 249.

[20] V. 14 relates their own words, in which the vow element is more emphatic:
ἀναθέματι ἀνεθεματίσαμεν ἑαυτοὺς μηδενὸς γεύσασθα κτλ., "We solemnly impre-
cated ourselves to taste nothing ...." V. 21 gives another version and says that
this band numbered over 40.

from Megara, c. II CE)²¹ with ἀνάθεμα inscribed on the back. The verb belongs chiefly to Greek-speaking Judaism and Christianity as translations of the Hebrew חרם, i.e., to dedicate to God in the sense of bringing under the divine curse or ban.²² In our passage it means "a curse in the sense of a vow or solemn obligation, the breach of which will bring them under the ban."²³ The proper understanding of this passage is that "the Jews pronounce themselves *anathema* (i.e., under the ban) *if* they eat or drink until they kill Paul."²⁴ The vow of abstinence solemnizes and empowers their commitment to their task. Thus the perspective here is practically identical with that in 1 Samuel.²⁵

---

²¹ A. Audollent, *Defixionum Tabellae* (Paris: Fontemoing, 1904).

²² N. Lohfink, "חרם," *TDOT*, 5.180-203. The LXX renders the *hrm* word group most often (about 35 times) with ἀνάθημα/ἀνάθεμα (for חרם), ἀναθεματίζειν (החרים); other renderings are less frequent; cf. also F. Blass, *Acta Apostolorum editio philologica* [Göttingen, 1895], 244). In classical Greek this word family had a long history of describing things dedicated to the gods, in that ἀνάθημα/ἀνάθεμα and ἀνατιθέναι are well established terms for votive offerings which filled pagan temples. Similar ideas were utilized in pagan magic, in that the magical act of cursing and sometimes the tablet itself on which the curse is recorded are spoken of in terms of a votive offering or object (cf. ἀνιεροῦν and ἀνατιθέναι in the family of defixiones from Cnidos, Audollent 1-13). Words such as παρακαταθήκη and παρακατατίθημι are also shared by the language of votive offerings and of magic for depositing things with the gods (cf. Rouse, *Greek Votive Offerings*, 324; Martinez, *P. Mich. 757*, 36-37). The LXX and early Christian usage of the ἀναθε- group is best described as a particular application of a religious/magical terminology well documented in pagan texts (in general see Rouse, *Greek Votive Offerings*, 323-24, 337-41; J. Behm, "ἀνάθεμα κτλ.," *TDNT*, 1.354f.).

²³ J. Behm, "ἀναθεματίζω, κτλ.," *TDNT*, 1.355f.

²⁴ Their failure to do so does not necessarily imply that they starved. Rabbinic treatises made provision for annulling vows on such occasions. See H. L. Strack and P. Billerbeck, *Kommentar zum Neuen Testament aus Talmud und Midrasch* (München: Beck, 1924), 2.767.

²⁵ The ἀναθε- words are used for self-binding or self-imprecation elsewhere in the NT. In Rom 9:3 Paul asserts, ηὐχόμην γὰρ ἀνάθεμα εἶναι αὐτὸς ἐγὼ ἀπὸ τοῦ Χριστοῦ ὑπὲρ τῶν ἀδελφῶν μου ... κατὰ σάρκα, "For I could wish myself to be a thing devoted apart from Christ for the sake of my brethren according to the flesh." In pronouncing *himself* devoted *from* a beneficial deity for the benefit of someone else, Paul intentionally reverses the normal magical formula of pronouncing *another* devoted *to* a baleful deity for one's own benefit (cf. Audollent 4A.1f. and Paul's own negative but ultimately redemptive formulae in I Cor 5:5 and I Tim 1:20). The apostle also includes himself in the ἀνάθεμα which he pronounces in Gal 1:8f. on any who preach a different gospel. On Mk 14:71, ἤρξατο ἀναθεματίζειν καὶ ὀμνύναι, "(Peter) began to curse and swear," J. Behm ('ἀναθεματίζω, κτλ.," 355) remarks, "ἀναθεματίζειν is intentionally left without an object to denote both that he curses himself if he lies and also the people if they make out that he is a disciple." Cf. also Enoch 6:4, which is similar in format to the *issar*:

The *issar* could entail abstention from many things besides food
and drink. It could include the renunciation of only certain kinds of
food, certain kinds of clothing, sleep, sex, speaking, bathing,
cutting hair, business dealings, entry into a house or town—
anything which, like fasting, produces isolation from normal
society.[26] A Hebrew psalmist prays (Ps 132.1-5), "Remember, O
Lord, in David's favor, all the hardships he endured; how he swore
to the Lord and vowed to the mighty one of Jacob, 'I will not
enter my house or get into my bed; I will not give sleep to my eyes
nor slumber to my eyelids, until I find a place for the Lord, a
dwelling place for the mighty one of Jacob.'"[27]

*   *   *

In light of the foregoing examples, I offer the following gener-
alizations concerning the nature and religious significance of self-
actualizing *issar*, many of which also apply to the subsequent
discussion of the "agonistic" type. I begin by comparing it with
two acts of religious devotion with which it has much in common,
fasting and oath-taking.

Abstinence from food and drink[28] never gained general importance as a cultic act or pious exercise in Greek and Roman religion,
occuring only in a limited number of contexts.[29] Nor was it vital in
ancient Egyptian religion.[30] It played a more important role in
Judaism, Christianity, and Greco-Oriental mystery religions.[31] In
most of its cultural expressions some common themes emerge, the
most prominent being isolation. Groups or individuals who fast
deny themselves for a prescribed period of time the most funda-

---

Ὁμόσωμεν ὅρκῳ πάντες καὶ ἀναθεματίσωμεν πάντες ἀλλήλους μὴ ἀποστρέψαι τὴν
γνώμην ταύτην, μέχρις οὗ ἂν τελέσωμεν αὐτὴν καὶ ποιήσωμεν τὸ πρᾶγμα τοῦτο.

[26] See Jeremias, *Die Abendmahlsworte Jesu*, 204f. = Eng. trans., 213.

[27] On this text see W. Kaiser "נדר," *TWAT*, 5.274.

[28] In general see Arbesmann, *Das Fasten*. Cf. also *idem*, "Fasten," *RAC*,
7.447-93; Ziehen, "νηστεία," 88-107; Behm, "νῆστις κτλ.," 924-35.

[29] M. Nilsson, *Geschichte der griechischen Religion*, 2 vols. (München:
Beck, I, 3rd ed. 1967; II 2nd ed. 1961), 1.94.

[30] H. Bonnet, "Speiseverbote," *Reallexikon der Ägyptischen Religions-
geschichte* (New York: Walter de Gruyter, 1952), 744-46; cf. H. Brunner,
"Enthaltsamkeit," *Lex. Äg.*, 1.1229ff.; Herod. 2.40.4;

[31] On the mystery religions, see Ziehen, "νηστεία," 92; Arbesmann, "Fasten,"
460-62. On Judaism, see Arbesmann, *op. cit.*, 451-56; Behm, "νῆστις κτλ.," 927-
31; Strack and Billerbeck, *Kommentar*, 4.77-114; On Christianity, see Arbesmann, *op. cit.*, 471-92; Behm, *op. cit.*, 931-35.

mental of human experiences and so isolate themselves from normal human society for devotion to prayer, repentence, study, mourning, or the like. Fasting, therefore, by nature is usually an ancillary discipline, which assists or empowers some other religious exercise.

The isolation of fasting often constitutes a necessary purifying process for experiences of divine encounter and disclosure.[32] It characterizes the spiritual discipline of shaman figures such as Abaris and Pythagoras.[33] Prophets and prophetesses of Greek oracular shrines abstain prior to their divine visitations.[34] Moses fasts "forty days and nights" before receiving the Ten Commandments,[35] as does Jesus before his testing in the wilderness.[36] Thus from the perspective of Greek religion, fasting ritualizes the self-emptying, or *ekstasis*, which is concurrent with the state of divine possession, or *enthousiasmos*. *Ekstasis* implies the abandonment of normalcy and good sense,[37] the exact charges which Odysseus

---

[32] Ziehen, "νηστεία," 93f.; Behm, "νῆστις κτλ.," 926-29; Arbesmann, "Fasten," 462f.; *idem.*, "Fasting and Prophecy in Pagan and Christian Antiquity," *Traditio* 7 (1949-51): 1-71.

[33] Herod. 4.36.1; Iamb. *vit. Pyth.* 141. For the later figure Apollonius of Tyana see Phil. *v. Ap.* 1.8 (vol. 1 p. 7,21ff. Kayser), 8.5 (vol. 1 p. 299,24f. Kayser). In some cases abstinence from only certain kinds of foods is involved.

[34] Cf. in general Arbesmann, *Das Fasten,* 97ff.; Ziehen, "νηστεία," 93f. The prophets of the oracle of Apollo at Clarus and the priestess of the same god's oracle of the Branchidae at Didyma fast one and three days respectively (Iamb. *myst.* 3.11 [125.15, 127.15]). For fasting in preparation for dream oracles, cf. Philostr. *vit. Ap.* 2.37, vol. 1 p. 79,20ff. Kayser (Amphiarios) and Strabo 14.44 (Pluto and Kore at Nysa). Closely related to fasting for mantic revelation is the use of fasting in magic of the Roman and Byzantine periods; typically, however, one must abstain only from certain foods: "I adjure you . . . not to eat swine flesh, and every kind of spirit and daimon will be subject to you," *PGM* IV 3078-81; cf. Arbesmann, *Das Fasten,* 63-67, and Ziehen, "νηστεία," 94.

[35] Ex 34:28; Deut 9:9. Similarly, Daniel fasted before receiving his visions (Dan 9:3; 10:2f., 12); cf. in later Jewish apocalytic 4 Ezra 5:13, 19f.; 6:31, 35 (cf. 9:23; 12:51); 2 Bar 9:2; 12:5; 20:5; 21:1ff.; 43:3; 47:2; see D. S. Russell, *The Method and Message of Jewish Apocalyptic* (Philadelphia: Westminster, 1964), 169-70.

[36] The attitude of Jesus toward fasting is complex; see Behm, "νῆστις κτλ.," 931-33.

[37] W. Burkert, *Greek Religion* (Cambridge: Harvard University Press, 1985), 110. Cf. Pla. *Phdr.* 249c-d, where Socrates describes the possessed philosopher as "abandoning (ἐξιστάμενος) the pursuits of normal people." Cf. also Iamb. *de myst.* 3.11 (125.14ff.) concerning the priest of the oracle at Clarus: καὶ πρὸ τοῦ πίνειν δὲ οὕτως ἀσιτεῖ τὴν ἡμέραν ὅλην καὶ νύκτα, καὶ ἐν ἱεροῖς τισιν ἀβάτοις τῷ πλήθει καθ' ἑαυτὸν ἀνακεχώρηκεν ἀρχόμενος ἐνθουσιᾶν, καὶ διὰ τῆς ἀποστάσεως καὶ ἀπαλλαγῆς τῶν ἀνθρωπίνων πραγμάτων ἄχραντον ἑαυτὸν εἰς ὑποδοχὴν τοῦ θεοῦ παρασκευάζει, "And thus before drinking (sc. of the sacred spring) he abstains

levels at Achilleus for the latter's mandate that the soldiers fast through the next battle. His rejection of food and drink is an aspect of his obsession and self-devotion to his task, which borders on a kind of μανία.[38] Yet, Athene's divine infusion notwithstanding, no real *enthousiasmos* accompanies this *ekstasis*. Achilleus' pledge of abstinence makes no pious claim to divine presence or possession.[39] Like the Jewish ἀναθεματίζειν, his words betray the bleaker image of a man under a curse. There is, however, a kind of manic possession here, borne of the ἀνάγκη, "necessity," which he imposes upon himself. His pledge of abstinence both consecrates him to his task and, by way of self-cursing, leaves him no choice but to accomplish it. As fasting clarifies the former aspect, the oath assists our understanding of the latter.

One who takes an oath does so under the threat of a self-imposed curse. In the the *Iliad* 3.298-300, the Achaians and Trojans, while pouring libations, finalize their oaths sworn on the occasion of the duel between Menelaos and Paris with the following:

Ζεῦ κύδιστε μέγιστε, καὶ ἀθάνατοι θεοὶ ἄλλοι
ὁππότεροι πρότεροι ὑπὲρ ὅρκια πημήνειαν,
ὧδέ σφ' ἐγκέφαλος χαμάδις ῥέοι ὡς ὅδε οἶνος.

---

from food for the entire day and night, and secludes himself in sanctuaries inaccesible to the crowd as he begins to be divinely possessed, and through separation and relief from human affairs he makes himself undefiled for the reception of the god." Cf. also R. Parker, *Miasma* (Oxford: Oxford University Press, 1983), 365.

[38] The warrior, like the prophet, is sometimes described as one possessed: "But he (sc. Diomedes) vehemently rages (μαίνεται), and no one can rival him in might" (Hom. *Il.* 6.100f.; cf. the θεία προθυμία of the mercenaries in Xen. *Hell.* 7.2.21). In Plato's *Symposium* Phaedrus employs this language in arguing that ideally the spirit which inspires the warrior is eros for his lover, by whose side he fights on the battle-field: οὐδεὶς οὕτω κακὸς ὅντινα οὐκ ἂν αὐτὸς ὁ Ἔρως ἔνθεον ποιήσειε πρὸς ἀρετήν, ὥστε ὅμοιον εἶναι τῷ ἀρίστῳ φύσει· καὶ ἀτεχνῶς, ὃ ἔφη Ὅμηρος, "μένος ἐμπνεῦσαι" ἐνίοις τῶν ἡρώων τὸν θεόν, τοῦτο ὁ Ἔρως τοῖς ἐρῶσι παρέχει γιγνόμενον παρ' αὐτοῦ, "No one is so cowardly that Eros by himself could not inspire to excellence, so that he is like one who is brave by nature. And most assuredly this, as Homer says, that a god 'breathes might' into some heroes, is what Eros provides for lovers, seeing that he is the origin of it" (179a-b).

[39] This is true for Homer himself. Later Greeks, such as Phaidros (*Sym.* 179e-180b), viewed the relationship between Achilleus and Patroklos as homosexual, and thus the μανία which empowers Achilleus at this point is that of ἔρως. In this context, Achilleus' abstinence could be understood as a form of love-sickness (on which see below).

"Zeus, illustrious, greatest, and you other immortal gods, whoever are first to attack in violation of the oaths, may their brains be spilled on the ground as this wine."

In the oath, persons or groups pronounce themselves accursed *if* the commitment *is not* fulfilled. In the *issar* they bind themselves to a vow of abstinence, which itself may be viewed as a kind of curse, *until* a goal *is* fulfilled. The oath-taker enforces a curse upon himself, if by his actions he brings about accursed circumstances; his state will parallel the evil he causes. The *issar*, however, presumes the existence of an accursed state of affairs in the present; for Achilleus, Patroclos' death unavenged; for Saul, incomplete revenge against the Philistines; for the Jewish conspirators, Paul's evangelism. In refusing what is most normal, the vow-taker protests the abnormality of the current situation and by abstaining makes himself parallel to the state of dearth which surrounds him, a situation which will only be righted by a decisive action to which he consecrates himself. Thus, the fasting of the *issar* is both self-imprecating and self-dedicating, in the same way as Hebrew חרם and its Greek equivalent ἀναθεματίζειν tread the tenuous boundary between "consecrate" and "curse."

To put it differently, both oath and *issar* involve a kind of self-cursing. The oath projects the curse entirely in the future and conditions it upon failing to accomplish the stated commitment, a failure which will bring about evil circumstances. The *issar* may include a non-specific future curse, but the differentiating factor is the pledge to abstain, which existentializes the curse and makes it a present experience to parallel the present evil, until some redemptive goal is accomplished.

As in the previously cited *Iliad* 3.298ff., the oath often involves direct appeals to deities. God or gods are invoked to witness the terms and, if need be, enforce the imprecations.[40] The upholding of oaths is the provenance of the supreme deity in both ancient Greece and Israel.[41] Other curse formulae connected with

---

[40] J. Plescia, *The Oath and Perjury in Ancient Greece* (Tallahassee: Florida State University Press, 1970), 2-3.

[41] For ὅρκιοι θεοί and particularly Ζεὺς ὅρκιος, see Plescia, *The Oath and Perjury*, 4-9; E. Ziebarth, "Eid," *RE*, 5.2.2076-79; Jessen, "Horkios, Horkioi," *RE* 8.2.2408f.; Schwabl, "Zeus I. Epiklesen," *RE*, 10A.345. The Torah mandates that oaths be taken by Yahweh alone (Deut 6:13; 10:20). The process of taking an oath itself was a solemn affirmation of Yahweh as the "one God." See J. Schneider, "ὅρκος," *TDNT*, 5.459.

oaths operate independently of invocations to gods.[42] Such is the case for many oaths which are based on sympathetic rituals, such as the following lines from a marble stele which preserves a late seventh-century BCE text concerning oaths taken by the founders of Libyan Cyrene:

κηρίνος πλάσσαντες κολοσὸς κατέκαιον ἐπαρεώμενοι πάντες συνενθόντες ... · τὸμ μὴ ἐμμένοντα τούτοις τοῖς ὁρκίοις ἀλλὰ παρβεῶντα καταλείβεσθαί νιν καὶ καταρρὲν ὥσπερ τὸς κολοσός, καὶ αὐτὸν καὶ γόνον καὶ χρήματα (44-49).

They all came together and, making wax effigies,[43] burned them, pronouncing grave imprecations, . . . that he who does not abide by these oaths but transgresses them melt and be consumed as the effigies, he and his offspring and his property.[44]

Such sympathetic formulae function without prayer, not because divine power is absent, but because the words and the sympathetic procedures themselves suffice to activate the realm in which divine power operates.[45] Indeed, such curse formulae, much like *voces*

---

[42] F. Büchsel, "κατάρα," *TDNT*, 1.449. In the Hebrew Bible, S. H. Blank ("The Curse," 73-82) notes that there are abundant examples both of curse formulae which do not mention God and which derive power through the spoken word alone, and curses which seek to enlist the help of Yahweh in fulfilling them, i.e., imprecatory prayers.

[43] For this meaning of κολοσσός, cf. Faraone, *CA* 10 (1991): 183 n. 65.

[44] *SEG* IX 3 = R. Meigg and D. Lewis, *A Selection of Greek Historical Inscriptions*, rev. ed. (Oxford: Oxford University Press, 1988), 5, pp. 5-9 with addendum. Most recently see C. A. Faraone, *CA* 10 (1991): 180f.; *idem*, "Molten Wax, Spilt Wine and Mutilated Animals: Sympathetic Magic in Near Eastern and Early Greek Oath Ceremonies," *JHS* 113 (1993): 60ff. Cf. also A. S. Gow's commentary on Theocritus 2.28, 2nd ed. (Cambridge: Cambridge University Press, 1952), 2.44. It is impossible to prove that the form of the oath curse without prayer or invocation of the gods was "older" or "original" as some scholars have suggested (W. Speyer, "Fluch," *RAC,* 7.1202; cf. Nilsson, *Geschichte*, 1.802f.). As our evidence stands the two forms were concurrent. Nor can it be said that the prayerless kind of cursing belongs to the realm of magic but cursing with prayer belongs to the realm of religion. This contention presupposes a dichotomy between the two which the evidence does not support. See in general Faraone, "The Agonistic Context," 4-10, 17-20; C. R. Phillips, "The Sociology of Religious Knowledge in the Roman Empire to AD 284," *ANRW*, 2.16.3 (1986), 2711-32; Faraone, "Molten Wax," 76-78.

[45] Cf. also the curse pronounced by Teucher in Soph. *Ai.* 1175-79. Speyer ("Fluch," 1202) also notes that no gods are invoked in the oaths in which the participants cast pieces of iron into the sea and swear to keep a covenant until the iron floats on the water (Herod. 1.165; Arist. *rep. Athen.* 23.5; Plutarch *Arist.* 25; Hor. *Epod.* 16.25f.). In such cases, however, when an author simply reports an

magicae in spells, undergo a kind of *hypostasis* and accomplish their own demands. Similarly, most of the cases of the *issar* cited above make no direct appeal, nor even reference to deities.[46] Many *issarim*, like many oaths, belong within this ancient tradition of prayerless cursing or self-cursing.

Although often they do not directly address deities, abstention vows could be used to exert pressure on gods, God, or others in authority. This brings us to the second distinctive *issar* type.

* * *

The "agonistic" *issar* displays a paradoxical transference. In a way similar to the self-actualizing vow, one pledges to abstain, but the actual ἀνάγκη falls on another. Through abstinence the vow-taker commits to a goal, but at the same time enters into an agonistic relationship with another, usually one who is in some position of authority, and pressures him to supply the means of achieving the goal. This form occurs frequently in the context of business dealings or contractual arrangements. We may take as a case in point a passage from the apocryphal book of Tobit. Raguel has just promised his daughter to Tobias in marriage and asserts that she is rightfully his. He then urges Tobias to sit down and partake of the fare set before him. His guest responds with the following vow: Οὐ μὴ φάγω ἐντεῦθεν οὐδὲ μὴ πίω, ἕως ἂν δι–αστήσῃς τὰ πρὸς ἐμέ, "I will neither eat thereof nor drink, until you settle my affairs" (7:12; ℵ recension, 250/175 BCE[47]). He refuses to eat or drink until marriage plans are finalized. The *issar* displays Tobias' resolution and demands action from another party in the context of a mutual agreement.[48]

---

oath without citing the *ipsissima verba*, we cannot be certain of the exact formula.

[46] Ps 132:1-5 (cited above) is an exception.

[47] BA says οὐ γεύσομαι οὐδὲν ὧδε, ἕως ἂν στήσητε καὶ σταθῆτε πρός με.

[48] The use of such vow formulations in the contexts of exerting pressure and invoking action range from the solemn and urgent, such as those above and that of the Demeter hymn below, to the most mudane and frivolous. With regard to the latter type, numerous rabbinical examples are collected by Jeremias, *Die Abend-mahlsworte Jesu*, 205f. (Eng., 213); cf. the trivializing use of oaths in later Judaism, against which Sir 23:9ff. complains (J. Schneider, "ὅρκος," *TDNT*, 5.461). Outside of Judaism, cf. a papyrus letter to a father in which his son demands that he send him a lyre, and warns, ἂμ μὴ πέμψῃς οὐ μὴ φάγω, οὐ μὴ πείνω· ταῦτα, "If you do not send it, I will never eat, I will never drink. So there!" (*P. Oxy.* I 119.13ff.).

The myth of Demeter offers some interesting variations on these themes. The author of her Homeric Hymn describes her rejection of Zeus' invitation (via Iris) to return to Olympus:

οὐ μὲν γάρ ποτ᾽ ἔφασκε θυώδεος Οὐλύμποιο
πρίν γ᾽ ἐπιβήσεσθαι, οὐ πρὶν γῆς καρπὸν ἀνήσειν
πρὶν ἴδοι ὀφθαλμοῖσιν ἐὴν εὐώπιδα κούρην (331-33).

For she claimed that she would never set foot on fragrant Olympus, nor let spring up earth's fruit, until she saw with her eyes her fair daughter.

These lines underscore two important *issar* motifs: first, Demeter, like David in the Psalm, swears not to go home until she realizes her goal.[49] She isolates herself to her commitment, which is the primary motif of the act of abstinence, regardless of what form it takes. Just as important, however, is the second part of her vow. Earlier in the narrative we learn that Demeter, upon discovering that her daughter had been abducted and given in marriage to Hades by Zeus, roams the earth fasting, mourning her daughter's absence, until cheered by the maidservant Iambe, she finally ends her fast by drinking the kykeon. Her comfort, however, does not last long. Soon after the princes of Eleusis build her great temple, she again begins to mourn, and I believe, although it is not explicitly stated, to fast. In the lines cited above we learn that, as Achilleus sought to impose his fasting upon the Achaians and king Saul upon the hosts of Israel, she incorporates the larger community of the human race into her abstinence. The focus of both her refusal to return home and the imposed fasting is not merely mourning; it sounds two important themes which we have previously seen in these vows, namely, desire for vengeance and invoking of action, in this case against Zeus and from Zeus. By imposing the curse of not eating upon the human race, she threatens Zeus with its extinction and the resultant loss of the honors of the cult.[50] Demeter, like Tobias, forces the authority in question to do business with her and ultimately to allow Persephone to return.

---

[49] Cf. Hom. *Od.* 5.177-79; when Kalypso invites Odysseus to build a raft and promises good provisions and fair wind for his journey home, he vows, οὐδ᾽ ἂν ἐγὼν ἀέκητι σέθεν σχεδίης ἐπιβαίην, εἰ μή μοι τλαίης γε, θεά, μέγαν ὅρκον ὀμόσσαι μή τί μοι αὐτῷ πῆμα κακὸν βουλευσέμεν ἄλλο, "Without your good will I have no intention of setting foot on a raft, unless, goddess, you can bring yourself to swear me a great oath that you will not devise some other evil mischief against me."

[50] See N. J. Richardson, *The Homeric Hymn to Demeter* (Oxford: Oxford University Press, 1974), 260-61 (n. on lines 311f.).

Centuries and worlds removed from this archaic, mythical setting, a woman of Roman Egypt named Eudaimonis, whose son is away at war, hopes for a similar result by use of a similar threat.[51] In a letter to her daughter (*P. Brem.* 63.25-28)[52] she vows, ἴσθι δὲ ὅτι οὐ μέλλω θεῷ σχολάζειν, εἰ μὴ πρότερον ἀπαρτίσω τὸν υἱόν μου, "Be assured that I will not concern myself with god, until (lit. "unless before") I receive back my son safely (?)"[53]

The distinction between the self-actualizing and agonistic *issar* is not always clearly drawn. What is arguably the most famous abstention vow combines aspects of both.[54] Among the exhaus-

---

[51] For the use of threats by humans against the gods, esp. in Egypt, see U. Wilcken, *Grundzüge und Chrestomathie der Papyruskunde* I.1 (Leipzig/Berlin, 1912), 125; Wm. Brashear, "Ein Neues Zauberensemble in München," *SAK* 19 (1992): 80 n. 7; and esp. R. K. Ritner, *The Mechanics of Ancient Egyptian Magical Practice*, Studies in Ancient Oriental Civilization, 54 (Chicago: The University of Chicago, 1993), 1, 5-6, 9, 21-22 with n. 92, *et passim* (see index, p. 311). Wilcken cites Porph. *Epist. ad Aneb.* 29, where the Neoplatonist expresses amazement at this practice as a peculiarity of Egyptian religion. There are, however, Greek, Roman, and even Christian parallels; cf. H. Bell, "Popular Religion in Egypt," *JEA* 34 (1948): 96; H. S. Versnel "Religious Mentality in Ancient Prayer," *Faith, Hope, and Worship*, ed. Versnel (Leiden: Brill, 1981), 37-42; and Martinez, *P. Mich. 757*, 69-74.

[52] =*Corpus Papyrorum Judaicarum*, ed. V. A. Tcherikover, A. Fuks, and M. Stern, 3 vols. (Cambridge: Harvard University Press, 1947-64), 2.442. Cf. another letter by the same Eudaimonis to her son (*P. Flor.* III 332): οὔτ[᾽ ἐ]λουσάμην [οὔ]τε προσεκύνησα θεοὺς φοβουμένη σου τὸ μετέωρον, "I have neither washed nor worshipped the gods, fearing your unfinished business," on which see Versnel, "Religious Mentality," 41 n. 169.

[53] In a text with much odd linguistic usage (see Wilcken's intro.) ἀπαρτίσω is especially enigmatic. Preisigke s.v. suggests "den Sohn ausrüsten" (i.e., equip him for [the Jewish] war). E. G. Turner renders simply, "see him through" (*CR* 11 [1961]: 226). The best sense is given by Wilcken's suggestion "ganz erhalte (d.h. heil aus dem Kriege zurückbekomme)"; similarly Versnel's "unless I have my son back in good health" ("Religious Mentality," 41 n. 168). Antikleia's description of Laertes refusing to sleep in his bed or wear decent clothing for as long as Odysseus was absent implies that he took a vow similar to that of Demeter and Eudaimonis (Hom. *Od.* 11.187-96).

[54] Jeremias and others before him have interpreted the following sayings as *issarim* or as within the *issar* tradition (*Die Abendmahlsworte Jesu*, 199-210 [Eng. trans., 207-18]). In the later editions of his book he prefers the less technical designation "Versichterklärung" to "Entsagungsgelübde," since Jesus does not actually use precise Hebrew terminology for vowing (such as "Corban" in Mk 7:11). Jeremias also mentions that it is Luke who has positioned these two pledges to abstain correctly, that is, the first before the beginning of the meal and the second immediately following at the passing of the first cup, as opposed to Mark, who places a single pronouncement after the "words of interpretation." For a critique of Jeremias' interpretation of this passage, see H. Patsch, *Abendmahl*

tively discussed "eucharistic words" of Jesus Christ are those uttered at Mk 14:25: ἀμὴν λέγω ὑμῖν ὅτι οὐκέτι οὐ μὴ πίω ἐκ τοῦ
γενήματος τῆς ἀμπέλου ἕως τῆς ἡμέρας ἐκείνης ὅταν αὐτὸ πίνω
καινὸν ἐν τῇ βασιλείᾳ τοῦ θεοῦ, "Truly I say to you, that never
more will I drink of the fruit of the vine until that day when I
drink it new in the kingdom of God." Compare with this the Lukan
account: λέγω γὰρ ὑμῖν ὅτι οὐ μὴ φάγω αὐτὸ ἕως ὅτου πληρωθῇ ἐν
τῇ βασιλείᾳ τοῦ θεοῦ. ... λέγω γὰρ ὑμῖν, [ὅτι] οὐ μὴ πίω ἀπὸ τοῦ
νῦν ἀπὸ τοῦ γενήματος τῆς ἀμπέλου ἕως οὗ ἡ βασιλεία τοῦ θεοῦ
ἔλθῃ. "For I say to you that I shall never eat it until it be fulfilled
in the kingdom of God. . . . For I say to you that from now on I
shall never drink of the fruit of the vine until the kingdom of God
come" (Lk 22:16, 18).

Phrases such as ". . . until I drink it new in the kingdom," ". . .
until it be fulfilled in the kingdom," ". . . until the kingdom of God
come," are surrogates for ". . . until God establishes his kingdom."[55] Thus on one level Jesus' vow falls within the agonistic
category, in that it invokes the action of another.[56] Like Demeter
and Eudaimonis, he displays earnest determination by withdrawing
from the sacred community. In abstaining from the passover meal
in general[57] and the bread and wine of the first Christian eucharist
in particular, he isolates himself from the most vital cultic activity
both of the old covenant in which he participated for his entire life
and the new covenant which he is initiating. Yet Jesus does not
assume the same kind of threatening posture as the goddess and
woman from Egypt. In fact, on another level Jesus consecrates
himself to the necessary action, making himself the instrument
through which God will establish the new order.

---

und historischer Jesus, Theologische Monographien 1 (Stuttgart: Calwer, 1972),
131ff.

[55] On this point see Jeremias, *Die Abendmahlsworte Jesu,* 203 n. 3 (Eng.
trans., 211 n. 5). Cf. in the Lord's Prayer, "Let thy kingdom come" (Mt 6:10, Lk
11:2).

[56] Similarly a fragment from *Gos. Heb.* concerning James, the brother of Jesus
(Hier. *de viris illustribus,* 2): *iuraverat ... Jacobus se non comesurum panem
..., donec videret eum resurgentem a dormientibus,* "James had sworn that he
would not partake of bread, until he saw him risen from among those who slept"
(in general cf. Jeremias, *Die Abendmahlsworte Jesu,* 207 with n. 1 [Eng. trans.,
215 with n. 4]). According to the account as it continues, the risen Jesus honored
his vow by appearing to him first.

[57] In the Lukan account, immediately before the vow, Jesus says, "I eagerly
longed to eat this passover with you" (22:15).

The consecration is also a curse. Jesus' words accentuate the notions of irrevocabilty and isolation. He seals his absolute commitment to the apocalyptic age with the vow that he will not partake of the sacred bread and wine until that age is ushered in. By cutting himself off from the holy meal of the cult he begins a process which will culminate in the supreme *anathema* of the crucifixion.[58] At the same time, however, by so extreme a display of determination and commitment to the coming kingdom, he struggles with God and invokes divine action in establishing it, the initial stages of which will be inaugurated by his own death and resurrection. Also, in keeping with basic *issar* themes, Jesus is recognizing that until the new age comes, the present state of affairs is indeed an accursed one. By his abstinence he dramatizes that recognition by paralleling himself with the accursed state; at the same time he consecrates himself to the divine intervention which will end it.[59]

---

[58] Jeremias continues to argue from the evidence of the early Christian passover fast that another central reason for Jesus' abstinence was as an act of mortification and prayer for Israel (*Die Abendmahlsworte Jesu*, 208-10 = Eng. trans., 216-18). But, the self-dedicating/imprecating nature of the abstention vow is in itself a sufficiently strong tradition to define what Jesus is doing without recourse to later developments within the Christian community. Nothing need soften the blow that Jesus is with these words surrendering himself to an accursed state.

[59] For all that these texts are culturally and chronologically diverse, a similar linguistic profile emerges, providing that we take into account the different means by which the Greek language expresses similar ideas at different stages in its development. The pledge to abstain is couched in terms of solemn and emphatic denial, which in the older epic language takes the form of the optative (+ ἄν) with (compounded or) intense negation (πρὶν δ' οὔ πως ἄν ... ἱείη ... οὐ πόσις οὐδὲ βρῶσις, *Il* . 19.209f.; οὐδ' ἄν ... ἀέκητι σέθεν ... ἐπιβαίην, *Od.* 5.177), which is further heightened by the intensive ἐγώ / ἔγωγε. For this usage of the optative see R. Kühner and B. Gerth, *Ausführliche Grammatik der griechischen Sprache*, 2 vols. (Hannover/Leipzig, 1898, 1904), 1.233; Schwyzer, *Griechische Grammatik*, 2.324; Jebb on Soph. *OT* 343; and esp. Slotty, *Der Gebrauch des Konjunktivs und Optativs*, 132f. (Homer), 143 (Attic); cf. also 93-99. In the koine examples which are related in direct speech (Tobit 7:12; Mk 14:25; Lk 22:16, 18; *P. Oxy.* I 119.13ff.), the dominant formula is the emphatic οὐ μὴ φάγω οὐ(δὲ) μὴ πίω. This idiom is classical (Kühner-Gerth, *op. cit.*, 2.221-23; Schwyzer, *op. cit.*, 2.317. For the origin of the construction see N. Turner, *Grammar of New Testament Greek*, vol. 3, Syntax [Edinburgh: T. & T. Clark, 1963], 96; esp. W. W. Goodwin, *Syntax of Greek Moods and Tenses* [New York: St. Martin's, 1889], 389ff.). In biblical Greek it was particularly adapted for oaths an asservations; cf. the 3rd person adaptation of the Nazarite vow in the prophecy of Gabriel to Zacharias concerning John in Lk 1:15: καὶ οἶνον καὶ σίκερα οὐ μὴ πίῃ. In general see Jeremias, *Die Abendmahlsworte Jesu*, 201f. (Eng. trans., 209f.); J. H. Moulton, *A Grammar of New Testament Greek*, vol. 1, Prolegomena, 3rd ed. (Edinburgh: T. & T. Clark, 1908), 187-92, and the fuller treatment in the German ed., *Einleitung in die Sprache des Neuen Testaments* (Heidelberg: Winter, 1911), 296-303;

*   *   *

Both types of *issarim* comprise abstinence and a state of necessity which the abstinence generates. In the self-actualizing type
both abstinence and ἀνάγκη belong to the vow-taker. In the agonistic vow, he imposes abstinence on himself, necessity on another. In Greek erotic magic of the Roman and Byzantine periods,
the operator of the spell inflicts both abstinence and ἀνάγκη on
another, namely, the beloved whom he seeks. I begin with a couple
of examples in which the formula is simple and straightforward:

καὶ μὴ ἐάσῃς αὐτὴν φαγῖν μήτε πῖν μήτε ὕπνου τυχῖν ἕως δὰν
(=ἀν) ἔλθῃ πρὸς ἐμὲ Διόσκ[ο]υρον, ὃγ ἔτεκε Θέκλα, ἤδη ἤδη
τ[α]χὺ ταχύ (P. Köln inv. no. 5514.8ff. [= *Suppl. Mag.* 43], IV CE).

And do not allow her to eat or drink or get sleep until she come to me,
Dioskouros, whom Thekla bore. Now, now, quickly, quickly.

καὶ μὴ δυνηθῇ μήτε πιεῖν μήτε φαγεῖν, ἄχρι οὗ ἔλθῃ πρὸς ἐμέ,
ἵνα με φιλῇ εἰς τὸν ἅπαντα χρόνον (*PGM* LXI 17-19 [III CE]).

and let her not be able either to drink or eat until she come to me, to love
me for all her life.

The formulae could also become quite elaborate:

ἀλλὰ μηδὲ 60 δυνηθῇ μήτε φαγῖν μήτε πῖν μήτε ὕπνου τυχῖν διὰ
παντὸς μήτε εὐσταθῖν ἢ ἰσυχάζιν τῇ ψυχῇ ἢ τὲς φρεσὶ ἐπαζη-
τοῦσα Ἐλουρίωνα ... ἕως οὗ ἐκπηδήσῃ ... πυρουμένη καὶ ἔρθῃ
πρὸς Ἐλουρίωνα ... φιλοῦσα, ἐρῶσα ... φίλτροις ἀκαταπαύστοις
καὶ ἀδιαλείπτοις καὶ παραμονίμοις ἐρωτικοῖς ... ἔρωτι θίῳ
(P.Mich. 757 [= *Suppl. Mag.* I 48] § J 9ff. [III/IV CE]).

And may she not be able to eat or drink or ever get sleep or enjoy good
health or peace in her soul or mind for her longing for Ailourion ... until

---

Turner, *op. cit.*, 95ff.; A. N. Jannaris, *An Historical Greek Grammar* (London:
MacMillan, 1897), 555. In all of the examples the grammar establishes a clear
delineation between two time frames: that in which the abstinence will occur and
the accomplishment of the goal which will terminate the vow and the abstinence.
These two periods are cast in sharper relief by various intensive expressions (πρίν
γ ... πρὶν ... πρίν, *h. Dem.* 332-33; νῦν μὲν ... ἅμα δ ἡελίῳ καταδύντι ... πρὶν δ
οὗ πως κτλ., *Il.* 19.206ff.; ἀπὸ τοῦ νῦν ... ἕως οὗ, Lk 22:18). This temporal
"bracketing" is vital in correlating the abstention vow and the erotic texts.

60 ἀλλὰ μηδέ: tab. αλλα μητε. See Martinez, *P. Mich. 757*, 59.

she leap up . . . burning with passion and come to Ailourion . . . loving, adoring, . . . with unceasing and relentless and constant loving affection . . . with a divine love.

Most documents which contain these phrases date in the third and fourth centuries CE.[61] The sentiments, however, also appear in two of the earliest magical papyri: P. Berol. 21243, ii.14-16 (=*Suppl. Mag.* II 72; Augustan age): μὴ πίοι . . . ἕως ἂν πρὸς ἐμὲ ἕως [c. 25], "May she not drink . . . until to me, until (text breaks off)"; *P.S.A.Athen.* 70 ii.5ff. (=*Suppl. Mag.* II 73; first cent. CE): ἐὰν καθεύδῃ μὴ [καθευδέτω, ἐὰν φάγῃ μὴ] φαγέτωι, ἐὰν πίν[ῃ μὴ πινέτω, ἕως ἔλθῃ πρὸς] ἐμέ, "If she is sleeping, let her not keep sleeping; if she is eating, let her not keep eating; if she is drinking, let her not keep drinking, until she comes to me" (trans. Daniel/Maltomini). Compare also a fragment of another first-century spell, *P. Monac.* II 28 (= *Suppl. Mag.* II 71) fr. 22, 4: ἀγρυπνίαν δότε τῇ δῖνα, "Give NN sleeplessness."[62] These texts provide sufficient testimony to the antiquity and persistence of these themes in Greek love magic. An important erotic motif lies behind them, which we should now consider.

Wasting away through sleeplessness and a lack of food and drink are all symptoms of love sickness, a malady which was well known to Hellenistic medicine and which acquired the status of a topos in the late Greek romantic tradition.[63] Galen describes the love sick as

---

[61] The texts known to me which contain similar phrases (i.e., some form of "may she not . . . until") with their paleographic dates are as follows: P. Berol. inv. 21243 ii.14ff. (*Suppl. Mag.* II 72; I); *P.S.A. Athen.* 70 ii.5ff. (*Suppl. Mag.* II 73; I); T. Cairo Mus. JdE 48217.20-24 (*Suppl. Mag.* I 46; II/III) Audollent 265A.8-10 (III); T. Köln inv. 2.25ff., 55-66 (*Suppl. Mag.* I 50; II/III); T. Louvre inv. 27145.20-24 (*Suppl. Mag.* I 47; II/III); *PGM* VII 610ff. (III); *PGM* LXI 17f. (late III); *P. Mich.* 757 §J.9ff. (*Suppl. Mag.* I 48; III/IV); *PGM* IV 372-79, 1425ff., 1510-31 (IV); *PGM* XXXVI 110ff., 147ff., cf. 356ff. (IV); P. Köln inv. 5514.8ff. (*Suppl. Mag.* I 43; IV); P. Köln inv. 3323.6f., 45ff. (*Suppl. Mag.* I 45; V). The following texts have similar prohibitions but lack the ἕως clause: Audollent 270.1ff. (II; Lat.); T. Cairo Mus. JdE 48217.10ff. (*Suppl. Mag.* I 46; II/III); T. Köln inv. 1.24ff. (*Suppl. Mag.* I 49; II/III); T. Köln inv. 2.55ff. (*Suppl. Mag.* I 50; II/III); T. Louvre inv. 27145.10f. (*Suppl. Mag.* I 47; II/III); Audollent 266.4ff. (III?; Lat.); *P. Laur.* III 57 (*Suppl. Mag.* II 82) frag. A.1 with Daniel/Maltomini's n. ad loc. (III); *P. Mich.* 757 §J.23f. (*Suppl. Mag.* I 48; III/IV); *PGM* IV 354ff. (IV). Cf. also the sentiment that the beloved must suffer fevered frenzy until she come to the lover (below n. 64).

[62] *Die Papyri der Bayerischen Staatsbibliothek München*, Band II, *Papiri letterari greci della Bayerische Staatsbibliothek di Monaco di Baviera*, ed. Antonio Carlini et al. (# 28 edited by P. Fabrini, F. Maltomini; Stuttgart: Teubner, 1986).

[63] Martinez, *P. Mich. 757*, 60; Winkler, "The Constraints of Eros," 222-24.

τοὺς δ' ἤτοι καταλεπτυνομένους ἢ ἀχροοῦντας ἢ ἀγρυπνοῦντας ἢ καὶ πυρέξαντας ἐπὶ προφάσεσιν ἐρωτικαῖς, "those who grow gaunt or pale or lose sleep or even get fevers for reasons of love" (*In Hipp. prog.* 1.4.18).[64] In *Daphnis and Chloe* 2.7.4, Philetas relates his past suffering over his love for Amaryllis: οὔτε τροφῆς ἐμεμνήμην οὔτε ποτὸν προσεφερόμην οὔτε ὕπνου ἡρούμην, "I could not think of food or take drink or get sleep."[65] It is obvious how verbally close these descriptions of love sickness are to the torments with which the lover curses the beloved victim in erotic magic.[66]

Hidden beneath the lover's desire that his beloved experience love sickness for him is his tormented longing to produce his own experience in her.[67] Here we have to do with another magical/erotic topos in which (as in the case of the "agonistic" *issar*) the notion of "transference" is important. Put simply, it is the operator who in reality is bound in hopeless passion, an illness which has robbed him of sleep and taken away his will to eat and drink. It has in effect alienated him from all meaningful human

---

[64] *Corpus Medicorum Graecorum* 5.9.2, ed. Diels, 207. *PGM* IV 132-37 describes the successful effects of a spell: νοσεῖ καὶ βούλεταί σοι λαλῆσαι - - - νοσεῖ ἢ καὶ τελευτᾷ, "she is sick and wants to talk with you, ... she is sick or even dying." In *PGM* XXXVI 356ff. the state which the lover wishes upon the beloved approaches a clinical description of the disease, similar to that of Galen: ποίησον αὐτὴν λεπτήν, χ[λωρ]άν, ἀσθενήν, ἄτοναν, ἀδύναμον ἐκ π[αντ]ὸς [τοῦ σ]ώματος αὐτῆς ἐ[νεργήματος]. Cf. also Galen's famous description of the woman who was sick with love for the dancer Pylades (*Prog.* VI 2ff., *Corpus Medicorum Graecorum* 5.8.1, ed. V. Nutton, 100-04). Many texts include fevered frenzy (πυρουμένη) among the symptoms (cf. *P. Mich.* 757 §§J-K.11, 35f.); in some texts this is the dominant idea; e.g., *PGM* IV 1527-31; XII 490-92; XXXVI 80-82.

[65] Cf. 1.13.6, τροφῆς ἠμέλει, νύκτωρ ἠγρύπνει, "(Chloe) did not care for food, at night she could not sleep." For parallels in other Greek romances, see Martinez, *P. Mich. 757,* 60.

[66] The motif also underlies Aristophanes' pathetic description of the two separated halves of the original human: ποθοῦν ἕκαστον τὸ ἥμισυ τὸ αὑτοῦ συνῄει, καὶ περιβάλλοντες τὰς χεῖρας καὶ συμπλεκόμενοι ἀλλήλοις, ἐπιθυμοῦντες συμφῦναι, ἀπέθνῃσκον ὑπὸ λιμοῦ καὶ τῆς ἄλλης ἀργίας, "Each pining away for its own half would come together, and embracing and intertwining with one another, longing to be grafted together, they would die from hunger and the other forms of neglect (Pla. *Sym.* 191a-b; τῆς ἄλλης ἀργίας = the other symptoms). Closely related, but not identical, is the sentiment that the lover's only food and drink is to be with the beloved (Pla. *Sym.* 211d).

[67] C. A. Faraone, "Clay Hardens and Wax Melts: Magical Role-reversal in Vergil's Eighth Eclogue," *CP* 84 (1989): 294-300; Winkler, "The Constraints of Eros," 225-28.

society, a dangerous state of isolation both death-like and deadly.[68] By the power of magic he now turns the tables;[69] he identifies her with himself, inflicting her with the same suffering which he has experienced, until she unites with him.[70] By so doing he imposes ἀνάγκη upon her: she will suffer as he suffers, until both experience the *remedium amoris* of sexual union.[71] In the self-actualizing *issar*, the vow-taker imposes ἀνάγκη on himself in the prohibition of eating and drinking, which in abstention vows has the character of a consecrating fast rather than a wasting disease. In matters of eros, however, some ancient minds do not make a sharp division between the two.

Euripides in the *Hippolytos* saw the relationship between the abstinence of love sickness and the fasting of ritual isolation and purity. The chorus describes Phaedra's suffering as follows:

τριτάταν δέ νιν κλύω | τάνδ' ἀβρωσίᾳ | στόματος ἁμέραν | Δάματρος ἀκτᾶς δέμας ἁγνὸν ἴσχειν | κρυπτῷ πάθει, θανάτου θέλουσαν | κέλσαι ποτὶ τέρμα δύστανον (135-40).

---

[68] For love sickness leading to suicide and death, see Winkler, "The Constraints of Eros," 222.

[69] As love sickness can cause the death of the lover, its transference can ultimately lead to the beloved's demise. See *PGM* IV 136-37, 2449-51, 2495; Winkler, "The Constraints of Eros," 242 n. 105. In Theokritos' second poem Simaitha's magic gives Delphis the choice to knock again on her door (line 6) or on Hades' (160, and see A. S. Gow's commentary, 2.62).

[70] Winkler ("The Constraints of Eros," 240 n. 71) points out that the texts in which we get a glimpse of the lover's own torment are rare. He cites in this connection T. Köln inv. 1.78 (*Suppl. Mag.* I 49). Add also the magical hymn of *PGM* IV 1400ff., where the spell-operator invokes Hekate-Persephone along with those who have died untimely and violent deaths, ὅπως αὐτὸν καρπίσησθε βασάνοις ἐχόμενον . . . ἄξατε οὖν αὐτὴν βασανιζομένην, "that you may prosper him who is possessed with torments, . . . then bring her in a state of torment" (1406-13). The importance of this magical role reversal/transference is not that it was the actual mindset of everyone who practiced erotic magic, but rather a romantic archetype which shaped the genre.

[71] A remarkable non-erotic parallel for this kind of transference occurs in the headache spell of P. Berol. inv. 21243 ii.26ff. (*Suppl. Mag.* II 72): "Osiris has a headache, Ammon has a pain in the temples of his head, Esenephthys has a pain all over her head. Osiris will not stop having a headache, Ammon will not stop having a pain in the temples of his head, Esenephthys will not stop having a pain all over her head until first he, NN stops completely (?) . . ." (trans. Daniel/Maltomini). The operator here threatens that the invoked deities will suffer as he suffers until they cure him.

And I hear that she for the third day now in fasting of mouth keeps her body pure from the grain of Demeter because of secret misery, longing to depart to the dreadful end of death.[72]

The poignancy of these lines consists in their play upon ἕκων and ἄκων. Euripides couches the involuntary affliction of love sickness in terms of a voluntary act of cultic observance. Phaedra is the unwilling victim of eros, but the loss of appetite associated with her disease is presented in the guise of a willing act of self-dedication and purification through fasting. This portrait mocks her desperation and ἀνάγκη, especially since the "purity" (ἀγνόν) of her "fast" mirrors the sexual purity of the one she desires, Hippolytos: λέχους γὰρ εἰς τόδ᾽ ἡμέρας ἀγνὸν δέμας, "To this moment my body is pure from marriage" (1003).[73]

Thus, it is a short leap from love as a disease to love as a sacred disease, a form of divine possession and holy madness. Plato in *Phaedrus* 244aff. asserts that the lover, like the prophet and poet, was possessed by a god-infused μανία, which he calls θεῖος ἔρως (266a). It was precisely this understanding which the medical tradition of Hippocrates (as represented by Galen) resisted:

μήτε οὖν τὴν ἐπιληψίαν οἰώμεθα θεῖον εἶναι νόσημα μήτε τὸν ἔρωτα· καὶ γὰρ καὶ τοῦτόν τινες ὑπολαμβάνοντες ἀληθῆ μὲν ἔγραψαν ἱστορίαν, ὡς Ἐρασίστρατος ἐφώρασε δι᾽ ἔρωτα τὸν τοῦ βασιλέως ἀρρωστοῦντα υἱόν, θεῖον δὲ οὐκ ἐδίδαξαν οὔθ᾽ ὑπὸ Ἐρασιστράτου καλούμενον οὔθ᾽ ὑπὸ Ἱπποκράτους οὔθ᾽ ὑπὸ ἄλλου τινὸς ἰατροῦ τὸν ἔρωτα (*In Hipp. prog.* 1.4.18).

So let us not conceive of either epilepsy or love as a divine disease. For even some who actually believe this to be true have recorded that Erasistratos discovered that the son of the king was love sick, but they did not

---

[72] On the entire passage and its difficulties, see W. S. Barrett, *Euripides Hippolytos* (Oxford: Oxford University Press, 1964), 187-88. I reproduce his text with a slight change of punctuation, deleting the comma after ἴσχειν and placing one after πάθει. The reading of the mss at 136, τάνδε κατ᾽ ἀμβροσίου, does not fit the meter or syntax of the rest of the sentence (it is, however, interesting to compare κατ᾽ ἀμβροσίου στόματος with Achilleus᾽ φίλον κατὰ λαιμόν in *Il.* 19.209).

[73] Hippolytos applies ἀγνός to himself also at 102. In general, the word group describes holiness connected with abstinence or avoidance; cf. *Hipp.* 315-16; Pla. *Leg.* 6.759c; Jos. *Ap.* 2.198; F. Hauck, "ἀγνός," *TDNT*, 1.122; Burkert, *Greek Religion*, 78, 271. For other examples of ἀγνός, ἀγνεύειν, κτλ. referring to abstinence from food and/or drink, cf. *PGM* IV 52-54; Plut. *de coh. ira* 464b; and other material cited by Arbesmann, *Das Fasten*, 9-10.

maintain that love was called divine by Erasistratos or Hippocrates or any other physician.[74]

It is probably magic rather than philosophy which the medical writer had in mind,[75] since the love which erotic spells mandate, frequently in the same context of the "neither eat nor drink until . . ." formula, is sometimes called ἔρως θεῖος or ἔρως / φιλία μανικός/ή.[76] In such phrases the full sense of words like θεῖος and μανικός far exceed translations such as "superhuman," "insane," or "obsessive." Particularly ἔρως θεῖος may at once mean love infused by divine or demonic agencies, or the kind of love which gods have for each other,[77] or the fervent devotion due only a god.[78] With regard to the last mentioned, no one will deny the close parallel between magical ἔρως θεῖος and the exclusive devotion demanded by Jesus in Lk 14:26:

εἴ τις ἔρχεται πρός με καὶ οὐ μισεῖ τὸν πατέρα ἑαυτοῦ καὶ τὴν μητέρα καὶ τὴν γυναῖκα καὶ τὰ τέκνα καὶ τοὺς ἀδελφοὺς καὶ τὰς ἀδελφὰς ἔτι τε καὶ τὴν ψυχὴν ἑαυτοῦ, οὐ δύναται εἶναί μου μαθητής.

---

[74] *Corpus Medicorum Graecorum* 5.9.2, ed. Diels, 206-07. Cf. also 1.4.19, p. 207.

[75] This is not the only point at which ancient medicine was at odds with magic. Cf. Hipp. *de morb. sacr.*, Littré vol. 6.260; Martinez, *P. Mich. 757*, 71-72.

[76] ἔρως θεῖος: with "neither eat nor drink etc." *P. Mich.* 757 §J.13, 25, §K.38 (*Supp. Mag.* I 48); P. Köln inv. 3323.48f., according to the corrected text of Daniel and Maltomini, *Supp. Mag.* I 45; without "neither eat nor drink etc." *PGM* X 7f.; XV 3. μανικός / μανιώδης with ἔρως / φιλία: P. Köln inv. 3323.7, 31, 49 (*Suppl. Mag.* I 45; in line 6, ὕπνω μὴ δυνηθῇ τυχῖν); Wm. Brashear, "Ein Neues Zauberensemble," 86f., lines 8, 18, 34, 50 (and cf. line 9, μὴ δυναμένη ὕπνου τυχεῖν).

[77] In this regard, ἔρως θεῖος between humans is sometimes demanded in terms of divine romantic archetypes: "Let NN love me ... as Isis loved Osiris," (*PGM* XXXVI 288f.; cf. Martinez, *P. Mich. 757*, 66f.) The opposite was also expressed paradigmatically; in Theok. 2.45-46 Samaitha prays, "(Whoever he may be with,) let him forget them, as, they say, in Dia Theseus once forgot lovely-tressed Ariadne."

[78] In Pla. *Sym.* 183a Pausanius characterizes the social behaviour which is permissible only for a lover as follows: ἱκετείας τε καὶ ἀντιβολήσεις ἐν ταῖς δεήσεσιν ποιούμενοι, καὶ ὅρκους ὀμνύντες, καὶ κοιμήσεις ἐπὶ θύραις, καὶ ἐθέλοντες δουλείας δουλεύειν οἵας οὐδ' ἂν δοῦλος οὐδείς, "Making supplications and prayers in their entreaties, and swearing oaths, and sleeping at his doors, and willingly performing acts of servitude, the likes of which not even a slave would do." It is no accident that such language also characterizes earnest religious devotion (see Bauer/Aland, *Wörterbuch zum Neuen Test.*, s.vv. δέησις, δουλεύω 2b).

If anyone comes to me and does not hate his father and mother and wife and children and brothers and sisters and even his own life as well, he cannot be my disciple.[79]

Compare the Lukan saying with P. Köln inv. 3323.46ff (=*Suppl. Mag.* I 45):

ποιήσατε αὐτὴν ... καταλῖψε πατέρα, μητέρα, ἀδελφούς, ἀδελ-
φάς, ἕως ἔλθη πρὸς ἐμέ, ... ἐρῶσά{ν} με θεῖον ἔρωτα ἀκατάπαυσ-
τον καὶ φιλίαν μανικήν.

Make her ... leave father and mother and brothers and sisters, until she come to me, ... loving me with an unceasing god-like love and frenzied devotion.[80]

When the curse not to eat or drink is viewed in this context, it assumes an expanded meaning, not only as the loss of appetite associated with love sickness, but also as an enforced purifying fast which accompanies an enforced state of possession. What the mantis (in preparation for prophecy) and the vow-taker undertake willingly, the user of love magic inflicts upon the beloved against her will. The result is the same: isolation from the land of the living. Thus the "neither eat not drink" prescriptions in the context of magically induced θεῖος ἔρως straddle the same tenuous boundary between isolating consecration and isolating imprecation as they do in the abstention vows. That disturbing semantic duplicity of Hebrew *hrm* (Greek ἀνάθεμα) of "consecrate" and "curse" apply to both applications of the formulae.

If there is a bright spot in this picture, it is that this isolation which erotic magic enforces, like that of the vow, is temporary. As the abstinence of the vow is terminated when the commitment is

---

[79] Cf. Matt 10:37, 19:29; Mk 10:29-30; Lk 14:26, 18:29; LXX Deut 33:9; Ex 32:25-29. Dionysiac ecstasy also causes domestic disruption: τὰς παρ' ἱστοῖς ἐκλιποῦσα κερκίδας ἐς μεῖζον' ἥκω, θήρας ἀγρεύειν χεροῖν, "I (sc. Agave) left the shuttles by the looms and have gone on to greater things, hunting wild beasts with my hands" (Eur. *Bak.* 1236f.; cf. 118).

[80] For leaving father, mother etc. cf. also Audollent, 230A.10ff.; 266.15ff.; *PGM* XV 4f.; LXI 29f.; IV 2756ff; and Pla. *Phdr.* 252a. For the religious dimensions of ἔρως in Plato, see R. Hackforth, *Plato's Phaedrus* (Cambridge: Cambridge University Press, 1952), 98. Compare also the Hebrew "Shema" (LXX Deut 6:4-5), and *P. Mich.* 757 §J.12 (*Suppl. Mag.* I 48), ἐρῶσα ἐξ ὅλης ψυχῆς, ἐξ ὅλου πνεύματος. In my comment on this passage (*P. Mich. 757*, 64-65) I argue that these phrases may have been influenced by the Shema, since that biblical text developed magical associations. Whereas this is certainly possible, we may have before us simply another case of the close correspondence between erotic motifs and the language of religious devotion.

fulfilled or the goal achieved, so ends the abstinence of eros when the beloved fulfills the desires of the lover; thus, the importance of "until . . . ."[81] She is then released and can again enjoy eating, drinking, and sleeping, as well as concourse with family and friends. But this normalcy may exist with him alone and never apart from him; thus erotic spells, like business deals in the documentary papyri, sometimes include phrases of binding finality, such as ἐπὶ τὸν λοιπὸν τῆς ζωῆς αὐτῆς χρόνον, "for the rest of her life."[82]

But this is not such a bright spot after all; it is rather part of the dramatic intensity and perilous urgency which the spell generates. In magic the issue of time looms large. The linguistic format of both love spells and abstention vows creates a kind of temporal bracketing: "I will not . . . until," "may she not . . . until." If the desired result is not procured within this framework, the implication is the destruction of the vow-taker or the beloved. Safety and normalcy abide on either side of the brackets. Within them is a threatening state of liminality, a no-man's land between well-being and destruction, life and death.[83] It is no wonder that love spells often climax with ἤδη ἤδη ταχὺ ταχύ, "Now, now, quickly, quickly." For the beloved, as with the vow-taker, time is running out.

---

[81] Cf. Jeremias, *Die Abendmahlsworte Jesu*, 202 n. 9 (Eng. trans., 210-11); Winkler, "The Constraints of Eros," 232.

[82] See *PGM* IV 405-06; VII 913-14; cf. XVI 24-25; LXI 17-19; Audollent 271.46; T. Köln inv. 1.79-80 (*Suppl. Mag.* I 49); T. Köln inv. 2.66-69 (*Suppl. Mag.* I 50); *P. Mich.* 757 §J.13-14 (*Suppl. Mag.* I 48) and Martinez, *P. Mich. 757*, 67 for other parallels between magic and business documents of the papyri. Cf. also in general Winkler, "The Constraints of Eros," 232-33. For the use of such phrases in other kinds of cursing spells, see H. S. Versnel, "'May he not be able to sacrifice . . . ,' Concerning a Curious Formula in Greek and Latin Curses," *ZPE* 58 (1985): 262 with n. 63. In this context the temporality of the "neither eat nor drink until" phrases is somewhat illusory. The implied threat, that the only factor which secures the beloved from a new onslaught of the disease is the presence of the lover, may indicate that the "binding finality" formulae create a kind of hedge about the ἔρως θεῖος and insure that it will indeed be "for the rest of her life."

[83] Similar, although not identical, is the state of P. Decius Mus having devoted himself to destruction as a sacrifice to procure the victory of his troops (Livy 8.9ff.), on which see H. S. Versnel, "Self-sacrifice, Compensation, and Anonymous Gods," *Le sacrifice dans l'antiquité*, Entretiens sur l'antiquité classique 27, ed. J. Rudhardt and O. Reverdin (Vandœuvres-Genève, 1980), 148-52. For the concept of the liminal as the stage for magical activity, see now S. I. Johnston, "Crossroads," *ZPE* 88 (1991): 217-24.

CHAPTER SEVENTEEN

DEFINING THE DREADFUL:
REMARKS ON THE GREEK CHILD-KILLING DEMON

Sarah Iles Johnston

At the beginning of his fifteenth *Idyll*, Theocritus portrays two women who are trying to get out of the house and have some fun at the annual festival for Adonis.[1] What holds them back is a child who, in the manner of all children about to be left behind with babysitters, is protesting loudly. Finally, in line 40, his exasperated mother says to him, "I will not take you with me, child. Mormo, the horse, bites!" (οὐκ ἀξῶ τυ, τέκνον. Μορμὼ δάκνει ἵππος). The reference to Mormo is intended to scare the child into quieting down. The scholiast on the passage implies that the mother is reminding the child that demons such as Mormo lurk outside in the dark; another scholiast explains that Mormo was the name of a *phasma* who killed children.[2]

In this essay, I will discuss not magic *per se,* but rather the nature of the beast against whom magic was directed—or at least, the nature of one beast: the child-killing demon.[3] I will react in particular to the works of two other scholars. The first is Walter Burkert's monograph on Oriental influences on Greek culture. Burkert briefly suggested there that two Greek child-killing demons named Lamia and Gello were derived from Near Eastern demons

---

[1] I am grateful for the helpful comments made by participants in the Kansas conference on Magic in the Ancient World after I delivered the oral version of this paper, particularly comments by David Frankfurter and JoAnn Scurlock. Work on the written version was facilitated by grants from The Melton Center for Jewish Studies at The Ohio State University and Ohio State's College of Humanities. This essay is offered to Oliver Phillips in thanks for his encouragement and instruction during my years at the University of Kansas.

[2] Schol. on Theoc. 15.40: [Ἡ μήτηρ] ἀπέστρεψε τὸν λόγον πρὸς τὸ παιδίον τὸ κλαῖον, καί φησιν, οὐκ ἄξω σε, τέκνον, μετ' ἐμοῦ, ὅτι ἡ μορμὼ ἵππος δάκνει. Schol. on Aristid. p. 41 Dindorf. Mormo frequently is identified with Lamia and Gello, two other child-killing demons (below, note 18). Cf. also the remarks of Erinn., *Distaff* line 25; Lib. *Or.* 30.38.12 and 33.42.7; Str. *Geo.* 1.2.8. 25 and 43; and Xen. *Hell.* 4.4.17.7, attesting to children's fear of Mormo.

[3] I include, however, an afterword on magical means of combatting this type of demon.

such as Lamashtu and Gallû.[4] One of my goals will be to evaluate
Burkert's suggestion: can the origin of any of the Greek child-
killing demon's traits securely be traced to the East? Need we seek
them there?

The second work is Jonathan Z. Smith's 1978 article "Towards
Interpreting Demonic Powers in Hellenistic and Roman Antiquity."[5] Smith suggested that the scholarly quest for the "roots" of
Greek demonology among other cultures, including those of the
Near East, was misguided; in fact, he noted, it placed scholars in
the same situation as the ancient Greeks themselves, who sought to
explain away anything dark or mysterious within their culture as
having been borrowed from the Persians, Egyptians, Chaldeans, *et
cetera*—as being anything but "Greek." Smith suggested that our
energies would be better spent examining how Greek and Roman
demonological beliefs functioned within those cultures themselves.
In particular, he developed the precepts set forth by Mary Douglas
in *Purity and Danger* by arguing that the demonic frequently
serves as a classificatory marker that is part of a larger system of
boundaries used to express or reinforce a society's values. Smith
sees this as working in one of two ways: "negative valence is
attached to things which escape place (the chaotic, the rebellious,
the distant) or things found just outside the place where they
properly belong (the hybrid, the deviant, the adjacent)." He goes
on to note that:

> The most frequent form of demons is that of a hybrid or monster, a pro-
> tean figure capable of a range of transformations or as a being with super-
> fluous parts. . . . the demonic is frequently characterized by the extremes
> of being either hard and cold (e.g., Satan's penis which is often described
> in witchcraft literature as being made of horn or iron and icy to the touch)
> or squishy and rotten (i.e., overheated). . . . To translate this range: de-
> mons are perceived as being either overdefined or underdetermined. De-
> mons serve as classificatory markers which signal what is strong and
> weak, controlled and exaggerated in a given society at a given moment.

Smith's suggestions apply well to the study of demons in general.
Before we consider the Greek child-killing demons, however, I

---

[4] W. Burkert, *The Orientalizing Revolution,* trans. Margaret E. Pinder and W.
Burkert (1984; Eng. trans. Cambridge: Harvard University Press, 1992), 82-87.
See also now David R. West, "Gello and Lamia: Two Hellenic Daemons of
Semitic Origin," *Ugarit-Forschung* 23 (1991): 361-68 (volume 23 was available
in early 1993; West's work kindly was brought to my attention by Richard
Beal).
[5] *ANRW,* 2.16.1 425-39.

would make some further observations about how demons reflect and reinforce the structures by which a culture organizes its physical and moral worlds.

Very frequently, the "displacement" of the demonic takes the form of liminality. That is, the demon is not merely outside of any single, given taxon, but situated squarely *between* two taxa that are considered to be mutually exclusive; the hybrid nature of demons, noted by Smith, is a form of this. The werewolf is a good example: it is far more frightening than either a normal wolf or a normal man would be precisely because it fails to adhere to the taxon either of "human" or of "animal." Such juxtapositions of animal and human are disconcerting because they suggest that one of the organizational grids that culture has imposed on the world is liable to flux. (On another level, such hybrids also are frightening because they typically possess the threatening characteristics of both their components: e.g., the wits of a man and the savagery of the wolf.) The common belief that the doorway is a gathering place for demons also expresses the liminal status of the demonic, for the threshold is neither inside nor outside of the house, it belongs to neither the interior sphere nor that of the outside world; crossroads—the interstices *between* three or four roads—also are demonic in many cultures.[6] Shape-shifting, a common demonic talent, is a diachronic form of hybridism: the demon does not display the traits of two or more taxa *simultaneously,* but his ability to change from human to horse to fire to tiger, *et cetera,* nonetheless prevents his secure categorization.

In challenging established taxa, of course, the association between liminality and the demonic helps to uphold those taxa by suggesting that anything falling between them is dangerous and must be avoided. Another way in which the demonic can challenge—and thus implicitly uphold—established taxa is by serving as a concave mirror for the human world, a mirror in which perfect inversions of behavioral or physical *desiderata* are held up to view.[7] In this paradigm, "normal" demonic behavior = abnormal human behavior. The worldwide tendency to portray witches and demons as indulging in incest and cannibalistic feasts is a good example of this. Such tales send the message that any individual

---

[6]See S. I. Johnston, "Crossroads," *Zeitschrift für Papyrologie und Epigraphik* 88 (1991): 217-24.

[7]This idea has been explored by some anthropologists, notably Rodney Needham (*Primordial Characters* [Charlottesville: University of Virginia Press, 1978], 23-50).

who wishes to retain membership within the human race—i.e., anyone who does not wish to be classed a demon or witch—must adhere to the established standards of behavior and appearance.

Often, an item, a person or a mode of behavior first is condemned as demonic because it aligns with one of these two paradigms of exclusion (it is either liminal or inverted), but subsequently, folk belief elaborates, adding to that item, person or mode of behavior qualities of the other paradigm. One of the simplest examples of this tendency already has been mentioned: demons, who by definition delight in harming people (and who thereby *invert* the rules of civilized human conduct), often are imagined to manifest themselves in physical forms that are *liminal* insofar as they are hybrid—the traditional picture of Satan, we recall, is that of a man with goat's horns, feet and tail. Herzfeld, in an article on contemporary rural Greek superstitions, gives an example of the opposite development, whereby a person who inverted one of the structures that underlay his society was suspected of having demonic powers. A man who refused to reciprocate coffee-house hospitality and who, instead, spent his time talking with tourists (in other words, a man who transgressed the boundaries of his group, preferring the things that were "outside" to those that were "inside"), was accused of having the "evil eye" (a desire and ability to harm the innocent).[8] Secondary expressions of either form of displacement—liminality or inversion—can be added to a demonic figure *ad infinitum,* each one moving it further and further from established norms and, thus, further and further condemning the behavior that made it demonic in the first place. The European tales of witches' sabbats that grew up during the thirteenth to seventeenth centuries are full of inventive examples: not only are the witches incestuous cannibals, but they walk on their hands, eat salt to quench their thirst, easily change themselves into animals to accomplish their ends, and dance back-to-back instead of face-to-face.

Having reviewed two ways of approaching the study of Greek demonology—Burkert's quest for Near Eastern precedents and Smith's attention to the way in which the demons functioned within a culture—we can now proceed to examine the Greek child-killing demon. Of course, Burkert's and Smith's methods need not be mutually exclusive. We should consider the possibility that *some* features of the Greek child-killer were borrowed from elsewhere in

---

[8] M. Herzfeld, "Meaning and Morality: A Semiotic Approach to Evil Eye Accusations in a Greek Village," *American Ethnologist* 8.3 (1981): 560-74.

the Mediterranean basin, but must we keep in mind that the recognition of such borrowings would become useful only if we took the further step of explaining how they upheld or toppled *existing* Greek taxonomies and beliefs. Until the question of *why* something was borrowed has been answered, we have advanced the discussion very little—constructing a genealogy is only the first step in understanding the peculiar quirks expressed by individual members within the Mediterranean family of religious beliefs. Sometimes when we ask the question "why," moreover, we may discover that what looked like a genealogical relationship need not have been one at all; upon deeper analysis we may discover that conditions within the Greek culture made the indigenous birth of a belief completely possible.

I have mentioned already the three most common names for Greek child-killing demons: Mormo, Lamia and Gello. These names, and their plurals *(mormones, lamiai, gelloudes),* can be used as common nouns, but as personal names they designate mythologically crystallized representatives of groups of demons.[9] Empousa *(empousai)* is another female demon often connected with these others by modern scholars, although, as I will discuss below, Empousa's role as a child-killing demon probably was slight and secondary to other aspects of her nature; her name is connected with attacks on children only twice and then only indirectly.[10] There is one more type of child-killing demon, whose name usually occurs in the plural, although it can be found occasionally in the singular: the *strix* or *striges.* It is likely that *"strix"* was originally a Roman name for the child-killing demon, which

---

[9] *"Mormo"* developed in ways that *"lamia"* and *"gello"* did not. First, the word *"mormo"* gave rise to a variation: *"mormolukê"* or *"mormolukia."* The word for "wolf" is present here; thus, we picture a sort of female werewolf (see further below). From *"mormolukê"* came *"mormolukeion."* This is used once by Lucian to refer to a monster (*Philops.* 23.5), but normally had the meaning of "mask"; cf. the development of *"gorgoneios"* from *"gorgô."* Some ancient sources connect *"mormolukeion"* specifically with theatrical masks (e.g., Ar. frg. 31 Edmonds).

[10] Gello is called an *"eidôlon* of Empousa" at Hsch. s.v. "Γελλώ" (Γ 308), which would seem to mean that Gello and Empousa were equated in ancient thought or that Gello was understood to be a type of *empousa.* The author of the *Vita Aeschines* (vol. 3 Reisk, p. 10) says that Aeschines' mother "was accustomed to rush out of dark places to frighten women and children, and was nicknamed Empousa, therefore, because Empousa was a νυκτερινὸν φάντασμα." (This may refer to Aeschines' mother's role in some mystery cult [C. Brown, "Empousa, Dionysus and the Mysteries: Aristophanes, *Frogs,* 285 ff." *Classical Quarterly* 41.1 (1991): 41-50]).

was adopted by the Greeks at some time before the first century
BCE[11] and made equivalent to their own *gello, lamia* and *mormo,*
but, as there is reason to believe that the *strix's* essential characteristics aligned with those already assigned to the Greek child-
killing demons (see below), I will include her. *Gelloudes,* and
probably other child-killers, too, were blamed for the deaths of
pregnant women and their fetuses as well as for the deaths of
children. The combination is logical, and is found in association
with child-killing demons throughout both the ancient and the
modern worlds: the demon who brings reproduction to an unhappy
end at one point in the process does so at other points as well.[12]

Let us start with some very general observations about how the
Greeks situated child-killing demons within their physical, moral
and social *kosmoi,* and how the demons, in turn, reinforced the
rules by which those *kosmoi* functioned. First, we can say that the
ancient placement of the characters called Lamia, Gello and
Mormo among the *eidola, daimones* and *phantasmata*—within the
ghostly or demonic realm, in other words—in itself reinforced the
standard Greek opinion as to what the proper role of a woman

---

[11] The second-century CE grammarian Festus (Müller, p. 314) passes down a
Greek iambic chant to avert the *striges*; he gives as his source the first-century
BCE Verrius Flaccus. The verses are reconstructed by T. Bergk, *Poetae Lyrici
Graeci,* vol. 3[4] (Leipzig: Teubner, 1882; reprint. 1914-15), frg. 26, and D. L.
Page, *Poetae Melici Graeci* (Oxford: Clarendon Press, 1962), frg. 859. Cf.
Müller's own reconstruction, however, which makes the verses dactylic hexame-
ter. See my remarks on the passage below. Cf. H. Versnel, "Polycrates and His
Ring: Two Neglected Aspects," *Studi storico-religiosi* 1(1978): 41-42; H.
Herter, "Böse Dämonen im frühgriechischen Volksglauben," *Rheinisches
Jahrbuch für Volkskunde* 1 (1950): 116-17; O. Weinreich, *Gebet und Wunder*
(Stuttgart: W. Kohlhammer, 1929), 12-13 n. 22; Wilamowitz, "Lesefrüchte 197a"
from *Hermes* 60 (1925), reprint. in *Kleine Schriften* 4 (Berlin: Akademie Verlag,
1962), 391-92; R. Heim, *Incantamenta Magica Graeca Latina* (Leipzig: Teub-
ner, 1892), 500-01.

[12] At *Kyran.* 2.40.38-39 Gello is called the night-wanderer who "strangles
babies and persecutes the woman in childbed." The Byzantine scholar Michael
Psellus reports that in his day, Gello was credited with killing pregnant women
and/or their fetuses as well as infants (ap. Leo Allatius, *de Graecorum hodie
quorundam opinationibus epistola* [Cologne: 1645], section 3). Some of the
magical stones listed in the *lithica* of Damigeron-Evax are said to protect both
infants and pregnant women, which suggests that the same type of demon was
responsible for both (1 [aetite], 31 [lynguros], 33 [galactite]). Cf. also my comments on ἐρυσμόν in the *h.Cer.* 230, below. For other Mediterranean examples of
this combination of functions, see the texts concerning Lamashtu collected by
West, "Gello"; the comments of G. Scholem, "Lilith," *EncJud* (Jerusalem, 1972),
2.245-49; and the description of the demon "Obizoth" in the *Testament of
Solomon* § 57.

was.[13] A female who would kill a child, or prevent its birth in the first place, ran completely contrary, of course, to the fecund and nurturing mother who was held up as the norm to which all women should aspire; attributing such behavior to demons emphasized its utter abnormality, and thus censured it. The etiological myths about child-killing demons delimited the acceptable behavior of a Greek woman even more strictly, however. Zenobius, explaining a phrase used by Sappho, tells Gello's story:

> "Fonder of children than Gello" is a saying used of those who died prematurely, or of those who are fond of children but ruin them by their upbringing. For Gello was a virgin, and because she died prematurely, the Lesbians say that her ghost haunts little children, and they attribute premature deaths to her (*Prov.* 3.3 = Sapph. frg. 178 Campbell; Campbell's Loeb translation, slightly adapted).

Lamia, in contrast, does not die a *parthenos,* but she similarly fails to reproduce and nurture successfully, because her children die early in life. A full, although euhemerizing, version of her story is given by Diodorus Siculus:

> At the base of this (Libyan mountain) was a large cave thickly covered with ivy and bryony, in which according to myth had been born Lamia, a queen of surpassing beauty. But on account of the savagery of her heart they say that the time that has elapsed since has transformed her face to a bestial aspect. For when all of the children that had been born to her had died, weighed down with her misfortune and envying the happiness of other women in their children, she ordered that newborn babies be snatched away from their mothers' arms and straightaway slain. Wherefore, among us even down to the present generation, the story of this woman remains among the children and her name is most terrifying to them (Diod. Sic. 20.41, 3-5 [Geer's Loeb translation, slightly adapted]; cf. Duris ap. *FGrH* 76 F 17 = Phot. and Suid. s.v. Lamia and the accounts of schol. Δ on Ar. *Vesp.* 1035; Apostol. ap. Leutsch *Paroim. Gr.* 2.497-98 and schol. Aristid. p. 41 Dindorf).

Of Mormo's myth, we have only scant remains, given by the scholiast to Aristides, p. 41 Dindorf:

---

[13] Explicitly stated by later sources such as Zen. *Prov.* 3.3; Hsch. s.v. Γελλώ, λάμια, μορμόνες; *Kyran.* 2.31.20 and 2.40.38; Choerob. in Cramer. Anecdot. Oxon. 2.239.13; schol. Aristid. p. 41 Dindorf; *Vita Aeschines* p. 10 Reisk; Eust. *Od.* 2.21.30; Hdn. *Epim.* 88.1. Also in *FGrHist* 338 F 2 (third-century BCE Idomeneus) and implicitly in such statements as that of Sophron, who calls Mormoluka (Doric for "Mormolukê") the "nurse of Acheron" (frg. 9 Kaibel).

[Aristides] speaks of Mormo, whose name frightens the children who hear it. They say that she was a Corinthian woman who, one evening, purposefully ate her own children and then flew away. Forever thereafter, whenever mothers want to scare their children, they invoke Mormo (author's translation).

The story is similar to that of Lamia, insofar as Mormo bears children but then fails to nurture them successfully to adulthood. This similarity is noted by the scholiast himself, who elsewhere in the passage calls Mormo a type of *lamia;* the scholiast to Theocritus *Idyll* 15.40 explains the poet's reference to Mormo by saying that "Mormo" is just another name for Lamia, as is "Gello," and then telling an abbreviated version of Diodorus' Libyan story.[14] Equations of two or all of these demons are found in other ancient sources as well. Such equations should not surprise us; after all, the "names" are in reality adjectives that describe the demons as "fearsome ones" *(mormones)* and "devourers" *(lamiai).*[15]

All of these *aitia* express the belief that child-killing demons have their origin in mortal women who failed to bear and nurture children successfully.[16] Thus, they suggest that it is not enough simply to hold back from the overtly inhuman act of killing children if a woman wants to retain membership in the human race—additionally, she must bear and nurture children. In other words, the *aitia* deliver the same message that a Greek woman heard from

---

[14] Elsewhere I have argued that the myth of "Mormo" as we see it in the scholiast to Aristides was influenced by the myth of Corinthian Medea, who purposely killed her children and then flew away in a dragon chariot (S. I. Johnston, "Corinthian Medea and the Cult of Hera Akraia," in J. J. Clauss and S. I. Johnston, eds., *Medea* (Princeton, 1996).

[15] On possible meanings of "empousa," see Waser, "Empusa," *PW,* 5.2 col. 2542. The original meaning of "Gello" is hard to determine, as it bears no similarity to any Greek root other than "gel-", which produces words that mean both "laugh" and "be an object of laughter." Some scholars associate "Gello" with the Sumerian/Akkadian "Gallû." See below, however; other scholars of Sumerian/Akkadian languages, such as E. Ebeling, have rejected the derivation.

[16] Similar explanations are given for the existence of child-killing demons in other cultures, particularly in the ancient Mediterranean (J. A. Scurlock, "Baby-snatching Demons, Restless Souls and the Dangers of Childbirth: Medico-Magical Means of Dealing with some of the Perils of Motherhood in Ancient Mesopotamia," *Incognita* 2 [1991]: 1-112; Th. H. Gaster, "A Canaanite Magical Text," *Orientalia* 11 [1942] 41-79). Egyptian texts mention "dead men and women" who come to attack the child; sometimes, a ghost wants to kiss the child or take it into her lap or arms, which may allude to the paradigm of the *aôros* woman (A. Erman, *Zaubersprüche für Mutter und Kind*, Abhandlungen der Königlichen Preussischen Akademie der Wissenschaften [Berlin, 1901], esp. 12-13, 32-33, 39, 40-45).

other sources: her goal in life was to become a mother. Failure or refusal to meet this goal amounted to virtually the same thing as an attack against the most important structure by which humanity organized itself: the family.[17] The weakening or destruction of the family would allow humanity to slide back to some primitive, lawless, bestial state, as myths frequently sought to demonstrate. Humanity would be human no more.

Zenobius and Hesychius specifically call Gello *aôros,* that is, "untimely dead," one who has died before completing her life on earth.[18] This term does not so much express Gello's failure to meet her reproductive obligations to others, such as those within her *oikos,* as the fact that she had failed to experience those things that defined her as a woman: parturition and nurture. *She herself* was incomplete; at the time of her death, she had not acquired the characteristics necessary to be considered a full member of the taxon "woman." Because of her death, she would never acquire them, she would never pass into completion. Although Lamia and Mormo are never explicitly called *aôroi,* it is logical to assume that they were considered to belong to this group as well, for if, as I have just noted, it was not by marriage *per se* but rather by childbirth and nurture that a female was understood to have fulfilled her obligations to the family and state, then it is probable that her

---

[17] Of course, the *aitia* associated with the demon also aligned well with the belief in demonic envy that was and still is very common in the Mediterranean basin: the sudden, inexplicable illnesses and deaths of children were attributed to demons who had cause to be envious of the children's successful mothers.

[18] Zen. *Prov.* 3.3; Hesych. s.v. "Gello" (he specifically understands her as a type of Empousa associated with virginal *aôroi:* Γελλώ εἴδωλον Ἐμπούσης· τὸ τῶν ἀώρων, τῶν παρθένων.) Cf. Suid. Γ 112, which seems to paraphrase Zenobius. For further discussion of *aôroi* and the related categories of *biaiothanatoi* and *ataphoi* (including their use in magic) cf. the author's article cited in n. 20 and see the following recent treatments (which include citations for important earlier treatments): D. Martinez, ed. and comm., *Michigan Papyri XVI: A Greek Love Charm from Egypt (P. Mich. 757)* (Atlanta: Scholars Press, 1991), 48-49; A. Henrichs, "Namenlosigkeit und Euphemismus: Zur Ambivalenz der chthonischen Mächte im attischen Drama," in *Fragmenta Dramatica. Beiträge zur Interpretation der griechischen Tragikerfragmente und ihrer Wirkungsgeschichte,* ed. H. Hofmann (Göttingen: Vandenhoeck & Ruprecht, 1991), part IV; W. Brashear, "Zauberformular," *Archiv für Papyrusforschung* 36 (1990): 49-74, esp. 53-55 and 69 (particularly concerned with their use in magic); R. Daniel, "Two Love Charms," *Zeitschrift für Papyrologie und Epigraphik* 19.3 (1975): 255-56; J. ter Vrugt-Lenz, *Mors Immatura* (Groningen: J.B. Wolters, 1960); J. H. Waszink "Biothanati," in Klauser, ed., *RAC,* 2 (1954), 391-94.

personal sense of completeness depended upon these accomplishments as well. Helen King has explored this topic in depth.[19]

Let us be exact about the ramifications of permanent exclusion
from the taxon of "completed woman." Death in this state exiles
the *aôros* woman not only from the world of the living, as all
deaths do, but also from the world of the dead, leaving her no
recourse but to wander restlessly between the two. This is expressed
in literary sources as early as *Odyssey* 11.13-41 by describing *aôroi*
as lingering at the border between the upper world and the Underworld.[20] Hesychius tells us that *mormones* were called *planeîes
daimones* (s.v. μορμόνας). The well-known importance of the
aôroi in magic rests upon the assumptions that, unimpeded by
Hades' gates, they could travel back and forth between the lower
and upper worlds more easily than a "fully dead" soul, and that,
unprotected by it, they were at the mercy of those who knew how
to invoke them. Successful death, in other words, just like successful life, was open only to the complete, to the taxonomically
perfect soul. Life and death themselves were *both* acceptable states
for the soul to exist in, even if death was a somewhat less desirable
state than life; it was in the margin between them that the real
problems lay. The Greeks structured their cosmos so as to place
one of the major sources of demonic interference—the *aôroi*—
between the two most mutually exclusive taxa that any culture
confronts: life and death. A comment by the Byzantine scholar
John Damascenus suggests that the eschatologically marginal status
of Greek child-killing demons, and perhaps of other *aôroi,* too, had
existential ramifications, for he says that *gelloudes* and *striges*
were believed to retain some, but not all, of their corporality.

The wanderings of the child-killing demon did take her into in
the world of the living, of course, where she made her presence
known in dreadful ways. Let us move on now to an examination of

---

[19] "Bound to Bleed: Artemis and Greek Women," in *Images of Women in
Antiquity,* eds. Averil Cameron and Amélie Kuhrt (Detroit: Wayne State Univer-
sity Press, 1983), 109-27. See also Charles Stewart, *Demons and the Devil:
Moral Imagination in Modern Greek Culture* (Princeton: Princeton University
Press, 1991), 173-77.

[20] On the Odyssean passage, see S. I. Johnston, "Penelope and the Erinyes:
Odyssey 20.61-82," *Helios* 21.2 (1994): 137-59; Jan Bremmer, *The Early Greek
Concept of the Soul* (Princeton: Princeton University Press, 1903), 103; R.
Lattimore, *Themes in Greek and Latin Epitaphs,* 2nd ed. (Urbana, 1962) 187; R.
Merkelbach, *Untersuchungen zur Odyssee,* 2nd ed. (Munich, 1969), 189; K.
Meuli, *Gesammelte Schriften,* vol. 1 (Basel and Stuttgart, 1975), 316.

her iconography—how were these demons imagined to manifest themselves?

There is no standard answer to this question, which, as Charles Stewart has discussed, is quite in accord with the nature of the demonic itself. In his study of the *exotiká* (demons) of the contemporary Greek countryside, Stewart notes that their physical traits and behavior patterns vary from locale to locale, from neighbor to neighbor, or even from one statement to the next during a conversation with a single individual. This is because the function of such traits and patterns is not to identify one demon definitively in contrast to all others, but rather to say something about the nature of the demon as it is being experienced by a specific person at a specific moment.[21] Demons are clay with which people mold images of their fears and anxieties; in order to express the fears and anxieties of the moment effectively, that clay must remain malleable. It is not until those who stand outside of a community begin to make lists of its demons (i.e., demonologies) for their own purposes that any real consistency of traits and imagery is obtained, and it is an artificial consistency, born from a scholar's desire to organize, a magician's desire to control or a missionary's desire to devalue and eventually overcome. For ancient Greek demons, this process began in earnest with the church fathers.

Of course, even if we ignore the artificial constructions of scholars, magicians and church fathers, and attend, so far as we can, only to the reports of those for whom the demons are a real and active force in the cosmos, some consistency of description will emerge over the long run. Some traits symbolize some anxieties better than others; thus, those traits are called into use more frequently than others when that particular anxiety is expressed. An example borrowed from Stewart will serve to illustrate this idea. Many different types of demons in contemporary Greece (including *lamies, khamotsároukhoi* and *neraïdes*) are frequently described as being part goat. Goats are notoriously difficult to manage; for a culture in which herding is important, therefore, the goat is a potent symbol of trouble and possible loss of livelihood. This rather broad connotation makes the goat a symbol suitable for a variety of demons. But other symbols, expressive of some-

---

[21] Stewart, *Demons*, chap. 6. A similar point can be made about ghost beliefs in virtually any culture; see for example, J. J. Winkler on the iconography of Greek and Roman ghosts ("Lollianos and the Desperadoes," *JHS* 100 [1980]: 155-81, esp. 158-165).

what different anxieties, are sometimes attached to the same
demons as is the goat symbol. A *neraïda* sometimes is described
not as a goatish woman but rather as a woman who has abnormally
elongated thighs; according to Stewart's analysis, this trait expresses her sexual deviancy and the danger she poses to married
men.[22] To pin down the symbol of the goat to one or two types of
demons, or to delineate an exact, standardized iconography for the
neraïda, would rob them of any power to express real, everyday
anxieties; under such circumstances, a demon becomes a quaint
remnant of a bygone culture rather than a vital idiom. The symbolic value of any trait associated with a demon, thus, must be
evaluated in isolation from the demon as well as in connection
with it.

The classicist faces two problems that Stewart does not. First,
our information is derived primarily from literary and artistic
products; the informant has taken special care in choosing what he
tells or shows us. A bigger problem is that our information is relatively meager: we cannot live among our subjects as Stewart did.
Neither problem is new to the classicist, but they do become more
acute when we are dealing with material that, as I have suggested, is
by its very nature fluid; any description of a demon that we possess
is just a single—and perhaps very deliberate—selection from a wide
range of possible traits. Nonetheless, some broad observations
about the significance of the child-killing demon's iconography
can be made.

As we might expect, like demons throughout the world, child-
killing demons generally are described as ugly—indeed, the
paroemiographers tell us that Lamia's ugliness was proverbial.
Mormo's name, which means "Frightful," conveys the same idea.[23]
Lamia is portrayed as having disgusting personal habits, too: Aristophanes describes her as farting in public (*Vesp.* 1177; cf. *Eccl.* 77
and Crates frg. 18 = schol. *Ar.* Eccl. 77) and as having filthy testicles (*Vesp.* 1035 = *Pax* 758).

This brings me to the next iconographic feature: Lamia was
imagined to be bisexual. Not only do we hear about her testicles in
Aristophanes' *Peace* and *Wasps,* but a scholiast on *Ecclesiazusae*

---

[22] Stewart, *Demons,* chap. 6.

[23] On Lamia's proverbial hideousness, see Ps. Diogenian. *ap.* Choirob. in
Crameri Anecdot. Oxon. 2.293, Duris *FGrH* 76 F 17; further at Schwenn,
"Lamia" *PW,* 12 col. 545. On Mormo as the essence of fearsomeness or *"mormo"*
as a synonym for *"phobos"*: Ar. *Equ.* 693; Xen. *Hell.* 4.4.17; schol. Ar. *Ach.* 582;
schol. Ar. *Pax* 474 and often elsewhere; Hesychius and Photius explain cognates
of *"mormo"* by cognates of *"phobos."*

77 tells us that the fifth-century comic poet Crates portrayed Lamia with a "staff" (σκυτάλη). In the *Lysistrata,* "σκυτάλη" is used as slang for "phallus" (line 991), and in a passage from the *Ecclesiazusae* that clearly alludes to the scene from Crates,[24] "σκύταλον" seems to be similarly used: some women are busily disguising themselves as men; one woman shows the others the splendid "σκύταλον" that she has stolen from her sleeping husband (lines 76-78); this follows immediately upon the other women's proud display of their "walking sticks" (βακτηρία; line 74). Stage business regarding that most essential piece of male comic-theatrical attire, the phallus, surely occurred here. A lekythos[25] dated to the fifth century shows a naked, ithyphallic[26] woman who, tied to a palm tree, is being tortured by satyrs. Her belly sags out over her groin, her breasts are horribly pendulous,[27] fang-like teeth make her appearance frightening as well as repulsive. Her facial features and hair follow the conventions used in antiquity to represent blacks. The palm tree and the negroid features suggest an African setting, which would align with the myths that made Libya Lamia's home (see below). The scholiast on *Ecclesiazusae* 77 tells us that Crates wrote a comedy called *Lamia;* scholars have suggested that the vase illustrates a scene from this or another satyr play about Lamia. (We know that Euripides, too, wrote a play about her; this would be slightly later than the lekythos, but bespeaks her popularity as a dramatic subject.[28])

Like her ugliness and dirtiness, Lamia's bisexuality obviously runs counter to the standard of the desirable woman. Moreover, as a sexual hybrid, Lamia is disconcerting in a way that she never could be as simply an ugly woman—or an ugly man—because she

---

[24] Aristophanes names the thieving woman's husband "Lamias"; one of the thief's friends asks whether the club she stole is the same one as her husband had when he farted.

[25] Lekythos in the National Museum of Athens, inv. 1129; discussed most recently by M. Halm-Tisserant ("Folklore et Superstition en Grèce Classique: Lamia Torturée?" *Kernos* 2 [1989]: 67-82), who cites the previous scholarship. The first to propose that the vase showed Lamia was M. Mayer, *Jahrbuch des Deutschen archäologischen Instituts* 7 (1892): 201.

[26] This feature first was noticed by Halm-Tisserant, p. 76. The paint on this portion of the vase is damaged, but incised lines still show the phallus. A satyr holds a torch just under the phallus.

[27] The modern Greek Lamia has monstrously large breasts (or else one monstrously large breast): B. Schmidt, *Das Volksleben der Neugriechen* (Leipzig: Teubner, 1871), 134.

[28] Frg. 922 Nauck = Diod. Sic. 20.41.6: τίς τοὐμὸν ὄνομα τοὐπονείδιστον βροτοῖς // οὐκ οἶδε Λαμίας τῆς Λιβυστικῆς γένος;

refuses to fit neatly into either of the sexual taxa. Shape-shifting
and partial theriomorphism, two other traits that, as was discussed
above, work to strand demons between taxa, frequently are associated with the Greek child-killing demon as well. Mormo is described
by the poetess Erinna as "having a face that changes constantly";
several ancient sources credit Empousa with the ability to turn
herself into various animals.[29] All of the child-killing demons were,
according to their myths, once women, and sometimes are portrayed as having retained human traits. Yet Lamia and Empousa
also are called *thêria*.[30] Empousa frequently is said to have the legs
of an ass, as is Mormo once.[31] Mormo's common alternative
name, *mormolukê*, implies a female werewolf; in the quotation
that opened this article, Theocritus associates Mormo with the
horse. Erinna's description of Mormo as "having big ears" and
"running around on all fours" would accord with either the wolf or
the horse. The *strix,* with which the Greeks were acquainted at least
as early as the first century BCE and probably earlier, frequently is
pictured as part woman and part owl or other bird of prey, a trait
that other Greek child-killing demons subsequently display: *lamiai*
are shown as birds in a fifth-century CE mosaic; several Byzantine
sources describe *gelloudes* as flying. The Greek association of
child-killing demons with nocturnal birds of prey is hinted at in a
myth that goes back at least to the sixth-century poetess Corinna:
the infanticidal Minyads become a νυκτερίς, a γλαῦξ and a βύξα
(or a κορώνη).[32]

---

[29] Erinn. *Distaff* 25-27; Ar. *Ran.* 288 ff. and scholiast on 293; D 18.130; Philostr. *VA* 2.4; Idomeneus of Lampsacus (fourth century BCE) = *FGrH* 338 F 2;
Lucian *Salt.* 19; Eust. ad *Od.* 4.401 and 460 (= pp. 1503.2 and 1504.62).

[30] Lamia: Nic. frg. 51 (Ant. Lib. 8), schol. E on Ar. *Vesp.* 1035, Diod. Sic.
20.41.2-6. Empousa: Ar. *Ran.* 288 ff.

[31] Empousa: Ps.-Plut. *Vit.Par.* 29 (312 E); schol. Ar. *Ec.* 1048 and *Ran.* 293,
294 and 296; Eustat. ad *Od.* 11.634 (1704.42); *Et. Mag.* s.v. ὀνόπολη. At Ar. *Ran.*
295 she is said to have a leg made of (or smeared with?) dung, which the scholiast specifically tells us was βολίτινον ὄνειον; this may have been a spoof of her
well known characteristic (cf. Waser, "Empusa," *PW,* 5.2 col. 2542). One of the
animals whose form she assumes in this scene is the ass. Mormo: schol. Aristid. p.
41 Dindorf.

[32] *Striges:* A. S. Scobie, "Strigiform Witches in Roman and Other Cultures,"
Fabula 19 (1978): 74-101; S. M. Oliphant, "The Story of the Strix," *TAPA* 44
and 45 (1913 and 1914): 133-49 and 49-63. *Lamiai:* a mosaic from Pesaro shows
two birds with human heads wearing Phrygian caps; the inscription reads
"LAMIE" (illustrated and discussed in G. Weicker, *Der Seelenvogel* [Leipzig:
Teubner, 1902], 33 and 208). *Gelloudes* as birds: e.g., Joannes Damascenus
(Migne, *PG* 94, 1064); Psellus, ap. Allatius, section 3. Byzantine *gelloudes* as
shape shifters in general, M. Gaster, "Two Thousand Years of a Charm Against

We can do more than simply note that such examples of theriomorphism situate the demons between taxa. Let us briefly consider the possible origins and, following Stewart's lead, the significance, of the four animals whose traits the child-killer borrows in extant sources: the bird of prey, the horse, the wolf and the ass.

The bird of prey: Lamashtu almost always is shown on amuletic plaques with the forelegs and claws of a bird of prey, and sometimes with wings, as well. Lilith, too, often is pictured with the features of an owl or other bird of prey.[33] However, we must not leap to the conclusion that the Greek demon owes her avian characteristics to the Eastern ones. Child-killing demons are associated with birds of prey—and particularly with nocturnal raptors such as the owl—not only in other areas of the Mediterranean basin but in many other parts of the world as well.[34] Moreover, many other types of Mediterranean demons have avian features—the Greek Harpies and Sirens, for example, are commonly represented as birds.[35] The association is logical: raptors—especially nocturnal raptors—are swift and unusually silent. It seems likely that any culture exposed to owls and their kin would come to associate them with the sudden sorts of illnesses and deaths that the demons were believed to inflict.

The horse: In Greece, the horse was strongly associated with Poseidon, a dark and marginal god, a god of the frightening sea and destructive earthquake.[36] According to myth and cultic tradition,

the Child-Stealing Witch," *Folklore* 11 (1900): 129-62. On the various versions of the myth of the Minyads' transformation, see W. Burkert, *Homo Necans*, trans. Peter Bing (1972; Eng. trans. Berkeley: University of California, 1983), 174-79.

[33] Reproductions or discussions of plaques that show Lamashtu with the feet and forelegs of a bird can be found in the articles cited below in notes 40, 60 and 63; one particularly good source of drawings is H. Klengel, "Neue Lamashtu-Amulette aus dem Vorderasiatischen Museum zu Berlin und dem British Museum," *Mitteilungen des Instituts für Orientforschung* 7 (1959/60): 334-55. On Lilith and other Near Eastern child-killing demons as birds of prey see Scholem, "Lilith," col. 246.

[34] See the survey by Scobie, "Strigiform," although his tendency to see all or most such beliefs as having their origin in the ancient Near East seems to me incorrect; and Gaster, "Canaanite," 45-48.

[35] Weicker, *Seelenvogel,* is still a useful survey of Greek and Roman examples of bird demons, and includes some other Mediterranean types. L. Malten, "Das Pferd im Totenglauben," *Jahrbuch des Deutschen Archäologischen Instituts* 29 (1914): 179-256, includes a discussion of Greek and Roman bird-like demons (pp. 239-50).

[36] Stories that made Lamia the mother of the sea monster Skylla (Stes. frg. 220

Medusa and Erinys (or Demeter-Erinys) each assumed the shape of a mare to become the consorts of Poseidon, and subsequently bore him the foals Pegasus and Areion.[37] At one time, Erinys and Medusa may have been chthonic goddesses with beneficent as well as maleficent sides, but from Homer onwards they represent the grim, horrific and threatening aspects of the chthonic world— appropriate mates and mothers for horses. It is true that, particularly when ridden, the horse can be a positive icon for the Greeks,[38] but its connection with the child-killing demon surely draws, instead, upon these darker and more violent connotations.

The wolf: It is scarcely necessary to comment on the significance of the wolf, an animal that still loomed as a threatening predator of both flocks and humans in Europe until quite recently. It was an animal that the Greeks particularly "liked to think with"; the wolf frequently was set in opposition to all that represented civilized culture, the story of Lykaon's cannibalistic feast being a famous example.[39] What does require some comment, perhaps, is the relationship between the *"mormo"* and the *"lukê"* of "Mormolukê." "Mormolukê" typically has been understood by modern scholars as simply a longer version of the name "Mormo," a version that delivers more information about the nature of the creature; the implication is that Mormo was a female werewolf. This causes problems for our understanding of Theocritus's description of Mormo as a horse. The key is to remember that "Mormo" began as a descriptive term—"the frightening one." The fact that no myth for Mormo survives, except one that seemingly was borrowed from Lamia and Medea (see note 14 above), suggests that "Mormo," in contrast to "Lamia" or "Gello," remained a

---

Campbell = schol. Ap. Rh. 4.828) and the daughter of Poseidon himself (Plut. *Pyth. Orac.* 398 C; Paus. 10.12.1; Clem. Al. *Strom.* 1.15.70) similarly linked the demon to the frightening, marginal area of the sea. In Byzantine traditions, the child-killing demon (usually called Gello) is chased to or found near the sea. See the stories collected by Gaster, "Two Thousand."

[37] Discussion of Poseidon and his hippomorphic consorts at S. I. Johnston, "Xanthus, Hera and the Erinyes," *TAPA* 122 (1992): 83-98, with notes to ancient sources and earlier secondary works. On Poseidon and the horse more generally, see W. Burkert, *Greek Religion*, trans. John Raffen (1977; Eng. trans. Oxford: Basil Blackwell, 1985), 138 with notes.

[38] S. I. Johnston, "Riders in the Sky: Cavalier Gods and Theurgic Salvation in the Second Century CE," *CP* 87 (1992): 303-21, esp. section 2.

[39] For a survey of the wolf's associations in ancient Greece, see Richard Buxton, "Wolves and Werewolves in Greek Thought," in J. Bremmer, ed., *Interpretations of Greek Mythology* (London and Sydney: Croonhelm, 1987), 60-79.

generic label for any frightening, child-killing demon, rather than becoming the name of a distinct entity. Given this—and given that demonological beliefs and iconography *must* remain fluid to serve any function—it is no surprise that "Mormo" could be conceived now as lupine, now as equine. We should remember, too, that Erinna described Mormo as changing constantly from one form to another. This expresses the disorienting, hybrid quality of a shape-shifter, but at the same time attests to a basic uncertainty as to which of many "four-legged creature with big ears" Mormo would choose to imitate. Perhaps in a given area, "Mormo" was associated primarily with one animal; the fact that the use of *"mormolukê"* before the Roman period is restricted to Athenian authors suggests that in Attica, she typically was imagined as part wolf. Elsewhere—perhaps in Sicily, Theocritus's home?—she typically may have been part horse. The paraphrase employed by the scholiast on Theocritus *Idyll* 15.40, "ἡ μορμὼ ἵππος δάκνει" (quoted in full in note 1) brings us very close to an imagined "Mormippos" indeed.

The ass: In contrast to the bird of prey, the horse and the wolf, the ass is not usually a demonic animal in ancient Greece or any-where else—worldwide, it typically has been associated with harm-less stupidity and stubbornness. There are two exceptions to this rule. The first is the familiar association of the ass with Egyptian Seth or Typhon. It is possible that this worked to confirm an existing association between the ass and Empousa, but it does not seem likely to have been the origin of Empousa's asinine traits. The second exception is more enticing, for it is Lamashtu. La-mashtu is often shown with ass's teeth and ass's ears on amuletic plaques, and these ears and teeth also are mentioned in ritual texts. Once, she is said to have an "ass's form." Once, she is adjured to "go away, like a savage ass!" Body parts of asses can be used in amulets against Lamashtu, which may be a case of *similia similibus* (see below).[40] It is tempting to trace Empousa's asininity back to Lamashtu, but the fact that it most often is expressed specifically by making Empousa's *feet or legs* asinine is problematic. Feet and legs are not among the parts of Lamashtu that are labelled or

---

[40] W. Farber, "Lamashtu," *Reallexikon der Assyriologie* 6 (Berlin and New York: de Gruyter, 1980-83), 44; Klengel, "Neue," *passim* ; Jean Nougayrol, "La Lamashtu a Ugarit," in *Ugaritica VI*, vol. 17 (Paris: Collège de France, 1969), 393-408, esp. 396; David W. Myhrman, "Die Labartu-Texte," *ZA* 16 (1902): 141-95, esp. 148 and 181.

shown as asinine in our sources; indeed, as noted above, Lamashtu usually has the feet and legs of a bird.[41]

Empousa's asininity must be interpreted with reference to another, and probably more dominant, aspect of her personality. As in many other cultures, the Greek child-killer not only was thought to attack infants and pregnant women, but also to seduce and then destroy young men. Thus, for example, when Empousa appears to Xanthias and Dionysus in the *Frogs,* she manifests herself, *inter alia,* as a beautiful girl (line 290). The lecherous old woman of Aristophanes' *Ecclesiazusae* (line 1056) is called an *empousa.* The demon that attempts to seduce a young philosopher in Philostratus' *Vita Apollonii* several times is called an *empousa*; Philostratus twice calls her a *lamia* and once a *mormolukia* as well (*VA* 4.25).

This combination of functions—seducing men and harming children—has survived today in the demons believed to inhabit the Greek countryside. Stewart discusses the fact that many of these demons are thought to look normal on top, but to have lower limbs that are defective in some way. Thus, modern *lamiai* are beautiful women with the legs or feet of an ass, or sometimes of a goat or cow. *Neraïdes* are said to have a single ass-leg or foot, or to have abnormally and displeasingly long legs. Modern *striges* have legs or feet that are turned backwards.

Stewart notes that feet and legs have erotic connotations in contemporary Greek thought, and suggests that the defectiveness of the demons' legs and feet, therefore, symbolizes the bestiality or perversity of their sexual conduct—such demons do not behave as "good" women should, sexually and reproductively.[42] Could we apply Stewart's interpretation to Empousa, too? This solution becomes appealing when we recall that the ancient Greeks associated both male and female asses not only with stupidity and stubborness, as many other cultures do, but also with excessive lust and extraordinary sexual ability. An illustration of this connection

---

[41] In the upper right-hand corner of amulets to avert Lamashtu there frequently appears a drawing of an ass's hoof and foreleg. This may represent some sort of offering, however, as do all of the other drawings that are distributed around the plaques (e.g., drawings of spindles, combs, fibulae). Some ritual texts promise Lamashtu an ass on which she can travel away from her victim; the foot and foreleg would be a convenient way of representing an entire animal that might be difficult to inscribe at small scale. Alternatively, as Erica Reiner has suggested to me, the drawing may allude to the use of fetlocks in ritual aversions and purifications. See, for example, a first-millennium spell recorded by R. Caplice, "Namburi Texts in the British Museum," *Orientalia* 40.2 (1971): 145 (line 46).

[42] Stewart, *Demons,* 180-83.

occurs already in Semonides' sixth-century BCE poem on women: god created different types of women from different animals; each displays the characteristics of its ancestor. The woman born of an "ash-grey ass . . . takes on any man when it comes to sex" (frg. 7.48-49). In Lucian's parody of the *Odyssey,* some sailors meet beautiful, ass-legged demons who intend to seduce and then consume them while they sleep (*Ver. Hist.* 2.46). The ass-legged demon who appears to Solomon in the *Testament* (line 1320) has the form of a beautiful woman above the knees; she, too, specializes in seducing and then devouring men. (As for the male ass's sexuality, I need mention only the mythic contest between Priapus and a male ass to determine which was the better endowed representative of his gender—a contest that Priapus lost.)[43] It is likely that Empousa's asinine legs and feet were intended to express her role as a seductress, rather than her role as child-killer, which in any case is less prominent in our sources.

Having analyzed the animals with which the demons are associated, we now might turn to the geographical and genealogical associations of one of them: Lamia. In one late source (schol. Ar. *Pax* 758), Lamia is called not the daughter of Poseidon, as she is in Plutarch (*Pyth. Orac.* 398 C), Pausanias (10.12.1) and Clement (*Strom.* 1.15.70), but the daughter of Belos; Burkert took this as an indication that the Greeks themselves recognized her Eastern origins, as "Belos" is a Hellenized form of the Babylonian "Baal". It seems more likely to me, however, that "Belos" functioned here as it does elsewhere in Greek myth—as a stop-gap name in foreign genealogies. In addition to Belos-the-father-of-Lamia, there was, for example, a mythological Belos who was the king of Tyre, a third of Lydia, a fourth of Persia and a fifth of Egypt.[44] All that "Belos" tells us about Lamia, in other words, is that the Greeks wanted to situate her outside their realm of normalcy and civilization. Similarly, Lamia usually is said to have come from Libya;[45]

---

[43] Contest with Priapus: Lact. *De Fals. Relig.* 1.22, *cf.* Hyg. 33. According to several sources, asses were sacrificed to Priapus: Ov. *F.* 1.391 and 440, 6.345; Lact. *Div. Inst.* 1.21; Myth. Vat. 3.6.26. Pindar *P.* 10.36 describes the asses which are sacrificed to Hyperborean Apollo as having "upright wantonness" (ὕβρις ὀρθία). Further on the ass as a symbol for lasciviousness or sexual prowess at Olck, "Esel," *PW,* 6.1 cols. 634-35. The ass-legged demon of *Test. Sol.* appears in many other demonological treatises; see Preisendanz, "'Ονοσκελίς," *PW,* 18.1 cols. 523-24.

[44] H. J. Rose, "Belus," *OCD,* 165.

[45] E. frg. 922 Nauck; Diod. Sic. 20.41, 3-5; cf. Duris ap. *FGrH* 76 F 17 = Phot. and Suid. s.v. Lamia; schol. Δ on Ar. *Vesp.* 1035 and Apostol. ap. Leutsch *Paroim. Gr.* 2.497-98; schol. Aristid. p. 41 Dindorf. Paus. 10.12.1 makes her the

Libya and other African lands usually function in myth as barbarian lands at the borders of the known world, far removed both geo-graphically and culturally from the civilized world of the Greeks.[46] The Greeks also portrayed *lamiai* as dwelling in the wild areas of their own landscapes—the woods, the glades (D.H. *Th.* 6). Analo-gously, Lamashtu is called a "foreigner" and is said to dwell in the swamps or mountains. Egyptian child-killers are believed to come out of Asia.[47]

The names of the child-killing demons also have been examined by scholars with a view to the East. Most recently, Burkert and West have suggested that "Gello" looks back to the Sumerian-Akkadian "Gallû," one type of Underworld demon. Some caution is necessary here, however, for "Gallû" denotes an all-purpose sort of *male* demon held responsible for a wide variety of problems and "Gello" a *female* demon with a very specific role. The relationship between them, if any, is thus limited strictly to a linguistic bor-rowing. It cannot be used to account for any of Gello's defining traits or her significance among the Greeks. Burkert, West and others also have suggested that "Lamia" was a development from "Lamashtu." But the scholiast on Aristophanes' *Wasps* 1035 and many modern scholars suggest that "Lamia" is derived from the same root as Greek words for "gullet" (*laimos* and *lamos*), and thus means something such as "She who swallows down" (discussed at Schwenn, "Lamia" *PW,* 12.1 col. 544; cf. Hor. *A.P.* 340 and the use of "lamia" to indicate a type of voracious shark at Arist. *HA* 540b18); the king of the cannibalistic Laestrygonians similarly is named "Lamos." "Lamia" probably began as an appellative noun that was later capitalized, so to speak, into a personal name, as in the case with many demonic names (e.g., "Harpy" from *"harpazein"*).[48]

---

mother, by Zeus, of the Libyan sibyl.

[46] A different idea is expressed by the scholium to Theoc. 15.40, which makes Lamia the queen of the cannibalistic Laestrygonians (although this surely draws on the fact that in *Od.* 10.81 and thereafter, "Lamos" is king of the Laestrygoni-ans).

[47] Myhrman, "Labartu," esp. 147-48; Erman, *Zaubersprüche,* 14, 22, 24, 41.

[48] Burkert, *Orientalizing,* and West, "Gello"; both cite earlier proponents. For further arguments against the derivation of Gello from Gallû, see E. Ebeling, "Dämonen," *Reallexikon der Assyriologie* 2 (Berlin and Leipzig: 1938), 109. The *Chicago Assyrian Dictionary* (G 19b) notes that the term "gallû" originally denoted a police official. I am grateful to JoAnn Scurlock for helpful discussions and letters concerning the nature of the Mesopotamian demons.

Having reached the end of our survey of the Greek child-killing demon's traits, I note that we have been able to interpret them without recourse to Near Eastern precedents. Instead, most of the traits have been shown to accord well with the premises that a society marginalizes that which is undesirable by labelling it demonic, and then further marginalizes the demonic by attaching to it other marginal traits such as bimorphism. Other traits are logical, for example, her associations with the bird of prey. Recent work, some of it by Burkert and some by other scholars represented in this volume, has argued persuasively that *ritual techniques* travelled extensively and easily around the Mediterranean basin in antiquity—with this premise, I strongly agree. But I hesitate to assume that demonic traits can travel as easily. Beliefs that express a culture's fears and desires, as demonological beliefs do, are more deeply embedded in that culture's cognitive map than are *technai*. Moreover, whereas new *technai* can be used in concert with old—can supplement the old—beliefs often cannot be. A new belief must either align closely with an old one—in which case it cannot be so new—or displace it completely. To seek *analogies* for Greek demonological beliefs within other cultures can be profitable in that comparisons sometimes point out to us certain features that would otherwise go unnoticed. But when we seek *genealogies* for them within other cultures, we usually will be on shakier ground, and will fail to reach conclusions that shed much light on Greek beliefs themselves.

*   *   *

Here I will survey techniques for averting the demons I have just described. It will be seen that, as was the case with most demonically-induced problems, aversion techniques existed from early times, but additional, foreign techniques subsequently were adopted, too.[49]

---

[49] In addition to the spells and amulets I discuss here, which are directed against demons, we also possess spells and amulets intended to protect the mother, fetus and newborn child against problems of unspecified origin; I will not discuss these because of constraints of space. In some cases, the intent of these spells seems to be a realignment of the woman's body (e.g., those to retain a "wandering womb") or some other sympathetic act (e.g., *PGM* 123 a 50). Discussion in J.-J. Aubert, "Threatened Wombs: Aspects of Ancient Uterine Magic," *GRBS* 30.3 (1989): 421-49 and A. A. Barb, "Diva Matrix," *Journal of the Warburg and Courtauld Institute* 16 (1953): 193-238.

Most of the archaic and classical information that we have about the aversion of these demons is allusive rather than descriptive, but we can say that the techniques are similar to other Greek magical practices; thus, plants and incantations are used frequently. When, in the *Homeric Hymn to Demeter,* Demeter describes how she will protect Demophon from demonic attack that brings many ills (ἐπηλυσίη πολυπήμων)[50] and, specifically, from a mysterious demonic force called "the undercutter" or "plant-cutter" (ὑποταμνόν, ὑλοτόμον), she says that she knows of an ἀντίτομον ("counter-cut," i.e., "counter-root" or "counter-plant") greater than the ὑποτάμνον or ὑλοτόμον and, more generally, that she knows an excellent means of averting such problems (ἐσθλὸν ἐρυσμόν) (lines 227-30):

θρέψω, κοὔ μιν ἔολπα κακοφραδίῃσι τιθήνης
οὔτ' ἄρ' ἐπηλυσίη δηλήσεται οὔθ' ὑποτάμνον·
οἶδα γὰρ ἀντίτομον μέγα φέρτερον ὑλοτόμοιο,
οἶδα δ' ἐπηλυσίης πολυπήμονος ἐσθλὸν ἐρυσμόν.

I will nurse him, nor do I expect that either a demonic attack or the "undercutter" will harm him due to his nurse's negligence; for I know a great antidote root, stronger than the "plant-cutter," and I know an excellent defence against the demonic attack that brings many ills.

Ἐρυσμόν is cognate with ἔρυμα, which suggests that it describes an object that was used as a "defense" against something. Like ἀντίτομον, it probably refers to a specific plant that Demeter will wield to protect the child, for in the only other place where it occurs, in later Greek, it is a name for a plant whose seeds are swallowed by women experiencing difficult labor.[51] As noted above, the same demons were thought to attack infants as attacked pregnant and parturient women; the same means of aversion, logically, could therefore be employed to protect the woman and the child.[52] Lines 227-30 of the Hymn noticeably echo magical incantations

---

[50] Discussion of ἐπηλυσίη as demonic attack in N. J. Richardson, ed., trans. and comm., *The Homeric Hymn to Demeter* (Oxford: Clarendon Press, 1974), 229-30; cf. *h.Merc.* 37.

[51] Paus. grammaticus frg. 182. *Cf.* "ἐρύθμος," a plant that also was called "ἐφιάλτον," and that was used to avert attacks of the demon Ephialtes.

[52] Cf. the hanging of buckthorn around doors and windows to avert *striges* in Roman magic: Ov. *F.* 6.101 ff; Phot. s.v. *rhamnos.* Psellus, ap. Leo Allatius, *de Graecorum* sections ii and iv (= K. N. Sathas, *Mesaionikê Bibliothekê* [Paris: 1876], 5.572-78) reports that in antiquity, herbs and other plants were hung in the labor room and nursery to avert demons.

in their chiasmus,[53] which suggests that Demeter may have employed chanted spells as well, similar to the one handed down by Festus (see below). Socrates described midwives as using *epaoidiai* to insure successful birth (Pl. *Theat.* 149 c-d), and in the *Phaedo* 77e, he tells Cebes that a child's fear of *mormolukeia* can be charmed away (ἐξεπᾴσητε) by the singing of spells (ἐπᾴδειν).

The more detailed aversion spells recorded in post-classical sources, like much Greco-Roman magic, show the influence of Egyptian and Near Eastern practices. Aetite, or "eagle stone," which is mentioned in several sources, is an interesting case in point. The *Kyranides,* a list of the magical properties of animals and plants that was compiled in Greek during the Imperial Age, says that, when worn, aetite protects the child in the womb and will not allow it to be miscarried (3.1.91-93). The Damigeron-Evax *lithica,* which probably was composed in the first century BCE, tells us that aetite prevents premature labor and then, when the proper time has arrived, facilitates parturition (1.5-7). "Aetite" was and still is the name of a hollow stone in which another, smaller stone is trapped—a special type of geode. The symbolism is obvious: a "pregnant stone" protects pregnant women. The *lithica* goes on to say that aetite also protects infants and young girls: "Amplius infantes et puellas conservat ... Limphaticisque et terroribus nefandis efficit ut nec visa somnientur nec frequenter cadant," "It greatly protects babies and young girls. ... it is efficacious against frenzies and unspeakable terrors so that neither will they be seen in dreams nor occur frequently" (1.13-15). The "nightmares" brought on by terrors sound like a rationalistic explanation for what folk belief would call the attacks of child-killing demons, who typically struck while the child was asleep. Aetite's use to protect children against such attacks probably was secondary to its obstetrical use, but such an extension is logical, when we recall that, in Greek belief, the same demons who attacked the pregnant mothers attacked the children.

We also know that aetite was used in Near Eastern obstetrical and pediatric magic. Because the logic behind aetite's obstetrical use seems obvious, we might presume that its deployment in each place developed independently.[54] The Greeks and Romans had

---

[53] Richardson, *Demeter*, 229. Also P. Maas, "ΕΠΕΝΙΚΤΟΣ," *Hesperia* 13.1 (1944): 36-37; *ibid.*, "The Phillina Papyrus," *JHS* 62 (1942): 33-34.

[54] On the Near Eastern uses of aetite—and its use in European obstetrics well into the seventeenth century—see A. A. Barb, "Birds and Medical Magic," *Journal of the Warburg and Courtauld Institute* 13 (1950): 316-22. Also, R. Campbell Thompson, *Dictionary of Assyrian Chemistry and Geology* (Oxford:

great difficulty explaining why they called the stone what they did, however. Pliny provided three different explanations, the most far-fetched being that the stone is the same color as an eagle's tail (*HN* 37§187; cf. 10§12 and 36§149; cf. further explanations in Barb, "Birds"). The real source of the name probably lies, as Barb suggested, in the fact that the Assyrian name for this stone was "aban eri." "Eru" can mean either "pregnant" or "eagle"; the Assyrians themselves punned upon this fact by making the eagle the means by which a mythical pregnancy drug was carried to a woman.[55] It seems likely that the Greeks first learned of aetite's obstetrical uses from Eastern sources and, when they adopted the stone, also adopted and translated the name. Whether the pediatric uses were associated with it already in the East, or were, rather, Greek additions, is unclear.

Other stones mentioned in the Greek *lithica* can be explained without recourse to the East; I describe only one here. Galactite was to be hung around the neck of a newborn to ward off the eyes of evil-planning "Megaira"; another *lithica* similarly says that galactite protects the infant from the "horrida mulier" who seeks to sap his strength; both "Megaira" (the "Begrudger") and "horrida mulier" would seem to refer to our child-killing demon.[56] These uses of galactite may have grown from galactite's other, less sensational uses in obstetrical and pediatric magic and medicine, where the logic behind the stone's use is self-evident: this stone that extrudes a milky-white liquid when it is soaked in water[57] was thought to increase the milk of herd animals such as goats and sheep and also of women. Perhaps it was believed that the same sort of demon that would obstruct milk also would obstruct delivery and attack the nursing child; perhaps the original, specifically associative values of the stone were forgotten, and galactite simply became a kind of stone that helped new mothers and babies, applied in a variety of situations.[58]

1936), 104-08.

[55] Barb, "Birds," 317-18.

[56] Orphic *lithica* 224-25, cf. Orphei *lithica kerygmata* 2.4 which says that it protects babies from *phthonos,* sickness and attacks. The *lithica* of Damigeron-Evax 34.21-28 says that a woman who is having trouble delivering should tie galactite to her right thigh with the wool of a fecund sheep.

[57] Orph. lith. 201-03 and other sources as given in the notes to Halleux and Schamp's edition.

[58] See also "lychnites" at *lithica* of Damigeron-Evax 28, *cf.* Psellus *Lap.* 13, p. 203; and "lynguros" at *lithica* of Damigeron-Evax 31; cf. Pliny *HN* 37§34 and

According to the *Kyranides*, Gello and other *nukterina synthêmata* could be averted either by wearing around the arm an amulet made of eyes taken from a living hyena and wrapped in a purple rag, or by sleeping on an ass's hide.[59] The amulet made of hyena's eyes probably played on the idea that the eyes of a nocturnal, sharp-sighted animal could avert the evil eye of a god or demon—*similia similibus*. Certainly, the hyena played an important role in Greco-Roman magic by the time of Pliny, who records a number of uses for hyena's body parts; a hyena's tooth, like its eyes, could avert night terrors and ghosts (*nocturnos pavores umbrarumque terrorem*), and skin from its forehead could avert the evil eye. The hyena was particularly useful in obstetrical and pediatric situations, judging from Pliny's remarks: *inter alia,* miscarriage could be averted by wearing white flesh from a hyena tied up in a gazelle skin with seven hyena hairs and a stag's penis (*HN* 28§27; cf. 28§29). Notably, the hyena is found throughout southwest Asia and northeast Africa but not at all in Europe; Greek and Roman authors most likely borrowed and adapted spells involving hyena parts from either Near Eastern or Egyptian sources. The author of the *Kyranides* or his source probably inserted the name of a child-killing demoness—Gello—with which he was familiar into a spell designed for obstetrical and pediatric problems in general.

Asses' bones and blood are familiar to us from the magical papyri; occasionally, we also encounter an ass's hide, used as a substitute for the papyrus on which a spell is to be written. Like the hyena, it also is an animal frequently encountered in the 28th book of Pliny's *Historia Naturalis* (see especially §77), and like the hyena, it has several obstetrical and pediatric uses. For example, an ass's liver, worn as an amulet, protects babies from epileptic fits, and an ass's hide protects sleeping babies from fears (*fecit infantes inpavidos*); this looks like a rationalized account of our spell against Gello from the *Kyranides* (*HN* 28§78). It probably is correct to explain most uses of ass parts in the magical papyri with reference to the asinine form of Seth-Typhon, for most of them draw on Egyptian sources. It is probable that this significance of the ass eventually became more broadly applied, too, so that it became a sort of all-purpose demonic animal, and its body parts became all-purpose amulets, *similia similibus*. Yet, in the case of

---

37§51 and Epiphanius, *de xii gemmis* 8, p. 197 Ruelle, and note 11 above.
[59] 2.31.20-23, 2. 40.35-38.

our spell to avert Gello, and perhaps in the case of some other obstetrical and pediatric uses of ass parts described by Pliny, we might look to techniques used against Lamashtu for precedent. A Mesopotamian practitioner seeking to avert Lamashtu from mother and child would take hair from the right side of a male ass, hair from the left side of a female ass and hair from an unspecified part of an ass foal. He would combine it with an insect and hang them in a bundle around the neck of the potential victim.[60]

I will finish this survey of aversion techniques with an iambic chant recorded by the second-century CE grammarian Festus, who gives the first-century BCE Verrius Flaccus as his source:

> Go away strix, you night-wandering one;
> go away from the people,
> you bird whose name is not to be mentioned.
> Go away upon swift ships.[61]

Clearly, as Weinreich[62] and others have pointed out, this is a variation of the *"apopompe"* or *"pheuge"* spells well known from other Greek and Roman sources, in which abstract evils such as hunger and famine, or animals that seem to represent diseases— dogs, wolves and beetles for example—are exorcised. But this passage is unusual in that it tells the demon to go away onto the *ship*. Rituals from the old, middle and new Babylonian periods (approx. 1750-600 BCE) attempted to send Lamashtu away by means of a ship, a donkey or both. The rituals involved dedicating small clay ships and/or donkeys to a statuette of Lamashtu, as well as provisions and gifts such as malt, food, water, spindles, sandals, fibulae and combs, which were supposed to keep her happy on her journey. Some ritual texts tell her to use the ship to "go across the river," which may mean the river that separated the land of the living from the land of the dead in Mesopotamian thought, or "go across the sea." This aversion ritual is reflected on amulets and plaques intended to keep Lamashtu away, which frequently show her standing either upon a ship or upon a donkey that itself stands on a ship, surrounded by the provisions and gifts that the worshipper has given.[63]

---

[60] Erle Lichty, "Demons and Population Control," *Expedition* 13.2 (1971): 22-26; Myhrman, "Labartu Texte," 151.

[61] Στρίγγ' ἀποπομπεῖν νυκτιβόαν, // στρίγγ' ἀπὸ λαῶν, // ὄρνιν ἀνωνύμιον / / ὠκυπόρους ἐπὶ νῆας. For the bibliography, see n. 11, above.

[62] Weinreich, *Gebet,* 10-20.

[63] An overview of the spells and plaques used to avert Lamashtu can be found in Farber, "Lamashtu." See also Nougayrol, "Lamashtu a Ugarit," esp. 397; H.

I suggest that the Greek spell's specific and unique command that the *strix* go away by means of ships reflects Greek acquaintance with the Lamashtu plaques and spells. Of all the ancient child-killers, it would have been particularly tempting to equate the *strix* with Lamashtu as she appears on the plaques, as one of her predominant iconographic traits there is that she—like a *strix*—has the legs and claws of a bird of prey.

Klengel, "Weitere Amulette gegen Lamashtu," *Mitteilungen des Instituts für Orientforschungen* 9 (1963): 24-29; B. Goldman, "The Asiatic Ancestry of the Greek Gorgon," *Berytus* 14 (1961): 1-23; F. Thureau-Dangin, "Rituel et Amulettes contre Labartu," *RA* 18 (1921): 161-98; Myhrman, "Labartu Texte." In Mesopotamian rituals, ghosts as well as Lamashtu are sent away in provisioned sailboats (J. A. Scurlock, "Magical Means of Dealing with Ghosts in Ancient Mesopotamia" [diss., University of Chicago, 1988], 32, 55, 64, 218, 235).

PART FIVE

MAGIC AND RITUAL POWER
IN ROMAN AND LATE ANTIQUITY

CHAPTER EIGHTEEN

SINGING AWAY SNAKEBITE: LUCAN'S MAGICAL CURES

Oliver Phillips

The Roman poet Lucan, who died in 65 CE as one of Nero's victims, has long entertained a reputation for his vivid, even bizarre, portrayal of magic. This reputation, however, largely rests on an episode of necromancy in the sixth book of his docu-drama epic about the Roman Civil War, the *Bellum ciuile* or the *Pharsalia*. In this striking segment of the poem—one of its longest episodes (*BC* 6.413-830)—Sextus, the unworthy son of the Optimate general Pompey, consults Erichto, the most notorious among the witches reputed to haunt Thessaly in northern Greece. The witch Erichto has been the subject of a number of concentrated studies, the most often cited probably one by A. Bourgery in 1928.[1] Bourgery limited himself to an intense examination of the necromancy in the sixth book and ignored other elements of magic in the epic. A fairly extensive progeny of studies has centered on or dealt in some measure with Erichto in the sixty-five years that have followed Bourgery.[2] Precisely this thorough treatment of one episode to the neglect or at least light treatment of another scene of magic in the epic persuaded me to look elsewhere in the poem.[3]

---

[1] "Lucain et la magie," *Revue des Etudes Latines* 6 (1928): 299-313.

[2] Anne-Marie Tupet gives a fairly detailed bibliography current up to 1974, along with a listing of some studies prior to Bourgery that he overlooked (*La magie dans la poésie latine I: Des origines à la fin du règne d'Auguste,* [Paris: Les Belles Lettres, 1976], 422-26). A more recent study by Richard Gordon also contains a fairly good summation of relevant bibliography up to the date of its publication ("Lucan's Erictho," *Homo Viator: Classical Essays for John Bramble,* eds. Michael Whitby, Philip Hardie, and Mary Whitby [Bristol: Bristol Classical Press, 1987; Oak Park: Bolchazy-Carducci, 1987], 231-41).

[3] W. R. Johnson remarks on the avoidance of the snake episode in "Lucan's strongest supporters" because it is "embarrassing" (*Momentary Monsters: Lucan and his Heroes,* Cornell Studies in Classical Philology 47, [Ithaca and London: Cornell University Press, 1987], 52). The subject is not really addressed at all by Mark P. O. Morford, though his book has a chapter on "Divination and Magic" (*The Poet Lucan: Studies in Rhetorical Epic* [Oxford: Blackwell, 1967], 59-74). Frederick M. Ahl deals with the snake episode twice, but the Psylli, who will become its final focus, as we shall see, are relegated to a

Consequently I have selected a long episode from the ninth book (*BC* 9.619-937) describing a westward march across North Africa undertaken by the Optimate politician, devotee of Stoicism, and army commander by default, the younger Cato, great-grandson of the more famous censor of the same name.   Following the account of Pompey's defeat at Pharsalus and assassination at Alexandria, described in the sixth and eighth books of the epic, Lucan tells how Cato undertook to rescue his cause's fortunes by leading troops westward across the Libyan desert from near Cyrene to the city of Leptis near Carthage.   After several preliminary passages Lucan recounts how Cato's army sets out across the sands with its commander on foot at the head of the column (*BC* 9.587-88).   The theme of poisonous serpents arises immediately as the army comes upon a water source infested by venomous snakes both on its banks and in the water itself (*BC* 9.607-10).   Cato, seeing that his troops fear that the snakes have transferred their toxin to the water (*BC* 9.611), assures them that the reptiles can poison only by injecting their venom into the bloodstream.   Further, he takes the first drink himself, an exception to his usual practice of drinking only after his troops have done so (*BC* 9.616-18).

To explain the presence of the snakes, Lucan recounts an etiological tale explaining how Africa came to have so many poisonous snakes.   When the Argive hero Perseus had cut off the Gorgon Medusa's head, blood dripped as the winged hero carried it homeward, and where the drops of blood fell, seventeen varieties of venomous snakes were born, all enumerated in detail (*BC* 9.619-733).

Now that Lucan is thoroughly warmed up to his subject, he turns to a series of baroque descriptions of the consequences of the bites of seven kinds of serpents.   He even gives the personal names of the soldiers bitten and sometimes their original homes (*BC* 9.734-838). This latter detail, as we shall see, will be in one instance of some relevance to our study.

The bite-ravaged army now feels despair, but just at this darkest moment in their fortunes hope arrives, as the following translation of Lucan's narrative will make clear:[4]

---

single note (*Lucan: an Introduction,* Cornell Studies in Classical Philology 39 [Ithaca and London: Cornell University Press, 1976], 72-74, 268-71, p. 271 n. 47).

[4] Translations throughout are my own.

At the last moment Fortune, herself wearied by such danger, brought aid to the miserable men. A nation uniquely immune to the savage bite of serpents inhabits these lands, the Marmarid Psylli. Their tongues are equal to powerful herbs, and their blood is secure and so powerful as not even to be affected by poison. The nature of the locale bade that they be unharmed though among serpents. They profited by placing their dwelling amid poison. They have made peace with death. So great is their confidence in their bloodline, that when a tiny infant falls to earth, out of apprehension that there is some admixture of foreign parentage, they test the questionable offspring with a fatal serpent.[5] . . . So the Psylli have proof of their offspring—any infant who has not shuddered at contact with snakes, any infant who has played with the serpents given him (is genuine). That race, content not only with their own welfare, watches out for strangers, and the Psyllan comes to everyone's aid against harmful monsters (*BC* 9.890-901, 906-11).

Lucan hereupon tells how the Psylli protect the Roman camp by fumigation, burning herbs, fragrant wood, and the horns of a stag to keep snakes away. While the plants and animal products protect the soldiers by night, for the hours of daylight, when they are on the march, they need help if bitten, and for this I return to a translation:

But if someone contracts mortal danger from a daytime misfortune, then take place the marvels of the magic race and the great battle of the Psylli with the poison that has been injected. First the Psyllan marks the limbs with a touch of his saliva, which restrains the venom and keeps it by the wound; then he rolls forth incantations with his frothing tongue in an unbroken murmur, and the progress of the wound does not grant a breathing space nor the approach of death allow the least silence. Often, in fact, the poison that has made its way to the blackened marrow flees when chanted over; but if any venom is reluctant to obey and resists when called forth and bidden to leave, then he bends over and licks the whitening wound with his mouth, drawing forth the venom. Then he dries the limbs with his teeth.[6] Moreover he successfully spits forth the fatal material that he has extracted from the chilly body; and the (other) Psyllans

---

[5] "Falls to earth" probably means simply "is born." Cf. *Iliad* 19.110 and our expression about "a mare dropping a foal."

[6] " . . . et siccat dentibus artus," perhaps meaning that the Psyllus removes the last of the venom from the wound or the surface of the sufferer's skin by pressure of his teeth.

readily recognize even by tasting (what the first Psyllan has spat out) which snake's bite it is he has overcome (*BC* 9.922-37).[7]

Once the Psylli have rescued the army, the poet abruptly terminates the journey at Leptis in a twelve-line epilogue (*BC* 9.938-49) and abandons Cato for the remainder of his incomplete epic, giving the impression that the colorful and colored events of the journey interested him much more than its goal.

Now we should examine several facets of the episode. First, who were the Psylli? Then, what were the antecedents of their snakebite treatment? Finally, why did Lucan regard the Psylli as magical?

In answer to the first question, Lucan's magical snake-charming Psylli, inhabitants of the Libyan desert, should have long since been extinct, according to the earliest account of them in Herodotus.[8] The fifth-century BCE historian has one of his most curious stories to tell of them, which I translate in its entirety:

> The Psylli are neighbors to the Nasamonians. They (the Psylli) perished in the following way. The south wind blew on them and dried up all their reservoirs of water. Their whole country, lying inside the Syrtes (sandy shoals on the North African shore), was waterless. They took counsel and by a common decision marched out in battle array against the south wind (—I'm telling you what the Libyans say!—), and when they were in the sand, the south wind blew and covered them. Since they perished, the Nasamonians possess the country (*Hist.* 4.173.1-8).

You will note that Herodotus does not connect them with snake charming. His account (in spite of the present-tense "*are* neighbors to the Nasamonians" in its first line) implies that he regarded them as no longer in existence.

But within two centuries of Herodotus we begin to find writers who regard them as still around, and almost every one of these

---

[7] The startling and unappetizing interpretation of the last two lines of Lucan's passage as indicated by the words in parentheses derives from A. E. Housman's critical apparatus to line 936 in his edition of the *Bellum ciuile* (1927, reprint; Oxford: Blackwell, 1950) and is now generally accepted.

[8] Hecataeus, a predecessor of Herodotus, spoke of the Psyllic Gulf of Libya (Felix Jacoby, *Die Fragmente der griechischen Historiker, I: Genealogie und Mythographie* [Leiden: E. J. Brill, 1957], fr. 332). No explicit indication survives that he mentioned the Psylli or their dealings with snakes, though Lionel Pearson claims that Herodotus used wording "very probably taken directly from the *Periegesis*" (*Early Ionian Historians* [Oxford: Oxford University Press, 1939], 91).

subsequent writers connects them with snake charming.[9]   The
major Hellenistic work on snakes, a didactic poem by Nicander, the
Theriaca, the "beast-lore" book, to be sure has nothing about the
Psylli in its extensive discussion of treatment of snakebite, but a
fragment of another work by this same second-century BCE writer
gives the basic notion of the Psylli that became widespread in the
ancient world:

> I have heard that in Libya the race of the Psylli themselves does not suffer
> at all from moldering bites of beasts, (the Psylli) whom beast-nourishing
> Syrtis feeds, and they aid also other people suffering from bites, not work-
> ing by roots of herbs, but by contact with their limbs (frg. apud Aristo-
> phanes Gramm. 32 1).[10]

The first-century BCE Roman scholar Varro adds the next element to our knowledge of the ancient beliefs about the Psylli. He
likens them to another snake-handling race, the Ophiogeneis of
Asia Minor, whose very name means "snake-born." He tells the
story that Lucan repeats, that these two peoples test the legitimacy of their children by allowing them contact with poisonous
snakes (*Antiquitates* 1.2.1).   A poet contemporary with Varro,
Gaius Helvius Cinna, whose works are lost except for fragments,
has left us a bit of a line about a Psyllus doing something to a
sleepy asp, the verb being lost (Cinna frg. apud Aulus Gellius
9.12.12.2). A more important poetic source comes in the generation following Caesar's death, this in the person of Aemilius
Macer, an older contemporary of Ovid.[11]   Ovid tells us in his
poetic review of his own life that Macer as an old man used to read
him a poem telling about "what serpent is harmful and what herb
helps" (*Tristia* 4.10.43). The "herb (that) helps" presumably helps
to treat snakebite, for we know that Macer did a verse adaptation
of Nicander's *Theriaca* into Latin, and he possibly moved the
Greek poet's reference to the Psylli into his rendering of the

---

[9] Aulus Gellius, to be sure, regards them as extinct, *Psyllos quondam fuisse
in terra Africa conterminos Nasamonibus* (16.11.3.4), but he clearly bases his
account entirely on Herodotus.

[10] Also quoted by Aelian, *Natura animalium* 16.28; frg. 32 in A. S. F. Gow
and A. F. Scholfield, *Nicander, the Poems and Poetical Fragments* (Cambridge:
University Press, 1953), 142.

[11] Initially noted in the late-ancient *Commenta bernensia,* ed. Hermann
Usener (Leipzig: Teubner, 1869; reprint, Hildesheim: Georg Olms, 1967, to *BC*
9.701). Some modern discussion in René Pichon (*Les sources de Lucain* [Paris:
Ernest Leroux, 1912], 41-42).

extant poem.[12]   Even from the scanty surviving fragments of
Macer's work we can see clearly that Lucan adapted a phrase from
the older man's poem about a snake that causes the ground to
smoke in his track from the power of his venom .[13]

Actually, a Roman need not have gone abroad to find a magical
people versed in dealing with snakes and snakebite, for in east
central Italy lived the Marsi, whose reputation in herpetology had
been around since the time of Ovid (*Med. Fac.* 39) and surely
much longer than that.   Lucan, however, for some reason wanted
to exclude them from the canon of snake handlers.   He does this
not by omission, as Bourgery suggests, but by expressly introducing
a Roman soldier from the Marsi, "Nasidius, a cultivator of a Marsian field" (*BC* 9.790) who was bitten by the prester, "the burning
snake," and died a hideous death.[14]   It would seem that Lucan
wanted to attribute the power of magic healing to the Psylli alone.
He never names the Ophiogeneis.

How the Psylli dealt with the snakes deserves some attention.
Consistent with what Nicander had said in the fragment quoted
earlier about the Psylli not using herbs to cure snakebite, Lucan's
Psylli use herbs and wood only to fumigate the area of the Roman
camp, not to treat bitten soldiers (*BC* 9.911-22).   In spite of what
Nicander said of the Libyan people in the fragment I cited, this is
not the way he recommended others proceed in the extant
Theriaca. There, in addition to preventative fumigation and other
botanical and zoological deterrents (35-114), he has specific herbal
remedies, and a few made from animal products, for treating the
victim, dozens of them extending over 221 lines of verse
(*Theriaca* 493-713).   The absence of any of this in Lucan is noteworthy.

Let me point out that when Lucan deals with treatments for
bites, he specifically calls the procedures magical, "the marvels of
a magic race," *magicae miracula gentis,* in the passage I cited
earlier (*BC* 9.923).   Lucan's wording gives me, for the moment at

---

[12] Willy Morel thinks that the poem by Nicander, from which the fragment
derives, had already disappeared by Macer's day and therefore could not have
been inserted in the version of the *Theriaca* ("Iologica," *Philologus* 83 [1928]:
351).

[13] Macer frg. 8 is clearly the model for *BC* 9.711 (*Fragmenta poetarum lati-
norum epicorum et lyricorum, praeter Ennium et Lucilium,* ed. Willy Morel, rev.
K. Büchner [Stuttgart: Teubner, 1982]).   There is nothing comparable in the
extant text and fragments of Nicander.

[14] A. Bourgery and Max Ponchont, *Lucain, La guerre civile (La pharsale),* 2
vols. (Paris: Les Belles Lettres, 1962), 2, note to 9.701.

least, a way of evading any in-depth confrontation with determining what constitutes magic. Provisionally I shall adopt a minimalist definition borrowed from Anne-Marie Tupet in her study of magic in Latin poetry:[15]

> In the face of the difficulty of ascertaining with certainty the particular features of magic, in the face of the ambiguity and indecision of its domains as well as of its aims and its procedures, it seems wiser to look for an exterior criterion and to have recourse to the authors. We shall consider as magic what the poets themselves recognize and present as such.

I shall not stick with this evasion for the entirety of the paper, but it is useful to recognize that Lucan considers in the category of magic every act the Psylli perform in the episode following the announcement of the "marvels of a magic race."

Lucan begins by saying, "First the Psyllan marks the limbs with a touch of his saliva, which restrains the venom and keeps it by the wound" (*BC* 9.925-26). Saliva magic has long been recognized by folklorists, and late in the nineteenth century its Greco-Roman manifestations were the subject of a study by Frank W. Nicholson.[16] He argued that saliva was thought to have primarily a prohibitive function, giving it its ability to inhibit the progress of the poison. The ancients regarded human saliva as particularly effective against snakes and even as being venomous. They thought that a human, particularly when fasting, could kill a snake by spitting into its mouth, a notion that persisted into the seventeenth century. As Anne-Marie Tupet reports, the belief was tested in a curious set of experiments some time before 1672.[17] The French royal physician and pharmacologist Moyse Charas proclaimed, "We have often spit into the mouths of several vipers, even when we were fasting, but the vipers a little afterwards

---

[15] Anne-Marie Tupet, *La magie* ... xi: "Devant la difficulté de reconnaître avec certitude les traits particuliers à la magie, devant l'ambiguïté et l'indécision des ses domaines, comme de ses objectifs et de ses procédés, il a paru plus sage de rechercher un critère extérieur, et de s'en remettre aux auteurs. Nous considérons donc comme magique ce que les poètes reconnaissent et présentent eux-mêmes comme tel."

[16] W. Crook, "Saliva," *Encyclopedia of Religion and Ethics,* ed. James Hastings (New York: Scribners, 1951), 11.100-04; G. Lanczkowski, "Speichel," in *RGG*, 3rd ed., 6.229-30; Frank W. Nicholson, "The Saliva Superstition in Classical Literature," *Harvard Studies in Classical Philology* 8 (1897): 23-40.

[17] *La magie . . . ,* p. 192, n. 4, citing Moyse Charas, *Nouvelles expériences sur la vipère* (Paris: the author and Jean d'Houry, 1672), 114: "Nous avons souvent craché dans la gueule de plusieurs vipères, mesme estant à jeûn, mais les vipères ont peu après rejetté notre salive, et n'en ont eu aucun mal."

spat out our saliva and suffered no harm from it." M. Charas'
willingness to risk a disastrous bite on the nose thus put the misap-
prehension to rest at last.

From his first mention of the Psylli Lucan had stressed the importance of their spoken formulae in the cure of snakebite. We
have seen that he introduced them by saying, "Their tongues are
equal to powerful herbs" (BC 9.893). True to that predication, the
Psyllan "then . . . rolls forth incantations with his frothing tongue
in an unbroken murmur, and the progress of the wound does not
grant a breathing space nor the approach of death allow the least
silence. Often, in fact, the poison that has made its way to the
blackened marrow flees when chanted over" (BC 9.927-31).

The place of chanted formulae in the ancient world is too well-
known and too extensively commented on to require much treatment at this point. Virgil in his magical eighth *Eclogue* has his
love-sick Simaetha, in recounting the powers of singing charms,
say, "By singing the cold snake in the meadow bursts" (71), but the
incantations are far older than that. Niek Veldhuis in the Netherlands is preparing for publication some charms against snakebite
from the Old Babylonian period.[18] In a period subsequent to Lucan, though perhaps reflecting far older folk practices, we find in
the Greek Magical Papyri a formula for killing a snake by words
and imitative action.[19] The same may be said for a Coptic wizard's
formula from the Michigan collection.[20]

Lucan's final curative procedure, standing in the last place in a
series as it does (BC 9.931-37), by the rhetorical and poetic practice of his day is meant to bear the chief emphasis in the episode.
This is the procedure of sucking the venom out, which I quoted
earlier:

> . . . but if any venom is reluctant to obey and resists when called forth
> and bidden to leave, then he bends over and licks the whitening wound

---

[18] Personal e-mail message, 2/19/92.

[19] "If you want to kill a snake: Say, 'Stay, for you are Aphyphis.' And taking a green palm branch and holding its heart, split it (longways) into two,
saying the name over it 7 times. At once the snake will be split or will break
open" (*The Greek Magical Papyri in Translation, Including the Demotic Spells*,
ed. Hans Dieter Betz [Chicago and London: The University of Chicago Press,
1986], 1.13.263-65).

[20] See Paul Allan Mirecki, "The Coptic Hoard of Spells from the University of
Michigan," in Marvin Meyer and Richard Smith, eds., *Ancient Christian Magic:
Coptic Texts of Ritual Power* (San Francisco: Harper Collins, 1994), 293-310;
idem, "The Coptic Wizard's Hoard," *HTR* 87 (in press).

with his mouth, drawing forth the venom, and he dries the limbs with his teeth, and he successfully spits forth the fatal material that he has extracted from the chilly body.

Of all the curative procedures Lucan and Nicander recommend, this is in fact the only one that would receive any attention in a modern first aid handbook, granted that it is now regarded as a last resort. Lucan clearly considers sucking out the poison as the crowning piece of the "marvels of a magic race," climaxing a sequence begun with saliva and incantation.[21] And to give a final punch to this miraculous procedure he assures us that the Psylli can identify by taste the sort of snake that caused the bite (BC 9.936-37).

In classifying the ability to suck out snake venom as magical, Lucan is less than consistent with what he had written earlier of Cato declaring that snake venom taken orally was harmless and thereupon drinking from the water in the snake-infested pool to prove his point (BC 9.607-618). At that moment the serpents' poison would seem harmless when taken orally. Our poet seems to have conveniently forgotten this when he tells of the Psylli, in whom the ability to suck out poison orally seems a form of magic. We would, however, be unreasonable to require adherence to consistency or toxicological accuracy from this most sensationalist of Roman poets. The purpose of the scene at the snake-infested pool is to enhance Cato's heroic stature. In this scene he wants to stress the marvelously anomalous physical constitution of the Psylli.

My remaining purpose is to move beyond Tupet's provisional classification of magic as being what Lucan expressly calls magic, *magicae miracula gentis* (BC 9.923), and to address the question of why the poet regards the Psylli as magical and his neighbors in Italy, the Marsi, as not. We should base our determination on the status of the Marsi and of the Psylli in Lucan's day. A magical people is socially, geographically, culturally, and politically marginalized.[22] But the Marsi were a native-born Italian military people and, since they had quit rebelling against Rome and since Italy had

---

[21] "Iologica," *Philologus* 33 (1928): 351-52. What Morel really wondered about was the placing of incantation "neben dem ganz rationellen noch heute empfohlenen Mittel des Aussaugens."

[22] Richard Gordon, "Aelian's Peony: the location of magic in Graeco-Roman tradition," *Comparative Criticism* 9, ed. E. S. Shaffer (Cambridge: Cambridge University Press, 1987), 66, 71-72.

become unified, served honorably and competently in the army.[23] Why not have Italians in uniform cure their comrades, or at least why not avoid the slight of having the Marsian Nasidius die of snakebite? The answer to this latter is, I think, that the Marsi were no longer marginalized, no longer different in Lucan's eyes, whereas the Psylli, a foreign, nomadic, little-known desert people, fit the requirements much better. On an individual scale the witch Erichto in the sixth book of the epic had been magical for similar reasons.[24] She was an old woman, in the remote north of Greece, living apart—the ultimate bag lady, only that her bag was filled with human body parts.

Similarly, I conclude that Lucan perceived the Psylli and their actions as magical because they appeared in his eyes as radically other, by genetic make-up as well as by habit, remote, on the periphery of the known world, and different from the normative standards of his culture.

---

[23] Earlier, of course, they had been quite otherwise. See Giulia Piccaluga, "I Marsi e gli Hirpi," *Magia: Studi di storia delle religioni in memoria di Raffaela Garosi* (Rome: Bulzoni, 1976), 209. My colleague, Prof. Anthony Corbeill, suggests that Lucan also might have shared Aulus Gellius' view that the Marsi lost their immunity by miscegenation, a mistake the Psylli avoided by the drastic trial by serpent to which they subject their new-born infants (16.11.2).

[24] See the analysis in Richard Gordon, "Lucan's Erictho," 231-41. He mentions the Marsi and the Psylli, 239.

CHAPTER NINETEEN

SATAN'S FALL IN COPTIC MAGIC

Jacques van der Vliet

Magical texts of all nations and periods are rich in mythological material.[1] This may be contained in a *historiola*, a piece of structured narrative incorporated within the magical spell.[2] The *historiola*, however, is but part of a broader phenomenon, that of the "mythical antecedent." By means of analogy, the mythical antecedent links the magician's present to an authoritative prototype with which it is supposed to merge in the course of the ritual action.[3] The manipulation of mythical paradigms is a widespread ritual procedure, not at all limited to magic, as a study of the Christian Eucharist would show. Plain narration is only one of the means to appeal to myth. Often myths are simply alluded to, for instance by referring to an appropriate mytheme or by merely quoting names of mythological characters (gods, demons, biblical personages). These allusions, themselves frequently garbled and obscure, present a major challenge to students of ancient magical texts, especially when a myth is otherwise unknown or imperfectly known. They raise, moreover, the question whether an *ad hoc* mythology could be concocted to fit the occasion.[4] How free were magicians to embroider upon, to change or even invent mythological material to make it suit their own purposes? Instead of dealing with these questions on a theoretical level, I propose to

---

[1] I wish to thank the University of Kansas Endowment Association Fund for its financial support during the Kansas conference on Magic in the Ancient World.
    [2] For a fuller treatment of the *historiola*, see D. Frankfurter's contribution in the present volume.
    [3] Some classic accounts of the procedures at work: G. van der Leeuw, "Die sog. 'epische Einleitung' der Zauberformeln," *Zeitschr. für Religionspsychologie* 6 (1933) 161-80; M. Eliade, *Traité d'histoire des religions* (Paris: Payot, 1964), 329-33; C. Lévi-Strauss, "L'efficacité symbolique," *Anthropologie structurale* (Paris: Plon, 1958), 205-26; and S. J. Tambiah, "Form and meaning of magical acts," *Culture, Thought, and Social Action* (Cambridge & London: Harvard University Press, 1985), 60-86.
    [4] Claimed, for example, for Egyptian magic by F. Lexa, *La magie dans l'Egypte antique* (Paris: Geuthner, 1925), 1.55-56.

look at the way in which a relatively well-known Judeo-Christian myth, that of the primeval fall of Satan and his angels, is received in Coptic magical spells from late antiquity. Even though examples are few in number, they can afford us some idea of what magicians may do with myths.[5]

*   *   *

Judaism, in the last few centuries BCE, saw the rise and diffusion of myths describing a primeval fall of angels to account for the existence of spiritual beings opposed to both God and the human race.[6] These myths acquired vital importance for the development of Christian theodicy and indeed for Christian doctrine as a whole, which may explain their rapid spread and durable impact. In Christian Egypt, too, they enjoyed great popularity. What may be the oldest of these myths, that of the angelic Watchers who fell through lust, deriving from Gen 6:1-6, was, in Coptic mainstream literature, soon superseded by two others.[7] According to both of these accounts the devil was originally an angel, even God's first creature (cf. Job 40:19, LXX, on Behemoth). He revolted against divine authority and was expelled from heaven to become the plague of humanity. Both, however, give different motives for his apostasy. In the first and best known myth, the story of Lucifer, it is the devil's pride which makes him aspire to be the equal of God and which triggers his fall. In the second myth, his fall is intimately connected with the creation of human being. The angels are summoned to adore Adam, God's own image and likeness, and Satan alone refuses. He claims to be superior to humanity both because of his priority, being created first, and because of his spiritual nature, Adam being created out of matter.

---

[5] The term "myth" is used here in a strictly neutral and technical sense to denote any more or less sacred narrative with authoritative and programmatic values, without any judgment on its veracity or inherent qualities.

[6] Cf. N. Forsyth, *The Old Enemy: Satan and the Combat Myth* (Princeton: Princeton University Press, 1987); E. Pagels, "The social history of Satan, the 'intimate enemy,'" *HTR* 84 (1991): 105-28, esp. 113-17.

[7] For what follows see J.-M. Rosenstiehl, "La chute de l'Ange," *Ecritures et traditions dans la littérature copte* (Cahiers de la Bibliothèque Copte 1; Louvain: Peeters, 1983): 37-60; cf. R. Stichel, "Die Verführung der Stammeltern durch Satanael," *Kulturelle Traditionen in Bulgarien*, ed. R. Lauer & P. Schreiner, Abh. Akad. Wissenschaften Göttingen, Phil.-hist. Klasse, 3. Folge, 177 (Göttingen: Vandenhoeck & Ruprecht, 1989), 116-28; M. E. Stone, "The Fall of Satan and Adam's Penance: Three notes on *The Books of Adam and Eve*," *JTS* 44 (1993): 144-48.

Both myths could claim some antiquity and both probably had their origin in Jewish *midrashim* of verses from the Hebrew Bible. Their ultimate fate within the Church, however, differed. The "Refusal-myth" was eventually rejected as "unorthodox," although it lost its authority only gradually. In Egypt it remained the object of polemical attacks until well into the 10th century. Probably it owed both its popularity and its "smell of unorthodoxy" to its occurrence in two widely read apocrypha, the *Life of Adam and Eve* and the *Questions of Bartholomew*.[8] The Lucifer-myth, on the other hand, prevailed, from the 3rd-4th century onward, as the "orthodox" version. Among the Fathers, Origen is credited for its classic formulation.[9] In a passage like *De principiis* I, 5, 4-5 (Crouzel & Simonetti, SC 252, 182-94) he succeeds in molding his exegesis of Isa 14 (on the king of Babylon), Ezek 28 (on the prince of Tyre) and Job 40-41 (on Leviathan) into a coherent account of diabolic nature and origins. These are indeed the very biblical texts which shaped the Coptic Lucifer-myth.

It is usual in earlier Christian tradition for the story of Satan's fall to take its place either in haggadic Adam-literature or in exegetical developments of the Genesis-story, for example in hexaemera. Coptic sources, however, following the lead of earlier Jewish accounts, turn it into a primarily angelological myth. As a rule, the real protagonists of the story are the great archangels whose popular cults represent a deeply rooted and typical aspect of Egyptian Christianity.[10] Even puristic Shenute (4th-5th cent.), when alluding to Satan's fall in his *Diatribe against the Devil*, betrays those characteristic angelological interests.[11] In Coptic as in older sources, the devil's great opponent is almost invariably St. Michael.[12] The Refusal-myth especially brings out in an effective

---

[8] For the *Life* in Coptic Egypt: M. Nagel, *La Vie grecque d'Adam et d'Eve: Apocalypse de Moïse* (Lille: Univ. de Lille III, 1974), 2. 101-04; M. Stone, *A History of the Literature of Adam and Eve* (Atlanta: Scholars Press, 1992), 39-41. For the *Questions*: J. van der Vliet, "Varia magica coptica," *Aeg* 71 (1991): 227-28; important general study: J.-D. Kaestli, "Où en est l'étude de l'"Evangile de Barthélémy,'" *RB* 95 (1988): 5-33.

[9] For a recent appraisal: Forsyth, *Enemy*, 369-72.

[10] Cf. C. D. G. Müller, *Die Engellehre der koptischen Kirche* (Wiesbaden: Harrassowitz, 1959); V. Saxer, "Jalons pour servir à l'histoire du culte de l'archange Saint Michel en Orient jusqu'à l'iconoclasme," *Noscere sancta: Misc. A. Amore*, ed. I. V. Janeiro (Rome: Pontificium Athenaeum Antonianum, 1985), 1.371-82; Th. Baumeister, "Die christlich geprägte Höhe," *RQ* 83 (1988): 199.

[11] Ed. P. du Bourguet, *Bull. Société d'Archéol. Copte* 16 (1961-62): 32-35.

[12] See W. Lueken, *Michael* (Göttingen: Vandenhoeck & Ruprecht, 1898), esp.

manner the contrary attitudes of both angels not only toward God but also—even primarily—toward humanity. Michael's prominent role accounts for the conspicuous military element in the Coptic myths of the fall. Often Satan is depicted as the original commander-in-chief of the heavenly armies, who was replaced by Michael only after his apostasy. He is a deserter as well as a rebel, and upon his fall he is stripped of the insignia of his angelic rank and given diabolic counterparts instead. His transgression is often the sign for general warfare between loyal and disloyal angels. This "first war in heaven," as it may be called, mirrors the eschatological war of Rev 12:7-9, Michael being the hero of both battles.[13] Satan's defeat can be solemnly sealed by Michael's investment with the highest commandership.

In spite of this angelological perspective, the Coptic myths did not lose their value as a model explaining the origins of evil and evil beings. Within the celestial world Satan's revolt gives rise to a dramatic split. For the first time good and bad powers find themselves opposed and even at war. The fall of the wicked angels, who are cast out of heaven, accounts for the genesis of a demonic order, an army of evil spirits haunting the lower world or inhabiting the pagan idols. For Satan, moreover, just as for humanity, the fall has deep ontological implications. As he turns away from God, he is not just kicked out of heaven, but he also becomes fundamentally "alien," excluded from divine grace.[14] This is well summed up by the *Apocalypse of Elijah*. There, Enoch and Elijah, returning at the end of time to combat the Antichrist, address the latter in the terms of the Lucifer-myth and thus mark him as the very villain who fell from heaven in the beginning. Their speech underlines his enmity towards "the angels and the thrones," his perennial "alienation" from the heavenly world, as well as the "change" (turning from light to darkness) which befell him and his kin.[15]

27-30, 106-11; J. P. Rohland, *Der Erzengel Michael, Arzt und Feldherr*, Beihefte *ZRGG* 19 (Leiden: Brill, 1977); Müller, *Engellehre*, esp. 8-19.

[13] Cf. A. van Lantschoot, "Un texte palimpseste de Vat. copte 65," *Mus* 60 (1947): 264 & 267 n. 8.

[14] "Alien" (Coptic: ⲩⲘⲘⲟ) may characterize both fallen Satan and fallen humanity; cf. G.J.M. Bartelink, "Ἀλλότριος und *alienus* als Teufels- und Dämonenbezeichnung," *Glotta* 58 (1980): 266-78.

[15] Sahidic: Steindorff, 124-26; Pietersma, 48. See now D. Frankfurter, *Elijah in Upper Egypt: The Apocalypse of Elijah and Early Egyptian Christianity*, Studies in Antiquity and Christianity (Minneapolis: Fortress Press, 1993), 127-40 and 317-19.

First of all, however, the fall of Satan is a prelude to the fall of humanity. The destitution of the devil and his host conditioned their perpetual animosity not only toward the loyal angels but also toward the human race. This is most evidently so in the Refusal-myth. Since Adam provided the occasion for Satan's downfall, Satan would naturally try to bring about Adam's fall. In popular apocryphal books like the *Life of Adam and Eve* and the *Questions of Bartholomew*, which inspired the Refusal-myth, the devil literally poisons man. In the latter work, Satan, cast down upon the earth, decides to avenge himself. He collects sweat from his breast and armpits and mingles it into the source of the rivers of Paradise. Drinking from this mixture, Eve gets infected with desire (ἐπιθυμία), which the *Life of Adam* calls "the root of all sin" (Greek 19:3; cf. Jas 1:15). Only now Satan can seduce her.[16] Egyptian magicians were well acquainted with the poisoning-myth of the *Questions of Bartholomew*. Thus, one Coptic love-spell (British Museum Or. 10376)[17] aims at provoking in a particular "daughter of Eve" "this desire (ἐπιθυμία) which Mastema[18] proclaimed loudly (?)[19] and which he threw down into the source of the four rivers and with which he drenched (?) . . . .[20] in order that the children of humanity would [drink] thereof and be filled with the devil's desire" (15-18). Another text (Heidelberg inv. nr. 518) directly invokes the devil who "went down into [the source of] the rivers and filled them with passion and desire and [. . . . .] and wickedness and love and longing and madness."[21] These texts bring us back to our subject: magic.

---

[16] *Questions* IV, 58-59 (Bonwetsch, 26). In the *Life of Adam* the snake deposits his poison on the fruit of the tree.

[17] W. E. Crum, "Magical texts in Coptic I," *JEA* 20 (1934): 51-53, pl. IX/2.

[18] In Coptic a popular name of Satan; cf. Müller, *Engellehre,* 77 n. 590.

[19] Emend -ⲁϣⲕⲁⲕ (ruled out by Crum, 52 n. 14)? See next note.

[20] An unintelligible word (ⲟⲕⲁⲕⲓ?); like the doubtful word in the preceding line it might be a magical name for Eden (in this text magical names are not marked by a *surligne*). For ⲁϥⲍⲟ- (thus?) perhaps read: ⲁϥⲧⲥⲟ- (the verb ⲧⲥⲟ would be technical in this context, as is shown by the Coptic translations of Gen 2:10; for ⲧⲥ/ⲍ change: W. E. Crum, in H. E. Winlock *et al., The Monastery of Epiphanius at Thebes* [New York: Metropolitan Museum, 1926], 1.245).

[21] F. Bilabel & A. Grohmann, *Griechische, koptische und arabische Texte zur Religion und religiösen Literatur in Ägyptens Spätzeit,* Veröffentlichungen aus den badischen Papyrus-Sammlungen 5 (Heidelberg: Universitätsbibliothek, 1934), 376, 32-34. The theme of water conveying sexual desire (ἐπιθυμία), which occurs in Gnostic texts too, is more fully discussed in my book *L'image du mal en Egypte* (in press).

*   *   *

The most straightforward account of Satan's fall in a magical spell is found in a text called *The Laudation of Michael the Archangel*, edited by A. M. Kropp after a lost Heidelberg manuscript (inv. nr. 1686).[22] Michael himself addresses God: "... I am Michael! It's me, indeed, who attended to the seven mysteries hidden in the heart of the Father which he performed on the day he created human being according to his likeness and his image (cf. Gen 1:26). After he had created Phausiêl, I came, I, Michael, with all my followers, and we worshipped Atôran, to wit the work of his hands. When we worshipped Arômachrim, that is Adam, Sanatael was disobedient to you. The first creature (ⲁⲣⲭⲏⲡⲗⲁⲥⲙⲁ)[23] you excluded from your holy glory. The son of perdition (cf. John 17:12; 2 Thess 2:3) you excluded from your holy glory, and you shook his foundations. He brought over them (sc. humanity) a great disease so that they did his will. Afterwards he overpowered the human beings whom you created. Afterwards <you> will heal them. Now then, my Lord, have mercy on your likeness and your image, and grant healing to everyone who will carry this holy laudation" (Kropp, 17, 32-44).

In this version of the Refusal-myth,[24] Michael and all his angels worship the newly created Adam, who receives several magical names. Only Satanael (here, with a metathesis found elsewhere, Sanatael)[25] refuses and is robbed of his celestial dignity. In revenge, he strikes humanity with disease in order to gain power over him. This account appears more or less directly dependent on the *Questions of Bartholomew*, one of the sources of the Refusal-myth. This seems to be the case, first of all, because of the name Satanael. According to the *Questions*, this was the angelic name of Satan which he bore before his fall (IV, 25; Bonwetsch, 22). Secondly, this dependence seems indicated by the reference to the "disease"

---

[22] *Der Lobpreis des Erzengels Michael* (Brussels: Fondation égyptologique Reine Elisabeth, 1966); for a second MS: M. Pezin, "Les manuscrits coptes inédits du Collège de France," *Ecriture et traditions dans la littérature copte,* Cahiers Bibliothèque Copte 1 (Louvain: Peeters, 1983), 24-25.

[23] In Coptic a frequent epithet of the devil, deriving from Job 40:19, LXX (on Behemoth); cf. A. M. Kropp, *Ausgewählte koptische Zaubertexte* (Brussels: Fondation égyptologique Reine Elisabeth, 1930-31), 3.50; Rosenstiehl, "Chute," 39 n. 18; 46 n. 55.

[24] Thus already Rosenstiehl, "Chute," 56.

[25] Thus too Ps.-Peter of Alex., *On Riches*, sah., ed. Pearson and Vivian, *Two Coptic Homilies*, 64. Satanael has been much discussed; some references in Stichel, "Verführung," 117 n. 5 & 120.

which Satan inflicted on humanity. Thirsty for revenge, Satan—as we saw—infected Eve with desire (ἐπιθυμία), which allowed him to seduce her. In the present spell, too, the "disease" serves as a way of forcing humanity to perform Satan's will, that is, to sin.

In our text, Michael pleads before God in his characteristic role of protector and advocate of the human race, thus counteracting the one who, according to the myth, is its prototypical detractor, the devil. His address reminds God of the high dignity of human-kind, on God's behest adored by the angels, and of the healing due to his violated image. The habitual military prowess of Michael does not come to the fore here, but rather his equally traditional care for human health.[26] The "image and likeness" formula, as a claim on divine protection (cf. Gen 1:26, but esp. Wis 2:23-24), is a standard element not only in angelic intercessory prayers for humanity, but in healing rituals and exorcisms as well.[27] The "disease" in the myth acquires a double meaning here: the focus shifts from the primordial, moral disease inflicted by Satan to any disease which might, at present or in the future, befall the bearer of the formula. The mention of "the son of perdition" may well be a reminiscence of another text implying divine protection, viz. Jesus' prayer in John 17, where "those watched over" are con-trasted as a body to the son of perdition who, alone, went to ruin (17:12).[28] The devil's exclusion is opposed to humanity's (desired) inclusion in divine protection.

At the magician's level, Michael's active sympathy is claimed on account of the strong bond which unites him with the human race from the very beginning. Michael is said to have "attended to the seven mysteries hidden in the heart of the Father which he performed on the day he created humankind" (32-33). In accor-dance, again, with the *Questions of Bartholomew* IV, 53 (Greek; Bonwetsch, 25), this phrase might be taken to refer to Michael fetching the elements (earth and water) out of which Adam's body

---

[26] Michael as a physician already in *Life of Adam & Eve* (Latin, ch. 41); see further: Rohland, *Michael*, esp. 27-32 (on the *Life*) & 80-86 (Coptic sources); Baumeister, "Höhe," 199.

[27] Examples in angelic prayer: *Life of Adam & Eve* (Greek, 33:5 & 35:2); M. Cramer, *Koptische Hymnologie* (Wiesbaden: Harrassowitz, 1969), 93 & 95 (Michael); in exorcism: *Vita Pachomii*, boh., ed. Lefort, CSCO 89, 152, 3-13.

[28] That John primarily refers to Judas is irrelevant: Judas is equated with the devil, cf. John 6:70; for discussion, see Forsyth, *Enemy*, 315-17, and J. V. Brown-son, "Neutralizing the intimate enemy: The portrayal of Judas in the Fourth Gospel," *Society of Biblical Literature 1992 Seminar Papers*, ed. E. H. Lover-ing, Jr. (Atlanta: Scholars Press, 1992), 49-60.

was to be fashioned.[29] The actual wording, however, is not so specific and suggests in a rather more vague sense his intimate involvement in the process of creating humanity.[30] Michael, moreover, proves to be familiar with three secret names of Adam, unknown to scripture and tradition alike. Details like these bring out the legitimacy of Michael's intervention on behalf of humanity, while at the same time enhancing, within the ritual context, the authority of the magician. The latter, by showing himself in the possession of "angelic" knowledge, raises himself to the superhuman level of his model.

A passage from the *Prayer of the Virgin in Bartos* in British Museum Or. 4714, edited by W. E. Crum,[31] appears likewise dependent on Coptic Michael-lore. Within a narrative framework, borrowed from the apocryphal acts of the Apostles, it presents a series of invocations put in the mouth of the Virgin Mary. Following a prayer to Christ, the archangels Gabriel and Michael appear at the Virgin's side. Gabriel introduces first himself, then his companion: "Mary said, 'Who is that one with the golden scepter (ῥάβδος) in his hand?' And he (Gabriel) said to her, 'That's Michael, the leader of the entire host of the angels.' She then raised a sweet voice and said, 'I conjure you today, Michael, I conjure you by my son, he who took the scepter from the hand of Mastema, and it was entrusted to you, and you were invested with a famous name.[32] I conjure you and I will not leave you at peace before you

---

[29] Elsewhere ascribed to Gabriel or to several angels; cf. L. Ginzberg, *The Legends of the Jews* (Philadelphia: Jewish Publication Society, 1946-47), 1.54-55; 5.71-73 (72 n. 15: seven substances employed in the composition of Adam's body); Kropp, *Zaubertexte,* 3.45-47. There is no trace here of the Gnostic development of this mytheme.

[30] The seven mysteries may be connected with the seven words exchanged between the Father and the Son when the latter descended into the world to create Adam (according to 49-50). The terminology, however, points to the divine performance of celestial liturgy, a motif dear to the author of the text (see especially 45-48 & 75-79). Adoring the "hidden mystery" is a principal liturgical task of the seven archangels (Müller, *Engellehre*, 9-10 and 138, nr. 15). According to l. 226, the seven archangels "stood by" when God created Adam. Actually, our phrase may mean nothing much more, *pace* Kropp, *Lobpreis,* 64.

[31] "A Coptic Palimpsest," *Proc. Society of Biblical Archaeology* 19 (1897): 210-18; for other versions (Coptic, Ethiopic, Arabic), see Crum's edition and A. M. Kropp, *Zaubertexte,* 2.125-45; *id., Oratio Mariae ad Bartos* (Giessen: Universitätsbibliothek, 1965); G. Viaud, *Magie et coutumes populaires chez les Coptes d'Egypte* (Sisteron: Editions Présence, 1978), 76-78.

[32] The Ethiopic version contains a more circumstantial description: R. Basset, *Les apocryphes éthiopiens. 5: Les prières de la Vierge à Bartos et au Golgotha* (Paris: Librairie de l'Art Indépendant, 1895), 15; text: C. Conti Rossini, "La

fulfill for me all the incantations of my tongue, to wit: this water here and this oil which are standing before me—it should become a cure in [the body?] of NN, son of NN, being like a renewal (?) in his bones, carrying away from him all diseases and all sufferings and all ailments and all snares of the enemy. May they leave everybody who washes himself with this water and this oil, through the power of God the Father, the Almighty. May all impure spirits withdraw from him and each of them go to its (proper) place through the power of our holy prayer'" (Crum, 213-14).

This invocation of Michael over water and oil has clear liturgical antecedents.[33] It opens with a piece of myth which recalls a familiar scene from Coptic angelological literature, viz. Michael's investment.[34] Following his apostasy and defeat, Satan was stripped of his rank and insignia, among which was his scepter.[35] These were given to Michael, who was made commander-in-chief "of the entire host of the angels" instead. His solemn installation was supposed to have taken place on the 12th of Hathôr, in the wake of Satan's fall (situated at sunset on the 11th). Although this train of thought was severely censured by, among others, the 6th-century bishop John of Parallos, Michael's investment on the 12th of Hathôr continued to be commemorated in Coptic liturgy.[36] In our spell, the "golden scepter" changing hands epitomizes his victory over the devil and his hosts. That this episode is evoked in a ritual against demonic diseases and "impure spirits" appears highly appropriate.

Another ritual against demons, *Rossi's Gnostic Tractate*, may likewise allude to the angels' primeval combat against the hosts of

---

redazione etiopica della Preghiera della Vergine fra i Parti," *Rendiconti Reale Accademia dei Lincei*, serie 5a, 5 (1896): 457-79.

[33] Cf. Kropp, *Zaubertexte*, 3.183-88. For its use in an Ethiopian church ritual, see Crum's edition, 211, referring to Basset, *Apocryphes*, 5.7-8.

[34] Thus already Müller, *Engellehre*, 34; cf. *id.*, 14-16 and Kropp, *Zaubertexte*, 3.79.

[35] The motif of Satan's lost panoply already in Shenute's *Diatribe against the Devil* (Du Bourguet, 34-35). For the scepter-motif, see among others Ps.-John the Evangelist, *Inthronizatio Michaelis*, ed. Müller, CSCO 225, 18 & 19; Ps.-Theodosius of Alex., *In Michaelem*, ed. E. A. W. Budge, *Miscellaneous Coptic Texts*, 338—supra; cf. the story of Euphemia, in Ps.-Severus of Antioch, *In Michaelem*, ed. Budge, *Saint Michael*, 115 & 121.

[36] See Müller, *Engellehre*, 147, nr. 34, *sub* VIII; Cramer, *Hymnologie*, 99. For John's criticism: A. van Lantschoot, "Fragments coptes d'une homélie de Jean de Parallos contre les livres hérétiques," *Miscellanea G. Mercati*, Studi e testi 121-26 (Vatican: Bibliotheca Apostolica Vaticana, 1946), 1.316-18, cf. 325-26.

Satan.[37] Here Gabriel is urged into action by refrain-like verses of this type: "stretch your bow against the first creature and all his forces; draw your sword against the first creature and all his powers" (10:15-18; Kropp, 70). The epithet "first creature" (ⲁⲣⲭⲏⲡⲗⲁⲥⲙⲁ) recalls Satan's original priority among the angels and thereby the drama of his fall. By its repeated use in this "battle-chant," the magician may have claimed the first war in heaven as a paradigm for the present one.[38]

If in the preceding examples, taken from spells against demons and diseases, the magician sides with the loyal angels, elsewhere he may have his reasons for choosing the opposite party. In a Berlin love-charm (P. 8320) demons and the devil himself are invoked in what may be called a "demonic epiclesis," pronounced over a philtre.[39] At the end of a series of demonic *voces*, which open the invocation,[40] there appears "Satanas, the devil, he who beat the earth with his staff against the living God, saying, 'I am a god too.'" The text continues, "I implore and invoke you all today that you may come for me over these [vessels?] which are presently in my hands in order that, at the moment I will give them to NN and she will eat or drink from them, you will bind her heart and her flesh to me for ever" (2-7).

Here "Satanas, the devil" is identified by an allusion to his rebellion against God, epitomized in the acts of beating the earth with his staff and proclaiming himself equal to God, "a god too." This last motif, as has been recognized by Rosenstiehl ("Chute," 40), pertains to the Lucifer-myth. It occurs in other Coptic versions of the myth of the fall as well[41] and derives from such key

---

[37] Text in Kropp, *Zaubertexte*, 1.63-78, after Carl Schmidt's copy of the lost Turin ms.; the same, with an English translation, in M. W. Meyer, *Rossi's "Gnostic" Tractate* (Inst. for Antiquity and Christianity Occasional Papers 13; Claremont: IAC, 1988). It is neither Gnostic nor a tractate!

[38] As was first suggested by Kropp, *Zaubertexte*, 3.82 & 95. Kropp surmised that these refrains originate from a hymn celebrating St. Michael. However, Gabriel's role as a warrior is well attested, see for example *1 Enoch* 40:9; Origen, *De principiis* I,8,1; Müller, *Engellehre*, 36-47.

[39] Text after A. Erman, in *Koptische Urkunden Berlin* 1, nr. 2; for more references, see my "Varia magica," 227 n. 49.

[40] Cf. that in Bilabel & Grohmann, *Texte*, 376, 28-29 (a comparable love-charm, invoking demons, pagan deities and eventually the devil himself). Variants also occur in other erotic *Bindezauber*.

[41] Ps.-Gregory of Naz., *In Michaelem*, ed. G. Lafontaine, *Mus* 92 (1979): 47 & 50; Ps.-Severian of Gabala, *In Michaelem*, Pierpont Morgan Library, M 602 (Depuydt, *Catalogue*, nr. 116, 5): f. 78 verso - 79 recto (photogr. ed., vol. 25, pl. 156-57).

texts as Isa 14:13-14 and especially Ezek 28:2 ("you became haughty and said, 'I am god'"). Beating the earth must have had the same provocative meaning. In a Coptic love-spell ascribed to Cyprian of Antioch, the latter describes how he challenged God by deliberately offensive and diabolical behavior.[42] Thus he snorted through his nose, a grave blasphemy imputed elsewhere specifically to the rebellious devil,[43] and "struck the earth with (his) foot."[44] Beating the earth, either with your feet or with a stick, was formally forbidden in Shenute's monasteries as a habit of "the Chaldeans" and of "lazy people lacking culture."[45] Shenute's "Chaldeans" could refer to magicians stamping the ground with their foot, a practice well attested by Demotic rituals.[46] From a traditional Egyptian point of view, the forbidden behavior had definitely Typhonian overtones.[47] Rather than referring to a specific mythical episode, the act of "beating the earth" brings out a boldness and a recklessness as befits the prototypical rebel.

An even more compact allusion occurs in another erotic spell, edited by W. E. Crum after Strasbourg ms. copte 135.[48] Here a spirit, invoked in order to make a rival impotent and prevent his intercourse with a certain girl, is thus addressed: "Keuentios-Patilos-Kous-Makous, he who fell from his invisible chariot (?)[49] and was cast[50] into outer darkness, bind and fasten the penis of (NN), son of (NN)" (2-5). Otherwise obscure names are connected with a mythical episode of fall and banishment in outer darkness, which scarcely fits anybody but the devil himself or one of his angels, as was already observed by Crum.[51] Riding a celestial ("invisible") chariot was part of Satan's former archangelic glory,[52] which stands in marked contrast to his present infernal

---

[42] Heidelberg inv. nr. 1684, 47-70 (Bilabel & Grohmann, *Texte*, 306-07).

[43] Cf. esp. Ps.-John, *Inthronizatio Michaelis*, Müller, CSCO 225, 12-14 & 13-15; J. Drescher, "Graeco-coptica," *Mus* 82 (1969): 90-92; 89 (1976): 319-20.

[44] l. 52-54; MS: ⲕⲉⲑⲁⲗⲓⲥⲓ, *l.*: ⲕⲉⲣⲁⲧⲓⳁⲱ, "to butt, gore" (ed.: ⲕⲁⲑⲁⲣⲓⳁⲱ).

[45] Shenute, frag. *De Vita monachorum XII*, ed. Leipoldt, CSCO 73, 81-82.

[46] Pap. London-Leiden V, 1; Pap. Louvre E 3229, ed. J. Johnson, *Enchoria* 7 (1977): 68 & 71.

[47] Cf. H. te Velde, *Seth, God of Confusion*, Probleme der Ägyptologie 6 (Leiden: Brill, 1967), 86-91 (about his murderous scepter and foot). In *PGM* XII, 368-69, Seth-Typhon "strikes the earth and shakes the world."

[48] "La magie copte," *Recueil Champollion* (Paris: Champion, 1922), 541-42; cf. Kropp, *Zaubertexte*, 2.228.

[49] Uncertain reading; ⳅⲁⲣⲙⲁ, "chariot," after Crum, "Magie," 542 n. 1.

[50] I amend ⲁⲩⲛⲟⲩϫⲉ <ⲙ>ⲙⲟϥ, changing the place of the pronouns.

[51] "Magie," 542, n. 1; cf. Kropp, *Zaubertexte*, 2.228, note *ad* 2-4; 3.96.

[52] Cf. Ps.-John, *Inthronizatio Michaelis*, fay., Müller, CSCO 225, 19: Mastema

confinement. In fact, such emphatic contrasts are a constitutive element of the myth of the fall from its very beginning (cf. Isa 14; Ezek 28). That "Keuentios" etc. are diabolical names is confirmed by other spells of aggressive erotic magic, which invoke diabolic assistance even more overtly.

In the last two texts, the allusions to the myth may be said to outline the character of a demon invoked. In the following examples, the myth is quoted once more in support of the ritualist's overall design. Quite explicit is a spell for separating a couple, a *diakopos*, from a Heidelberg manuscript (inv. nr. 1030).[53] It urges "Belso[bo]ul (Beelzeboul)[54] the strong one" to separate the two victims from each other "like Joseph and his brothers" (cf. Gen 37) and "like the devil who separated himself from God and the angels" (recto, 10-17). In Christian literature and art, the story of Joseph and his brothers had become, from Acts 7:9 and 1 Clem. 4:9 onwards, a stock theme exemplifying envy and hatred.[55] Satan's rebellion and fall are, according to the Coptic accounts, specifically acts of alienation and exclusion, ensuing lasting hostility. In separation spells like the present one, exactly these aspects acquire a paradigmatic value.

Another *diakopos*, Louvre E 14.250, edited by E. Drioton, shows the same principle at work.[56] It is written on a sheet of parchment cut in the form of the blade of a knife or sword. The actual text (there are drawings too) is made up of four formulae. Two (recto nr. 1 and verso) consist essentially of series of demons' names, followed by a request to cause discord between a man and a woman. A third one (recto nr. 2) addresses an unnamed demon who, following the burial of the phylactery near the gate of a

---

possessed a "chariot of light (ϩⲁⲣⲙⲁ ⲛⲟⲩⲁⲓⲛ)," which after his fall is transferred to Michael. Michael's chariot: *ibid.*, 24 & 25; *Laudation of Michael*, l. 3 (Kropp, 13). On the chariot's symbolism: M. Malinine, *et al.*, *Epistula Jacobi Apocrypha* (Zürich and Stuttgart: Rascher, 1968), 75-78.

[53] V. Stegemann, "Neue Zauber- und Gebetstexte," *Mus* 51 (1938): 74-82.

[54] Thus probably in 2-3; l. 1 perhaps contained one or two more names (a vignette shows two demons, personifying [?] respectively "destruction" and "hatred and dispersion"). For Beelzeboul's hand in envy, murder and war: *Testament of Solomon* 6:4 (McCown, 26*).

[55] In Coptic literature: J. Zandee, "Iosephus contra Apionem: An Apocryphal Story of Joseph in Coptic," *VC* 15 (1961): 193-213, esp. 212-13; Coptic textile depictions of Gen 37 are undoubtedly apotropaic scenes against envy (the evil eye), *pace* L. H. Abdel-Malik, "Joseph Tapestries and Related Coptic Textiles" (diss., Boston University, 1980), 103-12.

[56] "Parchemin magique copte," *Mus* 59 (1946): 479-89, pl. VI-VII.

pagan tomb, should mobilize the dead against the couple. The last one (recto nr. 3) invokes a demon named Apolle, plausibly a phantom of the Greek god Apollo who figures elsewhere in Coptic "black magic".[57] His image, laid under the head of the male victim, should again produce "hatred and separation." In the third and fourth spells the magician, urging the demon to do his job, identifies himself with a third person who claims expertise in separation. In the third spell these self-proclamations are heavily damaged[58]; in the fourth one they run thus: "I am the strong one (? – ⲕⲁⲣⲧⲁⲗⲟⲛ),[59] the one who separates a brother from his brother; it's me who separates a bride from her husband. I am the strong one (?), the one who separated Pharaoh from his nation through the multitude of his powers; it's me who incited Judas against Jesus so that he was crucified on the wood of the cross; it's me who soared up to heaven and exclaimed, 'eloï-eï-êlemas, I am a god too!'—I then, I implore and invoke you today, Apolle, in order that ... (etc.)" (26-33; Drioton, 485).

There can be little doubt that, to judge from his credentials, the expert in separation whose authority is claimed by the magician is none other than the devil himself. The "multitude of powers" through which he separated Pharaoh from his people definitely refers to the *Book of Jubilees'* characteristic rewriting of the Exodus story, which makes "Prince Mastema" responsible for Pharaoh's stubborn resistance and its evil consequences. Thus, according to *Jub.* 49:2, not God himself but "all the powers of Mastema" went out to smite the firstborn of Egypt (contrast Exod 12:12).[60] The treachery of Judas is directly ascribed, from Luke 22:3 and John 13:2 & 27 onwards, to the influence of Satan. Finally, the one who "soared up to heaven" (cf. Isa 14:13-14) and claimed to be "a god too" (cf. Ezek 28:2) must be Lucifer in person.[61] His rebellion which, as we saw before, was very much inter-

---

[57] E.g., Bilabel & Grohmann, *Texte*, 331, l. 52 (next to Zeus and demons).

[58] One may conjecture: "I am [the strong one, the one who] separates a friend from <his> friends; I am [the one who separated the waters of the] sea; I am the one who separates (NN), son of (NN), from (NN), daughter of (NN)" (13-15; Drioton, 482); l.14 could refer to Exod 14:21.

[59] Very uncertain translation. I hesitate to accept Drioton's reading χαρτάριον, "small leaf of papyrus," possibly designating the phylactery itself ("Parchemin," 486, n. *a*). With equal hesitation I propose to read καρτερόν (sc. δαιμόνιον or πνεῦμα), which as the epithet of an angel or demon would correspond to common Coptic ϫⲱⲱⲣⲉ, "strong one."

[60] Cf. M. Testuz, *Les idées religieuses du Livre des Jubilés* (Geneva: Droz; Paris: Minard, 1960), 81-86.

[61] As was recognized by Rosenstiehl, "Chute," 40. I can only guess why the

preted in terms of alienation and exclusion, here again takes a conspicuous place within the mythical paradigm of separation.

Strife and discord are also prominent in a *diakopos* from Pap. Schott-Reinhardt (Heidelberg inv. nr. 500/1).[62] It calls on two ass-headed (?) demons, who in a vignette are shown molesting a victim.[63] The invocation runs thus: "I conjure you today, Bakhoukh and Bikmn, two mighty ones, strong in their power, who contended and waged war with the angels and the cherubim so that they were cast out of heaven—similarly promise today the strife and war which occurred in their midst; [the ... of the angels][64] shall occur in the midst of NN and NN and you shall give them shouting and war and strife and separation—quickly!—between NN <and NN>! No peace whatever shall exist between them till eternity, through the power <of?> Gaiôr-Nôr-Nôrneôs-Abaôth-Meleuar-Pe (*sic?*). O great guardians, separate!" (7-23).

At least one of the demons invoked in this spell carries a traditional magical name. ⲂⲁⲬⲞⲨⲬ, usually interpreted as "Soul-of-darkness," is an Egyptian *vox*, familiar, with many variants, from earlier pagan magic.[65] Nevertheless, the ⲂⲁⲬⲞⲨⲬ and ⲂⲒⲔⲘⲚ of our spell are no stray "survivals." They acquired a new and specific mythical role. Their combat against "the angels and the cherubim," as a consequence of which they are thrown out of heaven, identifies them definitely as rebellious angels who, during that "first war in heaven," as it can be called, sided with Satan.[66] This

---

devil's exclamation is introduced by "eloï-eï-êlemas"; for the use of these words in Coptic magic, see Kropp, *Zaubertexte*, 3.128.

[62] Text: Bilabel & Grohmann, *Texte*, 329 & pl. 7 (left).

[63] This drawing is extensively discussed by I. Grumach, "On the history of a Coptic figura magica," *Proceedings Twelfth International Congress of Papyrology*, ed. D. H. Samuel (Toronto: Hakkert, 1970), 169-81.

[64] Traces only; the editor's conjectures are impossible.

[65] See, for instance, Pap. dem. mag. London-Leiden V, 8, Griffith & Thompson, with the note *ad loc.*; A. Audollent, *Defixionum Tabellae* (Paris: Fontemoing, 1904), 341, nr. 250 A, 1-2: "βαχα[χυχ .... qui es in Egipto magnu[s] demon ..."; *PGM* VII, 400 (invocation of an untimely dead); cf. Chr. Harrauer, *Meliouchos* (Wiener Studien, Beiheft 11; Wien: Österr. Akad. der Wissenschaften, 1987), 47 n. 50; possible variants in Coptic magic: Grumach, "History," 172-73. Speculations on the name ⲂⲒⲔⲘⲚ: *ibid.*

[66] No particular version of the myth of the fall seems to be envisaged. The emphasis on "strength" reminded Müller, *Engellehre*, 73 n. 563, of Gen 6:4. This is, however, a stock element of Greco-Egyptian magic; cf. V. Stegemann, "ⲞⲨⲚⲀⲞⲨⲰⲢⲈ ⲠⲚⲦⲈⲨϬⲞⲘ = stark," *Zeitschr. für Ägyptische Sprache u. Altertumskunde* 71 (1935): 81-85; Grumach, "History," 172 n. 32, and T. DuQuesne, *A Coptic Initiatory Invocation* (Thame Oxon: Darengo, 1991), 18-19 & 30-31,

celestial war serves as a paradigm for the domestic war which is invoked over the victims of our spell. As prototypical trouble-makers, these rebellious angels are direct successors to the turbulent god Seth-Typhon.[67] Indeed, although partly written in Arabic, our spell represents a remarkably traditional type. For its structure and terminology, it may be usefully compared with—for example—the far earlier Greek *diakopos* of *PGM* XII, 365-375, which has Seth for its protagonist.[68] The mythological background of Egyptian magic may have changed, far less so its aims and techniques.

A papyrus from Cologne, nr. 10.235, edited by M. Weber, ex-ploits in a more subtle way the disjunctive elements in the myth of Satan's fall.[69] In this spell the magician solicits the means to exert social influence, for both good and evil purposes (cf. l. 23), from a spirit whose name is lost.[70] The latter is thus addressed: "I invoke you today in order that you may come to me in this place wherein I am for you and that you reveal yourself to me, [that I see] you face to face and that you talk with me mouth to mouth,[71] together with your two decans, namely Archôn and Lamei,[72] and bring to

---

point out Typhonian connections. Neither are the "guardians" (ἐπίσκοπος) in the last line likely to refer to the ἐγρήγοροι of the Watcher-myth; the epithet ἐπίσκοπος too has its traditional background in Greco-Egyptian magic; see Th. Schermann, *Griechische Zauberpapyri und das Gemeinde- und Dankgebet im I. Kle-mensbriefe* (TU 34/2b; Leipzig: Hinrichs, 1909), 29; cf. H. W. Beyer, "ἐπισκέπτομαι," *TWNT,* 2.605-06.

[67] Emphasized by Grumach, "History," and DuQuesne (see previous note).

[68] On the Greek spell: D. F. Moke, "Eroticism in the Greek Magical Papyri" (diss., University of Minnesota, 1975), 259.

[69] "Ein koptischer Zaubertext aus der Kölner Papyrussammlung," *Enchoria* 2 (1972): 55-63, pl. 2-4 (my readings sometimes differ from Weber's). Related papyri in Cairo, Coptic Museum (cf. *Coptic Encyclopedia,* 5.1502), and in Yale (cf. *A Collection of Papyri* [New York: H. P. Kraus, 1964], 43, nr. 55) will be edited by Prof. B. Layton. Now see also M. W. Meyer and R. Smith, eds., *Ancient Christian Magic: Coptic Texts of Ritual Power* (San Francisco: Harper Collins, 1994), 243-44.

[70] The Cairo papyrus, cited in the preceding note, has ⲁⲃⲣⲁⲕ[. . .], perhaps one of the numerous variants of Abraxas / Abrasax.

[71] Cf. *Confessio Cypriani* (Coptic: Von Lemm, 11; Bilabel, 81): "I saw the devil face to face and through offerings caused him to reveal himself to me . . . I kissed him mouth to mouth and he talked with me (Bilabel: I talked with him)."

[72] "Decan" (δεκανός) is a common Coptic term for "demon, demon's assis-tant"; see H. Behlmer-Loprieno, "Zu einigen koptischen Dämonen," *Göttinger Miszellen* 82 (1984): 7-23. The same demonic trinity appears in the parallel spells, quoted above; a perhaps related one in the love-spell Leiden inv. F 1964/4.14, recto (ed. M. Green, "A late Coptic magical text," *Oudheidkundige Mededelingen* 66 [1987]: 42, pl. 1, top).

me the love and the favor and the peace which the Father gave to
his beloved, his only-begotten Son, when he came into the world,
while he said to him, 'Go in my peace and come again in my peace;
my peace which is mine I give unto you!' (cf. John 14:27). Again I
invoke you today in order that you may bring to me the disgrace
and the hatred which the Father pronounced upon the head of
Satan, to the effect that he excluded him and expelled him [. . .]"
(5-17).

Two diametrically opposed moments of separation are evoked:
Christ's mission into the world (a scene extrapolated from the
Gospel of John)[73] and Satan's fall from his celestial station. At
first sight, this antithesis may seem reminiscent of those ancient
series of paradigms which oppose divine reward to divine punishment (an old Christian example is 2 Peter 2:4-9). In such a context, the rebellious angels, who were cast down into hell (2 Peter
2:4; Jude 6), could be contrasted with Enoch, who was translated to
heaven (cf. Gen 5:24; Heb 11:5).[74] In the present case, however,
not reward and punishment as such are opposed, but the divine
feelings aroused by those two different scenes of farewell: love vs.
hatred, favor (χάρις) vs. disgrace. These pairs of opposites appear
again in the spell's final invocation, followed by a longer series
which includes "binding-unbinding," "killing-making alive,"
"collecting-dispersing," "establishing-expelling" (31-35). To make
the range of manipulatory faculties he wants to dispose of as
inclusive as possible, the magician asks for the two most sharply
opposed extremes of divine emotion. At the negative pole of this
rhetorical scheme, Satan's fall summarizes in mythological terms
rejection in its most complete and radical form.

*   *   *

In exploiting material from the myth of Satan's fall the Coptic
magicians invented very little. They merely adapted motifs from a

---

[73] For the Johannine quotes: Weber, 60-61. This scene represents a popular
motif in Coptic literature; see for example *Laudation of Michael*, 171-73 (Kropp,
39); *Apocryphon Bartholomaei* (Coptic: Budge, 13; Lacau, 53 & 57); Ps.-
Theodosius of Alex., *In Joh. bapt.*, ed. K. H. Kuhn, CSCO 268, 12-13; very
elaborate, but somewhat different: *Asc. Isa.* 10:7-16, which may have inspired the
Coptic fragment *apud* A. van Lantschoot, "Les textes palimpsestes de B. M., Or.
8802," *Mus* 41 (1928): 240-41.

[74] E.g., in a Greek exorcism, the *Prayer of Gregory the Wonderworker,* ed. A.
Strittmatter, *Orientalia Christiana* 26 (1932): 132, 6-8; in a Coptic homily:
Pachomius, *Catechesis*, ed. L. Th. Lefort, CSCO 159, 10, 5-6.

well-known myth to fit into the closely knitted micro-structure of the magical spell. Their often sophisticated adaptation of the myth shows that so-called magical texts had firm roots in literary culture. Whatever vagueness may sometimes obscure the identity of the mythical characters or the mythical (narrative) situation appears to stem from conventions imposed by the ritual context rather than from the magician's over-excited imagination or from imprecise knowledge. Thus the use of magical names which are unknown from other accounts of the myth of the fall will have been dictated by a ritual context in which the magician wished to impose his authority. Moreover, the myth is as a rule alluded to rather than recounted. A mere slogan ("I am a god too") may evoke the entire story more suggestively than a long abstract. A certain way of purposely blurring the mythical image is indeed proper to ritual and rhetorical discourse, as opposed to plain narrative. An instructive example is provided by a fragment of Shenute who, reprimanding his monks for unchastity, states that "Satan was thrown out of heaven for seeking to perpetrate his abominations."[75] He is not recounting an unknown variant of the myth of Satan's fall, but merely tells his audience that if they will be "seeking to perpetrate their abominations" within the monastery, they will be kicked out.

As for its exact role within the magical ritual, the myth of Satan's fall appears to be a multi-functional one. The devil, even when called by phantastic names, can be identified as that primeval mischief-maker by means of a reference to his myth. Although such a gloss may contribute but little to the ritual's argument, it brings out the devilishness of the personage invoked, and in curses and aggressive erotic spells this can be quite appropriate. Beside this labelling function, the myth acquired a twofold paradigmatic value. The first paradigm is closely connected with the figure of St. Michael as the traditional opponent of the devil. In exorcisms and healing formulae the myth represents the primordial defeat of evil spirits, which serves as a model for the magician's *hic et nunc*, where he too is fighting evil, demonic powers. The second paradigm takes another view: it presents the myth of the fall as the drama of the primordial split within the celestial world and features the ensuing exclusion and hostility. Exactly these aspects determine the magician's appeal to the myth in rituals aiming at separating people. Both the "exorcistic" and the "disjunctive" para-

---

[75] W. E. Crum, *Catalogue of the Coptic Manuscripts in the British Museum* (London: British Museum, 1905), 82, nr. 198.

digm draw upon characteristic aspects of the myth of Satan's fall
as it is known, in various traditional forms, through Coptic literature. Their use shows once more that magical spells, however
crudely they may have been copied, represent a world of learning.

CHAPTER TWENTY

MAGICAL BOWLS AND MANICHAEANS

Jason David BeDuhn

Magic bowls are apotropaic and exorcistic objects found pre-
dominantly in Mesopotamia. They are shallow bowls of varying
size, inscribed with binding spells and invocations, and dating
roughly from the 5th to 7th centuries CE.[1] The bowls have been
classified by their languages and scripts into four main types:
Judeo-Aramaic, Mandaean, and two varieties of Syriac. The
"magic" of the bowls, drawn from the available apotropaic and
exorcistic practices of the region, claims to protect a person,
family or household from demonic intrusion by declaring a "seal"
upon the particular persons or places which expels or incapacitates
evil forces.[2] This practice was "available" in the sense that no
institution had exclusive authority over its use, and it was adopted
by various religious practitioners in the service of their clientele.
The bowls survive, therefore, as artifacts of religious competition
and rival claims to power.[3] The variations in script and content
among the bowls show that the technique was employed by Jews,

---

[1] James A. Montgomery, *Aramaic Incantation Texts from Nippur*
(Philadelphia: University of Pennsylvania Press,1913), 103-04; *idem*, "The
Original Script of the Manichaeans on Texts in the Museum," *The Museum
Journal, University of Pennsylvania Museum* 3 (1912): 25.

[2] "The text of the bowls very often talks of chaining and pressing the evil entities; at the same time it may also bid them go away, leave the house and desist
from bothering the house owner. The bowl thus serves both to entrap the evil
powers and to reject them; there is no real contradiction between these two
propositions" (Joseph Naveh and Shaul Shaked, *Amulets and Magic Bowls:
Aramaic Incantations of Late Antiquity* [Leiden: Brill, 1985], 15). Self-
referential designations found in the bowl texts are "press" (*kibsha*) and "seal"
(*hatma*).

[3] A wonderful testimony to this milieu is Isbell's Judeo-Aramaic bowl 49:
"And there will cease from this dwelling and threshold of this Parrukdad the son
of Zebinta and of Qamoi the daughter of Zaraq, Aramean black-arts, Jewish black-
arts, Arabic black-arts, Persian black-arts, Indian black-arts, Greek black-arts,
black-arts of the Romans, black-arts which are practiced in the seventy languages,
either by woman or by man" (Charles D. Isbell, *Corpus of the Aramaic Incantation Bowls* [Missoula: Scholars Press, 1975], 113).

Mandaeans, Christians, and—perhaps—Manichaeans.[4]

Eighty years ago, James Montgomery of the University of Pennsylvania discovered that one of the two Syriac scripts found on the bowls was identical, for all intents and purposes, to the script used by the Manichaeans.[5] Because the content of the bowl inscriptions written in Manichaean script was not doctrinally significant, nor even definitively attributable to Manichaeans,[6] Montgomery's discovery has never been followed up and its ramifications for the history of Manichaeism have never seemed worth pursuing. But a reevaluation of Montgomery's discovery is overdue. Put simply, are these bowls Manichaean, and did the Manichaeans practice "magic"?

*   *   *

To the cultural establishment of the Roman and Sasanid Empires, the Manichaeans who came pouring into their respective realms from Mesopotamia in the 3rd century CE were both detested and feared, and they were subject to suspicion and suppression. As objects of loathing and dread, the Manichaeans had but two options by which to survive and advance. The first option was to assimilate, to mask strangeness and learn to speak with a famil-

---

[4] The various languages and scripts of the bowls are indicative of the "magicians" who prepared them; their clients are not necessarily of the same ethnic or religious community. In fact, the majority of the bowls were apparently prepared by Jewish "magicians" for Persian or non-Jewish Semitic clients (Naveh and Shaked, 17-18). In several cases, the same client has in his possession bowls from different traditions, hedging his bets, as it were, by covering himself with power from as many sources as he could arrange (see note 38).

[5] Montgomery, 1913: 32-34. Allotte de la Fuÿe apparently reached the same conclusion independently, but did not report his findings until 1924 ("Une coupe magique en écriture manichéenne," *CRAIBL* [1924]: 388-99). The Manichaean script is known from extensive texts in Iranian and Turkic languages recovered from Turfan and surrounding locales in Central Asia, smaller Syriac fragments recovered in Egypt, and a single crystal seal found in Mesopotamia reading, in Syriac, "Mar Mani, the Apostle of Jesus Christ."

[6] Montgomery concludes that "there are no Manichaean traces in the bowls" (1913: 35); cf. "Original Script . . . ," 28. But it should be pointed out that the position taken by Montgomery and merely repeated by all who have addressed the question since—that the script represents the source from which the Manichaeans developed their own—is untenable. The Manichaean script is traceable to the 3rd century, and hence predates the bowls by as much as three centuries. By the time the bowls were made, there was no surviving indigenous Mesopotamian scribal tradition unaffiliated with the major religious communities of the region. Therefore, the bowl script can only be derived *from* the Manichaean script.

iar accent. The Manichaeans were masters of assimilation, aggressive translators, consummate dissemblers. Their reputation in this respect is well established in the history of religions. The second option was to accentuate the exotic, cultivate dread, play upon fear and insinuate power barely held in check.[7]

The Manichaeans did indeed accentuate their exotic character, not only by claiming citizenship in a supercelestial paradise of light but also by embracing an earthly aura of antiquity, wrapping themselves in the geographic prestige of Babylon. In late antiquity "Babylon" had acquired the reputation of an exotic and portentous land.[8] This reputation held true not only in Greco-Roman but also Persian xenology; but in the west it was heightened by the addition of Persian exoticism to the ages-old legend of Babylon.[9]

Mani, a Parthian totally acculturated to Mesopotamia, used its reputation to best effect in his self-descriptive statements. A biographical text has him declare to the Persian emperor Shapur, "I am a doctor from Babylon" (M566 I), and in a self-revelatory poem, he emphasizes his links to the "gateway of God" (bab el): "I originated from the country of Babel and at the gate of truth I am placed ... I was led away from the country of Babel so that I should call out a call in the world" (M4). In the catechism he wrote for Shapur,[10] the Shabuhragan, Mani makes his Babylonian heritage key to his prophetic identity: "this revelation descended and this prophecy came in this last era in the figure of myself, Mani, the apostle of the true God in the country Babylon." This special relationship to exotic Babylon is promoted in western Manichaean sources as well. The Coptic Homilies call Mani "the great presbyter of the country of the great Babylon" (54,13-15) and "the

---

[7] A role of the exotic in the bowls is suggested by the observation that they appear in many cases to have been manufactured by "magicians" of one religious tradition for the use of people belonging to another religious tradition.

[8] See A. D. Nock, "Paul and the Magus," Essays on Religion and the Ancient World (Cambridge: Harvard University, 1972), 1.324.

[9] See, e.g., Lucian of Samosata, Menippus 6. Pseudonymous literatures of "Zoroaster," "Hystaspes," and "Ostanes" thrived in the Greco-Roman market. In the 2nd century, the Chaldaean Oracles did for Babylon what the Hermetic literature was doing simultaneously for Egypt—they rehabilitated the aura if not the substance of a politically subjugated but ancient culture.

[10] In this he follows an epistolary tradition in Hellenistic magical literature of "magician-to-king" instruction. See Jonathan Z. Smith, "The Temple and the Magician," in God's Christ and His People: Studies in Honor of Nils Alstrup Dahl, eds. J. Jervell and W. Meeks (Oslo: Universitetforl., 1976), 234. But this genre is itself the descendant of ancient Babylonian astrologer/priest-to-king correspondence.

interpreter of the country of the great Babylon" (61,14-17).

Mani's titles and claims were both prodigious and polyvalent. Religious titles in the ancient world in no way precluded scientific, medical or magical authority. The categories we take such trouble to distinguish were completely permeable in late antiquity. Jacob Neusner has described the rabbis of Mesopotamia in this way: "They were not merely teachers and judges, therefore, but 'holy men,' who talked to the dead, cursed or blessed effectually, mastered occult sciences, healed, and read the secrets of the stars."[11] Neusner's description is especially appropriate to our subject because of its Babylonian milieu. Mani's various titles place him as heir to the collective wisdom of Babylon.[12] Did this wisdom include bowl magic?

*   *   *

Did the Manichaeans practice magic? The opponents of Manichaeism, quite predictably, assert that they did. Both the Roman and Sasanid Empires were paranoid, aggressive socio-political orders. The Manichaeans became a disruptive presence in both realms by competing with sanctioned religious institutions and overturning established social norms.[13] Diocletian's rescript at the end of the 3rd century defined the Manichaeans as a "new and

---

[11] Jacob Neusner, *The Early Sasanian Period, A History of the Jews in Babylonia* (Leiden: Brill, 1966), 2.143-44.

[12] Likewise in rabbinic sources, where "the rabbi emerges as a wonder-working sage, master of ancient wisdom both of Israel and Babylonia, and privy to the occult. He was believed able to cast an evil eye, to consort with the dead, and to interpret the signs and omens not only of the stars but also of the animal and natural world ... His advice covered every aspect of human affairs ... He was learned in the medical traditions of his region, and achieved a wide reputation as an interpreter of physiological phenomena ... such a man would well find veneration among the people in his lifetime, and for the dust of his grave after death" (Neusner, 147). The figure of Samuel bears many of the same categorical ambiguities as Mani, his near contemporary, as already observed by Otakar Klíma, *Manis Zeit und Leben* (Prague: Tschechoslowakische Akademie der Wissenschaften, 1962), 145. "Like the other leading rabbis, Samuel was a sage, physician, astronomer, and magician. He interpreted omens; like Rav, was able to bring death upon those who made derogatory remarks about him, or angered him, and he was believed to (be) able to communicate with the dead ..." (Neusner, 2.137).

[13] Zoroastrian literature depicts the Manichaeans as the antithesis of Persian values, hating everything good, loving everything bad. In the terms of religious hyperbole, Mani was an incarnate demon (*druz astak—Denkart* 3.200). Ironically, the Romans considered Manichaeans to be every inch proper Persians, and for that very reason detested and abhorred.

unforeseen prodigy" from Persia, progressing into Roman territory like a shadow army, disturbing the peaceful and orderly life of virtuous citizens and overturning the god-given ordinances of Roman society with "perverse Persian laws." Even so, Diocletian did not use the term *mageia* in reference to the Manichaeans, but referred more broadly to "abhorrent practices" (*execrandas consuetudines*), using buzzwords like *venenis, malivolis,* and *maleficiorum*.[14] The anti-Manichaean rescript (*De maleficis et Manicheis*) was classified with those against astrologers (*mathematicis*) and sorcerers (*maleficis*).[15] It prescribed the burning of Manichaean leaders and books.[16]

Although the Christian emperors of subsequent administrations often employed the new category of "heresy" to marginalize the Manichaeans, they also retained the Diocletianic charges of magic against them.[17] Church polemic echoed the secular.[18] Epiphanius explicitly accuses the Manichaeans of magical practices (*Panarion* 66.10), and asserts that "they boast of their use of astrology and phylacteries, that is amulets, and other kinds of incantations and

---

[14] *venenum* = philtre, magical poison; *maleficus* = having to do with "black magic," harmful acts. See Ramsay MacMullen, *Enemies of the Roman Order* (Cambridge: Harvard University Press, 1966), 124-25; Theodor Mommsen, *Römisches Strafrecht* (Leipzig: Duncker and Humblot, 1899), 640.

[15] *Mosaicarum et Romanum Legum Collatio* 15,3. The anti-Manichaean edict fits into Diocletian's deliberate revival of Roman "patriotism" and traditional values, which first manifested itself in the legal sphere by the anti-astrology edict of 294, and culminated in the edict against the Christians in 302.

[16] Legal historians have yet to agree on the basis for Diocletian's violent suppression of the Manichaeans; some emphasize the religion's link to Persia, while others note its characterization as a "magical" practice. The punishments prescribed fit very closely those appropriate to sorcery (*Sententiae receptae Paulo tributae* 23.15-18); but burning was also applied to traitors (*Digest of Justinian* 48.19.8). The distinction may prove academic, since the foreign is by definition magical, the magical by definition foreign, and the common denominator of both tags is their sociopathic character. In any case, the punishments ordered for the Manichaeans *do not* fit those applied to "new sects or religious observances unknown to reasonable men" (*SrPt* 21).

[17] The edict of May 30, 428 (Theodosius and Valentinian to Florentius, Praetorian Prefect, 16.5.65) is most explicit: "[T]hose who have arrived at the lowest depths of wickedness, namely, the Manichaeans, shall nowhere on Roman soil have the right to assemble and pray ... since no opportunity must be left to any of them whereby an injury may be wrought upon the elements themselves." Cf. *Cod. Theod.* 9.16.5 against "magic arts employed to disturb the elements" issued by Constantius.

[18] Ambrosiaster (*Comment. ad II Ep. Tim.* 3,6) even quotes the edict of the (pagan, anti-Christian) emperor Diocletian in his characterization of Manichaeism.

chicanery" (66.13.6-7). Mani himself, Epiphanius adds, "was acquainted with, and wrapped up in, the practices of the magi" (66.88). C. H. Roberts points out an allusion to menstrual magic in an anonymous late 3rd-century epistle against the Manichaeans from Egypt, which warns that Christians must "be on our guard against these who with deceitful and lying words steal into our houses, and particularly against those women whom they call 'elect' and whom they hold in honor, manifestly because they require the menstrual blood for the abominations (*musagmata*) of their madness."[19]

In formulae of abjuration, converts from Manichaeism were instructed to recite, "I anathematize all the Manichaean books...as full of sorcery (*hoia goēteias ousan anapleō*) and paying homage to the devil their father" (*Seven Chapters* [*Cod. Vatopedinus*] 2,50). The convert must verbally reject "their abominable and magical prayers" (7,216f.)[20] and "their abominable and unclean and magic-filled mysteries" (7,219f.).[21] The polemical depiction of Mani which enjoyed the widest circulation in the church, the *Acta Archelai*, wraps the heresiarch quite literally in the mantle of a barbarian sorcerer.[22] The author calls Mani a "barbarian priest and crafty coadjutor of Mithras" (40) and reports a scandalous biography which makes him heir to a line of discredited conjurers.[23]

None of this should surprise us. The accusation of magic is a

---

[19] C. H. Roberts, *Theological and Literary Texts (Nos. 457-551)*, vol. 3 of *Catalogue of the Greek and Latin Papyri in the John Rylands University Library, Manchester* (Manchester: Manchester University Press, 1938), 45.

[20] *tais miarais autōn kai goēteutikais proseuchais.*

[21] *ta mysara toutōn kai akatharta kai goēteias plērē mystēria.* Cf. *Long Formula* [*Cod. Paris. Gr.* 1372]: "those abominable and unclean and magic-filled mysteries . . . and all those things which they perform impiously which are contained in the Manichaean, or rather magical, books" (1465D); "I anathematize and condemn all the Manichaeans and every book of theirs and every prayer, or rather sorcery" (1466D).

[22] "[F]or he wore a kind of shoe which is usually called in common speech the *trisole*; he had also a variegated cloak, somewhat ethereal (*aerina*) in appearance; in his hand he held a very sturdy staff of ebony wood; under his left arm he carried a Babylonian book; his legs were swathed in trousers of different colours, one leg in red and the other in leek-green; and his whole appearance was like that of an old Persian *artifex* or military magistrate (*dux bellorum*)" (14).

[23] Namely, Scythianus, who studied in Egypt, that seedbed of sorceries, and Terebinthus, who invoked magical names and was cast down from a roof by a spirit: 52ff. One should note likewise the clear association of Manichaeism with magic manifest in the trial of Priscillian of Avila (Henry Chadwick, *Priscillian of Avila: The Occult and the Charismatic in the Early Church* [Oxford: Clarendon, 1976]).

stock item of polemic, and "a form of social control used by those within the dominant social structure to label and exert control over those in the ambiguous and unstructured areas of society." In other words, "the charge of sorcery or magic is part of a constellation of accusations of antisocial behavior levelled at marginal or interstitial individuals and groups."[24] The heretical, the strange, the foreign is by definition the magical, because the designation "magic" marks every religious practice that is not "ours." So accusations of magic against the Manichaeans are to be expected. We can be just as confident that when examining Manichaean literature, we will find accusations and condemnations of magic aimed back the other way; and we do.[25] Very little historical weight can be given to such polemical characterizations.

For greater historical precision, it is necessary to avoid generic categories such as "magic," and to speak instead of specific practices of apotropaic or exorcistic character. Elsewhere I have demonstrated that Mani was as much physician as prophet, and that medical concepts and functions were part of both his identity and his ideology.[26] "Magical" practices must be added to this mix, since practices subject to the label "magic" were intrinsic to the majority of medical efforts in late antiquity. Such practices earned their polemical designation precisely because they were a set of techniques cut loose from sanctioned ideological moorings and transmitted across cultural boundaries. The same methods of mundane "salvation" were utilized by diametrically opposed parties of religious rivalry, but were considered "magic" only in the hands of an opponent or the culturally "other."

Manichaean literature shows Mani active in the role of exorcist and magical healer. In the Coptic Manichaean *Psalm-Book*, Mani's voice is characterized as "The cry of a physician, the cry of a spell-looser"[27] (220,26); he is directly addressed as a "spell-looser"

---

[24] David Aune, "Magic in Early Christianity," *ANRW,* 2.23.2: 1523.

[25] Manichaean ethical instruction from various points of missionary geography unanimously condemns the "black arts." The *Xuastuanift* confession, recited by congregated believers, classifies "black magic" (*yilwi*) as a sin (VIB). The prohibition (of *sihrun*) is repeated in the Manichaean moral code recorded in Arabic sources (e.g., *Fihrist*). In western Manichaean tracts, the prohibition is explicitly against *mageia*, and is given all the more force by the term's ambiguous reference to both "black arts" and the practices of the notoriously persecutory Zoroastrian hierarchy (cf. *Homilies* 11,15ff.; *Kephalaia* 31,25f.: "magic rites and spells of darkness"; 31,30: "magic rites of error"; 143,13ff.).

[26] "A Regimen for Salvation: Medical Models in Manichaean Asceticism," *Semeia* 58 (1992): 109-34.

[27] *p.hrau n.ou.seine p.hrau n.ou.balhik.*

(*balhik*) whose "healing is not of this earth" (221,1f.). He is depicted as speaking the following words to the arch-demoness of the world:

> I am the physician who heals, but you are the wounder that wounds. I am the spell-lifter (*p.ref.tihik*), but you are the striker, the one who lays low. (221,7f.)

Just as he first presented himself to the Persian court as "a doctor from Babylon," Mani made his last defense at court solely on the basis of his medical-magical services:

> Many and numerous were your servants whom I have [freed] of demons (*dyw*) and witches (*drwxs*). Many were those from whom I have averted the numerous kinds of fever. Many were those who were at the point of death, and I have revived them. (M3 V)

His disciples, too, displayed such powers.[28]

Some may suspect this to be pure performance, an appeal to benighted, superstitious masses by crafty missionaries. But a close examination of Manichaean doctrine reveals the degree to which this "magical" work was integral to the religion as a whole. Manichaeism portrays the world as a battleground between gods and demons, upon which the Manichaean elect roams, half warrior and half medic. The enemy is an army of 140 myriads of devils (*Xuastuanift* IB), and salvation depends on the overthrow of their control within the body.[29] In the *Cologne Mani Codex*, Mani makes the medical-magical power of laying on hands (*cheirothesia*) a centerpiece of his divine commission, fully equal to his doctrinal teachings (64,8-11; 70,1-4).

In all these sources, Mani is shown actively appropriating and using practices of power available to him from the fragmented and

---

[28] E.g., Adda on his mission to the Roman Empire: "He performed many miracles and (displayed) miraculous powers in those countries" (M2).

[29] The primordial awakening of human consciousness is depicted as an exorcism: "The bright Jesus came near to the ignorant Adam, and awakened him from the sleep of death in order that he might be saved from the many spirits. And like a man who is righteous and finds a man who is possessed by a powerful demon and appeases (*salli*) him by his art ('*ummanuta*), such was Adam like when the Beloved found him, when he was plunged in a heavy sleep, and made him move and shook him, and chased away from him the seducing demon, and took from him into bondage the great female archontess" (Theodore bar Konay, from Geo Widengren, *Mesopotamian Elements in Manichaeism* (Uppsala/Leipzig: A. B. Lundquistska/Otto Harrassowitz, 1946), 71. Widengren derives *salli* and '*ummanuta* from terms found in Babylonian exorcistic texts.

subjugated culture of late antique Mesopotamia.[30] He does not hesitate to sully his hands with techniques others had already condemned as "magical," i.e., cult.icly disenfranchised. With Mani as a role model, the Manichaeans revalorized practices which in their displaced, unsystematized and unsanctioned form were called "magic," and used them as integral practices of a religious system which was itself defined against other, rejected "magics."[31]

*　　*　　*

Montgomery identified nine bowls from Nippur written in a "Manichaean" script by at least three different hands.[32] Since his time, ten more Manichaean-script bowls have been identified.[33] Most of the bowls share a peculiar interior base design of a quartered circle, with each quarter marked with a cross or x. The bowl published by Allotte de la Fuÿe seems to identify this design as "le sceau de l'axe de la terre." The bowls are related to each other in other ways, by scribe, client,[34] or spell formulae.[35] The spells on

---

[30] Mani's self-presentation has tantalizing antecedents in the ancient Babylonian *asipu* or religious exorcist, and the magic bowls find roots in the *maklu* texts employed by such figures (Montgomery, 1913: 47). The Manichaeans also took up the astrological learning of Mesopotamia and developed it into an elaborate science of (mostly demonic) influences (e.g., *Kephalaion* 69).

[31] See *Kephalaion* 55 (143,13ff.).

[32] James A. Montgomery, "A Magical Bowl-Text and the Original Script of the Manichaeans," *JAOS* 32 (1912): 434-38 = Hamilton Text 1; "A Syriac Incantation with Christian Formula," *AJSL* 34 (1917/1918): 137-39 = Hamilton Text 2; Montgomery, 1913 (which Hamilton calls "1912"), Bowls 31-37 = Hamilton Texts 3-9.

[33] Allote de la Fuÿe, 1924; Javier Teixidor, "The Syriac Incantation Bowls in the Iraq Museum," *Sumer* 18 (1962): 51-62 (Hamilton has "1964") Iraq Museum 60960 = Hamilton Text 16; Victor Paul Hamilton, "Syriac Incantation Bowls" (diss., Brandeis, 1971), Texts 10, 17-21; Naveh and Shaked, Bowls 1 and 10. Hamilton Text 17 has been re-edited by Markham J. Geller, "Two Incantation Bowls Inscribed in Syriac and Aramaic," *BSOAS* 39 (1976): 422-27, Bowl A.

[34] Of Montgomery's bowls, 31 and 33 are written in the best hand. Both were made for Dadbeh bar Asmanducht, and 31 actually speaks of "these bowls." Bowl 31 declares its function for "sealing" his house and driving out "the Tormentor and the Curse and the very evil Dreams." Bowl 33 seals the wife and children of Dadbeh as well as his house, and makes reference to "Rab Jesus bar Perahia" through whose words "were subjected heaven and earth and the mountains; and through which were uprooted the heights, and through which were fettered (black) arts, demons and devils and satans and liliths and *latbe*; and through which he passed from this world and climbed above you to the height and brought counter-charms, a ruin to destruction ..." Bowl 32, written in a choppier hand, is nearly identical in content to Bowl 33, but was made for Dinoi bar

the bowls are concerned with "sealing" the bodies, families, homes

Ispandarmed. Bowl 35, in a similar hand, was made for the "sealing and guarding of the house and sons and property and body of Maiducht bath Kumboi"; but it contains an appended spell on behalf of Dinoi bar Ispandarmed, neatly tying up the relation between the bowls. Various angels and spirits, along with Moses, are invoked as Maiducht's guardians. Bowl 36, in a similar hand, has a unique text which reads, "The lord Shamesh has sent me against you, Sin has despatched me, Bel has appointed me, Nannai has commanded me, and Nebo has [clothed] me [with] his girdle, and Nirig (Nergal) has given me power to go against her, the evil spirit, against Dorib, whom they call the strangler." The spell is intended to produce a successful birth, and by its pantheon has definite ties to ancient indigenous Babylonian religion. Bowl 34, in a hand neither so crude as 32/35/36 nor as polished as 31/33, is "designated for the sealing of the house of Mihr-hormizd bar Mami by power of the virtue of Jesus the healer, by the virtue of my powerful cousin (?)." The power of the "sealing" is described as equivalent to the words by which God "subdued the earth and trees," and Moses' parting of the Red Sea is cited as an analogy. "Charmed and sealed is all evil that is in the body of Mihr-hormizd bar Mami and in his house (and) his wife and his sons and his daughters and his cattle and his property and in all his dwelling, by the signet of Arion son of Zand and by the seal of King Solomon son of David, etc." A spell is appended on behalf of Bahroi bath Bath-Sahde. Bowl 37, written for one Zaroi, is part of the set collated by Naveh and Shaked (see below). It has the same quartered circle on its interior base as all the other bowls written in Manichaean Syriac, but in place of the usual crosses or x's are written Hebrew *yôd-hês* as magical sigils.

35 Naveh and Shaked have collated the text of their Bowl 1 with Montgomery's Bowl 37 (Hamilton Text 9), Hamilton Text 10, as well as an Estrangelo-Syriac bowl (Hamilton Text 14): "Appointed is this bowl for the sealing and guarding of the house, dwelling and body of Huna son of Hupitay, that there should go out from him the tormentors, evil dreams, curses, vows, spells, magic practices, devils, demons, liliths, encroachments and terrors. The secret of heaven is buried in heaven, and the secret of the earth is buried in the earth. I say the secret of this house against all that there is in it: against devils, demons, spells, magic practices, all the messengers of idolatry, all troops, charms, goddesses, all the mighty devils, all the mighty Satans, all the mighty liliths. I tell you this word. He who accepts it, finds goodness, and he who is bad (and) does not accept the mystery words (*melle raze*), angels of wrath come against him, and sabres and swords stand before him and kill him. Fire surrounds him, and flame comes against him. Whoever listens to the word sits in the house, eats and feeds, drinks and pours drink, rejoices and causes joy, he is a brother to brethren and a friend to the dwellers of the house, he is a companion of children and is called educator, he is an associate of cattle and is called good fortune. Accept peace from your Father who is in heaven and sevenfold peace from male gods and from female goddesses. He who makes peace wins the suit. He who causes destruction is burnt in fire (several magical sigils and repetition of the text's opening lines). His sickness shall be pressed down, and a wall of pure steel shall surround Huna son of Kupitay. The sickness, devil and demon of Huna son of Kupitay shall be pressed down and he will be guarded by night and by day. Amen" (Naveh and Shaked, 124-32).

and property of the clients. The "seal" expels or blocks a host of demonic forces, including evil dreams and illnesses.[36]

In their details, these texts certainly do not match our expectations of normative Manichaean ideology. Jewish sacred words and religious authorities rejected by normative Manichaean teaching pepper the spells. But we should not preclude Manichaean authorship on such grounds without taking into consideration the possible influence of compositional conventions in the spells or of that messy, boundary-bending mix of traditions encountered whenever ordinary people get their hands on institutionally distinguished religions.[37] The appeals in Montgomery's bowl 34 to "Jesus the healer"—a common Manichaean name for Jesus (Isho Aryaman)[38]—and to "Michael the healer and Rafiel the reliever

---

[36] "MM May this bowl serve to guard the house of Chilai, son of his grandmother (?). May it cut off, anathematize and uproot bonds, chains, and ties, malediction and vow and incantation, vociferation, insult and sarcasm, sins of idolatry and adoration of false gods, the words of women, the terror of combat, the attack of sorcerers, the bandit of the road, the whirlwind of the desert, the sight of cadavres, the sound of the name *ai ai* and of the word *vei vei* son of death, nocturnal pollutions and day visions. May they be removed and hidden, and may they fall back upon their authors, their evokers, their artisans and their senders. May they vanish and be kept quiet, and may they be taken away very far from Chilai, son of his grandmother (?), and from his wife and his sons and his daughters and his house—by your name, you the four angels: by Chadiel, by Moudzahrit the great, by Afroum the powerful, and by Tsebab the strong. May they be guardians, aids, shields, ramparts. May they guard them, protect them and preserve them from the evil eye, from envious expectation, from the thought of a wicked heart, from the word of a deceitful tongue. May this house of Chilai, son of his grandmother (?), along with its walls, its thresholds, the top of its roof, his harvest, his field, his livestock and his health be sealed. May this Chilai, son of his grandmother (?) be bound and sealed. May the 360 bones of the body of this Chilai be bound and sealed by the bond of the ring of the sky and by the seal of the axis of the earth, against all evil devils, stained and polluted. Finally, may they not approach this Chilai, son of his grandmother (?)—by the name of Arar and Zemit and Ramram and Nasraseb. May he be bound and sealed by the seal of Haltoum the Nšna, the ram, and of Tsouts the lord (*nomina barbara*), amin amin selah" (Allotte de la Fuÿe, 394). The editor speculates the opening MM may stand for *Mar Mani*.

[37] For example, one bowl client, Dadbeh bar Asmanducht, appears on four bowls—two in Manichaean-script and two in the Judeo-Aramaic script. Here is a person who was clearly hedging his bets! Interestingly enough, his Judeo-Aramaic bowls have a stronger dualism and anti-cosmic tone than do the "Manichaean" bowls (Isbell, 71-74).

[38] Montgomery, 1913: 231ff. On Jesus Airyaman as "Jesus the healer," see Louis H. Gray, "Foundations of the Iranian Religions," *Journal of the K. R. Cama Oriental Institute* 15 (1929): 131. Most scholars of Manichaeism erroneously translate *airyaman* "friend" as if it were a common noun (and a Gnostic appellation), and not an identification with the Iranian deity Airyaman, god of

and Gabriel the servant of the Lord"—angels who are also prominent in Manichaean prayer texts—are in conformity with normative Manichaeism. These same spiritual personalities, however, are
common to several Near Eastern religious communities.[39] Such
parallels are not sufficiently definitive to resolve our doubts about
Manichaean authorship.

But unquestionably Manichaean texts recovered in Central Asia
display remarkable similarities to the bowls. M781, published by
W. B. Henning as one of "Two Manichaean Magical Texts,"[40]
contains a spell against fever which instructs, "cast a spell in water
. . . and ashes."[41] The text adds, "[if the spirit of fever] does not
go [of its own accord], then it will come out [of the body] of NN.
son of NN. and vanish in the name of the Lord Isho Aryaman,"
and includes a list of other spiritual beings, including Michael,
Raphael and Gabriel.[42] This text of certain Manichaean provenance follows the general compositional pattern of Montgomery's
bowl 34, and could be construed as instructions for the inscribing of
such a bowl, or a similar apotropaic device.[43] The second spell
found in M781 unleashes the Zoroastrian divinity Thraetona
("Fredon") who promises to smite "all the occult things (razan) of
the house, all the evil spirits of the house, all the wrathful 'robbers'
of the house."[44] Such a spell functions exactly like the bowl texts
and addresses the same concerns as those found in the bowls.

Another Manichaean magical text published by Henning is an
amulet (zawar) which bears on one side a list of demons (yaksas),
giving the name, hour, country, number, and food of each one.
The other side of the amulet reads,

> . . . in your name, by your will, at your command, and through your
> power, Lord Jesus Christ; in the name of Mar Mani the life-giver, the

---

exorcistic healing.

[39] Michael, Gabriel and Raphael are three of the most popular angels throughout late antiquity, and turn up together again on amulets from the Cairo Geniza
(Naveh and Shaked, 219, 225, 237) and in the PGM (90.1-13). They appear
together with Suriel in PGM 10.36-50.

[40] BSOAS 12 (1947): 39-66.

[41] According to Boyce's emendation.

[42] Henning, 40.

[43] The manuscript is not an actual "active" charm, but part of a spell book,
containing more than one spell and not naming an actual client.

[44] Henning, 40-41. Fredon commonly appears on Zoroastrian amulets against
disease. See K. R. Cama Memorial Volume: Essays on Iranian Subjects, ed. J. J.
Modi (Bombay: Fort Printing, 1900), 141-45.

apostle of the gods, and in the name of your holy, praised, blessed spirit, who smites all demons and powers of darkness; in the name of Michael, Sarael, Raphael, and Gabriel . . . of Qaftinus and Bar-Simus the apostle . . . in the name of Anel, Dadel, Abarel, Nisadel, and Rafel, who will smite all you demons (dyw'n), yaksas, she-devils (pryg'n), drujes, rak-sasas, idols of darkness, and spirits of evil. All ye sons of darkness and night, fear and terror, pain and sickness . . . and old age: from before the firm power and word . . . away from this man who wears it, flee ye . . . vanish, take flight, pass away . . . to a far place.[45]

Several of this text's angelic names also appear in the Manichaean text M20, published by Müller: "the lord Bar Simus," "Qaftinus the mighty," Raphael, Gabrael, Michael, Sarael.[46] The latter four appear as well in Manichaean narratives, such as Mani's *Book of the Giants*[47] and the Coptic *Kephalaia*, specifically as demon-conquering powers,[48] and in this capacity turn up again in the company of Fredon/Thraetona and other spiritual powers in the fascinating text M4. This latter manuscript is titled *Bar Simus Pevahišn*, "Invocation of Bar Simus," and invokes divine protection over the Manichaean Community:

Mihryazd, deliverer and merciful one, with Fredon the good and all the angels: may you protect and guard the religion, the holy, the blessed leader, the lords of the excellent names . . . May you all be glorified by the holy religion . . . (and) be a watcher of the inside and the outside, helper and protector. I invoke the angels, the strong, the powerful: Raphael, Michael, Gabrael, Sarael: by whom may we be protected from all adversity, and freed from the evil Ahriman.[49]

Such an invocation, in effect, applies the domestic protective techniques of amulets and bowls to the security of the entire religious community. When such magical evocations are called down as mantles of protection over the religious community itself, artificial divisions into "religious" and "magical" become meaningless.[50]

---

[45] Henning, 51.

[46] F. W. K. Müller, "Handschriften-reste in Estrangelo-schrift aus Turfan, Chinesisch-Turkistan, II," *AKPAW* (1904): 45-46.

[47] W. B. Henning, "The Book of the Giants," *BSOAS* 11 (1943): 54.

[48] On this theme in Manichaean literature, and its dependence on the Enoch cycle, see John C. Reeves, *Jewish Lore in Manichaean Cosmogony: Studies in the Book of Giants Traditions* (Cincinnati: Hebrew Union College Press, 1992).

[49] Müller, 55-56.

[50] Another Manichaean "magical" text (Fonds Pelliot M.914,1) can be found in Jean de Menasce, "Fragments manichéens de Paris," *W. B. Henning Memorial Volume*, eds. M. Boyce and I. Gershevitch (London: Lund Humphries, 1970),

But if we are looking for techniques that we can label "Manichaean magic," we are missing a fundamental point. Techniques such as the magic bowls are taken up and modified by synthesizing, syncretizing traditions, not made whole-cloth by those traditions. The existing technique already has its own conventions of composition, application and concern which are worked on by new encompassing systems but also resist such reshaping. Certain beings and words of power cross over all bowl types, others are peculiar to a single type. We can see tendencies in the bowls—e.g., the choice of script, vocabulary reflective of a particular community—but such tendencies do not instantly wash away the basic rules by which these devices are made and used.

So nothing in the Manichaean-script bowls (other than the script itself) definitively identifies them as Manichaean, and nothing in them precludes Manichaean composition. Yet we have seen from sources of unquestionable Manichaean provenance that the Manichaeans used apotropaic and exorcistic techniques, that they invoked apotropaic powers, and that they were concerned with "sealing" individuals and groups against demonic attack.[51] Regardless of our ability to identify the bowls definitively as the products of Manichaean hands, both the bowls and the Manichaean "magical" texts employ the same invocational technique and derive from a shared cultural environment and view of human existence.

*   *   *

Jonathan Z. Smith has observed that the Mediterranean world underwent a "rebellion" against cultural "paradigms" in the Hellenistic period, that "judged the cosmos, its gods, the human condition, and all structures of order to be evil and oppressive and sought to liberate man by annihilating or reversing these structures."[52] Manichaean ideology, in some ways the culmination of

---

303-06. Other "magical" Manichaean fragments are known, but have not been edited: M341b, M389, M5568, M7917, M8430.

[51] Analogous to such "magic" is the central Manichaean discipline of the "three seals"—of hands, mouth and breast—which are "knots" of control, regulating the transmission of power between the body and the (potentially dangerous) outside world: "these sure seals that are upon thee, O soul, by reason of which no demon can touch thee" (Psalm-Book 52.28-29).

[52] Jonathan Z. Smith, "Birth Upside Down or Right Side Up?" in *Map is Not Territory: Studies in the History of Religions* (Leiden: Brill, 1978), 151.

this rebellion, depicts the world as a devastated battlefield roamed by hostile forces. These forces were combatted by tools which we commonly call "magical"; the life of the Manichaean was an "exorcism interminable."[53]

Even while retaining a "locative" appeal to the authority of Babylon, Manichaeism manifests what Jonathan Z. Smith describes as a shift from the "locative" to the "utopian"—that is, rather than fix the world, Manichaeans seek to escape it by a transformation of themselves.[54] Peterson[55] and Segal[56] have both noted this attitude of escape and transformation in the materials of the Greek magical papyri; and this attitude is what some scholars have called the religious element in late antique magic. But we could just as well call it, in the case of Manichaeism, the magical element in the religion. The label is irrelevant: in either case we are dealing with specific techniques for overcoming demonic control, both on this earth and ultimately beyond it.

Narratives from the Near East in late antiquity show us a world intensely concerned with power and protection, and filled with rival purveyors of sacred security and "salvation." All sides of this religious rivalry employed rites which were liable to the tag "magic" at the hands of their opponents. Each religious commu-

---

[53] With apologies to Freud.

[54] "Within a 'utopian' world-view, it is man who is out of place, who is estranged from his true home 'on high.' The demons are 'in place'—they have their spheres, their realms, their 'houses.' And thus the ritual adjustments are directed against the practitioner rather than the demon. It is the man who will daringly attempt his own redirection or relocation (frequently, as in theurgic materials, by reinterpreting the older rites). It is the demons in their role as 'Watchers' ... who will either recognize him as an enemy or alien and seek to expel or destroy him or recognize him as belonging to the 'beyond' and become his 'ally.' The man proves his right to stand 'on high' by his *gnosis*, especially by demonstrating his knowledge of the demon's name and taxon" ("Towards Interpreting Demonic Powers in Hellenistic and Roman Antiquity," *ANRW*, 2.16.1: 438). Elements of both the "locative" and the "utopian" seem to be taken up into a third paradigm Smith identifies, where "the new center and chief means of access to the divine center will be a highly mobile holy man ..." (*ibid.*). This holy man will be " a magician, who will function, by and large, as an entrepreneur without fixed office ... Rather than celebration, purification and pilgrimage, the new rituals will be those of conversion, of initiation into the secret society or identification with the divine man. As a part of this fundamental shift, the archaic language and ideology of the cult will be revalorized" ("The Temple and the Magician," 238).

[55] E. Peterson, "Die Befreiung Adams aus der Anagke" in *Frühkirche, Judentum, und Gnosis* (Rome: Herder, 1959), 107ff.

[56] A. F. Segal, "Hellenistic Magic: Some Questions of Definition," in *Studies in Gnosticism and Hellenistic Religions presented to Gilles Quispel*, eds. R. van den Broek and M. J. Vermaseren (Leiden: Brill, 1981), 353f.

nity integrated into its system of identifying beliefs and practices available ritual acts which, when examined apart from that integration, looked to be mere "hocus-pocus." All parties to this spiritual competition are or are not liable to the charge of "magic" equally, since they often employed the very same ritual practices (such as the bowls). Within their respective religious systems, these practices were validated and legitimized, but from outside such systems the same practices were disparaged and condemned. The label of "magic" is a product of this context of rivalry, and once we step outside the rivalry the category entirely evaporates. What remains are various ritual acts, various rites of power which are "available" across the boundaries of individual religious communities, but which are customized by, and more or less integrated into, each community differently and, from their point of view, exclusively.

Manichaeism is itself an exorcistic and apotropaic practice, a technique of exorcising or suppressing demons in the body and "sealing" the body against renewed attacks. This technique should be construed not as a metaphor for some "spiritual" truth, but as an actual, "magical," literal transformation of the body.[57] The promise of such power must certainly have gained broad appeal in the late antique world awash in a sea of demons. The Manichaean elect could scarcely have avoided disseminating their power to the needs of their followers if they were to compete for allegiance with other powerful figures and institutions. They may have appropriated the concrete forms of such power dissemination, such as bowls or amulets, from the domestic practices of converts; or perhaps institutional Manichaeism itself developed out of just such practices. In either case, the exchange of power for support was no compromise of "higher" principles for the Manichaean elect; it was intrinsic to their role as the army of light on the battlefield called earth.

---

[57] See n. 26.

CHAPTER TWENTY-ONE

MAGIC, WOMEN, AND HERESY IN THE LATE EMPIRE: THE CASE OF THE PRISCILLIANISTS

Todd Breyfogle

In the summer of 385, Priscillian, bishop of Avila, was executed in Trier by the imperial arm on charges of sorcery, nocturnal orgies, and praying naked.[1] The case of the Priscillianists is unusual on several counts. First, many of Priscillian's followers were wealthy aristocratic women. Second, Priscillian was an established and powerful bishop, whose road to execution was marked not by explicit accusations of magic but by allegations that he subscribed to Gnostic and Manichaean heresies. This essay looks anew at the Priscillianist affair in an effort to tease out the curious relationships between magic, women, and heresy, and to ascertain what appeared magical to the fourth-century Christian mind.

On the whole, modern scholarship has either not addressed the specific questions of magic or has treated magic as a legal device in the persecution of heresy.[2] Heresy was not a capital crime, but magic was, prompting Gibbon's verdict that Priscillian was the first heretic to be executed by the state,[3] a judgment which has been frequently repeated.[4] More recent studies, however, have shown

---

[1] I would like to express my gratitude to Dr. N. B. McLynn, who supervised my initial research on Priscillian, and to H. M. D. Breyfogle, whose helpful suggestions substantially improved the text.

[2] The topic of magic was all but neglected in the major studies by E.-Ch. Babut, *Priscillien et le priscillienisme* (Paris: H. Champion, 1909); J. Davids, *De Orosio et Sancto Augustino Priscillianistarum Adversariis* (The Hague: A. N. Govers, 1930); and A. d'Alès, *Priscillien et l'Espagne Chrétienne à la fin du IVe siècle* (Paris: G. Beauchesne, 1936). See B. Vollmann's summary of magic and astrology in Priscillianism in "Priscillianus," *PWSup* 14 (1974): 536-39.

[3] Edward Gibbon, *The Decline and Fall of the Roman Empire* (New York: Modern Library, n.d.), 1.973-75.

[4] For example, W. H. C. Frend, *The Rise of Christianity* (Philadelphia: Fortress, 1984), 670; P. Brown, "The Diffusion of Manichaeism in the Roman Empire," in *Religion and Society in the Age of St. Augustine* (New York: Harper and Row, 1972), 94; N. Q. King, *The Emperor Theodosius and the Establishment of Christianity* (Philadelphia: Westminster Press, 1961), 51; and A. Piganiol, *L'empire chrétien: 325-395,* 2d ed. (Paris: Presses Universitaires de France, 1972), 228, 243-44.

that the affair was not as simple as Gibbon suggests. It is now clear that Priscillian's teachings and practices, though often unusual, fell within the tolerated norms of ancient Christian orthodoxy.[5] Thus, research has turned to sociological and anthropological theory for aid in explaining the accusations of magic and heresy which occasioned Priscillian's demise.[6] According to this latter approach, accusations of magic and Manichaeism functioned within a system of "community dynamics" as measures against those whom the community was unable to assimilate.[7]

The tools of anthropology have been a boon to historical research. But in the case of the Priscillianists, at least, rigid application of functionalist models has yielded two problems. First, it has led to the assumption that because the Priscillianists were accused of magic they must therefore have been marginal. Second, by focusing solely on conflicts of power, it has neglected the very real theological conflict, obscuring the Priscillianists' affinities with Manichaeism and Gnosticism.[8] That is to say, the functionalist approach has pre-empted the question of how Priscillianist practice and doctrine may actually have *appeared* magical and heretical to fourth-century observers.

The accusations of heresy and magic against Priscillian cannot be fully accounted for as a conflict between "articulate" and "inarticulate" power.[9] Priscillian was a well-educated urban aristocrat who with shrewd manipulation of the imperial power structure was able to frustrate his persecutor Ithacius at almost every turn.[10] Priscillian was openly supported by at least five fellow bishops, and possibly counted as informal supporters such prominent ecclesias-

---

[5] H. Chadwick, *Priscillian of Avila: The Occult and the Charismatic in the Early Church* (Oxford: Oxford University Press, 1976), is a characteristically erudite and thorough account. I have not yet seen A. B. J. M. Goosen, "Achtergronden van Priscillianus' Christelijke Ascese," (diss., Nijmegen, 1976).

[6] Raymond Van Dam, *Leadership and Community in Late Antique Gaul* (Berkeley: University of California Press, 1985), 88-114, brings modern anthropological theory to bear on his detailed assemblage of the historical evidence. The classic, groundbreaking application of modern anthropology to late antiquity is, of course, Peter Brown, "Sorcery, Demons and the Rise of Christianity: From Late Antiquity to the Middle Ages" in *Religion and Society*, 119-146.

[7] Van Dam, *Leadership*, 78-87, 102-03.

[8] For these affinities see below and Babut, *Priscillien*, 253-63; Davids, *De Orosio*, 117-20, 141-5; d'Alès, *Priscillien,* 92-93; Chadwick, *Priscillian*, 94-99, 194-98.

[9] The terms are P. Brown's, "Sorcery," 124.

[10] Sulpicius Severus, *Chron.* II.46.3, II.48.5-6 (*CSEL* 1), with A. Piganiol, *L'empire chrétien*, 254.

tical authorities as Martin of Tours, Paulinus of Nola, and Ambrose of Milan.[11] Among his followers were "many persons of noble station," including a renowned Spanish poet and the wealthy widow Euchrotia, whose husband had been a prominent professor at Bordeaux and friend of Ausonius (poet and consul in 379).[12] Far from being a social or religious anomaly who could not be assimilated by the existing community, Priscillian, both alive and dead, energized a tightly knit community which flourished in much of Spain and Gaul.[13] The sect survived well into the sixth century and has been tentatively linked with both the cult of St. James at Santiago de Compostella and the medieval Cathars.[14] Put simply, the Priscillianists were insiders, not outsiders; in social and political terms, the Priscillianists' battle was fought on level ground.

Thus, we must look again at the case of the Priscillianists in an attempt to determine why this bishop, famous for his female devotees, was mistaken as a purveyor of magic and heresy. In charting a possible matrix of relationships between magic, women and heresy, I hope to shed greater light not only on the Priscillianist affair, but also, through tentative generalization, on how

---

[11] Explicitly Priscillianist bishops were Instantius, Salvianus, Hyginus, Symposius, and Vegetinus (Sulp. Sev., *Chron.* II.46.8, II.47.3, II.51.1-10; Priscillian, *Tract.* II.40, 1-2; Chadwick, *Priscillian*, "Exemplar professionum," 237-38). Martin and Ambrose objected to the secular trying of ecclesiastical matters but may well have had deeper sympathies with their fellow ascetic (Sulp. Sev., *Chron.* II.50.4-6, *Dial.* III.11-13; Ambrose, *ep.* 24.12, also *ep.* 21). On Paulinus' possible Priscillianist associations see Babut, *Priscillien*, 213; W. H. C. Frend, "The two worlds of Paulinus of Nola," in *Latin Literature of the Fourth Century*, ed. J. W. Binns (London: Routledge, 1971), 100-33; but also J. T. Lienhard, *Paulinus of Nola and Early Western Monasticism* (Köln: P. Hanstein, 1977), 52-57.

[12] Sulp. Sev., *Chron.* II.46.5. The poet Latronianus, beheaded with Priscillian at Trier (*Chron.* II.51.3), is lauded by Jerome (*De vir. illus.* 122); see further *Prosopography of the Later Roman Empire*, eds. Jones *et al.* (Cambridge: Cambridge University Press, 1971), 1.496. On the career of Euchrotia's husband Delphidius, see Ausonius, *Comm. Prof. Burd.* 5 and *PLRE* 1.246. The Priscillianists' substantial wealth is attested by Pacatus, *Paneg. Theod.* 29; Sulp. Sev., *Dial.* III.11.10-11.

[13] Almost fifty years after Priscillian's death, the Priscillianists could be infiltrated only by outright deceit; see Constantius to Augustine, *ep.* 11* (ed. J. Divjak, *CSEL* 88 [1981]: 51-70).

[14] Priscillianism was of prime concern to the Council of Braga in 563 (*PL* 84.561-68). On the survival of Priscillianism in the fifth and sixth centuries see Chadwick, *Priscillian*, 170-233. Santiago de Compostella: B. Vollmann, "Priscillianus," 517. Cathars: L. Varga, "Les Cathares sont-ils des Neomanicheens ou des Neagnostiques?" *RHR* 120 (1939): 175-93. For the Priscillianist writings in Ireland see J. Hillgarth, *Visigothic Spain, Byzantium and the Irish* (London: Variorum, 1985), 167-94, 442-56.

magic, women and heresy were related in the late fourth-century mind.

The evidence is somewhat problematic. For the most part, we are dependent upon texts outside of the Priscillianist circle. Councils and chronicles—both contemporary with and several centuries after the affair—are hostile to the Priscillianists almost without exception.[15] The Priscillianist texts themselves, discovered in Würzburg just over one hundred years ago, can hardly be called magical texts in any remotely conventional sense. The field is thus tricky, and many conclusions will be more approximations than demonstrable certainties.

The earliest source of our information on the teachings and practices of Priscillian is the Council of Saragossa, held probably in October of 380.[16] The canons of the council make no mention of magic, but are nonetheless of great interest as our earliest and probably most accurate external account of the beliefs and practices that later were to be construed as magical. The council's initial concern is social and ecclesiastical impropriety. Canon 1 censures women for visiting the houses of men to whom they are not related to attend "readings" (*lectio*) for the purpose of "instruction and discussion." The readings themselves are apparently not suspect. But canon 7 implies that unauthorized persons are being permitted to teach. And the unauthorized teachers may have included laymen and possibly laywomen; the Priscillianist writings affirm the spiritual equality both of clergy and laity and of men and women.[17]

The central concern of the Council of Saragossa, however, was unconventional religious practices: fasting on Sunday and withdrawing from consecrated churches during Lent (canon 2), accepting but not consuming the Eucharist in church (canon 3), and abandoning the churches and walking barefoot during Advent and Epiphany (canon 4). While magic is not specifically alleged, many of these charges may have carried with them connotations of magic in a fourth-century milieu.[18]

---

[15] For this reason, in part, my account concentrates on the evidence closest to the affair both in time and geography. Chadwick, *Priscillian*, gives a full account of all the relevant ancient and medieval sources.

[16] *PL* 84.315-18. The council drew bishops from as far away as Aquitaine.

[17] E.g., Prisc., *Tract*. I.28, 14-24, *Canones* 55, 61, 39, 48.

[18] The other canons decry the acceptance of excommunicants at the altar (5), excommunicate clergy who abandon their duties to become monks (6), and censure virgins who take vows of celibacy and service before the age of forty, or who do not do so formally in the presence of a bishop (8).

Fasting on Sunday—a feast day of celebration—would have smacked of ascetical excess as well as Manichaeism, and may have been seen as having magical associations not identified with asceticism more generally.[19] Fasting was held to have magical potency and was an important preliminary part of pagan and Christian rites and visions, as well as theurgic possession by the divine.[20] The Priscillianists' habit of fasting on a feast day prompted great abhorrence.[21] Those outside the sect may have suspected an alternate purpose—magical ritual in conjunction with the traditional mass.

The withdrawal from established churches carried even more serious connotations of magic. Canon 2 expresses suspicions about the apparent Priscillianist practice of retiring to mountain hideaways and stealing away to strange villas. Several imperial rescripts condemn those who spurn Catholic congregations, whether for heretical or pious purposes.[22] How far these laws applied to Priscillian is not clear, for as bishop he was of course the authority of the local Catholic congregation.[23] Imperial legislation issued in 382 forbids the convocation of "secret and hidden assemblies (*occultos ... latentesque conventus*)," and an earlier rescript permitted "ceremonies of a bygone perversion" to be conducted, provided they were done so openly (*libera luce*).[24] The Priscillianists'

---

[19] On the Manichaean practice of fasting on Sundays, see Augustine, *ep.* 36.27.

[20] Pliny (*NH* 26.60.93) describes a cure which requires the patient to fast and a poultice to be applied by a naked and fasting maiden. On fasting and visions see *Herm. Vis.* 2.2.1, 3.1.1, 3.10.6-7; Synesius, *De Insomniis* 11 (*PG* 66.1311); Iamblicus, *De myst.* 3.2, 3.11; *PGM* VII.664, 704, 740; XII.107. The evidence for fasting as preliminary to both pagan and Christian rites is thoroughly assembled, with commentary, by R. Arbesmann, "Fasting and Prophecy in Pagan and Christian Antiquity," *Traditio* 7 (1949-51): 1-71; also E. R. Dodds, *The Greeks and the Irrational* (Berkeley: University of California Press, 1951), ch. 4; R. Lane Fox, *Pagans and Christians* (New York: Knopf, 1987), 102-67, 375-418.

[21] E.g., Augustine, *ep.* 36.27: ". . . fasting on Sunday is considered utterly revolting (*ut ieiunium diei dominici horribilius haberetur*)." Even today Roman Catholics regard fasting on a feast day as an affront.

[22] *Codex Theodosianus* 16.5.9 (382), 16.4.6 (404), 16.5.15 (388).

[23] *CTh.* 16.5.5 (379) condemns teachers of perverse doctrines, even if the teachers are ordained priests or deacons, or claim episcopal support. The rescript (Gratian to Hesperius) may have been directed against the Priscillianists, then under the supervision of bishops Instantius and Salvianus (Sulp. Sev., *Chron.* II.46.7). Hesperius, Praetorian Prefect in Gaul in 378-79, may have had jurisdiction over Spain (*PLRE* 1.427-28).

[24] *CTh.* 16.5.9 (382); *CTh.* 9.16.2 (319). See also *CTh.* 16.5.7 (381) which forbids Manichees to establish "*conventicula oppidorum*" for their "*feralium mysteriorum.*"

meetings thus had the appearance of secrecy, one of the strongest determinants of magic in the Roman world. The countryside and mountains were considered to be the location of illicit activity generally.[25] If the Priscillianists retired regularly and in secret to country villas and mountain cells, it is not surprising that they were suspected of magical practices.

It is likely that the Council also saw magical connotations in the alleged Priscillianist practice of not immediately consuming the eucharistic elements. As early as the second century Justin Martyr felt compelled to defend the eucharistic rite against charges of magic, and Clement of Alexandria speaks of the transformation of the bread into "spiritual power."[26] Long venerated as the central Christian mystery reserved only for those initiated through baptism, the celebration of the Eucharist became more elaborate in the fourth century and took on a stronger sense of the effects of consecration.[27] John Chrysostom described the Lord's Table as a place of "terror and shuddering" worthy of great awe and veneration, and Ambrose viewed the consecration of the elements as effecting a real change in the bread and wine.[28] The consecrated elements themselves were thus increasingly considered to possess stronger and stronger supernatural power.[29] Consecrated elements are known to have been taken home by early modern Christian

---

[25] See *CTh.* 16.10.16 (399), where country temples are referred to as "the material basis for all superstition." Many rescripts forbid heretical or superstitious assemblies "within the towns": *CTh.* 16.5.6 (381), 16.5.11 (383), 16.5.30-35 (396-402). Rescripts of 425 banish heretics 100 miles from Rome to protect the city from contagion (*CTh.* 16.5.62, 16.5.64). See also R. Van Dam, *Leadership and Community*, 67-68.

[26] Justin Martyr, *Apol.* 61-2, 65-7, with H. Chadwick, "Justin Martyr's Defense of Christianity" *BJRL* 47 (1965): 279; Clement of Alexandria, *Excerpta ex Theodoto* 82.

[27] Hippolytus, *Apos. Trad.* 23.14, 32.1, 32.1-4; Ambrose, *De myst.* I.2; G. Dix, *The Shape of the Liturgy* (Glasgow: Dacre, 1945), 199; H. Chadwick, *The Early Church* (Baltimore: Penguin, 1967), 261-71.

[28] Chrysostom cited in Chadwick, *Early Church*, 267. Ambrose, *De sacramentis*, IV.iv.15: "that things previously existing should, without ceasing to exist, be changed into something else (*ut sint quae erant et in aliud commutentur*)"; see also the helpful note by J. H. Srawley, ed., *On the Sacraments and On the Mysteries* (London: SPCK, 1950), 37-42, 87-88; also *De sacr.* IV.iv.16, IV.v.23, VI.i.1 and *De myst.* IX.58. For Ambrosian "transfiguration" as the precursor for the much later doctrine of "transubstantiation" see E. Mazza, *Mystagogy: A Theology of Liturgy in the Patristic Age* (New York: Pueblo, 1989), 171.

[29] The understanding of the Holy Spirit's presence at the consecration is described by Dix, *Shape*, 275-80.

peasants for use as cures or in gardens as inducements for great growth.[30] Unfortunately, the Priscillianist texts give us no specific information as to how regular (or official) this practice was, nor do they provide us with a detailed understanding of Priscillian's eucharistic theology.[31] Nevertheless, the consumption of the consecrated elements outside the walls of the church was probably seen as magical by the council.

The practice of going barefoot, condemned by canon 4, was a recognized form of ascetic denial. But going barefoot was a more complicated issue in antiquity than we moderns might imagine.[32] Several late fourth- and early fifth-century sources make it clear that opinions differed strongly as to whether Christians were forbidden to wear shoes.[33] At least one sect that preached that Christians were required to remove their shoes, after the examples of Moses and Isaiah, was declared heretical.[34] Going barefoot was also widely considered to have strong associations with pagan ritual and to increase magical power. The Pythagoreans held that sacrifice must be offered with bare feet, and some Roman processions were conducted without shoes.[35] Going about with unshod feet may also have evoked suspicions of pantheism and thus pagan nature worship and nature magic.

What is most striking about many of the canons of Saragossa, however, is the fact that the Council is at pains to proscribe certain practices not in themselves, but at particular times during the ecclesiastical calendar. Hence, the Council does not condemn fasting *per se*, but on Sundays (*die dominica*). So too, the second canon is concerned that the Priscillianists were forsaking established churches for their mountain hideaways during Lent (*quadragesimarum die*). Going barefoot, canon 4 emphasizes, as

---

[30] See K. V. Thomas, *Religion and the Decline of Magic* (London: Penguin, 1971), 38, though such a broad chronological and geographical comparison is suggestive rather than conclusive. Examples of taking the eucharistic elements home: Justin Martyr, *Apol.* I.65; Hipp., *Apos. Trad.* 26.15-16; Sozomen, *HE* 8.5.

[31] The Priscillianist Tractate XI has been convincingly identified as an early Spanish Illatio by Stephen Coombs, "Thematic Correspondences in Iberogallic, Egyptian and Ethiopian Eucharistic Prayers," *Ostkirchliche Studien* 38 (1989): 281-310.

[32] For much of what follows I am endebted to Chadwick's thorough account of bare feet (*Priscillian*, 17-20).

[33] Gaudentius, *Tract. V in Exod.* (*CSEL* 68. 43-48); Ambrose, *Expl. Ps. 118* 17. 17 (*PL* 15.1446).

[34] Filastrius 81 (*CSEL* 38.43). Augustine objects on exegetical grounds (*De haer.* 68).

[35] Suetonius, *Aug.* 100.4; Iamblichus, *Vita Pyth.* 85, 105.

well as forsaking the churches and other practices are anathematized only during the second half of Advent and all of Epiphany (*viginti et uno die quo a XVI Kalendas Januarias usque in diem Epiphaniae*). As we have seen, the practices condemned at Saragossa had strong associations with magic and indecency. But what most concerned the Council was the proximity of these practices to high Christian holy celebrations such as Christmas and Easter. While "orthodox" or at least permissible in themselves, many of the Priscillianists' deeds smacked too strongly of pagan magic when practiced concurrently with the most important Christian celebrations.[36]

Whether the Priscillianists themselves crossed the line into magic is difficult to say.[37] Though suspicious of Priscillian's activities, the Council of Saragossa found itself similarly uncertain; the Council did not make specific accusations of magic, and Priscillian was not censured by name on any count.[38]

In the years after Saragossa, Spain and southern Gaul saw a continuation of Priscillian's remarkable success. Driven from Spain by imperial command, Priscillian traveled to Rome and Milan and succeeded in having the rescript overturned. His episcopal nemesis, Ithacius, fled to Trier where soon a change in imperial politics would halt the Priscillianists' success. The usurpation of the throne by Maximus allowed Ithacius to resume his persecution. Priscillian and his followers were compelled to attend the council of Bordeaux in 384. Upon Priscillian's appeal to the emperor, the proceedings were resumed under imperial jurisdiction in Trier in 385.[39]

---

[36] Not surprisingly, the Church was concerned to preserve the purity of its mysteries. Imperial legislation consequently forbids heretics to "contaminate with profane mind the mystery of Almighty God (*profanaque mente omnipotentis dei contaminare mysterium*)" (*CTh.* 16.5.26 [395]) and to "present the false appearance of mysteries (*mysteriorum simulationem ad injuriam verae religionis aptare*)" (*CTh.* 16.5.15 [388]).

[37] Such a judgment begs the question of defining magic and of its utility as a social scientific term, a dispute which I cannot engage here. In charting what appeared magical to the fourth-century mind I have throughout employed working definitions, though some of the conclusions of this study will have implications for the theoretical debate.

[38] *PL* 84.515; Prisc., *Tract.* II.35.16-22, II.40.7-8, II.42.19ff; Sulp. Sev., *Chron.* II.47.2-3, is mistaken.

[39] Sulp. Sev., *Chron.* II.49.5-II.50.1. The year of the trial at Trier is disputed: Chadwick, *Priscillian*, 132-38; A. R. Birley, "Magnus Maximus and the Persecution of Heresy," *BJRL* 66 (1983): 29-33. I part company with both for reasons outside the scope of this paper.

Unfortunately, the proceedings of Bordeaux and Trier do not survive. Sulpicius Severus does not record the specific complaints lodged against Priscillian at Bordeaux, but he does tell us the charges on which Priscillian was convicted at Trier. In these charges we find the most explicit conjunction of magic, women and heresy.

Unlike most sorcery trials, Priscillian was given not one but two full and lengthy trials at Trier. The occurrence of a second trial suggests that Trier was not a kangaroo court and that the prosecution had difficulty proving its case. But the double dose of due process was undoubtedly not welcomed by Priscillian; capital cases regularly employed torture and this case seems to have been no exception.[40] In the end, Sulpicius writes, Priscillian was convicted of "sorcery (*maleficii*), nor did he disavow that he had studied obscene doctrines (*obscenis doctrinis*), that he had convened, by night, assemblies of vile and indecent women (*turpium feminarum*) and that he was accustomed to pray while naked."[41] Sorcery was a capital charge, and much more than peasant agricultural magic must have been proven to merit execution.[42]

It is likely that the seriousness of the charges derived from their conjunction. Separately, the charges may have merited only defrocking or exile. Together, they constituted a dangerous threat. The study of "obscene doctrines" need not be taken in a strictly religious sense, though neither should that sense be excluded. Legislation concerning magic and astrology tolerated the holding of "forbidden doctrines" but strongly condemned the teaching of such doctrines.[43] That Priscillian had studied these doctrines smacked of the promulgation of a magical sect with all its conspiratorial overtones. The same imperial rescript of 370 equated the learning of magical doctrines with teaching them, and punished both by death. Priscillian was said to have been instructed by the disciples of a certain Marcus from Egypt, long recognized as a center of ancient magic.[44] In the eyes of his accusers, Priscillian was educated in a

---

[40] Sulp. Sev., *Chron.* II.50.7-II.51.3; Pacatus, *Paneg. Theod.* 29; Chadwick, *Priscillian*, 139. On legal aspects of the case see K. Girardet, "Trier 385, Der Prozess gegen die Priszillianer," *Chiron* 4 (1974): 576-608; A. Rousselle, "Quelques Aspects Politiques de l'Affaire Priscillianiste," *REA* 83 (1981): 85-96.

[41] Sulp. Sev., *Chron.* II.50.8.

[42] *CTh.* 9.16.5 (357), 9.16.7 (364). See also Amm. Marc. 28.1.1-56; Paulinus, *Vita Ambr.* 20.

[43] *CTh.* 9.16.8 (370).

[44] Sulp. Sev., *Chron.* II.46.2. On Marcus see V. C. De Clerq, "Ossius of Cor-

magical sect, and in the words of an imperial rescript of 358, people "imbued with magical contamination (*magicis contaminibus adsuetus*)" should not escape torture and death, even if they were of high rank.[45]

We saw above how secret assemblies compounded suspicions of magic. Assemblies at nighttime—such as those evidently practiced by the Priscillianists—greatly multiplied the appearance of magic. A rescript of 364 threatens with death those who engage in "wicked prayers (*nefarias preces*)" or "magic preparations (*magicos apparatus*)" which take place "during the nighttime."[46] The further text of the rescript makes it clear that such nighttime assemblies were strongly associated with sacrifices to demonic forces. Had the Priscillianists gathered only during the day, the appearance of nefarious activity may have been reduced.

Added to this, Priscillian was accused of praying naked. Nudity in antiquity was held to increase the potency of magic to a degree even greater than that accomplished by bare feet.[47] Praying naked also evoked religious objections. Jerome chided Vigilantius for not covering himself before praying for safety during an earthquake, and a monk's improper attire after a bath drew a sharp response from Martin. In both cases, nudity was not only immodest but presumed a sinlessness that obtained only before the fall.[48]

If the Priscillianists were naked at secret nighttime meetings at which women were present, it is no surprise that charges of immorality were leveled. We have noted already the suggestion of improper reading groups raised by the first canon of the Council of Saragossa. Knaves often pretended priestly station for purposes of seduction, and even pious priests took care not to visit women unchaperoned.[49] Moreover, adultery was frequently held to be the result of magical intervention through the use of love spells and

---

dova and the Origins of Priscillianism," *Studia Patristica* 1 (=*Texte und Untersuchungen* 63, 1957): 601-06. On Egypt's reputation as a magical center see Jerome, *In Esaiam* 5 on 19:11-13 (*CChr.* 73.175); *Vita Hilarionis* 21 (*PL* 23.28). It is interesting that Coombs, "Thematic Correspondences," 304-08, notes the similarity between the Spanish rite (the earliest example being the Priscillianist) and the Ethiopian and Libyan rites.

[45] *CTh.* 9.16.6 (358). Senators were subsequently exempted from torture (*CTh.* 9.35.3 [377]).

[46] *CTh.* 9.16.7 (364).

[47] Again, I am indebted to the evidence collected by Chadwick, *Priscillian*, 18-19, 140.

[48] Jerome, *Contra Vigilantium* 11 (*PL* 23.348-49); Sulp. Sev., *Dial.* III.14.8-9.

[49] Jerome, *ep.* 125.6, *ep.* 22.14-16, 28; Possidius, *Vita Augustini*, 26-27.

the like.[50] Women formed a large part of the Priscillianist party, and it is no surprise that Priscillian would have been seen as a seducer of "silly women laden down by sins."[51] Indeed, Priscillian was said to have had an illicit affair with Euchrotia's daughter Procula, whose pregnancy was terminated by the use of certain plants.[52]

In addition to immorality, the presence of women evoked both heretical and magical connotations. Priscillian was taught, we are told, by a wealthy Spanish woman named Agape, a disciple of Marcus the Egyptian and a purveyor of both magical and heretical doctrine.[53] Women were often associated with pernicious doctrines in Christian antiquity, at least in part because of their presumed weakness of mind and character, though we must remember that positive appraisals of female ability are also common.[54] The relationship between women, heresy, and moral turpitude among the Priscillianists is highlighted by the fact that the Manichees were widely believed to practice ritual orgies, to have meetings at which men and women prayed together naked, and to mix semen (a common ingredient in magical potions) with the eucharistic bread.[55] And, like the Priscillianists, the Manichees were suspected of magic. The close relation of heresy to moral turpitude is further emphasized by the fact that the moral and the religious were closely related for ancient philosophy generally. Not only Christians but Neoplatonists, Epicureans, and Stoics held that one's

---

[50] Amm. Marc., 28.1, 16.8. For examples of love spells from the Greek magical papyri see J. Winkler, "The Constraints of Eros," in *Magika Hiera: Ancient Greek Magic and Religion*, eds. C. Faraone and D. Obbink (New York: Oxford University Press, 1991), 214-43.

[51] 2 Tim 3:6, cited by Jerome, *ep.* 133.4 (referring to heretics generally).

[52] Sulp. Sev., *Chron.* II.48.4. Ausonius attests to the infamy of the rumor (*Comm. Prof. Burd.* 5).

[53] Sulp. Sev., *Chron.* II.46.2.

[54] Jerome (*ep.* 133.4) charts the central role of women in the promulgation of many heresies (Priscillianism included); also *ep.* 130.17. See also R. Kraemer, *Her Share of the Blessings: Women's Religions among Pagans, Jews, and Christians in the Greco-Roman World* (New York: Oxford University Press, 1992), 157-73, and bibliography. For positive appraisals: Jerome, *ep.* 127.5-10; and generally the rich picture painted by P. Brown, *The Body and Society* (London: Faber, 1989), 145-54, 341-427.

[55] Ambrose, *ep.* 50.14: Manichees "mingle and unite sacrilege with impiety." Also Augustine, *De haer.* 46.61-81, *De moribus*, II.70; Anastasius Sinaita, *In Hexaem.* 7; other sources conveniently noted by Chadwick, *Priscillian*, 140-43. Jerome, *ep.* 133.3: "[The Priscillianists] shut themselves up alone with women and justify their sinful embraces by quoting lines [from Vergil]" (trans. NPNF 2d ser. vol. 6, 274). For semen as magical ingredient, *PGM* XII.401-44.

beliefs constituted a way of life; a defect in belief necessarily entailed a defect in morals.[56]

There is also considerable ancient evidence that women were
thought to have possessed special or unusual powers. According to
Pliny, women—naked and *sine menstruis*—can secure the safety of
sailors. Menstruous women, Pliny continues, can drive away hail-
storms and other bad weather by standing naked. Women even had
the power of pesticides: when menstruous naked women walked
through cornfields, agricultural pests fell dead.[57] The womb, menstrual blood, and especially fresh embryos had magical power.[58]
Some measures were taken to moderate the presence of women in
the mass; women stood apart from men in the *ecclesia,* and menstruous women were not to be baptized.[59]

The large number of women prominent in religious life in the
fourth-century West suggests that women may not have been
regarded as practitioners of magic in themselves. Nonetheless, it is
significant that none of the miracles recorded by the biographers
of Martin, Ambrose, or Augustine involves a woman.[60] The mere
presence of women seems to have increased the possibility of
magic. Given the Priscillianist teaching of the equality of men and
women and of clergy and laity, it is not inconceivable that Priscillianist women celebrated the Eucharist.[61] We have no evidence of
women celebrants among the Priscillianists, but the prospect of a
woman celebrating the Eucharist at secret nighttime nude gatherings would be a terrifying prospect indeed for a fourth-century
observer. Like fasting and bare feet, then, it was the proximity of
women to "orthodox" religious activities that compounded the
appearance of both magic and heresy.

To supplement the Council of Saragossa and Sulpicius' account
of Bordeaux and Trier we have the Priscillianist texts them-

---

56 See generally P. Hadot, *Exercises Spirituels et Philosophie Antique*
(Paris: Etudes augustiniennes, 1981), 13-74, 217-27; also J. Pigeaud, *La
Maladie de l'Ame* (Paris: Société d'édition "Les Belles Lettres," 1981).

57 Pliny, *NH* 28.23.77-8.

58 J.-J. Aubert, "Threatened Wombs: Aspects of Ancient Uterine Magic,"
GRBS 30 (1989): 421-49.

59 Hippolytus, *Apos. Trad.* 18.2, 20.6; Paulinus, *Vita Ambr.* 11.

60 The few exceptions are clearly based on biblical models: Sulp. Sev., *Vita
Mart.* 16, *Dial.* III.2 (two young girls), and *Dial.* III.9 (a woman, cf. Matt 9:20-
23); likewise Paulinus, *Vita Ambr.* 10.

61 R. Kraemer, *Her Share of the Blessings,* 174-98, contends that the early
church had women celebrants. For the opposite conclusion see R. Gryson, *The
Ministry of Women in the Early Church* (Collegeville: Liturgical Press, 1976),
who briefly discusses the Priscillianists (100-02).

selves.[62] Of particular interest here are what have come down to us as the first two of the Würzburg Tractates: the *Liber apologeticus*, submitted to the Council of Saragossa, and the *Liber ad Damasum*, a similar defense of orthodoxy submitted to Pope Damasus as part of an unsuccessful Priscillianist appeal.[63] Both Tractates are over-whelmingly concerned with demonstrating Priscillian's orthodoxy, but the very brief mention of magic gives us a clearer picture of the relationship between magic, women, and heresy.

Priscillian mentions the "crimes of sacrilege" (*sacrilegii nefas*) of which he has not, he emphasizes, been formally accused: harvest rituals involving "magical incantations (*magicis praecantationi-bus*)" and "evil invocations (*maledictis*)" to the sun and moon.[64] The relatively benign nature of this accusation of agricultural magic led Chadwick to speculate that Priscillian had probably been present at a peasant harvest rite.[65] What Chadwick suggests is not impossible; Priscillian's followers included "many common peo-ple," and the success of crops was of prime interest to most nobles and farmers alike.[66] But while magic in general was not uncommon among the wealthy and well-educated of the late fourth century, it would indeed be odd for peasant agricultural magic to have played a prominent part in the religious lives of the many well-educated Priscillianists.[67]

A charge of agricultural (i.e., "white") magic, moreover, would have had little shock value.[68] Most important, such a charge was of

---

[62] For a full listing of the extant Priscillianist texts see Chadwick, *Priscillian*, xiii.

[63] The eleven Priscillianist Tractates were discovered in a codex in the library at Würzburg in 1885 by G. Schepss, and are edited by him in *CSEL* 18 (1889), together with the Priscillianist *Canones*. Schepss' edition is reprinted, with additional emendations, in *PLSup* II.1413-1483 (Tractates) and 1391-1413 (*Canones*). That the first Tractate was submitted to Saragossa was originally argued by Babut, *Priscillien*, 143, and is endorsed by Chadwick who believes it is of Priscillian's authorship (*Priscillian*, 33, 47-51, 69).

[64] Prisc., *Tract.* I.23, 22 - I.24, 3.

[65] Chadwick, *Priscillian*, 54.

[66] Sulp. Sev., *Chron.* II.46.5.

[67] On magic among the well-educated, see Amm. Marc. 28.1.1-56, 28.4, 29.1-2, with J. Matthews, *The Roman Empire of Ammianus* (Baltimore: Johns Hopkins University Press, 1989), 209-26. A. A. Barb, "The Survival of Magic Arts," in A. Momigliano, *The Conflict between Paganism and Christianity in the Fourth Century* (Oxford: Clarendon, 1964), 100-25 is still helpful on fourth-century magic generally.

[68] Particularly given the general corruption among the Spanish clergy: Inno-cent I, *ep.* 3.4.7 (*PL* 20.490-91); E.-Ch. Babut, *Priscillien*, 92-96; also Sulpicius' description of Ithacius, *Chron.* II.50.2-3.

little importance from both a legal and an ecclesiastical point of view. An imperial rescript of the early fourth century explicitly exempted from prosecution magic used innocently in rural areas to prevent the natural destruction of crops by rain or hail. The church, for its part, was intent on extending its mission to the countryside by demonstrating Christ's power—sometimes in the form of a holy man—in the protection of crops and animals. The presence of Martin of Tours protected nearby farms from a hail-storm, and cattle were apparently branded with the sign of the cross to preserve them from plague.[69]

Perhaps more troubling was an amulet worn by Priscillian and described in the first Tractate. The amulet bore the name of Christ in Hebrew, Greek, and Latin, with the words "King of kings and Lord of lords," together with the image of a lion.[70] Such an amulet is not at all unusual; a large number of Christian amulets survive, and the Priscillianist amulet is illustrative of superstition common to pagans and Christians alike.[71] The title itself occurs several times in scripture, and the occurrence of Christ's name in Hebrew, Greek and Latin (as Priscillian himself reminds us) recalls the inscription above Christ at his crucifixion.[72] The amulet is clearly designed to emphasize Christ's supreme power in warding off hostile demonic and magical forces. The lion is both an emblem of great strength and an appellation of Christ, "the Lion of the tribe of Judah" who has conquered and is worthy to break the seven seals of the scroll.[73] The Apocalypse frequently identifies the Lion with the Lamb to denote Christ the conquering sacrifice.[74] Recording

---

[69] *CTh.* 9.16.3 (317-319). On Martin: Sulp. Sev., *Dial.* III.7. On the brand, see A. Riese, *Anthologia Latina*, ed. F. Buecheler (Stuttgart: Teubner, 1982), II.i.338.

[70] Prisc., *Tract.* I.26, 2-14.

[71] See N. Brox, "Magie und Aberglaube an den Anfängen des Christenismus," *TTZ* 83 (1974): 157-80; C. D. G. Müller, "Geister: Volksglaube," *RAC* 9 (1975): 761-97. Thomas Aquinas gives qualified approval of amulets (*Summa Theologiae,* 2a2ae.96.4).

[72] 1 Tim 6:15; Rev 19:16; for the reverse order see Rev 17:14. All of the passages emphasize the absolute sovereignty of the Christian God. A similar phrase, "God of Gods and Lord of Kings," is found at Dan 2:47, where Nebuchadnezzar speaks of God as "a revealer of mysteries." Many ancient manuscripts of Luke 23:38 record that the inscription "This is the King of the Jews" was written in Greek, Latin, and Hebrew letters.

[73] Rev 5:5; cf. *Tract.* I.26, 12. On the strength of lions: Num 23:24, Judg 14:18, Jer 49:19.

[74] R. Bauckham, "The *Figurae* of John of Patmos," in *Prophecy and Millenarianism,* ed. A. Williams (Harlow, Essex: Longman, 1980), 107-25.

Christ's name in three languages was undoubtedly intended to strengthen the potency of the amulet.[75]

The lion appears in the zodiac, of course, but is also frequently found in Gnostic texts and in Gnostic interpretations of canonical scripture.[76] In Gnostic writings, the lion represents in turn the Yahweh of the Hebrew Bible, the tyrannical persecutor, a figure of demonic powers and death, and is associated with the Egyptian solar deities Horus and Heliorus. Priscillian is himself apparently aware of this—he takes pains to defend his use of the lion image ("*sed nobis leo non est deus*") by means of allegorical interpretation.[77] The Gnostic mythological tradition also associated the lion with the lord of creation and, especially among Gnostic ascetics, with sexual desire and cosmogenic sexual passion. Indeed, the lion was regarded as particularly sexually charged quite apart from Gnostic circles and would have reinforced the perception of Priscillianist immorality.[78] For our purposes, then, the amulet becomes symbolic of the intersection of Christianity (the proclamation of Christ as "King of kings"), magic (the amulet itself), heresy (the Gnostic lion) and women (the lion of lust).

The third Priscillianist Tractate (*Liber de fide et de apocryphis*) does not specifically mention magic but nonetheless enriches our understanding of the relationship between magic, women, and heresy.[79] The Priscillianist devotion to the reading of apocryphal scriptures itself smacked of heresy, and Manichaeism in particular.[80] But the importance of the apocryphal—and canonical—scriptures for Priscillian lay in their symbolic function as texts for allegorical exegesis. Priscillian's exegesis included a marked fasci-

---

[75] See generally the insightful article by J. Dillon, "The Magical Power of Names in Origen and Later Platonism," in *Origeniana Tertia*, eds. R. Hanson and H. Crouzel (Roma: Edizioni dell'Ateneo, 1985), 203-16. Clem. Alex., *Excerpta ex Theodoto* 82: "the power of the name [of God]" transforms the bread into "spiritual power." On the Priscillianist fascination with names: Prisc., *Tract.* I.27, 15 - I.28, 13).

[76] E.g., the Gospel of Thomas, saying 7. For much of what follows see the comprehensive analysis by H. Jackson, *The Lion Becomes Man: The Gnostic Leontomorphic Creator and the Platonic Tradition*, SBL Diss. Ser. (Atlanta: Scholars Press, 1985), 13-23, 45-53, 59-74, 108-11.

[77] Prisc., *Tract.* I.26, 13-16.

[78] Jackson, *The Lion Becomes Man*, 211-13. Pliny speaks of the "*magna ... libido coitus*" of lions (*NH* 8.17.42); see also Origen, *Hom. Luc.* 8.3 (on Luke 1:46).

[79] Priscillian, *Tract.* III.44-56, defends the careful use of apocryphal scriptures as orthodox.

[80] E.g., Augustine, *ep.* 36.28; also Chadwick, *Priscillian*, 77-85.

nation with numerology, not exclusively the domain of magicians in the ancient world but closely linked with them.[81] Further intimations of magic are present in the Apocryphal Acts of the Apostles, on which the Priscillianists relied, where epiphanies are frequently induced by fasting. Women are especially prominent in the Apocryphal Acts, making the Priscillianist defense of apocryphal scriptures triply dubious in the eyes of critics.[82]

The peculiar character of the Priscillianist conjunction of magic, women, and heresy is made clear when we compare Priscillian to his contemporaries. St. Jerome, driven from Rome in the 380s by considerable opposition, was never formally accused of magic though he had a large following of ascetic aristocratic women and was later tainted by Origenism.[83] The venerable St. Ambrose was associated with no fewer than 12 deaths—many more than any recorded Roman *maleficus*—yet he suffered no indictment for magic.[84] The miracles of St. Martin of Tours frequently bear resemblance to pagan nature magic.[85] Nonetheless, in spite of severe opposition to Martin's asceticism, the bishop of Tours faced no accusations of magic but was instead revered as a holy man, indicating just how difficult it is to distinguish between holy man and magician in late antiquity.

Given the marked opposition which Jerome, Ambrose, and Martin encountered, a functionalist model would lead us to expect charges of magic against them; we do well to remember that their enduring reputations were peppered at the time with the most dangerous fluctuations. Nonetheless, most of Priscillian's contemporaries escaped the shadow of sorcery; only three other fourth-century bishops were accused of magic.[86] Indeed, what is most striking about accusations of magic in this period is the marked *infrequency* with which they are leveled.

Priscillian's conviction at Trier has invariably been seen in modern scholarship as something of a surprise—an unfortunate

---

81 On Priscillianist exegesis see Babut, *Priscillien*, 115-35. On numerology and astrology: Prisc., *Tract.* V, *Tract.* VI; Davids, *De Orosio*, 180-218. Cf. Augustine, *ep.* 55.1-32.

82 On women in the Apocryphal Acts see Brown, *Body and Society*, 153-59; Kraemer, "Ecstatics and Ascetics," (Ph.D. diss., Princeton, 1976), 134-67.

83 For suggestions of informal accusations: Jerome, *eps.* 45.2, 54.2; *ep.* 45.

84 Brown, "Sorcery," 129-30. For accounts of five of the deaths, see Paulinus, *Vita Ambr.* 16, 18, 54.

85 E.g., Sulp. Sev., *Vita Mart.* 11-13, 19, 21, *Dial.* II.2, II.5.

86 The others are Ossius of Cordoba, by the Synod of Serdica in 342 (*CSEL* 65.66), Eusebius of Emesa (Socrates, *HE* 2.9), and Athanasius (see below).

outcome derived primarily from political circumstance or social conflict.[87] Looking closely at the accusations of magic, however, our discussion has revealed a strong line of continuity from Saragossa to Trier. Far from being last-minute inventions, the charges of magic were persistent concerns for Priscillian's opponents. What was insinuated at the council in 380 was made explicit by the trial in 385. Saragossa alleged heresy with tinges of magic; Trier convicted on charges of magic tinged with heresy. And while social and political pressures played substantial roles, no purely social explanation will suffice.

We cannot exclude the possibility that the conflict stemmed from a legitimate dispute over what constituted the appropriate ritual and intellectual forms of worshiping and speaking about God.[88] The motives behind the prosecution of Priscillian surely involved matters of personality and power, but fear of the proximity of tainted teachings and practices to orthodox worship suggests that genuine theological differences were of substantial importance.

That Priscillian himself saw the conflict in largely theological terms is clear from his defense, where the question of magic is subsumed beneath the much larger question of cosmology and the "object" of religious devotion. The first two Tractates, remarkably silent on the question of magic, are dominated by the rejection of every conceivable heresy. Priscillian's rhetoric operates on a thoroughly theological plane. We would expect Priscillian to claim Catholic orthodoxy, but the two Tractates make clear two purposes: to refute the religious implications of the "crimes of sacrilege" alleged against him, and to rebuke those theoretical views of the cosmos which invite the actual veneration of demons and give authority to astrology.[89]

One gathers from Priscillian's defense that magic concerned less the rituals themselves than the supernatural being (or beings) to whom one performed those rituals. That is, magic was seen as a matter of idolatry, as we see in Priscillian's denunciation of the Manichees: "not heretics, but idolaters and wicked servants of the Sun and Moon" (*non hereticos, sed idolatras et maleficos servos*

---

[87] A. Rousselle, "Quelques Aspects," 85-96; A. R. Birley, "Magnus Maximus," 13-43.

[88] See H. D. Betz, "Magic and Mystery in the Greek Magical Papyri," in *Magika Hiera*, 247: "We will have to recognize that our dilemma of defining magic versus religion will simply remain unsolvable if we do not allow theological questions to play their role."

[89] Priscillian, *Tract.* I.4, 2, I.7, 26, I.8, 12, I.14, 13.

Solis et Lunae). The implication is that heretics worship the same God wrongly, while magicians (like idolaters) worship another god entirely.[90] In a world in which matters of doctrine—whether pagan philosophy or Christian teaching—profoundly affected the way one lived one's life, and in which the state of one's soul was of the utmost importance, it is of little surprise that Priscillian would see theological disavowals as encompassing a disavowal of magic. It is against this backdrop that the denials of the first Tractate becomes less of a puzzle and more clearly part of a calculated argument, directed in part against suspicions of magic.

Magic, then, was a subset of broader theological concerns. Yet it would be incorrect to conclude that the distinction between magic and orthodoxy was the divide between "our God" and "their god." For to view magicians and heretics in the single category of social outsiders does nothing to distinguish heretics from magicians. There is abundant evidence for heretics who were not magicians (nor was pagan magic strictly "heretical" until it touched Christian circles). Indeed, it is striking that in the Arian controversy the accusations of magic were lodged not against Arius, but against his "orthodox" opponent Athanasius, who was twice run out of Alexandria under the shadow of sorcery.[91]

Can we go further in isolating the theological elements involved in the peculiar combination of Priscillianist practices and doctrines which contributed to suspicions of magic? The Priscillianist doctrine of the soul, vegetarian and ascetical practices, and intense interest in numerology and astrology suggest a Neoplatonic milieu.[92] Neoplatonic influence on Priscillian would not be surprising given its provenance among educated aristocrats and the acknowledged dependence of the Priscillianist writings on Hilary of Poitiers, a convert from Neoplatonism.[93] We have seen how the Priscillianist practices of fasting and going barefoot resemble pagan

---

[90] Priscillian, *Tract.* II.39, 9-10; cf. Origen, *De principiis*, 3.3.3-4.

[91] Sozomen, *HE* 4.10: Socrates, *HE* 1.27-35; Amm. Marc. 15.7.7-8. The charge against Athanasius derived in part from his breaking of the crystal chalice (Sozomen, *HE* 2.23-25).

[92] On vegetarianism: Prisc., *Can.* 35; Augustine, *De haer.* 70; also Jerome, *eps.* 22.9, 54.11, 127.4; Augustine, *ep.* 55.36. Tractate XI is certainly panentheist and is of Neoplatonic tone. For Neoplatonic interest in vegetarianism: Porphyry, *Vita Plotini* 2, and *De abstinentia*; and in numerology and astrology: Ps-Iamblichus, *The Theology of Arithmetic* (Grand Rapids: Phanes, 1988); and D. J. O'Meara, *Pythagoras Revived: Mathematics and Philosophy in Late Antiquity* (Oxford: Clarendon, 1989).

[93] For dependence on Hilary see Chadwick, *Priscillian*, 11, 65-67, 70-74, *et passim*.

practices and theurgic preparations for visions of the divine. Priscillian does not seem to have participated in pagan rites, but his emphasis of earthly mortification and divine encounter may have involved pagan methods. And if the Neoplatonic element is present in Priscillianist thought and practice, the Priscillianists may well have been viewed as having theurgical affinities, thus incurring the charges of both heresy and magic.[94] In the absence of detailed examination along these lines (and such an examination would be useful indeed), this must remain the most speculative of suspicions. But the possible proximity of theurgic Neoplatonism to Christian worship fits well with our analysis of the relationship between magic, women, and heresy.

Conjectures of Neoplatonism aside, Priscillianist asceticism and theological position are rightly seen as mystical.[95] And while many will object that I have merely substituted one ill-defined term for another, it seems to me that mysticism is much more firmly rooted in human experience generally and is less likely than magic to have strictly pejorative connotations.[96] And while a very fine line often separates magic and heresy on the one hand from mysticism on the other, my suspicion is that much of Priscillian's intellectual and religious appeal came from the latter rather than the former.

How, then, are we to understand the puzzling relationship between magic, women, and heresy? The answer lies, in part, in recognizing a genuine theological difference between Priscillian and his accusers. My suggestion is that the Priscillianist teachings and practices inclined to a mysticism which, to unsympathetic observ-

---

[94] On the ancient confusion of philosophers with magicians, see Apuleius, *Apologia*, 27; Socrates, *HE* 5.16, 3.1, 3.21. On the vexing relationship between Neoplatonic philosophy and theurgy, see G. Luck, "Theurgy and Forms of Worship in Neoplatonism," in *Religion, Science, and Magic: In Concert and in Conflict*, eds. J. Neusner *et al.* (New York: Oxford University Press, 1989), 185-225; also E. R. Dodds, *Greeks and the Irrational*, 283-311. Not all Neoplatonist philosophers were theurgists, and not all theurgists were philosophers. Many Christian Neoplatonists, among them Victorinus, Ambrose and Augustine, seem to have avoided the theurgical side of fourth century Neoplatonism.

[95] "[M]ysticism is the attempt here and now to partake of the eternal Reality which normally we expect fully to share only after death": E. Goodenough, *Jewish Symbols in the Greco-Roman Period* (New York: Pantheon, 1953), 1.266. On asceticism linked with mysticism in Priscillian, see Babut, *Priscillien*, 109-15.

[96] B. McGinn, "Appendix: Theorical Foundations. The Modern Study of Mysticism," in *The Foundations of Mysticism: Origins to the Fifth Century* (New York: Crossroad, 1991), 265-343, is a most helpful survey.

ers already hostile to asceticism, appeared both heretical and magical. It is easy to see how fasting in conjunction with the Eucharist, nighttime worship services, and mountain retreats would be seen as mystical piety by the Priscillianists, while judged to be heresy and pagan magic by opponents.

It is significant that none of our sources attributes malicious "black magic" to Priscillian, and he probably did not practice "magic" in any way that we usually understand the term. The crucial point is that, to many of his contemporaries, he *appeared* to practice magic, for the reasons we have discussed. Any one of the Priscillianist practices—most of which were practiced singly by other prominent bishops—would have been insignificant on its own. It was the conjunction of these practices—fasting, going barefoot, meeting with women—with high Christian holy days, particularly in secret and at night, that was viewed as problematic. Imbedded in a theology directed towards a life of earthly denial and heavenly encounter, the Priscillianists were too close, when viewed from a distance by unsympathetic eyes, to abominable heresy and the abhorrent practice of pagan magic.

Undoubtedly, the accounts of the Priscillianist affair which emphasize the vagaries of orthodoxy and the importance of community dynamics have helped to extend our understanding of magic in antiquity. Our efforts at contextualization and desire to escape Whig historiography are indeed laudable. But in the case of the Priscillianists, the richer matrix of magic, women and heresy has been obscured by approaches which have neglected to consider fully "the deeper substratum of convictions about the nature of the universe."[97] We do well to remember that the issues, especially in the history of religions, are at least as much ontological as social, though not exclusively so. As Gibbon pointed out so keenly, "[Priscillian's] bishopric (in Old Castile) is now worth 20,000 ducats a-year . . . and is therefore much less likely to produce the author of a new heresy."[98]

---

[97] H. Geertz, "An Anthropology of Religion and Magic, I" *Journal of Interdisciplinary History*, 6/1 (Summer 1975): 71-91.
[98] Gibbon, *Decline*, 973 n. 53.

CONCLUSION

MYTH, MAGIC, AND
THE POWER OF THE WORD

CHAPTER TWENTY-TWO

NARRATING POWER:
THE THEORY AND PRACTICE OF THE MAGICAL
HISTORIOLA IN RITUAL SPELLS

David Frankfurter

"Narrating Power" carries a double meaning.[1] First, when one "narrates" or utters a spell, the words uttered draw power into the world and towards (or against) an object in the world. This is perhaps the fundamental principle of magical or ritual speech. Scholars like Stanley Tambiah have developed its utility for the study of magic by connecting the idea of verbal power to the notion of the so-called *illocution,* or efficacious statement, in Speech Acts theory.[2]

But I intend an additional sense to "narrating power": a "power" intrinsic to any narrative, any story, uttered in a ritual context, and the idea that the mere recounting of certain stories situates or directs their "narrative" power into this world. Egyptologists have

---

[1] *Abbreviations*: Borghouts = J. F. Borghouts, *Ancient Egyptian Magical Texts*, Nisaba 9 (Leiden: Brill, 1978); *PGM* = Karl Preisendanz, ed., *Papyri Graecae magicae: Die griechischen Zauberpapryi*, 2 vols., 2nd ed. Albert Henrichs (Stuttgart: Teubner, 1972), trans. and expanded in *The Greek Magical Papyri in Translation*, vol. 1: *Texts*, ed. Hans Dieter Betz (Chicago & London: University of Chicago Press, 1986); Heim = Richard Heim, *Incantamenta Magica Graeca Latina*, Jahrbücher für classische Philologie Supp. 19 (Leipzig: Teubner, 1893); Kropp = Angelicus M. Kropp, *Ausgewählte koptische Zaubertexte*, 3 vols. (Brussels: Fondation égyptologique reine Elisabeth, 1931).

[2] J. L. Austin, *How to do Things with Words*, 2nd ed., J. O. Urmson and Marina Sbisà (Cambridge: Harvard University Press, 1975); John R. Searle, " A Taxonomy of Illocutionary Acts," *Language, Mind, and Knowledge*, Minnesota Studies in the Philosophy of Science 7, ed. Keith Gunderson (Minneapolis: University of Minnesota Press, 1975), 344-69; S. J. Tambiah, "The Magical Power of Words," *Man* 3 (1968): 175-208; *idem*, "Form and Meaning of Magical Acts: A Point of View," *Modes of Thought*, ed. Robin Horton and Ruth Finnegan (London: Faber & Faber, 1973), 199-229; Wade T. Wheelock, "The Problem of Ritual Language: From Information to Situation," *JAAR* 50 (1982): 49-69. Cf. Bronislaw Malinowski, *Coral Gardens and their Magic*, vol. 2 (Bloomington: Indiana University Press, 1965); compare his *Magic, Science, and Religion* (Boston: Beacon Press, 1948), 54-55. Also see Steven T. Katz, "Mystical Speech and Mystical Meaning," *Mysticism and Language*, ed. *idem* (New York: Oxford, 1992), 20-24.

long been familiar with this concept of narrative, since ancient
Egyptian ritual traditionally involved the recitation of mythic
narratives as a kind of instrumental praxis, but also because Egyptians had a highly nuanced sense of the power of the spoken word.[3]

Historiola is the long-standing term for an abbreviated narrative
that is incorporated into a magical spell. In the following essay I
will describe both the mechanisms by which *historiolae* were assumed to work as ritual utterances and the permutations of its
form. Ultimately I hope this essay will be part of a larger enterprise in the description and classification of magical language.

*   *   *

Let me begin by offering some illustrations of what is meant by
historiola. One of the most striking examples appears among the
parallels that Alexander Heidel adduced for the Babylonian creation "epic," the *Enuma Elish*. It is an incantation for toothache,
beginning, "After Anu had created the heaven, (And) the heaven
had created the earth," and following this sequence down to the
creation of the worm. The worm proceeds to declare his preference for teeth and jawbones instead of the figs and apricots offered
by the god Ea, at which point Ea, or the ritualist, or most likely
both, declare, "Because thou hast said this, O worm, May Ea smite
thee with the might of his hand!"[4] Then the inscription gives
instructions for how to recite the spell and what to put on the
tooth. The recitation of the cosmogony itself is therefore meant
to heal the tooth.

A contrast to this cosmogonic *historiola* is the Greek Philinna
papyrus, whose portentous references do not appear to have specific mythological antecedents: "The son of the most august
goddess, the initiate, was scorched. On the highest mount he was
scorched. The fire gulped down seven springs of wolves, seven of
bears, seven of lions, but seven dark-eyed maidens drew water with

---

[3] George Foucart, s.v., "Names (Egyptian)," *Hastings' Encyclopedia of Re-
ligion and Ethics* (New York: C. Scribner's Sons, 1911), 9.151-55; Serge
Sauneron, "Le monde du magicien Egyptien," *Le monde du sorcier*, Sources
orientales 7 (Paris: Editions du Seuil, 1966), 32-34, 49; Robert K. Ritner, *The
Mechanics of Ancient Egyptian Magical Practice*, Studies in Ancient Oriental
Civilization 54 (Chicago: Oriental Institute, 1993), 35-49, 73-110.

[4] Alexander Heidel, *The Babylonian Genesis*, 2nd ed. (Chicago & London:
University of Chicago Press, 1951), 72-73.

dark blue jugs and quieted the untiring fire" (*PGM* XX).[5] Concluding in this way, the spell contains *neither* precise mythological
allusions *nor* ritual indications. But we can begin to see four basic
structural aspects of the *historiola* in the Philinna papyrus: (1) the
past tense suggests that it describes events in mythic time; (2) in
contrast to the Babylonian toothache spell, the Philinna papyrus
shows that a *historiola* need not explicitly reflect a well-known
mythological discourse like a cosmogony; (3) the lack of explicit
application, in the Philinna spell, to a "real-world" situation suggests that the narrative's power is invoked by implicit analogy; and
(4) the fact that this is the entire spell—lacking not only application, but also invocation or *voces magicae* —demonstrates that
the magical power of the Philinna spell and its analogues is, indeed,
contained within the narrative itself, not sacred names, symbols, or
commands.

These principles operate similarly in Egyptian magical spells. A
spell against crocodiles begins like a folktale:

> Isis struck with her wing; she closed the mouth of the river. She caused
> the fishes to lie down on the mud-shoal; the waves do not immerse it.
> Isis became weary <on> the water; Isis arose on the water, her tears fal-
> ling into the water. See, Horus has had intercourse with his mother Isis!
> Her tears are falling into the water. . . . It is Isis that has recited, it is not
> a crocodile that has done so. Protection! Protection has arrived!
> (Borghouts #129)

Another spell, intended to facilitate bird-catching, reads,
"Horus, son of Isis, ascended a hill in order to sleep. He sang his
melodies, spread his nets, caught a falcon, a *bank*-bird, a mountain
pelican."[6] Other spells, such as those inscribed on magical stelae
and statue bases, give lengthy and impassioned accounts of Horus'
scorpion-sting in the Nile marshes, and his successful cure by the
magical powers and incantations of the gods Isis, Re, and Thoth.
These stories are told as events in mythic time, but are punctuated
with dramatic monologues delivered by the various deities, giving
the narrative a strong "presence" if heard aloud. Indeed, it seems
that the central "act" in the Egyptian *historiola* is not so much a

---

[5] Cf. P. Maas, "The Philinna Papyrus," *JHS* 62 (1942): 33-38; Ludwig
Koenen, "Der brennende Horosknabe," *Chronique d'Egypte* 37 (1962): 167-74;
Christopher Faraone, "The *Mystodokos* and the Dark-Eyed Maidens: Multicul-
tural Influences on a Late-Hellenistic Incantation," in this volume.

[6] Berlin 8313, II = Kropp #III (2.10-11); cf. L. Kákosy, "Remarks on the Interpretation of a Coptic Magical Text," *Acta Orientalia Hungaricae* 13 (1961):
325-28.

gesture or movement but a god's utterance of a name or spell—
thus, reciting divine dialogue takes on a special significance.[7] Of
course, few people could read these spells for themselves; instead,
people tapped their contagious power by pouring water over the
hieroglyphs or merely touching the stele.[8] Thus the power of the
story was also accessible through the concrete letters that told it.

A particularly large number of *historiolae* are collected from
Christian regions. A Coptic amulet against snakebite declares,
"Christ was born on the 29th of Choiak (or Dec. 25). He came
descending upon the earth. He passed judgment on all the poisonous serpents."[9] A Coptic obstetrical ritual includes the following to
be recited: "[Jesus] came wandering [on] the Mount of Olives . . .
He found a deer in distress . . . while she gave birth. [She said],
'Hail, O son of the virgin . . . Come to me today and help in my
hour of need.' (But) he turned his eyes to her and said, 'You cannot endure my glory . . . but when I depart I will send you Michael
the archangel.'"[10] A Coptic sex-spell includes the following story:
"Mastema . . . threw [Eve] down into the source of the four rivers.
He [washed?] in it, so that the children of humankind should [drink
f]rom it and be filled with the devil's passion. N.N. son of N.N.
(that is, the client) drank fr[om] it, (and) he has been filled with
the devil's passion." This spell proceeds to invoke certain supernatural beings to fetch his beloved.[11] A Syriac healing spell summa-

---

[7] Cf. Ritner, *Ancient Egyptian Magical Practice*, 40-45.

[8] See translations and discussions by E. A. Wallis Budge, *Egyptian Magic*,
Books on Egypt and Chaldea 2 (London: Kegan Paul, Trench, Trübner, & Co.,
1901; repr. ed. New York: Dover, 1971), 130-36, cf. 147-53; A. Moret, "Horus
sauveur," *Revue de l'histoire des religions* 72 (1915): 213-87; Adolf Klasens, *A
Magical Statue Base (Socle Behague) in the Museum of Antiquities at Leiden*
(Leiden: Brill, 1952); E. Jelínková-Reymond, *Les inscriptions de la statue
guérisseuse de Djed-Her-le-Sauveur* (Cairo: IFAO, 1956), 1-84; Borghouts
##87, 90-95, 101, 104; and literature review by Robert S. Bianchi, *Cleopatra's
Egypt: Age of the Ptolemies* (Brooklyn: Brooklyn Museum, 1988), 204-5 (cat.
##98-99).

[9] P. Yale 1792, in George M. Parássoglou, "A Christian Amulet Against
Snakebite," *Studia Papyrologica* 13 (1974): 107-10. The amulet then quotes
Psalm 119: "Thy word, O Lord, is the lamp of my feet; and it is the light of my
way."

[10] Berlin 8313^r I = Kropp XVII (2.64-65). Instructions for a childbearing amulet in the *PGM* require that the following be written on a potsherd and placed on
the right thigh: "Come out of your tomb, Christ is calling you!" (*PGM*
CXXIII.49-50).

[11] B. M. Hay 10376, ll. 15-19, in Crum, "Magical Texts in Coptic–I," *JEA* 20
(1934): 51-53; cf. *Quest.Barth*. 59.

rizes the Christian annunciation and visitation stories in order to
cure a specific ailment:

> Zardōsht the prophet prophesied saying: A time will come, when they
> will see a star in the heavens having the likeness of a mother with a son
> in her arms. The time came and they saw the star. Twelve kings set out
> from Persia to go to Jerusalem. They saw king Herod, who said to them:
> "Whence come ye, and whither are ye going?" They answered: "A king
> has been born in Bethlehem, and we have come to worship him." Then
> the star fell down in front of them; they went and worshipped the boy
> who had been born. They opened their treasure chests and brought him
> offerings: gold and myrrh and frankincense. They asked for a set of swad-
> dling clothes; they then went to Persia, made a great fire, and threw the
> swaddling clothes of our Lord upon the fire. Before the swaddling clothes
> of our Lord the fire went out. In this manner may the [disease] go out and
> leave, and be plucked from the body of N.N. the son of N.N. and all the
> evil boils, (just) as that fire went out in the presence of the swaddling
> clothes of our Lord. Amen.[12]

Here certainly we can see that the *historiolae* are not merely
economical, instrumental speech like *voces magicae*, but stories
told for their own sake, as gatherings of lore for the sake of some
special need.

*   *   *

What is happening through all these narratives? What is the
"theory" of the *historiola*? At the very least it is clear that *historiolae* as forms of religious speech involve a "mythic" dimension
of action; a "this-worldly" or human realm of problems or needs;
and the speech act itself, which draws from the mythic dimension
to apply to the human dimension. One might also note that *historiolae* most often are employed in healing spells (as opposed to
love or curse spells), perhaps because situations of illness, accident,
and childbirth were so dire in antiquity as to require more dramatic
invocations of divine power than were possible with mere directives, prayers or commands.

Under various names the *historiola* has long been recognized in
folklore and religious studies, although discussions have taken quite

---

[12] Richard Gottheil, "References to Zoroaster in Syriac and Arabic Literature," *Classical Studies in Honor of Henry Drisler* (New York and London:
Macmillan and Co., 1894), 31, in Joseph Bidez and Franz Cumont, *Les mages
hellénisés*, 2 vols. (Paris: "Les Belles Lettres," 1938), 2.133-34 (= #S19).

different approaches to the phenomenon. In his entry on "Segen" in the *Handwörterbuch des deutschen Aberglaubens,* the German folklorist F. Ohrt concentrated on the dynamics of its formal structure, consisting of (1) characters, (2) situation and focal action or words, and (3) application to the present condition.[13] The *situation* is often a crisis (e.g., a deer in labor, swaddling clothes before the fire); and yet in many spells the recounting of this critical event is missing, so that the spell merely reports the focal words of power as they were delivered *in illo tempore*, without any frame or explanation. The *focal action or words* may appear in the spell as a past accomplishment, subsequently to be applied to the present, or as direct speech (such as the "living" dialogues between Isis and Nephthys in Egyptian spells), which effectively collapses the story with the reality of the performance.

The *application*, Ohrt notes, functions linguistically like a simile: ". . . thus, just like the accomplishment described, so also let it happen now." In one form of application the *historiola* concludes with an invocation or prayer that is framed as the culminating speech of a character in the story (e.g., ". . . (that you, impaling object,) come out by the power of this prayer that Maria the virgin spoke outside the tomb: . . . ," from a Coptic spell).[14] By uttering the same vital invocation as the character in the story, the practitioner or client taps into the power of the entire story. However, the specific declaration to apply the *historiola* may be only implicit, such as an amulet inscribed with a healing account (or image) alone: a person in need of the same healing enacts the "application" by the very act of wearing it.[15]

Ohrt's observations are based on the important principle that the *historiola* form is meant to replicate speech—in this case the oral "telling" of the *historiola* during a healing ritual—even in the case of those archaic examples extant only in written texts such as amulets or stelae. In the ancient preparation of inscribed amulets the order in which one *uttered* the words of power and *inscribed* them on papyrus, leather, or other medium could vary. The in-

---

[13] Cf. F. Ohrt, "Segen," *Handwörterbuch des deutschen Aberglaubens* (Berlin/Leipzig: De Gruyter, 1935/36), 7.1590-91.

[14] P. Rylands 102, ed. Walter E. Crum, *Catalogue of the Coptic Manuscripts in the Collection of the John Rylands Library, Manchester* (Manchester: University Press, 1909), 52-53; cf. Kropp XXVI.

[15] For a linguistic analysis of implicit *historiolae* see Thomas A. Sebeok and Frances J. Ingemann, *Studies in Cheremis: The Supernatural*, Viking Fund Publications in Anthropology 22 (New York: Wenner-Gren Foundation, 1956), 287-89.

scription of the spell, however, generally functioned to "lock in" the power of the uttered words for ongoing effect.[16] In the case of those spells found in ancient ritual manuals the words of power—*voces magicae*, invocations and prayers, *historiolae*—are often clearly designated as oral utterance, separate from the instructions for preparing the accompanying amulets.[17] This "oral" nature of *historiolae* requires that they be interpreted as oral performance rather than as written text. One must remember that in a semi- or non-literate society written words are usually not sacred semantically but rather visually—as concrete symbols.[18]

In classics and religious studies *historiolae* (though rarely by this name) have been scrutinized for their relationship to myth. So, for example, many classicists have regarded *historiolae* merely as applied derivations of more well-known narratives or macro-myths. If they find no evidence of a macro-myth, they conclude that the *historiola* must be, in Arthur Darby Nock's terms, "invented *ad hoc* and recounted in magic with complete assurance as though canonical."[19] But it is to the credit of historians of religions that the *historiola* has been unpacked as a functional aspect of ritual and not just derivative mythology. Van der Leeuw described a form of ritual speech called the "magical antecedent":

> An event that occurred in prehistoric times, and which now possesses a mythical eternity and typicalness, is *by the power of the formula* rendered present in the literal sense and made actual and fruitful.[20]

By this scheme it is the performative aspect of the *historiola*—its very utterance or inscription—that holds power; its function is

---

[16] See, e.g., Roy Kotansky, "Incantations and Prayers for Salvation on Inscribed Greek Amulets," *Magika Hiera: Ancient Greek Magic and Religion*, ed. Christopher A. Faraone and Dirk Obbink (New York: Oxford, 1991), 107-37.

[17] E.g., *PGM* IV.2622-2707 typically distinguishes "the name (to be) written" (2636) and the *logos*, the spell to be uttered (2639).

[18] See David Frankfurter, "The Magic of Writing and the Writing of Magic: The Power of the Word in Egyptian and Greek Traditions," *Helios* 21 (1994): 189-221.

[19] Arthur Darby Nock, *Essays on Religion and the Ancient World*, 2 vols., ed. Zeph Stewart (Oxford: Clarendon, 1972), 1.271. Compare J. F. Borghouts, "Magical Texts," *Textes et langages de l'Egypte pharaonique*, 3 vols. (Paris: IFAO, 1974), 3.17: "Magical texts are a most important *source* for Egyptian mythology, though the latter is freely *adapted*—not to say *invented*—to suit the occasion" (emphases mine).

[20] G. Van der Leeuw, *Religion in Essence and Manifestation*, tr. J. E. Turner (London: George Allen & Unwin, 1964; repr. ed. Princeton: Princeton University Press, 1986), 424, emphasis mine.

to "render present" a distinctly separate event from the mythic past. Mircea Eliade refined this perspective to allow more slippage between the two "periods" of mythic time and the human present. Moreover, Eliade placed the "power" of the *historiola* not in the formula *per se* as Van der Leeuw, but in the very contents of the narrative: a citation of events and acts performed in cosmogonic time (like the Babylonian toothache spell). That is, narrative that describes "creative" miracle intrinsically contains the power of that creative miracle. And thus the recitation of such narrative for magical purposes draws those powers into present circumstances: "the patient," Eliade suggests, "is penetrated by the gigantic forces that, *in illo tempore*, made the Creation possible."[21] (Of course, one need not limit this idea to cosmogonic *historiolae*, which were Eliade's own interest.)[22]

Insofar as "magic" at the very least concerns the manipulation of power, both Van der Leeuw's and Eliade's descriptions of *historiolae* offer quite useful outlines of the invocation of mythic episodes for their particular demonstrations of power. In fact, by understanding the *historiola* as the performative transmission of power from a mythic realm articulated in narrative to the human present, we might instructively include under the same rubric two other popular forms of amulets in antiquity: *iconographic vignettes* (such as the holy rider figure or scenes from Christian legend) and the quotations and citations of *scripture* so common in Jewish and Christian amulets. Both express mythic episodes as *continually* powerful. The iconography on amulets and pilgrims' *eulogia*, as Gary Vikan has shown, functioned specifically to draw sacred power from a "myth" represented (e.g., a saint's *legenda* or gospel stories) into the realm of the wearer.[23] While many such amulets held generalized, apotropaic value, at least as many were designed for specific ailments and problems.[24]

---

[21] Mircea Eliade, *Myth and Reality*, tr. Willard R. Trask (New York: Harper & Row, 1963), 25, cf. 21-38. See also S. G. F. Brandon, *History, Time and Deity* (Manchester: University Press, 1965), chap. 2, esp. 20-21.

[22] Cf. William Brashear's definition: "a legend, a mythical event, even a tale composed *ad hoc*, by recounting which the magician reactivates the bygone archetypical situation (*'in illo tempore'*) for his use in the present situation" (*Magica Varia*, Papyrologica Bruxellensia 25 [Brussels: Fondation égyptologique reine Elisabeth, 1991], 19).

[23] See esp. Gary Vikan, "Art, Medicine, and Magic in Early Byzantium," *Dumbarton Oaks Papers* 38 (1984): 65-86.

[24] Cf. Herbert Jennings Rose, "A Blood-Staunching Amulet," *HTR* 44 (1951): 59-60.

The "power" inherent in sacred scripture could be tapped simply by writing gospel *incipits*. However, more often there was an analogical relationship between the contents of, say, a psalm or a saying of Jesus, and the apotropaic or curative function for which the amulet was intended.[25] The psalm or scriptural quotation, therefore, worked not only by its magical writing, but also as a *historiola*, invoking a specific power that was performed and guaranteed *in illo tempore*.[26] So not only through *historiolae* but also through talismanic iconography and scripture quotations a "myth" might convey power to present human situations.

Yet the problem with the Van der Leeuw-Eliade approach is precisely that it leaves unexamined the nature of this analogy that the *historiola* establishes between mythic time and present circumstances. That is, it is not simply undifferentiated power that is unleashed through *historiolae*, but precedence or paradigm. Here it is useful to bring in Malinowski's concept of the myth as a charter for present institutions: that a myth by definition functions to

---

[25] See Joshua Trachtenberg, *Jewish Magic and Superstition: A Study in Folk Religion* (New York: Behrman, 1939; repr. New York: Atheneum, 1982), 104-13; Alessandro Biondi, "Le citazioni bibliche nei papiri magici cristiani greci," *Studia papyrologica* 20 (1981): 93-127; E. A. Judge, "The Magical Use of Scripture in the Papyri," *Perspectives on Language and Text*, ed. Edgar W. Conrad and Edward G. Newing (Winona Lake: Eisenbrauns, 1987), 339-49; Lawrence H. Schiffman and Michael D. Swartz, *Hebrew and Aramaic Incantation Texts from the Cairo Genizah: Selected Texts from Taylor-Schechter Box K1*, Semitic Texts and Studies 1 (Sheffield: JSOT, 1992), 37-40, 58. On the use of gospel *incipits* see John Chrysostom, *Hom.* 19.14; P. Mich. 1559, ed. Gerald M. Browne, *Michigan Coptic Texts* (Barcelona: Papyrologica Castroctaviana, 1979), 43-45 (#12); and the pierced stone in the Bodleian Library with the four gospels' incipits in Coptic, mentioned by W. E. Crum, "La magie copte: nouveaux textes," *Recueil d'études égyptologiques dédiées à la mémoire de Jean-François Champollion* (Paris: Champion, 1933), 544, but now edited by P. A. Mirecki (forthcoming). Other texts from Christian tradition include Heb 1:1 and Gen 1:1-5 (P. Amherst 3a, in Herbert Musurillo, "Early Christian Economy," *Chronique d'Egypte* 31 [1956]: 124-26); Ps 119 (P. Yale 1792 in Parássoglou, "Christian Amulet Against Snakebite"); and GTh 6c (reported by H.-Ch. Puech, "Un logion de Jésus sur bandelette funéraire," *RHR* 147 [1955]: 126-29). The psalms were by far the most frequently employed on both Jewish and Christian amulets: see Trachtenberg, *Jewish Magic and Superstition*, 109, 112-13; the Arabic Christian ms. ed. by Nessim Henry Henein and Thierry Bianquis, *La magie par les psaumes*, Bibliothèque d'études coptes 12 (Cairo: IFAO, 1975); and Claire Préaux, "Une amulette chrétienne aux Musées royaux d'art et d'histoire de Bruxelles," *Chronique d'Egypte* 10 (1935): 361-70.

[26] Compare "scriptural" uses of Homeric verses in *PGM* IV.467-74, 820-34; VII.1-148.

articulate precedent for present circumstances.[27] The mythic time in which precedents and paradigms are set is typically the past, but not necessarily, as we see in the wide variety of Egyptian spells which use a kind of dramatic present through dialogue. The *historiola's* link between times is not as important as its link between a human dimension where action is open-ended and a mythic dimension where actions are completed and tensions have been resolved. The *historiola*, as one Egyptologist puts it, "formulates a rule that will exert an authority of its own on the events to follow."[28] And this is obviously a dialectical process: confronted with an unresolved situation, the ritualist formulates, out of traditional terms and characters, a precedent in which the same situation is resolved. We might describe the process as a kind of "active analogizing."[29]

*   *   *

How then is the mythic paradigm, once "narrated" or developed in a *historiola*, assumed to work? Here I believe we can get some light from Speech-Acts theory. To begin with, I think we can agree, following Malinowski and Tambiah, that the very words of magical spells—and ritual speech in general—are meant to be efficacious, and are in fact efficacious in the social context of ritual.[30] That is, the utterance "performs" the action desired. This principle is vividly confirmed for Egyptian ritual because of the very concept of "utterance," "word," "written letter," and even "magic" itself in ancient Egypt; and it is probably true for all the Mediterranean cultures which drew upon Egyptian magic. In the terms of J. L. Austin, therefore, the magical spell becomes a performative utterance, insofar as "the uttering of the words is . . . usually a, or even *the* leading incident in the performance of the act . . . the performance of which is also the object of the utterance."[31]

---

[27] Malinowski, *Magic, Science, and Religion*, 63-64; *idem, Sex, Culture, and Myth* (New York: Harcourt, Brace, & World, 1962), 291, 303-04.

[28] Jørgen Podemann Sørensen, "The Argument in Ancient Egyptian Magical Formulae," *Acta Orientalia* 45 (1984): 8.

[29] Cf. Serge Sauneron, "Aspects et sort d'un thème magique égyptien: Les menaces incluant les dieux," *Bulletin de la société française d'égyptologie* 8 (Nov. 1951): 12; compare *idem*, "Le monde du magicien égyptien," *Le monde du sorcier*, Sources orientales 7 (Paris: Editions du Seuil, 1966), 36-42. Sauneron tends to overstate the ritualist's use of threats to motivate divine power and action.

[30] Tambiah, "The Magical Power of Words."

[31] Austin, *How to Do Things With Words*, 8.

But there is a considerable difference between, on the one hand, a spell which commands or directs ("I have spoken your signs and symbols. Therefore, lord, do the so-and-so deed by necessity, lest I shake heaven," *PGM* III.536-37), and, on the other hand, one which simply declares a situation as *fait accompli* ("A foolish woman was sitting on a fountain, and she was holding a foolish infant in her lap. The mountains dry up, the valleys dry up, the veins dry up, even those full of blood," Heim 111). A more evocative example of this *declarative* type of ritual utterance is the announcement on Easter morning: "Christ is risen!" It creates *and simultaneously recognizes* a certain reality.[32] In this particular genus of speech act, a broadening of Searle's "declarative" category that Wade Wheelock designated "situating speech," such an utterance as the *historiola* not only changes a particular element of the environment, it transforms the entire environment into a mythic situation.[33]

The difference between the directive utterance and the declarative utterance seems to revolve around the active presence and authority of the ritualist or speaker. In the case of the directive utterance, which includes *both* prayer *and* magical command, the speaker's mind-set, preparation, traditional status, and purity are of paramount importance since the force of that utterance explicitly comes from that "I" who says the words. On the other hand, the authority of the declarative utterance—at least insofar as it pertains to the *historiola*—derives from the content itself: the mythic events that are recounted.[34] A good example of the *historiola's* power independent of its speaker's status may be the magical stelae and statue bases in Egypt, whose power to heal was commonly available to anyone who could pour water over them or touch them, since the power rested in the Isis-Horus narrative itself rather than in a priest's recitation of it.[35]

---

[32] In general see Searle, "Taxonomy of Illocutionary Acts," 355-56 (directives), 358-61 (declaratives). Compare Anders Jeffner's "performative" category of religious language (ostensibly developed independently of Austin), *The Study of Religious Language* (London: SCM, 1972), 11-12 & chap. 4.

[33] See Wheelock, "The Problem of Ritual Language," esp. 58.

[34] Compare Searle, "Taxonomy of Illocutionary Acts," 359-60 on requirements that the speaker occupy an appropriate status to complete a declarative speech act successfully.

[35] See P. Lacau, "Les statues 'guérisseuses' dans l'ancienne Egypte," *Académie des inscriptions et belles-lettres, Commission de la fondation Piot, Monuments et Mémoires* 25 (1921/22): 189-209; Keith C. Seele, "Horus on the Crocodiles," *JNES* 6 (1947): 43-52; Jean-Claude Goyon, "L'Eau dans la médecine pharaonique et copte," *L'homme et l'eau en Méditerranée et au proche*

* * *

This analysis of the speech-acts involved in magical spells aids us not only in the understanding of the dynamics of ancient magic, but also in the taxonomy of magical speech overall. If, as I have been arguing, the *historiola*, as a declarative utterance, "works" in a fundamentally different manner from the directive spell or invocation, then perhaps we should consider what to do with those spells which employ *historiolae* as part of a *similia similibus* formula—"just as . . . so also . . . ."—for this formula puts the analogy between myth and application right out on the table.

For example: "Christ, who has multiplied the stars in the sky and the water in the sea, multiply also the fruits in the vineyard of Paul," reads an inscribed tablet from Sicily.[36] "As Typhon is the adversary of Helios, so inflame the heart and soul of Amoneios" (*PGM* XXXIIa.1), reads a Greco-Egyptian love-spell.[37] In referring to "myths" like Christ's creation of the cosmos or Typhon's hostility to the sun, these spells are surely different from the kinds of instrumentally analogical formulae that we find in curse tablets, which draw upon concrete images like the coldness of lead, the heat of a fire, or the limpness of a rag on a dunghill to bind, kill, or

---

orient 1, Travaux de la Maison de l'Orient 2 (Lyon: GIS–Maison de l'Orient, 1981), 147-50; Claude Traunecker, "Une Chapelle de magie guérisseuse sur le parvis du temple de Mout à Karnak," *JARCE* 20 (1985): 65-92; Robert K. Ritner, "Horus on the Crocodiles: A Juncture of Religion and Magic in Late Dynastic Egypt," *Religion and Philosophy in Ancient Egypt*, Yale Egyptological Studies 3, ed. William Kelly Simpson (New Haven: Yale University, 1989), 103-16.

[36] D. R. Jordan, "Two Christian Prayers from Southeastern Sicily," *GRBS* 25 (1984): 297-302.

[37] This is one of a rare species of *Typhon*-versus-Re images (as opposed to the traditional opposition of *Apophis* vs. Re) used in Greco-Egyptian spells: compare P. B. M. 10588^V B, ll. 6-8, in H. I. Bell, A. D. Nock, and Herbert Thompson, "Magical Texts from a Bilingual Papyrus in the British Museum," *Proceedings of the British Academy* (1931): 252-53, 255, 274-79 (= Nock, *Essays*, 1.271-76); Arthur S. Hunt, "An Incantation in the Ashmolean Museum," *JEA* 15 (1929): 155-57; O. Guéraud, "Deux textes magiques du Musée du Caire," *Mélanges Maspero* 2, MIFAO 67 (Cairo: IFAO, 1934-37), 201-06; and cf. P. Mich. 593, 13.4-10, in W. H. Worrell, "A Coptic Wizard's Hoard," *American Journal of Semitic Languages* 46 (1929/30): 251; and Paul Allan Mirecki, "The Coptic Hoard of Spells from the University of Michigan," in Marvin Meyer and Richard Smith, eds., *Ancient Christian Magic: Coptic Texts of Ritual Power* (San Francisco: Harper Collins, 1994), 293-310, and Mirecki's fuller translation "The Coptic Wizard's Hoard," in *HTR* 87 (in press).

otherwise "persuasively" transform their victims.[38] The last two spells do, in fact, invoke mythic narratives to drive their spells, rather than material objects. However, the *similia similibus* structure essentially *subordinates* the narrative portion of the spell to a directive utterance, the part that states, "so also let it be that ...." Thus the *historiola*, if we can still call it that, works in these cases as a guarantee or rationale, an explicit precedent, for the directive utterance, the command, which is the central speech-act in these spells.

I would therefore make a preliminary distinction between those *historiolae* that function by virtue of their narrative—what I would call *historiolae* proper—and those that function as a subsidiary invocation to a directive utterance, a command or prayer—what we might call "clausal *historiolae*."[39] But having made this distinction, I want to point out that few *historiolae* remain entirely aloof from the human, performative context—entirely implicit in their analogy to the present problem.

*   *   *

The *historiola* invariably includes some specific links with the immediate ritual context in which it is uttered. The Egyptologist Podemann Sørensen has identified five of these links in Egyptian spells, but we can see them operative throughout ancient magical traditions.[40]

First, and most characteristically Egyptian, the ritualist himself may, in the course of narrating, enter the narrative by identifying himself as a god. The effect is, therefore, a collapsing of bounda-

---

[38] Cf. Christopher A. Faraone, "Hermes but no Marrow: Another Look at a Puzzling Magical Spell," *ZPE* 72 (1988): 279-86; *idem*, "The Agonistic Context of Early Greek Binding Spells," *Magika Hiera: Ancient Greek Magic and Religion*, ed. C. Faraone and Dirk Obbink (New York: Oxford University Press, 1991), 7-8; Sebeok and Ingemann, *Studies in Cheremis: The Supernatural*, 292-96, on categorization of *similia similibus* formulae. Faraone ("Hermes but no Marrow," 284) proposes that the articulation of mythical precedent in *historiolae* is invariably expressed in past tense (e.g., aorist), thus *distinguishing* it from most examples of *similia similibus* formulae. But as the Egyptian spells illustrate, the linguistic representation of the "realm" of mythic precedent can be in any tense (just as "myth" in traditional cultures is rarely so distinct from mundane time as the aorist would imply). The *similia similibus* formula should thus be viewed as one possible way of "applying" *historiolae*.

[39] Cf. Kropp, 3.218 (§374).

[40] Podemann Sørensen, "The Argument in Ancient Egyptian Magical Formulae," 9-13.

ries between the human situation and the mythical dimension; the *historiola* is effective not by analogy or precedent but by becoming dynamically real within the ritual context. A similar effect may be achieved in those spells using dramatic dialogue:

"Your son Horus has been burnt in the desert!"

"Is there water there?"

"There is no water there!"

"Water is in my mouth, an Inundation is between my thighs. It is to extinguish the fire that I have arrived. Break out, burn!" (Borghouts #35)

Come out of your tomb, Christ is calling you! (*PGM* XXIIIa.49)

In both cases the mythical context of the speech is established in the performative situation simply by virtue of reciting the speech. Its inscription on an amulet would presumably imply the same dynamic.

Second, the *historiola* itself may be, or include, an account of the genesis and initial use of a specific incantation within it, which is then used by the ritualist and/or written on an amulet. Ohrt had noted that a prayer or spell uttered by a character in a *historiola* would link mythical and performative dimensions when that same prayer or spell was uttered by the ritualist or the client. In late antiquity such a magical "pedigree" or "genealogy" had broad usage even beyond the framing of specific spells: from a Coptic spell that begins "The binding words, which Elijah the prophet spoke upon the holy mountain . . . ,"[41] to the introduction of the magical ascent text *Sefer HaRazim*, which traces the very text's origin back to Noah.

Third, in a similar vein, the *historiola* may account for a substance used in the accompanying ritual. In an Egyptian childbirth spell the god Horus describes a statue of the god Bes such as is required in the ritual itself (Borghouts #60, cf. 61). An Old Coptic spell for sexual gratification describes how the goddess Isis is advised to procure "a double iron nail with a . . . head, a thin base, a strong point, and light iron. Bring it before me, dip it in the blood

---

[41] P. Heidelberg 1682, 11. 29-30, in Bilabel-Grohman, 1934:394. See in general Malinowski, *Magic, Science, and Religion*, 55-57, 64; A.-J. Festugière, *La Révélation d'Hermès trismégiste*, 3 vols. (2nd ed.; Paris: "Les Belles Lettres," 1950), 1.309-54; Kropp, 3.219-24 (§§376-82).

of Osiris, and hand it over" (*PGM* IV.110-13). It is reasonable to assume that the accompanying ritual included some such instrument, even though this is not explicitly indicated in the extant instructions.[42] In these cases it is the instrumental presence of the images in the rituals that "situates" the mythical dimension within the performative setting.

Fourth, the link may be made with details of the specific *problem* to be resolved. A Coptic spell describes the nature and origin of the lance which pierced Jesus' side at Golgotha, and then proceeds to identify the lance with a penetrating object in the patient's eye.[43] Egyptian spells describe real scorpion poisoning in detail, but attribute the scorpion to the god Seth and locate the suffering in the child Horus. Thus the affliction itself is rendered mythical through a series of declarations, and consequently the power to cure the affliction also must belong to the realm of myth.

Fifth, a link may be made by explicitly mentioning, *within the narrative*, the body of the patient or even his or her name. A common aspect of healing ritual in ancient Egypt was the "mythical re-definition" of parts of the body as different gods, who then themselves act in the *historiola*. A spell to protect breasts begins, "These here are the breast(s) which Isis suffered from in Khemmis . . . " (Borghouts #64). But throughout Christian spells we find actual names included as *dramatis personae* in the recitation of *historiolae* or their preparation in amulets.[44] A. A. Barb has discussed a medieval Greek charm against headaches that tells how "Migraine came out from the sea rioting and roaring, and our Lord Jesus Christ came to meet it"; when Jesus asks why Migraine brings so many ailments to humankind, he replies, "We are going to sit down in the head of the servant of God, so-and-so"— that is, the name of the patient. At this point Jesus himself commands,

---

[42] Cf. "blood of Osiris" as wine in *PDM* xiv.440-41. *PGM* IV.115ff commences an instrumental *similia similibus* formula "persuasively," comparing the beloved's state to a fire to be made in a ritual brazier. This might suggest that the initial *historiola* in ll. 94-114 derives from another context (perhaps a revenge spell?). In *PGM* XII such "mythical" ingredients as "Blood of Hephaistos," "Semen of Hermes," and "Semen of Ammon" are translated into more common ritual substances (XII.401-44).

[43] P. Rylands 102, in W. E. Crum, *Catalogue of the Coptic Manuscripts in the Collection of the John Rylands Library, Manchester* (Manchester: Manchester University Press, 1909), 52-53 = Kropp, 2.80 (#XXVI).

[44] Cf. Ohrt, "Segen," 1591.

Look here, do not go into my servant, but be off altogether and go into
the wild mountains and settle in a bull's head. There you may eat flesh,
there drink blood, there ruin the eyes, there darken the head, seethe and
wriggle. But if you do not obey me I shall destroy you there on the burning mountain where no dog barks and the cock does not crow.[45]

With the mythic and human dimensions so thoroughly shuffled
as they are in this spell, we can see that the "active analogizing"
involved in the coining of *historiolae* is really a form of dynamic
story-telling, a "bricolage" of environment, tradition, and ritual
speech.

*   *   *

This brings me to a final point in the analysis of the *historiola*:
the question of the sources to which they seem to appeal. The
traditional approach to *historiolae* has always seen them as extrac-
tions or applications of pre-existent "myths," such that if one had
the *historiola* one might dig down to the myth it came from. Barb
and others have displayed their scholarly prowess by unveiling the
"myth" behind some otherwise unrecognizable *historiolae*.[46] Yet it
is quite obvious that some *historiolae* refer to no over-arching
macro-myths at all, but are compilations and syntheses of diverse
lore. Even the Christian spells cannot be said to be direct citations
of, or even allusions to, gospel texts.

I would say that, as long as we regard *historiolae* as referring in
some sense to a mythic dimension, we may need to redefine what
we mean by "myth" in the first place. In many cultures "myths" as
coherent narratives describing supernatural events do not exist
except as ritual librettos which are implicitly or explicitly oriented
toward the ritual context and its goals.[47] For example, the so-called
"myth" of Isis' rescue of the poisoned Horus to which the magical
stelae seem to refer is *only* extant in such magical spells, as an
extended *historiola*. That is to say, myths only exist in the form
of ritual applications; the *historiolae* "are" the myths, rather than

---

[45] F. Pradel, *Griechische und süditalienische Gebete ... des Mittelalters*,
Religionsgeschichtliche Versuche und Vorarbeiten III/3 (Giessen, 1907), 15-16,
cit. A. A. Barb, "Antaura: The Mermaid and the Devil's Grandmother," *Journal
of the Warburg and Courtauld Institutes* 29 (1966): 2-3.

[46] See esp. "Antaura," 11.

[47] See C. J. Bleeker, *Egyptian Festivals*, NumenSupp 13 (Leiden: Brill, 1967),
11-12, 15-18; Ritner, "Horus on the Crocodiles," 113; and now John Baines,
"Egyptian Myth and Discourse: Myth, Gods, and the Early Written and
Iconographic Record," *JNES* 50 (1991): 81-105.

derivatives of them; and the "canonical" myths to which scholars like Barb appeal are literary contrivances, masking the diversity and even incoherence of the actual traditions.[48] It is a helpful corrective to consider Malinowski's term for *historiolae*, "myths of magic," since by his scheme each recitation of precedent for an applied purpose carries independent value as "myth." Likewise the structuralist vision of a myth as the sum-total of all narrative variants, themselves *only* extant in such performance-specific genres as *historiolae*, eliminates the quest for the putative *Ur-* or archetypal myth, since by this conception "the" myth never appears.[49]

Yet the concept of a "myth" or macro-narrative somehow transcendent of the *historiola* is not entirely an analytical or romantic construct. The one who composes the *historiola* certainly considers himself or herself to be, in Theodore Ludwig's terms, "fit(ting) the specific human circumstance into the larger pattern of sacred existence and power as known in the religion of the people."[50] Thus at one level, *historiolae* bespeak *tradition* broadly conceived; and it is this "traditional" factor, the *historiola's* recognizability, which establishes the *historiola's* performative value and power—renders its utterance "felicitous" according to Speech-Acts analysis.[51]

But in another sense, *historiolae* are deliberate acts of *blending* that tradition—the symbols and motifs that constitute local authority and power—with *both* "the specific human circumstances" and broader, more abstract concepts of power, cosmology, transformation, and identity. Indeed, they represent a hypostasiza-

---

[48] Cf. Marcel Détienne, "Myth and Writing: The Mythographers," *Mythologies*, 2 vols., ed. Yves Bonnefoy, re-ed. Wendy Doniger (Chicago & London: University of Chicago Press, 1991), 1.10.

[49] E.g., Claude Lévi-Strauss, "The Structural Study of Myth," *Myth: A Symposium*, ed. Thomas Sebeok (Bloomington: Indiana University Press, 1955), 92: "We define the myth as consisting of all its versions"; and *idem*, *The Raw and the Cooked*, tr. John and Doreen Weightman (New York: Harper & Row, 1969), 13: "Each myth taken separately exists as the limited application of a pattern, which is gradually revealed by the relations of reciprocal intelligibility discerned between several myths." Cf. Détienne, "Myth and Writing," 10-11.

[50] Theodore Ludwig, "Incantation," *Hidden Truths: Magic, Alchemy, and the Occult*, ed. Lawrence Sullivan (New York: MacMillan, 1987), 195.

[51] Cf. Plutarch, *De Iside et Osiride* 65: when people hear the details of Isis' delivery of Harpocrates they "put their love and trust in them, choosing from this source the most credible account on the basis of what is well-known and familiar" (tr. Griffiths, *Plutarch's De Iside et Osiride* [Cardiff: University of Wales Press, 1970], 221).

tion, a coming into being, of the very world-view of a culture, particularly as this world-view might pertain to the resolution of human misfortune. Mary Mills' recent definition of myth as a "basic cosmic framework ... [which] indicates where cosmic power resides, what it is called, and so how it can be used" (in ritual), provides a descriptive model for the present problem, since *historiolae* become a distinct *level* of discourse, one which applies or directs cosmic power, while myth itself remains the general "framework."[52] However, I would extend Mill's model into several tiers: (1) the abstract set of concepts and relations that might crystallize around or into (2) certain figures, names, places, or folklore motifs according to a culture's current circumstances, and then come into being within (3) a variety of performative settings according to a variety of forms that range from priestly liturgy (like the *Enuma Elish*) to scribal mythography (like Plutarch) to *historiolae*, drama, sculpture, or painting. These latter genres are merely the *articulations* of myth; the myth itself remains at the *pre*-articulate level, a condensation of social structure, morality, and existential concerns at the broadest level. The diverse articulations of a myth vary in scope and complexity according to their forms or genres of composition; the forms and genres, in turn, are immediately dependent upon the performative context: healing rite, festival recitation, amulet, etc.

Finally, the specific terms, symbols, and motifs of composition (my level [2]) do not themselves constitute "myth" but rather the *authoritative discourse of precedent* in a given region at a certain time: stories, prayers, heroes and gods—a discourse that would certainly evolve through time (and particularly as a culture converted to Christianity or Islam). The concept "myth" therefore serves as a theoretical explanation of structural resemblances, links, and overall relationships among *historiolae*, liturgical recitations, texts, and other forms of mythical expression.

*   *   *

How would this approach to myth work in the cases we have examined? The Philinna spell, far from being dependent on any single macro-myth, is evidently a pastiche of mysterious images and Mediterranean motifs composed ingeniously to "tap into"

---

[52] Mary E. Mills, *Human Agents of Cosmic Power in Hellenistic Judaism and the Synoptic Tradition*, JSNTSupp 41 (Sheffield: JSOT, 1990), 30, cf. 28-29 on an approximate description of *historiolae*.

several authoritative symbol systems (perhaps most deliberately an Egyptian one).[53] Similarly Barb's "Antaura" spell and its medieval analogue are singular examples of *historiola* artistry, evoking a traditional "world" of precedent through the image of an evil mermaid, rather than a line of descent to ancient Babylonian demonology. It is important to recognize that, whatever the history of the motifs, *historiolae* themselves function in a present that requires only that they be recognizable.

In their sometimes blatant syncretism the Christian spells have always posed an interesting test of one's concept of "myth." In the case of P.Yale 1792, "Christ was born on the 29th of Choiak. He came descending upon the earth. He passed judgment on all the poisonous serpents," we see *not* a synthesis or epitome of written gospels or a syncretistic use of Horus cycles, but the author's creation of a prototype of divine power over serpents (the myth) out of the symbols and motifs of contemporaneous Christian folklore (the local discourse of authority and precedent). Similarly, behind *PGM* CXXIII, "Come out of your tomb, Christ is calling you," lies *not* one of the extant (canonical or extra-canonical) accounts of Christ's empty tomb or harrowing of hell but a general tradition of the hero Christ liberating the dead. Beyond the Christian story one might trace this *historiola* to a broader (and indigenous Egyptian) concept of divine power over human death—what I would call the myth, the essential paradigm this *historiola* is articulating. Thus its articulation within a local Christian discourse gives the spell immediate authority, while its application for childbirth determines what details should be invoked.

One can similarly explain the persistence of indigenous (pagan) gods and their stories in Coptic and other Christian spells (e.g., Hs. Schmidt 1 and 2). Scholars have alternated between taking these as evidence of a still-pagan or syncretistic world-view on the one hand, and dismissing them as culturally meaningless on the other.[54] But one might better regard the use and deployment of these names as a "bricolage," at the first level (performance), of symbols and motifs from the second level (the local discourse of authority

---

[53] See Faraone, "The *Mystodokos* and the Dark-Eyed Maidens: Multicultural Influences on a Late-Hellenistic Incantation," in this volume. Obviously by the present scheme the search for any "influences" is superfluous, particularly in light of the commonness of the motifs.

[54] Although note the more qualified conclusions of Kropp (3.5-9) and Walter Beltz, "Zur Morphologie koptischer Zaubertexte," *Coptic Studies: Acts of the Third International Congress of Coptic Studies*, ed. Wlodzimierz Godlewski (Warsaw: PWN, 1990), 56-57.

and precedent), that articulates the "myth" of divine accomplishment in a certain realm of human experience (like love, in the case of the Schmidt spells, or snakebite in others). The use of indigenous names and motifs simply indicates their continuing availability and authority. The choice, that is, of Christ or Horus for a particular spell, depends on what was believed necessary and workable at one point in time in one client-"doctor" relationship, *not* on the presently dominant god in public ritual. The *historiola* that results from this process is indeed an *ad hoc* composition by its very nature—one that will vary substantially from the more elaborate narratives used in church and temple—but it is a composition that successfully "narrates power."

PLATES

NEW GREEK MAGICAL AND
DIVINATORY TEXTS IN BERLIN

P. Berol. 21300 (↓)

P. Berol. 21300 (→)

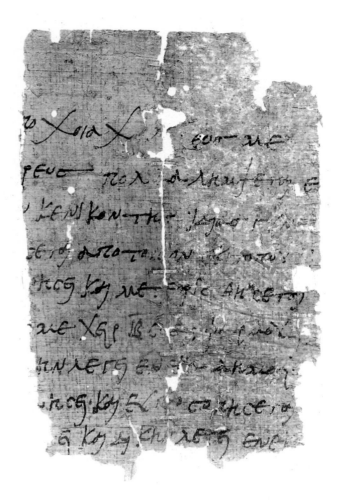

P. Berol. 21198 (→)

41 42 43 44 45

P. Berol. 21336 (→)   P. Berol. 21336 (↓)

P. Berol. 21337 (→)

P. Berol. 21341 (→)

P. Berol. 21341 (↓)

P. Berol. 21358 (→)   P. Berol. 21358 (↓)

P. Berol. 21316 (↓)

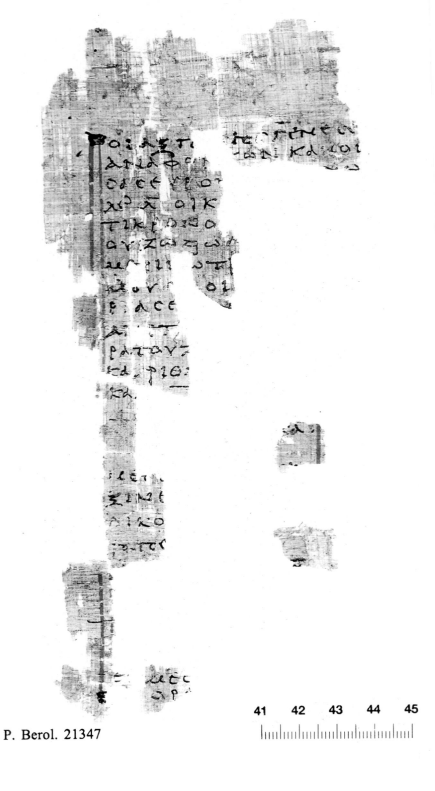